ANNOTATED TEACHER'S EDITION

FOURTH • EDITION

SPEECH
Exploring Communication

J. Regis O'Connor
Western Kentucky University

National Textbook Company
a division of NTC/Contemporary Publishing Group
Lincolnwood, Illinois USA

Reviewers
We are grateful to the following teachers who reviewed the *Annotated Teacher's Edition*
and offered their suggestions and insights:

Heidi Knable
Everett School District
Mill Creek, Washington

Jim Long
Plano High School
Plano, Texas

Darlene Musso
Plantation High School
Plantation, Florida

Development
Word Management, Inc.

Design
Anderson Creative Services

ISBN : 0-8442-5851-2

Published by National Textbook Company,
a division of NTC/Contemporary Publishing Group, Inc.,
4255 West Touhy Avenue,
Lincolnwood (Chicago), Illinois 60712-1975 U.S.A.
© 1996 by NTC/Contemporary Publishing Group, Inc.
All rights reserved. No part of this book may be reproduced,
stored in a retrieval system, or transmitted in any form or by any means,
electronic, mechanical, photocopying, recording or otherwise,
without prior permission of the publisher.
Manufactured in Canada.
Library of Congress Catalog Card Number : 95-69501

9 0 1 2 3 4 TCP 8 7 6 5 4 3

ANNOTATED TEACHER'S EDITION

FOURTH • EDITION

SPEECH
Exploring Communication

J. Regis O'Connor
Western Kentucky University

National Textbook Company
a division of NTC/Contemporary Publishing Group
Lincolnwood, Illinois USA

Reviewers
We are grateful to the following teachers who reviewed the *Annotated Teacher's Edition* and offered their suggestions and insights:

Heidi Knable
Everett School District
Mill Creek, Washington

Jim Long
Plano High School
Plano, Texas

Darlene Musso
Plantation High School
Plantation, Florida

Development
Word Management, Inc.

Design
Anderson Creative Services

ISBN: 0-8442-5851-2

Published by National Textbook Company,
a division of NTC/Contemporary Publishing Group, Inc.,
4255 West Touhy Avenue,
Lincolnwood (Chicago), Illinois 60712-1975 U.S.A.
© 1996 by NTC/Contemporary Publishing Group, Inc.
All rights reserved. No part of this book may be reproduced,
stored in a retrieval system, or transmitted in any form or by any means,
electronic, mechanical, photocopying, recording or otherwise,
without prior permission of the publisher.
Manufactured in Canada.
Library of Congress Catalog Card Number: 95-69501

9 0 1 2 3 4 TCP 9 8 7 6 5 4 3

THE #1 SELLER—
NOW BETTER THAN EVER!

NEW! • Content for the 21st Century

NEW! • "Ethically Speaking" Feature

NEW! • Speech Activities

NEW! • *Annotated Teacher's Edition* with on-page information and suggestions where you need them

NEW! • Ancillaries include:
- Portfolio Products
- Computerized Assessment Strategies
- Speech Library
- Self-Help Videos for Students

• Solid experience at work in the classroom

Dear Teacher:

Speech: Exploring Communication has become the most successful high school program in speech because students' speaking and listening skills improve dramatically with its use.

You will find your tasks made easier with the updated content in the student text and the diverse suggestions provided in this all-new *Annotated Teacher's Edition.* Let me acquaint you with the program's philosophy, the organization of the student text, and the easy-to-use features of this *Annotated Teacher's Edition.*

Philosophy   High school students are struggling with issues of communication with parents, peers, authority figures, and employers. **Speech: Exploring Communication** offers students an opportunity to develop effective speaking and listening skills to solve these and other challenges throughout life. Through **Speech: Exploring Communication** students become conscious of the process of speech communication and develop skills to improve the process and enhance their success in achieving speech-related goals.

Student Text   High school students learn best when they are active, involved in the process, and "doing" something. **Speech: Exploring Communication** is a student-centered text that offers frequent opportunities for activities and skill development. It follows the simple two-pronged strategy of *explain,* then *do.* This easy two-step approach is implemented in each of the seventeen chapters of the text. Students appreciate the short manageable sections that explain the speech process. Special features, including "Career Close-Up" and "Ethically Speaking," demonstrate how communication skills apply to the real world.

Annotated Teacher's Edition   Both experienced and beginning speech teachers will welcome the wealth of on-page information and the variety of teaching suggestions. Check out *Amazing Facts!* to motivate, and perhaps astound, your students. Emergency help is provided with *Substitute Teacher Tips*, and *15-Second Skill Opportunities* give students quick, nonthreatening opportunities to develop skills in the classroom without lengthy preparation. Veteran teachers will wish they had had this kind of support when they were starting out; beginners will be grateful to all those teachers who have shared comments, suggestions, and classroom experience for this teacher's edition.

Additional Resources   In addition to the *Annotated Teacher's Edition,* we think you will find many ways to use the following: Portfolio Product Activities, Assessment Strategies Test Book, Speech Library, Video Kit, Speech Strategies and Answer Key, Computerized TestMaker, and an Audiocassette. Please see page 10T for a description of these products.

I am confident that you will find **Speech: Exploring Communication,** with its *Annotated Teacher's Edition* and other ancillaries, a useful and creative tool. If you have comments or questions, please feel free to write to me at: National Textbook Company, 4255 West Touhy Avenue, Lincolnwood, IL 60646-1975.

J. Regis O'Connor

STUDENT EDITION FEATURES

This leading speech book uses a two-step "explain" and "do" approach.

Text explanations include:
- Words and terms defined and used in context of narration
- Guided reading that helps students preview content
- Graphic organizers and visually appealing photos and charts

Active learning opportunities include:
- Activities
- Cooperative learning projects
- Stand-up skill development opportunities
- Speech Appendix

Real-life applications include:
- "Career Close-Up" featuring communication on the job
- "Ethically Speaking" examining speech values and priorities throughout life
- "Speaking in Action" featuring speech activities outside of class
- Work and technology-based references

Critical and creative thinking opportunities include:
- Chapter activities that encourage analysis and synthesis
- Projects that extend chapter content
- Sequential questions and activities that apply communication skills

Students quickly become confident speech communicators.

5T

TEACHER EDITION FEATURES

● PREPARE

- *Unit* and *Chapter Planners* help you manage precious classroom time
- *Performance Objectives* clarify goals and promote accountability
- *Portfolio Products* suggestions suit individual, group, and class activities
- *SCA Guidelines* suggest skill standards widely endorsed in speech classrooms
- *Professional Resources* suggest additional print and multimedia materials

> Solid teaching strategies that focus on the essentials.
> •Prepare •Teach
> •Apply •Assess

● TEACH

- *Substitute Teacher Tip* provides suggestions for immediate classroom use
- *Amazing Facts!* provide interesting and motivational information
- *Links to Past Learning* relates speech concepts to prior knowledge
- *Motivation* creates student interest in explanation of topic that follows with relevant application
- *Enrichment, Extension,* and *Assessment* suggestions are also included
- *Curricular Connections* suggest ways to integrate speech instruction with other areas of the curriculum

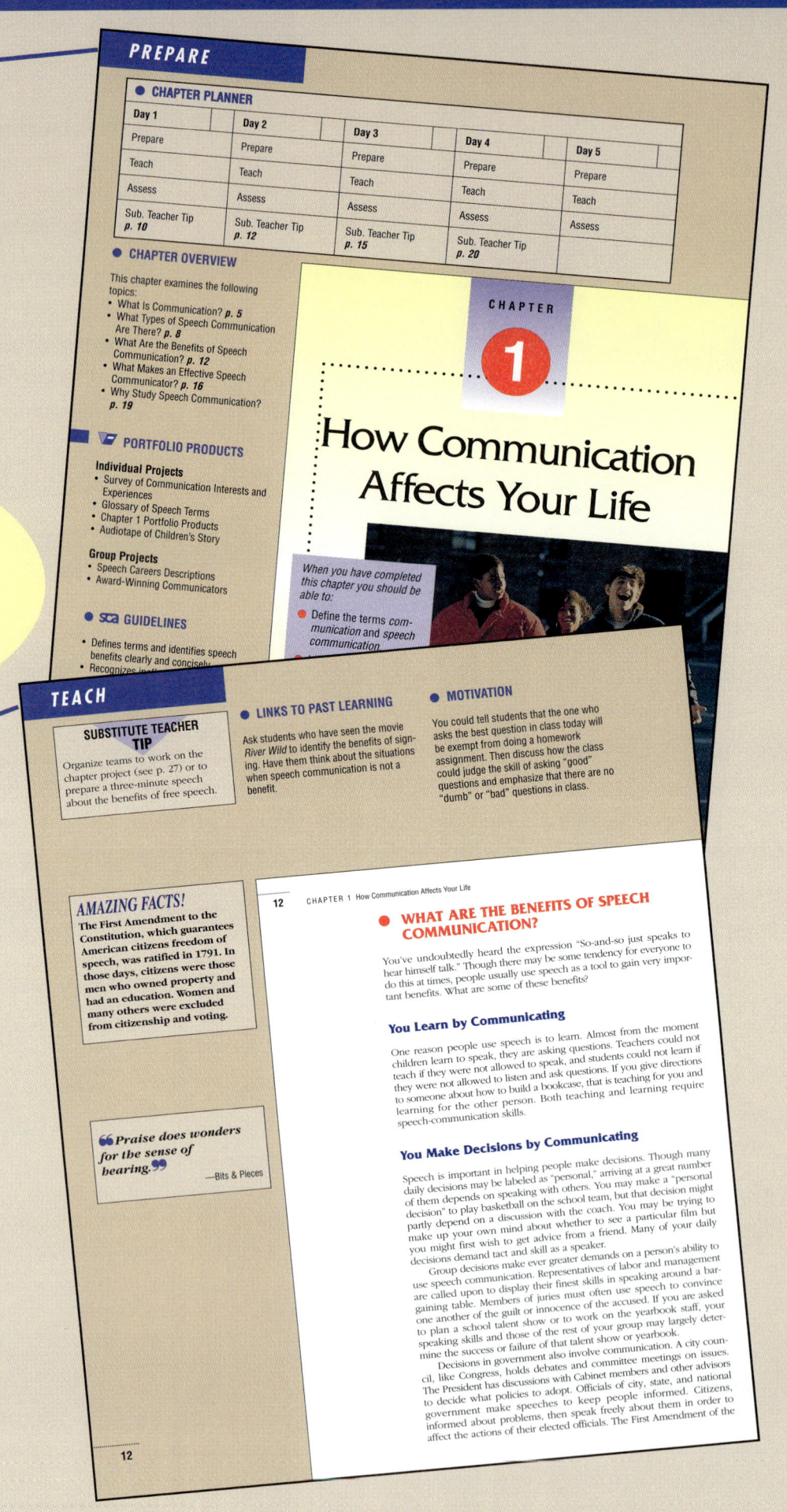

6T

● **APPLY**

- "Career Close-Up" features demonstrate how communication skills are essential to many fascinating careers
- "Ethically Speaking" features showcase the need for responsible communication
- "Speaking in Action" features are activities aimed at enhancing speech skills outside the classroom
- *Skill Application* suggestions offer students practical applications for skills relating to the specific topics

● **ASSESS**

- *Student Performance Competencies* are identified to promote accountability for performance
- *SCA Guidelines* suggest national competencies for high school students
- *Portfolio Assessment* is encouraged through a wide variety of projects that reflect average, enhanced, and superior performance
- *Assessment Strategies* for individuals and groups are suggested
- *Answers* are conveniently provided on-page with explanations

7T

LEARNING STYLES

LEARNING STYLES

Something for everyone! Diverse students learn in diverse ways. A full menu of teaching suggestions for the various learning styles of your students promotes successful speech comunication for *all* students.

- *Cooperative Learning* suggestions encourage small-group and team-building projects and activities

- *Multicultural Learning* suggests ways that students from a variety of ethnic backgrounds can learn from their heritage and apply their background successfully in today's world

- *Visual Learning* suggestions help students convert verbal explanations to a visual process that presents information or activities in an alternate form

- *Kinesic Learning* emphasizes techniques that promote more effective speech communication through body language and gestures

8T

SKILLS AND APPLICATIONS

● SKILL DEVELOPMENT

Practice makes perfect! Students make amazing progress in speech skills and self-confidence. There are many opportunities for students to target specific skills and gain practice and confidence that will serve them throughout life. These practical suggestions are found in the side columns and include the following:

- *15-Second Skill Opportunity* suggests easy stand-up speech opportunities in the classroom requiring little preparation. Repeated practice quickly reduces speech anxiety while building better skills and enhancing self-confidence

- *Critical Thinking* activities raise significant questions or suggest projects that sharpen students' skills in higher level learning

- *Feedback* suggestions give students guidelines and practice in giving each other positive and critical feedback

- *Active Listening* skills are encouraged in a variety of contexts

● SKILL APPLICATION

Life-long learning for home, work, and as citizens at the polls. Students learn how to apply the process of speech communication in a variety of real-life situations.

- *Media Literacy* suggestions alert students to the many diverse media communications in everyday life

- *Citizens Speak Out* features provide activities for students to gain practice in voicing opinions and making decisions that affect the common good

- *Debate* suggestions help students use logic and persuasion to express a point of view about significant real-life issues

9T

RESOURCE MATERIALS

NEW! Unsurpassed Resource Materials to Put Help at Your Fingertips!

● **PORTFOLIO PRODUCT ACTIVITIES**—*Classroom-tested Projects and Activities*

This collection of BLM activities provides useful applications for the development of speech skills for every chapter. When completed, these surveys, evaluations, and activities can become part of the student's individual portfolio.

● **ASSESSMENT STRATEGIES TEST BOOK**—*Chapter and Unit Tests and Final Exam*

This duplication master book provides easy-to-use one page (two-sided) print forms containing test questions for every chapter and unit as well as a final exam. These questions are keyed to each chapter objective and coded for ability levels.

● **COMPUTERIZED TESTMAKER**—*Customized Test Questions*

This is a computerized test question data bank that allows you to select and rearrange test questions to accommodate the specific needs of every class. The convenient, easy-to-use testmaker comes with technical assistance from the "experts" when backup support is necessary. Available in both MAC and PC formats.

● **SPEECH LIBRARY**—*Primary Source Materials*

This resource provides short, suitable speech selections for student use with each chapter to give students practice with classic expressions of speech.

● **VIDEO KIT**—*Tutorial and Self-Help Videos for Student Instruction*

Two twenty-two-minute videos include short segments that demonstrate simple techniques students can use to enhance their communication skills in real-life situations. These topics include: "How to Tame Speech Anxiety," "How to Interview," "How to Become an Active Listener," "How to Build Confidence," "How to Prepare a Speech," and "How to Use Visual Aids." Worksheets accompany each video segment.

● **AUDIOCASSETTE**—*Recordings of Memorable Speeches*

This audiocassette allows students to hear the inspiring words of famous speeches and apply effective speech techniques to their own presentations. In addition, those with limited experience with English can use the guided vocabulary instruction to gain understanding and practice in the correct use of special words and terms used in the student text. Worksheets accompany the audiocassette.

● **SPEECH STRATEGIES AND ANSWER KEY**—*Classroom Suggestions and Complete Answers*

This resource provides plentiful suggestions for extending your teaching, indicates possible scope and sequence options to suit various time allotments, and presents complete answers for all the questions and activities found on the Chapter Review pages.

FOURTH • EDITION

SPEECH
Exploring Communication

J. Regis O'Connor
Western Kentucky University

National Textbook Company
a division of NTC/Contemporary Publishing Group
Lincolnwood, Illinois USA

Contents

UNIT 1 Elements of Communication 2

1 How Communication Affects Your Life 4

ACTIVITY Appreciating Human Communication 5
WHAT IS COMMUNICATION? 5
ACTIVITY Daily Communication 8
WHAT TYPES OF SPEECH COMMUNICATION ARE THERE? 8
ACTIVITY Enjoyment of Speaking 10
Ethically Speaking Ethics in Communication 11
WHAT ARE THE BENEFITS OF SPEECH COMMUNICATION? 12
ACTIVITY Speech and Careers 15
WHAT MAKES AN EFFECTIVE SPEECH COMMUNICATOR? 16
Career Close-Up High School Teacher 18
WHY STUDY SPEECH COMMUNICATION? 19
ACTIVITY Effective Speech Communication 21
CHAPTER REVIEW 22

2 The Process of Communication 28

ACTIVITY Steps in the Communication Process 29
AN OVERVIEW OF THE COMMUNICATION PROCESS 30
ACTIVITY Ineffective Speech Communication 32
DECIDING TO COMMUNICATE 32
ACTIVITY Memory 35
CHOOSING SYMBOLS 35
ACTIVITY Using Communication Other Than Words 42
Career Close-Up Peace Corps Volunteer 43
VOCALIZING 44
ACTIVITY Proper Breathing Techniques 46
RECEPTION 47
Speaking in Action Communicating with the Hearing Impaired 49
FEEDBACK 50
ACTIVITY Reception and Feedback 51
CHAPTER REVIEW 52

3. Listening 58

ACTIVITY Hearing versus Listening 59
REASONS FOR LEARNING EFFECTIVE LISTENING 60
ACTIVITY Taking Listening Personally 62
RECOGNIZING BARRIERS TO LISTENING 63
ACTIVITY Classroom Distractions 67
BECOMING AN ACTIVE LISTENER 67
ACTIVITY Being an Active Listener 73
Career Close-Up Medical Secretary 74
CRITICAL LISTENING AND THINKING 75
ACTIVITY Identifying Logical Fallacies 81
CHAPTER REVIEW 82

UNIT 2 Interpersonal and Group Communication 88

4. One-to-One Communication 90

ACTIVITY Types of One-to-One Communication 91
THE VERBAL ASPECTS OF CONVERSATION 91
ACTIVITY Practicing Clarity in Conversation 95
THE NONVERBAL ASPECTS OF CONVERSATION 96
ACTIVITY Discussing Aspects of Conversation 102
SPEAKING ON THE TELEPHONE 102
TAKING PART IN AN INTERVIEW 104
Career Close-Up Travel Agent 107
ACTIVITY Role Playing Interviews 111
CHAPTER REVIEW 112

5. Group Discussion 118

ACTIVITY Reports from Student Groups 119
THE NATURE OF GROUP DISCUSSION 119
ACTIVITY Describing Group Communication 123
FACTORS AFFECTING GROUP DISCUSSION 123
ACTIVITY Working with Groups 127
HOW GROUPS BEHAVE 127
Speaking in Action The Crippled Ship 132
ACTIVITY Task and Maintenance Messages 133
PREPARING TO PARTICIPATE IN A GROUP 133
Career Close-Up Systems Analyst 137
ACTIVITY Preparing for a Group Discussion 138
LEADING A GROUP 139
ACTIVITY Conducting a Group Discussion 142

Contents

HANDLING CONFLICT IN GROUPS 142
ACTIVITY Handling Conflict 146
OUTCOMES OF DISCUSSION 146
ACTIVITY Decision Outcomes 147
ALTERNATIVES TO GROUP DISCUSSION 147
ACTIVITY Using the Nominal Technique 149
CHAPTER REVIEW 150

UNIT 3 Preparing for Public Speaking 156

6 Building Confidence 158

ACTIVITY Defining and Describing Stage Fright 159
UNDERSTANDING STAGE FRIGHT 160
CONTROLLING YOUR NERVOUSNESS 164
Career Close-Up Candidate for Public Office 167
ACTIVITY Controlling Stage Fright 171
ACTIVITY Critiquing Classmates' "Talks" 175
CHAPTER REVIEW 176

7 Preparing Your Speech 182

ACTIVITY Four Cornerstones of Speech Preparation 183
FOCUSING ON YOUR TOPIC 184
ACTIVITY Choosing Topics for a Class Speech 186
ACTIVITY Narrowing Your Topic 190
RESEARCHING YOUR TOPIC 191
Career Close-Up Public Relations Specialist 197
Speaking in Action Researching through Interviews 201
Ethically Speaking Crediting Your Sources 203
ACTIVITY Using Reference Materials 205
ORGANIZING AND OUTLINING YOUR SPEECH 205
ACTIVITY Making a "Delivery" Outline 214
REHEARSING 214
ACTIVITY Rehearsing with a Friend 217
CHAPTER REVIEW 218

8 Choosing Effective Language 224

ACTIVITY Written versus Spoken Language 225
DIFFERENCES BETWEEN WRITTEN AND SPOKEN LANGUAGE 227
MAKING SPOKEN LANGUAGE CLEAR 228
ACTIVITY Using Simple Language 230
ACTIVITY Economy of Language 232
CREATING LEVELS OF EMPHASIS 233

Ethically Speaking Intensity of Language and Image 235
ACTIVITY Finding Language Devices 236
Career Close-Up Lobbyist 239
USING FIGURES OF SPEECH 240
ACTIVITY Finding Figures of Speech 242
Speaking in Action Student Speech 243
AVOIDING COMMON PROBLEMS 244
CHAPTER REVIEW 248

9 Delivering Your Speech 254

ACTIVITY Pros and Cons of Speech Delivery Methods 255
USING DIFFERENT METHODS OF DELIVERY 255
ACTIVITY Extemporaneous Speech 259
RECOGNIZING NONVERBAL ASPECTS OF DELIVERING A SPEECH 260
ACTIVITY Gesturing 266
Career Close-Up Interpreter 271
ACTIVITY Discovering Your Best Average Volume 273
SPECIAL PROBLEMS OF DELIVERING A SPEECH 273
ACTIVITY Dealing with Distractions 277
ANALYZING AND EVALUATING SPEECHES 278
CHAPTER REVIEW 282

UNIT 4 Types of Public Speaking 288

10 Speaking to Inform 290

ACTIVITY Defining Informative Speaking 291
TYPES OF INFORMATIVE SPEECHES 292
BEGINNING AN INFORMATIVE SPEECH 295
ACTIVITY Sample Attention Devices 300
IMPARTING THE MESSAGE OF AN INFORMATIVE SPEECH 305
Career Close-Up Park Ranger 310
ACTIVITY Reacting to Feedback 312
CONCLUDING AN INFORMATIVE SPEECH 312
ACTIVITY Making Conclusions Work 316
CONDUCTING A QUESTION-AND-ANSWER PERIOD 317
USING VISUAL AIDS 319
Ethically Speaking Using Visual Aids Responsibly 329
ACTIVITY Judging Visual Aids 331
ANALYZING AND EVALUATING INFORMATIVE SPEECHES 331
Speaking in Action Speech to a Civic Club 332
CHAPTER REVIEW 340

Contents

11 Speaking to Persuade 346

ACTIVITY Persuasive Mini-Speech 347
TYPES OF PERSUASIVE SPEECHES 347
THREE SOURCES OF PERSUASION 350
ACTIVITY Types of Persuasive Speeches 350
PATHOS: ANALYZING THE NEEDS OF YOUR LISTENERS 350
ACTIVITY Audience Analysis 356
ETHOS: ESTABLISHING YOUR PRESTIGE 356
Career Close-Up Social Worker 359
ACTIVITY Critiquing Ethos 362
LOGOS: BEING LOGICAL 362
ACTIVITY Presenting Evidence 365
Speaking in Action Speech Contest 366
BEING RESPONSIBLE 367
Ethically Speaking Telling the Whole Story 368
ANALYZING AND EVALUATING PERSUASIVE SPEECHES 369
CHAPTER REVIEW 374

12 Other Kinds of Speaking 380

ACTIVITY Identifying "Other" Kinds of Speaking 381
SPEECHES FOCUSED ON PERSONS 382
ACTIVITY Speeches of Introduction 385
Career Close-Up Coach 392
ACTIVITY Commemorative Speeches 393
SPEECHES FOR SPECIAL OCCASIONS 393
ACTIVITY Giving a Commencement Speech 395
ACTIVITY Speeches to Entertain 400
SALES PRESENTATIONS 400
Speaking in Action Class Shopping Trip 403
IMPROMPTU SPEAKING 404
ACTIVITY Impromptu Speeches 405
CHAPTER REVIEW 406

UNIT 5 Debate and Parliamentary Procedure 412

13 Debate 414

ACTIVITY Debate versus Discussion 415
THE NATURE OF DEBATE 415
ACTIVITY Writing Debate Propositions 417
PREPARING TO DEBATE 418
ACTIVITY Using Evidence and Reasoning 426

USING DIFFERENT STRATEGIES 426
Ethically Speaking Using Quotations Responsibly 427
Career Close-Up Trial Lawyer 433
MEETING THE OPPOSITION 435
ACTIVITY Keeping a Flow Sheet 441
CHAPTER REVIEW 442

14 Parliamentary Procedure 448

ACTIVITY Challenge Quiz on Parliamentary Procedure 449
BASIC PRINCIPLES 450
HOLDING A MEETING 451
ACTIVITY Basic Definitions 453
ACTIVITY Duties of the Chair 455
MOTIONS 455
Career Close-Up Health Services Administrator 461
ACTIVITY Defining Subsidiary Motions 462
ACTIVITY Defining Privileged and Incidental Motions 467
CHAPTER REVIEW 468

UNIT 6 Mass Communication 474

15 Radio and Television 476

THE NATURE OF RADIO AND TELEVISION 477
THE DEVELOPMENT OF ELECTRONIC MEDIA 478
Career Close-Up Radio Announcer 485
THE PURPOSES OF RADIO AND TELEVISION 486
ACTIVITY Exploring the Influence of Radio and Television 488
PERFORMING ON RADIO AND TELEVISION 489
PRODUCING FOR RADIO AND TELEVISION 492
ACTIVITY Creating a Newscast 493
CHAPTER REVIEW 494

UNIT 7 Performing Arts 500

16 Oral Interpretation 502

A BRIEF HISTORY OF ORAL INTERPRETATION 504
TYPES OF MATERIAL FOR ORAL INTERPRETATION 506
ACTIVITY Working with Poetry 507
CHOOSING MATERIAL FOR ORAL INTERPRETATION 508
ACTIVITY Finding Beauty in a Selection 511
INTERPRETING YOUR SELECTION 513

Career Close-Up Children's Librarian   518
ACTIVITY   Analyzing Literature   524
TWO FINAL STEPS: INTRODUCTION AND PRACTICE   524
ACTIVITY   Delivery of an Oral Interpretation   529
CHAPTER REVIEW   530
SELECTIONS TO INTERPRET ORALLY   536

17 Drama   538

THE NATURE OF DRAMA   539
A BRIEF HISTORY OF DRAMA   540
DEVELOPING A CHARACTER   543
Career Close-Up Actors   546
ACTIVITY   Experimenting with Movement   551
ACTIVITY   Developing Character Through Improvisation   555
ORGANIZING A THEATRICAL EVENT   555
ACTIVITY   The Importance of Organizing   561
PRODUCING A THEATRICAL EVENT   561
CHAPTER REVIEW   566

Appendix of Speeches   572

INFORMATIVE/COMMEMORATIVE SPEECH
   Address on the Anniversary of Lincoln's Birth
   Carl Sandburg   572
PERSUASIVE SPEECH
   Woman's Right to Suffrage   *Susan B. Anthony*   576
INSPIRATIONAL SPEECH
   Choice and Change   *Barbara Bush*   577
SPEECH OF INSPIRATION AND PERSUASION
   I Have a Dream   *Martin Luther King, Jr.*   580
EULOGY
   Max Planck in Memoriam   *Albert Einstein*   583
SPEECH OF DEDICATION
   The Gettysburg Address   *President Abraham Lincoln*   584
COMMENCEMENT ADDRESS
   Saving Our Cities   *Tom Gerety*   585
SPEECH IN TRIBUTE
   To Thurgood Marshall   *Carol Moseley-Braun*   588
MOTIVATIONAL SPEECH
   The Quest for Shared Values   *Robert A. Plane*   590

GLOSSARY   593

INDEX   602

TEXT CREDITS   611

PHOTO CREDITS   613

PREPARE

● **PERFORMANCE OBJECTIVES**

- Participates in daily 15-second skill drills when asked
- Applies active listening strategies to work-related situations
- Speaks clearly and distinctly when contributing to public discussions

● **sca GUIDELINES**

- Expresses information clearly and concisely
- Recognizes when another does not understand a message and takes appropriate measures to correct the message delivery
- Organizes messages so that others can understand them

● **UNIT FOCUS**

Unit 1 introduces the process of communication and describes and defines this common and important activity. The unit stresses the importance of active listening as well.

● **CONTENTS**

1. How Communication Affects Your Life *pp. 4-27*
2. The Process of Communication *pp. 28-57*
3. Listening *pp. 58-87*

▼ **UNIT PORTFOLIOS**

Individual Portfolios
- Flow Chart of the Communication Process
- Illustrated Chart of the Impact of Communication at Home or at School
- Audiotape Identifying Listening Strategies
- Chapter Portfolio Products

Group Portfolios
- Video Segment Demonstrating Some Do's and Don'ts of Active Listening
- Taped Examples of Communication Styles

Class Portfolios
- Classroom Rules for Listening and Learning
- School Guidelines for Large Group Assemblies

UNIT 1

ELEMENTS OF COMMUNICATION

PREPARE

● UNIT PLANNER

Chapters	Time Management	● ANCILLARY RESOURCES				
1 How Communication Affects Your Life *pp. 4-27*	Week 1	✔	✔	✔		
2 The Process of Communication *pp. 28-57*	Week 2	✔	✔	✔		✔
3 Listening *pp. 58-87*	Week 3	✔	✔	✔	✔	

● PROFESSIONAL RESOURCES

Print
Agee, W. K. *Introduction to Mass Communications.* 10th ed. New York: Harper-Collins, 1990.

Allen, R. R., S. Clay Wilmington, and Jo Spraue. *Communication in the Secondary School: A Pedagogy.* 3rd ed. Scottsdale, AZ: Gorsuch Scarisbrick, 1990.

Civikly, Jean. *Classroom Communication.* Dubuque, IA: William C. Brown, 1992.

Cooper, Pamela, ed. *Activities for Teaching Speaking and Listening: Grades 7–12.* Annandale, VA: Speech Communication Association, 1991.

Reid, Loren Dudley. *Speaking Well.* New York: McGraw-Hill Book Co., 1992.

Film
Open the Door: A System for Better Communication (11 min, color; Cally Curtis) 1986.

Video
Speak Up: Skills of Oral Communication (60 min, color; Guidance Associates) 1989.

---

1 How Communication Affects Your Life

2 The Process of Communication

3 Listening

Ancillary Resource Key

▼ = Portfolio Product Activities
📄 = Tests/Answer Key
📕 = Speech Library
📼 = Self-Help Videos
🎞 = Audiotape

3

PREPARE

● CHAPTER PLANNER

Day 1	Day 2	Day 3	Day 4	Day 5
Prepare	Prepare	Prepare	Prepare	Prepare
Teach	Teach	Teach	Teach	Teach
Assess	Assess	Assess	Assess	Assess
Sub. Teacher Tip *p. 10*	Sub. Teacher Tip *p. 12*	Sub. Teacher Tip *p. 15*	Sub. Teacher Tip *p. 20*	

● CHAPTER OVERVIEW

This chapter examines the following topics:
- What Is Communication? *p. 5*
- What Types of Speech Communication Are There? *p. 8*
- What Are the Benefits of Speech Communication? *p. 12*
- What Makes an Effective Speech Communicator? *p. 16*
- Why Study Speech Communication? *p. 19*

▽ PORTFOLIO PRODUCTS

Individual Projects
- Survey of Communication Interests and Experiences
- Glossary of Speech Terms
- Chapter 1 Portfolio Products
- Audiotape of Children's Story

Group Projects
- Speech Careers Descriptions
- Award-Winning Communicators

● sca GUIDELINES

- Defines terms and identifies speech benefits clearly and concisely
- Recognizes ineffective speech communications and makes appropriate adjustments
- Provides real-life examples of the importance of speech communications

---

CHAPTER

1

How Communication Affects Your Life

When you have completed this chapter you should be able to:

● Define the terms *communication* and *speech communication*.

● Identify some specific benefits of improving your speech communication.

● State the skills that make an effective speech communicator.

● Understand the importance of speech communication in your life.

TEACH

● **MOTIVATION**

Take a poll of the number of students who have pet dogs and those who have pet cats. Ask each group to describe how dogs communicate when they are hungry and how cats tell their owners they are hungry. Identify similarities and differences. Suggest that groups of people communicate in different ways and also that individuals have unique styles of communicating.

● **LINKS TO PAST LEARNING**

Encourage students to remember the longest speech they ever heard in person. Discuss their impressions.

AMAZING FACTS!

The longest speech made in the United Nations lasted 4 hours and 29 minutes. The speech was made by President Fidel Castro of Cuba on September 26, 1960.

What Is Communication? 5

ACTIVITY

Appreciating Human Communication

In small groups of five to seven members, hold brief discussions on the questions, "How does your pet dog or cat's communication differ from that of humans? What powers do we have that enable us to communicate at a much higher level than animals?" Elect one member of your group to report your group's findings to the entire class.

Imagine yourself in a world without communication. You would be able to see and smell and taste and feel. But you would not be able to get your ideas across to others. You would also be unable to take in ideas that other people wished to express to you. In a very real sense, you would be isolated in a silence even more profound than that felt by a person who was deaf or mute.

Communication is a complex process, but one that is full of rewards. By taking part in the Activity that opens this chapter, you should have developed an appreciation for the special gift we humans have in our ability to speak. Now that you realize the incredible range and power of human communication, you'll want to begin searching for those rewards—specific ways in which you can improve your own speech communication.

● **WHAT IS COMMUNICATION?**

Communication is the process of sending and receiving messages to achieve understanding. You have undoubtedly heard the expression "Say what you mean and mean what you say." Saying what you mean

The communication process involves a sender transmitting a message to a receiver.

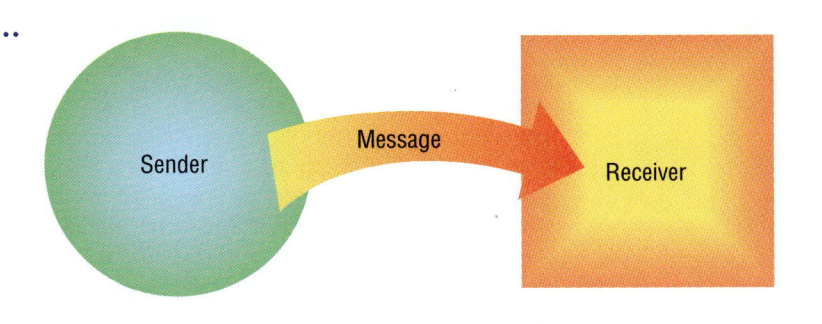

Sender → Message → Receiver

● **LEARNING STYLES**

🌐 **Multicultural Learning**

Students could reinforce the differences between sender and receiver by examining excerpts of speeches made in Japan, Germany, England, South Africa, and Mexico. Ask them to compare and contrast the use of gestures, and the speed and tone of speech that they may be aware of. Extend the activity by asking students to comment on regional speech differences in the U.S.

● **SKILL DEVELOPMENT**

⏱ **15-Second Skill Opportunity**

You could use an opener like this: Write on the chalkboard "The most important communication I could hear today is . . . ." Give students a moment to reflect on how they would complete the sentence. Ask students (or volunteers) to stand, face the class, and complete the sentence using gestures, tone, and timing for emphasis.

TEACH

● **RETEACHING**

To emphasize the need to repeat and reinforce communication, ask students to imagine that they are parents requesting a child to take out the garbage. This is the third request. Discuss how they would communicate differently and more effectively with the child.

● **SKILL DEVELOPMENT**

Critical Thinking
Ask students to identify at least ten types of communication they give and receive each day. Have them list three things those communications have in common and three things that make them different.

---

6   CHAPTER 1 How Communication Affects Your Life

Whether exchanging information with a classmate or addressing a large audience, you are sending and receiving messages—you are communicating.

is precisely what communication is all about. Anytime you speak a sentence, make a gesture, or merely grunt, you are "saying" you have some idea in your mind that you wish to transfer to another person. Words, body movements, facial expressions, and voice tones are all symbols you select in your attempts to transmit the meaning in your mind to the mind of your receiver.

How Do People Communicate?

Human beings use various means of communication. You can show that you agree with someone just by nodding your head. You can walk in such a way as to indicate something about your personality or the way you feel. You can also communicate something about yourself to almost everyone you meet by what you wear. These are all examples of **nonverbal** communication.

Human beings, however, communicate best through speaking and writing. These are **verbal** forms of communication. By using words to stand for, or to symbolize, the ideas they have in their minds, people can transfer the meaning of those ideas to other people. That is what communication between people is all about—getting the meaning of thoughts one person has in his or her mind into the mind of another as clearly and accurately as possible. When people do this by transmitting words with their voices, it is called **speech communication**.

TEACH

● CURRICULAR CONNECTIONS

Writing
Ask students to write a script suitable for use in the suggestion about renewing a prescription over the phone. Some students could do the prescription renewal activity using the written script and some could speak spontaneously. Ask students to discuss which requests (from the written script or the spontaneous conversation) were more effective.

> *Well I'll tell you what a phone is for. It's not for looking someone in the eyeball and saying I love you.*
> —Louise Mattage

● SKILL DEVELOPMENT

15-Second Skill Opportunity
Explain to students that phone calls are part of our daily communication. Suggest that renewing a medical prescription is a common communication. Ask students to assume the role of one of the following—a parent, a doctor, or a CEO—and role-play the phone request. Compare phone communications with face-to-face speech.

Feedback
Other students should guess which role the student has played in the activity above and explain how they identified the role. Discuss the typical communication patterns of parents, professionals, and business people. Suggest that students also have some common communication patterns and discuss those in class.

What Is Communication? 7

How Is Speech Communication Used in Everyday Life?

You have probably heard and used the word *communication* many times, but have you ever thought about the many different ways people communicate through speech every day? Take time now to follow a typical high-school student through one day's activities.

6:45 a.m.	Awakes to a radio-alarm clock; listens to news, weather report, two commercials, and two musical recordings while getting ready for school.
7:15 a.m.	Eats breakfast; makes plans for baby-sitting that evening for younger sister while parents attend League of Women Voters' meeting to hear speeches by mayoral candidates.
7:30 a.m.	Leaves for school; meets new classmate on corner and describes school to him.
7:50 a.m.	Arrives at school; introduces friends to new classmate before directing him to his homeroom.
8:00 a.m.	School starts; listens to announcements over the public-address system; attends class where English teacher explains homonyms; watches a movie about the presidency of Theodore Roosevelt; takes a Spanish grammar test.
12:00 noon	Eats lunch in cafeteria with friends.
12:30 p.m.	Attends gym class and listens to instruction on the rules of volleyball; has conference with guidance counselor about next year's schedule; receives advice from art teacher on how to improve posters being made by class to advertise school play; conducts an experiment that demonstrates osmosis in science class.
3:00 p.m.	Attends school newspaper staff meeting to plan layout of next edition.
4:30 p.m.	Walks home with friend; stops to buy CD heard on radio that morning.
5:30 p.m.	Arrives home; calls classmate to plan oral report on the causes of lead poisoning; calls family doctor to make appointment to interview her on number of cases of lead poisoning she has treated over the years.
6:00 p.m.	Walks dog, eats dinner, takes out trash.
7:30 p.m.	Listens to parents give instructions on when sister should be put to bed and where they can be reached in an emergency.
8:00 p.m.	Reads sister a story about astronauts before putting her to bed.
8:30 p.m.	Does homework.
9:30 p.m.	Watches television before getting ready for bed.

TEACH

> **"The mind is like a TV set—when it goes blank, it's a good idea to turn off the sound."**
>
> — Communication Briefings

● **ASSESSMENT STRATEGY**

You could tape the role-played requests to renew the prescriptions and play them back to the class. Ask students to evaluate each in terms of clarity and tone. The evaluations could be written or oral.

● **SKILL DEVELOPMENT**

Active Listening
Ask students how a pharmacist listens to the request over the phone to renew a prescription. Most will notice that the pharmacist will take notes or use a memo pad. Have students write and design a pad that pharmacists could use to record the essential information when renewing a prescription. As an alternative, some students could do this as a computer activity and write and design a screen to record the essential information.

● **SKILL APPLICATION**

Phone Calls
Ask students to imagine that they have to call their parent's doctor to report a very high fever and request a prescription. Their parent is too sick to make the call personally. Discuss what information they should try to get from the parent to anticipate the questions of the doctor. What information and preparation will they need for this call?

---

8   CHAPTER 1   How Communication Affects Your Life

ACTIVITY

Daily Communication

Throughout this course, you will be keeping a speech notebook in which you will record ideas, thoughts, and feelings about how you communicate. Here is your first activity to begin your notebook.

Write down your own schedule for a typical day following the example on page 7. Identify all your activities that involve communication. Estimate the number of hours per day that you spend using some form of communication.

Communication played a large part in this student's day. Your life is also filled with communication situations. Actually, communication is so constant and widespread, you cannot escape its influence. Whenever you are awake and in the presence of others, you are communicating. Even though you may not be speaking to others, your appearance, eyes, and movements all represent communication.

● **WHAT TYPES OF SPEECH COMMUNICATION ARE THERE?**

The events in the life of the typical student given in the last section are all examples of **interpersonal communication.** You also communicate when alone, through a kind of inward talking to yourself called **intrapersonal communication.** This book is specifically about interpersonal communication—talk that takes place between two or more human beings. You will find that many different types of interpersonal communication exist.

One-To-One Communication

One-to-one communication involves talking with one other person. Included here are face-to-face conversations, telephone conversations, and interviews. Usually the sender and receiver switch roles often during one-to-one communication. The student whose day was described in the previous section was engaging in this type of communication when telling a new classmate about the school and when conferring with the guidance counselor. If you study the list of events, you will undoubtedly find many other examples of one-to-one communication in the student's day. Chapter 4 explores this very important type of communication in more detail.

TEACH

● **EXTENSION**

Committee and club meetings are a fact of adult life. Ask students to describe a recent club meeting they attended. Discuss how future club meetings could be improved. Identify strategies for improving group communications.

● **SKILL APPLICATION**

Media Literacy
Have students give examples of the best and the worst public communicators they have heard on television. Identify the criteria they use to judge the best and the worst. You could begin a chart on the chalkboard using the labels "Good Communicators" and "Bad Communicators." Invite students to add to the descriptions of each. Students could add to their portfolio products by developing "Eagle" and "Turkey" awards for the best and worst public communicators. Guide students to identify criteria they use to judge public communicators.

What Types of Speech Communication Are There?   **9**

Group communication includes planning meetings and gatherings for discussion of issues that are of mutual concern.

Group Discussion

Group discussion is a second type of interpersonal communication. It involves three or more people with a common purpose. The purpose may be to solve a common problem, to make a decision, or to answer a question that interests all the members of the group. Each member of a group generally has an opportunity to communicate.

Group communication includes such things as committee meetings, conferences, and workshops. Most group discussions take place in fairly small groups of fewer than fifteen members. The student you read about took part in a group discussion when plans were made for baby-sitting. A review of the student's day will uncover a number of other examples of group discussion. Group discussion is widely used because it offers one of the most effective ways of reaching decisions. Chapter 5 will explore this type of communication in depth. Later on, Chapters 13 and 14 will deal with *debate* and *parliamentary procedure*.

Public Communication

Public communication is a type of interpersonal communication in which one or more people communicate with an audience. A typical example of public communication is **public speaking**. At least since the

9

TEACH

> **SUBSTITUTE TEACHER TIP**
>
> On the chalkboard write teachers, attorneys, preachers, and politicians. Ask students to provide examples for each category. Ask students to role-play how members in each category would introduce themselves at a school board meeting. Discuss differences in their styles of public speaking.

● **LEARNING STYLES**

Cooperative Learning

Organize four groups to represent each of the four types of communication: 1) one-to-one; 2) group; 3) public; and 4) mass. Each group could identify a portfolio project that would demonstrate each process of communication visually or audibly.

● **ACTIVITY**

Ask students to prepare a bedtime story or a library story hour presentation for small children. Encourage them to think of how to use distinctive voices for each of the story characters. Ask what they remember from such activities. What made them enjoyable? Ask students to provide examples of how the oral interpretation of bedtime stories became more enjoyable for the listeners. These stories could be taped and could become a portfolio product.

● **RETEACHING**

To summarize the four types of communication, you could use four pieces of poster board or newsprint with each piece labeled. Have a supply of newspapers or magazines available for students to select an article or picture that represents each type of communication and make a collage for it.

---

time of Aristotle and Isocrates, public speakers have had a powerful influence on society. Teachers, attorneys, preachers, politicians, and many others have used this form of interpersonal communication to reach large numbers of people through the spoken word. Often those who have developed their skill at public speaking have found they have become better all-around communicators. Thus, this book devotes Chapters 6 through 11 to helping you acquire the ability to use this important form of public communication. In addition, models of various types of speeches are presented in the Appendix of Speeches, which appears at the end of the book.

Two others forms of public communication are **oral interpretation of literature** and **drama.** Oral interpretation of literature is a performing-art form in which literature is read aloud to an audience. Reading a story to a young child is perhaps the simplest example of oral interpretation of literature. Drama is a performing art that uses both language and action to present a picture of human life to an audience. The number of actors can vary from one to as many as the stage will hold. Chapters 16 and 17 will deal with these forms of public communication.

Mass Communication

In **mass communication** one person or perhaps several senders communicate with a large number of listeners. Usually these listeners are not physically present when the sending takes place. Newspapers and magazines are examples of mass communication. Because this book deals with speech communication, however, the types discussed here will be those of radio and television rather than written communication. Mass communication differs from the other types of communication because the receiver can "turn off" the sender at will, often by the simple push of a button. As you know, this is seldom possible in face-to-face communication. Chapter 15 will consider radio and television in depth.

● **ACTIVITY**

Enjoyment of Speaking

Hold an informal class discussion in which class members tell which of the four types of speech communication they most *enjoy* taking part in, and why. Remember, you are a participant in communication when you are the listener as well as when you are the speaker. In the case of mass communication, most of us participate almost exclusively as listeners.

APPLY

● MOTIVATION

Students will be aware of many ethics issues that affect students in the classroom. To begin the discussion, you might describe a story involving a high school academic decathlon coach and his team that prepared for national competition. The school team scored very well in the test, but later it was discovered that the coach had secured a copy of the test answers and helped the team perform well by cheating. Ask students what they think about the responsibilities of the teacher and team members and if one is more responsible than the other. Have students suggest appropriate strategies for dealing with the coach and the team.

● LEARNING STYLES

Multicultural Learning

You could invite small groups of students to discuss how various cultures would perceive the responsibilities of students on the academic decathlon team to communicate unethical practices in the situation described above. Encourage students to explore the differences, if any, in the male-female communication patterns.

● SKILL APPLICATION

Citizens Speak Out

Invite small groups of students to role-play a situation where one of them witnesses another student distributing an answer key to an important test before the exam. Each student in the group should be given the opportunity to speak to the student involved. Discuss the responsibility of the individual to speak out in an effective way in the face of unethical practices.

ETHICALLY SPEAKING

Ethics in Communication

As you make your way through this textbook, learning to communicate *effectively*, it will also be important for you to learn to communicate *ethically*. The ethics of communication is a concept that is difficult to define. It relates to considerations of what's *fair and unfair, right and wrong;* it means communicating in a way that conforms to high moral standards. When you communicate ethically, you not only get your ideas and opinions across to your listeners, but you do so in a way that does not violate the rights or sensitivities of others, does not misrepresent or distort the facts, does not mislead or influence your listeners on the basis of flimsy or one-sided arguments.

A variety of communication situations—in this class and in other communication activities—might raise ethical questions or present ethical dilemmas. When you use other people's ideas and information, do you always need to give them credit? When you are trying to persuade others to agree with your position, do you need to give equal time to opposing positions? When you hear someone spreading false information, is it necessary to challenge their facts or should you mind your own business? Is it acceptable to present information in a way that makes the most forceful argument even if it slightly colors the truth? These are the kinds of ethical questions you will face as you seek to cultivate communication skills that are both effective and ethical. From time to time throughout this textbook we will examine issues of this nature in a feature called *Ethically Speaking*.

In ethical communication, you get your ideas across to listeners without violating their rights, without misrepresentation, and without misleading them.

TEACH

SUBSTITUTE TEACHER TIP

Organize teams to work on the chapter project (see p. 27) or to prepare a three-minute speech about the benefits of free speech.

● **LINKS TO PAST LEARNING**

Ask students who have seen the movie *River Wild* to identify the benefits of signing. Have them think about the situations when speech communication is not a benefit.

● **MOTIVATION**

You could tell students that the one who asks the best question in class today will be exempt from doing a homework assignment. Then discuss how the class could judge the skill of asking "good" questions and emphasize that there are no "dumb" or "bad" questions in class.

AMAZING FACTS!

The First Amendment to the Constitution, which guarantees American citizens freedom of speech, was ratified in 1791. In those days, citizens were those men who owned property and had an education. Women and many others were excluded from citizenship and voting.

> ❝Praise does wonders for the sense of hearing.❞
> —Bits & Pieces

CHAPTER 1 How Communication Affects Your Life

● **WHAT ARE THE BENEFITS OF SPEECH COMMUNICATION?**

You've undoubtedly heard the expression "So-and-so just speaks to hear himself talk." Though there may be some tendency for everyone to do this at times, people usually use speech as a tool to gain very important benefits. What are some of these benefits?

You Learn by Communicating

One reason people use speech is to learn. Almost from the moment children learn to speak, they are asking questions. Teachers could not teach if they were not allowed to speak, and students could not learn if they were not allowed to listen and ask questions. If you give directions to someone about how to build a bookcase, that is teaching for you and learning for the other person. Both teaching and learning require speech-communication skills.

You Make Decisions by Communicating

Speech is important in helping people make decisions. Though many daily decisions may be labeled as "personal," arriving at a great number of them depends on speaking with others. You may make a "personal decision" to play basketball on the school team, but that decision might partly depend on a discussion with the coach. You may be trying to make up your own mind about whether to see a particular film but you might first wish to get advice from a friend. Many of your daily decisions demand tact and skill as a speaker.

Group decisions make ever greater demands on a person's ability to use speech communication. Representatives of labor and management are called upon to display their finest skills in speaking around a bargaining table. Members of juries must often use speech to convince one another of the guilt or innocence of the accused. If you are asked to plan a school talent show or to work on the yearbook staff, your speaking skills and those of the rest of your group may largely determine the success or failure of that talent show or yearbook.

Decisions in government also involve communication. A city council, like Congress, holds debates and committee meetings on issues. The President has discussions with Cabinet members and other advisors to decide what policies to adopt. Officials of city, state, and national government make speeches to keep people informed. Citizens informed about problems, then speak freely about them in order to affect the actions of their elected officials. The First Amendment of the

- **EXTENSION**

The class could attend or ask to video a meeting of the local government. Review the video in class and/or discuss the speech styles reflected in the meeting. Ask students to develop criteria to evaluate the speech performance of the government officials.

> *"It's all that the young can do for the old, to shock them and keep them up to date."*
> —George Bernard Shaw

Constitution of the United States guarantees such freedom of speech. With freedom, however, comes the responsibility to exercise it wisely. The freedom to say what you think does not give you the right to distort the truth or to harm others by your words. It does, however, give you the chance to try to persuade others to share your views and to reach the decisions you favor.

You Find Pleasure in Communicating

Another important use of speech is for pleasure. Human beings enjoy good conversation and the company of others. Psychological studies have shown that people need to interact with others to remain healthy and happy. The wider your experiences are and the better your skill at relating them, the more enjoyable you can be as a conversationalist. Whether face-to-face or over the telephone, good conversation can be one of life's most enjoyable pastimes.

Your Future Depends on Communicating

Speech communication skills are vital to your future. Learning is likely to continue throughout your life. Though you may not "learn something new every day," you probably will average that much during your lifetime. In learning, both in and out of school, communication is the key tool. Lee Iacocca, the dynamic former chairman of Chrysler Corporation, has said: "The most important thing I learned in school was how to communicate....You can have brilliant ideas, but if you can't get them across, your brains won't get you anywhere."

You are bound to spend a major portion of your adult working life communicating with others. You may not become involved in all forms of speech communication, but you will certainly be engaged in some of them. How well you succeed in communicating may have a great deal to do with how happy and successful you are in your future career.

Accurate directions, instructions, and information must often be communicated through the spoken word. Directions explaining how to perform a task or instructions about new methods and equipment require the giving and receiving of correct information by word of mouth.

In some jobs, speech communication is required to convince others. Salespeople must be persuasive in promoting their product or service. Managers must be capable of motivating their workers verbally. Elected officials must constantly convince the public that they are adequately doing their job.

- **SKILL DEVELOPMENT**

Decision by Committee
Four groups of students could represent the interests of the freshman, sophomore, junior, and senior classes to decide whether four credits of math/science should be required for graduation. You could select other topics of schoolwide interest. Each group should prepare a three-minute presentation for their position on the issue. Each group casts a vote. In the event of a tie, the teacher's vote could be the tie-breaker.

TEACH

> ❝The most important thing I learned in school was how to communicate.❞
>
> —Lee Iacocca

● ASSESSMENT STRATEGY

Students could make a checklist of five items that represent important characteristics of good speech communication. Then they could evaluate their own performance as a speech communicator. After the evaluation, they could target one characteristic they want to improve in the coming week. This checklist could be placed in their portfolios and their weekly progress charted.

● LEARNING STYLES

Limited English Proficiency

Ask students to provide directions from school to their homes for a stranger in town. The stranger is unfamiliar with your neighborhood and is not fluent with your language. Have students practice giving oral directions. Then ask them to write the directions. Discuss whether they prefer getting oral or written directions to an unfamiliar place.

● SKILL DEVELOPMENT

🕐 15-Second Skill Opportunity

Ask students to imagine that they want to call to invite someone to go to a movie this weekend. Have them think about what they will say on the phone in the first 15 seconds of that conversation. Ask for volunteers to stand and role-play those first 15 seconds on the phone.

On the Job

Discuss the Menninger Clinic study and ask students if they think they know anyone who has lost a job because of ineffective communication skills. Survey the number of students who have jobs. Ask students with part-time jobs how they get feedback on the quality of work they perform. Discuss ways students could ask to receive feedback from their supervisors. Various situations could be role-played.

---

14   CHAPTER 1   How Communication Affects Your Life

Communication skills—both clear speaking and careful listening—are critical to success in virtually every professional field.

Studies conducted by the Menninger Clinic discovered that 70 percent of the workers who lose their jobs do so because they fail to communicate clearly, not because they do not have the technical knowledge to perform their work. In another study over a thousand people were asked to evaluate the importance of training in speech communication for themselves. Included in the group were accountants, homemakers, unskilled laborers, sales clerks, and professional people. Seventy-five percent of the group responded that skill in speaking was important or essential to their work. Ninety percent of the executives interviewed said speech training was particularly important to them.

Business and industry are realizing more every day the importance of having employees who are skilled communicators. Most professional people such as attorneys, clergy, doctors, and teachers must use speech extensively in their work. Unless you, too, develop skill in speaking, your success in life may be severely limited.

Careful listening is just as important to your future as is clear speaking. In a recent survey, California business leaders were asked what skills they looked for in college graduates seeking jobs. Almost 80 percent placed listening skills in their top five choices. A majority reported that listening was the most important skill for those seeking employment.

TEACH

● **RETEACHING**

Students could work in pairs to take turns asking and answering the question: "What are the benefits of speech communication?"

● **CURRICULAR CONNECTIONS**

Math
For each career listed in the feature, ask students to identify how many hours in a 40-hour work week they think would be spent in oral communication and in written communication. This information could be charted in a bar graph.

SUBSTITUTE TEACHER TIP

Students could role-play a job interview process in which some students demonstrate poor listening skills and others demonstrate good listening skills. Discuss why a majority of employers valued the importance of good listening skills.

"You don't need an M.B.A. from Harvard to figure out how to lose money."

—Royal Little

● **LEARNING STYLES**

Multicultural Learning
Discuss whether men or women are better communicators in the workplace. Encourage examples and help students relate generalizations to specifics and avoid stereotypes. Ask if men or women are better communicators on the phone and discuss students' examples and reasons.

Cooperative Learning
Different groups of students could gather information about careers students are most likely to pursue in the 21st century. The importance of global communication in those careers should be explored.

What Are the Benefits of Speech Communication? **15**

Careers

The following is a list of some of the careers for which communication skills are important.

Auctioneer	Narrator
Audiologist	News reporter
Children's librarian	Police officer
City manager	Public information officer
Clergy	Public relations representative
Clinical psychologist	Receptionist
Commentator	Salesperson
County agricultural agent	Sales manager
Director	Social worker
Directory assistance operator	Speech pathologist
Disc jockey	Speech writer
Drama teacher	Sports announcer
Employment interviewer	Stage manager
Fund raiser	Survey worker (Interviewer)
Hotel front-office clerk	Teacher
Interpreter	Training representative
Labor relations manager	Travel guide

In each chapter of this book you will find a Career Close-up. Notice, as you read them, the great number of careers that are connected by the common tool of speech communication.

● **ACTIVITY**

Speech and Careers
In small groups, each person should present his or her career goals to the other members of the group. Mention how speech communication is important in that career.

TEACH

● MOTIVATION

Play a tape or video excerpt of a famous speech such as Martin Luther King Jr.'s "I Have a Dream" speech. (See p. 580 in the Appendix.) Discuss how hearing a speech has a different impact than merely reading a speech.

● LINKS TO PAST LEARNING

Ask students to recall "sermons" they have heard. They could provide examples from their parents or church or synagogue. Ask them to describe effective sermons.

● ENRICHMENT

For each of the characteristics identified in this section, ask students to identify its opposite. Then ask students to give examples of speakers who have each quality.

● SKILL DEVELOPMENT

Creative Thinking
Have students make a list of the eight characteristics mentioned on pp. 16–17. Then ask them to make a list of the five characteristics they think are most important in an effective speech communicator. Compare their lists. Then suggest that students rank these characteristics in order of their importance.

● WHAT MAKES AN EFFECTIVE SPEECH COMMUNICATOR?

Throughout history the people who have had the greatest impact on other people's lives have been those skilled in speaking. In the United States, Thomas Jefferson, Abraham Lincoln, Susan B. Anthony, Franklin D. Roosevelt, Eleanor Roosevelt, and Martin Luther King, Jr. were all effective communicators, able to speak with power and persuasiveness. As you have read, developing skill in speech communication is also important in your own life. What are the skills that make someone an effective communicator?

Sincerity   Effective speech communicators must be sincere. That is, they must themselves believe in what they say. Other people must believe they mean what they say in order for communication to be successful in the long run.

Knowledge   Effective speech communicators must speak knowledgeably. Whether talking in a small group meeting, giving a public speech to a large crowd, or in one-to-one conversation, speakers should know enough about the subject to make it worthwhile for people to listen. At times this requires much research and preparation on a speaker's part. At other times, little advance preparation is needed. In any case, to be an effective speaker you must be able to speak with confidence and knowledge about your subject.

Organization   Effective speech communicators must be well organized. Some speakers are like the man who jumped on a horse and rode off first in one direction then in another. The rider wound up going nowhere and it definitely confused the horse! A clear message begins with a definite purpose and proceeds in a single direction to the end.

Listening   Effective speech communicators must know how and when to listen. At least half of the oral communication process involves listening. Occasionally you may talk to yourself, but most often you expect someone to be listening when you speak. Effective communicators know they may learn more during their listening time than when they are speaking. Good listening is often neglected, but a good speaker will remember this important "flip side" of the speaking process.

Confidence   Effective speech communicators must be confident. Building confidence as a speaker and controlling stage fright are not accomplished overnight. But a course in speech, and experience in communicating with others are two of the best ways to achieve the

TEACH

● **MOTIVATION**

The number of schools and business seminars that offer courses and workshops on better communication has increased dramatically in the past decade. Use your local phone book to count the number of communication-related businesses there are in your area.

● **CURRICULAR CONNECTIONS**

Language Arts
Choosing the best words for a particular audience is a difficult task. Give students practice in proper word selection by suggesting various occasions to them. Ask them to list two or three appropriate words to use for wishing a grandparent a happy birthday, asking for permission to use the family car, or congratulating a friend on a great test score.

What Makes an Effective Speech Communicator?

needed confidence. Chapter 6 points out a number of ways in which you can control stage fright and build confidence for speaking.

Language Effective speech communicators must use language carefully. A speaker's choice of words can make the difference in whether or not the message is received and understood as the speaker intends it to be. Learning to choose the best words to suit a particular audience and occasion is one of the most difficult tasks for a speaker. It is also what separates great speakers from the rest.

Nonverbal Communication Effective speech communicators must make good use of nonverbal communication. Speakers "say" a great deal with the tone of their voice, their body movements, and their eyes. Even clothes and grooming communicate to others. Good communicators are aware of what they are communicating nonverbally as well as verbally.

Goal Setting Effective speech communicators will generally be able to reach certain goals. When an effective speaker presents information about a topic, the receivers will almost always know more about the topic after listening than they did before. If a skilled speaker tries to convince an audience to accept his or her solution to a problem, the listeners will generally be partially or fully convinced.

Effective athletic coaches are capable speech communicators. Much of their message is nonverbal.

● **SKILL DEVELOPMENT**

15-Second Skill Opportunity
Have students imagine that they coach a junior high school basketball team. The team is losing by 20 points in the 4th quarter, with 5 seconds remaining. You have called a time out. What will you tell your team in 15 seconds? Ask volunteers to deliver their pep talk to the class.

Gestures
Ask students to think of the simple word, "yes," and all the ways it can be said. Have students say the word with a specific situation in mind. Encourage them to use gestures and tone of voice to convey the meaning of the situation. Listening students could guess the circumstances surrounding the "yes."

● **LEARNING STYLES**

Limited English Proficiency
Students with limited proficiency in English could be paired with other students to develop "flashcards" with a common American expression on one side and synonyms or similar terms on the reverse side of the card. A dictionary or thesaurus could be used. For example: Side A, "Congratulations;" Side B, "You did very well!" In this way, students can learn from each other.

APPLY

● **EXTENSION**

Students could ask their parents to describe their best high school teacher and identify the characteristics that they admired most in that teacher.

● **CURRICULAR CONNECTIONS**

Language Arts
Students could survey teachers at school and ask them what communication skills they think are most important in high school teaching. Teachers could be encouraged to talk about where and how they learned those communication skills. Feature a teacher's interview. Include and display a photograph, if possible, and a quote.

● **SKILL APPLICATION**

Media Literacy
Students could conduct a class or school-wide poll to determine the students' choice for most effective teacher in the school. Have the class, or cooperative learning groups, prepare a press release for submission to the local paper. The press release could include a photo, brief biography of the teacher, and a description of the class, or school activity.

Citizens Speak Out
Ask students to imagine that they have been requested to introduce the "Teacher of the Year" to a school assembly, to which the press and community leaders have been invited. Students could write out their introduction and practice before the class.

CAREER CLOSE-UP

High School Teacher

Communication skills are basic to the teaching profession. In addition to their expertise in particular subjects, teachers constantly communicate with their students both by speaking and by listening.

High school teachers have a bachelor's degree with courses concentrating in education and their subject area. Today most teachers continue their education by attaining a master's degree.

Good high school educators have an extensive knowledge of their subject. They also teach in a clear, well-organized way so that students will understand the subject's basic facts and concepts. Because excessive use of technical terms often confuses students, teachers explain the subject matter simply and in language the student will understand.

An ability to listen is another invaluable skill for teachers. By listening and being attentive to students' ideas, misunderstandings, and problems, teachers gain the information they need to design more effective teaching strategies. Instructors communicate new ideas well by being sensitive to students' needs and learning styles.

Teachers listen actively to student comments and respond enthusiastically to student concerns and questions. In this way student and teacher communicate to attain educational goals.

Teachers are also called on to communicate with groups outside the classroom. As spokespersons for other educators, as advocates for student concerns, and as advisors or experts in their subject area, teachers continually meet the challenge to renew ideas and information through communication.

Through clear, organized presentation of the basic facts of the subject area, as well as by listening attentively and actively, teachers assist students in attaining their educational goals.

TEACH

● MOTIVATION

Pairs of students could work together to answer the nine questions. First, each should answer the questions individually, then answer the questions for his or her partner. The pairs could compare answers.

● LINKS TO PAST LEARNING

Ask students to recall a New Year's Resolution that they once made and discuss how the goal was achieved. Each student could select one of the areas mentioned in this introduction and target it as a goal for improvement.

● LEARNING STYLES

Audio Learning
Ask students to pick one of the questions asked and prepare to read it aloud for the class. The rest of the class should close their books as they listen to each question read. Ask the listeners to identify the word they heard most emphatically or distinctly after each has read a question.

At the end of each chapter you will find a checklist highlighting some important points for improving your speech communication. The checklist is a good way for you to review what you have learned in the chapter about being an effective communicator.

● WHY STUDY SPEECH COMMUNICATION?

The benefits of good speech communication are clear. It can help you learn, make decisions, enjoy yourself, and succeed in your chosen career. The eight basic skills for becoming an effective communicator, as listed on pages 16–17, are also clear. With these factors in mind, you may ask why you should take a course to practice something you have been doing every day for years? Why not just continue speaking, keeping these eight factors in mind?

The answer is that speech communication is not that simple. Many people have problems communicating with others in various situations. Note the following questions, and answer them for yourself:

- Do you sometimes have trouble choosing the best words to express your ideas?
- Have you ever spoken without preparing your remarks carefully?
- Do you ever have difficulty paying attention when others speak?
- Do people ever ask you to repeat something because they could not hear or understand what you said the first time?
- Have you ever been asked to give a speech or act in a play and refused out of timidity?
- Have some of your in-class reports over the years fallen a bit flat because of the way you presented them?
- Do you sometimes feel that your friends do not listen to what you say?
- Can you argue effectively and logically with someone?
- Do you have difficulty remembering a speaker's main points several hours after hearing a speech?

If you answered "Yes" to any of the questions listed, a speech course can help you. Perhaps you can think of other reasons for studying speech communication, as well. Even if you are already an effective speaker, improvement is always possible.

TEACH

> **SUBSTITUTE TEACHER TIP**
>
> Ask each student to stand and give name, grade level, and favorite color or song. Then discuss the fact that although each student provided the same information, some communicated better than others. Identify those characteristics that made some students better communicators than others.

● **LEARNING STYLES**

Visual Learning
Review the photos in this chapter and ask students to make a list of each one and describe the content of each communication pictured. Discuss which types of communication are most common for students and adults.

CHAPTER 1 How Communication Affects Your Life

Mastery of the basic skills of speech communication will be invaluable to you both now and in all aspects of your adult life.

This course will provide you with opportunities to practice oral communication in a variety of speaking situations. Some of them may be new to you. Interviewing, group discussion, public speaking, debating, oral interpretation of literature, and drama are among the types of situations included.

As you progress through the course, you will learn to identify your assets and your liabilities as a speech communicator. Listen carefully to your teacher's and classmates' comments. Do not assume your ways of speaking are necessarily the only ways or the best ways. Some of your methods may prove to be best. It will be reassuring to hear people say so. Other methods that you now use may not be best. This is where you can gain the most from a speech course. Make a determined effort

TEACH

● **ASSESSMENT STRATEGY**

Have students make a checklist of things they want to learn in this course. Suggest they write a list of 5-10 goals they want to achieve. Keep this checklist in their portfolios and record progress regularly. Encourage self-evaluation as well as peer and teacher evaluations.

> *Progress, man's distinctive mark alone, Not God's, and not the beasts': God is, they are; Man partly is and wholly hopes to be.*
> —Robert Browning

● **LEARNING STYLES**

Technology Tools
Ask students to think about communication tools that are currently available that might help them improve their communication skills. Then encourage their imagination by asking them to describe something that might be invented to address each of the challenges mentioned in this section.

Why Study Speech Communication? 21

Speaking effectively and logically is essential to persuasive oral communication.

to rid your speech of those habits that make you a less effective communicator. Being able to speak and being skilled at speaking are two very different things. This course can help you develop the skills you need to become a better speech communicator.

● **ACTIVITY**

Effective Speech Communication

In your speech notebook, write the eight "Effective Communicator Skill" key terms from pages 16 and 17. Next to each term, write whether or not you need to make improvements in that skill. Keep this list for review periodically in this course to check your progress.

● **ACTIVITY**

You might suggest that at the end of each speech class each student use the eight key words to evaluate their own performance as a communicator. After one week of daily evaluation, students could develop their own progress reports.

21

ASSESS

- **STUDENT PERFORMANCE COMPETENCIES**
  - Defines terms
  - Identifies benefits of speech communication
  - Lists skills of effective speech communicators
  - Understands the importance of speech

- **sca GUIDELINES**
  - Defines terms and identifies speech benefits clearly and concisely
  - Recognizes ineffective speech communications and makes appropriate adjustments
  - Provides real-life examples of the importance of speech communications

PORTFOLIO ASSESSMENT

Standard
- Completed Survey of Communication Interests
- Compiled Glossary of Speech Terms
- Completed Assignments, Quizzes, Projects, and Chapter 1 Test

Enrichment
- Bar Chart Display of Communication Time
- Turkey Awards for Worst Public Communicators
- Active Listening Activity Product (memo pad or computer screen)
- Audiotape of Children's Story

Challenge
- Written or Taped Introduction for the "Teacher of the Year" Award
- Careers in Speech Communications Job Descriptions
- Audiotape of Speech Library Selection

CHAPTER 1 REVIEW

SUMMARY

Without communication people would truly be isolated, unable to give and receive ideas. Civilization itself would be impossible.

What Is Communication? Communication is the process of sending and receiving messages to achieve understanding. When this process takes place orally, it is called speech communication. People may also communicate in writing and in nonverbal ways through gestures, movement, and dress. All aspects of your life are likely to involve communication of one form or another. Even "talking" silently to yourself is a form of communication, called intrapersonal communication.

What Types of Speech Communication Are There? Interpersonal communication (communication involving more than one person) can be divided into four different categories. One-to-one communication involves give and take between two people. Group discussion involves three or more people communicating and exchanging ideas. Public communication takes place when one or more speakers address a larger audience. Mass communication calls for one or more speakers and a very large audience, usually at a distance from the speaker. Television and radio fall into this last category. Though you will not be continually involved in all of these forms of communication, you are certain to be involved in some of them every day.

What Are the Benefits of Speech Communication? Communication is a very necessary part of learning and decision-making. It also adds enjoyment to people's lives and can play an important role in helping a person achieve success in almost any career.

What Makes an Effective Speech Communicator? Effective speech communicators must have several important skills. They must be sincere and thoroughly knowledgeable about what they are saying. They must be well organized, know how and when to listen, and be able to use language effectively. In addition, they must make good use of nonverbal communication and achieve the desired results from their audience.

ASSESS

● **ASSESSMENT STRATEGIES**

Individual Assessment
- Participates in practice activities daily or weekly
- Completes classwork
- Demonstrates knowledge of content through questions, discussion, quizzes, and Chapter 1 test
- Displays improved speech skills as targeted in this chapter

Group Assessment
- Sets and achieves goals
- Demonstrates cooperative learning activities
- Supports efforts of team and class members
- Provides encouragement and feedback to members

Why Study Speech Communication? A course in speech communication will give you a chance to practice the skills needed to become an effective speaker under the careful guidance of your teacher. A determined effort on your part will rid you of any poor speech habits you may have acquired and sharpen those positive ones you possess.

VOCABULARY

Define each term in a complete sentence.

communication
nonverbal
verbal
speech communication
intrapersonal communication
interpersonal communication
one-to-one communication
group discussion
public communication
public speaking
oral interpretation of literature
drama
mass communication

CHECKLIST

Effective Communicator Skills

1. Be sincere and say what you mean, both in words and in gestures.
2. Speak knowledgeably. Know your topic.
3. Have a clear speaking purpose.
4. Organize your thoughts.
5. Develop good listening skills.
6. Build your confidence and control stage fright.
7. Use language carefully by learning to choose the most appropriate words.
8. Use nonverbal language, such as tone of voice, body movement, and eye contact.
9. Set goals for communicating and reach them whenever it is possible.

ASSESS

● **ANSWERS**

See the Answer Key for more complete answers.

REVIEW QUESTIONS
1. Communication is the process of sending and receiving messages to achieve understanding.
2. People communicate through nonverbal means such as gestures, body language, music, art, and dance. People also communicate through writing.
3. These interpersonal communications include: *one-to-one communication, group discussion, public communication, and mass communication.*
4. The public speaker addresses the audience in person, while the mass communicator is removed from the audience in space and often in time.
5. Four goals are learning, decision-making, pleasure, and achieving success.
6. Teaching, listening, and asking questions all require speech skills.
7. Answers will vary. (1) Governments hold debates to consider various issues; (2) leaders often hold discussions with advisers; (3) government officials make speeches; (4) lawyers present arguments, ask questions, and give speeches in court; (5) jury members listen carefully to evidence and then discuss this evidence; (6) judges must listen carefully to evidence and render verbal decisions.
8. People use speech (1) to learn and to teach by asking questions and by listening, (2) to make decisions, and (3) for pleasure.
9. Answers will vary. Effective speaking is essential to lawyers, doctors, teachers, salespeople, nurses, counselors, politicians, broadcast journalists, actors, and entertainers.
10. Characteristics of an effective speaker include sincerity, knowledge, organization, listening ability, and confidence.

DISCUSSION QUESTIONS

The following code is used to designate discussion questions and activities as suitable for students of varying ability levels:
- ▼ = below average to average
- ◆ = average to above average
- ■ = all students

1. ■ You might begin discussion by using the example of heads of state embroiled in a territorial dispute who refuse to meet to settle it. Ask your students to provide other examples of communication resulting from a refusal to communicate. Discussion should lead naturally to other aspects involving appearance, clothing, and body language. Discuss the impact of wearing of uniforms.
2. ◆ Discuss the communication skills required in specific jobs. Point our that in many jobs all four kinds of communication are important. Students who have held jobs on their own will be able to provide numerous examples of situations in which problems arose because of poor communication skills.
3. ▼ Make sure that students understand that much of the time in a speech class will be spent in performance activities. Make sure that students understand the importance of courtesy toward others in the class. Students must listen carefully to one another, avoid destructive criticism, and generally work toward establishing an atmosphere in which all students can feel at ease.

24

CHAPTER 1 REVIEW

REVIEW QUESTIONS

1. Define communication.
2. Name several other forms of communication that people often use besides speech communication.
3. Name four general kinds of interpersonal communication.
4. Describe two major differences between public communication and mass communication.
5. Name four important goals that people can achieve through the use of speech communication.
6. Describe how speech communication relates to learning.
7. Give three reasons why speech communication is important in government and courts of law.
8. Name some ways in which people can make use of speech communication.
9. Name several careers in which skill in speaking is essential.
10. List several characteristics necessary to an effective speech communicator.

? DISCUSSION QUESTIONS

1. A well-known saying states, "You cannot NOT communicate." Have a class discussion focusing on the message of this saying. Think about these questions as you discuss: Do we reveal our feelings unintentionally? How does *not* talking to someone reveal our feelings? What impressions do we make on others by our personal appearance, our clothes, or our posture?
2. The Menninger Clinic study and the survey of California business leaders both point to the importance of speaking and listening skills on the job. As a class, cite five specific kinds of interaction that occur in business in which speaking skills are critical. Then cite five specific ways that listening skills are vital. Compile a list of ways in which you believe employees could lose their jobs because of poor communication skills.
3. Take part in a class discussion on the topic "How will this speech class be different from most of my other classes?" Give consideration to the role of your teacher as well as your own role in this class. Will each of you behave differently than in most other classes? To what extent is it important to know the members of this class well In what ways will you learn information about subjects other than speech communication theory?

4. There are a number of differences between conversation, group discussion, and public speaking, on the one hand, and oral interpretation and drama on the other. In a discussion with your classmates, identify these differences. Which have to do with the different characteristics of each type of communication? Which have to do mainly with people's attitudes toward them? Describe any elements that these types of communication have in common. In what ways are they alike?

5. As a class, discuss ways in which students can affect others through communication. Focus first on the immediate environment—the classroom. Then expand the discussion to include other people and situations, both in and out of school. Discuss the possible benefits to you and others that might result from improved communication skills.

CRITICAL THINKING

1. Analysis In small groups, review the skills of an effective communicator. Make certain that everyone in the group understands the exact definition of each of the criteria. Then answer the following questions: Which skill is most easily developed? Which skill is most difficult to develop? Which skill is easiest to observe? Which skill is most difficult to assess? Which skill should receive the most attention in this class? Why? As each group reports to the class, try to reach a consensus.

2. Synthesis History has been changed by great communicators. Discuss with your classmates various figures from U.S. history who used effective communication skills to alter the course our country followed. Give specific names and events based on your knowledge of history. Discuss why communication skills were able to affect events.

ACTIVITIES

In-Class

1. In pairs, role-play a conversation using as little nonverbal communication as possible. Then, as a class, discuss these questions: How difficult is it to omit gestures, facial expressions, etc.? How much of your message is lost to the receiver? Did you experience misunder-

---

ASSESS

4. Explain that the steps in comparison and contrast are as follows: (a) List the characteristics. (b) Look for similarities and differences. Advanced students might be asked to classify the types of speech communication in several ways, according to number of speakers, size of audience, allowance for feedback, and so forth.
5. Have students begin by listing important people in their lives— teachers, friends, relatives, employers, and others. Ask students to think about ways in which they might improve their communication with important people in their lives.

CRITICAL THINKING

1. **Analysis** Ask students to keep their books open to pages 16 and 17 as they discuss these questions. Each group should arrive at a group decision about each question, first by holding a brief discussion, and then by taking a vote. One student in each group should act as group leader, directing the course of discussion. Emphasize the importance of establishing an agenda for a group discussion.
2. **Synthesis** Students could gather information about the communication skills of the following historical figures:

   Abraham Lincoln
   Susan B. Anthony
   John F. Kennedy
   Franklin D. Roosevelt
   Dr. Martin Luther King, Jr.

   Tell students to use as many sources of information as possible, including history textbooks and encyclopedia articles.

   Discuss which contemporary public figures are the most effective communicators and why.

ACTIVITIES

In-Class

1. Students should be instructed to keep their arms to the sides and to maintain blank expressions on their faces. Most students will find these instructions difficult to carry out because of the unconscious nature of most nonverbal communication. When students do slip into nonverbal signals, discuss the meaning of these signals.

ASSESS

2. Most students will have heard speeches delivered in school and at least portions of speeches delivered on television or radio.
3. Ask students to take notes during the speaker's presentation. Students should also jot down questions to ask after the presentation.
4. Explain the division of a speech into introduction, body, and conclusion. Ask students to prepare a written introduction and conclusion to their speeches. If you wish to do so, have each speaker discuss one career instead of three.

Out-of-Class
1. You may also wish to have members of the speech squad visit your class to explain what they do and to perform.
2. Ask students to deliver short speeches to report their findings.
3. Have students reenact these nonverbal signals in class and ask other students to interpret the signals.
4. Explain the following basic interviewing skills: (1) preparing a list of questions beforehand, (2) setting up an appointment, (3) treating the interviewee with courtesy, and (4) recording the responses.
5. Listening to a conversation between two other people is acceptable only if the two other people are aware that such listening is taking place.

CHAPTER 1 REVIEW

standing on the part of the receiver? How did the feedback differ from times when you used nonverbal signals?

2. In small groups, discuss what you think about public speaking. Have you heard a famous person speak? Have you done any public speaking? Would you like to be a public speaker? If so, what kind of public speaker interests you: a politician, a diplomat, a teacher, etc.? Take notes in your notebook on what you learn from your group.

3. Invite to class a popular radio disc jockey or local television personality. Ask him or her to share information about the speech training that is required for a career in mass communication.

4. Give a short speech in class in which you identify three careers that seem attractive to you at this time. Describe the speaking and listening skills that will be required in each career.

Out-of-Class

1. Attend a meeting of the forensics squad of your school. Observe their preparation, and talk with members to discover extracurricular contests that are available in public speaking, debate, oral interpretation, and drama. What differences exist in types of performance? What differences can you discern in type of preparation? Which activity appeals to you most? Why? What do you think these students will gain from competitive speech activities? What carry-over from these activities do you see in the adult world?

2. Attend a courtroom trial, a session of the U.S. Congress, a meeting of your state legislature, your city council, your local school committee, or any other governing body and report briefly to the class about your visit. What forms of speech communication were used? Which communicators did you think were most effective? Why? Present your findings to the class.

3. Make a list of as many types of nonverbal communication as you can think of. For one hour of the day, focus your attention on the many ways that you and others are using nonverbal signals. Take notes, jotting down your observations in your notebook.

4. Choose a career from the *Careers* list on page 15 or any other career that interests you. Interview someone in that career. Ask that person how important communication skills have been in that field, what kind of special training in communications is necessary or would have been helpful to him or her. Prepare a brief report for the class.

5. Observe closely one-to-one conversations both out of school and in school. Jot down notes in your notebook on how often the participants switch roles from sender to receiver.

6. Practice one-to-one communication by phoning a friend or by speaking face-to-face with a classmate or family member. Do you see room for improvement in your communication skills? Make an entry in your notebook about your experience and self-evaluation.

CHAPTER PROJECT

Form four groups in class, as follows: (a) one-to-one communication, (b) group discussion, (c) public communication, and (d) mass communication. Each group should then clip pictures from magazines showing people engaging in the type of speech communication your group is responsible for. The group task will be to lay out and design an attractive poster collage depicting the assigned area of communication. Display these posters in the classroom.

ASSESS

6. You may wish to have students record several such communication experiences over a period of a week or so.

CHAPTER PROJECT
- Have each group use a brainstorming technique to develop a list of situations, that involve the type of communication that the group is to research.

PREPARE

● CHAPTER PLANNER

Day 1	Day 2	Day 3	Day 4	Day 5
Prepare	Prepare	Prepare	Prepare	Prepare
Teach	Teach	Teach	Teach	Teach
Assess	Assess	Assess	Assess	Assess
Sub. Teacher Tip *p. 33*		Sub. Teacher Tip *p. 38*	Sub. Teacher Tip *p. 46*	Sub. Teacher Tip *p. 47*

● CHAPTER OVERVIEW

This chapter examines the following topics:
- An Overview of the Communication Process *p. 30*
- Deciding to Communicate *p. 32*
- Choosing Symbols *p. 35*
- Vocalizing *p. 44*
- Reception *p. 47*
- Feedback *p. 50*

▽ PORTFOLIO PRODUCTS

Individual Projects
- Glossary of Speech Terms
- Collection of International Symbols
- American Sign Language Demonstration
- Chapter 2 Portfolio Products

Group Projects
- Taped Speech
- Role-play Communication Scenes
- Nonverbal Signals
- Diagram of Shared Experiences
- Feedback Checklist
- Flow Chart: Anatomy of Speech

● sca GUIDELINES

- Produces and responds to spoken English and nonverbal forms of communication
- Uses appropriate volume and intonation when asking questions
- Uses nonverbal cues to indicate understanding or lack of understanding in the classroom

CHAPTER 2

The Process of Communication

When you have completed this chapter you should be able to:

● Explain the basic elements of the communication process.

● Describe the two functions of memory and the role of thinking in the communication process.

● State how the importance of shared interests relates to the communication process.

● Explain the nature of nonverbal communication and define the general categories of nonverbal symbols.

TEACH

● **LINKS TO PAST LEARNING**

You could write on the chalkboard "Think Before You Speak" and ask students to give examples when they wish they had followed this advice.

AMAZING FACTS!

Few people are able to speak articulately at a sustained rate of more than 300 words per minute.

● **ACTIVITY**

You could award the "class brain for a day" a visible symbol of that honor such as a medal or button. You could increase the incentive by excusing the "brain" from doing a homework assignment or portfolio project.

The Process of Communication 29

● **ACTIVITY**

Steps in the Communication Process

This chapter describes five basic steps that make up the process of human communication. Before you read further in the chapter, close your books, and see which class member can first predict what those steps are. When you think you know all five steps, raise your hand. Whoever can first describe all five aloud is "class brain for a day."

Now that you have begun thinking about the steps in the communication process, recall for a moment a recent conversation you have had with someone. It may have been with a classmate, a friend, a teacher, or one of your parents. No matter who the other person was, or what the topic, both of you talked automatically. You concentrated on the meanings being exchanged and probably never gave a thought to the process you were using. However, if you had some way of recalling how you felt when you first learned to talk at about age two, you would be much more aware of how difficult and complex the communication process really is. In fact, it is so complex, it's amazing that humans communicate with one another at all.

The successful exchange of ideas is critical to a study session with a classmate as well as to a committee meeting of a school organization.

29

TEACH

> **"Words are what hold society together."**
> —Stuart Chase

● LEARNING STYLES

Kinesic Learning
Ask students to pantomime the request to use the family car this evening. Students could think of the gestures and symbols they will use repeatedly to represent the key elements in the request, such as *car, please, gas, time.*

Limited English Proficiency
Encourage students to make a list of the English words they want to use to request the use of the family car for the evening. These students could write out the request in the language they often use at home. Then, with the help of the vocabulary they identified above, they could write out the request in English. Have these students practice with students who use English proficiently at home.

CHAPTER 2 The Process of Communication

As you read this chapter you will explore the process of communication. You might ask, "Why should I analyze something I do so naturally? If I concentrate too hard on my speech, I might wind up not being able to speak at all!" There is not much danger of this happening, and a great deal can be gained from looking closely at the communication process. Even though you communicate naturally and automatically, examining each part of the process can help you see how your personal communication skills can be improved.

● AN OVERVIEW OF THE COMMUNICATION PROCESS

Communication is the process we humans use to achieve understanding. When you want others to understand what is in your mind, you choose "words" to form your message, then "say" the message to your intended receiver. The receiver must "read" the message as it comes in if he or she is to understand the ideas you are trying to get across. Then the receiver reacts to your ideas. Often the whole process takes place in a few seconds, but a great deal happens in those few seconds! Let's take a step-by-step look at the process.

The process begins when you decide to communicate. Let's imagine you want to ask your dad for the use of the family car this evening. You

The communication process involves the sender, or "sayer," and the receiver, or "reader," of the message.

have a purpose you want to achieve that requires you to talk with your dad. You will probably spend some time mentally rehearsing what you will say to your father in order to achieve your purpose of getting the car. When you actually begin speaking with him, you are changing the communication purpose in your mind into a message that your dad can see and hear. Your message consists of symbols, such as words, which stand for the ideas you wish to get across. Of course, the symbols are not the things they represent. Rather they are a code through which you can bring ideas such as "the family car" to your dad's mind as you talk with him. Words are by no means the only symbols we use to communicate either. As we shall see later in this chapter, nonverbal symbols often make up more of our message than words do.

While you are in the role of **sender**, your dad is the **receiver** of your message. If you ever hope to get your request to use the car across to him, he must also take an active part in the communication process. His first job is to interpret the symbols you are sending. This involves more than his simply hearing you. He must actively listen to your message and constantly turn your word-symbols into meaningful ideas in his mind. Then, once he understands your message, he must react to it in some way. His reaction is known as **feedback**, and is an important step in the communication process. Once he has decoded the message, he can't help but react—he is bound to provide you with some form of feedback. Even if he does not say a word in response and just sits there staring at you, that in itself is a reaction. Then it's up to you to interpret his reaction and decide whether you wish to start another cycle of communication in response.

If we put all this together, we might say that *communication is the process by which a sender encodes a message using symbols which a receiver then decodes to achieve understanding. The receiver then reacts using feedback to let the sender know how well the message has been received. The whole purpose of this process is to achieve greater understanding.*

Feedback always occurs during the communication process.

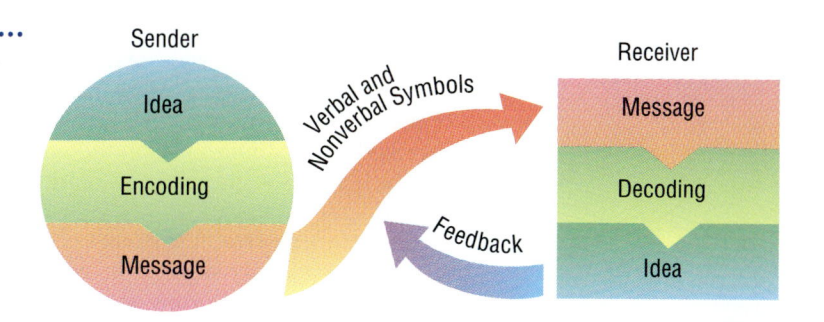

Sender: Idea, Encoding, Message
Verbal and Nonverbal Symbols
Receiver: Message, Decoding, Idea
Feedback

TEACH

● **SKILL DEVELOPMENT**

15-Second Skill Opportunity
Organize the class into two groups: one to role-play parents; the other, students. Ask each in the student group to pick one of the following to ask for the car: *"I need the car tonight,"* or, *"May I use the car tonight to go to the movie with Pat?"* or *"I wanna use the car."* Ask each in the parent group to select one of the following responses: *"Are you crazy?"* or *"Sure,"* or *"We are going to visit Uncle Joe."* Give pairs of students 15 seconds to send, receive, and provide feedback, or respond, to the request.

● **LEARNING STYLES**

Audio Learning
Have students repeat the sentence they choose from the selections given above with several variations of tone, volume, and gestures. These variations could be tape recorded and played back for evaluations.

Visual Learning
Write the important words *sender, receiver, message,* and *feedback* on the chalkboard. Some students might want to illustrate this process in a cartoon or diagram that uses the same labels.

TEACH

AMAZING FACTS!
The memory is an amazing thing. Consider Mamoon Tariq (from Pakistan) who memorized a deck of shuffled cards in 44.62 seconds at the Florida Institute of Technology on June 14, 1993!

● ACTIVITY
Use the Activity to discuss how the hearing impaired are affected by the communication process. Some students might volunteer to wear ear muffs or ear plugs for some time in class or while watching TV at home. Discuss the experience. Identify various electronic devices that assist the hearing impaired.

● LEARNING STYLES

Beyond the Classroom
You might invite a hearing impaired person or speech therapist to talk to the class about how hearing difficulties are diagnosed. Discuss the various compensation strategies for hearing impaired people.

Cooperative Learning
Two groups of students could work to learn about the memory function of humans and computers. Each group could list those functions and compare information. Each group could decide on a portfolio project to represent this information.

● SKILL DEVELOPMENT

Creative Thinking
Ask students to estimate the amount of time they spend listening to music every day. This information could be recorded in the form of a chart or graph. Then ask students to try to imagine a world without music. Discuss how our lives would be different and encourage students to think of ways we could compensate if we did not have music.

32

32　CHAPTER 2　The Process of Communication

● ACTIVITY

Ineffective Speech Communication
Volunteer to step in front of the class and state an idea—any idea that can be expressed in just three or four sentences. While relating your idea, intentionally use some part of the communication process poorly. For example, you might use poor articulation or you might speak so softly as to be difficult to hear in the back of the room. When you finish stating your idea, ask the class to identify what part of the communication process was ineffective.

Now, let's look at each step in the communication process in more detail. As you read through the rest of the chapter, remember that having a clear understanding of how you communicate can improve your personal skill as a communicator.

● DECIDING TO COMMUNICATE

Communication begins with an idea in your head which you decide you want to get into someone else's head. When you think of communication, you may first think of moving mouths, but that is only one step in the communication process. Before a person's mouth can move with meaning, the person's brain must have decided what ideas the mouth should express. You may have heard the expression "Be certain your brain is in gear before putting your mouth in motion." Actually humans *must* have their brains in gear before they can even begin to speak. Thus, the first step in communicating with another consists of having ideas in your head.

The Two Functions of Memory

Where do people get ideas? From infancy you begin collecting bits of information through your senses—sight, hearing, touch, smell, and taste. Human brains are like computers in many respects. As bits of information are received by the brain through the senses, they are put into the **memory**, which serves as the brain's storage bin, for later use in communicating.

But a person's memory differs from a computer's memory. For one thing, a computer can only store in its memory items that are intentionally put there. A human's memory will store items of information

Deciding to Communicate   33

picked up both consciously and subconsciously. Have you ever done something or said something that later puzzled you? You could not figure out why or how you could have done or said that particular thing. Undoubtedly, at that moment, information or experience from your past, which had been stored in your memory, influenced what you did or said.

A second major difference between computer and human memories is that a computer can recall any information entered into its memory, no matter how much material has been entered or how long ago. A human, on the other hand, can often experience what is called "loss of memory." Actually, what people experience is a loss of recall ability rather than a loss of memory. Have you ever *known* there was a joke you wanted to insert in a conversation but couldn't remember how it started or how the punch line went? That joke was stored in your memory, but you simply could not recall it at that moment. Later, when the pressure to recall the joke was gone, you probably remembered it with ease. Knowing that everyone experiences this difficulty at times can make you more tolerant of yourself and others who experience this problem during communication.

In addition to storing information and experiences, your brain also stores the words needed to express these ideas. Words are symbols that stand for ideas or experiences. Sometime during your early childhood, you adopted language as your primary means of thinking and communicating. Now, when you have an idea you wish to communicate, your brain scans its store of available words (your vocabulary) for the symbol that best identifies that idea. Although this process takes place in fractions of a second, it is quite complex. During this short period, you must decide on a word (a symbol) that best identifies your idea not only for yourself but for your receiver as well.

Reasoning

Your brain has another function besides storing ideas and the words that represent them in your memory. That function is **thinking**, or **reasoning**. Animals have memories, but humans have a highly developed ability to put two or more ideas together and produce a new idea. This ability to reason gives humans a tremendous advantage over other forms of life. Thus, you have two major advantages over other living beings. You can put ideas together by thinking, and you can label your ideas with words.

The process by which you obtain, store, reject, and combine ideas constitutes intrapersonal communication—a kind of subconscious talking you carry on continually within yourself. Having ideas is the start of interpersonal communication—communicating with others.

TEACH

SUBSTITUTE TEACHER TIP
Ask students to remember the last good, clean joke they heard. Can they remember who told the joke? Can they remember the punch line? Ask volunteers to share a family joke or one they heard on TV. Discuss the qualities of a good joke and identify the comedians students think are funny and why.

● **LEARNING STYLES**

Beyond the Classroom
Small groups could be given a page from the phone book and a set amount of time to memorize as many phone numbers as possible. Compare each group's ability to memorize. Discuss why some people find it easier to memorize numbers and others are more comfortable memorizing words—and some do not like to memorize anything at all. Identify those things that students would find useful to memorize (for example: social security number, password to computer, PIN).

● **SKILL DEVELOPMENT**

15-Second Skill Opportunity
Write the phrase "The last good idea I had was…." Have students think about how they would complete the sentence. Have students stand, face the class, and articulate the entire sentence. Encourage students to question each other about what they did with their good ideas.

● **SKILL APPLICATION**

Making Conversation
Someone once said that good conversation is like lettuce—both need to be crisp and fresh. Ask students to imagine that they want to speak to a person they have not met, perhaps someone they see at the video store. Give them the opportunity to think of what they would want to say as a first sentence to get the other person's attention and attract interest in continuing a conversation. Suggest that they write out that first sentence of the conversation. Share those opening lines with the class.

TEACH

● **ENRICHMENT**

To explore the fields of experience that might be shared by members of class, consider the following. In each of these categories, ask students to use their experience and write down the most common and most unusual (a) food they have eaten; (b) place they have visited; (c) animal they have seen. Share their answers and compile a list of the "most common" foods, places, and animals. Then list the most unusual examples. Ask volunteers to share details about their most unusual examples.

● **CURRICULAR CONNECTIONS**

Math/Science
Some students might want to investigate the research into the functions of the right and left brain. The differences between the two areas could be diagrammed and students could be surveyed to determine which area of the brain most influences their learning and communicating.

● **SKILL DEVELOPMENT**

Critical Thinking
Ask students to think about the research presented about the arrangement of chairs as a stimulant to conversation. Suggest that students think of a way to determine the impact of standing versus sitting on conversation. Small groups of students could be asked to participate in the "research." Students could also suggest a variety of chair patterns for the class.

● **LEARNING STYLES**

Cooperative Learning
Have students meet in small groups and share information about the longest phone conversations they have had. Each student could identify the length of time and at least five topics of conversation. Compare and contrast information and compile class results.

Visual Learning
Some students could develop their own diagram to illustrate the shared fields of experience process. Display these for the class. Students or groups might want to include these as portfolio products.

CHAPTER 2 The Process of Communication

Needing to Communicate

Reasons for deciding to communicate with another vary greatly. For many people the mere presence of others is often sufficient reason to begin a conversation. People are social creatures by nature and feel a need for a certain amount of communication. If you are the type who starts a conversation with a stranger in a dentist's office, you may have a strong need to interact with others. People who have an above-average urge to communicate will strike up more conversations with strangers than will persons without such a strong need. Sometimes people who seem to lack such a need to communicate may, instead, have a fear of being rejected by others. People having this fear seldom start a conversation with a stranger unless some other stronger need drives them to do so.

Research has indicated that the angle at which chairs are arranged can help people overcome fear of rejection and begin communicating. Seats which face one another on a 45–degree angle encourage conversation more than side-by-side seats, facing the same direction. Having some unusual object in the room, such as an abstract art print, can also make conversation between two strangers more likely, even if both are highly sensitive to rejection. The object appears to serve as an ice breaker, providing an excuse to talk about something impersonal.

Sharing Common Experiences and Interests

Have you ever tried to talk with someone who has never even heard about your topic before? For example, have you tried to explain to a younger brother or sister what a yo-yo is like and what fancy tricks can be done with one if he or she had never seen a yo-yo? People who do not share the same knowledge do not have the same **fields of experience.** Wilbur Schramm developed a model of communication which stresses how important shared fields of experience are to effective

A signal, or message, readily gets from one person to the other when it is about an experience both people share.

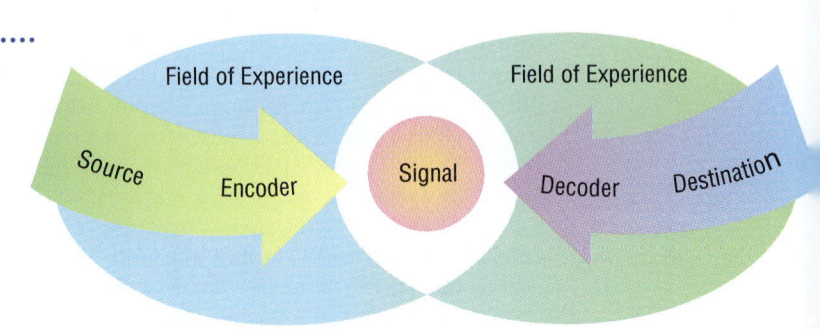

● LINKS TO PAST LEARNING

To reinforce the concept that common interests are linked to the communication process, ask students to think of their lives in three segments. Ask them to label a sheet of paper with three categories—1 to 5 years, 5 to 10 years, and 10 to 15 years. Ask students to list five friends they had in each age group. Then ask them to list the things they did and the things they talked about for each age category. Discuss how some interests continue over a lifetime and others change. Encourage them to predict what current interests will probably endure throughout their lives.

AMAZING FACTS!

The lymphocytes have the longest memory of any cell in our bodies. These cells, part of our immune system, never forget an enemy. For example, if you get measles as a child, the lymphocytes will recognize and destroy this virus even 70 years later!

● LEARNING STYLES

Cooperative Learning
Have small groups of students share what they find difficult to remember. As each student shares this information, the rest of the group will serve as a "think tank" to suggest creative ways to help the individual remember what is shared.

Beyond the Classroom
You might invite a parent or community professional who works with memory impaired people to speak to the class. Some students may have a relative with Alzheimer's disease and be able to interview care providers about symptoms and supervision.

● SKILL DEVELOPMENT

Vocabulary
Have students make a list of all the words in boldface and write a definition for each.

Choosing Symbols **35**

communication. The model shows that people communicate most easily about those topics with which both are already familiar.

Having common interests is one of the most frequent reasons for deciding to communicate. Did you ever notice how quickly the time slips by when you are having a phone conversation with one of your friends? Or what brief phone conversations you usually have with someone who doesn't share any of your interests?

Sometimes your common interests with others can last a long time. Generally, family members and friends share common interests during their entire lifetimes. Even after long separations they find it easy to communicate with each other on many subjects.

With other people, however, you may find common interests for only a short period of time. You find it easy to talk with a classmate about a school play in which you are both performing. But when the play is over, you may decide that you do not have any other common interests. Carrying on a conversation with a salesperson is interesting to you both only until your business is completed. Then you may never have an occasion to communicate with that person again. Whether short-lived or enduring, common interests are an important reason for deciding to communicate.

● ACTIVITY

Memory
In small groups, discuss the frustrations of a memory lapse. Share experiences in which you have forgotten names or information for a test or even the punch line of a joke. Describe the circumstances and try to assess why you had the memory lapse.

● CHOOSING SYMBOLS

Once you have decided to communicate with someone, the next step is to use symbols to **encode** your ideas. It might be nice if there were some method of simply pouring the ideas from your head into someone else's, but there isn't. You must transfer ideas into a symbol system, or **code,** known to both you and your receiver, and then hope that the receiver will **decode,** or translate, the symbols correctly. Of course, if the symbols are unknown to your receiver, you will fail to communicate.

TEACH

AMAZING FACTS!
Gon Yangling, 26, has memorized more than 15,000 phone numbers in China.

● **LEARNING STYLES**

Visual Learning
Ask students to sketch the $20,000 sports car mentioned in the text. Have students compare drawings. They will notice that the same words are represented differently by each student. Discuss what it would take for each student to sketch the same picture.

Cooperative Learning
Provide small groups of students with a section of the newspaper and ask them to identify examples of injustice (or justice) found in the news. Have the group discuss what could be done to pursue justice in the example they selected. Then, have groups exchange the examples selected and discuss how justice could be pursued. When all groups have examined the examples, ask a representative of each group to describe the example and the suggestions of the group to achieve justice. Compare approaches. Discuss why a term like "justice" is so difficult to define.

Imagine yourself conversing with someone who understands English but who knows nothing about roller coasters. If you suggest riding on a roller coaster, the person will have no idea what you are talking about and will be unable to decode your message or respond to it.

You use symbols every day for a variety of purposes. A **symbol** can be a word, a gesture, eye contact, dress—anything that stands for an idea and is used to communicate. Since words are the symbols most often used, they will be explored in more detail first.

Language Symbols

Words are language symbols. They are also called **verbal symbols**. In certain respects language is like money. Language is a medium of exchange for ideas as money is a medium of exchange for goods and services. Putting a price on a new car is a way of making money represent that type of car. You've heard people make remarks such as "Oh, yes, she just bought a $20,000 sports car." In somewhat the same way, language represents, or symbolizes, the ideas people have in their minds. Notice that the phrase *$20,000 sports car* is not the same thing as the actual *sports car*. It is merely one way of representing a type of automobile. Words are not the ideas they represent. They are only a way of symbolizing those ideas.

People often think that a word will represent the identical idea in a receiver's mind that it represents in their own. Unfortunately, this seldom is the case. Have you ever found yourself talking to a friend about a person named Tom, only to discover that your receiver had a different Tom in mind during the first few moments of the conversation? Or consider the different images evoked by a word like *justice*. One person may picture the traditional symbol of a blindfolded woman holding a scale. Another may see a courtroom scene. A third might envision a criminal in prison. Some of these impressions are positive, others negative. Some are practical, others theoretical. Some are general, others specific. It is important to remember that words are symbols that can evoke different meanings in different minds. This realization will prevent much miscommunication.

Actually most words do have a basic meaning. This meaning is known as a **denotation.** The denotative meaning of the word *vacation*, for example, is a time of rest and freedom from work or study. Differences in meaning represented by the same word are largely because of connotation. **Connotation** refers to the meanings people attach to words that are beyond the dictionary meaning. They are meanings that come to different people because of their different past associations with an idea. Connotative meanings are emotionally charged. For example, when someone uses the word *vacation* in front of an audience

TEACH

● **CURRICULAR CONNECTIONS**

Language Arts
Students can add to their collection of vocabulary words the terms printed in boldface. Encourage them to define these terms and suggest synonyms. These words include:

encode	code	verbal symbols	denotation
decode	symbol	connotation	nonverbal symbols
		kinesics	proxemics
		paralanguage	volume
		pitch	speaking rate
		voice quality	stress

● **LEARNING STYLES**

Limited English Proficiency
Provide the following list of paired words, which mean the same but have different connotations. Have students explain the differences and give examples of when each could be used.

friend	pal
sweat	perspiration
film	movie
athlete	jock
food	cuisine
guy	gentleman
kid	child

Choosing Symbols   **37**

each member of the audience may attach his or her own meaning to that idea. For someone who doesn't like to leave work or study, the connotation may be quite negative. For someone who enjoys travel and change, the impression will be agreeable. Even though all the listeners share the same basic meaning, their strong associations with the word can often be more important than the basic meaning.

Thus, if you wish to communicate clearly, you must be careful in choosing the words to encode your ideas. You must remember that some of the people you speak to will not know the meaning of a word that comes to your mind. Even if they do know the meaning of the word, they may attach a different connotative meaning to it. In most cases, however, your meaning will be clear if you use simple words, and adjust your vocabulary for the listener or listeners you are addressing on each occasion.

Nonverbal Symbols

Nonverbal symbols include all of the ways you encode your ideas without words. You may smile or nod to show you agree with someone. Tapping your foot may indicate that you are impatient. People who study nonverbal communication claim that well over half of the meaning exchanged in face-to-face communication comes from nonverbal symbols rather than from words.

"Are you certain?" "I don't believe you!" Nonverbal symbols include all the ways we communicate without words.

37

TEACH

SUBSTITUTE TEACHER TIP

Have students select one of the photos in the chapter and rewrite a caption for it based on what they think is being shown visually.

● **LEARNING STYLES**

Kinesic Learning
Have students consider the importance of body language by acting out the following scenarios and discuss the meaning of each.
(a) Stand straight, cross arms, tap your foot.
(b) Bury your head in your hands.
(c) Shake fist angrily.
(d) Smile in exaggerated way.

● **SKILL DEVELOPMENT**

15-Second Skill Opportunity
List the following on the chalkboard.

Boredom   Surprise
Fear   Anger
Impatience Curiosity

Place a chair in front of the class and ask students to demonstrate various ways to sit in the chair to convey one of the words on the board. Or place words in a hat, have a drawing, and let the class guess based on student demonstrations.

CHAPTER 2 The Process of Communication

Nonverbal symbols communicate a bit differently than verbal symbols. First, it is often more difficult to attach a definite meaning to a nonverbal symbol than to a word. Suppose you are talking with a friend, and your friend frowns at something you say. You will probably get a negative impression from the frown, but you may not be able to decide whether the frown means lack of understanding, disagreement, or something else. If your friend yawns while you are talking, it may mean boredom with what you are saying, or it may simply mean your friend is sleepy. Second, we receive feelings more than ideas from nonverbal symbols. If you ask a friend to go to the movies, and the friend responds with "I'd really like to go with you, but...." while trying to avoid looking you straight in the eye, you will probably get the *feeling* that your friend really doesn't want to go to the movies with you. The words say the idea "I'd really like to go with you" but the eyes express the feeling "I don't want to go with you."

Kinesics What are some of the most common nonverbal symbols? One category is body motions. The study of the use of body motions to communicate is called **kinesics.** Rolling one's eyes, frowning, staring, laughing, gesturing, crossing one's legs, or any similar body movements fall into this category. Unless you stop and think about it, you may not realize how much people depend on body motion to help them communicate. People in business often hold initial job interviews over the phone, but they will seldom decide to hire a person until that person has been interviewed face-to-face. They want to see how a job candidate "moves" as well as hear the person speak before making a decision. People express a great deal with their movements. They can communicate nervousness or calmness, intensity or relaxation, even sincerity or hypocrisy. In some cultures parents can often tell if little children are lying simply by whether or not the children are willing to look them in the eye. In other cultures children indicate respect for their elders by deliberately not looking directly into their eyes.

A highly specialized form of body motion communication is the sign language used by the deaf and those who communicate with them. Some people claim it is not an instance of nonverbal communication since particular hand and finger movements simply stand for words. If you have ever seen sign language used by someone to whom it is second nature, however, you soon recognize it for the beautiful form of communication that it is—a painting of pictures in the air that can move and thrill you as it creates understanding.

Proxemics A second category of nonverbal symbols involves the use of space to communicate. The study of spatial communication is called **proxemics.** People (usually without realizing it) arrange the

Choosing Symbols **39**

The study of spatial communication—the physical closeness with which we interact—or proxemics reveals a great deal about our relationships.

distance between themselves and those with whom they are talking in such a way that the degree of closeness communicates in itself. When people are good friends, they usually express this by standing or sitting closer to each other than they would with strangers or new acquaintances. Closeness can also be a signal that a person wants to discuss personal matters. Greater distances indicate that the discussion is to be on an impersonal level. The table on page 40 shows approximate distances most Americans use for typical communication situations.

The way in which space is arranged in homes, offices, schools, and at other public places can communicate certain ideas. The Gateway Arch on the riverfront in St. Louis, Missouri, symbolizes the gateway to the West. The Astrodome in Houston, Texas, indicates the existence of big-time sports. The size and shape of your school's classrooms point out the present or past philosophy of education in your school system. The furnishings in your home give visitors an idea of your lifestyle.

Arrangements of furniture within a room, or space allotments within a building also communicate. Have you noticed that top executives generally have larger and more splendid offices than other employees? This is arranged to say to a visitor or a client: "This person has high status in this company. This person is important." People in their homes try

TEACH

● **LEARNING STYLES**

Multicultural Learning
Some cultures consider it impolite to look at an older person directly in the eyes. In other cultures, it is considered impolite to avoid looking at the speaker directly. Encourage students to share customs that reflect various cultural values. Ask students who have traveled to explain customs of communication in countries or regions they have visited.

● **SKILL DEVELOPMENT**

15-Second Skill Opportunity
To develop skills in the use of body motion, ask students to prepare a 15-second communication depicting an elderly person's difficulty in making a phone call. Students cannot use words, but can only convey the scene through kinesics.

● **LEARNING STYLES**

Cooperative Learning
Invite an instructor in sign language to teach the class some basic expressions. Then ask small groups to develop a signing for five sentences they would use if they wanted to be excused from doing homework. Signing could be shared with the class.

TEACH

● LEARNING STYLES

Multicultural Learning
Ask students to consider how the use of space is often conditioned by a culture's geography and customs. Discuss how much space a family of six would require in New York City, in Mexico City, or in Tokyo.

Cooperative Learning
Ask each group to create a diagram of the school stage and show the placement of the maximum number of people on that stage for a musical performance. Share the diagrams with the class.

Visual Learning
Ask students to imagine how the classroom furniture could be rearranged to facilitate communication. Students could make a scale drawing of the room and its furnishings. Some students may have access to CAD equipment and be able to show a variety of possibilities.

Visual Learning
Students could expand or illustrate the chart on this page and think of a title for the chart.

CHAPTER 2 The Process of Communication

People use distance to signal the kind of communication they want or expect.

Distance	Typical Situation
touching to 18 inches (10 to 46 cm)	giving comfort or aid, whispering, conversing with close friends and family
18 inches to 4 feet (46 to 120 cm)	talking with friends or business associates, instructing in a sport
4 feet to 12 feet (1.2 to 3.6 meters)	discussing impersonal or business matters with someone in authority, taking part in a small group discussion
12 feet to 25 feet or more (3.6 to 7.6 meters or more)	public speaking, teaching a class, leading a pep rally

to arrange their furniture to create the most inviting atmosphere for conversation and relaxation. Notice how space is used constantly to communicate in many different ways.

Paralanguage A third category of symbols that many researchers include as part of nonverbal communication is called paralanguage. **Paralanguage** consists of the ways in which you say words. It includes volume, pitch, speaking rate, and voice quality. **Volume** indicates how loudly or softly you are speaking. **Pitch** is how high or low the sounds of your voice are. **Speaking rate** is how fast or slowly you are speaking. **Voice quality** is what makes people able to recognize you by your voice alone. Volume, pitch, and speaking rate change according to the particular speaking situation. Your voice quality, however, usually remains the same whatever the situation.

Volume and pitch work together to create **stress**—the amount of emphasis you place on different words in a sentence. By changing the words that are stressed in a sentence, you can change the meaning of

TEACH

● **ASSESSMENT STRATEGY**

Use the stress exercise described in the text on pp. 40-41. Ask students to evaluate their speech using the checklist developed from the boldface terms in this section.

▽ **PORTFOLIO PROJECT**

Students could make an illustrated dictionary of all the terms mentioned in this chapter.

● **CURRICULAR CONNECTIONS**

Language Arts
Have students determine the meaning of "para" as a prefix and make a list of words that begin with "para." Discuss how a knowledge of the meaning of the prefix enhances the meaning of the term.

● **LEARNING STYLES**

Audio Learning
To demonstrate the impact of volume on communication, read the first sentence of the "Gettysburg Address" (p. 584) to the class with a steady volume. Ask a student to do the same. Then repeat the line, increasing your volume for "all men are created equal." Ask all students to think of ways to vary volume to emphasize those words. Then ask for volunteers to demonstrate various volumes.

Technology Tools
Ask students to identify electronic devices that amplify or reduce volume. Talk about the importance of volume in hearing music and the care that students often give to selecting amplification equipment.

Audio Learning
Develop a checklist using the elements of paralanguage identified here. Ask each student to prepare a reading of a paragraph from a book or newspaper. Tape record each reading.

Choosing Symbols **41**

the sentence. Consider the different ideas expressed in the following statements:

"*I* like him very much."

"I like *him* very much."

"I like him *very* much."

Using the same words, but changing the patterns of volume and pitch can make the words carry three quite different meanings.

Changes in the speaking rate can also change the meaning of your message. If you wished to be assured that a friend felt certain about a matter, which speaking rate would give you more confidence?

"I feel sure about that."

"I…feel…sure about…that."

The first sentence, spoken more rapidly, would cause most listeners to have greater confidence in their friend's "sureness."

In addition, paralanguage includes a number of specific sounds people make (coughing, grunting, saying "uh" or "er") as well as the silent pauses between words or sounds. Yawning, sighing, hissing, or snoring are also forms of paralanguage.

Unintentional Communication

Not all communication is intentional. At times you send a message (often through nonverbal means) that you do not mean to send, or that you are not even aware of sending. Edward T. Hall, a noted researcher in cross-cultural communication, tells the story of a United States diplomat in a foreign country who set up an appointment to meet with representatives of the local government. In the United States, the accepted method for keeping such an appointment is to arrive either slightly ahead of the stated time or no more than three or four minutes after it. Arriving any later than that demands an apology in our culture. The United States diplomat, however, was in a country where it was expected that a person might be as late as forty-five minutes without a word of apology or explanation. When the local residents arrived nearly an hour late and made no apology, the United States diplomat took it as an insult. But they had not intended to insult him or the United States and were probably not even aware that anything was wrong! This is an example of unintentional communication, using *time* as the channel of expression.

TEACH

● **ENRICHMENT**

Time is often used as a form of communication. Ask students to provide examples of being early, late, and on time, and discuss the impact of each in the American culture.

● **SKILL DEVELOPMENT**

15-Second Skill Opportunity
Ask students to prepare an explanation to a supervisor for being 15 minutes late for a job because they missed the bus. Volunteers can present their explanations to the class.

● **LEARNING STYLES**

Multicultural Learning
Ask students to provide examples from various cultures to demonstrate the variety of approaches to time as a form of communication.

Visual Learning
Ask students to develop illustrations to emphasize the labels used in the diagram on this page. Cartoon characters, for instance, could be used to clarify the meaning and provide examples of the communication process.

● **ACTIVITY**

The nonverbal communication message of each group could be videotaped and reviewed by the class as a whole. Develop a checklist of factors you want to focus on to evaluate the effectiveness of the nonverbal communication.

---

42   CHAPTER 2   The Process of Communication

The process of communication is complex. This model shows factors that typically affect every message and every sender and receiver of messages. A mix-up at any point can disrupt the whole process.

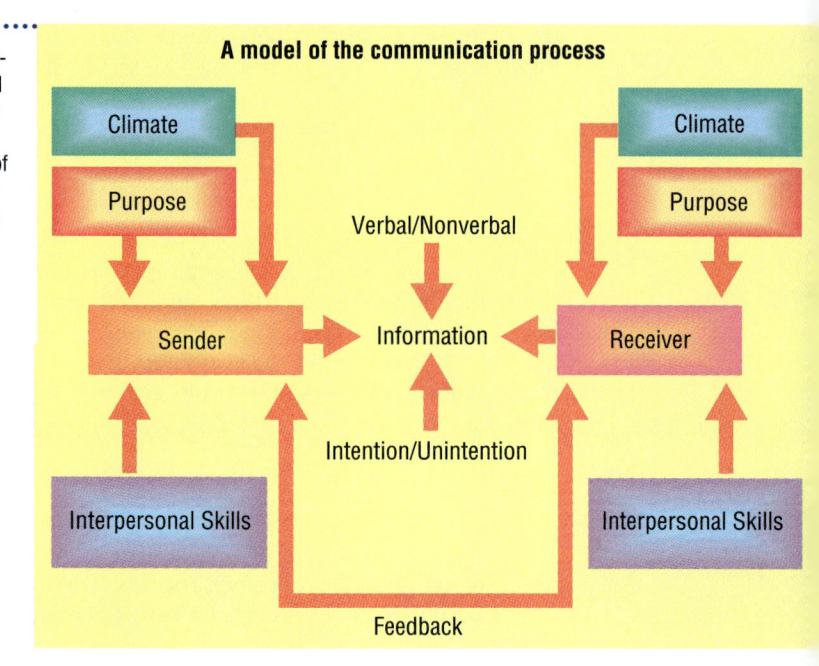

A model of the communication process

Climate → Purpose → Sender → Information ← Receiver ← Purpose ← Climate
Verbal/Nonverbal
Intention/Unintention
Interpersonal Skills — Feedback — Interpersonal Skills

Similarly, mix-ups can occur if we use space, body movements, clothing, touching, eye contact, or language without full realization of the effect they may have on the receiver. In some parts of the world, people stand very close and often touch one another when discussing business or other impersonal matters. Americans, however, usually do not do this. They generally consider touching or standing too close to be violations of their space.

● **ACTIVITY**

Using Communication Other Than Words
In teams of two, take turns with a classmate giving a message using numbers or letters of the alphabet instead of words. Your message may be a funny story, a secret, some exciting news, a sad event, etc. Use stress, pitch, rate, and volume to help communicate your message. You may also use nonverbal communication. Then, as a class, discuss how successful each team was at relaying a certain mood or attitude. Which was more effective, the vocal inflection of the numbers or letters, or the nonverbal? Were they more effective when both were used? Was there any unintentional communication?

● **EXTENSION**

A Peace Corps volunteer could be invited to speak to the class and address issues of communication in a foreign land. Some members of the class might write the Peace Corps at 1990 K Street NW, Washington, D.C. 20526 to obtain information and/or applications.

● **CURRICULAR CONNECTIONS**

History
Students could trace the history of the Peace Corps from its creation by President Kennedy. Its history could be presented chronologically in a timeline. A world map could also be developed with a legend to indicate the nations that have received Peace Corps volunteers.

APPLY

"And so, my fellow Americans, ask not what your country can do for you; ask what you can do for your country."

—John F. Kennedy

● **SKILL APPLICATION**

Media Literacy
Students could prepare a press release to highlight the accomplishments of local Peace Corps volunteers. The press release could include quotations or excerpts from interviews of Peace Corps volunteers by members of the class.

CAREER CLOSE-UP

Peace Corps Volunteer

Peace Corps volunteers devote two years to working in developing nations, promoting world peace. The only essential prerequisites are a willingness to become totally involved in a foreign culture, to work hard despite difficult conditions, and to further understanding between cultures. Because people with every imaginable skill are needed (teachers, engineers, agricultural specialists, etc.), there are no absolute educational requirements. However, 96% of volunteers have attended college. Once accepted, a volunteer participates in a 3–week training program prior to foreign assignment.

The Peace Corps is based on the belief that communication is the key to achieving world peace and understanding. When volunteers have only thirteen weeks to learn the language of their community, they cannot rely on language alone to communicate. Volunteers are taught to supplement the use of language with such nonverbal symbols as nods, smiles, hand motions, and facial expressions to communicate their enthusiasm and willingness to help.

Peace Corps volunteers also become skilled in monitoring feedback during conversations in their communities. Volunteers study facial expressions and body language to determine whether they are being understood or whether they have unintentionally communicated something. In this way, misunderstandings can be corrected before any harm is done.

The discovery that communication is much more than the simple exchange of words is a truth that emerges from the Peace Corps experience. Through the skillful use of verbal and nonverbal communication, volunteers find there are a multitude of ways to express good will.

Among the many skills communicated by Peace Corps volunteers are those related to personal health and well-being.

43

TEACH

AMAZING FACTS!
According to *The Oxford Companion to the English Language*, 22 organs are required to produce speech. And that list does not include the brain!

● **ENRICHMENT**

Play a segment of an aria from an opera and ask students to try and count the seconds before the singer takes another breath. Use the aria to discuss breath control. A similar discussion could take place after listening to a jazz piece with a sax or trumpet solo.

● **SKILL DEVELOPMENT**

15-Second Skill Opportunity
Write the first line of Robert Browning's famous poem "Soliloquy of the Spanish Cloister" on the chalkboard: "Grrr— there go, my heart's abhorrence!" Ask students to prepare to say that line expressing the character's hatred of another.

● **LEARNING STYLES**

Limited English Proficiency
Some of the technical terms used and explained in this section may not be familiar to some students. List the following on the chalkboard and help students understand their meaning by using the dictionary, oral pronunciations, and frequent repetition in class.

diaphragm   trachea
vocal cords   larynx
resonators   pharynx
nasal cavity articulators
articulation

---

44 CHAPTER 2 The Process of Communication

● **VOCALIZING**

Once you have chosen the ideas you wish to communicate and the word symbols through which to express those ideas, it is time to set your vocal mechanism in action. Have you ever laid a wide blade of grass between your thumbs and blown against it to produce a shrill vibrating sound? If you have, you know something about how speech sounds are made. Your lungs provide a flow of air as you exhale which can be forced through your vocal cords causing them to vibrate. This produces sound which in turn passes through your throat and past your tongue, lower jaw, and lips, where it is molded into vowel and consonant sounds to produce speech. Let's look at each part of the speech mechanism step by step.

Getting Enough Air

Your lungs are like an air compressor that is always running. At the base of your rib cage you have a thick muscle called the **diaphragm**. As you inhale, the diaphragm lowers, creating a larger chest cavity and a partial vacuum. Air rushes in. When you exhale, the center of your diaphragm rises, making the diaphragm again dome shaped, and forcing air out the **trachea**, or windpipe. This happens naturally, and usually without your being aware of it, when you are breathing. To produce

Vocalizing involves your respiratory system and your resonating chambers.

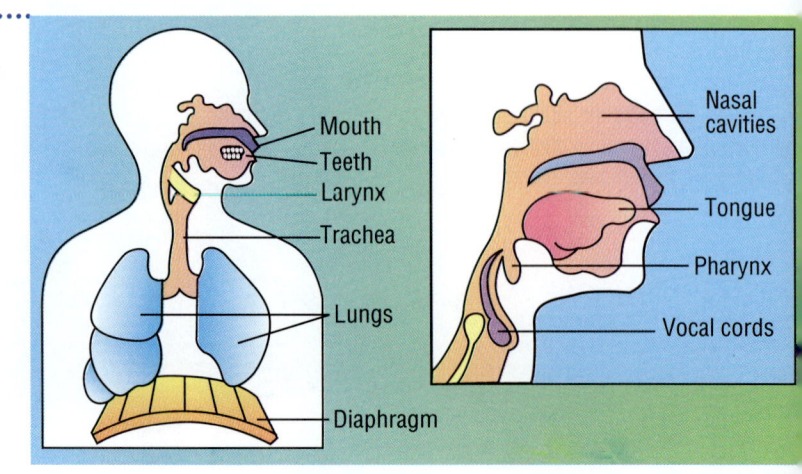

TEACH

● **LINKS TO PAST LEARNING**

Students could be asked to recall examples of times when they tried to hold their breath as long as possible. Discuss the sensations they had after expelling their breath. You might also talk about times that individuals have "lost their voices" because of laryngitis. Locate the larynx on the diagram and ask students to place their hand over their own larynx.

● **CURRICULAR CONNECTIONS**

Math/Science
Compare the diagram of the organs required for speech here with a similar diagram in a biology text. Note similarities and differences. Students could number the organs in the sequence in which they are used in the process of vocalization.

Math/Science
Borrow models of the head and thorax from the biology department. Ask the biology teacher to demonstrate or explain speech mechanisms and the production of sounds. This demonstration could be videotaped for repeated use.

● **SKILL DEVELOPMENT**

15-Second Skill Opportunity
Ask students to select one vowel sound and practice vocalizing it with high to low tones. Ask volunteers to practice. Identify students with the greatest range and discuss the physical composition of the speech organs that make such a range possible.

---

speech, however, you need an extra large supply of air, particularly when you speak to a large group. So you must concentrate more on your breathing process to "pump up the air pressure" in your lungs. Becoming aware of how quickly and completely the diaphragm can fill the lungs with air can aid you in producing a forceful voice at a moment's notice.

The larger the group you are addressing, the more conscious you need to be of your breathing. When giving a public speech without a microphone to a large audience, you should remember two things about breathing. First, you should inhale through your nose rather than through your mouth, using your diaphragm to fill your lungs with air. Second, as you speak, pace your exhalation so that you will have enough air to complete longer thoughts without having to steal a breath at awkward moments.

Treating Your Vocal Cords with Care

Vocal cords vibrate to produce sound. As you begin to speak, these two folds of membrane located in your voice box, or **larynx,** tighten and move closer together, creating a narrow slit. When exhaled air is forced through this slit, the cords vibrate and produce sound, in much the same way that blowing air between your thumb and a blade of grass produces sound. Since women's vocal cords are usually a bit shorter and thinner than men's, women's voices produce a higher pitched sound. It is important not to strain your vocal cords by prolonged yelling or by constantly trying to make yourself heard above loud noises. Excessive coughing or clearing of your throat when it is clogged by a cold may also damage the vocal mechanism.

Making Use of Resonators

The sound produced by your vocal cords is weak and thin. Before the sound waves leave your mouth, however, they pass through several resonating chambers. These **resonators** are your **pharynx** (the back part of the throat), your **nasal cavities,** and your mouth. Each acts much as a hollow chamber does to amplify or increase sound. If you have ever spoken inside a stairwell or tunnel, you know how much a chamber can increase the sound of your voice. Fortunately, your built-in resonating chambers are always handy to boost the level of your vocal sounds.

TEACH

SUBSTITUTE TEACHER TIP

Practice proper articulation by asking students to read out loud one paragraph from a text or newspaper. This could be done in small groups or in front of the entire class. Have students develop a checklist to evaluate proper articulation. The group could provide feedback to each student who reads a passage.

● LEARNING STYLES

Audio Learning
Proper articulation and pronunciation of words takes effort. List on the chalkboard some commonly mispronounced words. You could include the following.

going	goin
specific	pacific
when	wen

Model the correct articulation for the students and then ask them to practice out loud in pairs, standing up. When the pair has determined that they articulate the words correctly, they may sit down. When most or all are seated, call on volunteers to demonstrate proper articulation.

● ACTIVITY

You might try to add more interest to the Activity by introducing a stop watch and having students time the length of the "ooh" they can produce. The number of seconds can be recorded and tabulated in the form of a bar graph. Students could also use the classroom clock and do the activity in pairs.

CHAPTER 2 The Process of Communication

Articulating Clearly

You are probably beginning to notice that the production of vocal sounds occurs in a kind of assembly-line fashion. The process begins with breath in the lungs and ends with the emergence of words from your mouth. The final step on this assembly line is the forming of sounds produced into recognizable symbols—words. This is the job of the articulators. The **articulators** are the tongue, teeth, lower jaw, and soft palate. By the movement of these organs into various positions, sound waves are molded into the vowels and consonants that form words. Sometimes speakers allow their **articulation** to become lazy. By not moving their articulators vigorously enough, they begin to produce "goin" for "going," "pacific" for "specific," and "wen" for "when." When they use their articulators correctly, however, speakers are able to produce clear, crisp sounds that are easily heard.

Once you begin to study it, you realize that the process of vocalizing—the producing of vocal sounds—is a very complicated one. Because it happens so rapidly in actual communication, you are rarely conscious of the individual steps. When you consider that vocalization is just one part of the total communication process, you realize how amazing human beings are. Look at the illustration on page 44 and notice how many different parts of the body are involved in vocalizing.

Now that you have looked at each part of the sending side of the communication process, let's put it all together in the form of a model. The one shown on page 47 is simply a way of picturing what occurs when a person begins to communicate.

● ACTIVITY

Proper Breathing Techniques
Practice breathing for public speaking. Stand up and place your hands at the base of your rib cage. Inhale deeply through your nose. You should feel your hands rise as you inhale, indicating that you are filling your lungs with air. Now say a loud, continuous "ooh" for as long as you can. Notice how your hands gradually sink in as you lose your supply of air. You may also be able to feel your diaphragm and rib muscles tightening near the end of your "ooh." For speaking, you must be able to regulate the flow of outgoing air so you will not run out at an awkward moment.

TEACH

● **LINKS TO PAST LEARNING**

Ask students to recall a family conversation where members are retelling a story of a family event and one of the participants disagrees with the storyteller's version. Discuss why the communication process involves both sending and receiving messages and often there is room for misunderstanding and misperceptions.

SUBSTITUTE TEACHER TIP

Ask students to describe the last time they had poor reception on a TV program. Discuss what steps were required to correct the problem. Ask if there could be a connection between the reception involved in interpersonal reception of messages and TV reception.

● **SKILL DEVELOPMENT**

Feedback
Ask pairs of students to work together so that one describes a family or friend's pet to the other. The other will try to draw the pet based only on the description given. The students will compare the drawing with the description and discuss how modifications would be made to bring the drawing closer to reality.

Reception 47

● **RECEPTION**

Perhaps when defining sound in your science class, your teacher asked you the question. "If a tree falls in a remote forest and no person or animal is close enough to hear it, is there any sound?" The answer depends, of course, on how you define *sound*. But if you are talking about interpersonal communication and ask "If no one hears or sees a person sending symbols, is communication occurring?" the answer is "No!" Communication is a two-way process. When someone is sending, but no one is receiving, the only thing that is occurring is *sending*, not communication. Interpersonal communication is the process of using symbols to evoke a meaning in someone else's mind, similar to a meaning you have in your own.

So far this chapter has only dealt with the sending half of the communication process. **Reception** is a kind of mirror image of this first half. When senders select certain ideas from their memory bins and change them into sound or sights, the resulting messages go out across space to receivers' ears or eyes. The receivers then attempt to connect

When the communication process is activated, both the mind and body respond.

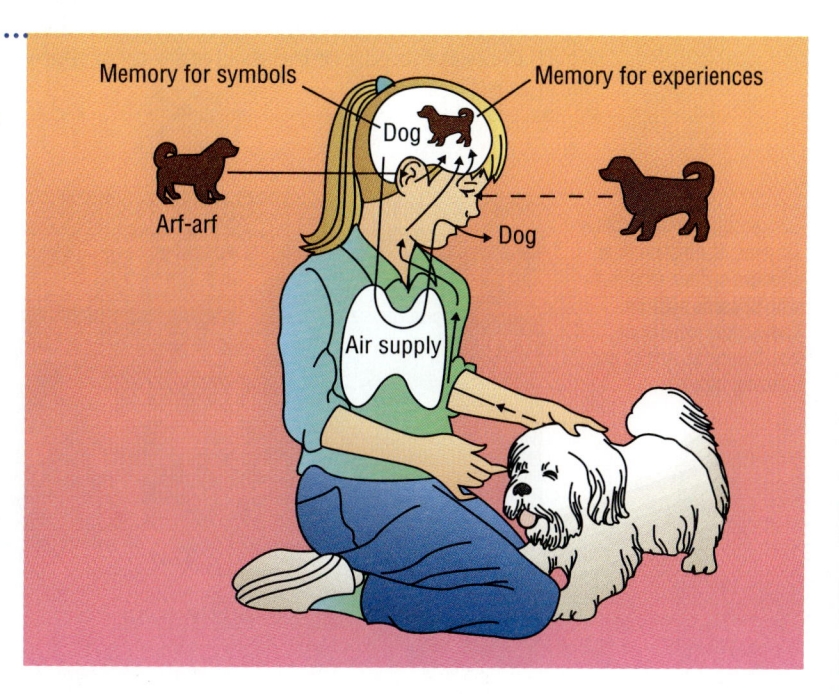

TEACH

> **"Learning, that cobweb of the brain"**
> —Samuel Butler

● **LEARNING STYLES**

Multicultural Learning
Use the example in the text of the English and French words *waiter* and *garçon*. Examine how many word symbols can be listed for a common object like *table*, based on the language experiences of the students in the classroom.

● **SKILL DEVELOPMENT**

Creative Thinking
Use the illustration to encourage students to think of what is being said and what is heard in the photo. Ask students to write a sentence for each person shown that represents what each is saying or receiving.

---

48 CHAPTER 2 The Process of Communication

the symbols they receive with experiences in their own minds. This process is called decoding. To the extent that the senders and receivers have similar backgrounds and experiences, they will probably achieve shared meanings. If the receivers have no experience of something the senders are describing or are not familiar with the symbols the senders use, communication will fail. If someone speaks to you in a language you do not understand, communication is difficult, at times impossible. The problem, of course, is primarily that you and the sender do not share enough verbal symbols for things. If you were looking at pictures, you might both understand the same basic idea—that of someone serving food, for example. But while you would use the English language symbol *waiter* to represent this concept, a person from France would use the symbol *garçon*. Unless you speak French, the word symbol used wouldn't mean anything to you.

Many people think that when communication fails it is always the fault of the sender. Actually, the receiver shares part of the responsibility for incomplete communication. Placing all the blame for poor communication on the sender is a bit like having a broken TV set and blaming your local channel because you can't see your favorite program. Besides an effective sender, communication involves a receiver who has sufficient knowledge, experience, and vocabulary to be able to tune in on different kinds of messages. It also involves good listening habits on the part of the receiver, a topic that will be considered in the next chapter.

Successful communication requires, in addition to an effective sender, receivers who possess sufficient knowledge, experience, and vocabulary, as well as good listening habits.

APPLY

● **ENRICHMENT**

Invite a representative from the phone company to come to the class or provide literature to the class to identify ways to communicate with the hearing impaired.

Speaking IN ACTION

Communicating with the Hearing Impaired

Situation
Imagine you are about to visit your grandmother who is ninety and lives in a nursing home. This kind older person whom you love has been able to hear a little bit less each time you have visited her over the last several years, and you have become increasingly saddened *and* a little more frustrated with each visit. But now that you know more about the process of communication, you decide to practice some of the suggestions in this chapter to make this upcoming talk more enjoyable for both of you.

Preparation
You begin planning for your visit by realizing that you are facing a major challenge, since your grandmother now understands only about one out of three words you say on the first try. You are determined to use every communication tool at your disposal to improve that average.

Start by planning to mention some topics that you know she will recall and will enjoy discussing. Many of these may be about things that happened early in her life, before you were born—events you have heard her mention before. Doing so will motivate her to listen as carefully as she can, and may help her hear *two* out of every three words instead of just one in three. Plan to speak slowly, and to articulate clearly to help her catch as many sounds as possible. When she doesn't hear a key word, try to have a synonym ready that might come through her hearing aid more clearly. Come prepared to use lots of gestures, facial expressions, and body movements that support and accent the messages you are sending with your words. Remember to sit close to her, facing her so she can see your lips move at all times, and nearer the side on which she wears her hearing aid. Remind yourself not to yell, but to speak slowly in a normal conversational volume. If she seems not to hear at all at that volume, increase it slightly until you find her best level. Plan to let your feelings come through in your voice tones as well as through your body movements. Finally, recognizing from your past experience that there will be times when she simply won't get an idea despite your best efforts, bring a pencil and notepad along on which you can jot key words to get her back on track.

Delivery
Team up with a classmate who will play the role of your grandmother (or grandfather). The classmate's job is to realistically play the role of an alert, but very hearing-impaired elderly person who will challenge your best communication efforts. Then you can switch roles.

If you actually know a hearing-impaired relative or friend, you could brighten that person's day enormously by preparing yourself to communicate as clearly as possible when you next visit her or him.

● **SKILL APPLICATION**

Making Conversation
Ask students to make a list of three topics they know they can discuss with their grandmother. Have students compare lists. Those with similar topics could work together as pairs.

The partners should identify several key words for each topic and make a list of several synonyms for each.

Partners should take turns practicing one sentence at a time for volume and articulation.

Partners could role-play one topic of conversation with their grandmother. Suggest ways for partners to provide feedback.

● **SKILL DEVELOPMENT**

15-Second Skill Opportunity
Ask students to think about how they would want to complete the sentence "The best thing about my grandmother (or grandfather) is...." Volunteers can stand and face the class to complete the sentence.

49

TEACH

AMAZING FACTS!
The day after Western Union opened its office, the Pony Express closed its business.

PORTFOLIO PRODUCTS

Students could select a way to depict the feedback process. Options might include (a) a diagram that identifies and labels various parts of the process, (b) a video that contrasts situations where feedback is given and not given, or (c) a checklist that identifies elements in the feedback process.

SKILL DEVELOPMENT

15-Second Skill Opportunity
Ask students to think about the kind of feedback they would like to receive from their teachers or parents to help them achieve a specific goal. Invite volunteers to share the description of the feedback they would like.

LEARNING STYLES

Cooperative Learning
Each group could take a different communication situation and brainstorm ways that feedback could be given to improve the performance of the communicators. Situations could include any of the following: (a) a school assembly, (b) a family birthday celebration, (c) a performance review on the job, or (d) a ratings week for a TV station.

Audio Learning
Students could role-play a phone conversation that uses tone of voice to convey feedback. Encourage students to use various tones of voice to explore a range of messages. Students could pursue a situation of their own choosing or you could suggest that the phone conversation convey the news of the death of a family pet.

Beyond the Classroom
Several parents could be invited to the class to participate in a discussion of feedback as a technique for improving communication. Role-playing with role reversals might be an activity that both parents and students would enjoy.

---

50 CHAPTER 2 The Process of Communication

FEEDBACK

The next time you have a casual conversation with a good friend, try this little experiment on her or him: Every time your friend talks, you stop reacting in any way. Do not say any words, or even utter any sounds. Do not nod or shake your head or move your hands, arms, or any part of your body. Do not even look into your friend's eyes, but stare off to the side of his or her left ear. If your friend is like most of us, he or she will soon ask what is wrong with you, or why you're not paying attention. As a matter of fact you may have been paying close attention, but you were not showing that you were! The signals that a receiver continuously gives to a sender indicating how well the message is being received are known as **feedback.** Feedback is terribly important for senders, since it allows them to discover such matters as whether they are speaking too fast, using words that are too complex, or even whether they are offending or angering their receivers.

Feedback can consist of words, nonverbal symbols, or both. Feedback makes it possible for speakers to judge how well they are communicating. Whenever anyone sends a message to another person some sort of feedback takes place. Sometimes it is easy for the speaker to detect. For example, the listener is asleep. The audience begins to walk out during a public speech. The interviewer leans forward and says "Good, tell me more!"

Feedback, which can consist of words, nonverbal symbols, or both, is extremely important because it signals to the sender how well the message is being received.

Feedback 51

At other times feedback is less obvious. TV news commentators, unable to see their listeners, must rely on mail or phone surveys to discover how the audience responds to their broadcasts. A person talking on the telephone must frequently rely on an occasional "uh-huh" to know the listener is still there. But no matter how difficult some feedback is to detect, it is always present whenever communication occurs. Short of leaving the presence of a sender, it is impossible for a receiver *not* to provide feedback. Even when a receiver sits perfectly still, says nothing, and keeps a deadpan expression on her or his face, the sender can read this as a lack of interest. The receiver has supplied feedback.

In face-to-face conversation, interviews, and small group discussion, a good balance of verbal and nonverbal feedback is possible. A good receiver will maintain a sufficient level of both forms of feedback to inform senders constantly about how effectively they are getting their ideas across.

When talking on the telephone, however, the sender cannot see the receiver, so the feedback is primarily verbal. The word *primarily* is necessary because nonverbal feedback, in the form of paralanguage, may be used at times as feedback over the phone. A change in the tone of voice or in the speaking rate, silence, and sounds that are not words are available to the listener as forms of feedback.

In public speaking, the usual form of feedback is nonverbal. This is because, if a large number of audience members began responding aloud, it would soon be impossible to hear the speaker. So most audiences confine their feedback to kinesic symbols—smiles, frowns, and nods of their heads. Some paralanguage, consisting of yawns, occasional boos or hisses, and clapping, may also be used as feedback.

Performers on radio or television sometimes receive feedback from a studio audience. Feedback from the audience at home will often be in the form of telephone calls or letters. This type of feedback usually reaches the sender after the performance. It cannot help the speaker adapt the message to the receivers during the performance.

ACTIVITY

Reception and Feedback

Divide into teams of two. Practice giving feedback by role-playing with your partner. Ask this person to talk about something or someone he or she enjoys a great deal. This might be a favorite hobby, a favorite rock singer, or a particular sport. Be attentive while the person is speaking, giving positive feedback. Now role-play again, but this time give negative feedback. Reverse roles so that you are doing the talking and your partner is giving the feedback. Each team should then report the results to the class.

TEACH

● LEARNING STYLES

Kinesic Learning
Feedback from an audience is usually expressed in nonverbal forms. Small groups of students could be asked to role-play an audience attending a talk show. One group could be encouraged to develop three kinesic symbols that reflect boredom, that reflect enthusiasm, or that reflect disagreement. Discuss the different gestures and symbols chosen.

● SKILL DEVELOPMENT

15-Second Skill Opportunity
Distribute copies of this excerpt from *The Ghost* and ask students to give a dramatic reading.

Great use they have, when in the hands
Of one, like me, who understands,
Who understands the time, and place,
The persons, manner, and the grace,
Which fools neglect; so that we find,
If all the requisites are join'd
From whence a perfect joke must spring,
A joke's a very serious thing.
—Charles Churchill

● ACTIVITY

After the role-playing is completed, ask each student to list reactions to both situations as a sender and as a listener. Conduct a class discussion on responses and reactions given by students.

51

ASSESS

● **STUDENT PERFORMANCE COMPETENCIES**

- Explains elements in communication process
- Describes two functions of memory and the role of thinking in the communication process
- Explains and uses verbal and nonverbal forms of communication
- Improves the process of vocalizing and articulation

● **sca GUIDELINES**

- Produces and responds to spoken English and nonverbal forms of communication
- Uses appropriate volume and intonation when asking questions
- Uses nonverbal cues to indicate understanding or lack of understanding in the classroom

▽ **PORTFOLIO ASSESSMENT**

Standard
- Diagrammed the communication process
- Compiled glossary of speech terms
- Completed assignments, quizzes, projects, and Chapter 2 test

Enrichment
- Timeline of Shared Interests Throughout Life
- Diagram of Vocalization Process
- Representation of Feedback Process

Challenge
- Hearing Impaired Project
- Interview of Peace Corps Volunteer

CHAPTER 2 REVIEW

● **SUMMARY**

People usually take the process of human communication for granted. However, a close look reveals its complexity and the reasons for communication breakdowns. Studying this process in detail can also uncover opportunities for people to sharpen their communication skills.

Communicating for Understanding Communication is the process people use to understand one another. The sender transmits symbols—words and nonverbal signals—to the receiver. The receiver must decode the message and react to it by providing feedback to the sender.

Deciding to Communicate Communication begins in your brain with an idea. Your brain stores information, including words, in your memory and enables you to reason. People communicate for different reasons, but sharing common interests is a major one.

Choosing Symbols You must encode your ideas in order to exchange them. Code systems consist of verbal and nonverbal symbols. For communication to succeed, the symbols you choose must mean similar things to your receiver. Language is the symbol code used most frequently. However, nonverbal symbols, such as kinesics, proxemics, and paralanguage, are frequently used together with language.

Vocalizing Vocalizing begins with the diaphragm forcing air through the trachea during exhalation. As this air is forced between your vocal cords, the cords vibrate, producing sound waves. The pharynx, mouth, and nasal cavities act as resonating chambers, amplifying the sound. Finally, as the sound passes the lower palate, tongue, lower jaw, teeth, and lips it is formed into the vowels and consonants that make up words.

Reception Reception is half of the communication process. Once the message leaves the sender, the receiver picks it up and decodes it into ideas. Unless the experiences and vocabulary of sender and receiver are similar, communication is difficult and sometimes impossible.

Feedback Communication is never complete without feedback. Feedback is the total of all receivers' responses that tells senders how they are "getting through." Feedback may be either verbal or nonverbal, or it may be a mixture of the two.

ASSESS

● **ASSESSMENT STRATEGIES**

Individual Assessment
- Participates in practice activities daily or weekly
- Completes classwork
- Demonstrates knowledge of content through questions, discussion, role-playing, quizzes, and tests
- Displays improvement in targeted speech skills

Group Assessment
- Demonstrates cooperative learning activities
- Supports efforts of team and class members
- Provides encouragement and feedback regularly

VOCABULARY

Define each term in a complete sentence.

memory	pitch
thinking	speaking rate
reasoning	voice quality
fields of experience	stress
encode	diaphragm
code	trachea
decode	vocal cords
symbol	larynx
verbal symbols	resonators
denotation	pharynx
connotation	nasal cavities
nonverbal symbols	articulators
kinesics	articulation
proxemics	reception
paralanguage	feedback
volume	

✔ CHECKLIST

Sender and Receiver Skills

1. Develop an understanding of the communication process to help your communication skills.
2. Remember that people have different needs to communicate.
3. Choose words carefully; they can evoke different meanings for each individual.
4. Recognize the importance of nonverbal symbols.
5. Adjust your volume, pitch, and speaking rate to the particular speaking situation.
6. Take care not to send the wrong message unintentionally.
7. Use appropriate breathing and crisp articulation.
8. Be a responsive listener. Provide both verbal and nonverbal feedback to the sender.

REVIEW QUESTIONS

1. Explain where communication originates.
2. Name the functions of the brain that are most important to communication.

● **ANSWERS**

See the Answer Key for more complete answers.

REVIEW QUESTIONS
1. Communication originates in a person's brain.
2. Memory, reasoning, and symbols all play important roles in communication.

ASSESS

3. "Loss of memory" means the inability to recall particular words or facts.
4. People communicate when they have ideas, a need to communicate, and a potential receiver with common interests.
5. Words are the basic symbols of communication.
6. Denotation is the basic or literal meaning of a word.
7. A connotation is a significance attached to a word that goes beyond the word's basic, or denotative, meaning.
8. Three types of nonverbal communication are kinesics, proxemics, and paralanguage.
9. Vocalization involves the lungs, diaphragm, and trachea, the vocal cords and larynx, the pharynx, nasal cavities, and mouth, and the tongue, teeth, lower jaw, and soft palate. The Answer Key provides information about functions.
10. Feedback is a response given to a message.

DISCUSSION QUESTIONS
The following code is used to designate discussion questions and activities as suitable for students of varying ability levels:
- ▼ = below average to average
- ◆ = average to above average
- ■ = all students

1. ▼ Have students discuss these questions in small groups.
2. ■ Remind students that nonverbal messages include facial expressions and body movements, or kinesics, and spatial relations, or proxemics.
3. ■ Have students generalize their observations and apply these to other communication situations such as group discussion or public speaking.
4. ◆ Explain that many animals establish territories in various ways. Tigers claw certain boundary markers, leaving scratch marks that other tigers will recognize.

54

CHAPTER 2 REVIEW

3. Explain what "loss of memory" means in everyday situations.
4. Name three factors that influence most people's decision to communicate.
5. Name the basic symbols of communication.
6. Define denotation.
7. Define connotation.
8. Name and give examples of three kinds of nonverbal communication that people use.
9. Name and give the functions of the parts of the body that are involved in the vocalization process.
10. Define feedback.

? DISCUSSION QUESTIONS

1. Ask some of your classmates to describe what they think of when you say the following words: "dog," "tree," "house." How many different responses do you get? What kind of dog, tree, or house do *you* picture? Discuss how past experiences create present images and thoughts. List ways you can be sure that the sender and the receiver are discussing the same ideas.

2. In small groups, discuss instances you have experienced in which conflict occurred because of nonverbal messages you either gave or received. Include tone of voice, and facial expressions. Discuss ways to clarify nonverbal messages.

3. Discuss with your classmates the importance of volume as a factor in communication. Does it offend you when a person speaks to you in a loud voice? Do you form an unfavorable opinion about someone who speaks in a very soft voice? If so, what sort of judgment do you make?

4. Territoriality is an aspect of proxemics that explains our attachment (even possessiveness) of our space. Discuss ways that you claim your territory. How do you feel if someone else sits at "your" desk in school? Do you have a particular chair at the dinner table? Is "your" room open territory for others in your home or do you keep the door closed or locked? In what ways do we "mark" our territory if we have to leave our seat in an auditorium? Include in your discussion any circumstances under which you have willingly given up claim to "your" territory.

54

ASSESS

CRITICAL THINKING

1. Analysis Analyze your need to communicate with others. Think about the following: Why do you need to communicate? With whom do you need to communicate? Are you nervous about communicating with certain people? Jot down your answers to these questions in your notebook. Then jot down possible resolutions of problems. Save your notes for reference later on.

2. Evaluation In small groups, discuss whether the clothes people wear make a difference in what others think of them. To what extent does choice of clothing reflect self image? To what extent are people stereotyped according to appearance? Be sure to give reasons for your opinions. Do you think it is correct to judge people by their clothing? At the end of the discussion each group will hand in two or three statements about the importance of appearance.

ACTIVITIES

In-Class

1. Seated in a circle, each of you will tell the class your name and one bit of personal information. ("My name is Rosa, and I collect seashells.") The second person will repeat the information just given, then give new information about himself or herself. ("Her name is Rosa; she collects seashells. My name is Jeremy, and I play the guitar.") The third and all other participants will continue the process. Clearly, if you are a student near the end of the exercise you will have to recall as many as 30 names and personal facts. Your task will be more difficult, but you will have the reinforcement of everyone before you.

2. Put three columns on the board: POSITIVE, NEGATIVE, and NEUTRAL. As a class, suggest words that are related to each other but that have different connotative factors for each category. Place each word in the proper column. See how many different words you can come up with.

3. Engage in a game of "charades" to discover the frustrations of total reliance on nonverbal symbols. Form two groups. Each group will write titles of books, movies, songs, and TV programs on small sheets of paper to be distributed to the opposing team. A maximum time limit should be set for each player, and a careful record kept of time for each team. No mouthing, pointing, or pantomiming of letters is allowed.

CRITICAL THINKING

1. Analysis Guide students to recognize that communications plays a role in meeting most human needs. Students should identify people in their lives with whom they wish to improve their communication.

2. Evaluation You may wish to point out that, regrettable as such judgments may be, people nonetheless do judge others by their clothing. Due to the demand created by the increase in white collar service jobs, many books on the subject of "dressing for success" have been published in recent years.

ACTIVITIES
In-Class

1. Divide students into groups of five to fifteen, depending on the level of difficulty that you expect them to have with this exercise.

2. Follow the procedure described in the assignment. Have students use each word in the context of a sentence or situation.

3. Provide students with a set of nonverbal symbols to use, including symbols for *book, movie, song, television,* and *sounds like.*

ASSESS

4. Use simple or complicated shapes to vary the difficulty of the activity to suit students of various ability levels.
5. Have students learn and present dialogues in sign language.

Out-of-Class
1. Check the students' notebooks to make sure that they have grasped the intent of the assignment.
2. Have students record the words they spoke, list the articulators used, and describe the differences in voice quality when some of the resonators were impeded.
3. Have each of the students prepare a display, such as a poster, showing the photos and their findings.

CHAPTER 2 REVIEW

4. Try a "one-way/two-way" communication exercise. Working in pairs, one of you will be the *sender;* the other will be the *receiver.* The sender should think of a diagram of a geometric design and then explain to the receiver what to draw. The receiver will attempt to draw on his or her own paper what is being described. In the first phase of the exercise (one-way), the sender will describe the design as quickly and as accurately as possible; the receiver cannot ask questions or call for clarification. In the second phase of the exercise (two-way), the receiver should turn the paper over and begin a new drawing on the back. As many questions as necessary are allowed.

Each phase should be timed. When all teams have finished, have a class discussion about the activity. Identify the advantages and disadvantages of one-way and of two-way communication. Discuss the confidence and frustrations of both sender and receiver in each phase.

5. Invite to class a specialist proficient at sign language. Ask him or her to share with you the graphic movement of the language and to explain how it is taught to others. Learn to communicate using several of the basic signs.

Out-of-Class

1. Turn the sound off completely on your home television set, so that you pick up only the picture. Watch for three minutes, seeing how much you can understand. Then turn the sound up and close your eyes so that you only hear the words. Can you understand more or less during this three-minute period? Which way gets more of the message to you as the audience? Make notes in your notebook on the types of verbal and nonverbal communication you missed when you only watched the picture, and what types of nonverbal communication you missed when only listening to the sound.

2. Say several different words aloud concentrating on how each part of the vocalization process works. Remember to practice good breathing habits. Can you feel your vocal cords vibrate? Which of the articulators are you using with a particular word? Block some of the resonators by holding your nose. How different is the quality of your voice?

3. Take photos of several people of various backgrounds, occupations, and ages. These people could be friends or family members, at home or at work. They can be young children playing in a playground, or classmates participating in sports. Using at least five of these photos, list the best ways to communicate with the people in them. Share your findings with a small group. Then participate in a class discussion on how communication might break down with each

CHAPTER PROJECT

In small groups compose a newspaper article entitled, "Twelk Sighted Near Campus." Give special attention to details of the physical characteristics and mannerisms of the "twelk." Design a lively plot that tells of the sighting and that provides the reader concrete information about who, when, and where. When finished, one group member should read the story aloud to the class.

As a class, compare the various stories. What can you learn about ways that we differ in interpreting word symbols? Discuss how this experience might be similar to times when people do not have a common understanding of a "real" English word.

ASSESS

CHAPTER PROJECT
- When discussing results, note whether the students' articles report communication given to or received from the "twelk."

PREPARE

● CHAPTER PLANNER

Day 1	Day 2	Day 3	Day 4	Day 5
Prepare	Prepare	Prepare	Prepare	Prepare
Teach	Teach	Teach	Teach	Teach
Assess	Assess	Assess	Assess	Assess
Sub. Teacher Tip *p. 60*	Sub. Teacher Tip *p. 65*	Sub. Teacher Tip *p. 69*	Sub. Teacher Tip *p. 75*	

● CHAPTER OVERVIEW

This chapter examines the following topics:
- Reasons for Learning Effective Listening *p. 60*
- Recognizing Barriers to Listening *p. 63*
- Becoming an Active Listener *p. 67*
- Critical Listening and Thinking *p. 75*

▼ PORTFOLIO PRODUCTS

Individual Projects
- Audio Tape to Demonstrate Good Listening Skills
- Glossary of Speech Terms
- Chapter 3 Portfolio Products

Group Projects
- Television Segment in Format of Choice
- Crisis "Hotline" Dialog
- Interview Analysis

● sca GUIDELINES

- Listens to oral instructions to perform designated task
- Identifies key points in oral communications

CHAPTER

3

Listening

When you have completed this chapter you should be able to:

● Explain the difference between hearing and listening.

● State the barriers to effective listening and identify ways to overcome them.

● Describe several major responsibilities of an active listener.

● Identify several ways to improve your ability to analyze and interpret a message.

TEACH

● **LINKS TO PAST LEARNING**

Students could be asked to talk about a rumor they have heard about a famous person or important event. Discuss the relationship of what they have heard to probable reality. Begin to identify some of the factors that cause distortion in retelling information.

● **ACTIVITY**

You could award the student with the best "photographic memory" a coupon worth a discount of $1.00 at the school bookstore. Or you might prepare a Certificate of Recognition that could be given to the student.

Listening 59

ACTIVITY

Hearing versus Listening

This exercise will demonstrate how ineffective many of us are as listeners. Seven students should step outside the classroom and close the door behind them. Your teacher will ask the rest of the class to turn to the photograph on page 303 in this textbook. Then one student will be called in from the hall, asked to sit in one of two chairs facing each other at the front of the classroom, and be given a copy of the text opened to the photo on page 303. This student will be asked to describe everything about the photo to a second person brought in from the hall, who will be asked, in turn, to describe it to a third person from memory (without looking at the photo). The rest of the students will be called in one by one and asked to continue the process. The class members who remained in the room from the start should notice a number of changes occurring in the description of the photo as it is passed from one person to another in the communication chain. When the demonstration is complete, discuss why the final description of the photo differed from the first description. What did the experiment show you about our abilities as listeners?

If you are like most people, you probably think a good communicator is someone who can speak well. Speaking, however, is just part of the total process of communication. In order for speakers to get their messages across, someone must also be listening. If details of the picture described in the opening activity were gradually forgotten as the retelling moved from one student to another, it was most likely due to a lack of careful listening. Yet your classmates who were brave enough to participate in the exercise are probably as equally alert listeners as yourself, or the average person.

Listening is not an easy task. "Doesn't everyone know how to listen?" you might ask. The answer is "No." Effective listening involves more than just **hearing,** or the reception of sound. Hearing and listening are often confused. People think that if they can hear automatically, they can listen automatically. But this is simply not true. To be a good listener your must also understand and interpret sound in a meaningful way. A good deal of thinking must go on in effective listening.

When messages are misunderstood, it is easy to blame the speaker. The listener, however, must share the responsibility for effective communication. It takes a lot of concentration and effort to be a good listener. Statistics show, in fact, that most people are poor listeners. The average person misses about 75 percent of what he or she hears.

59

TEACH

SUBSTITUTE TEACHER TIP
If a daily newspaper is available, you could distribute pages to pairs of students and ask them to find an example of effective listening as reported in any section of the paper.

● **CURRICULAR CONNECTIONS**

Language Arts
Students could be asked to listen to a tape of a recorded 911 conversation they heard on a TV news program and transcribe the message. Discuss why it is important to listen carefully to such messages and suggest some of the difficulties in communicating in emergency situations.

● **SKILL DEVELOPMENT**

Critical Thinking
Students could be asked to list all of the reasons for effective listening as presented by the headings in this section. Then, next to each heading, they could write or tell an example of each benefit suggested by the heading.

● **LEARNING STYLES**

Audio Learning
Play a segment of a tape on a fast and slow speed. Discuss with students how they adjust their listening when someone speaks slower or faster than what they expect.

Multicultural Learning
Students who are learning a language other than the language spoken at home might be encouraged to talk about why speakers of a "foreign" language always seem to be speaking so fast to those unfamiliar with the language. The class might discuss which languages seem to be spoken at the fastest pace.

---

60   CHAPTER 3   Listening

Learning to listen involves self-motivation, a good deal of thinking, and practice.

The encouraging fact is that no one has to remain a poor listener. Listening, like speaking, reading, or writing, is a skill that can be learned. Learning to listen, however, takes self-motivation and practice.

This chapter will give you information about the benefits of learning to listen effectively. It will also describe the most common barriers to good listening, and give you a few basic steps to follow in becoming a better or more active listener. You will also receive hints on how to remember what you hear, how to analyze the speaker's logic, and how to interpret nonverbal messages.

● **REASONS FOR LEARNING EFFECTIVE LISTENING**

Why learn to listen? There are many good reasons. As you read through the ones discussed here, think carefully about how each applies to you. The more reasons you can find to improve your listening behavior, the easier it will be to learn and practice good listening skills.

You Will Avoid Misunderstandings

Has one of your teachers ever asked for a homework assignment that you didn't realize was due? Have you ever been introduced to someone and then a few minutes later called the person by the wrong name? Misunderstandings such as these are easy to avoid when you become an active listener.

Reasons for Learning Effective Listening

You will also be able to do things right the first time when you learn to listen effectively. If friends give you directions or tell you where and when to meet them, you won't have to ask for a recap or phone later with questions if you know how to listen well. You will be able, if you listen actively, to spend your energy on productive activities. You won't have to worry about how you are going to solve the problems created by poor listening.

In addition, practicing good listening skills may help you become more confident. You will know that you can understand and interpret correctly what other people say to you. People will learn to depend upon you.

You Will Get Along Better with Others

No one likes to talk to someone who doesn't listen. Think about the people you know. Which of them do you enjoy talking to? You probably most enjoy talking to those who seem honestly interested in what you have to say.

Listening attentively to your friends shows that you sincerely care about them, too. It is a very high compliment when you listen to another person. Just by listening you can give a speaker a feeling of confidence and self worth.

Good listening skills contribute to clear communication as well as to success in school and on the job.

TEACH

● **LEARNING STYLES**

Cooperative Learning
Ask small groups of students to work on one of the benefits of effective listening as mentioned on pp. 60–62. The groups could also be encouraged to identify a benefit not listed here. Ask each group to prepare a demonstration of the benefit they have selected. The demonstration could be a role-played situation, a tape, a cartoon, or another project of their choosing. Encourage the group to include their project in a group portfolio.

● **SKILL DEVELOPMENT**

On the Job
Ask students to imagine that they have been invited to a job interview at a company they select from your local phone book. This company could be located in an unfamiliar part of the community. Have students imagine calling the company to ask for directions. Encourage students to think of what they will need to have and do in order to listen effectively to the telephone instructions.

Feedback
To encourage a candid discussion of the importance of listening and the mistakes that can happen as a result of poor listening skills, you might share a personal anecdote about an embarrassing moment that happened because of miscommunication. With your example, you could invite volunteers to share an anecdote about things that happened to them when they were daydreaming or did not pay enough attention to something being said.

TEACH

● RETEACHING

To reinforce the idea that listening is an integral part of communication you might ask students to keep a log for 24 hours. Students could note activities they engaged in during the specified period. Each activity could be coded as a listening or speaking communication.

● ENRICHMENT

From the log of daily activities students could list the amount of time spent listening every day. The list could include listening to tapes, TV, and phone conversations. The students could compile the information and make a bar graph to show the relative amounts of time spent on various listening activities.

● ASSESSMENT STRATEGY

You might ask students to nominate another student for the "Best Listener" award in your classroom. When students nominate a classmate for the award, encourage them to give a reason why that person might receive the award. Encourage students to provide an example, or anecdote, that supports their nomination.

● ACTIVITY

The barriers to listening could be listed on the chalkboard in the form of a report card. As the barriers are introduced and examples explained, students could be encouraged to "grade" themselves on which barrier is the greatest challenge to them. Encourage them to share their "best" and "worst" obstacles to effective listening.

---

62   CHAPTER 3 Listening

You Will Learn More about the World

You probably spend a lot more of your time speaking and listening than reading and writing. Therefore, most of what you know comes from what people tell you. Television and radio as well as conversations with friends, parents, and teachers, all contribute to your understanding of your immediate environment and the world in general. The more knowledge you gain, the more you will be able to enjoy and appreciate the things around you.

It is difficult to carry on a conversation with another person if your knowledge is limited. Active listening will help you acquire a storehouse of helpful and interesting information, and it will enable you to relate better to people with a variety of interests.

You Will Be More Successful in School and on the Job

Listening skills are very important in school. Grades and interest in school activities usually improve when students make an effort to develop their ability to listen.

Good listening skills can also favorably affect your future. Regardless of what your career plans are, you have a better chance of getting the job you want and being successful at it if you know how to listen. One salesperson analyzed a typical work day and discovered that one third of the salary received was for listening.

Think for a minute about all the jobs that require good listening skills. Telephone operators, nurses, auto mechanics, teachers, and lawyers must all be able to listen carefully in order to do a good job.

● ACTIVITY

Taking Listening Personally

As your teacher talks with you about the next major section of this chapter, "Recognizing Barriers to Listening" (p. 63), ask yourself to what extent you are hampered in your everyday listening by each of those barriers. "Do I allow distractions to interfere with my listening?" "Does daydreaming sometimes prevent my catching much of what people are saying?" "Am I sometimes close-minded when listening to certain people?" When your teacher has finished discussing each of the barriers, be prepared to tell the class which barrier you find the greatest roadblock for you as a listener.

RECOGNIZING BARRIERS TO LISTENING

What would happen if a telephone operator kept giving callers the wrong number, or if a nurse didn't follow a doctor's instructions and wrote down the wrong medication? Consider a lawyer or judge who didn't pay attention to most of what went on in the courtroom. It is difficult to think of any job where good listening would not be an asset. In some jobs, it may even be a key ingredient in saving lives.

● RECOGNIZING BARRIERS TO LISTENING

At one time or another, you have probably had the nerve-wracking experience of trying to carry on a conversation with someone in a noisy room. The sounds of traffic, machinery, or even a dance band can produce such a racket that it is often impossible to hear what the other person is saying. Or perhaps you have tried to call someone long distance on the telephone and could hardly hear them over the static on the line. Noises such as these can cut off communication entirely.

Noise, however, is only one possible barrier to communication. Anything that blocks or distorts the message that a speaker is trying to get across to a listener is a barrier to the communication process. Barriers can come from problems caused by the environment, the speaker, or the listener. Whatever the original source of the problem, a good listener should make every effort to overcome it.

Being able to recognize barriers is the first step toward overcoming them. In the next few pages, you will look at five different types of barriers as well as ideas for combating them.

Distractions

There are almost always **distractions** when people communicate. Some distractions are environmental. Perhaps there are people talking close by. A radio may be playing or a television may be on. Even the temperature of the room or the time of day may influence your ability to keep your mind on the speaker's message.

Another type of distraction can come from the speaker. Have you ever heard someone remark after listening to a public speech, "I'm not sure what was said, but the speaker spoke beautifully"? Actually, this is not a compliment. If the *way* the speaker delivered the message is all the receiver can remember, something is wrong.

Good listeners must learn to keep their minds on the basic message, not on the speaker's delivery. Whenever you find yourself concentrating on how relaxed a speaker looks, how smooth a speaker's gestures seem, or how pleasant someone's voice sounds, force your mind back

---

TEACH

AMAZING FACTS!
Czar Nicholas I of Russia had asked the great pianist, Liszt, to play at court. During the performance, Liszt saw the Czar talking to an aide. Liszt quit playing. When the Czar sent a message asking Liszt why he was not playing, Liszt said: "When the Czar speaks, everyone should be silent."

● LEARNING STYLES

Cooperative Learning
Teams of students could discuss the kinds of announcements that are typically made over the school PA system. Each team could identify the barriers to listening to these messages. Encourage each group to brainstorm strategies that could improve PA announcements. Share these suggestions with the entire class.

Limited English Proficiency
Ask students to imagine that they are exchange students from an Asian country. They have just boarded a plane to come to the U.S. Discuss what those exchange students would want to hear and what might prevent them from listening carefully.

● SKILL DEVELOPMENT

15-Second Skill Opportunity
To demonstrate the effect of distractions on a speaker, ask students to prepare a short talk about a topic that interests them. Privately, ask several students in class to create some distractions such as coughing, sneezing, yawning, or clearing their throats upon receiving a visual signal from you. After a student has given a speech delivered with these distractions, ask the speaker as well as the class to comment on how these verbal and nonverbal actions influenced communication.

TEACH

AMAZING FACTS!
The fastest public speech on record was made by President Kennedy in December, 1961, with a verbal burst in excess of 300 words per minute.

● **LEARNING STYLES**

Audio Learning
Pairs or small groups of students might want to practice speaking as fast as they can. They could use stopwatches and read a passage to the others and have the effort timed. These could be taped for comparison. Compile a list of fastest times. Discuss why articulation is difficult at high speed. Encourage students to express their reactions to people who speak too fast.

● **SKILL DEVELOPMENT**

15-Second Skill Opportunity
Ask students to listen to a radio or TV program for 15 seconds with their eyes closed. Discuss what they remember hearing with their eyes closed. Then repeat the activity, but this time ask students to listen for 15 seconds with their eyes open and reading something. Discuss what they remember hearing. Encourage them to compare the experiences.

CHAPTER 3 Listening

to the content. Effective listening means concentrating on *what* the speaker says rather than on *how* it is said.

Whenever you feel yourself being distracted, whether it be by the conversations of other people, the temperature of the room, or the speaker, you should mentally remind yourself to listen. It helps if, as you enter the room for a meeting, speech, or play, you remind yourself that you aren't going to let anything distract your attention from the message you came to hear. Of course, this is easier to decide than to carry out. With real determination, however, you will gradually become better at overcoming distractions of all types.

Daydreaming

Another very common barrier to listening is daydreaming. Daydreaming is really a form of internal distraction. Your mind wanders off and you miss much of what the speaker is saying. One of the reasons this happens is that people can think much more rapidly than they can speak.

The average public speaker articulates at the rate of about 150 words per minute. Research has shown, however, that listeners can understand the message just as well when the rate is as fast as 380 words per minute—more than double that of normal speech! Just think if your teachers could learn to speak at the rate of 380 words per

One of the barriers to listening is daydreaming, a form of internal distraction that can cause you to miss much of what is being said.

● **CURRICULAR CONNECTIONS**

Language Arts
Students could gather letters to the editor from the local newspaper or a national magazine. Compare the letters with signatures only with those that contain both a signature and title. Discuss the impact of having a title attached to an opinion. The discussion could be enlarged to include the pros and cons of titles as a measure of status and credibility in our society. Some students could design their own business cards that would identify the title they would like to have.

SUBSTITUTE TEACHER TIP

You might bring in a copy of one of the tabloid newspapers and write one of the headlines on the chalkboard. Discuss what it would take to make the statement credible to the majority of students.

---

minute, you could learn about as much as you do now and be out of school before noon each day! Unfortunately, speakers cannot articulate at such a high rate of speed.

This big difference between comprehension speed and speaking rate makes it easy for people to acquire bad listening habits. Since listeners can often complete a sentence mentally before a speaker can complete it verbally, they may get bored and begin to think about something else. Instead of daydreaming, however, good listeners learn to use this extra time to concentrate on what they are hearing. Rather than letting yourself daydream about tomorrow's football game or the history exam you have next period, use your bonus time to summarize to yourself the main points the speaker is making. Think about the topic being discussed and ask yourself questions that will keep your mind on the subject.

Close-Mindedness

Try to recall some of the most recent arguments you have had. What were they about? Did you go into the discussions prepared to fight immediately to support your side, or did you really make an attempt to listen first to what the other person had to say? Were you prepared in any way to let the other person convince you that she or he was right?

When people disagree, they often become so involved with defending their own positions that they forget to listen to the facts that the other person presents. Responsible listeners, however, keep an open mind until they have heard all of the information. They listen to and weigh the merits of someone else's opinion, no matter how strong their own opinions may be.

People who refuse to expose themselves to ideas that are different from their own are basically **close-minded.** Such people may not even be willing to attend a speech by a candidate from another political party or to read a newspaper article that supports a position with which they disagree.

An **open-minded** person, on the other hand, does more listening than speaking. An open-minded person has the attitude, "I hold a certain opinion which I believe is true, but I am willing to listen carefully to the ideas and opinions of others before I make my final decision."

As a good listener, you should try to be open-minded and suspend judgment until you have heard all of the facts. Carefully consider all the information that is presented. Seek out situations in which you will hear views that are different from your own so that you will have a chance to practice careful listening. Certainly, when you get an opportunity to speak you will want the same kind of consideration and genuine listening from those who do not agree with you.

TEACH

❝*Some minds are like concrete; mixed up and permanently set.*❞
—Rev. Ralph Sander

● **SKILL APPLICATION**

Debate
Use an issue that is getting widespread attention at school or is a matter of public concern and ask students to prepare an affirmative or negative argument about it. Encourage students to examine the information or experience it would take to get them to change their minds about something.

● **LEARNING STYLES**

Visual Learning
Some students might present a cartoon representation depicting an open-minded person and a close-minded person in contrast and in the context of their participation at a school board meeting.

TEACH

> *I heard that you were a very great man, but I don't think so. I heard your speech and understood every word you said.*
> —Davy Crockett to Daniel Webster

● **RETEACHING**

You could represent each of the barriers to listening as a wall around a treasure chest. You might ask students to draw this image or represent the image on poster board. Near each wall, have students draw a toolbox that contains each of the suggestions mentioned in the text as a strategy for knocking down the barrier to listening. Encourage students to add other suggestions to their toolbox.

● **ASSESSMENT STRATEGY**

Students could be asked to identify what they perceive as the major obstacle to better listening. Once the obstacle has been identified, suggest that they write down two strategies for reducing or eliminating that barrier. Encourage them to think about how they would reward themselves for better listening skills.

---

66 CHAPTER 3 Listening

Overemphasizing the Source

If you heard a speech calling for more lenient treatment of juvenile offenders in our courts, would you be more convinced if it was presented by (1) a juvenile court judge, (2) a criminal, or (3) an ordinary citizen? When an experiment was conducted using this exact situation, the researchers found that those listeners who thought a judge was presenting the information were much more favorable in their attitude toward juvenile criminals than those who were told that the speech was being given by a criminal or an ordinary citizen. Those who thought the speaker was a criminal accepted the message least.

What does this experiment tell you about listening? For one thing, it tells you that people seem to accept a message more favorably from a person they respect than from a person whose reputation they question. However, it also points out the danger of paying too much attention to the source of a message and too little to the message itself.

Although you will naturally be influenced by your feelings about the speaker or your knowledge about the speaker's reputation, as a responsible listener you must be careful to evaluate what is being said apart from who is saying it. A message should not be judged entirely on the basis of how you feel about the speaker.

The next time you attend a public speaking event, you might take some time before the speech begins to analyze your feelings about the speaker as a message source. Do you like the speaker? Do you think the speaker is reliable? What do you know about the speaker's background?

If you listen only to things that are easy for you to understand, you may miss the opportunity to improve your listening ability.

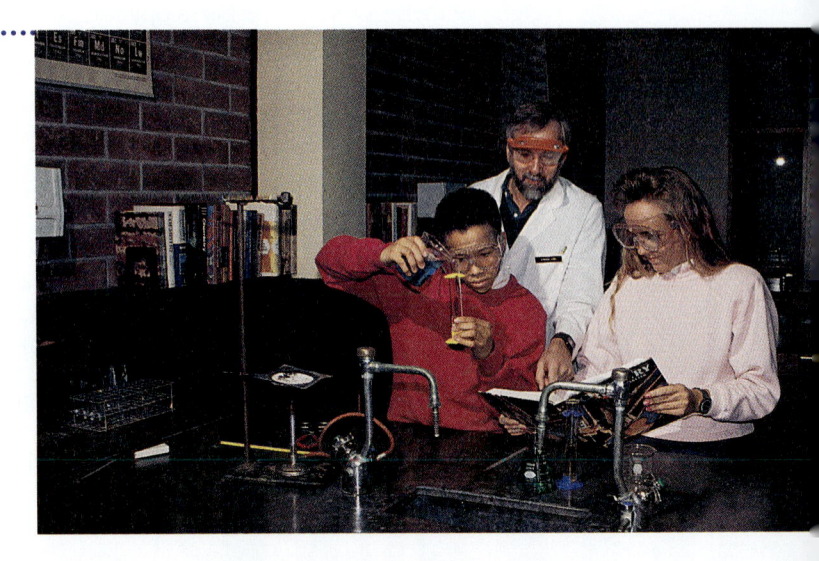

66

● LINKS TO PAST LEARNING

The Scout motto "Be Prepared" has many applications. You might ask those students who are, or who have been, in scouting programs what they were taught about that motto. Encourage them to provide examples of when being prepared was a real advantage.

> **"One of the best ways to persuade others is with your ears — by listening to them."**
>
> —Dean Rusk

● ACTIVITY

Classroom Distractions

As a class, sit quietly with your eyes closed and listen. Make a mental note of all the sounds you hear. After a few minutes help compile a list on the board. Which sounds were most distracting? Brainstorm with your classmates on how these distractions can be overcome.

● ACTIVITY

Students can be encouraged to think of ways to reduce or eliminate distractions. They might brainstorm suggestions in small groups and share ideas with the entire class. You might ask them to discuss how people who live near major airports can deal with the distractions of frequent airplane noise.

● SKILL DEVELOPMENT

Creative Thinking
You might share with the class an example or two of an annoying situation in which a person arrived late for a listening activity such as a college lecture, a play, or a movie. Encourage students to express how they felt when they were inconvenienced by someone's tardiness or rude behavior. Take one of the scenarios described in class discussion and ask students to think of several alternate ways to deal with those who are late or rude during a performance. The class could draw up a list of Do's and Don'ts for proper theater etiquette and make illustrated posters.

If the score is very low or high—if you have a most unfavorable or very high opinion of the speaker—you will know that you must be very careful in making judgments about what the speaker has to say.

Listening Only to What Is Easy to Understand

Another common barrier to good listening is listening only to what is easy to understand. If you become accustomed to "turning off" whenever you become confused, it won't be long before this behavior becomes a habit. If you avoid material that is difficult and only expose yourself to things that are already easy for you, you will never have the opportunity to improve your listening ability.

If you have studied a foreign language, you know that the first time you listen to someone speaking in that language it sounds very confusing. It is easy to become frustrated and give up because you get lost very quickly. As you practice and become more familiar with the foreign sounds, however, you soon begin to *enjoy* hearing that language.

The more often you challenge yourself by listening to difficult material, the better you will be at following and understanding what you hear.

● BECOMING AN ACTIVE LISTENER

To become a good listener you should be ready to do some hard work. Remember that as a listener you have certain responsibilities both to yourself and to the speaker. Not only must you avoid the barriers to listening that were just discussed, but you must also actively do your part to insure that you get the most out of each listening experience.

TEACH

AMAZING FACTS!

The English language has about 616,500 words plus 400,000 technical terms, the most in any language. It is doubtful that any individual uses more than 60,000 words. Shakespeare used a vocabulary of about 33,000 words.

PORTFOLIO PRODUCTS

Some students or a cooperative learning group might prepare a crossword puzzle that incorporates speech terms used in this text. The puzzle could be duplicated for all students to use.

CURRICULAR CONNECTIONS

Language Arts

Suggest that students make cluster vocabulary lists. They could take a topic or any subject they are studying and make a list of 10 words that are commonly used to talk about that subject. These lists could be shared and displayed.

SKILL DEVELOPMENT

15-Second Skill Opportunity

Students will gain practice in active listening if they learn to ask at least one question in each class, workshop, or club meeting they attend. Ask them to prepare one question they will ask in this or another class. Encourage volunteers to raise thoughtful questions and share them with the class.

LEARNING STYLES

Multicultural Learning

You might share the following story and then ask students what vocabulary they think a visitor to the U.S. would need in order to travel from Maine to California.

Erich Maria Remarque, author of *All Quiet on the Western Front*, met an American in Berlin. Speaking in German, she asked Remarque why he had never traveled to the U.S. He replied that he knew only a few sentences in English. They were: "How do you do? I love you. Forgive me. Forget me. Ham and eggs, please."

The young woman exclaimed, "Why, with that vocabulary you could tour my country from Maine to California."

---

68 CHAPTER 3 Listening

Prepare to Listen

In order to hear and understand everything a speaker has to say, be ready to listen from the very beginning. This means arriving early enough to get a good seat at a play or getting to a meeting on time. If you go into a class after the teacher has already begun the day's work, you not only interrupt your classmates but you create a difficult situation for yourself. You then have to try to make sense out of what is being discussed without having heard the introductory remarks.

If you know that you will be doing a lot of listening, it is a good idea to get sufficient rest beforehand. If you are tired, hungry, or upset, it is much harder to focus on the message than if you listen when you are alert and rested.

Finding out as much as you can beforehand about a speaker's topic, the plot of a play, or the agenda of a meeting are other ways you can prepare yourself to listen. If you have thought in advance about some of the ideas you will be hearing, you can better understand what the speaker is talking about. You become like a runner who has used warm-up exercises before jogging. The runner can perform better because he or she has made a smooth transition from a relaxed to an active state. Sometimes, of course, it is not possible to discover information about a topic ahead of time. But do not overlook opportunities to prepare yourself to listen more effectively.

Expand Your Vocabulary

One aid that will help you to understand better and benefit more from what you hear is the development of a good vocabulary. Words are symbols that a speaker uses to convey ideas. In order for the ideas to reach their destination, however, the listener must also be familiar with the words the speaker has chosen. You can think of good listeners as being similar to good carpenters—the more tools they know how to use, the better the job they can do. The more words listeners have at their command, the more effective they can be. If your listening vocabulary is limited, so is your ability to learn new and useful things.

Can you define *epitome? regurgitate? calcify?* If you don't know the meaning of words such as these, you might consider spending some time each day expanding your vocabulary. Whenever you hear a word or phrase that is unfamiliar, find out its meaning right away. Then search for opportunities to use the new word in your conversations during the next several days. Using the unfamiliar word yourself will implant it firmly in your memory so that its meaning will be easily recognized the next time you hear it used.

Becoming an Active Listener 69

Apply the Message to Yourself

As an active listener, you must also apply the speaker's message to yourself as you listen. Search your mind for circumstances under which you could use the information you are hearing. Find something in what is being said that arouses your interest.

When you have freely chosen to get involved in some listening situation, you should have no difficulty in applying the message to yourself. If you like surfing, you should find it easy to relate to a speech on Big Sur. Many times, however, you will find yourself in a situation where the subject is not of great interest to you. Your tendency then, as an unwilling participant, may be to escape from listening.

Deciding not to listen in any situation is like betting the speaker will have nothing helpful to say to you. Either way you lose. Why spend your time and not get any personal benefits? Practice searching for ideas that can apply to you and your interests, regardless of the topic. You may be surprised at how many ways you will be able to relate what the speaker is saying to your own needs. Constantly ask yourself questions such as:

- Do I believe what this speaker is saying?
- How can I put this information to use?
- Do I feel differently about this subject than the speaker does?

Taking notes in outline form is an excellent method of identifying a speaker's main ideas.

TEACH

SUBSTITUTE TEACHER TIP

You could bring in a newspaper or magazine and have students note the titles of articles. The title, or headline, is a succinct summary of the main idea of the article. Ask students to write alternate headlines or titles that reflect the main idea of the article.

● **SKILL DEVELOPMENT**

Main Idea
To help students identify the main idea presented in written and oral communications, ask a volunteer to restate the main point made in the class at 15-minute intervals. Others could be asked to identify the central point another student has just made in class.

Outlining
Students could use an outline format to identify the major points they would want to develop for a topic that interests them. Suggest that the title of the topic they select be a clue to the main point they want to make.

TEACH

● **LEARNING STYLES**

Visual Learning
Suggest that students use two different colored markers to distinguish main ideas from supporting ideas when they read material or highlight notes. You could practice with them to show them how to distinguish major and supporting information in a paragraph from a magazine or book.

Cooperative Learning
Have students meet in small groups to talk about a topic of interest. If students need suggestions, they might talk about a favorite pet, animal at the zoo, or vacation they would like to take. Each student could talk for one minute. When finished, the student could ask another in the group to summarize the main idea. Everyone in each group could have the experience of speaking and summarizing.

● **SKILL APPLICATION**

Citizens Speak Out
Students could watch a political speaker and list all the nonverbal clues the speaker provides to indicate the main point of the speech. If a political speaker is not easily available, students could watch a speaker on a TV talk show. Discuss the variety of nonverbal clues that are used to emphasize the main idea.

CHAPTER 3 Listening

Pick Out the Central Ideas

Many people, untrained in listening, become fascinated by stories, examples, and statistics and lose sight of the **central idea** a speaker is trying to communicate. Good listeners, on the other hand, who have learned to pick out the key ideas, have less difficulty in understanding what they hear because they know that they should not waste time trying to remember *all* the less important details.

Most well-organized public speeches contain very few main ideas, often no more than two or three. A play usually contains one main plot and perhaps a few subplots. The same is true of literary selections that are read aloud. Therefore, if you begin to look for these main ideas, you will have a better understanding of the speaker's primary message. Other facts and details presented by the speaker, instead of confusing the issue, can be used to clarify these central points.

Learning to identify main ideas takes practice. A public speaker often mentions main ideas near the beginning and end of her or his remarks. Thus, when listening to a public speech, pay close attention to the speaker's introduction and conclusion, since there the speech's purpose and main points usually stand out in clear fashion. The rest of the speech may develop these central ideas by giving reasons for them. If you hear the same idea mentioned several times, you can be quite sure the speaker considers it an important point. Listen carefully for words and phrases such as "first," "second," "most important," "to summarize," and "remember." These verbal cues usually indicate an important point is coming next.

One good way to identify main ideas in formal speaking situations is to take notes in outline form. Most speakers organize their message in some way. If you make an effort, you are likely to become very good at recognizing different organizational styles and picking out main points. Outlining will also help you identify the relationships between ideas.

The organization of ideas in conversations tends to be somewhat less logical, mainly because ideas are generally not organized in advance. Locating the speaker's main ideas in informal communication situations is therefore more difficult. But this problem can be offset by the increased opportunity you have to give feedback to the speaker and to participate in the communication.

When you listen to another person in an informal setting such as a one-to-one conversation, a group discussion, or a meeting, practice restating in your mind what you feel were the main ideas expressed. Then ask the speaker whether you are correct. This is particularly helpful when you are discussing a controversial topic with another person, since it is even more difficult to listen well to someone with whom you disagree. In one-to-one and small group situations it is important to

Becoming an Active Listener

use this opportunity to ask questions during the conversation to insure that you understand the main points being made.

Almost all speakers will appreciate a listener who focuses on the main message they are trying to present rather than on the small details used to illustrate their points. Learning to pick out a speaker's main ideas is one of the most useful listening skills you can acquire.

Provide Feedback

Good listeners encourage the speaker by providing feedback—by actively responding to what they hear. Signs of attention and interest help a speaker present the message in the most effective way possible. Most public speakers, for instance, even prefer frowns and the shaking of heads to blank stares or drowsy eyelids. At least the frowns let a public speaker know the listeners are following what is being said. If the audience makes no response, speakers have no way of judging whether they are speaking successfully.

It is just as important and much easier to give feedback when the communication situation is less formal. Feedback is extremely valuable in meetings, group discussions, or one-to-one conversations. Remember that when you ask a question, nod your head, or laugh, you are helping the speaker get the message across. Unless speakers know what your reaction is to their words, they cannot tell whether or not they are accomplishing their purposes.

Feedback, in the form of signs of attention and interest, is the most useful response for speakers. Even frowns or shaking heads are preferable to no reaction at all.

TEACH

"The true art of memory is the art of attention."
—Samuel Johnson

● **SKILL DEVELOPMENT**

Feedback
Ask students to imagine that they have a friend who has the irritating habit of interrupting a conversation or another's sentence. Discuss the type of feedback that would be appropriate to give the friend.

15-Second Skill Opportunity
Ask volunteers to stand and give their name, address, and telephone number. Then ask the students who are able to remember and repeat the address and phone number to explain how they are able to remember what they hear.

● **LEARNING STYLES**

Visual Learning
Ask students to stand and speak a sentence with their eyes closed. They could remain standing until they think they can describe student response to their statements. Discuss how feedback can be expressed without the ability to read facial expressions or body language.

Multicultural Learning
You could invite students to discuss how different cultures suggest appropriate types of feedback. You could begin by asking how various cultures provide praise to a young student for successful completion of a high school education. Provide various examples of how praise is communicated in several cultures.

TEACH

● **RETEACHING**

Review each of the suggestions for becoming a better listener and then ask students to name a classmate who seems to have the best skills in each area. You could award each student selected by the class a Certificate of Recognition.

● **ENRICHMENT**

Some students might enjoy reading and reporting on a mystery story. They could explain the main idea and then identify the verbal and visual clues that the "hero" pursued to arrest the "villain."

CHAPTER 3 Listening

Whenever you listen to any speaker, think about what types of feedback are appropriate. The following list suggests some of the more common ways in which listeners can let the speaker know that they are following the message.

- Look the speaker directly in the eyes much of the time.
- Nod your head slightly to indicate understanding or agreement.
- Frown or shake your head to show you disagree or don't understand.
- Smile or laugh at humorous remarks the speaker makes.
- In informal communications, occasionally interject a word of encouragement such as "Yes," or "I see."
- If seated, maintain an upright, alert posture. Don't slouch in your chair.
- In informal communications, lean forward to show interest in what the speaker is saying.

It is also important that your feedback be clear enough so that the speaker can easily interpret it. In many instances, the feedback you provide as a listener will be nonverbal. Nonverbal signs are very easy to misread. Thus, you must take extra care to insure that you are sending the message you intend through your facial expression, body posture, and eye contact.

Remember What You Hear

If one of the main reasons for learning to be a better listener is to acquire new information, it is important that you be able to remember what you hear.

You receive so many messages each day that you probably have a hard time sorting them out and deciding which ones should be remembered. Think for a moment about how many people spoke to you yesterday. Now, how many of their messages can you remember in detail? Unless you have an exceptional memory, you probably don't remember as many as you would like. It takes a conscious effort to remember what you hear, but it is worthwhile because that is the only way the information you receive will be useful to you.

One of the surest ways to remember something is to have a strong reason to remember it. The famous detective of fiction, Sherlock Holmes, once told his friend Watson that he knew nothing of the solar

Becoming an Active Listener 73

system. When Watson expressed astonishment that Holmes was unaware that the earth traveled around the sun, Holmes explained that he remembered only what was important to him: "What the deuce is it to me?" he interrupted impatiently. "You say that we go round the sun. If we went round the moon it would not make a pennyworth of difference to me or to my work." Though Holmes seemed a bit extreme in choosing what to forget, he was certainly motivated to remember what was important.

Did you ever notice how attentive everyone in a class becomes when a teacher says, "This will be on the exam"? Of course it's easier to listen closely when you are strongly motivated. When the conversation is boring or the meeting is dull, a good listener must rise to the challenge. There are many occasions when you have to *find* good reasons to remember.

Another way to remember something is to connect new information you are hearing with something you already know. This is called the **process of association.** An example of this process of association would be if a speaker claims that a certain part of the ocean is 15,000 feet (4600 meters) deep. You want to remember that number. If you already know that Mt. Whitney is approximately 15,000 feet (4600 meters) in altitude, you can associate the ocean depth with the height of the mountain. Later, you will likely remember the ocean depth by recalling, "Oh yes, that was about the same as the height of Mt. Whitney."

● ACTIVITY

Being an Active Listener

Five students should leave the room. A member of the class will then tell a story or incident that includes several important details. The students who left earlier will be called back into the classroom *one at a time*. The teacher will then select a student from the class to tell the story to the first one who returns. This student will tell what he or she heard to the next student who reenters the classroom, and so on, until all five have heard the story from the student preceding them into the room. The last student to return will tell the final version of the incident or story to the class.

Take notes in your notebook on how many errors have occurred since the original telling. Participate in a class discussion on how or why these errors in listening took place.

TEACH

> *"All you have to do to entertain some people is to listen."*
>
> —Anonymous

● **LEARNING STYLES**

Beyond the Classroom
You might invite a school counselor or psychologist to speak to the class about the active listening techniques used to understand a student's or client's message. Discuss which of these techniques might be useful in ordinary communication.

● **ACTIVITY**

You may wish to begin this Activity with a short printed anecdote rather than a student anecdote. If so, distribute copies for students to use. The students can use the printed version to compare with the oral version. Students could be asked to identify the significant details of the story and make a note of those that are consistently remembered.

73

APPLY

● EXTENSION

Ask a medical secretary to speak to the class about the importance of listening skills. If this is difficult to arrange, some students could interview a medical secretary in person or by phone. Develop interview questions that explore the importance of listening and communication. Have students share their interviews with the class.

● SKILL APPLICATION

Phone Calls
Ask students to role-play several phone conversations a medical secretary might have with patients calling to make appointments, report a medical emergency, or request a referral to a medical specialist.

● CURRICULAR CONNECTIONS

Math/Science
Students could make a cluster list of technical terms that a medical secretary would often use. Discuss how a medical secretary, or any person working with technical language, learns the pronunciation and meaning of terms uncommon to others outside the profession. Try to get students to imagine how the math and science required for the medical profession will change within the next five years. Talk about how medical secretaries would train to keep themselves current in their profession.

CAREER CLOSE-UP

Medical Secretary

The medical secretary, an integral part of the physician's office, is usually the first person whom the patient contacts. The medical secretary acts as a receptionist, takes simple patient histories, transcribes medical records, manages insurance claims, and bills patients. Medical secretaries must be high-school graduates who have studied the secretarial sciences and English. One- and two-year associate degree programs are also available.

Good communications skills are an important part of the medical secretary's role. Despite many distractions, he or she listens carefully as patients relate symptoms or other problems. Active listening involves more than providing a receptive ear, however. The secretary needs to ask pertinent questions so that the nature and severity of a problem can be gauged. He or she also restates information back to the patient to make sure there is complete understanding. Since patients are sometimes frightened or in pain, a secretary needs to convey calm and capable assurance by speaking in even vocal tones and using reassuring nods and gestures. These techniques communicate to patients that their problems are receiving competent attention.

Developing good communications skills enables a genuine understanding of patients and their problems to a medical practice. Thus, physician and patient relationships improve. Medical secretaries who communicate effectively become invaluable members of the health care team by providing an all-important link between patient and doctor.

Through professionalism and good communications skills, the medical secretary both inspires trust and provides an essential link between patient and physician.

TEACH

● LINKS TO PAST LEARNING

Ask students to share stories of "really dumb" remarks or arguments that they have heard that defy logic. Discuss what makes people believe outlandish things or say things that defy logic.

● CURRICULAR CONNECTIONS

Language Arts
Students could be encouraged to compile a dictionary of the terms used in this section. Learning about how expressions came into popular usage is interesting, and students can share their findings with the rest of the class.

SUBSTITUTE TEACHER TIP

Encourage students to ask and discuss the question, "What's missing here?" as they examine a newspaper article or watch a TV program. Suggest ways individuals can obtain missing information about events or products. Discuss the amount of time it would take to get the missing information.

> **"**To avoid criticism, do nothing, say nothing, be nothing.**"**
> —Elbert Hubbard

● LEARNING STYLES

Cooperative Learning
Bring examples of printed advertising for groups to examine. Ask each group to identify the logical fallacies and propaganda arguments.

● CRITICAL LISTENING AND THINKING

Although picking out main ideas, knowing the definitions of the words being used, and making good use of your memory are important, there is a great deal more you must do to be an effective listener. A good listener must also be able to interpret the sender's message. This can be done by considering factors such as motives, reasoning, and nonverbal communication. The active listener must be a critical listener. A **critical listener** is one who analyzes and interprets messages carefully. Your ability to analyze and interpret a message correctly depends upon how carefully you listen for what is "behind" the speaker's words.

You might remember that in *Alice in Wonderland* things weren't always what they seemed. The same is often true in real life. It is up to you as a good listener to consider all factors involved in a particular message so that you are in a position to decide on the value and meaning of what you hear.

Listen for Faulty Reasoning

Part of your responsibility as a listener is to analyze what you hear. Listeners who believe everything they are told can get into a lot of trouble. Be especially alert when listening to messages that are meant to persuade you. Be prepared for the speaker who has not constructed an argument using sound reasoning but depends on misleading you.

Thus, in order to make intelligent decisions about the information that comes to you, you need to analyze the speaker's methods. Clever speakers will often seem to be giving you the facts when really they are misleading you with deceptive reasoning. It is important to be alert for false methods of reasoning, which are called **logical fallacies.** Descriptions of a few of the most common fallacies follow.

Name calling is the term used for the faulty reasoning involved when a speaker gives a person or idea a bad label without providing any evidence to prove what is said. When you hear a speaker call someone a criminal, a cheater, or a liar, don't be misled. Make sure the speaker gives good reasons for using such labels.

Card stacking is a method whereby the speaker, instead of presenting all of the important evidence, tells the audience only those facts that support the point she or he is trying to make. The speaker leaves out the bad aspects of the idea and neglects to point out the benefits any alternatives may have.

The **bandwagon technique** gets its name from the fact that the speaker asks the listeners to "jump on the bandwagon," to become part of a supposedly overwhelming group in favor of some person, product,

TEACH

> **From listening comes wisdom; and from speaking, repentance.**
> —Italian Proverb

● **LEARNING STYLES**

Visual Learning
Ask students to make a list of TV commercials that accompany a program that they watch frequently. Ask them to develop a chart that would include the following information: Name of Product, Length of Commercial, Main Idea of Commercial, Logical Fallacy Used in Commercial. These charts could be shared and displayed in the class.

Cooperative Learning
Small groups of students could identify some of the leading spokespersons used in commercial advertising. Encourage each group to pick a product and agree upon a spokesperson for that product. Have the group discuss the kind of testimonial or endorsement they would want from the spokesperson. Discuss what type of audience is most influenced by testimonials.

CHAPTER 3 Listening

or idea. The speaker tries to convince you that because everyone else doing something—using a certain shampoo or voting for a particul candidate, for example—you should do it too or you will regret bein left out. Television commercials use this approach often. Watch for it

A **glittering generality** is a word or phrase that is so vague th everyone can agree on its value but no one is really sure exactly wh it means. Politicians may say they are in favor of "freedom of speech" "equal rights." Later, however, you may discover that what they mea by these terms is different from your own interpretation of the words

A **testimonial** is the opinion of some well-known person on a pa ticular subject. However, the person, although famous, may not be a expert on that subject. Is a movie star really more knowledgeable abo dish detergent than anyone else? Whenever you hear a testimonia make sure that you ask yourself, "Is this person really in a position know the facts?"

In the fallacy called **begging the question,** speakers never real prove the points they are trying to make. They take it for granted (ar sometimes may want you to, also) that their ideas are true without pr viding proof. Suppose a speaker says, "Juana is the best president o student council ever had. We should reelect her." If no reasons a given for believing Juana to be the best council president ever, t speaker is guilty of begging the question.

The term **non sequitur** is a Latin phrase meaning "It does not fo low." A speaker guilty of a *non sequitur* may provide evidence to bac up a statement, but if you examine the evidence you will find that does not really prove the point. Suppose you were to campaign fo class president by stating that you were the best candidate and the emphasizing how well you played tennis or how good you were Chinese cooking; you would be guilty of this kind of faulty reasonin

A **hasty generalization** occurs when the speaker does not real have enough evidence to support the broad conclusion drawn. Suppos during a recent visit to Denver, Colorado, friends of yours ate at thre restaurants. When you ask them about the trip, they tell you Denv restaurants are terrible. Drawing the conclusion that all restaurants Denver are bad just because the three they ate in were unsatisfactory not good reasoning. Hasty generalizations are a very common type faulty reasoning. You can often spot them by listening for telltale word such as "everyone," "always," "never," "all the time," and "nobody."

The fallacies of begging the question, *non sequitur*, and hasty ge eralization often occur not because speakers are attempting to deceiv their audiences but because they have not given enough thought their arguments. Good listeners, though, will insist on sound reasonin in the messages they hear. It is up to you, as a listener, to detect thes common faults and logical fallacies.

Consider the Source

You have probably heard someone who disagreed with what another person had just said react by scowling, "Consider the source!" Such an attack on the speaker instead of his or her words is often unjustified, but the careful listener does need to pay close attention to the motives, biases, backgrounds, and viewpoints of the speakers he or she hears.

Consider, for example, a salesman trying to convince you to buy a new car. Though every feature he points out may be every bit as good as he says, listen for those features he fails to mention. He may be omitting them because he knows the competition is superior regarding those features. Ask him questions about areas where you feel his presentation was unclear. Make him provide you with solid evidence (facts, figures, examples from unbiased sources) that his cars are indeed safer, more economical, and more dependable than the competition's. Remember that, as a salesman, he is naturally going to be blind to certain defects in his own product, and biased against those of the competition. One of his primary motives is to sell cars. That is also his job, and he needs to be good at it. As the listener (customer) your job is to realize that the salesman has some purposes and motives that differ from your own. You need to listen "between the lines"!

Part of "considering the source" means learning to distinguish between facts and opinions. A fact is that which the speaker proves to you with sound evidence—with examples, statistics, and testimony. An opinion, on the other hand, is just that—something the speaker *thinks*

Whether buying a car or a computer, you need to be aware of the salesperson's motives and biases so that you can distinguish between facts and opinions.

TEACH

AMAZING FACTS!
The longest running TV commercial character was Jan Miner, who played "Madge the Manicurist" from 1965 to 1991.

● SKILL DEVELOPMENT

15-Second Skill Opportunity
Ask students to think about the first sentence they would say to a used-car salesperson to inquire about a specific car in the price range they have identified. Suggest to students that their first sentence will indicate to the salesperson the seriousness and intelligence of the potential buyer and will influence the kind of time and information the salesperson will provide. Ask for volunteers to stand up and deliver their first sentence in this situation. Others in the class can provide feedback about the effectiveness of the inquiry.

TEACH

● LINKS TO PAST LEARNING

Many students are probably turning their thoughts to selecting an appropriate college. Some of them will have a variety of brochures. Ask students to bring some of those brochures to class. Some colleges have prepared video presentations for prospective students. If those are available, visual learners could use the video version.

● LEARNING STYLES

Visual Learning
After hearing testimony at a high-profile trial, a relative of the crime victim gave a thumbs-up sign. Discuss the impact of that nonverbal cue to the jury and others in the courtroom. Ask students to think about what the judge in the trial would rule about the use of nonverbal cues in court.

Kinesic Learning
Ask students how they think animal trainers use nonverbal cues for training purposes. Encourage students to think of, and demonstrate, several nonverbal cues that might be used effectively in the training of guide dogs.

Ask students to review the definition of propaganda and look for examples of this technique in the college brochures. Discuss how "considering your sources" will empower students to make more reasonable decisions about colleges.

● ENRICHMENT

Some friends of Johnny Carson played a practical joke on him when they staged a party in London and hired actors to pretend to speak British English with proper intonation and expression. The actors, however, were just speaking gibberish. Some students might enjoy playing a practical joke on another friend by using inflections and tone of voice that would suggest something other than the meaning of the words they use.

---

78   CHAPTER 3 Listening

and *says* is a fact, but fails to prove with evidence. One of the chief characteristics of **propaganda** is the stating of opinions as though they were proven facts. Opinions sometimes turn out to be factual, but as a listener you are never in a position to know unless the speaker provides you with the evidence.

Finally, when "considering your sources," be wary of accepting the speaker's message because of his or her status, fame, or position. Well-known, famous, and highly intelligent people make mistakes just as the rest of us do. Judge each message on its own merits. When listening to someone you respect highly, try to separate the speaker from the message. Do the same when listening to someone whom you distrust or dislike. Valid, truthful, and helpful messages can come from those whom you may not hold in high regard.

Recognize Nonverbal Cues

In order to arrive at an accurate interpretation of a message, it is important to focus not only on a speaker's verbal message but also on the speaker's nonverbal communication. Analyzing nonverbal communication can give you important information about the speaker's attitude

In addition to words, this caller supplements her message with varying vocal tones, volume, and rate, as well as pausing, laughing, and other forms of paralanguage.

▱ PORTFOLIO PRODUCTS

Students could make a checklist from the nonverbal elements listed in the narrative. The checklist could be duplicated and used to help assess communication in the classroom.

TEACH

● SKILL DEVELOPMENT

🕒 15-Second Skill Opportunity

You could ask students to brainstorm to create a list of emotions that they are familiar with. The list could include anger, fear, apprehension, love, impatience, surprise, etc. These could be recorded on the chalkboard. Then ask students to select one of the emotions listed and say the sentence, "I think Mrs. Jones is a fair person," to convey the emotion they selected. The other students in the class could guess which emotion the speaker is trying to convey.

Critical Listening and Thinking   79

emotional state, and motives. You will discover that the nonverbal portion of a message carries considerable impact in projecting the overall meaning.

A good speaker strives to use gestures, facial expressions, and a tone of voice that support and reinforce the verbal message. Sometimes, however, a speaker's verbal and nonverbal messages contradict. A good listener will recognize this and interpret the speaker's meaning by considering both the words and the nonverbal cues. Think for a moment of a parent scolding a small child. Along with a stern look and a serious voice, the child hears, "Johnny, we don't use crayons on the wall!" The words are important, but Johnny may cry as much because of the vocal tones and facial expressions as because of what is said.

Every communication situation combines nonverbal elements with verbal. Even a telephone conversation includes vocal tones, volume, speaking rate, pausing, laughing, and other forms of paralanguage. In Chapter 2 you learned that paralanguage is the *way* something is said rather than the words themselves. Thus it is considered a form of nonverbal communication. If you pay close attention while listening you will discover that the stress a person uses to say different words can make a big difference in the meaning you receive. Imagine having a telephone conversation with a classmate about your school's principal. Your friend makes the statement "I think Ms. Jones is a fair person." If you had received these words in written form, you would not know whether your friend means that, in her opinion, Ms. Jones is only an "average" person, or whether she means Ms. Jones treats everyone equally. However, your friend's vocal stress on *fair* makes the meaning immediately obvious. Tone of voice is also important. Through tone a speaker can indicate sarcasm, disgust, anger, or other feelings that cannot be conveyed through words alone.

While paying close attention to the speaker's words, the careful listener must also be alert to the importance of all forms of nonverbal communication. The following list includes some of the elements you should take into account:

- movements
- gestures
- eye contact
- paralanguage (stress, voice tone, speaking rate, pauses, etc.)
- proxemics (how close the speaker is to the listener or listeners)
- body posture

By keeping all the senses tuned in, an active listener will pick up much more than those listeners who attend only to the speaker's words.

TEACH

> Q "Where's that mule I told you to have shod?"
>
> A "Whoops! I thought you said 'shot'."

● **LINKS TO PAST LEARNING**

Ask students to provide examples of how misunderstandings have caused them trouble or embarrassment. You could use the examples to suggest ways that getting feedback would have avoided or improved the situation.

● **LEARNING STYLES**

Visual Learning
Some students might show the feedback process as a flow chart. Encourage them to use cartoon characters and dialogue to illustrate the process. Display these flow charts in class. Some may want to include them in their assessment portfolio.

80

---

80 CHAPTER 3 Listening

Use Feedback to Check Your Interpretation

Have you ever had a good friend ask you "What's the matter?" even though you had not said anything was wrong? Paying attention to nonverbal cues, as you know, is essential in order to understand fully a communicator's message. It is, however, very easy to misinterpret nonverbal communication. In the preceding example, your somber expression and slow movements, which your friend interpreted as an indication that you were unhappy, may have simply been the result of not getting enough sleep. Your friend, expecting to see your usual smiling face and fast walk, may easily have misread the nonverbal signs you were sending.

Although verbal messages create less of a problem, they too can be misinterpreted. If your teacher says, "The exam will be coming up soon," you may not worry because you assume you have another weekend in which to study. When your teacher announces later that day that the exam will be tomorrow, you may be upset. Such problems in communication happen all the time.

Checking your understanding and interpretation of both verbal and nonverbal messages can help to avoid breakdowns in communication.

In order to avoid these breakdowns in communication it is important to check your understanding and interpretation of the messages you receive. Ask the speaker questions. Restate what you think the speaker has said so that you know whether or not your interpretation is correct. If your sister says, "I'll be back in a little while," you might ask, "Do you expect to be back before noon?" to be sure you understand what she means.

Many problems and misunderstandings can be avoided if you remember your responsibility as an active listener and do not expect the speaker to do all of the work. Remember that listening is an active process and requires that you do your part to improve the communication process.

ACTIVITY

Identifying Logical Fallacies

Pretend you are trying to help a politician who is running for local office. Role-play a situation in class in which you try to persuade a classmate to vote for your candidate. Use one of the logical fallacies listed on pages 75 and 76. When you have finished ask your classmates to comment on your technique. Are they able to tell which logical fallacy you used?

TEACH

SKILL DEVELOPMENT

Feedback
Suggest to students that class instruction might be improved if they could identify several of the best activities they have experienced in previous classes. Encourage them to share those experiences and discuss how some of them could be replicated.

ACTIVITY

Cooperative learning groups could choose a specific political candidate. If possible, they could obtain campaign literature from their candidate. Ask each group to campaign for their candidate. Students might create slogans, placards, or buttons. They could deliver "speeches" to support their candidate using one or more of the techniques mentioned in this section.

ASSESS

● STUDENT PERFORMANCE COMPETENCIES

- Explains the difference between *hearing* and *listening*
- States several reasons for learning to listen well
- Lists ways to improve listening skills
- Identifies several ways to improve ability to analyze and interpret messages

● sca GUIDELINES

- Listens to oral instructions to perform designated task
- Identifies key points in oral communications

▽ PORTFOLIO ASSESSMENT

Standard
- Completed checklist to help evaluate good listening skills
- Compiled glossary of speech terms
- Completed assignments, quizzes, projects, and Chapter 3 test

Enrichment
- Interview of Medical Secretary
- Flow Chart Illustrating the Feedback Process

Challenge
- Advertising Analysis for Logical Fallacies
- Tape of a Communication Delivered Using Nonverbal Messages Only

---

CHAPTER 3 REVIEW

● SUMMARY

Listening to speech involves much more than simply hearing. Listening is a learned process that requires a search for understanding and a careful interpretation of the speaker's words. People often fail to recognize the importance of listening, even though it is just as essential to communication as speaking.

Benefits of Learning to Listen Effectively Important benefits flow from improving your listening skills. A good listener avoids misunderstandings, learns many interesting and useful things, and attracts those who enjoy talking to someone who listens. People who work at listening are also more successful in their jobs because they can follow directions and relate easily to other people.

Recognizing Barriers to Listening Recognize barriers to listening, such as distractions and daydreaming, and learn to overcome them by concentrating on the speaker's ideas, suspending your judgments, and keeping an open mind until you have heard all of the facts. In addition, avoid overemphasizing a message's source and listening only to what is easy to understand.

Becoming an Active Listener An active listener does everything possible to bring about effective communication. Get into shape to listen. Research the subject beforehand, arrive on time, well-rested, and ready to listen, and expand your vocabulary in order to improve your listening comprehension. Pick out the speaker's main ideas, relate them to your interests, and provide feedback so that the speaker knows you are receiving the message. Then strive to understand and remember what you hear, so that the information will have value for you.

Interpreting the Message An active listener also listens critically and analyzes the speaker's verbal techniques and logic. The bandwagon technique, card stacking, and testimonials are just a few of the logical fallacies a clever speaker may use to persuade you of something. So a good listener must always "consider the source" of the messages, recognize speakers' motives and viewpoints, learn to distinguish fact from opinion, and judge the validity of messages separately from their sources. Just as a speaker's message is conveyed verbally and nonverbally, the effective listener provides verbal and nonverbal feedback to the speaker to make sure the message is interpreted correctly.

ASSESS

● **ASSESSMENT STRATEGIES**

Individual Assessment
- Participates in practice activities daily or weekly
- Completes classwork
- Demonstrates knowledge of content through questions, discussion, role-playing, feedback, quizzes, and tests
- Displays improvement in targeted speech skills

Group Assessment
- Participates in cooperative learning activities
- Supports efforts of team and class members
- Provides encouragement and feedback regularly

VOCABULARY

Define each term in a complete sentence.

listening
hearing
distractions
close-minded
open-minded
central idea
process of association
critical listener
logical fallacies

name calling
card stacking
bandwagon technique
glittering generality
testimonial
begging the question
non sequitur
hasty generalization
propaganda

✓ CHECKLIST

Listening Skills

1. Communicate with the speaker by concentrating and making an effort to listen.
2. Give others confidence by showing that you are listening attentively.
3. Keep your mind on the basic message, not on distractions or the speaker's delivery.
4. Keep an open mind to the speaker until you've heard all the information. Remember the merits of other opinions.
5. Be prepared to learn difficult material; listen even when it is not easy to understand.
6. Prepare to listen by arriving early, well-rested, and informed about the topic.
7. Expand your vocabulary so that you will understand what is being discussed.
8. Train yourself to pick out the central ideas. Take notes if helpful.
9. Remember what you hear; use the process of association to improve your memory.
10. Check your understanding of the speaker's message by asking questions and restating ideas.

ASSESS

● **ANSWERS**

See the Answer Key for more complete answers.

REVIEW QUESTIONS
1. Hearing is the reception of sound. Listening is the understanding and interpreting of sound in a meaningful way.
2. Active listening combines hearing with understanding and meaningful interpretation.
3. Active listening can help a person avoid misunderstandings, learn about the world, get along better with others, and succeed in school and on the job.
4. Barriers to effective listening include external distractions, daydreaming, close-mindedness, overemphasizing the source, and listening only to what is easy to understand.
5. To counteract distractions, concentrate on what the speaker says, ask questions, listen to and evaluate what the speaker says, and analyze and evaluate the message, not the speaker.
6. To become a better speaker, prepare to listen, apply the message, and provide feedback.
7. Techniques for improving one's ability to interpret messages include listening for central ideas, expanding one's own vocabulary, and using memory devices to ensure that what is heard will be remembered.
8. In interpreting a speaker's message, a person must consider the speaker's words, use of logic, nonverbal cues, and responses to feedback.
9. The fallacies discussed in this chapter are name calling, card stacking, the bandwagon technique, glittering generalities, testimonials, begging the question, non sequiturs, and hasty generalizations.
10. In interpreting a speaker's message, a person should consider movements, gestures, eye contact, paralanguage, proxemics, and body posture.

DISCUSSION QUESTIONS
The following code is used to designate discussion questions and activities as suitable for students of varying ability levels:
- ▼ = below average to average
- ◆ = average to above average
- ■ = all students

1. ▼ Encourage students to refer to the jobs discussed in Chapter 1 and to establish the kinds of communication situations that each job involves.
2. ■ Have students refer to the text for review of nonverbal signals and feedback.
3. ■ Have the students refer to page 73 for review of the process of association.

84

CHAPTER 3 REVIEW

📔 REVIEW QUESTIONS

1. Define *hearing* and then define *listening*.
2. Name the elements that must be added to hearing in order to achieve active listening.
3. Name several things you can accomplish by means of active listening.
4. Name several barriers that may sometimes interfere with effective listening.
5. State what you can do to overcome the barriers you listed in question 4 above.
6. Name three techniques you can use to become a better listener.
7. Name three skills you can use to understand a speaker's message more easily.
8. Name four factors that you must consider in interpreting a speaker's message.
9. Name five logical fallacies used in deceptive reasoning.
10. Name the nonverbal elements that you should consider whenever interpreting a speaker's message.

❓ DISCUSSION QUESTIONS

1. As a class, discuss five different jobs that involve critical listening skills. Describe what kind of information would need to be transmitted in each type of job. Discuss the possible consequences of not listening attentively while doing each job.
2. As a class, discuss the types of nonverbal signals that you recognize when your listener: (a) agrees with the message, (b) disagrees with the message, (c) is not interested in the message, and (d) does not understand the message. Which type of feedback are we most likely to respond to? Which are we least likely to respond to? Which nonverbal signals are confusing? Why?
3. Discuss the ways in which you use the process of association to study for tests. How do you memorize information that must be retained for a test? Do you use special tactics to memorize items in sequence (such as the position of the planets or the lines and spaces on a music staff)? Jot down in your notebook any new and helpful ideas you gain from your classmates.

84

ASSESS

CRITICAL THINKING

1. Analysis   In small groups, discuss the types of nonverbal signals that you recognize when your listener: (a) agrees with the message, (b) disagrees with the message, (c) is not interested in the message, and (d) does not understand the message. Which type of feedback are we most likely to respond to? Least likely to respond to? Why? Report your opinions to the rest of the class.

2. Synthesis   In small groups, discuss your favorite radio or TV commentator. Explain to your group why you enjoy listening to this person. If the commentator is on TV, explain whether it is also helpful to be able to see him or her. Gather together your group's ideas to share with the class.

ACTIVITIES

In-Class

1. In small groups, role-play a conversation or personal argument in which each participant gives only one side of an issue and provides a series of reasons to support the position he or she favors. List the logical fallacies that are used by each. Discuss with your group which fallacies were easy to detect and which were difficult.

2. Three or four students will role-play a conversation in which one or more participants exhibit a severe case of close-mindedness. Analyze the communication/thinking patterns of each person. Note any person's failure to process or respond to information that could have opened up solutions or new viewpoints. Your teacher will list these on the board as they are discussed by the class.

3. Listen to a cassette or to a classmate giving an oral presentation on nonfiction material that is theoretical rather than narrative in style. Take notes on the material. Your teacher will give an open-note test on this material. Did you note the information that you needed to pass the test? Write a self-evaluation of your note-taking abilities.

4. Check your ability to pick out the main ideas in a message by outlining one of the next in-class speeches. Write down the speaker's main ideas in outline form as you listen. After the speech, compare your listening outline with the speaker's outline. How well did you pick out the main ideas?

CRITICAL THINKING
1. **Analysis** Students should complete a list of nonverbal signals and then role-play situations listed in the assignment.
2. **Synthesis** Ask students to explain what body language can tell a listener about a speaker's personality and attitudes.

ACTIVITIES
In-Class
1. Help students to come up with topics for their conversations. Have students pair up and write scripts for their conversations. Then have students rehearse their scripts and present their staged conversations before the class.
2. Have students choose conversation topics from a newspaper or newsmagazine.
3. After students have heard the recording or presentation, ask them the following questions: How does the speaker organize the topic? What does the speaker do to emphasize important issues?
4. Assign topics for short speeches to your class.

ASSESS

Out-of-Class
1. This activity is optional if you have had students do similar activities.
2. Point out to students that this is one of the surest and easiest ways to make dramatic improvements in one's interpersonal relations. The positive feedback that students give to others will be returned to them tenfold.
3. Have students record their observations in their speech notebooks. This activity also provides an opportunity to discuss how a discussion leader can ensure that group members are, in fact, listening to one another.
4. Discuss with students the messages conveyed by such elements of paralanguage as volume, pitch, pausing, tone, vocal quality, and stress.
5. This activity addresses an important aspect of listening: preparation.
6. Stress to your class the importance of remembering names when interacting with others in school or on the job.

CHAPTER 3 REVIEW

Out-of-Class

1. Using old magazines, put together a collage on poster board that illustrates the numerous ways in which logical fallacies appear in advertisements. Share your project by giving an oral report.

2. The next time you have a discussion with relatives or friends, try this: Look them in the eye frequently, nod in understanding or agreement, maintain an alert posture, and show a genuine interest in what they are saying. Do you notice any difference in their speaking when you provide positive feedback? If so, what changes can you identify? Make a notebook entry identifying ways to improve communication through the use of positive feedback.

3. Watch a television talk show. Evaluate the listening of each participant. Note nonverbal signals that indicate whether good listening is or is not occurring. Is there any misunderstanding that occurs in the conversation? Are there any obvious distractions? Does the host share time with the guests or dominate the conversation?

4. Listen on the radio to a number of disc jockeys from different types of programs: rock, country-western, easy listening, classical, etc. Analyze the different styles of communication that you hear. What image is each projecting? Write your findings as a notebook entry. Be prepared to discuss your analysis in class.

5. The next time you plan to attend a movie, a speech, or a play, or watch a special television show, practice the following techniques for preparing to listen. Discover as much as you can about the speech topic, play script, or program in advance. Find out what you can about the speaker or actors. Arrive early and choose a good seat. Bring with you a strong determination to listen well. Observe the extent to which such preparation enhances your participation in the event.

6. Practice the following technique to remember the first names of the next five people to whom you are introduced. As you meet each one, concentrate on the person's name by repeating it to yourself immediately after hearing it. Several moments later, and again at the end of your conversation, intentionally use the name aloud in your conversation with the person. Does this technique help plant a person's name in your mind? Does using the person's name during conversation affect his or her response to you?

ASSESS

CHAPTER PROJECT

Join one of four groups in your class. Each group will write and enact a 10–minute television segment that portrays the importance of listening skills. Each segment should include both a "feature" and commercials. Group I will use a "serial" format. Group II will use a talk-show format. Group III will use a children's-show format. Group IV will use a newscast format, including an editorial commentary.

Each group's project should reflect the major points emphasized in this chapter: benefits of effective listening, barriers to listening, strategies to promote active listening, ways to achieve better understanding through improved listening, and methods of improving analysis and interpretation of messages.

At the end of each group's presentation, the class will analyze the content, evaluating the level of success of the production.

CHAPTER PROJECT
- Have each group address itself to one or two specific aspects of listening. For example, the group doing the newscast and editorial commentary might report on a sports negotiation session that failed because one of the participants refused to be open-minded enough to listen to the proposals made by negotiators on the other side.

PREPARE

● PERFORMANCE OBJECTIVES

- Participates in daily 15-second skill drills when asked
- Explains and uses important nonverbal forms of communication
- Uses the telephone effectively in social and business environments
- Uses group discussion techniques effectively

● sca GUIDELINES

- Expresses ideas and information clearly and concisely
- Asks questions to obtain information
- Summarizes information

● UNIT FOCUS

Unit 2 focuses on interpersonal and group communication and provides examples and strategies for improvement in both areas.

● CONTENTS

4 **One-to-One Communication** *pp. 90–117*
5 **Group Discussion** *pp. 118–155*

▽ UNIT PORTFOLIOS

Individual Portfolios
- Classified Ad with Job Description
- Resume
- Job Interview Evaluation Form
- Video of Mock Interview Process
- Chapter Portfolio Products

Group Portfolios
- Symposium Agenda
- Symposium Publicity
- Speaker Evaluation Form

Class Portfolios
- Symposium Presentation for School
- Press Release for School Symposium

UNIT 2

INTERPERSONAL AND GROUP COMMUNICATION

PREPARE

● UNIT PLANNER | ● ANCILLARY RESOURCES

Chapters	Time Management	📁	📄	📕	📼	🎙️
4 One-to-One Communication *pp. 90-117*	Week 1	✔	✔	✔	✔	
5 Group Discussion *pp. 118-155*	Week 2	✔	✔	✔		

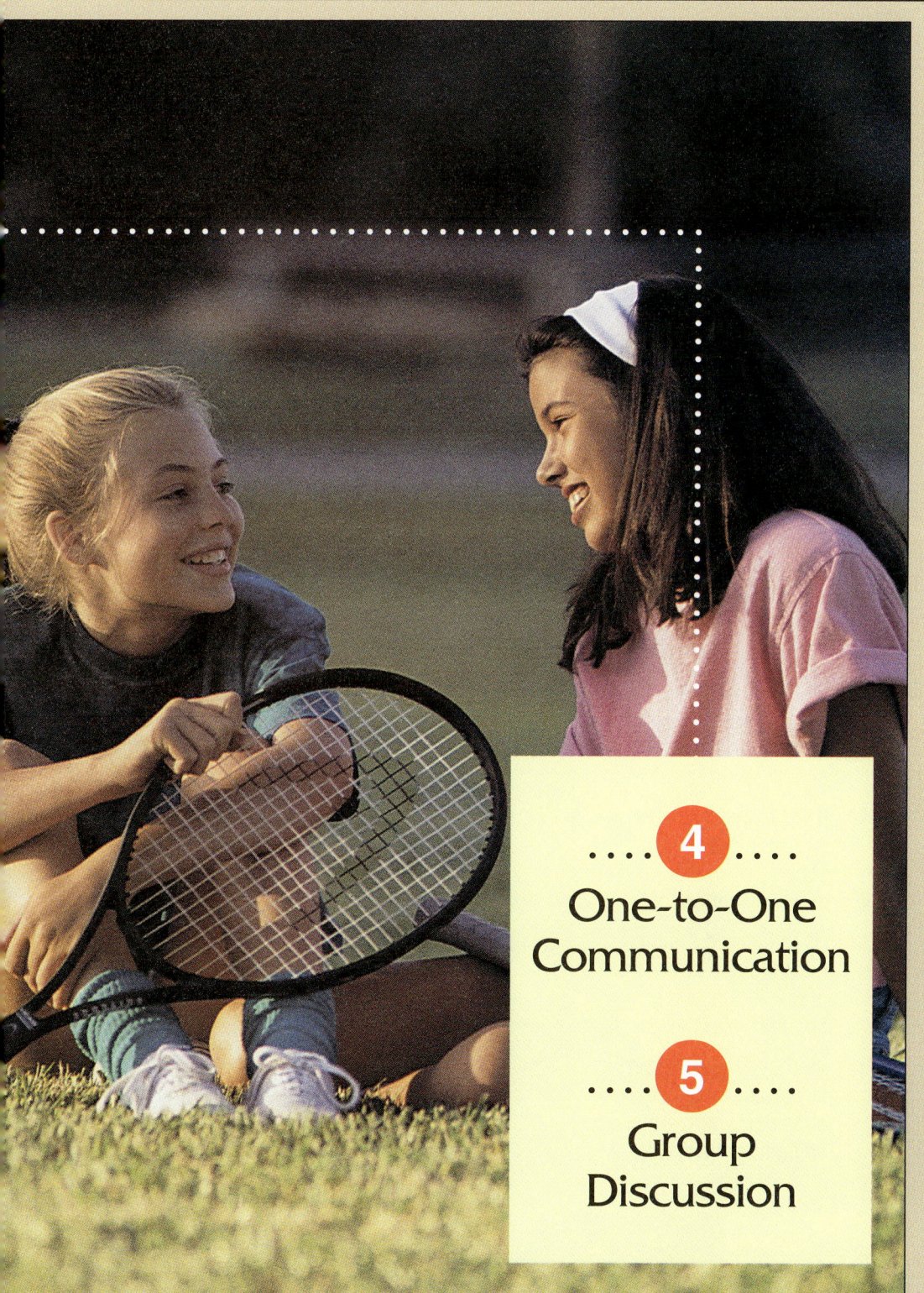

● PROFESSIONAL RESOURCES

Print

Barker, L., et.al. *Groups in Process; An Introduction to Small Group Communication.* 4th ed. Englewood Cliffs, New Jersey: Prentice-Hall Inc., 1990.

Burgoon, Judee K., David B. Buller, and W. Gill Woodall. *Nonverbal Communication: The Unspoken Dialogue.* New York: HarperCollins, 1989.

Hocker, J., and W. Wilmot. *Interpersonal Conflict.* 3rd ed. Dubuque, IA: Wm. C. Brown, 1991.

Video

Communication: Person to Person. Contact Series I: Communications and the Media (Scholastic Book Services, Englewood Cliffs, NJ).

Interpersonal Communication (22 min, color; Michigan State University, Audiovisual Department, East Lansing, MI 48824).

Small Group Communication (24 min, color; Michigan State University, Audiovisual Department, East Lansing, MI 48824).

4
One-to-One Communication

5
Group Discussion

Ancillary Resource Key

- 📁 = Portfolio Product Activities
- 📄 = Tests/Answer Key
- 📕 = Speech Library
- 📼 = Self-Help Videos
- 🎙️ = Audiotape

PREPARE

CHAPTER PLANNER

Day 1	Day 2	Day 3	Day 4	Day 5
Prepare	Prepare	Prepare	Prepare	Prepare
Teach	Teach	Teach	Teach	Teach
Assess	Assess	Assess	Assess	Assess
Sub. Teacher Tip *p. 94*	Sub. Teacher Tip *p. 100*	Sub. Teacher Tip *p. 101*	Sub. Teacher Tip *p. 106*	Sub. Teacher Tip *p. 107*

CHAPTER OVERVIEW

This chapter examines the following topics:
- The Verbal Aspects of Conversation *p. 91*
- The Nonverbal Aspects of Conversation *p. 96*
- Speaking on the Telephone *p. 102*
- Taking Part in an Interview *p. 104*

PORTFOLIO PRODUCTS

Individual Projects
- Glossary of Speech Terms
- Telephone Memo Pad
- Interview Questions
- Chapter 4 Portfolio Products

Group Projects
- Classified Ad with Job Description
- Tape or Transcript of Telephone Interview
- Tape of Mock Job Interview

sca GUIDELINES

- Uses the telephone appropriately to make social and business calls
- Introduces self properly at the beginning of a job interview
- Explains job requirements to an applicant
- Speaks with appropriate rate, clarity, and volume when conducting an interview
- Summarizes information for use in social and business environments

CHAPTER 4

One-to-One Communication

When you have completed this chapter you should be able to:

- Describe several factors involved in becoming an effective communicator.
- Identify and explain the important nonverbal aspects of one-to-one communication.
- Describe and practice effective use of the telephone in social and business situations.
- Identify at least three important factors to consider when you are being interviewed for a job.

TEACH

● **LINKS TO PAST LEARNING**

Ask students to tally the number of person-to-person conversations, telephone conversations, and job interviews they have had in the past week. They could develop a simple bar graph to illustrate the frequency of each. Compare all bar graphs in the class and discuss which kind of communication seems most important to their personal, social, and business lives.

> *"Speech is a faculty given to man to conceal his thoughts."*
> —Talleyrand

● **ACTIVITY**

Types of One-to-One Communication

Team up with a classmate and briefly demonstrate some form of one-to-one communication. Your teacher will give you time to prepare your brief demonstration, then you and your partner will be asked to engage in a short conversation, a mock telephone call, or a portion of a job interview in front of the class. After at least one conversation, one phone call, and one interview have been demonstrated, hold a class discussion comparing and contrasting these three types of one-to-one communication. Which of the three relies most on nonverbal communication? How do the purposes of each differ? Which form imposes the greatest restriction on feedback?

● **ACTIVITY**

You might have three stacks of different colored paper or index cards at the classroom door and ask each student to select a color when they enter. Once class has started, you could indicate that one color represents "conversation," another is for "telephone," and the third is for "interview." Give students a few minutes to work with a partner to prepare a brief example of the type of communication they selected through the color code. Ask volunteers to demonstrate their example. You might offer "bonus points" to those who volunteer.

● **LEARNING STYLES**

Audio Learning
You might play a section of dialogue from a play that students are studying or might be interested in. You might discuss whatever differences students associate with the terms *dialogue* and *conversation*. Discuss why it might be easier to hear dialogue than to read it in a play.

In Chapter 1 you were asked to list the various kinds of communication events in which you participated during a single day. Chances are good that your list was fairly lengthy and included many different kinds of communication situations. Which events from that list occupied most of your communication time? If you're like most people, the forms of one-to-one communication accounted for the majority of your time that day and most other days as well.

One-to-one communication plays a very important part in almost everyone's life. As you learned from the Activity at the start of this chapter, it occurs most often in face-to-face conversations, and in telephone calls and interviews. Speaking with just one other person demands speech skills that differ from those needed for other types of communication. These special skills are the subject of this chapter.

● **THE VERBAL ASPECTS OF CONVERSATION**

Face-to-face conversation, as you have already discovered, is the most common form of one-to-one communication. **Conversation** consists of talk about various matters of common interest to both of the people involved. There is often no single goal or topic. Conversations, unlike many other types of communication, are usually not planned or rehearsed beforehand. But good conversation requires adherence to a few rules, which you should be aware of if you wish to be an interesting person to talk with.

TEACH

● **RETEACHING**

The text makes the point that simply repeating what has already been said seldom helps clarify meaning. Ask students to think of two different ways to say "I need help." Ask volunteers to share these variations with the class.

● **LEARNING STYLES**

Cooperative Learning
Give small groups of students time to talk informally. Explain that, at the end of the time allotted for conversation, members of the groups will be asked to introduce each other to the class. Their introductions should provide as much information as possible. At the end of the introductions, discuss why some students were able to find out more information than others.

● **SKILL DEVELOPMENT**

15-Second Skill Opportunity
To demonstrate the need to send and receive messages accurately, ask students to work in pairs and answer the question, "What did you say the homework assignment is?"

---

92 CHAPTER 4 One-to-One Communication

One-to-one conversation demands speech skills that differ from those needed for other types of communication.

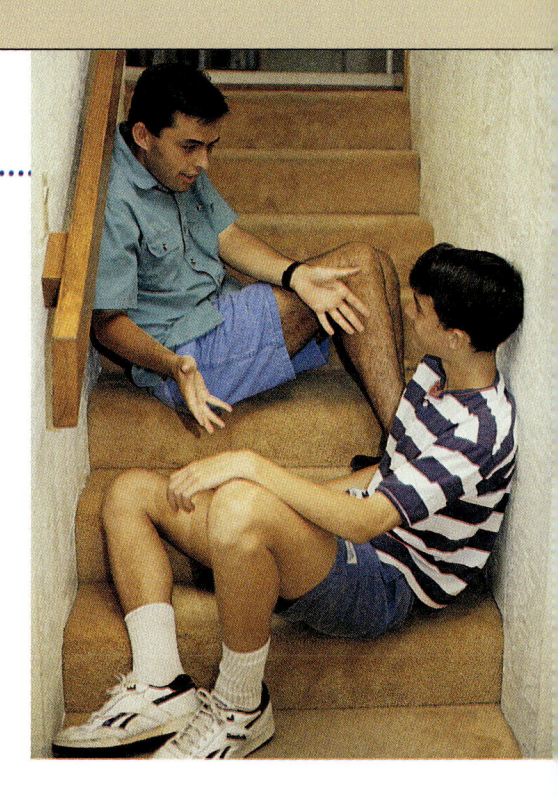

Send and Receive Messages Accurately

As in all types of communication, an important aspect of conversation is accuracy—the accurate sending and receiving of messages. Careful thought in advance about what you will say and how you will say it is not possible with unplanned conversations. But, on the other hand, having only one receiver makes it possible for you to adapt your words and topics to that particular person as you speak.

Choose words you are sure your receiver will understand. Your choices should largely depend on who your listener is. Your listener's age and experience must be considered, as well as the particular communication situation. You would not use technical words in describing automobile engines to someone not familiar with them, for example. Rather, you would explain what you mean in simple words, adding definitions for any technical terms you found necessary to include.

Close attention to the feedback you receive can help you make sure the listener understands you. If your listener looks puzzled, unhappy, or displeased, perhaps you will need to clarify your meaning.

You can rephrase an idea in a different way if your listener doesn't seem to understand what you mean. Giving an example or story as an illustration of what you mean is another way to clarify your message. Merely repeating what you have already said seldom helps to make your meaning clear.

● **CURRICULAR CONNECTIONS**

Writing
Ask students to write a script for a conversation that might be suitable for use on a TV program they usually watch. The script might be role-played for the class. The conversation could be evaluated according to the criteria identified in this section.

Careful choice of words, close attention to feedback, rephrasing, and careful listening skills are techniques that are essential to the accurate sending and receiving of messages.

Sometimes a speaker presents ideas too rapidly for another person to follow. Don't assume that your listener will understand your reasoning. Present your ideas in a logical, step-by-step way so that the other person will see how you reached your conclusions.

Listen carefully during conversation. Listening helps assure your understanding of the speaker's ideas. Concentrate on the ideas you are hearing and learn as much as you can. Remember that listening makes up one half of the communication process.

Nothing is more difficult for a speaker during a two-person conversation than having to speak to someone who does not seem to be listening. Provide supportive feedback while listening. Look interested in what the other person is saying. Smile, frown, or nod at appropriate times. Ask questions to clarify points of which you are not sure. It is by your feedback that you show your interest and understanding.

Be Courteous

Good conversation involves taking turns. Some of the most unsatisfactory conversations are those in which one party talks like a jackhammer and the other person simply sits there and takes a pounding. Of course, no one wants to have a conversation in which each person's speaking time is clocked with a stopwatch. But unless each speaker is willing to yield the floor regularly to the other, what starts out to be a conversation soon turns into a public speech with an audience of one. You have

TEACH

> **SUBSTITUTE TEACHER TIP**
>
> Bring to class a magazine photo or advertisement showing two people. Have students imagine a conversation between the people shown. Students could be asked to write out or vocalize that conversation.

● **SKILL APPLICATION**

Making Conversation
Encourage students to think about the art of making conversation and the occasions when this would be a useful skill. Have students work in pairs to role-play a situation where two students are shopping in an electronics store and want to strike up a conversation.

● **LEARNING STYLES**

Audio Learning
Ask students to watch a favorite TV program to evaluate the depicted conversation. Students could rank the conversational performance of various actors on the program.

CHAPTER 4 One-to-One Communication

probably had conversations with people about whom you later thought: "Talking with him sure involves taking turns. He takes *all* the turns!"

Avoid interrupting to express an idea of your own while the other person is speaking. If what you have to say is valuable, it can wait until it is your turn to speak. Be careful, too, not to interrupt your listening to plan your next comment as long as the other person continues to speak. You may miss an important point he or she is making, and your inattention will eventually become apparent.

It is much easier for people to accept criticism about a situation than about themselves. When disagreeing with someone, avoid verbally attacking that person's character or motives. Unlike a letter that can be destroyed before it's mailed, words, once they have been spoken, cannot be unsaid. Try to explain how you feel about the issue calmly and logically without hurting the other person's feelings. Emotional outbursts of anger rarely lead to improved relationships between people.

Try to be open-minded. People often change their opinions after receiving new information. Even if you still disagree after hearing different ideas, show respect for the other person's point of view. That person, in turn, will then be more likely to give your ideas a fair hearing since he or she has already been shown the same courtesy.

Be Able to Speak on a Number of Topics

Conversation deals with topics of interest to both people involved. In order to carry on stimulating conversations you should try to develop a variety of interests. More people will seek your company if you can converse on a wide range of topics intelligently. Sports, music, politics, current events, fashion, communication, hobbies, school, and energy conversation are all possibilities. If, on the other hand, you are viewed as someone who talks only about your hobby or favorite sport, you will soon find yourself having fewer and fewer conversations.

When you change the subject during a conversation, use words or phrases to relate the new topic to the previous one. In this way your conversation will flow smoothly. Jumping from one unrelated topic to another without discussing any one of them thoroughly makes conversations less meaningful.

Of course, good conversation does not deal only with topics of interest to you. It deals with topics of interest to the other person as well. In conversations with friends, you should regularly attempt to bring up subjects you know the other person finds fascinating, even though these may not be your favorites. With new acquaintances, search for topics of common interest. When the other person brings up a subject that is new to you, listen carefully. Good conversation can be one of the most pleasant ways of learning about new ideas. No one likes conversationalists who constantly talk about *I* topics—topics that relate only to themselves and their interests. Neither do most people enjoy a steady flow of one-upmanship or put-downs. The person who constantly tries to "top" the other's remark, or who frequently makes mean remarks, even in fun, is not long appreciated.

Learn to Enjoy Conversation

Good conversation is an art you can develop. During periods when you are the speaker, speak dynamically and enthusiastically. No one likes to listen to someone who converses in a flat, dull monotone with a deadpan face and no gestures of any kind. To develop the art of conversation, let your enthusiasm for your topic show in your voice and body movements.

Try to make the conversation interesting and pleasant for everyone involved. Avoid talking too much about yourself. Using pet phrases and exclamations too often also makes conversation less interesting. Choose good standard language forms that will make your message clear and lively. Illustrate your ideas with stories your listeners will find relevant and fascinating.

Finally, learn to enjoy face-to-face conversation. You will find that it can provide one of life's most pleasant means of both teaching and learning. In addition, friendships can be established and deepened through good conversation. For those who take the trouble to develop conversation as an art, it can provide an enjoyable form of recreation and relaxation.

● **ACTIVITY**

Practicing Clarity in Conversation
The class should form into teams of two. One student should explain something that is of particular interest to him or her. This explanation might be about a hobby, a sport, a game, or the workings of a particular machine. Watch for feedback from your partner. Does he or she understand your explanation? Now reverse roles. You listen to your partner's explanation and then provide feedback. Do you both feel that you have learned something? Record in your notebook what you spoke about, what feedback you received, and what communication problems occurred, if any.

TEACH

> *Gratiano speaks an infinite deal of nothing; his reasons are as two grains of wheat hid in two bushels of chaff; you shall seek all day ere you find them, and when you have them they are not worth the search.*
> —Shakespeare

● **SKILL DEVELOPMENT**

On the Job
Two students could role-play the situation where they are waiting at a bus stop. One of them is going to a job interview and wants to make sure this is the correct stop and the bus goes to a convenient location for the interview.

● **LEARNING STYLES**

Limited English Proficiency
Ask students to list five topics that they feel comfortable speaking about. For each topic, suggest that they write down several words that they would probably use in the conversation. Then have students list five additional topics they would like to be able to talk about. Pair up students with similar topics and have students share words that would probably be useful in a conversation about each topic.

● **ACTIVITY**

A variation on this Activity could involve pairs of students reading directions from a product that has to be assembled. One student could read the directions and the other student could try to repeat them. The student who has the printed copy of directions can "correct" the student who is listening to the directions. At the end of the activity, ask students to comment on the differences between reading and listening to directions.

TEACH

AMAZING FACTS!
Rebel X.C. of Chicago, IL rapped 674 syllables in 54.9 seconds at a recording studio on August 27, 1992.

● **ASSESSMENT STRATEGY**

To demonstrate some of the techniques described in this section, bring a photo from a teen fashion magazine to class or ask students to bring in samples. Ask students to comment, in a tactful and courteous way, on the outfit the person in the photo is wearing.

● **RETEACHING**

You may want to review the terms *kinesics, proxemics,* and *paralanguage* with students.

● **LEARNING STYLES**

Kinesic Learning
To convey the importance of nonverbal communication in the way people respond to each other, ask students to demonstrate the following. You could prepare four slips of paper with each one describing an appearance and emotion. Ask volunteers to select a slip of paper and, without saying a word, try to convey the impression suggested on the paper. Students could describe their impressions through the nonverbal clues the volunteers supplied. The four descriptions are:
(a) Confident teenager, well dressed, waiting in a lobby for a job interview
(b) Nervous teenager, in jeans waiting in front of the principal's office
(c) Hesitant teenager in a car lot looking over used cars and hoping to negotiate a good price with a salesperson
(d) Teenager waiting outside a convenience store when police car arrives

---

96   CHAPTER 4   One-to-One Communication

● **THE NONVERBAL ASPECTS OF CONVERSATION**

Most forms of one-to-one communication rely heavily on the nonverbal means of communication. As you read in Chapter 2, researchers agree that in face-to-face communication over half of the meaning is carried by nonverbal signals. Even in telephone conversations, much of the message is transmitted through vocal tones, pauses, and sounds that are not words. Imagine how dull a face-to-face conversation with one of your friends would be if your friend stood at attention while speaking, looked straight ahead, never moved a muscle, and spoke in the monotone voice of a robot. Nonverbal communication—body movement, timing, eye contact, and vocal variety—add feeling and life to the words in a message.

Although nonverbal forms of communication account for a large proportion of meaning, they cannot convey as specific a message as words do. If someone smiles at you, you are likely to react in a generally positive way, but you may not be certain whether the smile means friendliness, agreement, understanding, or respect.

While nonverbal communication is not as specific in meaning as verbal communication, it often makes a deeper and longer-lasting impression. Review in your mind the last five times you were intro

In the interest of practicality and rapid communication, the traffic officer utilizes nonverbal signals as a substitute for words.

duced to new acquaintances. Your first impressions were probably based largely on such matters as the amount of enthusiasm shown, the facial expressions used, the ways in which the persons moved and gestured as they spoke, and the warmth of their smiles. If you are like most people, you have remembered those nonverbal signals better than what the people said.

Sometimes nonverbal communication acts as a substitute for language. This usually occurs in situations where words would be impractical or too time consuming. A jet pilot, for example, relies on the ground crew's hand signals to park a roaring plane.

More often, however, nonverbal communication occurs together with language as an aid to total communication. Nodding one's head while saying "Yes, I'll go with you" can strengthen that "Yes." The tone of your voice may deepen the impression that you're angry. Keeping these general principles about nonverbal communication in mind, look now at some specific types of nonverbal communication in one-to-one communication situations.

Using Body Motion (Kinesics)

If you have ever seen a good pantomimist perform, you know how much can be communicated through body motion, or kinesics. Marcel Marceau or Red Skelton could create a mood or tell a story simply through body movement, gesture, and facial expression. Most people similarly pantomime a bit in their everyday conversation.

What kinds of kinesic communication do people regularly use? One of the most powerful tools of nonverbal communication is found in the eyes. Strong messages about your feelings and attitudes are conveyed by how you look at another when speaking, how frequently you look, and how long you gaze into another's eyes. In the American culture, such people as employers and parents seem to expect great amounts of eye contact from a listener. They appear to want the other person in face-to-face communication to look them in the eyes regularly. However, when speaking, the person in authority often does not provide steady or regular eye contact to the listener. There is one predictable moment, though, when both parties are likely to establish eye contact. This is when either is about to finish speaking and yield the floor to the other. Eye contact at this point appears to serve as the major signal that the person is about to finish speaking.

When conversing with another—even someone in authority—it is important to avoid the extremes of too much or too little eye contact. Not looking at the speaker frequently enough may be taken as a sign of lack of interest. Looking too much at the other party may distract the person. Research has shown that in two-person conversations, speakers

TEACH

● **LEARNING STYLES**

Multicultural Learning
Discuss the universal language of specific nonverbal communication. Provide some examples, such as a smile or a shake of the head, to begin the discussion. Encourage students to give additional examples. Ask students to imagine situations where nonverbal communication would be sufficient to conduct a transaction. Could students order a meal or learn directions to a hotel in a foreign country without knowing the language?

Kinesic Learning
Encourage students to pantomime a situation involving nonverbal communication. You may want to use one of the examples mentioned already. You might show a film clip of Marcel Marceau or Charlie Chaplin to demonstrate excellent use of body motion, or kinesics.

TEACH

AMAZING FACTS!
The Atlantic giant squid has the largest eye of any creature, living or dead. Its eyes have been measured at almost 16 inches in diameter!

● **ENRICHMENT**

Ask students to find examples of "shifty eyes" either in advertising, in movie scenes, or in the school cafeteria. Discuss what they mean by "shifty eyes," the occasions they notice it, and typical reactions to it. Students could discuss probable causes and whether or not they would ever be accused of having shifty eyes.

● **CURRICULAR CONNECTIONS**

Math/Science
Some students could trace the development of photographic lenses and compare the capabilities of lenses to the human eye. A timeline of significant developments in photography could be generated and displayed.

"Eyes will not see when the heart wishes them to be blind."
—Seneca

● **SKILL DEVELOPMENT**

15-Second Skill Opportunity
Ask students to identify a favorite movie actor and describe a scene in which the actor used a gesture to convey or reinforce communication.

---

98   CHAPTER 4   One-to-One Communication

Dancers, like mimes, rely on the language of kinesics to communicate mood and story.

gaze at their listeners an average of 38 to 41 percent of the total conversation time. Listeners look at speakers about 62 to 75 percent of the total time. An unwillingness to look an interviewer in the eyes, for example, will probably leave a very negative impression, even though the interviewee's answers may be excellent.

Your eyes may be a most effective means of body-motion communication, but they have their greatest impact when viewed as part of a larger tool of nonverbal expression—the face. Your facial muscles can be arranged in an almost infinite variety of positions to express a wide range of emotions. They can also show the degree of interest you have in a conversation, and even give certain information about your personality. Though your face is capable of displaying a blend of different emotions, at any one time you are more likely to show single emotions such as anger, sadness, fear, surprise, happiness, or disgust with the greatest accuracy. It is important for you to be aware of your expressions and the messages they continually communicate to others.

Another widely used form of body-motion communication in two-person interaction consists of arm-hand movements. You can use your arms and hands to describe, locate, emphasize, and symbolize. Of course, some people "talk" more with their hands and arms than others. You probably have seen any number of persons making arm-hand gestures when talking on the phone. Holding some people's arms would make it nearly impossible for them to speak.

As with any form of communication, however, extremes in using arm-hand movements should be avoided. The interviewee who sits perfectly still, hands in lap, and never moves a muscle during a half-hour interview is likely to be seen as lacking in dynamism and drive. O

TEACH

● RETEACHING

You could place a strip of tape on the floor of your classroom and mark the tape at inch and foot intervals. Ask students to volunteer to demonstrate the intervals they feel most comfortable with in a variety of situations. Discuss the comfortable space between student and teacher, between student and adult stranger, between male and female strangers, and between girlfriend and boyfriend.

● CURRICULAR CONNECTIONS

Writing
Take a dialog excerpt from a play that students have studied and suggest that they write the gestures and stage direction for a stage presentation using that dialog.

● LEARNING STYLES

Multicultural Learning
Some students might look into the seating arrangement at the United Nations and indicate the placement of seats for the General Assembly. Discuss why seating arrangements are an important consideration in communication in business meetings, dinner gatherings, and international diplomacy.

Cooperative Learning
You might give to small groups of students a list of ten names taken from the political, sports, or movie arena. The names should include individuals who are known not to get along. Ask each group to imagine that they are planning a business meeting or social dinner for the public figures. They should plan the seating arrangements for that event.

● SKILL DEVELOPMENT

On the Job
Ask students to imagine that they are going to participate in a weekly team meeting at the company they work for. They will be meeting around a conference table. Ask them to think about the best and the worst places to sit during that meeting.

The Nonverbal Aspects of Conversation 99

the other hand, the conversationalist whose arms are continually waving about with the velocity of a windmill may distract the listener's attention from the basic verbal message. Arm and hand movements should grow out of a natural urge to complete the total communication process. They should never be forced, but instead reflect the real communication goals of the person using them.

Using Space (Proxemics)

In Chapter 2 you read about how much closer two friends will sit when talking than two strangers will. This is just one way in which people use space to communicate nonverbally. The study of spatial communication, or proxemics, can tell you a great deal about a level of communication that is often carried on subconsciously in two-person communication. It seems that all people leave an invisible territory around them that they consider their own private domain. Whom you allow to invade your territory, how closely, and for how long, says much about your feelings and reactions towards others.

Family members or close friends generally allow close proximity when talking. Allowing another to sit close enough to touch you and being relaxed about it says to the other person "I like you, I trust you, I am willing to take you into my close confidence." On the other hand, sitting too close during a business interview or while talking with a new acquaintance may cause problems. Giving the other person too little breathing room may make that person feel uncomfortable. Americans like to reserve close distances for those they know well. Chapter 2 discussed basic distances, used in various communication situations.

You have probably met some people who regularly invade your space. A new acquaintance may stand so close while talking that your noses nearly touch. A student may take the seat right next to yours at the library study table when many other seats are available. These are usually unintentional instances of bothersome communication, but they can be annoying nevertheless. When such space invasion occurs, many people back away, turn their backs slightly to a seated invader, or lay their forearms on the table as a barrier to the intruder. While these signals may seem readily understandable to everyone—a kind of universal language—such is not the case.

Edward T. Hall, who has studied the different uses that people from various cultures make of space, reported many incidents in which diplomats from other countries repeatedly approached too close for the comfort of Americans. Every time a foreign diplomat got too close, the American backed up a step. The other, thinking the American was losing interest in their conversation, approached again. In a short time they often found themselves at the other end of the room.

TEACH

SUBSTITUTE TEACHER TIP

Ask students to make a list of each hour in their day. Then ask students to remember how they used the time in each hour yesterday. Have them identify the hour that seemed the longest and the hour that seemed the shortest. Discuss what makes time seem to go fast or slowly.

> *Time will reveal everything. It is a babbler, and speaks even when not asked.*
>
> —Euripides

• SKILL DEVELOPMENT

15-Second Skill Opportunity
Ask students to think about how they manage their time and to identify one aspect they would like to improve about their use of time. Ask volunteers to share a time management resolution with the class.

---

100   CHAPTER 4 One-to-One Communication

The way in which individuals use spatial communication reveals a great deal about their feelings toward each other.

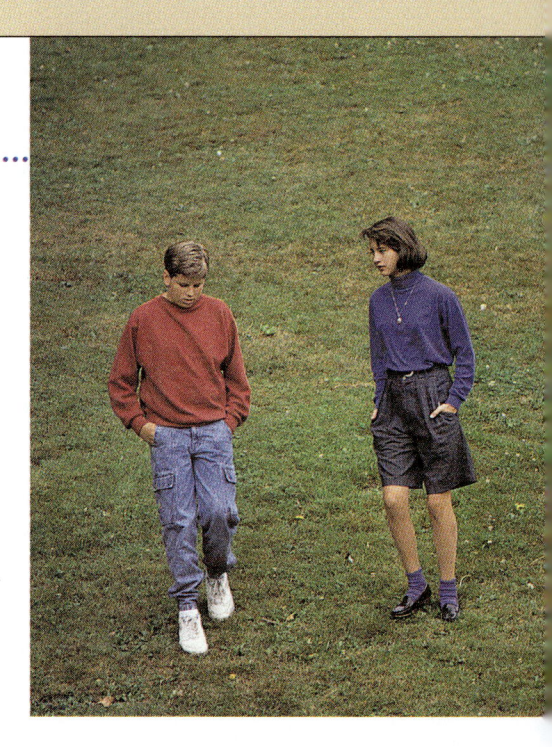

The foreigner had "chased" the American across the room without either being conscious of it. Since moving in too closely often causes embarrassment, it usually hinders communication. Watch your use of space so you don't make others uncomfortable. If others invade your space, realize that it is probably unintentional.

Using Time

Have you ever considered what an enormous impact time has on your life? You eat at certain times. You sleep for certain lengths of time. You often ask what time it is. You clock your life through birthdays and anniversaries. Time also has a great impact on communication.

Suppose one of your classmates says, "Did you hear? John just spent an hour and a half in the principal's office!" You know immediately John and the principal were not just chatting about the weather. The length of their conversation tells you their business must have been significant. Suppose one of your teachers announces "This test will only take five minutes." You can assume that the test you are about to take won't cover the entire book.

Executives frequently use time to tell visitors how highly they regard them and their visit. Those whose prestige is not great or whose business is not considered pressing may "cool their heels" in the outer office while the executive finishes up a few other matters. Allowing frequent interruptions such as telephone calls during a conversation may also make the other person feel less important.

Using Appearance

Appearance also acts as a nonverbal form of communication in two-person communication. One of the chief reasons businesspeople hold job interviews is their desire to see what kind of appearance a person makes before deciding to hire her or him. People are inclined to make snap judgments about others the first time they meet based largely on personal appearance. Hair style, clothing, height, weight, neatness—all communicate something about you, whether you like it or not. The visual image you present influences others' interpretation of your personality, your character, your intelligence, and your likeability. Sometimes these first impressions can be totally incorrect, but once made, they are very hard to erase.

You need not constantly go about looking as if you had just stepped out of a fashion magazine. Rather, the key ingredients for a favorable appearance are being neat and well-groomed. They are particularly essential for a good interview. If you are clean and carefully dressed, you will make a good first impression. At all times you will find these two things can have a marked influence on the opinions of others.

Using Paralanguage

Paralanguage refers to forms of communication connected with vocal sounds. It concerns how words are produced vocally, but does not include the words themselves. Suppose, for example, you scream at someone with whom you are angry "I've told you not to do that!" Your voice volume, the high pitch (tone) of your voice, and your rapid rate of speaking are all part of your paralanguage. These vocal characteristics communicate anger more clearly than do the words themselves. On the other hand, suppose you calmly answer a simple question. Your vocal cues are quite different. You use a lower volume, a lower pitch, and a slower rate. Again your calm attitude is conveyed less by what you say than by how you say it.

A common problem for many people during one-to-one communication is the habit of frequently inserting vocalized pauses into their speech. A **vocalized pause** consists of filling the spaces between words with non-meaningful sounds, such as "uh," "er," "like," or "you know." A certain number of vocalized pauses are acceptable, since they occur naturally in nearly everyone's speech. If they occur regularly and

---

TEACH

SUBSTITUTE TEACHER TIP
Bring to class several photographs from a newspaper or magazine that show people dressed in a variety of styles. Ask students to think of five words to describe each person pictured based on the clothing each is wearing. Discuss why people tend to make judgments about others based on what they are wearing.

> **"** Personal appearance is a helpful factor in business success. **"**
>
> **"** Yes, and business success is a helpful factor in personal appearance. **"**

● SKILL APPLICATION

Debate
You might want the class to discuss the advantages and disadvantages of a policy that restricts the type of clothing that can be worn at school.

● LEARNING STYLES

Audio Learning
You might ask a student to volunteer to be a "bell-ringer" during class. Give the student a small bell and have him or her ring it each time the student hears a vocalized pause such as "uh" in the course of class.

TEACH

● **RETEACHING**

Ask students to use the photos in this section and either discuss or write a summary of the nonverbal aspects of communication based on these visuals.

● **SKILL DEVELOPMENT**

15-Second Skill Opportunity

Ask students to stand and role-play a telephone call to invite their grandparent(s) to dinner on Sunday.

● **ACTIVITY**

This Activity provides an excellent opportunity for students to identify and correct undesirable conversational traits. For each of the elements of conversation, have the class determine the most desirable alternatives. Make lists of these on the board. Suggest that students make a personal list of improvement strategies for their portfolio.

CHAPTER 4 One-to-One Communication

frequently, however, they are likely to make a negative impression on the listener. They can lead the listener to perceive the speaker as insecure, unsure of the information, possibly deceitful, or even stupid. Vocalized pausing is usually just a bad habit. Once a speaker is aware of it, such pausing can be cured with patience and concentration.

As you can see, paralanguage can be very important in one-to-one communication. It enables a listener to reach conclusions such as "He's tired," or "She's angry," or "She's kidding." Paying close attention to the type of information paralanguage conveys can make the difference between successful or unsuccessful communication.

● **ACTIVITY**

Discussing Aspects of Conversation

With a partner, role-play several face-to-face conversations. Vary the setting in which the conversation takes place. Settings might include a supermarket, a home, a bank, a classroom, or a bus. The situation might involve strangers, family members, friends, or teachers. After each role-play, the class will discuss the appropriateness and effectiveness of word choice, feedback, body movement, use of space, and other verbal and nonverbal techniques used in the conversation.

● **SPEAKING ON THE TELEPHONE**

The telephone is a marvelous aid to human communication. Until such time as picturephones or some other new form of visual technology comes into widespread use, however, people must continue to rely totally on their voices when communicating over the phone. This means that telephone conversations are often more difficult than face-to-face conversations. Thus, a special effort is called for in order to make telephone conversation efficient, courteous, and pleasant.

Follow Conversational Rules for Social Calls

The telephone is very useful for extending invitations, deepening friendships, correcting misunderstandings, or simply enjoying good conversation. The telephone is especially valuable when distance makes face-to-face conversation impractical. For these purposes efficiency is somewhat less important than courtesy and friendliness. Most of the

TEACH

● **CURRICULAR CONNECTIONS**

Math/Science
Use a world time zone map and provide students with a list of several countries that they need to telephone for business purposes. Ask students to figure out what time they would have to call from their office here in order to talk with someone in the designated country at 2:00 P.M. local time.

AMAZING FACTS!
The United States has 812 telephones for every 1,000 people. Nicaragua has 61 phones for every 1,000 people.

● **LEARNING STYLES**

Technology Tools
Many businesses rely on telemarketing to increase their sales. Imagine that you have just sat down to dinner and the phone rings with a telemarketer asking if you want a salesperson to speak to you about replacing your windows. Discuss polite responses to the request. Some students could write a script for those telemarketers that could be evaluated by other students.

● **SKILL DEVELOPMENT**

15-Second Skill Opportunity
Ask students how many of them are commonly using answering machines or voice-mail. Students could role-play leaving a message on a friend's answering machine. Others could role-play leaving a message on a business answering machine to request an interview in response to a "Help Wanted" sign in its window. Compare and contrast the messages and develop guidelines for each type of phone conversation.

Speaking on the Telephone   **103**

rules for face-to-face conversations also apply to telephone conversations as well.

When you are the caller, you are disturbing the privacy of another person's home. Thus, you should make social calls at times when you are least likely to disturb the family or individual. Early in the morning, late at night, or at mealtimes are generally poor times to call.

Always identify yourself as soon as someone answers. Give your name first and then ask to speak to the person you are calling. When someone answers the phone, say, for example, "Hello. This is Joe Lincoln. May I please speak with Maria?"

When the person with whom you wish to talk reaches the phone, introduce yourself again. If the purpose of your call is to extend an invitation or correct a misunderstanding, you will want to make some brief opening comments before proceeding with your main purpose for calling. If you called simply to visit, use a more relaxed approach.

Avoid tying up the line for long periods of time. Others may be expecting a call or wish to make a call of their own. If you are the caller you are responsible for bringing the conversation to a close. Always be sensitive and avoid extending the conversation too long.

Follow More Formal Rules for Business Calls

Business calls are made for specific purposes. They may be made to give or receive information, to sell or buy a product or service, to make appointments, or to resolve problems. When making business calls, efficiency is of great importance. All businesses exist in order to make a

making business calls, it important to identify ourself, request your party, ake a brief statement of ourtesy, and state your usiness promptly.

103

TEACH

AMAZING FACTS!
More calls are made between the USA and Canada than between any other countries. In 1991 there were over 3.3 billion minutes of two-way phone traffic between the two.

● LEARNING STYLES

Multicultural Learning
Ask students to learn about the polite way to answer the phone in a variety of countries. Suggest that they contact the local phone company or various long-distance carriers to request information about calls overseas.

● SKILL DEVELOPMENT

On the Job
Ask students to provide a list of three schools or companies they would like to apply to after they finish high school. They should be encouraged to describe the company or school "culture" of each and develop three questions they would like to ask during an application interview.

CHAPTER 4 One-to-One Communication

profit. Wasting time on the telephone during business hours involves greater expense and less profit.

One way to increase efficiency is to be sure of the number you are calling. If you are not sure of the number, look it up. Another way to be efficient is to be prepared. Have any materials you intend to refer to or relay to your party at hand before placing your call. Also have writing materials ready to write down any information you may receive.

As soon as you reach the number, identify yourself, then ask for your party. Make a brief opening statement of courtesy, then relate your business immediately. Speak directly into the mouthpiece using conversational volume. Don't forget that your vocal tones, rate, and articulation all play a part in conveying your message.

● TAKING PART IN AN INTERVIEW

There are many different kinds of interviews. When interviews are mentioned, most people are likely to think first of the face-to-face communication held when someone is seeking employment—the job interview. But workers are interviewed periodically after they have been on the job for awhile. People with problems are interviewed by psychological counselors. Government officials are interviewed by news reporters seeking information. Couples are interviewed by members of the clergy before getting married. Students are interviewed by guidance counselors, teachers, and sometimes principals about their schedules, grades, or behavior. People applying for admission to a vocational school or college are usually interviewed before they are accepted. At some time in your life you will certainly take part in a face-to-face interview.

Unlike conversation, an **interview** is a more formal kind of communication event with a particular and definite goal in mind. An interview may last a few minutes or may continue for several days, but it is ordinarily planned in advance and directed toward a definite outcome.

Being Interviewed

Interviews are held with people seeking all kinds of jobs. These include positions in private industry, in government service, in schools, and in professional offices such as those of lawyers and doctors. Since many of the principles involved in job interviews are typical of other forms of interviewing, and since practically everyone engages in a job interview at least once in his or her life, emphasis here will be given to this type of interview.

TEACH

● **ENRICHMENT**

Invite a human resource person from a local company to talk to the class about interviewing practices and strategies. Students could prepare questions they would like to ask the visitor.

● **LEARNING STYLES**

Visual Learning
Members of the class could role-play and videotape interview experiences. Use the videos to identify strengths and weaknesses of various interviews.

● **SKILL APPLICATION**

Interviews
Encourage students to ask various adults about the most difficult interview question they ever had to face. Share those questions in class and discuss possible responses.

Taking Part in an Interview **105**

or a job interview, thorough preparation includes becoming informed about the organization and being ready to pose specific questions about responsibilities, salary, and advancement opportunities.

Prepare Thoroughly If you are seeking employment, you are the **interviewee.** A good job interview demands three things of the interviewee: thorough preparation, active participation, and good follow-up. Thorough preparation includes finding out all you can about the organization, the job, and the interviewer beforehand. It means preparing answers to the types of questions you can expect to be asked. It means readying questions of your own to ask the interviewer about aspects of the job and organization that interest you or may be unclear to you.

Some form of correspondence often takes place before a job interview. In this correspondence, ask for any brochures or other written information about the company. Read it carefully when it arrives. Educate yourself about the firm's history, its products or services, and its size. Try to discover who will conduct your interview and his or her name beforehand.

Though there are frequently unexpected questions during an interview, most job interviewers ask a number of similar questions. Here are some you should prepare answers to beforehand:

- Why do you want to work for this company?
- What experience have you had that prepares you for this position?
- What kind of grades did you receive in school? (Or what grades have you earned thus far in school?)

105

TEACH

SUBSTITUTE TEACHER TIP

Bring to class the classified ad section from the Sunday newspaper. Ask each student to choose a job from the classified section and write down his or her job qualifications for the selected job. Discuss questions that students might be asked in the interview process.

● SKILL DEVELOPMENT

15-Second Skill Opportunity

Ask students to select one of the interview questions listed here and prepare a response.

● LEARNING STYLES

Cooperative Learning

Give groups of four students various interview situations. Have two students in each group role-play a successful interview and the other two role-play an unsuccessful interview. Students could assess each other's performance.

● CURRICULAR CONNECTIONS

Language Arts

Ask students to make a list of interview questions they would anticipate for a specific job they identify. Then ask students to work with a partner, exchange their list of questions, and try to answer the partner's questions.

Language Arts/History

Have students choose famous people from the past whom they would like to interview. Ask them to develop at least five questions they would like to ask each interviewee. Share these questions with the class. Discuss what makes some questions better than others.

- What would you expect as a starting salary?
- If you are hired for this job, how long would you expect to stay with this company?
- What are your long-range career goals? (Or what do you expect to be doing five years from now?)
- What hobbies or outside interests do you have?
- How much do you know about this firm?
- What do you feel are your major strengths for this job?

Laws have been passed to insure equal treatment for all people applying for jobs. Because of these laws, you will probably not be asked any questions about your national origin, race, sex, religion, or marital status. Physical and mental handicaps usually are discussed only if they might relate to the performance or the duties of the job. Age can be discussed only if the interviewee is a minor or over seventy. If you should be asked questions you feel are improper, politely refuse to answer them.

A good interviewer will give you the opportunity to ask questions during an interview. Actually, your ability to ask intelligent questions will probably make a more positive impression on the interviewer than your answers to the interviewer's own questions. If it appears that the interviewer is about to close the interview without giving you such an opportunity, ask for it. Here are sample questions of the type you may wish to ask:

- What would my specific duties be?
- Can you tell me a little bit about the people with whom I would be working directly, including my immediate superior?
- What kinds of fringe benefits accompany this position?
- At what salary would I start? (Ask this late in the interview if it has not already come up.)
- What is the likelihood I would be asked to move to another town to keep my job or get a promotion? Would the company pay moving expenses?

Several of these questions apply mainly to an interview for a full-time position after graduation. However, even during brief interviews for summer employment, you will want to ask questions about duties, hours, fringe benefits, and wages. Don't be timid about such matters. You have a right to know about them before you accept a job, and your expectations will align more closely with the realities of the job.

● ENRICHMENT

Invite a travel agent to speak to the class about the importance of communication in his or her work. Students could prepare questions to ask the speaker.

APPLY

SUBSTITUTE TEACHER TIP
Use the Yellow Pages to identify several travel agencies in your area. Ask students to select one of the agencies and prepare a list of three questions they would like to ask the agency about communication practices in a country of their choice.

AMAZING FACTS!
The largest passport processing center in the U.S. is in Portsmouth, NH. It can handle 6,000 passports a day.

CAREER CLOSE-UP

Travel Agent

While travel agents need many complex abilities in order to unravel the maze of international travel for their clients, superior communication skills are their most valuable attribute. A high school diploma is the minimum requirement for employment, but most agencies prefer candidates who have had 2–4 years of college, including courses in foreign languages, English, and public speaking.

Travel agents will not survive in this competitive industry without the ability to relate well to clients. Since most of their business is conducted by telephone, agents must master this difficult form of one-to-one communication. As a result, they often need to rely on their voices alone to convey the helpful enthusiasm they want to project. With the skillful use of vocal tones, pauses, and other sounds to supplement their speech, telephone communication becomes more powerful.

Effective travel agents make a client feel special by listening carefully during conversations and responding to each concern. Because travel details are often complicated, agents strive to present information logically. They repeat information back to the client when necessary and listen for feedback that indicates understanding or need for more information.

Successful travel agents develop a large clientele because they make the effort to practice skillfully the art of one-to-one communication. Although many agents try to be attentive, their clients will not perceive them as caring unless they dynamically communicate this attention through every telephone and personal contact.

One-to-one communication skills are the principal asset employed by the travel agent in order to convey enthusiasm to clients.

● LEARNING STYLES

❋ **Cooperative Learning**
Have small groups of students identify the ten places they would most like to visit in the U.S. Have them do the same for the ten most popular places to visit abroad. Compare group choices. Each group could develop a travel brochure or poster to advertise the appeal of the places selected.

107

107

TEACH

● ENRICHMENT

Invite the school counselor to talk to the class about developing suitable résumés. You might display sample résumés that students could use. Some students might want to contact alumni of your school and ask about the résumés they developed in college or on their first jobs.

● CURRICULAR CONNECTIONS

Writing
Suggest that each student would benefit from drafting a résumé to focus their attention on their accomplishments and objectives. Review the standard parts of a résumé and suggest ways that students could emphasize their school and part-time work experience.

Writing
Ask students to write a thank-you note as a follow-up to a job interview. They could work in pairs and share the notes with a partner. Invite feedback and identify the strengths and weaknesses of the note.

CHAPTER 4 One-to-One Communication

Be an Active Participant Your skill at verbal and nonverbal communication probably creates the single most important impression during an interview. The following suggestions will help to make th impression a favorable one.

Be on time for the interview. Several minutes early is perfect acceptable. Five minutes late could spell disaster.

Be certain your appearance is neat, clean, and generally conserv tive. Good grooming applies to any job interview, even if the job itse requires work clothes and getting dirty. Sit in a relaxed manner, but not slouch. You want to appear alert, but not overly tense. Do not fi get in your seat.

Answer the interviewer's questions completely, but do not ramb Once you have answered a question fully, stop. At the other extrem avoid single-word answers, such as "Yes" or "No." The interview wants to hear you talk. Do not try to bluff. If you do not understand question, ask the interviewer to explain it. If you do not know th answer to a question, say so. If you are a "C" student, don't claim to a "B" student.

Emphasize any of your past experiences that show you have bee in a position of responsibility or leadership, no matter how insignil cant they may seem. If you were class president in school, for exan ple, mention it. If you have been a summer-camp counselor, mentic that.

Speak in a voice that can be easily heard, but that is not too loud fo the size of the room. Speak clearly. Show enthusiasm through you voice by varying volume, pitch, and rate of speaking.

Listen carefully to everything the interviewer says. Be sure to mai tain regular eye contact with the interviewer as you listen. Keep a plea ant, interested expression on your face during the interview. You w make the best impression if you seem to be enjoying the interview an the challenge it provides.

Follow up If you are not offered a job at the close of the interviev correct follow-up may determine whether you will get it later. This ge erally consists of mailing a business letter to the interviewer the ne day. In the letter, thank the person for the opportunity of being inte viewed and enclose your résumé if you have not previously presente it. A **résumé** is a neatly typed summary giving your name, addres education, and previous work experience. Close the letter by offering send any additional information the interviewer may want about yo Emphasize the fact that you hope to hear from the interviewer as soc as possible.

If you are offered the job during the interview, write a letter than ing the interviewer. Express your intention to do the job well.

Taking Part in an Interview

Conducting an Interview

The interview is often a source of information. Businesspeople, government officials, and news reporters use interviews to gather material. Students conduct interviews when preparing material for reports or speeches. Suppose you need information about accidents involving bicycles for a report you plan on bicycle safety. Interviewing a local police officer about bicycle accidents would be a possible source of information for that topic. Experts in many fields are generally available in every community.

There is one main difference between being an interviewee and being an interviewer. The interviewer must manage the interview.

Prepare Thoroughly After deciding what information you need, choose the person you wish to interview. Preferably, choose the best available expert on the subject. For example, if you need information about city government, and the mayor is unavailable because of a busy schedule, try contacting a member of the city council or someone working for a city agency who might be able to help you. A citizen involved in city affairs could also prove to be a good source of information.

Once you have located someone to consult, make an appointment for the interview. Be courteous. Tell the person why you wish an interview. Arrange a time and place convenient for the interviewee. Be sure

courage an interviewee express his or her views lly.

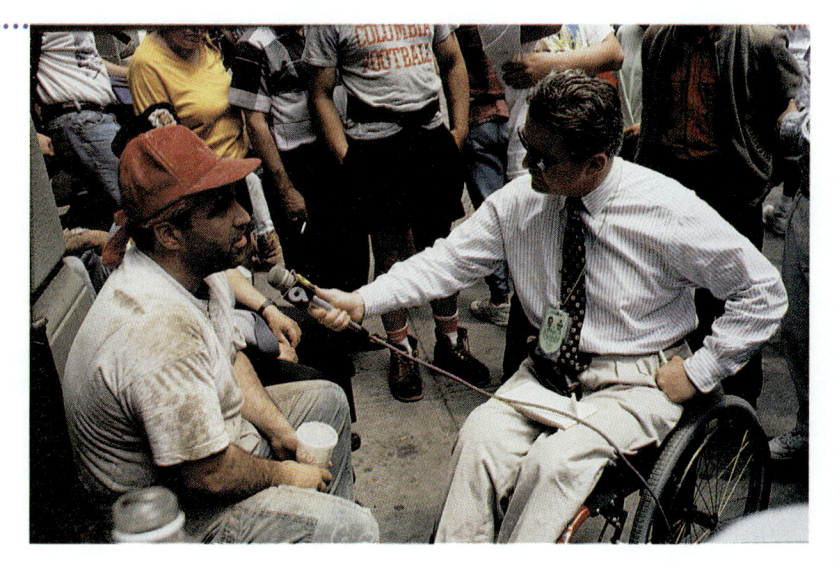

TEACH

"When I applied for a job, the manager had the nerve to ask if my punctuation was good."

"What did you say?"

"I said I had never been late for work in my life."

● SKILL APPLICATION

Media Literacy
Ask students to watch a news broadcast on television and make a chart in order to list and compare the interviews conducted by reporters. The chart could contain the names of the interviewer and the interviewee and the time spent during the broadcast on the interview. Students could identify the topic of the interview and record the question(s) and answer(s). After students have watched the interview, encourage them to evaluate the performance of both the interviewer and the interviewee. Discuss the criteria they would use to make comparisons.

● SKILL DEVELOPMENT

15-Second Skill Opportunity
Students realize that sports newscasters seldom have much time to ask an athlete a question. Have students identify an athlete they would like to interview and think of the best questions they would like to ask. Ask volunteers to share that interview question with the class and identify the athlete they have chosen.

● SKILL APPLICATION

Citizens Speak Out
Ask students to identify the politician they most like or dislike. Ask them to imagine that the politician will be at your school auditorium for a town meeting tomorrow. Ask students to practice asking and responding to political interview questions.

TEACH

● **LEARNING STYLES**

❋ **Cooperative Learning**
The art and skill of asking questions improve with practice. Ask small groups of students to talk about the "dumbest" questions they can recall. Discuss why the questions seemed dumb. Then ask each student in the group to write a question they would like to ask the principal. Each could share the question with the group, and ask the group to select the question they think is the best to share with the class.

● **SKILL DEVELOPMENT**

Feedback
Ask students to imagine that they have just finished an interview. No job has been offered; no school entrance has been promised as a result of the interview. Encourage students to think about how they would know if the interview went well or not. What would they consider positive or negative signs? Discuss the kind of feedback they would appreciate after participating in an interview. What question(s) could they ask to obtain that kind of feedback?

110

---

110   CHAPTER 4   One-to-One Communication

Student interviews may involve the election of class officers as well as leaders of other school organizations.

to thank the person before concluding your conversation. Be poli even if the person refuses to grant you an interview.

Next you will need to study material available on your topic. A informed interviewer always does a better job. Also study any bac ground information you can find about the person to be interviewe Know all you can about the subject and the person with whom you w be speaking. Thorough research is the foundation of a good interviev

Finally, make a list of questions to ask during the interview. Remen ber that your interviewee's time is valuable. Do not plan to ask que tions that could easily be answered by consulting books, public record or other sources. Avoid questions that can be answered with only yes or no.

Manage the Interview Carefully   As the person conducting th interview, you are responsible for managing it well. Make sure yo appearance will make a good impression. Arrive promptly. Greet yo interviewee with a firm handshake and express your pleasure at beir able to talk with him or her.

Start the interview by explaining its purpose. Try to make the inte viewee relaxed and comfortable. People are more likely to speak free if they feel at ease. Do not follow your list of questions too closel Perhaps your interviewee will say something that will suggest que tions you had not considered in advance. Go ahead and follow u Without straying too far from the subject, encourage the interviewee express his or her views fully. Perhaps the interviewee will want to a: you some questions. Constantly be aware of the nonverbal aspects

● RETEACHING

Suggest that students make a list of the guidelines presented here about how to conduct successful interviews. Then, ask them to select the guidelines they consider most important and write a list of the "Ten Commandments" for good interviews. These Ten Commandments could be illustrated and displayed for the class.

Taking Part in an Interview 111

your interview. Maintain frequent eye contact. Smile frequently and show your interest. Give encouragement by nodding. Sit close enough to converse easily.

Using a tape recorder during the interview will assure that the information you gather will be accurate. Be sure, however, to ask permission of the interviewee before using a tape recorder. Once you have permission to use it, test the recorder to be sure it is working properly and place it so that the recording will be clear. If the interviewee refuses to allow you to use a tape recorder or is made uncomfortable by its presence, don't use it.

If you are unable to use a tape recorder, take notes of important points. Try to do this without interrupting the flow of conversation. You may wish to record several quotations to be included in your report. It would be a good idea to repeat these to the interviewee to be sure each quotation is exact.

End the interview when you have the information you need. If you notice that the other person is tired or anxious to get on with other matters, try to conclude quickly. Do not overstay your welcome. Conclude by expressing your thanks. Tell the interviewee how helpful he or she has been.

Follow Up   People like to know they have helped others. Follow up by sharing the outcome of your interview with the interviewee. You may send the person a copy of your report or speech. Include a letter thanking the interviewee again for the help you were given.

Write a letter even if a copy of the material using the interview is not available. Perhaps you can explain how you used the interview in your presentation. You may include favorable reactions from your readers or listeners. Remember to express your thanks before concluding.

● ACTIVITY

Role-Playing Interviews

With an assigned partner, prepare to role-play a job interview in front of your speech class. Decide upon the company setting in which the interview is taking place, the position title of the interviewer, and the job description for which the applicant is being interviewed. Agree upon the topics you will talk about in your 5–7 minute interview, but *do not plan a script of the specific questions and answers*. Your teacher may wish to make this a graded assignment for all the class members, an exercise for extra credit for those who wish to participate, or an ungraded assignment for those wanting the experience. The class may be asked to discuss the strengths and weakness of each interview.

● LEARNING STYLES

Audio Learning
Ask students to tape an interview that is role-played or a conversation with a family member or friend. Play the taped interview or conversation in class and ask members of the class to comment on the nonverbal aspects of the interview. Discuss the tone, pitch, and speed of the voices and how these elements affect the conversation.

● SKILL DEVELOPMENT

15-Second Skill Opportunity
Emphasize the importance of ending an interview on a positive note so that a lasting impression is made that will benefit the interviewee. Ask students to think of what they would want an interviewer to remember about them as a result of an interview. Then, have them practice a concluding sentence that would convey the impression they want.

● ACTIVITY

These role-played interviews could be recorded as a video or audiotape for review purposes. Before the role-played interviews take place, suggest that the students visit a book store or use the library computer to examine the number and titles of books available on the interview process. List some of those titles on the chalkboard and ask students to imagine what the emphasis of the book might be, based on the title.

TEACH

ASSESS

STUDENT PERFORMANCE COMPETENCIES

- Demonstrates how kinesics, proxemics, time, appearance, and paralanguage are used in effective communication
- Prepares for interviews through research, appearance, and questions
- Uses conversational skills in social and business situations

sca GUIDELINES

- Uses the telephone appropriately to make social and business calls
- Introduces self properly at the beginning of a job interview
- Explains job requirements to an applicant
- Speaks with appropriate rate, clarity, and volume when conducting an interview
- Summarizes information for use in social and business environments

PORTFOLIO ASSESSMENT

Standard
- Glossary of Speech Terms
- Written Interview Questions
- Completed Assignments, Quizzes, Projects, and Chapter 4 Test

Enrichment
- Ten Commandments of Interviews
- Telephone Time Zone Charts
- Travel and Communication Challenges
- Taped Answering Machine or E-mail Message

Challenge
- Travel Agent Interview
- Taped Interview Analysis
- Interview Follow-Up
- Stage Direction to Suggest Gestures and Space for Dialogue in Play

CHAPTER 4 REVIEW

SUMMARY

One-to-one communication accounts for much of our daily communication. Most of us spend more time engaged in face-to-face conversation than in the other forms of speaking. While we take one-to-one conversation pretty much for granted, it involves certain special characteristics and rules.

The Verbal Aspects of Conversation Good conversation demands accuracy, courtesy, and a genuine interest in a range of topics. You should also learn to enjoy the art of conversation. The checklist can help you evaluate the effectiveness of your own conversational style.

The Nonverbal Aspects of Conversation Most forms of one-to-one communication rely heavily on the nonverbal channels. Sometimes nonverbal signals substitute for words. More often they occur together with spoken language to complement, emphasize, and sometimes contradict what is being said.

Body motion is very important in one-to-one communication. Eye contact can signal when a speaker is about to yield the floor to the listener. Too little eye contact can indicate a lack of interest. Too much can be distracting. People also use space during two-person conversations to signal greater or lesser degrees of intimacy. Being on time for meetings or interviews, giving sufficient time to conversations, and not allowing frequent interruptions during a discussion all speak clearly of your attitudes towards others. Neatness of appearance can often be a deciding factor in the outcome of a job interview. Finally, your speaking rate, voice pitch, volume, and vocalized pauses may sometimes make a greater impact than your words themselves.

Speaking on the Telephone Telephone conversation depends on the voice alone to convey the message. Whether using the telephone for social or business conversation, you must remember the importance of efficiency, courtesy, and friendliness.

Taking Part in an Interview Though there are many types of interviews, the job interview is the kind most commonly encountered. Being interviewed for a job demands careful preparation, active participation, and good follow-up. Conducting an interview also requires all of these things as well as careful management.

ASSESS

ASSESSMENT STRATEGIES

Individual Assessment
- Participates in practice activities daily or weekly
- Completes classwork
- Demonstrates knowledge of content through questions, discussion, quizzes, and tests
- Displays improved speech skills in the use of the telephone and interview process

Group Assessment
- Sets and achieves goals
- Develops cooperative learning projects
- Supports efforts of team and class members
- Provides encouragement and feedback to members

VOCABULARY

Define each term in a complete sentence.

one-to-one communication
conversation
vocalized pause
interview
interviewee
résumé

CHECKLIST

One-to-One Communication Skills

1. Choose words you are sure your receiver will understand.
2. Pay close attention to the feedback you receive in one-to-one communication.
3. Present your ideas in logical steps so that your receiver will be able to see clearly how you reached your conclusion.
4. Be a careful listener when you are conversing. Concentrate on what the other person is saying, and provide supportive feedback.
5. Be aware that good conversation involves taking turns. At the same time, show respect for the other person's point of view whether or not you agree with him or her.
6. Use body motion when conversing, but avoid making exaggerated gestures.
7. Be aware of the importance of space when conversing. Adapt yourself to the person to whom you are speaking by maintaining an appropriate distance.
8. Be punctual for appointments.
9. Be neat and well-groomed, especially when you participate in interviews.
10. Speak clearly and avoid vocalized pauses.

REVIEW QUESTIONS

1. Name three common examples of one-to-one communication.
2. List three rules for having a good conversation.
3. Identify three ways to send messages accurately during conversation.
4. Name several nonverbal aspects of conversation.

ANSWERS

See the Answer Key for more complete answers.

REVIEW QUESTIONS

1. Common examples of one-to-one communication include conversations, telephone calls, and interviews.
2. Basic guidelines for having a good conversation include sending and receiving messages accurately, being courteous, and speaking on a variety of related topics of interest to both parties.
3. To ensure the accurate sending of messages, one should choose words the receiver will understand, pay attention to feedback, and present ideas logically.
4. Nonverbal aspects of conversation include kinesics, proxemics, time, appearance, and paralanguage.

ASSESS

5. Telephone conversation is more difficult because the speakers cannot make use of nonverbal elements of communication.
6. These elements include tone, speaking rate, and articulation.
7. Students should refer to pp.105-106 for a list of kinds of questions that might be asked.
8. Students should be ready to ask questions such as those on pp.105-106.
9. An interviewer will likely be influenced by what the interviewee says and by the interviewee's promptness, appearance, courtesy, attention, enthusiasm, and interest.
10. A job interview should be followed by a thank-you letter and, if one has not already been submitted, a résumé.

DISCUSSION QUESTIONS

The following code is used to designate discussion questions and activities as suitable for students of varying ability levels:

▼ = below average to average
◆ = average to above average
■ = all students

1. Have students make a list of possible ways
▼ to correct these problems.
2. Begin this activity by having students para-
◆ phrase the two quotations. Encourage students to recognize the importance of listening to people who are "older and wiser."
3. You might wish to have students review the
■ discussion of proxemics in Chapter 2 before conducting this activity.

CRITICAL THINKING

1. **Analysis** You may wish to have students
■ do this in small groups.

114

CHAPTER 4 REVIEW

5. State why telephone conversation is more difficult than face-to-face conversation.
6. List several speech elements that carry your message in a telephone conversation.
7. Describe several kinds of questions that you should be prepared to answer during a job interview.
8. Identify the kinds of questions you should be prepared to ask in a job interview.
9. Describe several factors that may influence the impression you make on the interviewer during a job interview.
10. Describe how you should follow up on a job interview.

? DISCUSSION QUESTIONS

1. Identify and discuss common problems that occur in one-to-one communication situations, such as interrupting, wandering attention, and not allowing the other person to speak. How can these problems be overcome if you are involved in a conversation with someone who allows these things to happen?
2. Study the following quotations.
   A single conversation across the table with a wise man is worth a month's study of books. (Chinese Proverb)
   Conversation is the laboratory and workshop of the student. (Ralph Waldo Emerson)
   Explain what each quotation means. Share with your classmates experiences you have had conversing with someone whom you consider to be "older and wiser." How did you feel about these conversations? Were you intimidated or made uncomfortable by the older person?
3. As a class, identify the various ways that individuals lay claim to space or their own territory at school and at home. Consider "your" desk in each class, "your" locker, "your" books, and "your" personal items at school. Consider "your" room, "your" place at the dining table, "your" place in the family car, and "your" favorite chair. In your speech notebook, make a list of your personal spaces at home, at school, and wherever else you spend a great deal of time.

△ CRITICAL THINKING

1. **Analysis** Discuss the similarities and differences between a one-to-one conversation and an interview. How is the informal situation like the formal one? How do they differ?

ASSESS

2. Evaluation Discuss what purpose a job interview serves for both the employer and the candidate for employment. Do you feel that it accomplishes more than the sending of a résumé? As an employer, how can it help you to evaluate a candidate? As a candidate, how can it help you evaluate the employer and the job?

ACTIVITIES

In-Class

1. Join one of three groups in your class. Group I will focus on facial expressions by collecting magazine pictures, designing a collage, and writing word balloons over each face in the collage. Group II will follow the same procedure but will concentrate on pictures depicting various forms of body language: posture, kneeling, running, reaching, etc. The group will decide what specific messages are being sent with kinesics. Group III will also follow the same procedure but will gather and display pictures that show spacial relationships. Then the group will decide what messages are being sent by the figures' use of space.

   When the collages are complete, one member of each group will present an oral report, sharing the collage and explaining the ideas that were formulated in the group that designed it.

2. Form small groups. Each group should set up a display in the classroom that is made up of various personal items. The class then visits each display. Each individual should visualize a "person" based on the items in the display. Each member of the class should then write a brief description of the "person." Discuss each "person" you have imagined with your classmates.

3. If videotape equipment is available, someone will videotape a class period during which members of the class are working in small groups. The tape will not include an audio recording. The class will view the tape and analyze the nonverbal signals communicated by the various members of the small groups. Which signals are sent without the person being aware of them? Which signals seem to be sent intentionally?

4. In small groups, develop one of the following three skits. Each skit will involve two speakers: a caller and a receiver of a telephone call. (a) Situation 1: Call someone you have just met to invite him or her to see a movie with you. (b) Situation 2: Call a dentist's office to make an appointment. (c) Situation 3: Call to announce that you are unable to honor a promise to babysit on a Saturday evening. The skits may be serious or humorous, but each should make an important

---

2. Evaluation Ask students to create imaginary job descriptions and then to make lists of questions to be asked by interviewers and interviewees.

ACTIVITIES
In-Class
1. Ask students to bring magazines or magazine pictures for use in this assignment.
2. Conducting this activity will help students to understand that much communication is nonverbal.
3. You could video, without the sound, small groups at work. Discuss nonverbal signals given intentionally or unintentionally by members of the group.
4. Have students evaluate the speakers in the skits.

ASSESS

5. Have students prepare lists independently.
◆ Then have them work in small groups to come up with tentative master lists. Each group should present its list to the class and combine these to make a final master list.

Out-of-Class
1. Have students evaluate themselves.
■ Encourage students to be frank about the difficulties experienced in these conversations.
2. Have students refer to the material on prox-
▼ emics in the text before doing this activity.
3. You may wish to make the meetings of this
■ club a regular part of your class.
4. When students make their reports to the
◆ class, have them imitate the characteristics that they rate.

116

CHAPTER 4 REVIEW

point about telephone usage. Present each skit in class and discuss the lessons to be learned from each.

5. In small groups, design a Pre-interview Checklist. Include making arrangements for the interview, doing research, designing questions, and making plans to record the information. Lists from each group will be combined into a master list to be written on the chalkboard. You may then copy it in your speech notebook.

Out-of-Class

1. Have a conversation this week with someone outside your family or peer group. Choose an older person or young child with whom you do not normally communicate. Write an entry in your speech notebook about this experience. Include facts about both the conversation and your response to the conversation. Consider how easy or difficult it was to keep the conversation going. How do you think the other person felt about the experience?

2. In one of your classes that has no assigned seating, sit at a desk normally occupied by someone else. Observe how that student reacts to your being in "his" or "her" space. How do you feel when someone violates "your" space? How does the other student react when you return to your "own" seat? Record the other student's reactions in your speech notebook.

3. Organize a Conversation Club that meets periodically to discuss certain topics of interest to members. Assign a specific topic for each meeting. You may want to encourage those people who share a common interest to become members. For example, there may be a number of people in your English class who enjoy reading. Your club could then devote each meeting to a particular type of literature.

4. Make a "nonverbal communication profile" of a television news commentator from one of the major networks. Watch facial expressions, eye behavior, and appearance. Listen for vocal tones, speaking rate, volume, and voice quality. Keep lists of your positive and negative impressions of the commentator for a period of two weeks. Report your impressions to the class.

ASSESS

💡 CHAPTER PROJECT

Divide the class into two groups. One group will invent a company and assign jobs in the company to those who are members of the group. Each person with an assigned job will then write an advertisement for a new position that he or she would supervise. Post these ads on the class bulletin board or in some other suitable location.

Each member of the second group should then read the ads and select a job to apply for. Then, one at a time, the person applying for a job will role-play an interview with the person offering the job. (Before the interview, you may also wish to role-play a telephone call that obtains preliminary information about the job and sets up an interview.) Do all of this realistically by preparing a résumé, developing questions beforehand, and dressing appropriately.

When all interviews are completed, conduct a class discussion about the experience. Was it more difficult or was it easier than expected? Did practice help?

CHAPTER PROJECT

- To prepare students for this activity, you may wish to describe the various departments in a hypothetical company (production, accounting, personnel, payroll, marketing, etc.). You might also wish to provide students with model job descriptions. Have students evaluate conversations and interviews as they carry out this project.

PREPARE

● CHAPTER PLANNER

Day 1	Day 2	Day 3	Day 4	Day 5
Prepare	Prepare	Prepare	Prepare	Prepare
Teach	Teach	Teach	Teach	Teach
Assess	Assess	Assess	Assess	Assess
Sub. Teacher Tips *pp. 123, 125*	Sub. Teacher Tips *pp. 129, 131*	Sub. Teacher Tip *p. 135*	Sub. Teacher Tips *pp. 140, 144*	Sub. Teacher Tip *p. 149*

● CHAPTER OVERVIEW

This chapter examines the following topics:
- The Nature of Group Discussion *p. 119*
- Factors Affecting Group Discussion *p. 123*
- How Groups Behave *p. 127*
- Preparing to Participate in a Group *p. 133*
- Leading a Group *p. 139*
- Handling Conflict in Groups *p. 142*
- Outcomes of Discussion *p. 146*
- Alternatives to Group Discussion *p. 147*

▽ PORTFOLIO PRODUCTS

Individual Projects
- Glossary of Speech Terms
- Agenda for Group Discussion
- Publicity for Group Meeting
- Chapter 5 Portfolio Products

Group Projects
- Taped Question and Answer Segment of Group Meeting
- Debate of Selected Topic
- Media Publicity for Group Meeting

● sca GUIDELINES

- Expresses ideas clearly in a group meeting
- Expresses and defends position in a group forum
- Uses several forms of organization to explain point of view
- Answers questions about public issues
- Summarizes arguments for and against controversial public issues

CHAPTER 5

Group Discussion

When you have completed this chapter you should be able to:

● Explain and give examples of the important role of group communication in life today.

● Describe various types and forms of group discussion.

● Describe several factors that affect group discussion.

● Explain ways to prepare for group discussion.

● Describe three aspects of group leadership.

TEACH

● **MOTIVATION**

Take a poll of students in the class and ask each to identify the number of clubs and associations each belongs to. Encourage them to consider groups at churches, synagogues, and other places in addition to school. Tally the number and figure out the class average. You might award "bonus points" to students who volunteer time with younger students or the elderly.

● **LINKS TO PAST LEARNING**

Ask students to share descriptions of televised sessions of local, state, or federal legislatures. Discuss the issues that were the topic of debate or discussion. Ask students to share their impressions of the legislators' ability to listen to and debate the issues.

● **ACTIVITY**

Ask students to prepare several questions to ask a guest speaker. Suggest that the class evaluate their own performance as a group as they respond to the speaker. Identify areas for improvement. Save these suggestions and use them at the conclusion of the chapter to measure improvement in group participation skills.

The Nature of Group Discussion 119

● **ACTIVITY**

Reports from Student Groups

Ask class members who have experience in group communication (a member of a school council, an officer of a club, a leader of a Scout troop, a staff member for the school paper) to report to the class what they learned about group interaction through their participation in such groups. Ask the speakers what they discovered about the importance of prior preparation for group meetings, what form of leadership they consider best for group meetings, and what the major benefits of deciding matters by using group discussion are.

Group discussion is rapidly becoming one of the most widely used forms of interpersonal communication in modern society. In the world of business, managers may spend up to fifty percent of their time in meetings. Public meetings may be held to discuss the budget proposed by a school board or a city's new zoning laws. Students may be asked to carry out assignments in small groups.

As shown by the opening Activity, people communicate in groups for several purposes. Often groups meet in order to solve a problem or to reach a decision. Groups may also meet to share information, such as self-help groups, religious study groups, and workshops. As in one-to-one conversation, there is often no single goal or topic and no planning of a group's social conversation beforehand. The rules for successful group conversation are similar to those presented for one-to-one conversation in Chapter 4. Therefore, in this chapter the focus will be on group discussion used to arrive at decisions and to share information, rather than on group conversation.

● **THE NATURE OF GROUP DISCUSSION**

Group discussion occurs any time three or more people meet to solve a common problem, arrive at a decision, or answer a question of mutual interest.

The idea of *cooperation* is basic to discussion. It means that the members of the group must share a desire to achieve a common goal. They may not all wish to achieve that goal in exactly the same way. But they must be willing to devote their energies to reaching a group solution, rather than to promoting their own individual solutions or opinions.

119

TEACH

> **"No speech can be entirely bad if it is short."**
>
> —Anonymous

● TEACHING

Make a chart on the chalkboard with the boldface labels identifying types of group discussions. Ask students to add characteristics of each type based on the text explanation. Have students identify the audience and purpose of each.

● LEARNING STYLES

Cooperative Learning

Ask students if they prefer working on a problem by themselves or with a group. Let those who prefer to work independently do so and organize small groups for the others. Then encourage students to identify what they consider to be the biggest problem connected with the school cafeteria. Give the individuals and small groups a specific amount of time to come up with at least two possible solutions to the problem they identified. Share all suggestions. Then discuss the process by which individuals and small groups arrived at the solutions.

● SKILL DEVELOPMENT

15-Second Skill Opportunity

Ask students to think about the worst club, group, or committee meeting they ever attended. Ask volunteers to stand and explain the "who, what, when, where, and why" relative to that experience. Then ask other students to offer suggestions that might have helped change the character of the meeting.

CHAPTER 5 Group Discussion

Each group member must be prepared to listen as well as to argue.

This does not mean that there won't be differences of opinion in group discussion. Rather, it means that each member must enter the group with an open mind, genuinely prepared to listen as well as to argue.

Discussion groups are generally formed for a definite purpose, to achieve a particular and sometimes urgent goal. Ordinarily, such a goal can be reached only when the members are *prepared*. If a member has prepared actively to participate and achieve the group's goal, she or he can not only help the group reach a decision but can also have considerable influence in forming the group's decision.

Types of Group Discussion

Discussion groups can be classified by their *purpose* and their *audience*. Groups classified by purpose usually meet for one of two reasons: **decision-making** or **enlightenment.** A board of directors of a corporation generally meets to decide upon action for the future. A group of TV commentators discussing unemployment on a news broadcast, on the other hand, generally has the enlightenment of the listeners as its primary purpose. Determining whether a discussion group exists for the purpose of decision-making or for enlightenment is one of the basic ways of classifying different types of groups.

Groups can also be classified by their audience, that is whether they are engaged in closed-group or public discussion. If the members of the group are communicating only with each other, the discussion is a **closed-group discussion.** If they are also communicating with listeners outside the group, the discussion is a **public discussion.** It is

In a typical closed-group discussion, city planners exchange ideas on relatively limited subjects.

public discussion even if the audience is not physically present, as in the case of a TV or radio broadcast.

These types of discussion can, of course, occur in combination. When a group of students meets to study together before a big exam, it is a closed-group, enlightenment discussion. If those same students were gathered to plan a dance, the format would be a closed-group, decision-making one. When city council members discuss recreation facilities available in their city in front of an audience it is a public, enlightenment discussion. Suppose the council members were to discuss whether they should build a new city hall or repair the old one. If an audience was present, the discussion would be a public, decision-making one.

Forms of Discussion Groups

Probably the most common form for closed-group discussion is the committee. A **committee** is a small subgroup of a larger organization that has been given a specific task or set of tasks to perform. The committee is often used for decision-making. Some committees have only the power to recommend action or policy to the larger body of which they are a part. Others can actually make a decision or carry out a task. A board of directors for a corporation is a special kind of elected committee. They have been given the authority to carry out decision-making tasks for the owners of the corporation.

TEACH

"If you want to kill any idea in the world today, get a committee working on it."

—C. F. Kettering

LEARNING STYLES

Cooperative Learning
Organize teams of students so that each group represents a major commercial television network. The task of each group is to determine the lineup of programs for Tuesday evenings that would bring in the most revenue and capture the greatest viewing audience.

Visual Learning
To emphasize the two major purposes for group discussion, consider the following: Develop a large chart on the chalkboard with the labels "To Know" and "To Do." Ask students to name several things that are common in their lives and indicate whether these things relate to something they need to know or do. Compare the length of the lists and the examples. Discuss if there are more things to know or do in their lives.

TEACH

● **CURRICULAR CONNECTIONS**

Language Arts
Have students look in the newspaper for listings of meetings or conventions that will be held in your area. Make a list of these meetings and identify the groups that sponsor them. Students could write or call these groups for additional information. Students could determine if these meetings are a closed-group or public discussion.

● **LEARNING STYLES**

Cooperative Learning
For each of the types of discussion mentioned in this section, organize a small group. The groups should each research and demonstrate one of the forms of discussion. Each group could be given a specific amount of time to demonstrate for the entire class how their form of discussion works.

Limited English Proficiency
Some students might want to make a list of all the terms in boldface in this section. Each term could be written on an index card. On the reverse side of the card, the explanation of the term with an example could be developed. Students could work in pairs to gain practice in matching definitions and examples.

CHAPTER 5 Group Discussion

Another common form of closed-group discussion is the **round-table discussion.** Perhaps you remember King Arthur's Round Table. It was, according to legend, a circular table around which King Arthur and his knights discussed their adventures. The purpose of the circular shape of the table was to prevent arguments about each knight's relative importance in the group. During a round-table discussion, a circular table is often used for the same reason. Although the term *round table* is sometimes used to apply to almost any type of closed-group discussion, it most often means a closed-group session in which information-sharing or enlightenment of those taking part is the object. For example, a literary club would be using a round-table form if its members met to discuss the latest novel.

Public discussion often takes the form of a panel. A **panel** is a group that discusses a topic in front of an audience. The panel's purpose could be either enlightenment or decision-making. In either case they are discussing for the benefit of an audience as well as for themselves.

A similar form of public discussion is the **symposium.** In a symposium, one group member gives a short, uninterrupted speech, which is followed by a speech from the next member, and so on until all members have spoken. A symposium, then, is really a series of short public speeches generally given by experts, and is thus not a true group discussion. In a symposium, the free interaction of ideas that is so important in group discussion does not exist.

Either the panel or the symposium can be opened up to questions or comments from the audience. When this is done, the form is called either a **panel-forum** or a **symposium-forum.** This arrangement can be quite effective with live or radio and television audiences where listeners or viewers can call in questions or reactions by telephone.

When public discussion takes the form of a symposium that is open to members of the audience, it becomes a symposium-forum.

ACTIVITY

Describing Group Communication

Hold a class discussion on these two questions: What is the difference between *types* of group discussion and *forms* of discussion groups? How many different types of group discussion are possible? List on the blackboard as many concrete examples of panels, symposiums, panel-forums, and symposium-forums as you have seen or been a part of as a participant.

● FACTORS AFFECTING GROUP DISCUSSION

Several factors affect whether or not a group discussion is successful. Two of these concern the formation of cliques within a group and the imposition of personal goals on a group. Four other factors deal with more concrete issues: group size, physical environment, seating arrangement, and the time when meetings are held.

Size of the Group

At least three people must be present in order to have a group discussion. Discussion groups seldom have more than fifteen members, however. Each member of a discussion group must have the opportunity to take part in the discussion. Too many members can cause verbal traffic jams, preventing the group from arriving at a decision. The group size that seems to work best for most situations is five or seven—not six! If a group has an even number of members, a vote on an issue would result in a tie, and the discussion would be deadlocked. If the group has an odd number, a tie could not occur.

Cliques Within a Group

When a clique develops within a group, it is almost certain to hamper the group's success. A **clique** consists of a few of the group members (often two or three) who become a separate group within the larger group. They may do so by talking among themselves much of the time, often about topics unrelated to the discussion. Or they may try to dominate the discussion, talking so much that other members have little

---

TEACH

SUBSTITUTE TEACHER TIP

Take a poll of the number and type of meetings the parents of the students attend every week. Tally the results by type of group meeting mentioned in the text. Ask students to think about the amount of time spent in meetings in the work place. Talk about the factors that influence the amount of time spent in group work on the job.

● ACTIVITY

You might emphasize how the nature of the audience and the purpose of a group could influence the *type* and the *form* of a group presentation. You might give a variety of examples and ask students to think of what type of group discussion might be most appropriate. Examples could include: (a) doctors presenting new research about AIDS, (b) parents complaining about a school policy, (c) an advertising agency working on a new TV campaign.

● LEARNING STYLES

Visual Learning
Some students might be interested in making cartoon representations that depict each of the types of group discussion mentioned in this section. Other students might collect examples from commercial cartoons or political commentary that refer to any of the types of group discussions mentioned.

Cooperative Learning
Ask teams of students to consider the following problem, *The Bridge,* and arrive at a solution. Compare the solutions of each group. A busy bridge is found to have structural damage, and only three more vehicles may safely cross it before it collapses. Many vehicles are lined up and want to cross. The group must decide which of the following will be allowed passage. (a) an express mail truck; (b) an ambulance with a stroke victim; (c) a CIA agent tracking a terrorist; (d) a diplomat going to an emergency meeting of the National Security Council; (e) a fire truck going to put out a fire at a major oil refinery.

TEACH

AMAZING FACTS!
A general meeting of AT&T stockholders brought 20,109 people together in 1961. This is a world record!

LINKS TO PAST LEARNING

Look at the definition of *clique* in the text and ask students to give examples of cliques at work. Encourage comments on why they get started and what peers can do to minimize their influence.

CURRICULAR CONNECTIONS

Math/Science
Ask students to gather information about the numbers of members in each of the clubs sponsored by the school. Include information about the distribution in freshman, sophomore, junior, and senior classes. Ask students to review the data and make generalizations about the influence of size of membership on school life.

SKILL DEVELOPMENT

15-Second Skill Opportunity
Ask students to imagine that they are recruiting freshmen to join a school club they belong to. Have volunteers give a brief "sales pitch" to encourage a prospect to join their club.

LEARNING STYLES

Kinesic Learning
Organize various sized groups of students to discuss the questions below. Groups should be both large and small. Arbitrarily assign some groups to sit on the floor for the discussion. Give each group 15 minutes and then ask each to comment on the effects of the seating arrangements on the discussion. Questions to discuss: (a) What is the most important reason for finishing high school? (b) For what reasons do students select electives?

CHAPTER 5 Group Discussion

chance to speak. Sometimes they will laugh and joke when the majority of the group is seriously trying to discuss the topic.

When a clique develops, someone outside it needs to exert leadership to halt its negative influence. Sometimes this can be done by encouraging everyone in the discussion group to participate. When the clique gets the group away from the subject, a leader needs to remind the members what the current topic is. In those cases where the clique is causing a constant, or major disruption, strong leadership must be exerted. This may mean calling on the members of the clique by name and asking them to stop the interference. In extreme cases, the other members of the group may need to expel the clique from the group.

Personal Goals of Members

People take part in groups to achieve some kind of common goal. The goal may be to make a joint decision, to solve a mutual problem, or to share information. In addition, each member of a group generally wishes to achieve certain personal goals. These may include a position of leadership, a feeling of comradeship, or a desire for security. Sometimes fulfilling personal goals helps to achieve group goals. At other times, personal goals may become barriers to group goals.

A personal goal involving leadership can have a strong effect on a group. Many people prefer to lead rather than follow. But it is difficult for several in a group to lead at the same time. In new groups, members sometimes spend so much of their discussion time in power plays for leadership that the group has no energy left to solve a problem or reach a decision. When a group forms, there is often a period of time during which the group must either elect leaders or wait for leaders to emerge naturally. This is normal. It is only when the group allows personal matters to overshadow group goals that jockeying for leadership positions must be controlled. The controlling of power plays is never easy. It requires a willingness on the part of those members seeking leadership to recognize the needs of the entire group and to place those needs ahead of a personal goal.

A member's need for acceptance by the group is another personal goal that can affect group discussion. Sometimes, the desire to be liked and accepted will cause a member to give way to majority influence. Research has shown that a person will go along with what he or she thinks is a majority opinion, even when it is directly opposite to his or her own view of the situation. Occasionally, two or three very persuasive members of a group can cause their opinion to seem like the majority opinion, when actually it is not. If other members of the group then "tag along," what is a minority view can become the group's decision or policy. To avoid this each member of a group should be sure that his or

TEACH

● **TEACHING**

Ask students to suggest how a group leader might restore cohesiveness to a situation in which a clique has become disruptive.

● **CURRICULAR CONNECTIONS**

Writing
Ask students to make a list of the ten most important qualities a leader can have. For each characteristic, ask students to provide a historical and a contemporary example.

SUBSTITUTE TEACHER TIP

Ask students to name as many members of Congress as they can. List each on the chalkboard. Ask students to think about the leadership qualities they think are important in Congress. Using these criteria, ask students to evaluate the performance of each politician as a congressional leader.

"All for one and one for all."
—Dumas

● **SKILL DEVELOPMENT**

15-Second Skill Opportunity
Ask students to think of a group or association they would like to join. Ask volunteers to practice requesting information about membership.

● **LEARNING STYLES**

Multicultural Learning
Review the story of, or show film clips from, *The Three Musketeers*. Ask students to think of modern examples of small groups working together for the benefit of all. Encourage students to share examples from various cultures represented in the classroom. Most cultures have similar stories and heroes.

Factors Affecting Group Discussion **125**

her opinion is heard and understood. No member should ever agree with another's opinion unless convinced it is the best solution the group can produce.

A third personal goal that involves a group's cohesiveness can also affect discussion. **Cohesiveness** is a kind of group spirit. The cohesiveness of the Three Musketeers, characters in the novel by Alexandre Dumas, was indicated by their motto, "All for one and one for all." When a group has cohesiveness, each member is dedicated to the unity of the group. The attainment of this personal goal of dedication allows a person to draw strength from being a member of a productive group. When cohesiveness is low, members generally put little effort into their discussions. Meetings may be carried on politely but are boring. They often end quickly. Important decisions are usually made hastily with practically no disagreement or weighing of evidence. With little cohesiveness, members do not really care about the group or its decisions, so they tend to make poor decisions. The only solution for this lack of cohesiveness is for members to become dedicated to the group and begin to be active and concerned about its goals. They must participate fully in the group's discussions and devote their energies to achieving quality solutions to group problems.

Physical Environment

The physical setting in which a group meets can affect its discussion. Members should try to avoid communication barriers caused by meeting in an unsuitable environment. For example, the temperature of the room should not be so high that members have trouble staying awake. On the other hand, the temperature should not be so low that people are uncomfortable.

A comfortable setting that affords privacy and quiet is the most conducive to successful group communication.

125

TEACH

AMAZING FACTS!
Researchers have studied the impact of various colors on human moods and behavior. Most people find blue rooms to be tranquil.

● **CURRICULAR CONNECTIONS**

Math/Science
Ask students to research the influence that sound waves and particular types of music have on children, especially infants.

● **LEARNING STYLES**

Audio Learning
Some students find silence disturbing; others think loud music makes it difficult to concentrate. Ask students to identify the most disturbing audio distraction they can think of. Compile a list on the chalkboard and identify the loudest and softest sounds.

Visual Learning
Ask students to design a classroom that would be especially conducive to group discussion. Encourage them to make scale models and display these for the class.

---

126   CHAPTER 5 Group Discussion

Noise and visual distractions can prevent a successful discussion too. Doors or windows may have to be closed to keep outside noises or the activities of others from distracting group members. Conversations within the group which are not related to the discussion question should also be discouraged. The time for social conversation is before or after group discussion. A quiet, uncluttered room that offers privacy is the best environment for group discussion.

Seating Arrangement

As you read in Chapter 2, it is important to consider proxemics, or the use of space, when communicating with others. In discussion, comfortable seating arrangements can sometimes mean the difference between whether or not a group reaches its goal. Chairs should be placed close enough to make discussion easy. On the other hand, group members should not be made uncomfortable by being so close that they feel their personal space has been invaded.

Good seating arrangements will make it possible for each group member to maintain eye contact with every other member. Being able to look at each other helps to keep members actively engaged in the discussion process.

Time for Discussion

The best group discussions are held at times when members are most alert. Avoid scheduling a discussion just before lunch or at the end of a busy day. People who are hungry or tired are less able to reason well.

A short break from a lengthy meeting will often refocus the attention of participants and allow them to return refreshed.

TEACH

● TEACHING

To emphasize the importance of the seating arrangement in the classroom, ask students to make a chart assigning a specific seat for each person. Display their seating charts and ask students to explain why they think their arrangement is best.

● LINKS TO PAST LEARNING

Ask students who have attended a live performance of a play or music group to describe the seating arrangements in the theater. What would they consider to be "the best seats in the house" and why?

> *"Take time to think—it is the source of wisdom."*
> —The Milwaukee Road Magazine

Groups should be sure there is enough time to share the information or to reach the decision called for by the discussion question. If the goal cannot be reached in one meeting, members should hold the next session as soon as possible. Members of the discussion group will remember better what was done at the first session if the second one follows shortly afterward. Summarizing what happened at the first meeting will also help members pick up where they left off.

If a discussion is expected to be lengthy, members may need a short break. After moving about and relaxing for a few minutes, a group is often able to resolve issues more successfully.

● ACTIVITY

Working with Groups

Your class will be divided into two halves. One half of the class will work on its own as individuals and the other half will work in groups of from five to seven members. Both the individuals and the groups will consider television commercials and will try to determine the characteristic that effective and memorable commercials have. Both the individuals and the groups will consider this topic for a period of time. The individuals will report their findings in class, and a leader chosen by each group will also report findings. As a class, discuss whether working together gave better results than working individually. Why or why not?

● HOW GROUPS BEHAVE

You have probably noticed, as you have participated in discussion groups, that some group members behave very differently than others do. You may also have noticed that a particular student acts differently as a member of the debate squad than he or she does as a staff member on the school paper. You may even have recognized that *you* take different roles and behave quite differently depending on the particular group with which you are involved at a given time. Some groups succeed in accomplishing their goals, while others do not. Some seem to experience little controversy, while others appear to be constantly in turmoil. Just as it is important to recognize such differences in the behavior of groups and their members, it is also important to know why some groups succeed and others do not. To do so, you need to know about two aspects of group behavior—the relationship between the group task and group maintenance, and the life cycle of groups.

● LEARNING STYLES

Cooperative Learning

Ask students to imagine that keeping school open throughout the entire calendar year is being proposed. Groups of students should suggest the best time to discuss the issue and give reasons for their choice of time.

● ACTIVITY

Ask students to think about the pros and cons of working together in groups and working individually. A common practice is to assess, or evaluate, individual performance. Ask students what they think of giving a group, or class, grade.

TEACH

> *"A camel is a horse designed by committee!"*

● **LINKS TO PAST LEARNING**

Ask students to reflect on experiences of learning in a group and learning one-to-one. Tally the numbers that preferred each style. Encourage discussion about the relative merits of each type.

● **TEACHING**

For each of the sentences in the dialogue, ask students to code it with a "T" if it is a task message and an "M" if it is a maintenance message.

---

128   CHAPTER 5 Group Discussion

Task Versus Maintenance

Imagine you are behind a two-way mirror observing a group of your fellow students planning the upcoming senior prom. You can see and hear them, but they are unaware of your presence. Here's an excerpt of what you hear:

Jennifer: Can we get back to what we are going to do about the drinking and driving problem that was so bad last year?

Brad: Wait a minute! I don't think we've finished with the question about the music yet. Did we definitely decide on the band?

Roger: Yes we did. About a half hour ago we finally took a vote, remember? You didn't vote for the Four Horsemen like most of us did, but it is settled. I agree with Jennifer. We need to talk about keeping people from driving while drunk.

Kimberly: Well, I've heard that a lot of schools have started a kind of taxi service where several juniors drive home those who can't drive themselves. Maybe we could try something like that this year.

Susan: Just how does that work, Kim? Do the juniors volunteer to do the driving? And who decides who is drunk enough to need a ride? It sounds like a good idea, but I'd like to know more about it.

Jennifer: Brad, don't you have a cousin at Southern High where they tried something like that last year? Do you know what they did and how well it worked?

This little peek at a discussion group highlights the constant flipping back and forth between task and maintenance messages that the typical group engages in. **Task messages** are those primarily designed to help the group achieve its goals or complete its task. **Maintenance messages** are mainly for the purpose of keeping relationships among the group members harmonious so there is a positive climate in the group. In our prom-planning group, Jennifer began with a task message, that of refocusing the group's attention on the specific topic of handling drunk drivers. This type of task message has been labeled "initiating." When Brad attempted to sidetrack the group onto the topic of the band, Roger reminded him and the group as a whole that that matter had already been agreed upon by an earlier vote. Roger was using a maintenance message known as "standard setting"—pointing out standards of procedure that the group has already agreed upon, such as following majority opinion. Kimberly then used the task message known as "giving information or opinion" when she asked the group to consider the taxi service idea she had heard about. Susan responded with another

TEACH

● **RETEACHING**

Ask students to use the major headings in this section to list the main ideas emphasized here. Then, for each major point, ask students to imagine they are a photo researcher or illustrator and their job is to think of an illustration or photo that would get the main point across.

SUBSTITUTE TEACHER TIP

Use photos of groups in the text and ask students to write an imaginary dialogue for each photo. Students should identify the topic under discussion and suggest a possible comment for each of the people pictured.

● **SKILL DEVELOPMENT**

15-Second Skill Opportunity
Ask students to give an example of any of the types of messages mentioned in this section. List these on the chalkboard to help students focus on the differences among them.

● **LEARNING STYLES**

Limited English Proficiency
Encourage pairs of students to work on the terms and phrases in the table on this page and to think of synonyms and alternate expressions for each. Students could develop an alternate vocabulary to describe similar communications.

How Groups Behave 129

Task and maintenance messages help groups work smoothly towards goals.

Task Messages

Initiating—messages that propose a general group task or goal; suggestions for how the group should proceed; ideas for solving a problem

Seeking Information or Opinions—messages that ask for information or facts; requests for ideas, estimates, or suggestions

Giving Information or Opinion—messages that offer facts or information; statements of opinion, belief, or suggestion

Clarifying and Elaborating—statements that help clear up confusion or define terms; messages that indicate alternatives and issues before the group

Summarizing—messages that pull together ideas shared by group members; restating group problems, suggestions, and conclusions

Consensus Testing—messages that ask whether the group is approaching agreement or nearing decision

Maintenance Messages

Harmonizing—messages designed to reduce group tension, to reconcile disagreements, or to get members to explore differences

Gate Keeping—messages to encourage the participation of other group members, help keep channels of communication open, and promote sharing

Encouraging—messages to show friendliness to other group members; facial expressions or remarks that show acceptance, warmth and responsiveness

Compromising—remarks that show a willingness to admit errors, give in, or modify one's position

Standard Setting and Testing—remarks made to determine whether the group is satisfied with its procedures; pointing out rules or norms the group may wish to adopt or has already adopted

TEACH

▼ PORTFOLIO PRODUCT

Students could make an evaluation chart listing the various types of task and maintenance messages. They could record examples of these messages and evaluate the frequency with which each type is made. They could be encouraged to rate themselves in each area.

● CURRICULAR CONNECTIONS

Writing
Ask students to examine the explanation of various types of messages. Make a list of the courses that students are taking and ask students to think about the average frequency of each type of message in each course.

● LEARNING STYLES

Cooperative Learning
Have students participate in discussion groups to explore the topic "What can be done about violence in the United States today?" At the end of the designated time for discussion, ask students to reflect on the various task and maintenance messages they heard. Encourage them to provide examples of each.

CHAPTER 5 Group Discussion

task message, "seeking information or opinions," when she asked for more details about Kimberly's suggestion. Finally, Jennifer used the maintenance message called "gate keeping" by trying to draw Brad back to discussion of the drunk driving. "Gate keeping" messages are those designed to keep everyone in the group involved in the topic and to promote a sharing atmosphere. Notice that Jennifer's final remark to Brad was not only a maintenance message designed to draw Brad back into the discussion. It also served as a task message of "seeking information or opinions" to further the group's progress towards a decision about how to handle drunk drivers.

Once you realize that not all messages spoken in group meetings are directly related to the content of the discussion, but that some are designed to accomplish very necessary maintenance functions, you will understand better why groups behave as they do. On page 129 are two lists describing several of the most common types of task and maintenance messages encountered in groups. The next time you find yourself involved in a group discussion, watch and listen for them.

The Life Cycle of Groups

Discussion groups seem to experience life cycles just as individuals do. As each of us develops and matures from infancy through adolescence into adulthood, so groups go through similar stages of progress. One writer has identified and labeled four stages in the life cycle of discussion groups: **Forming, Storming, Norming,** and **Performing.** During each stage, group members must attend to four aspects of the group's life if the group is to reach its goals and achieve its task. They must, of course, attend to the task itself; they must monitor the relationships among the individual members of the group; they must pay attention to behavior patterns of the group as a whole; and they must attend to the leadership of the group. Let's see what typically happens during each stage of group life.

Forming This stage is like infancy. When members of a new group first come together, each person listens to the others as they state their reasons for being a part of the group, and what they hope the group's goals and accomplishments will be. Individual members are anxious as they try to discover whether they will feel comfortable in this group and will be accepted. Everyone is polite. No one emphasizes differences of opinion during the forming stage. Rather, everyone is searching for as much similarity of views and goals as possible. Members are also looking for leadership and guidance during this first stage, much as the infant is dependent on parents for guidance. If no designated leadership already exists, members will quickly move to establish it. The forming

TEACH

● **LINKS TO PAST LEARNING**

Ask students to identify four stages in the life cycle of a flower or animal. Encourage them to think of "catchy" labels for each stage. They might make a time line showing that life cycle and indicating the relative length of each stage.

● **CURRICULAR CONNECTIONS**

Writing
Some students might research some of the oldest groups in our history. Or they could use the Republican and Democratic political parties as examples. Have students develop a timeline that would show the four life-cycle stages in the history of either party.

SUBSTITUTE TEACHER TIP

Use the flow chart and ask students to develop an icon or illustration to represent each of the four stages.

How Groups Behave

stage may be smooth and pleasant for a group when members find they have compatible goals and interpersonal styles. It can also produce much tension and anxiety if members find little similarity and compatibility.

Storming Once a group discovers sufficient similarity of goals and personalities in the first stage, it is ready to move into the storming stage, that is, the adolescent stage that is usually the most difficult stage in the life of a group. Here, individual members challenge differences of goals and approaches as part of an effort to express their individuality and to wield power and influence over the group. Often the designated leadership is challenged while members struggle with wanting to have sufficient control over the direction of the group. It is also during this storming stage that the group is trying to create order and establish the operating rules for its decision-making. This state is a time of maximum struggle for the group as members wrestle with both the demands of their task and issues of power and influence within the group. This stage can be frustrating, but will help the group learn to confront and resolve conflict.

Norming Once the group begins to resolve the conflicts over who is to exert influence and what procedures it will use to accomplish its goals, it moves into the calmer stage called norming. Here the group becomes a cohesive unit, ready to tackle its task. Members are now learning to function effectively as a group, trusting each other as they negotiate the best ways of working out the group's goals. They are beginning to share leadership functions as they allow members with special insights and knowledge to lead at appropriate places in the discussion. They are learning to trust one another as the group as a whole begins to experience success.

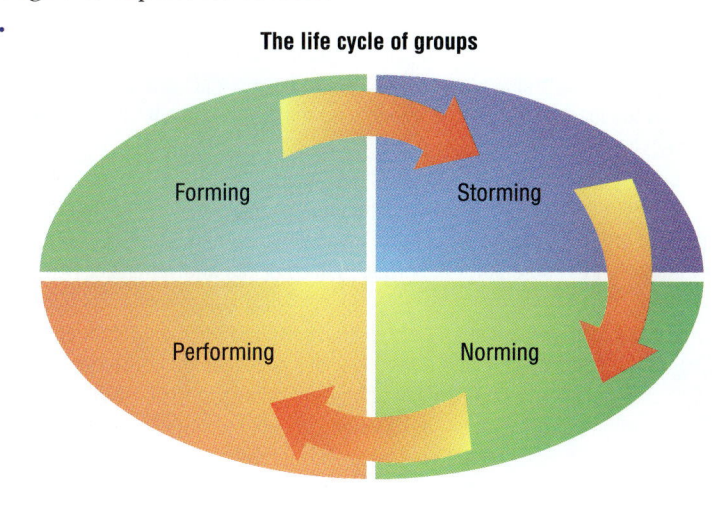

> *"A person who talks much is sometimes right."*
> —Spanish proverb

● **LEARNING STYLES**

Cooperative Learning
Ask groups of students to discuss how they would define success. After the specific period of time, ask each group to consider these questions: (a) Did they see evidence of the four stages of group formation? (b) How did group leadership emerge? (c) Did all the stages develop, and if so, in what order?

life cycle of forming, storming, norming, and performing is the group equivalent of childhood, adolescence, and adulthood.

The life cycle of groups

Forming → Storming → Norming → Performing

APPLY

● **LINKS TO PAST LEARNING**

This feature lends itself to many variations. You could emphasize any of the following in using this activity: (a) leadership selection and change; (b) persuasive speaking techniques; or (c) the four phases of group development.

● **SKILL DEVELOPMENT**

Critical Thinking
You could suggest that students consider the differences between appointed and elected leaders. Ask them to name examples, good and bad, of each type. Discuss the style of leadership they think would be most effective in crisis situations such as the one described.

● **SKILL APPLICATION**

Citizens Speak Out
Ask students to think of effective techniques for convincing others to endorse their personal point of view. Discuss how they feel when someone disagrees with a strongly held personal opinion. You could role-play various ways to disagree.

● **LEARNING STYLES**

✻ **Cooperative Learning**
Students might record their group discussion and play back the comments to help them distinguish the four phases of group participation.

Speaking IN ACTION

The Crippled Ship

Situation
You are one of seven survivors on a passenger ship that has hit an iceberg in the North Atlantic. The captain, all crew members, and all but you seven have perished. Your radio has been lost, and the ship is without power. It is obvious that within several hours at most the ship will break apart and sink. Only one small lifeboat is in working condition, and it is clearly capable of holding only four of you, along with sufficient food and wraps to keep the four alive for seventy-two hours. The group of seven knows it will have to make the awful decision of which three must be left behind on the ship to die. The seven survivors are: a healthy 30-year-old Jewish rabbi, a retired male physician, a 32-year-old female counselor, an eight-months-pregnant woman, and a well-to-do middle-aged couple and their eight-year-old daughter.

Preparation
Seven members of the class will volunteer to play the roles of the seven survivors. Each of you will be given time to prepare individually for this upcoming life-and-death discussion. Begin your individual preparation by deciding on the most important criteria that you feel should serve as the bases for the group's decisions. In this case, such criteria might consist of matters such as the age of each of the survivors, their physical ability to help the four survive once in the lifeboat, their medical condition, and their relationships to one another. Only when you have decided upon what you consider the fairest criteria should you begin thinking about which of the seven people should be left behind. Though you will come to the discussion with some tentative ideas of your own, you should also come prepared to keep an open mind about all seven survivors as you listen carefully to the others.

Discussion
When the discussion itself begins, the group should first select its leader. As you do this, try to choose on the basis of *real* personality and leadership qualities rather than according to the role that person is playing as a survivor. Once the leader is picked, however, you may treat one another as though you were the seven people described above.

When conflict develops during the discussion, look first to your chosen leader to handle it. If the leader is unable to deal with the conflict effectively, some other member should step in and provide the necessary leadership. The group should try to achieve unanimous agreement on which four survivors go and which three stay behind. If at some point the group is deadlocked and will never agree, then and only then should you take a vote.

Attempt each time you speak to be logical. Use sound reasoning and factual evidence. As a listener, keep an open ear for logical fallacies, and point them out in a clear yet courteous manner when you get the opportunity. Don't ever go along with the ideas of other members simply for the sake of being agreeable. If you disagree with something another member has said, say so, but not offensively. Never interrupt another speaker.

When deliberation concludes, the other class members may wish to discuss when each of the four phases of forming, storming, norming, and performing occurred.

● **CURRICULAR CONNECTIONS**

Math/Science
Ask students to think about the "norms" that represent both conscious and unconscious behavior or expectations that students in various high schools or colleges have. Discuss the possibility that what is thought to be the "norm" at one school may not be the "norm" at another. Research the process by which "norms" are determined.

● **SKILL DEVELOPMENT**

15-Second Skill Opportunity
Ask students to formulate a response to the proposal that young people should postpone entering college for several years after high school. Ask volunteers to share their comments with the class or in small groups

● **ACTIVITY**

You might appoint two groups to listen with special care to the tape. One group could listen for all task messages; the other could concentrate on the maintenance messages. Each group could transcribe appropriate examples from the excerpt. A third group of students might comment on the selections made by each group.

Performing In this final stage, trust and even affection among members blossom. As the group efficiently works out the details of its task, members feel a strong bond of unity, that is, each member feels that he or she is a key part of this unique group. They are now able to work together effectively and harmoniously as they complete their task.

Just as a person cannot skip infancy or adolescence on the way to adulthood, so groups appear to be unable to skip the forming and storming stages on their way to the adult stages of norming and performing. The next time you find yourself part of a discussion group which is having a "stormy" time, recall that this is a necessary step in the life cycle of any group.

● **ACTIVITY**

Task and Maintenance Messages
Play a brief excerpt from an audio tape of a group discussion. It might be from last year's speech class, a portion of a meeting of the school council, or a segment of your school board's deliberations. It need be only about five minutes long. As your teacher plays it two or three times, see if you can note each of the task and maintenance messages. Afterwards, compare your lists in a class discussion.

● **PREPARING TO PARTICIPATE IN A GROUP**

Many opportunities for discussion in groups exist in school situations. Members of student government, clubs, and teams use discussion groups to share information and to solve problems. A classroom group discussing a bill pending in the state legislature may report its recommendation in a persuasive letter to lawmakers.

A successful discussion should be planned in advance. Sometimes a leader of the group or several of the group's members will make plans for the discussion. Another very good way to plan is for all members of the group to hold a prediscussion meeting. During the planning stage, members of the group can choose the topic they want to talk about. They can decide on the type of question they want to discuss and take time to word the question carefully. Finally, they can write an outline or list of questions about the topic. This outline or list can then serve as a guide during the discussion.

TEACH

> *Someone once asked Daniel Webster how long he had worked on his great reply to Hayne. Webster replied, 'Twenty years.'*

● **RETEACHING**

You might suggest that students make an outline of the main points made in this section. They could use the major headings found in bold type.

● **LINKS TO PAST LEARNING**

Ask students to share feelings they might have if they came to class or a test unprepared. Discuss how preparation can relieve some of the anxiety surrounding difficult tasks.

● **LEARNING STYLES**

Cooperative Learning
Ask small groups of students to decide on a topic all members want to discuss. Provide a limited amount of time for the task. After the topic is selected, encourage the group to make a list, or outline at least three aspects of the topic that they would like addressed.

CHAPTER 5 Group Discussion

If all members are not present during the planning meeting, those who did not attend should be notified of the question to be discussed. They should also be given the outline to guide them in doing research on the topic.

Choose a Topic

The first step in making a discussion a success is to choose a suitable topic. A topic for group discussion should be interesting, significant, and manageable.

A well-chosen topic must be of interest to at least several persons. The members of the group themselves will participate best when the topic is of interest to the group as a whole as well as to each individual member. If the discussion is to be a public one, the subject should already be of interest to the audience or be one about which they can become interested.

It is not enough, though, that the topic be interesting. It should also be significant. The topic should affect the lives of the group members and of the audience, if one is present at the time of the discussion. For example, it might be interesting, but not very significant, for a high school group to discuss the question "How can sales managers develop better on-the-job relationships with their sales representatives?" Such a topic would lack a sense of immediacy for most or all of the students involved.

Finally, a well-chosen topic must be manageable. Discussion is a slow process at best. A group should not attempt, for example, to solve the world's economic problems in one hour. Groups should choose a topic that can be discussed thoroughly in the time allotted.

Decide What Type of Question to Discuss

After an interesting, significant, and manageable topic has been chosen, it should be worded in the form of a question. Groups usually discuss one of three types of questions. These are questions of fact, questions of value, or questions of policy. **Questions of fact** deal with whether a situation exists, under what circumstances it exists, or how it may be defined. "Is the United States' use of nuclear power on the decline?" is basically a question of fact.

Questions of value go a step beyond those of fact. While questions of fact deal with the existence of something, **questions of value** revolve around the worth of the object, person, or situation. A question of value emphasizes whether a thing is good or bad, desirable or undesirable, promising or hopeless. If a question requires judgments of worth, it is

TEACH

● TEACHING

After reading the section on choosing a topic, ask students to identify the criteria that are mentioned. List these on the chalkboard. Encourage students to think of additional criteria or guidelines for selecting topics for a group discussion.

● RETEACHING

Using the questions developed in Cooperative Learning, ask students to rephrase a question of fact so that it becomes a question of policy. Various examples can be pursued by the class.

> **SUBSTITUTE TEACHER TIP**
>
> Bring a newspaper or magazine to class and list the topics covered in the headlines or table of contents. Ask students to pick their favorite two topics and indicate why those topics are of interest to them.

● LEARNING STYLES

✳ Cooperative Learning

Organize teams of students so that each group represents one of the types of questions mentioned in the section. The team "questions of fact" could develop ten examples of this type of question. The other groups should do the same. Share examples with the entire class and reinforce the differences.

● SKILL APPLICATION

Debate

Invite a member of the debate team to talk to the class about the debate topic for the year. Share information abut how the topic is chosen and how the team begins to gather information to prepare a convincing debate.

Preparing to Participate in a Group **135**

usually called a question of value. "Is the two-party system the best political system for the United States?" would be a question of value.

Questions of policy are usually the most complex type of discussion questions. Questions of policy are also those most commonly discussed. **Questions of policy** are questions that are directed toward a course of physical or mental action. Questions such as "How much and what kind of support should our school give to its drama program?" and "What role should the federal government assume in the fight against industrial pollution of our waterways?" are questions of policy. These often include the word *should*. A group does not necessarily need to have the power to put its decision into action in order to discuss such a question. Many groups that can only recommend action may nevertheless have great influence on policy decisions.

Word the Question Carefully

As soon as a question is chosen, someone needs to narrow it down by wording it in clear, concise, and unbiased language. Many discussions become cloudy, and many more fail to achieve productive results, because no one has taken the time to state the question in a careful way.

In wording a discussion question, the most important thing to remember is that it should *be worded as a question,* not as a statement. Furthermore, it should usually be worded so that it has three or more possible answers. A question such as "Should taxes be cut?" allows only a "Yes" or "No" answer. This tends to turn the discussion into a debate, with two group factions, each arguing for its own opinion. A better way to phrase this question would be: "How should our government revamp the tax system?" With the question phrased in this manner, the question of taxes becomes just one of several possible solutions to be considered.

A well-worded question should also *be clear.* Avoid unclear questions such as "What about our school system?" This is not a question of fact, value, or policy. A group would not get very far if they tried to discuss such a vague question. The words within a discussion question must also be clear. Group members should agree on definitions for all the words used in each question. Suppose your group is to discuss the question "What action should our representatives in Congress take regarding international terrorism?" The phrase *international terrorism* should be defined before the discussion in started.

Conciseness is also important in a properly worded discussion question. Extremely long and involved wording can confuse, rather than clarify, a group session. Picture yourself trying to discuss the following question: "What kinds of required subjects, such as Math, English, and History, and what kinds of electives, such as Band, Debate, and Typing

135

TEACH

> **"The weaker the argument, the stronger the words."**
> —Anonymous

● **LINKS TO PAST LEARNING**

Ask students to think of the worst interview question they can remember from a talk show. Encourage some to share their examples and discuss why they thought the question(s) was so bad.

● **ASSESSMENT STRATEGY**

Ask small groups of students to think of at least three questions about the material in this chapter that would be suitable for asking on a test. Compare each group's questions and discuss which questions are clear and concise.

● **LEARNING STYLES**

Limited English Proficiency
Provide an example of a vague question such as "What about the weather?" or "What about our grading system?" Have students work in pairs or in small groups and think of several different ways to phrase the question to clarify the meaning.

CHAPTER 5 Group Discussion

should high-school students be made to take or be allowed to take at various grade levels?" This exaggerated example could be discussed better with the wording: "Which subjects should be required and which should be elective in grades nine through twelve?"

Finally, if you are given the responsibility for wording a discussion question, be sure that your wording is not one-sided or **biased.** Suppose you were opposed to raising money for a class trip by having a bake sale. You would display your bias if you used wording such as "How can we earn money for the trip without selling anything?" On the other hand, "How can we earn money for the trip?" would be asking an unbiased question.

Prepare the Outline

If you were driving from New York to California for the first time, you would probably use a road map. You would plot the best route beforehand, and decide about how far you would drive each day. If you were planning a leisurely vacation, however, you might not adhere to a strict schedule. Whenever an interesting side trip presented itself, you might depart from your planned route. A discussion outline serves much the same purpose as a road map does on a vacation. It provides the necessary guidance to keep the group moving toward its goal. But it should never be followed so rigidly that it stifles creative thinking among the members. Just as leisurely vacation travelers readjust their plans, so a discussion group should feel free to depart slightly from its outline because of changing conditions.

Since questions of policy are most common, the emphasis here will be on preparing an outline for such a question. A policy question generally demands an outline with three main divisions or phases:

1. Analysis of the background and causes of the problem or situation.
2. Consideration, evaluation, and comparison of alternatives or various possible solutions.
3. Agreement and disagreement about the best solution or action to take.

Most policy discussions will include each of these phases, usually outlined in the above order. The actual discussion, however, might sometimes move briefly into one of the latter phases before an earlier one is completed.

The discussion outline could easily be drawn up by the entire group in a prediscussion meeting. Outlines are general in nature. Questions rather than statements are used in main heads and subheads. Before the

APPLY

● ENRICHMENT

A systems analyst could be invited to class to describe the computer communication systems that are commonly used in many businesses. The career counselor at school could provide information about training requirements for this career.

▽ PORTFOLIO PRODUCTS

Students could review a classified ad for a systems analyst and develop a response to that ad. The response could be a résumé and cover letter that would identify the characteristics an employer would be looking for and the communication skills that would be useful.

● CURRICULAR CONNECTIONS

Math/Science
Some students could research the numbers of companies that use systems analysts as part of their regular communication system. Projections for the job market for this career could also be made.

CAREER CLOSE-UP

Systems Analyst

Systems analysts design and maintain information (computer) systems for businesses, government agencies, and other organizations using a variety of computers and data processing tools. To complete any task, analysts must be able to work effectively with groups of people. They meet with programmers, managers, and other employees to create information systems and find solutions to problems. Educational requirements for this profession include a bachelor's degree in computer sciences, electrical engineering, or business administration.

Because analysts realize they must have everyone's cooperation to achieve their goals, they cultivate group discussion before a meeting takes place by sending employees detailed information about a meeting's agenda, requesting their suggestions, and contacting them personally to let them know their contribution is needed.

During group discussions, the analyst actively encourages group members to speak openly. He or she listens carefully and responds to employees' and managers' proposals and opinions. Brainstorming, another important technique analysts use, focuses a group on producing creative ideas instead of evaluating them, thus generating many more potential solutions.

As technology becomes increasingly complex, one person cannot solve every computer problem. The analyst's use of group discussion to utilize each employee's expertise toward the solution of problems is precisely what makes these specialists so valuable to businesses.

By planning for communication and with careful attention to detail, the systems analyst encourages solution of complex problems through group discussions.

TEACH

> *How a minority,
> Reaching a majority,
> Seizing authority,
> Hates a minority!*
>
> —L.H. Robbins

● **CURRICULAR CONNECTIONS**

Language Arts
Prepare a generic outline format for distribution and use it in the class. Give students practice recognizing the outline format in newspaper and magazine articles by giving them such an article and asking them to fill in the outline format from information in and the organization of the article.

● **SKILL APPLICATION**

Debate
Organize teams of students to debate an issue of local political interest. Suggest that students would want to emphasize a maximum of three points as they prepare their speech.

● **SKILL DEVELOPMENT**

15-Second Skill Opportunity
Ask students to select one of the three points regarding outlines and prepare a short statement that exemplifies one of the three divisions of the outline.

● **ACTIVITY**

Ask students to develop a form to keep track of the references they use to gather information about the topic they select. The form should include title, author, and date of publication.

CHAPTER 5 Group Discussion

actual discussion, a leader may want to draw up a more specific outline consisting of questions within each phase which will be used to stimulate group members' thinking during the discussion. It is probably best the leader's detailed outline is not distributed to the members in advance. Answers will then occur freely and naturally during the discussion. However, in some forms of public discussion, such as radio or television programs, it may be necessary to give the members of the group a preview of the kinds of questions that they will be asked to deal with.

Research the Topic

All members of a group should prepare for discussion by doing research on the topic. The first step in doing research is to think carefully about the topic and the prepared basic outline. Search your memory for any experience or knowledge you may already have that relates to the question to be discussed.

If you are discussing a question of fact, you will need information on the background and causes of the problem. Use newspapers, magazines, books, or interviews to gather the information you need.

When discussing a question of value, you will need to do more than collect information. You will have to analyze that information in order to compare and judge various possible solutions.

Discussing a policy question also requires the gathering of information and then the consideration of all alternatives, as well as ideas, before choosing a solution or course of action. You probably will have decided upon a solution you favor before taking part in the actual discussion. Be prepared to support your opinions with facts and sound reasoning. Remember to keep an open mind when listening to the opinions of others.

● **ACTIVITY**

Preparing for a Group Discussion
Form into groups of from five to seven members. Choose a topic for a future group discussion. Consider only those topics that every member of the group is interested in. It may be school-related, a topic of local interest, or a topic that is international in nature. Decide upon the wording of the discussion question and upon the kind of research that is needed to gather information about the question. Each person in the group should then do individual research on the topic. Save your research information in your notebook for the next Activity.

TEACH

● **RETEACHING**

Ask the class which students think they are ready to participate in a group discussion. For those that respond with a "yes," ask them why they think they are ready. List their answers on the chalkboard. For those who do not think they are ready to participate in a group discussion, ask them for the reasons for their reluctance. Encourage them to identify the information or skills they would like to have before they participate in group discussion. Have them prepare a course of action and a timeline for the accomplishment of the tasks they identify.

AMAZING FACTS!
The largest public library in the United States is the Harold Washington Library Center which opened in Chicago, IL, in 1991. It contains over 70 miles of bookshelves.

● **LEARNING STYLES**

Audio/Visual Learning
Ask students to label themselves as people who like to learn primarily through seeing a demonstration or through hearing an explanation. Ask them to select one of the topics from those suggested in the preceding activity and list resources that could help them learn through either visual or audio means.

● **SKILL DEVELOPMENT**

Research
List several topics on the chalkboard and include some unfamiliar areas. Ask students to brainstorm at least three reference sources to begin research for more information about the topic.

Leading a Group **139**

● **LEADING A GROUP**

In most groups, certain members exercise greater degrees of influence than do others. Such influence is referred to as group leadership. Researchers used to feel that leadership ability was something that certain people had and others did not. If you had it, you turned out to be a group leader. If you didn't, you would only be a follower in practically any group in which you found yourself.

The more recent view is not quite so simple. It holds that a given group possesses a kind of group personality, called **syntality.** Syntality is like an individual's personality. Whenever any group member says or does something that has a major influence upon group syntality, that person is exercising leadership in the group. A member's influence or leadership of the group can vary from day to day.

Different Forms of Leadership

In some discussion groups all the leadership tasks are handled by a single group member. Jean may already be president of a club, so all the leadership functions of that group naturally fall to her. Mark may be elected by group members to serve as leader of a different group. Ricardo may be named leader of a committee by the principal. If all the leadership duties fall to a single individual, that person is called an **appointed leader.** An appointed leader is usually a very busy person during the discussion.

Some discussion experts suggest dividing the functions of the leader among several, or even among all, of the group members. One may begin the discussion. Another may keep participation balanced and the discussion moving toward its goal. A third may tone down arguments that arise. Another may watch the time limit and conclude the discussion with a summary. Whenever this shared form of leadership is arranged beforehand, it is also a form of *appointed leadership*.

Still other researchers have found it is best not to appoint or assign any particular duties to anyone. Ideally, all the group participants should understand what leadership functions are necessary. If they do, some group member will handle each function of leadership as the need for it arises during the discussion. This natural form of leadership is known as **emergent leadership.**

Leadership Roles

A discussion has three basic parts—a beginning, a middle, and an end. Whenever any group member fulfills one of the functions of beginning

TEACH

SUBSTITUTE TEACHER TIP

Many cartoons poke fun at the various types of leadership in government or business. Bring in some samples of these cartoons and encourage students to identify the type of leadership that is the subject of the cartoon.

> **"** The way of superior people is threefold; virtuous, they are free from anxieties; wise, they are free from perplexities; bold, they are free from fear. **"**
>
> —Confucius

● SKILL DEVELOPMENT

15-Second Skill Opportunity
Ask students to think about the leadership qualities that would best suit a new high school principal or college president. Ask volunteers to stand and identify those characteristics for the class.

● TEACHING

List the various types of leadership on the chalkboard and ask students to name several contemporary people who exemplify each type.

● CURRICULAR CONNECTIONS

Writing
Ask students to select a historical leader they admire and write a letter to that person, summarizing his or her accomplishments and identifying the reason for admiration.

---

140   CHAPTER 5 Group Discussion

the discussion, regulating communication, or concluding it, he or she will be acting as a leader at that particular moment.

Beginning the Discussion   The introduction of group members to each other and to the audience, if the discussion is public, is of primary concern at the beginning of a discussion. Effective leadership and group cohesiveness depend on members being acquainted with each other. Any time two or more people you know come together, the question should pop into your mind "Do these people know each other?" If the answer is "No," your immediate task is one of making introductions.

The rules for properly introducing people taking part in group discussion are the same as those used on social occasions. They are based first on age, then sex, and then status. When introducing persons of different ages, begin by mentioning the older person's name first. "Mr. O'Rourke, I'd like you to meet Janice Schmidt, a reporter on our school newspaper." When introducing persons of opposite sex, mention the woman's or girl's name first. "Mimi Rivera, may I introduce my teammate, Greg Chiang." If there is a difference in the status of the two individuals, begin with the person of higher rank. "President Franklin, allow me to introduce Jesse Stoner, our newest member." Introduce members of a group to an audience in order from left to right so the audience can locate each person as he or she is introduced.

The second task when you begin a group discussion is to introduce the topic. The group will have already worded the topic for discussion as a question. The question should be repeated to the group and, if the discussion is public, introduced to the audience. Stating the question at the start of the discussion will prevent uncertainty about the subject to be discussed.

Finally, enough background information about the question should be given to show why the group has assembled to discuss it. Assume seven members of your class are about to begin an in-class panel discussion. The topic is "Energy." If you were chosen as leader, you could begin the discussion briefly and effectively by opening the discussion like this:

"For the remainder of the period today, our panel is going to discuss the question 'What sources of energy should the people of this country use during the rest of this century?' As you know, we are all concerned about the suitability of nuclear power and the diminishing resources of oil and gas as sources of energy for our nation. Today we will compare these sources with other energy sources such as the sun, wind, and coal to find the best possible combination to use for the next twenty years."

• TEACHING

Invite two students to come to the front of the class and pretend that they do not know each other. Introduce them to each other in the proper way, following the procedures explained in the text. Model the proper introduction techniques for them. Then give each of them practice and ask them to introduce you to another member of the class.

AMAZING FACTS!
The record number of hands shaken by an elected leader was 8,513 by President Theodore Roosevelt at a New Year's Day White House presentation in 1907.

• SKILL DEVELOPMENT

15-Second Skill Opportunity
Give each student the opportunity to introduce another person to the class. They could imagine that they are introducing their parents to other parents at a school function.

• LEARNING STYLES

Multicultural Learning
Each culture has accepted ways of introducing strangers to each other. Ask students to share experiences of these customs with the entire class. Some of these introductions could be role-played for the group. Discuss why it is important to know the proper forms of introduction in the United States as well as in any country in the world.

Cooperative Learning
Ask small groups to discuss the topic of energy sources as described in the text. Then, leave the room for several minutes. On returning, survey the class to determine if and how leaders emerged. Discuss the factors that facilitate the development of leadership.

Regulating Communication Several leadership tasks must be attended to during the central part of any discussion. All members should feel free to speak their minds fully and frankly. This means that the leader must not only invite but also encourage members to contribute to the discussion. The leader should promote the idea that each individual's ideas are valuable and need to be aired. Encouraging such participation is frequently done by means of a general statement early in the discussion. Then, if the need arises, the leader may use more specific urging at necessary points along the way.

Keeping participation balanced during discussion is another leadership task. In any group some members are going to talk more than others. This is all right as long as no one monopolizes the discussion, and no one sits back and says nothing. The leader must exercise tact when suppressing those who talk too much. An appropriate comment might be "Sam, that's a very interesting point you just made. I wonder what some of the rest of us think about that. Sarah, what is your opinion?" But the leader must be careful not to embarrass or put a quiet member on the spot by suddenly asking "Mike, what do you think?" A better approach might be "This seems to be a critical point we are discussing. Why don't we get everyone's opinion on this?" Then, by starting with other people, the leader gives the quiet member time to plan ideas and words.

A leader must also be prepared to step in when two or more members of the group begin to argue. Progress cannot be made in a discussion that becomes an argument. This is especially true if those who are arguing freeze everyone else out or begin to deal in personal attacks. Group morale and productivity will quickly decline. When this occurs, the leader must step in with a comment such as "David, Maureen, I think each of your positions is pretty clear to all of us. Perhaps we need to hear some other opinions on this matter. Leon, do you have an opinion about this you'd like to share with us?" By taking the floor away from those arguing, you can often stop an argument.

Leaders are expected to keep the discussion on the track. This means recognizing a major detour from the prepared outline as it develops and gently reminding the group that it is getting off onto a side issue. An excellent way for a leader to keep the discussion moving towards its goal is by inserting brief summaries for the group after they finish discussing each major part of the outline.

Sometimes a few group members may have excellent ideas, but they aren't very successful in expressing them clearly to the group. When this happens, it becomes the leader's job to save each worthwhile idea. A leader may say something like "I think that's a fine idea, Maxine! If I understand you correctly, you're saying…." If you restate the idea in clearer terms, others will be able to understand it.

TEACH

AMAZING FACTS!
Forty-five of the world's 191 sovereign states do not have republican leaders, but are led by monarchs or hereditary sheiks.

● TEACHING
Encourage students to identify all the functions a group leader is expected to perform in the course of a meeting. List these on the chalkboard. Discuss those functions that the class think are the easiest to perform as well as those they think are the most difficult. Ask students to develop suggestions for making the difficult tasks easier.

● RETEACHING
Have students make a list of all the major headings in the section on leading a group. Then ask them to identify the three most important guidelines from those that are included in this section. Discuss their comfort level with the three guidelines they selected and determine if further explanation or practice is needed.

● SKILL DEVELOPMENT
15-Second Skill Opportunity
Ask students to think of a way to encourage a shy or hostile person to participate in a group discussion. Encourage volunteers to stand and state the nonthreatening question or encouraging comment for the entire class.

● LEARNING STYLES
Limited English Proficiency
Many people for whom English is a second language do not feel comfortable making comments or asking questions in a group. Discuss possible strategies that a group leader could use to encourage participation of all members of the group.

● ACTIVITY
In small groups, ask each to select a leader for a group discussion. Give each group five minutes for this task and then compare the process each group used.

● SKILL DEVELOPMENT
Conflict Resolution
Ask volunteers to represent the people selling and buying the car as described in the text narrative. Role-play the situation so that the price of the car is the area of conflict. In one version of the demonstration, ask students not to resolve the price conflict. In a second demonstration, ask students to negotiate the conflict successfully. Invite the class to discuss the key elements in the successful negotiation.

---

142 CHAPTER 5 Group Discussion

Finally, leaders are responsible for watching the time limit. This ca be an especially important leadership function in public discussior such as those produced for radio or television.

Concluding the Discussion There are two major concluding fur tions of leadership. First, when leaders feel the group has adequate covered the discussion question or a preset time limit has almost bee reached, leaders should summarize the major ideas and outcomes of t discussion. At the same time they must be careful not to overload t summary with their own ideas. Second, leaders should save enoug time for group members to disagree with the summary or to insert minority opinion if they wish.

● ACTIVITY
Conducting a Group Discussion
Using the topic that you researched in the previous Activity, conduct a group discussion. Choose a leader who must be able to use the knowledge of task and maintenance messages presented earlier in this chapter. At the end of the discussion, the participants should be prepared to provide useful feedback about the techniques of the group leader, their own participation in the discussion, and the reaction of the audience. Summarize your reactions to your own participation in your speech notebook.

● HANDLING CONFLICT IN GROUPS

Ideally groups make decisions by members' sharing ideas through cal and reasoned communication. We all recognize, however, that in t real worlds of business, government, industry, and even the famil meetings frequently involve much conflict, and communication that often neither calm nor reasoned. Though it is natural for members decision-making groups to come to a meeting with some conflictir goals and problems, how they go about handling their conflicts ca determine whether they all win or all lose by the time they part con pany. Consider the example of a couple who wishes to sell their ca They are asking $1,000 for it. Another couple becomes interested i buying the car, but say they can offer only $800 for it. The two couple share an interest in completing the sale. The first couple has alread bought a new car and wants to sell the old car quickly to help pay fo the new one. The second couple sees the car as their dream car. But th

TEACH

● **LINKS TO PAST LEARNING**

Conflict is an everyday part of life. Ask students to share an example of conflict that they witnessed in the past week. Discuss how the conflict was resolved and suggest that there could be more options available to them for resolving conflict.

● **CURRICULAR CONNECTIONS**

Writing
Ask students to identify a historical conflict of long standing such as the conflict in Northern Ireland or the conflict over Palestine. Students could develop a plan for the resolution of that conflict and prepare a written report on the topic providing historical background and suggestions for improvement.

> ❝Speeches cannot be long enough for the speakers, nor short enough for the hearers.❞
> —Perry

● **LEARNING STYLES**

Multicultural Learning
Different cultures handle conflict or differences of opinion in ways that are not common in the United States. Discuss some of those practices or use the example of looking a person directly in the eyes and the effect that eye contact has in heightening or resolving conflict.

● **SKILL APPLICATION**

Citizens Speak Out
Review the issues that divided baseball team owners and baseball players in the 1994–95 strike. Organize the class into three groups—one to represent the owners; one to represent the ball players; one to represent mediators. Ask the owners' and players' groups to develop a set of guidelines for themselves about the areas they would be willing to negotiate or compromise, and submit their lists to the mediator group. The mediator group may not share this information. Ask representatives from each group to come to a conference table and try to resolve the conflict.

---

two parties also have a major area of conflict to deal with—the sale price. If they handle the conflict successfully, they will both win a great deal of what they want. If they cannot come to agreement on some sale price, they will both lose in important ways.

When such conflict arises, as it does regularly in many areas of life, skill in group communication provides one of the major keys to success. When nations are threatening war against one another, experienced diplomats are asked to try to settle the matter through negotiation. When labor and management cannot agree on a contract, they use bargaining and mediation in the hope of avoiding strikes and layoffs which mean lost income and wages for both sides. Within the family, meetings may be held in attempts to reduce conflict among parents and children. When conflict arises, as it frequently does in groups, success in handling it depends largely on how well you can apply several communication skills.

Identify the Warrants of the Opposition When two viewpoints develop in a group, or members seem to be locking into conflict over an issue, the first communication skill you need to call into action is that of careful listening. This is because it will be difficult, if not impossible, to manage the conflict until you understand its causes. Too many times, unfortunately, once people realize they have a conflict with another person or group, they immediately begin stating only their *position* on the question, and avoid telling their reasons, or **warrants,** for holding that position. On the following page is an example.

Applying communication skills leads to the successful handling of most group conflict, whatever the setting or disagreement.

TEACH

> **SUBSTITUTE TEACHER TIP**
>
> Bring to class a sample warranty from any household product. If possible, make copies and distribute them to the students. Ask students to read the warranty and put it into their own words. Discuss the use of the terms "warrant" and "warranty."

> *"Behind every argument is someone's ignorance."*
> —Louis Brandeis

● **LEARNING STYLES**

Audio Learning
To help students develop better listening skills, tape record a paragraph read by you from a book or newspaper. Ask students to listen carefully to the recording. Prepare a second segment in which one of the sentences is omitted from the recording. Ask students to listen carefully to the second reading and try to identify the sentence that was omitted.

● **SKILL DEVELOPMENT**

15-Second Skill Opportunity
Invite students to role-play the situation involving Jim, Kyle, and Coach Martin as described on this page in the text. Then invite another group of students to provide another version of the situation showing better listening or questioning skills on the part of any of the characters.

CHAPTER 5 Group Discussion

Jim, the manager of his school's baseball team, needed additional storage space for uniforms. Therefore, he went to the school secretary and requested the key to a storage room next to the gymnasium. The secretary told Jim that another student, Kyle, had already requested use of the storage room. Jim was furious. Coach Martin had promised Jim use of that room. Jim went to Kyle and demanded the key. Kyle refused, and a loud argument followed. Hearing the noise, Coach Martin rushed into the room. "Okay," said the coach. "Suppose you tell me what the problem is."

"Beats me," said Kyle. "I just went to the secretary and got the storage room key, as you told me to do. Now Jim here wants to take the key away from me."

"And, Kyle, do you remember why I asked you to get the key?" said the coach. He smiled knowingly.

"Sure," said Kyle. "You said you needed it for somebody who wanted to store some uniforms."

"Oh," said Jim with embarrassment. "Sorry."

Had the two boys shared with one another their reasons for wanting the key, they would have avoided an unnecessary disagreement. When you find yourself on one side of a question, first listen for the other side's interest in taking their position. Listen for their "why." When you think you understand the other side's point of view, tell them what you think their reasons are for taking their position. When you do that, they get the feeling they are not wasting their time talking to you. Careful listening builds trust between the two sides.

Explain the Warrants of Your Position Of course you also need to communicate the warrants, or grounds, on which your position is based. Just as you may not know precisely the warrants of your opponents' position, they can only guess at the warrants of your position unless you explain these warrants carefully. Since your interests are driving you to take your position, you should not be timid about sharing these interests. Explain them in specific, concrete terms with the sense of urgency in your voice that you feel inside.

Many times, once people understand that you too have legitimate reasons for your viewpoint, they become more willing to give you a more open-minded hearing. This is especially true if you can also show them that both of you share certain interests in common, as was the case in the example of the boys and the storage room. In that example, the interests of both sides corresponded perfectly.

Respect Your Opponents' Interests While it is entirely appropriate to attack a *problem* vigorously, you should carefully avoid attacking the *people* on the other side, as Jim did in the example. Actually,

TEACH

● **TEACHING**

Ask students to prepare a statement with 2 to 4 reasons why they would support an increase in the minimum wage. Then ask students to stand and read or give their statement. After the statement, ask another student to summarize the points the first student made. Then ask the first student if the second student summarized the position accurately. Ask the first student to identify points that were missing. Students could also consider emphasis in the "translation" of remarks.

AMAZING FACTS!

The world's greatest linguist was Harold Williams (1876–1928), of New Zealand. As a boy he spoke 58 languages and many dialects fluently. He was the only person to attend the League of Nations and talk with every delegate in his or her own language!

● **LEARNING STYLES**

Visual Learning
Use the chart to describe two procedures for dealing with complicated issues. Suggest that students develop charts using cartoon characters and dialog to illustrate each.

Handling Conflict in Groups   145

is not enough to avoid attacking others. You also need to show clearly that you personally support them. Let your opponents know that you respect them. Be courteous, and show your appreciation for their time and effort in trying to work with you towards the best solution.

Work for a Reasonable Solution   Push hard and continuously for decisions based on reason. Work to convince the other side that everyone will benefit more in the long run by an agreement worked out by following fair procedures and fair standards. Perhaps you have heard the age-old method for dividing a pie fairly between two children. You allow one child to cut the pie, and the other to choose the first piece. Though not all complex discussion problems lend themselves to such clear-cut solutions, there is much to be gained by a constant search for solutions that meet the important needs of both parties. At the same time that you are insisting that the other side listen to reason, you must constantly be willing to accept their statements that strike you as reasonable. When both parties are willing to use objective, factual bases for arriving at solutions, the chances of both winning are markedly increased.

Maintain Dialogue   As elementary as this sounds, you would probably be amazed to know how often people clam up as soon as they realize there is a conflict. Since we feel uncomfortable with disagreement, we often simply give up searching for an acceptable solution in our effort to relieve the discomfort. When that happens, everyone loses. If the couples who couldn't agree on price when trying to negotiate the sale of a car simply parted company as soon as they learned they were

To avoid conflicts, participants in a group discussion should address themselves to issues rather than to the personalities and motivations of other group members.

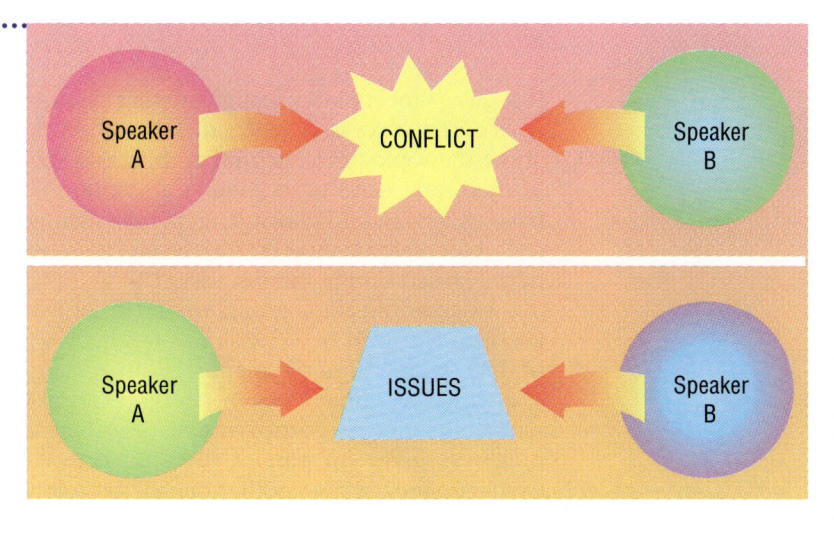

145

TEACH

> *"Salesmanship is what happens after the customer says 'no!'"*
> —Bumper Sticker

● **RETEACHING**

Ask students to prepare a poster to emphasize one of the conflict resolution techniques presented in this section. These posters could be displayed and could become one of the portfolio products for the chapter.

● **LINKS TO PAST LEARNING**

Ask each student to think of an example of a decision that affected his or her own life. Invite volunteers to share that decision with the class and identify how it was reached.

● **SKILL DEVELOPMENT**

Creative Thinking

Challenge small groups of students to develop a conflict resolution/defense system for a space colony. They should attempt to define the defense goals for the colony and indicate strategies for maintaining peace. Penalties for infractions should be clearly stated. Ask students to discuss how they propose to gain the support of the colonists for their conflict resolution system.

● **ACTIVITY**

Controversial issues are often difficult to discuss. You might suggest that the class examine the arguments on both sides of the abortion issue. Discuss why this issue often becomes an emotionally charged topic and is difficult to discuss. Identify the warrants for both sides.

● **SKILL DEVELOPMENT**

On the Job

Ask students to imagine or describe a situation in which two employees do not get along in their work. Their conflicts influence the ability of their team to work together. Discuss strategies for managing the two employees and for enhancing the performance of the team.

146

---

146   CHAPTER 5 Group Discussion

$200 apart, the sellers would lose an opportunity to make an early sale, and the buyers a chance to get their dream car. All too often when a division develops within a discussion group, people on each side spend most of their time talking among themselves about "the unreasonable position of those other people" rather than communicating with the other side. Holding such mutual agreement parties makes people feel good, but does nothing to solve the conflict. Actually, it frequently serves to deepen the disagreement when the two sides *do* get back together. Only by facing the disagreement with the other side can you ever hope to arrive at an equitable solution.

● **ACTIVITY**

Handling Conflict

As a class, select a current controversial topic on which two parties need to come to agreement, but are experiencing conflict in trying to bring the matter to a successful outcome. It could be a conflict between nations, between political parties, or within your own school. After everyone has had time to study and research the warrants of both sides, divide the class into two negotiating teams to discuss the matter. Remember to identify the warrants of the other side, explain your own side's warrants clearly, respect your opposition's interests, work for a reasonable solution, and maintain dialogue.

● **OUTCOMES OF DISCUSSION**

If a group meets in an enlightenment discussion (see page 120), it is considered successful when members have learned new information about the topic from each other. It is also successful if members have learned new ways of looking at a situation because of the ideas they have exchanged. In concluding an enlightenment discussion, it is often useful for each member to give a brief summary of the new ideas they have learned during the discussion.

A decision-making group, on the other hand, is successful when its problem is solved or a decision is reached. A group can do this in one of three ways. All of the members can agree on a solution or decision. This is called **consensus.** A decision can also be reached when the members agree to **compromise.** That is, each member or group of members gives up part of the solution or decision they want. In exchange they retain another part of the solution they favor. A **major**

TEACH

● **ENRICHMENT**

Some students could review the voting records of selected members of Congress and present the data to the class. Indicate if the individual's vote sided with the majority or minority in Congress. Discuss how minority interests protect their rights within the framework of majority rule.

● **CURRICULAR CONNECTIONS**

Writing
Ask students to review the Great Compromise to the U.S. Constitution. They could prepare a chart that would indicate the issue(s) involved and the original position of both sides. The chart should also show the compromise that allowed each side to benefit in some degree.

> *"Rhetoric is nothing but reason well dressed, and argument put in order."*
> —Jeremy Collier

● **LEARNING STYLES**

Multicultural Learning
Select students to represent the 15 nations of the United Nations Security Council. Ask them to consider an international issue, assuming the viewpoint of the nation they represent on the council. Discuss how the national interests of each are integrated into the international commitment to the charter of the UN.

● **SKILL APPLICATION**

Debate
Students might want to debate the advantages and disadvantages of autocratic and democratic decisions.

● **ACTIVITY**

Ask each group to develop a suitable portfolio product that demonstrates how they made the group decision targeted in the Activity.

Alternatives to Group Discussion **147**

ity vote is the third way of reaching a decision. The solution or decision favored by over half of the members becomes the solution or decision for the entire group.

Consensus is the most desirable of the three possible outcomes. When everyone genuinely agrees on a single solution, everyone is happier and more committed to helping carry out the group's decision. Unfortunately, consensus is not the most common outcome of group discussion. Compromise and majority votes are frequently necessary. However, compromise and majority votes, when they arise out of honest differences of opinion, are better than false consensus. **False consensus** occurs when several group members keep serious disagreement to themselves and "go along just to make it unanimous." False consensus is an outcome that usually does the group more harm than good.

● **ACTIVITY**

Decision Outcomes
Divide the class into groups of five to seven members to hold a series of decision-making discussions. Class members not participating in a given discussion should pay close attention to how the group achieves its decision. Did they achieve consensus? May it have been a *false* consensus? Was there compromise involved? Did the outcome require a majority vote? Following each group's discussion, comment on the advantages and disadvantages of the decision process used.

● **ALTERNATIVES TO GROUP DISCUSSION**

This chapter has dealt primarily with the form of group communication called group discussion. Group discussion is one of the most widely used forms of group communication in everyday life. However, group discussion can be a rather slow and difficult process, especially when the group is large. Let's look briefly at two alternative forms of group communication—brainstorming and the nominal technique. Each has certain advantages over group discussion in certain situations.

Brainstorming

Brainstorming is a technique sometimes used in business when it is desirable to produce a large number of creative ideas in a short period of time. Like group discussion, **brainstorming** usually involves three or

TEACH

> **"The fact that the people who create are good workers tends to be lost."**
>
> —A.H. Maslow

● **RETEACHING**

Ask students to select an example of conflict either at school or at work and to identify three of the techniques presented in this section as strategies for resolving the conflict. They should list all the menu options available to them in the conflict resolution process and indicate why they selected the ones they did.

● **TEACHING**

Brainstorming is a practice that encourages creativity and alternate thinking. Give students practice with brainstorming by asking them to think of at least five things they could do if they did not have to go to school tomorrow.

● **SKILL DEVELOPMENT**

15-Second Skill Opportunity
To show how one idea leads to another, explain that you will start the brainstorming process with a suggestion and ask for someone else in the class to offer an additional suggestion triggered by the first. Try to extend the chain of suggestions as far as you can within a total time frame of 5 minutes. Ask one student to record the suggestions and the number of students who participate in the process.

● **LEARNING STYLES**

Audio/Visual Learning
During the brainstorming activity ask one student to list the suggestions on the chalkboard and another student to record the brainstorming session on tape. Discuss whether students would prefer using the list on the chalkboard or listening to the tape to begin the nominal technique.

CHAPTER 5 Group Discussion

Because the purpose of brainstorming is only to generate ideas, criticism is not allowed during such a session.

more people who meet to solve a problem or to share information. A brainstorming session, however, consists of rapidly throwing ideas out on the table, without taking time to evaluate each idea as it is spoken. Since the purpose is only to generate ideas, criticism of any ideas presented is not allowed during a brainstorming session. Group members are encouraged to mention any idea about the topic that occurs to them, even if it seems unusual. The purpose is for each member's idea to spark additional ideas in other members. Brainstorming is only a first step in solving a problem or reaching a decision, however. The ideas are recorded, but not evaluated during the brainstorming session. Evaluating and sorting through the ideas occurs during a later group-discussion session. Sometimes the group discussion of ideas is conducted by the same members who participated in the brainstorming session. Sometimes a different group takes part.

The Nominal Technique

The nominal technique is an alternative form of group communication designed to reduce two problems that often arise in group discussion. One of these problems is the amount of time group discussion takes. The second is the fact that a few members may try to dominate a group discussion. Others may not get a word in edgewise.

TEACH

● TEACHING

Have the class conduct a brainstorming session to identify and rank ten problems facing the United States. Students should consider the number of people affected by each problem and the amount of money required for the solution.

● RETEACHING

Ask students to imagine that they have to teach this chapter (or section) to the seventh graders in your local middle school. The school has been divided over the issue of curfews during the school week. Have students develop a "lesson plan" that will help those younger students use group discussion techniques to solve their conflicts.

SUBSTITUTE TEACHER TIP

Ask students to use the nominal technique described here. Suggest several "problems" for the group to consider. These problems could be taken from the headlines of the current newspaper.

Alternatives to Group Discussion **149**

A group using the **nominal technique** begins by asking each member to write down a list of possible solutions to the group's problem. There should be no more than seven to nine members in the group, and this first step should take only about 10 to 15 minutes. Each member is then asked to state one idea from her or his list. Each idea stated is listed so that all may see the entire list. The group may ask for a second or third idea from each member. The list may be public, depending on the size of the group and the number of ideas desired. The third step consists of a brief discussion of the ideas on the board. This discussion is primarily to clarify, but may also involve some evaluation of the ideas. Next a secret vote is conducted with each member ranking the ideas in order of personal preference. Finally the rankings are tabulated, and the solution with the highest ranking becomes the group's solution.

The nominal techniques may reduce the amount of time needed to reach a decision and may prevent a few members from dominating the whole group. However, the nominal technique does not permit an in-depth discussion of a problem. Such a discussion usually produces the wisest decision.

> **"Prejudices are what rule the vulgar crowd."**
> —Voltaire

● LEARNING STYLES

Cooperative Learning

Organize small groups of students and explain that each group will receive an imaginary $10,000 to solve one of the major problems facing your school. The group should use the nominal technique to decide how to use the money. After the process is completed, each group should identify the project they selected and explain the process they used to arrive at the decision.

● ACTIVITY

Using the Nominal Technique

Have a group of seven class members use the nominal technique to decide the issue discussed by the two teams during the Activity on page 146. Carefully follow the steps listed in the text for using the nominal technique. Once the decision is made, discuss whether the nominal technique shortened the decision time, reduced the chances that a few group members would dominate the interaction, or both. Were there other advantages of using the nominal technique?

● ACTIVITY

To compare the process and benefits of the nominal technique with other group techniques, suggest that students prepare a chart that lists each technique, defines the term, and explains how the process works. The advantages and disadvantages for each should also be noted.

ASSESS

STUDENT PERFORMANCE COMPETENCIES

- Identifies various types of group discussions
- Explains ways to prepare for group discussions
- Describes types of groups leaders and their responsibilities
- Practices techniques for avoiding or reducing conflicts in discussion
- Uses problem-solving and group decision-making techniques

sca GUIDELINES

- Expresses ideas clearly in a group discussion
- Expresses and defends position in group meeting
- Uses several forms of organization to explain point of view
- Answers questions about public issues
- Summarizes arguments for and against controversial public issues

PORTFOLIO ASSESSMENT

Standard
- Glossary of Speech Terms
- Chart of Group Discussion Formats
- Flow Chart for Conflict Resolution
- Outline of Topic for Group Discussion
- Completed Assignments, Quizzes, Projects, and Chapter 5 Test

Enrichment
- Historical Leaders Analysis
- Congressional Leaders Analysis
- Posters or Cartoon(s) Illustrating Some Aspect of Conflict Resolution
- Timeline for the Four Stages of any Group

Challenge
- Debate of a Public Issue or Local Controversial Issue
- Report on Conflict Resolution Strategies for a Contemporary or Historical Conflict
- Survey of Political Opinion with "Norm" Data
- Guidelines for Reduction of Conflict on the Job

CHAPTER 5 REVIEW

SUMMARY

Group discussion is rapidly becoming one of the most widely used forms of interpersonal communication. This chapter has focused on group discussion used to arrive at decisions and to share information.

The Nature of Group Discussion In group discussion, three or more people meet to solve a common problem, reach a decision, or answer a question of mutual interest. It may be closed, or it may be public if members interact with an audience.

Factors Affecting Group Discussion Group size, physical environment, seating arrangement, and time of day all affect discussion. A clique can hinder group success, as can the personal goals of members.

How Groups Behave Behavior patterns can determine a group's success or failure. Leaders must constantly communicate both task and maintenance messages in order to progress toward group goals and must keep harmony among members. The life cycle of groups—forming, storming, norming, and performing—also affects their behavior.

Preparing to Participate in a Group The topic must be interesting, manageable, and phrased as a clear, unbiased question of fact, value, or policy. A detailed outline must be prepared to keep the group on track.

Leading a Group Leadership affects a group's overall personality. Leadership activities include introducing group members and the topic; encouraging full participation, suppressing arguments, keeping the discussion on track, and clarifying ideas; and watching the time limit, summarizing the discussion, and eliciting opinions.

Handling Conflict in Groups Handling group conflict involves listening to the other side; expressing your interests; attacking problems, not people; using reason and being open to reason; and talking the conflict through to resolution.

Outcomes of Discussion For enlightenment groups, success means knowing more about the topic after discussion than before. For decision-making groups, it means reaching a decision by consensus, compromise, or majority vote.

ASSESS

● **ASSESSMENT STRATEGIES**

Individual Assessment
- Participates in practice activities daily or weekly
- Demonstrates knowledge of content through questions, discussion, quizzes, and tests
- Displays improved skills in participation in group discussions

Group Assessment
- Sets and achieves goals
- Identifies ways that group leaders develop
- Practices several techniques for arriving at group decisions
- Supports efforts of group leader and team members
- Provides encouragement and feedback to members

Alternatives to Group Discussion For decision-making, group discussion may be too slow or else dominated by a few members. Two alternatives, *brainstorming* and the *nominal technique,* can often help.

VOCABULARY

Define each term in a complete sentence.

group discussion	norming
decision-making group	performing
enlightenment group	question of fact
closed-group discussion	question of value
public discussion	question of policy
committee	biased
round-table discussion	syntality
panel	appointed leader
symposium	emergent leadership
panel-forum	consensus
symposium-forum	compromise
clique	majority vote
cohesiveness	false consensus
task messages	brainstorming
maintenance messages	nominal technique
forming	warrant
storming	

CHECKLIST

Group-Discussion Skills

1. Understand the purposes for communicating in groups.
2. Be prepared to participate actively in group discussions.
3. Avoid forming cliques or personal goals that hinder group success.
4. Know how to bring the group back to the subject.
5. Be aware of task and maintenance messages within a group.
6. Take group life cycles into account during discussions.
7. Research the topic beforehand.
8. Practice ways to handle and resolve group conflict.

ASSESS

● **ANSWERS**

See the Answer Key for more complete answers.

REVIEW QUESTIONS
1. The main purposes of group discussion are decision-making and enlightenment.
2. Committee meeting and roundtable discussion are both types of closed-group discussion.
3. The best number of participants for a group discussion is five to seven people.
4. A desire to lead, a strong need for acceptance, and a desire to remain apart are personal goals that can interfere with a productive group discussion.
5. Questions of fact, questions of value, and questions of policy are the three main types of discussion questions.
6. Yes or no questions tend to lead to statements or to shouting matches.
7. The responsibilities of a group leader at the beginning of a discussion are to introduce the members of the group, to introduce the topic, and to present any background information that may be needed.
8. During the discussion, the leader should intervene to invite and encourage participation, to prevent arguments, to keep the discussion on track, to restate unclear ideas, and to make other members aware of time limitations.
9. The leader should summarize the major ideas and outcomes and allow time for minority opinions or concluding arguments.
10. A group decision may be reached by *consensus, compromise,* or *majority vote.*

DISCUSSION QUESTIONS
The following code is used to designate discussion questions and activities as suitable for students of varying ability levels:
   ▼ = below average to average
   ◆ = average to above average
   ■ = all students
1. ▼ Groups should use techniques outlined in the chapter to develop a topic list. Ask them to choose the final list by consensus, compromise, or majority vote.
2. ■ Have students review the text section on leadership and role-play, contrasting styles of leadership in a skit portraying a discussion group.
3. ■ Students could make a chart to identify the advantages and disadvantages of the three types of methods.

152

CHAPTER 5 REVIEW

📝 REVIEW QUESTIONS

1. Describe the main purposes of any group discussion.
2. Name the two types of closed-group discussion.
3. State the size limitations that are recommended for effective group discussion.
4. Name some personal goals that may interfere with a productive group discussion.
5. Describe the three main types of discussion questions.
6. State why discussion questions answerable by "yes" or "no" should be avoided.
7. Identify the kinds of activities a leader should always perform at the beginning of a group discussion.
8. State under what circumstances a group leader should intervene.
9. Identify the responsibilities of a leader when concluding a group discussion.
10. Name three possible methods by which a group may arrive at a decision.

❓ DISCUSSION QUESTIONS

1. As a class, identify ten topics for class discussions and write them on the chalkboard. Discuss each topic to be sure it is of interest to a large number of students in your class. If few students are interested in the topic, eliminate it. Check the wording of each remaining topic to be sure it meets the topic guidelines presented in this chapter. Copy the final list in your speech notebook. The list can be used in future class discussions.
2. What constitutes leadership? What qualities are most important in the student leader? As a class, determine whether you prefer appointed or emergent leadership. Why? Then design a critique sheet that can be used to evaluate a group discussion leader.
3. Discuss with your class the three methods that can be used to reach agreement in a group: consensus, compromise, and majority vote. What are the advantages and disadvantages of each method? Which method does your class prefer? Under what conditions might one method work better than either of the other methods? Why?

ASSESS

CRITICAL THINKING

1. Analysis Discuss the life cycle of groups. Apply the theory to groups that you belonged to. Explain what happened at each stage of the cycle that you have witnessed. Is the theory accurate? Are there any other stages that you would add?

2. Evaluation Do you believe that leadership is a talent that one is born with, or is it an ability that can be acquired and developed? In answering this question, think of all of the aspects of group behavior that you have learned about.

ACTIVITIES

In-Class

1. Form into small groups of from five to seven people. Imagine that you live in a coastal community that is threatened by an approaching storm. Residents must be evacuated inland to safer ground. You and the other members of your group belong to a committee that is charged with the responsibility of organizing the evacuation. You have the resources of the community at your disposal, but people in the area live in houses that are spread over a wide area. You have only thirty minutes to come up with an appropriate plan.

After your group has discussed the problem and come up with a solution, discuss the following: Who became the group leader? How did that come about? Did everyone participate in the discussion? Did the group move through the normal stages of growth? Which stage was the most difficult? Compare your results with the other groups in the class.

2. When your class begins to give public speeches, the problem of scheduling is sure to arise. Form into groups of from five to seven people and attempt to solve the problem before it arises. Each group should discuss the following questions: What is the best method for determining speaking order? What should be done to keep the class on schedule if assigned speakers are absent? What is an appropriate penalty for not being prepared to give a speech on an assigned day?

CRITICAL THINKING
1. **Analysis** Ask students to explain how it might be possible for groups to omit one or more stages under certain circumstances.
2. **Evaluation** Assign an essay or report on leadership—its development and its role in decision-making.

ACTIVITIES
In-Class
1. Groups should demonstrate an ability to choose a leader, work together effectively, divide and accept responsibility, handle conflict, and organize a clear plan in the time period allowed.
2. As a class, combine group suggestions to develop a class speech schedule form and to discuss the group discussion methods that made the end result possible.

ASSESS

3. After the discussion, write task and maintenance messages on the board. Evaluate the contribution of each message to the efficiency and outcome of the discussion.

Out-of-Class
1. This activity provides an opportunity for students to see the information outlined in the chapter come to life in the real world.
2. Students should be specific and detailed in the interview in order to develop a true picture of the role group discussions play in the world of work.
3. Ask students to break topics into categories (questions of fact, policy, and value). Post a comprehensive class list.
4. Post articles in each category.

CHAPTER 5 REVIEW

Your group will report its scheduling recommendations to the rest of the class in the form of an oral statement. The class as a whole will then decide by consensus, compromise, or majority vote on all three issues. This decision could be applied to the scheduling of future public speaking assignments.

3. Ask several students in class to be a part of a group discussion on a topic of their choice. The rest of the class can watch the discussion, taking notes on the task and maintenance messages used during the discussion. As a class, review and analyze the discussion.

Out-of-Class

1. Observe a panel discussion by either attending a meeting of your local school board or city or town council or by watching a panel on television. Take careful notes, especially in terms of task/maintenance messages. Afterwards, analyze the dynamics of the communication experience, giving special attention to the task/maintenance factors. Based on these criteria, which participants were most effective as group members? Place your analysis in your speech notebook. Share your findings with your classmates.

2. Interview an adult who is in a job or a career that you find interesting. Ask the interviewee about group discussions that occur in that occupation. Find out about how the processes and outcomes of group discussions are affected by such factors as goal setting, type of leadership, and life cycle stages. Be certain that you gather information on informal discussions, as well as formal ones. Write your findings in your notebook.

3. Compile a list of ten topics that interest you and that you would like to discuss in class. Make your list as diverse as possible. Include topics that cover a wide area of interest. File the list in your notebook for quick reference when discussion topics are being considered in class.

4. Look through a local newspaper for accounts of discussions of various current issues. Clip the articles and label them "value" or "policy" questions. Bring the articles to class and share them with your fellow classmates.

CHAPTER PROJECT

Plan a symposium-forum for a special audience. Complete this project in the following ten steps.

1. Form a committee to choose five topics that are of interest to particular audiences. For example, a symposium on "Contemporary U.S. Poets" would interest an American literature class; a symposium on "U.S./Franco Relations, Now and in the Past" would appeal to a government class. If you prefer to develop a program for an audience outside the classroom, consider a program that might interest your parents, such as "Speech Training: Not *a* Basic—*the* Basic" or a program that might appeal to incoming students at your school, such as "Life at ——— High School."
2. As a class, choose the "best" topic by one of the three methods of group decision-making. (Make certain the topic is well-worded and in the form of a question.)
3. Select from five to seven participants for the symposium.
4. Decide who will lead the symposium, using one of the two methods described in your text.
5. As a class, develop an outline for the discussion and assign subtopics to the participants.
6. Have each participant research his or her specific area of the topic.
7. The participants will then meet to discuss their research and to make minor adjustments, if necessary, in the outline.
8. The participants practice the symposium in class. Those not directly involved in the presentation must keep a written critique of the presentation. These will be submitted to the participants.
9. Publicize the event if it is to be a public performance. Invite an audience if it is to be a special-interest program.
10. Present the symposium before your audience.

ASSESS

CHAPTER PROJECT
- This activity gives students an opportunity to use all the skills for groups that are outlined in the chapter. Students should delegate responsibility, choose a leader, develop and research a topic, handle conflict, and reach a compromise or consensus. Use care to assign students to tasks that are commensurate with ability.

PREPARE

● PERFORMANCE OBJECTIVES

- Participates in daily 15-second skill drills when asked
- Applies specific skills to overcoming stage fright
- Uses research skills
- Expresses ideas clearly and concisely
- Gives concise and accurate directions
- Summarizes messages
- Performs social rituals
- Expresses feelings to others
- Describes differences in opinion
- Uses voice effectively

● sca GUIDELINES

- Uses words, pronunciation, and grammar appropriate for situation
- Identifies main ideas in messages
- Organizes messages so that others can understand them
- Distinguishes facts from opinions
- Distinguishes between informative and persuasive messages
- Expresses and defends point of view with evidence

● UNIT FOCUS

Unit 3 discusses ways to prepare for public speaking. It describes ways of dealing with stage fright and explains how to choose a topic and deliver an effective speech.

● CONTENTS

6 **Building Confidence** *pp. 158–181*
7 **Preparing Your Speech** *pp. 182–223*
8 **Choosing Effective Language** *pp. 224–253*
9 **Delivering Your Speech** *pp. 254–287*

▼ UNIT PORTFOLIOS

Individual Portfolios
- Humorous Remarks List
- Use of Humor Checklist
- Interruption Cartoons
- Knowledge, Interests, and Opinion Inventory
- School Issues Survey
- Information Note Cards
- Monroe's Motivated Sequence Cartoons
- Simplifying Pretentious Terms
- Pamphlet of Devices for Creating Emphasis
- Do's and Don'ts for Speech
- Conclusions
- Strategies for Dealing with Interruptions
- Chapter Portfolio Products

Group Portfolios
- Newspaper and Newsmagazine Articles
- Dress Code Guidelines

Class Portfolios
- Situations for Four Kinds of Speech Deliveries

UNIT 3

PREPARING FOR PUBLIC SPEAKING

PREPARE

● UNIT PLANNER

● ANCILLARY RESOURCES

Chapters	Time Management	📁	📄	📕	📼	🎧
6 Building Confidence *pp. 158–181*	Week 1	✔	✔	✔	✔	✔
7 Preparing Your Speech *pp. 182–223*	Week 2	✔	✔	✔	✔	✔
8 Choosing Effective Language *pp. 224–253*	Week 3	✔	✔	✔	✔	✔
9 Delivering Your Speech *pp. 254–287*	Week 4	✔	✔	✔	✔	✔

● PROFESSIONAL RESOURCES

PRINT

Ayres, Joe, and Tom Hopf. *Coping with Speech Anxiety.* Norwood, NJ: Ablex Publishing Corporation, 1993.

Byrns, James H. *Speak for Yourself: An Introduction to Public Speaking.* 3rd ed. New York: McGraw-Hill, 1994.

Crannell, Kenneth C. *Voice and Articulation.* 2nd ed. Belmont, CA: Wadsworth Publishing Company, 1991.

Verdeber, Rudolph. *Essentials of Informative Speaking: Theory and Contexts.* Belmont, CA: Wadsworth Publishing Company, 1994.

Film/Video

Aids to Speaking (Film, 15 min, 16 mm color; Coronet/MTI Film and Video).

Planning Your Speech Film (Film, 13 min, 16 mm color; Centron Corporation).

Speaking Effectively: To One or One Thousand (Film, 21 min, color; CRM Films).

Verbal Communication: The Power of Words (Film, 30 min, color; CRM Films).

Ancillary Resource Key

📁 = Portfolio Product Activities
📄 = Tests/Answer Key
📕 = Speech Library
📼 = Self-Help Videos
🎧 = Audiotape

---

6 Building Confidence

7 Preparing Your Speech

8 Choosing Effective Language

9 Delivering Your Speech

PREPARE

● CHAPTER PLANNER

Day 1	Day 2	Day 3	Day 4	Day 5
Prepare	Prepare	Prepare	Prepare	Prepare
Teach	Teach	Teach	Teach	Teach
Assess	Assess	Assess	Assess	Assess
	Sub. Teacher Tip *p. 162*		Sub. Teacher Tip *p. 173*	

● CHAPTER OVERVIEW

This chapter examines the following topics:
- Understanding Stage Fright *p. 160*
- Controlling Your Nervousness *p. 164*

▼ PORTFOLIO PRODUCTS

Individual Projects
- Glossary of Speech Terms
- Techniques for Reducing Stage Fright
- Chapter 6 Portfolio Products

Group Projects
- Guidelines for Building Confidence
- Confidence Awards

● sca GUIDELINES

- Understands suggestions to control stage fright
- Uses nonverbal signs in speeches to help overcome stage fright
- Expresses ideas clearly and concisely when giving speech critiques

158

CHAPTER

6

Building Confidence

When you have completed this chapter you should be able to:

- Define the term *stage fright* and state its causes.
- Explain how to control stage fright to help you become an effective speaker.
- Describe some specific methods for gaining confidence.
- Understand the importance of humor and body movements in gaining confidence for speaking.
- Understand the importance of speech critiques in becoming a more confident speaker.

TEACH

● **LINKS TO PAST LEARNING**

Ask students to think back on how they felt when they had to describe an item for a "show and tell" presentation in preschool or in kindergarten. Ask them to explain why they had these feelings.

AMAZING FACTS!
A recent survey revealed that most Americans would rather die than give a speech. When asked what they feared the most, death was fourth on the list, while giving a speech was first.

● **ACTIVITY**

After students have described instances where they have experienced stage fright, ask them to think of what they did to overcome these feelings. Call on volunteers to describe methods that they used to cope with these feelings. If appropriate, some students might demonstrate the techniques.

● **LEARNING STYLES**

Visual Learning
Ask students to recall a time when they saw a speaker or other type of performer experience stage fright. Have them explain what visual clues the speaker or performer gave that indicated to the audience that he or she was experiencing stage fright.

Building Confidence 159

● **ACTIVITY**

Defining and Describing Stage Fright
Begin by holding a class discussion in which you define stage fright. Why does it start? What is it that makes us so tense about speaking in front of an audience? Does it affect people engaged in situations other than public speaking?

Once you have identified the root cause of stage fright, you next need to describe the feelings that come along with it—butterflies in the stomach, for example. In alphabetical order by last name, each class member should step in front of the class and briefly tell about some earlier occasion on which she or he experienced some of the feelings of stage fright, and what those feelings were.

"The human brain is a wonderful thing. It starts working the moment you are born and never stops until you stand up to speak in public." This quote from well-known entertainer George Jessel illustrates what is probably the most common problem faced by those who give public speeches—the problem of **stage fright.**

Until now you have been learning about and participating in the "calmer" forms of speaking. As you begin your study of *public speaking* you probably feel less calm about standing alone in front of the class than you did about doing an interview or taking part in a small group meeting. That age-old scourge of public speakers, stage fright, may begin to bother you even before your teacher assigns your first speech. Hopefully the opening Activity has not only helped you *understand* stage fright a bit better, but has also begun to help you *learn how to handle it* when in front of an audience. Ultimately, stage fright is something you best learn to control by being thrust into public speaking situations. If you didn't realize it, you just gave a short public speech!

Stage fright is a significant problem for most beginning speakers—an obstacle that can make the difference between success or failure in accomplishing your speech purpose. In this chapter you will face stage fright squarely. You will explore its causes, see what effects it can have (*good* as well as bad), and learn methods for controlling it. Once you can view stage fright as a normal part of a public speaking experience, you are ready to begin building the kind of confidence you need to be an effective speaker.

TEACH

AMAZING FACTS!

One problem that Demosthenes, the great Greek orator, had was his posture. To improve it, he practiced speaking before a mirror with two swords hanging from the ceiling. The points of the swords touched his shoulders. If he made any awkward movements, the swords would stab him!

> *Any actor who claims he is immune to stage fright is either lying, or else he's no actor.*
>
> —Otis Skinner

● SKILL DEVELOPMENT

15-Second Skill Opportunity

Have students imagine that they are at a party at which they know only one or two people. Ask students to introduce themselves to one person at the party whom they don't know. Ask volunteers to present their introduction to the class. Discuss with students whether stage fright is a feeling they might experience in this type of situation.

● LEARNING STYLES

Audio/Visual Learning

Adlai Stevenson and Abraham Lincoln were two famous speakers who suffered terribly from stage fright. Both would start a speech stiffly but would become more animated as the speech progressed. Ask students to imagine how the "Gettysburg Address" might have sounded as Lincoln delivered it, overcoming his anxiety as he became impassioned on this topic. Have volunteers demonstrate the speech to the class. Use the Appendix, p. 584.

160

● MOTIVATION

Write the following on the board: "Public Speaking and Other Coronary Threats." Tell students that this is the title of a speech given by a vice president of a company. Have students discuss what this speech implies about public speaking. Ask students if they can relate it to their own experiences.

● CURRICULAR CONNECTIONS

Math

Survey the class to find out who experiences and who does not experience stage fright in activities such as public speaking, athletic events, or performing in plays. Have students illustrate their findings in the form of a circle graph.

---

160   CHAPTER 6 Building Confidence

● UNDERSTANDING STAGE FRIGHT

Of course, you may be one of those people who do not experience stage fright. Some speakers feel as relaxed in front of a large audience as they do chatting with a few friends around the dinner table. If you really feel this way, be happy about it, but do not get overconfident. Being free of stage fright does not automatically make a person a better public speaker than one who suffers from it.

Most People Experience Stage Fright

An old saying goes "misery loves company." If you have been feeling that you are the only one in your class who gets sweaty palms and a queasy stomach at the very thought of giving a speech, you couldn't be more wrong! As a matter of fact, you are part of the majority. Research figures show that over half of the beginning speakers surveyed reported stage fright, and very few experienced speakers were totally free of nervousness. If you were to poll the members of your speech class right now, probably 80 to 90 percent would report some form of nervousness about giving a public speech.

Although the term stage fright is often reserved for public speakers and actors, these same symptoms are also common among tennis and baseball players, concert pianists, and circus clowns—in other words, among most people who must give a public performance of any kind. Nor are these uneasy feelings reserved for inexperienced speakers and performers. Many famous persons, seasoned in appearing before the public, have reported stage fright. Even Sir Winston Churchill, considered one of the most influential speakers of this century, once confessed that he had stage fright when delivering his speeches. The major difference in the effect stage fright has on a beginner and on an experienced speaker comes from how each handles the nervousness once it occurs. Although there is no substitute for platform experience in learning to control stage fright, speakers can start to build confidence with their first speech if they begin correctly.

Why Stage Fright Occurs

The first step in building speaker-confidence is understanding why you usually feel nervous when speaking in public (or even while *preparing* to speak in public). Stage fright affects most people in physical ways—sweaty palms, queasy stomach, dry mouth, excessive perspiration, increased heart rate, shortness of breath. But the beginnings of stage fright are mental, not physical. When you are preparing to give a public speech, a strong psychological **tension** can build up within you

● **EXTENSION**

Ask students to write letters to well-known personalities asking about how stage fright affects their performance and how they control it.

● **CURRICULAR CONNECTIONS**

Science
Have students find more information about the physical aspects of stage fright—the role of adrenaline, heart rate, breathing rate. Students should research the connection between the brain and the rest of the body in creating stage fright sensations. Students could use a diagram to present their research to the class.

TEACH

"Fear defeats more people than any other one thing in the world."
—Ralph Waldo Emerson

● **SKILL DEVELOPMENT**

Creative Thinking
Review the idea that tension is generated from conflict. Ask students to illustrate other specific examples of conflict, such as, "I want to do well on the SAT so that I can go to XYZ University. If I do badly on the SAT, I can't possibly gain admission to XYZ University." Have students give other examples of conflict involving nonspeech activities such as athletics and social events.

15-Second Skill Opportunity
Have students role-play changing their demeanors from timid, stooped, and unsure to self-confident, erect, and certain of success. Ask for observations about how action and emotion can work together.

Understanding Stage Fright   **161**

Sir Winston Churchill, who admitted to stage fright, is considered one of the most influential and inspiring speakers of the twentieth century.

This tension comes from two conflicting realizations: (1) I desperately want to perform well and make a good impression, and (2) I may not be very successful. Your realization that all eyes will be focused on you and that you will be the center of attention intensifies the desire for success and the fear of failure and embarrassment. Most students find it difficult, if not impossible, to take a nonchalant, "so what" attitude about the outcome of speeches they are about to give.

This mental tension carries over to your body, readying you physically as well as mentally to perform well. Just before the start of an important test or athletic event, you have probably experienced this same kind of mental conflict and physical tension. You wanted to succeed so badly you could almost taste it, but you also feared failure and defeat. Once the test or event got underway, however, what happened? Probably you were able to use that tension to think more clearly and perform better. Some coaches of athletic teams check their players' palms before a big game to help them decide on the starting lineup. The players with sweaty palms have the right tension. They are "up" for the game.

Controlled Stage Fright Is Helpful

You can make good use of tension when you are preparing to deliver a speech. Such internal tension causes your muscles to tighten, your heart and breathing rates to increase, and more adrenaline and oxygen to pump throughout your body. The result is that your brain and body muscles become "supercharged." Your body is carrying out its natural function of preparing you to meet a special situation.

161

TEACH

SUBSTITUTE TEACHER TIP

Students could work in pairs to role-play controlled stage fright and runaway stage fright. First, the pairs could come up with a situation and then demonstrate how a controlled stage fright situation could be dealt with.

● **LINKS TO PAST LEARNING**

Students could give examples of Olympic athletes who did poorly in their performances as a result of anxiety. Ask students what might have caused the stage fright in these athletes.

● **RETEACHING**

To show an understanding of stage fright, students could use the vocabulary words in this section in a poster that illustrates what stage fright is, the different types of stage fright, and the role of lack of confidence and overconfidence in producing runaway stage fright. Discuss students' posters.

● **LEARNING STYLES**

Cooperative Learning

Students could work in small groups to brainstorm thoughts that produce lack of confidence before a speech. Possible responses might include "I'm going to look stupid" and "I'm going to forget the speech." Then students could come up with ways of dealing with these thoughts, such as telling themselves they're well prepared. Students could make a list of these solutions and add the list to their portfolio products.

---

162   CHAPTER 6 Building Confidence

The symptoms of stage fright are common not only among public speakers but also among most people who give public performances of any kind.

Good public speakers can take this result of stage fright and make it work for them by learning how to control it and channel it properly. Well-known speakers have reported that their most successful speeches have been those they were most nervous about beforehand. On other occasions when they were less concerned about making a good impression, or felt overconfident, their presentations fell flat. The simple realization that stage fright is natural before a speech—and actually an aid to sharper thinking—can itself be a means of controlling it. **Controlled stage fright** can then aid you in becoming a successful speaker.

Uncontrolled Stage Fright Can Be Harmful

Inexperienced speakers, unused to feeling the symptoms of stage fright, often think that their dry throat or sweaty palms spell certain doom for their speech. The greater these feelings become the more intense the stage-fright symptoms become. This in turn leads to more worry, which leads to worse symptoms, and so on, and so on. The result is **runaway stage fright.** Its effects are quite different from controlled stage fright and may ruin a well-prepared speech.

TEACH

● **EXTENSION**

Students could brainstorm and list some humorous remarks a speaker might make if he or she does fumble a line, such as "Let me try that again in English." Students could add their list to their portfolio products.

● **MOTIVATION**

Students could work in pairs to answer the question "How do I go about controlling my stage fright?" Students could create a list titled "Tips for Controlling Stage Fright." Discuss pairs' suggestions with the class.

● **LINKS TO PAST LEARNING**

Ask students to recall speeches they have heard for which the speaker was clearly unprepared. Ask them to list the things the speaker did that indicated that he or she was unprepared.

● **SKILL DEVELOPMENT**

Feedback
Students could give a two-minute speech about some aspect of public speaking that gives them stage fright. They could explain it in detail, telling why they find it frightening and what they might do to overcome the stage fright. They could ask their classmates for other techniques that they might use to overcome their fear.

Runaway stage fright takes one of two forms. The first form is born of **lack of confidence** and usually strikes before the speech begins. Many times the speaker who experiences this form is actually well-prepared for the speech, but has allowed the symptoms of stage fright to snowball. As a result, self-confidence is at a very low point by the time the speech begins, and this leads to runaway stage fright. The second form arises from poor preparation combined with **overconfidence** and ordinarily does not occur until after the speech has begun. Read in a quote from Mark Twain's famous story how Tom Sawyer suffered great embarrassment when he experienced this form of runaway stage fright.

> Tom Sawyer stepped forward with conceited confidence and soared into the unquenchable and indestructible 'Give me liberty or give me death' speech, with fine fury and frantic gesticulation, and broke down in the middle of it. A ghastly stage fright seized him, his legs quaked under him and he was like to choke.

As you have read, this second form strikes suddenly and takes the speaker by surprise. Inadequate preparation does not always surface during introductory remarks, but it may become very obvious once a speaker has reached the body of the speech. At that point, a moment of forgetfulness is all that is necessary to trigger sudden stage fright.

Since both too little confidence and overconfidence can initiate stage fright, the wise speaker must aim for that critical degree of self-assurance that comes from thorough preparation, mixed with a realization of the unpredictable nature of a public speaking situation.

Stage Fright Feels Worse Than It Looks

Stage fright is a problem that is much more noticeable to the speaker than to others. Beginning speakers sometimes experience the feelings caused by stage fright so intensely they fail to realize that their listeners aren't nearly so aware of their nervousness. The audience can't see or hear your tightening stomach muscles, nor will they ordinarily notice your sweaty palms or dry mouth. They might notice a slight tremor in your voice occasionally or a faster-than-normal breathing rate, but even these symptoms bother the speaker much more than the listeners. Realizing this fact can make a big difference for some stage-fright sufferers.

Chronic victims of stage fright are generally not content to worry only about their possible inability to speak clearly or remember ideas. They like to worry in big bundles, so they also get concerned about what kind of impression their stage-fright symptoms will make on the audience. For such giant-economy-size worriers, it should be comforting to realize that stage fright always feels much worse than it appears to

TEACH

● **SKILL DEVELOPMENT**

Creative Thinking
Ask students to use the four steps for being prepared (p. 164) and give examples of what could be done in each step. Have students create a pamphlet that illustrates the examples for each step.

● **LEARNING STYLES**

Beyond the Classroom
Invite community representatives such as a minister, public official, or salesperson to sit on a panel for your class. Students could prepare questions for the panel that address how the guests prepare speeches, how they handle interruptions, and how they handle forgetting parts of a speech.

---

164   CHAPTER 6   Building Confidence

others. Unless speakers foolishly call specific attention to their stage fright by comments such as "I'm so nervous, I'm sure this speech isn't making much sense," the audience will often be unaware that the speakers are nervous.

● **CONTROLLING YOUR NERVOUSNESS**

Before you began reading this chapter you very likely imagined that the best way to deal with stage fright was to rid yourself of it. By now you know that a limited amount of stage fright can be helpful. The trick is to control that amount—not to get rid of it entirely. The next question, then, is "How do I go about controlling my stage fright?"

Prepare Thoroughly

One effective method for controlling stage fright is to prepare thoroughly for each public speech. Since most stage fright comes from a fear of not succeeding in front of the audience, thorough preparation can guarantee that about 90 percent of your speech will go smoothly. When you are the speaker, you are the person with the greatest control over what occurs during the speech. Make sure you are well prepared.

1. Study your topic.
2. Analyze the needs of your audience.
3. Research and outline the ideas of your speech.
4. Rehearse your presentation sufficiently.

Study and research of your topic can build confidence as you prepare for a speech.

If you do all these things, you will have little reason to fear that something unplanned or unpleasant will happen. Thus you can begin your speech with confidence.

The possibility always exists that something unexpectedly disturbing will occur (a loud noise, a heckler, a fire drill), but such interruptions occur very infrequently. Just keeping in mind this possibility will keep you sufficiently alert, but not allow you to become overconfident.

Thorough preparation can not only give you the right level of confidence *before* your speech begins but also support you once you have started speaking. One of the greatest fears of most beginning speakers is the fear of forgetting part of their speech. Once you have gained some experience at giving speeches, you will realize this is not such a serious problem as it may first seem. For one thing, the audience ordinarily does not know in advance what you intend to say, so even if you leave out a large section of your planned speech, no one is the wiser. (Don't call attention to an omission by mentioning you have forgotten something or by appearing confused.) Second, most speakers have note cards available during their speech to help jog their memories if they forget a point. Finally, forgetting is seldom a problem if a speaker has rehearsed thoroughly and correctly. You will see in the next chapter that correct preparation does not mean word-for-word memorization of your speech. If you try to do this, you put a tremendous burden on your memory and are likely to forget.

Relax Before You Speak

Even when thoroughly prepared, many speakers experience physical tension shortly before they are to speak. Some can feel their neck muscles tightening. Others will experience tense stomach muscles. Some may have problems with their facial muscles. Though these are symptoms rather than causes of stage fright, speakers quite frequently find it helpful to relax physically before beginning a speech. Relaxing one's body is a way of convincing oneself that things aren't really hopeless.

Listed her are several relaxation techniques that will help reduce the physical symptoms of stage fright. They should be done as close to the start of a speech as possible, without being noticeable to your audience. Most of these techniques can be done privately just before you join your listeners.

1. Force yourself to yawn widely several times. Fill your lungs with air each time by breathing deeply.
2. Let your head hang down as far as possible on your chest for several moments. Then slowly rotate it in a full circle, at the same time allowing your eyelids to droop lazily. Let your mouth and

TEACH

● **SKILL DEVELOPMENT**

Critical Thinking
Ask students why memorizing a speech is not an effective way of giving one.

Creative Thinking
In small groups, have students brainstorm possible interruptions during a speech. Ask them to divide the interruptions into two categories—minor (coughing, latecomer entering, desk scraping) and major (audio equipment failure, being introduced by the wrong name). Have them suggest how a speaker might handle such events. Students could make cartoons that illustrate interruptions and ways of handling them. They could add these cartoons to their portfolio products.

● **LEARNING STYLES**

Kinesic Learning
Ask students to work in pairs to practice the three relaxation techniques. Pairs should help each other perform the techniques accurately. In addition, you could have students stand and practice deep-breathing techniques. This can provide students with more oxygen, which can lessen apprehension and make projection less difficult.

TEACH

● **LINKS TO PAST LEARNING**

Ask students what relaxation techniques they use to prepare for an athletic event or for a performance such as a musical recital.

● **CURRICULAR CONNECTIONS**

Science
Health students could find out about other relaxation techniques they could use to deal with various stresses in their lives. Have them report on these techniques to the class. Discuss how many of these techniques students use.

---

lower jaw hang open loosely. Repeat this rolling motion five or six times, very slowly.

3. Sit in a slumped position in a chair as if you were a rag doll. Allow your arms to dangle beside the chair, your head to slump on your chest, and your mouth to hang open. Then tighten all muscles one at a time, starting with your toes and working up your body to your neck. Next, gradually relax each set of muscles, starting at the top and working back down to your toes. Repeat this process several times.

Realize Audiences Tend to Be Sympathetic

Audiences are usually sympathetic to the problem of stage fright. Most listeners realize that they could have the same feelings if they were the one at the podium, and they show by their sympathetic treatment of the speaker that they would expect the same charity in return. Audiences want to see speakers succeed, not fail. To the extent that listeners do notice symptoms of stage fright, they will usually react in a friendly and encouraging fashion.

Develop the Right Attitude

If you are like most speakers you are destined to feel some of the symptoms of stage fright before every speech. Since it is probably impossible to prevent these symptoms from occurring, the key to success lies in your mental attitude toward the feelings. Once the butterflies-in-the-stomach and the shaking knees begin, train yourself to think in the following sequence:

1. Since the time for my speech is getting near, what I'm feeling are symptoms of stage fright.
2. This is my body's way of preparing me to meet a special speech situation.
3. Once my speech begins, this tension will serve as a spring to sharpen my thinking and give vitality to my presentation.

If you look upon stage fright as something positive, you are less likely to experience the kind of runaway stage fright that befalls speakers who see it as a totally negative experience. Controlled stage fright will then aid you in becoming a successful speaker.

APPLY

● **ENRICHMENT**

Invite a politician to the class. Have students ask questions and find out other information about political life.

● **LEARNING STYLES**

✻ **Cooperative Learning**
In small groups, have students make a chart comparing the skills needed by a candidate for public office with the skills needed by a student in a public speaking course.

● **SKILL DEVELOPMENT**

Critical Thinking
Many politicians begin their careers by participating in speech activities in high school. Ask students why a person who enjoys communication would be drawn to the field of politics.

CAREER CLOSE-UP

Candidate For Public Office

Political candidates must become polished public speakers in order to gain the public favor necessary to win an election. The pressure to succeed drives many candidates to develop speaking skills quickly, often within a few months.

Most candidates experience some of the symptoms of stage fright, especially at the beginning of their campaigns. Those who thoroughly research and study the issues they plan to speak about, however, can face an audience with increased confidence. Altering a talk according to the group being addressed is another excellent technique candidates use to attract an audience's attention. A successful speech to a local businessmen's group, for example, would include a knowledgeable discussion of business-related issues.

Using humor at the beginning of a speech also helps candidates capture audience attention. An audience's enthusiastic response to humor often gives speakers the impetus to continue with more assurance. Effective speakers also practice the use of gestures and platform movement to help them communicate a message more forcefully. Making direct eye contact with listeners and using appropriate gestures are skills that candidates must practice repeatedly to be effective.

Fortunately for political candidates, their campaigning necessitates frequent public speaking. With this additional practice, they can increase their speaking skills by experimenting, rehearsing, and mastering the art of public speaking—abilities that will serve them well throughout their political careers.

The ability to face an audience confidently, with well-researched and specific content, is basic to the successful political career.

TEACH

> *Of the three elements in speech making—speaker, subject and persons addressed—it is the last one, the hearer, that determines the speech's end and object.*
>
> —Aristotle

● **SKILL APPLICATION**

Citizens Speak Out
Students could come up with a list of topics that they would like to speak about. Encourage them to come up with topics that they feel enthusiastic about and would want to share with others

● **SKILL DEVELOPMENT**

15-Second Skill Opportunity
It is important to be sure the audience is following the ideas presented in a speech. Ask students to imagine that a salesperson does not understand their requests. Have each student come up with a request. Ask for volunteers to role-play in 15 seconds how they could make the salesperson understand.

● **LEARNING STYLES**

Multicultural Learning
Ask students what speakers could do to prepare for a speech to an audience that is of an ethnic background other than their own.

Concentrate on Your Topic

Many beginning speakers lack confidence because they are thinkin too much about themselves: "Will I do as well as that last speaker whe my turn comes?" "Should I be making more gestures?" "My mouth feel dry." Instead, begin to develop a positive attitude. Say to yourself: " have a topic that I really want to share with these listeners. I want t make certain they are informed (persuaded, entertained), and I will d everything in my power to assure that they are." Once you begin trul thinking in those terms, the worst symptoms of stage fright are likely t disappear.

How can you begin developing such an attitude? For one thing choose your speech topics carefully. Select something you are gen uinely interested in and let your speech be an opportunity to shar your enthusiasm for that topic with your audience. Don't get up in fron of your audience with the feeling "I *have* to give a speech today," bu with the feeling "I have a speech to give today!"

Concentrate on Your Audience

While you are actually delivering your speech, search the faces of you audience to make certain they are following your ideas and to se whether the listeners agree with your ideas. If you perceive boredor growing among your listeners, change tactics and attempt to regai their attention and interest.

Of course, in any audience, some listeners will appear more inter ested than others. It is perfectly all right to give more of your attentio while speaking to the interested listeners. Their obvious appreciation fc your speech can be a great confidence-builder for you.

Some speakers make the mistake of attempting to interest the mos bored or disgusted-looking member of the audience. Nearly every aud ence will have one or two such people. If you change your tactics t suit them, you may be ruining what was a highly rewarding speech fc 90 percent of your listeners. Only when a large portion of your audienc is showing signs of boredom or disinterest should you begin changin your approach.

If you concentrate on looking for audience feedback and making a appropriate response to it, you will have little time to think about you self. As you think less about yourself, your stage fright will be cor trolled and your confidence will increase.

● **LINKS TO PAST LEARNING**

Ask students to recall speeches they have heard in which humor did not work. Ask them to explain why they think it failed. Have them decide if the reasons that it failed had anything to do with the precautions listed here.

● **ASSESSMENT STRATEGY**

Students could use the four precautions listed on page 169 as a checklist to evaluate the use of humor in the speech they gave to introduce a political candidate. After the evaluation, they could target ways to improve the use of humor in their speeches. Students could place this checklist in their portfolios and chart their progress.

> *Wit is a sword; it is meant to make people feel the point as well as see it.*
>
> —G.K. Chesterton

● **SKILL APPLICATION**

Citizens Speak Out
Students could use humor when giving a speech. Have students prepare a short speech in which they introduce a political candidate by summarizing some of the candidate's positions on political issues. Call on students to present their speeches, focusing on their use of humor.

Controlling Your Nervousness   169

Inject a Little Humor

Humor has long been used as a means of reducing tension between speaker and audience. Getting a laugh from an audience builds confidence rapidly; a speaker is assured that there is little to fear from the listeners. Once your speech has begun, injecting a bit of humor, particularly near the beginning, relaxes you more effectively than anything else. If not overdone, humor can actually relax your audience as well. When using humor, observe these precautions:

1. Prepare humor thoroughly beforehand, making certain that it will be understood and appreciated by this particular audience. A joke that falls flat can destroy a speaker's confidence rather than build it.
2. Use humor mainly during the speech introduction, sprinkling lesser amounts throughout the remainder of the speech.
3. Do not overuse humor.
4. Avoid offensive jokes.

Move About, Use Gestures, and Make Eye Contact

Believe it or not, moving while delivering a speech can help reduce nervous tension as well as the other symptoms of stage fright. Have you ever narrowly missed being in a car accident? If so, you probably noticed that right after your near miss you were trembling. Your body was getting rid of the tension that had built up suddenly when you saw the accident coming. In much the same way, movement of one's body while speaking helps dissipate some of the tension the speaker feels.

Any movements you make should be suited to the speech and the audience. All kinds of movement will reduce tension, but some forms look pretty ridiculous during a public speech. Beginning speakers, in a subconscious attempt to reduce stage fright, occasionally use movements that tend to distract the listeners from the message. Among these awkward movements several have become fairly common, and might be given names.

The Ping-Pong Pacers constantly pace to and fro in front of the audience until the listeners appear to be viewing a ping-pong tournament. The Lectern Leeches grab the sides of the lectern so tightly their knuckles turn white. The Hair-Tossers, whose hair may not really be in

TEACH

> *"There was speech in their dumbness, language in their very gesture."*
> —Shakespeare, *The Winter's Tale*

● **LEARNING STYLES**

Visual Learning
Call on students to demonstrate the awkward movements that can distract from a speech. Ask students if there are other speakers they have seen whose movements tend to distract the audience from the speech.

Multicultural Learning
Ask students to investigate movements and gestures that are particular to certain cultures. Discuss with them why this kind of knowledge would be important for someone giving a speech to a particular cultural group.

---

170   CHAPTER 6   Building Confidence

their eyes, regularly toss their heads to get it out of the way. The Pencil Twirlers manage to draw all eyes to a pencil, paper clip, rubber band, or note card they are folding, spindling, or mutilating as they speak.

Movements that help communicate your message nonverbally are the only kind you should strive to make while speaking. Such movements release nervous tension just as effectively as the distracting ones but have the added advantage of helping you get your message across. Chapter 9 on delivery will present communicative body movements in detail. For the time being, however, notice that they fall into three broad categories:

Total Body Movement Except for very formal occasions, a speaker should occasionally change positions on the platform. Moving the entire body is called **platform movement.** Such movement looks best when it is made on a diagonal: not directly on a forward-backward axis, nor completely on a side-to-side axis, but between the two. Total body movement is especially appropriate when a speaker is making a major transition in thought patterns or when it is desirable to get closer to one part of the audience where attention seems to be flagging. Movement can also be useful in simply providing variety after a speaker has been in one position for some time. Naturally any amount of total body movement that resembles the antics of a Ping-Pong Pacer is too much.

Gestures Although some people tend to "talk with their hands" more than others do, most beginning public speakers tend to be too "quiet" with their arms and hands. Practicing specific gestures for a particular

Gestures during public speaking should be natural and appear "unrehearsed."

AMAZING FACTS!
Providing facial expressions should be a reasonable accomplishment. The human face is capable of some 250,000 expressions!

point in a speech is not wise. Gestures during a live performance should not look practiced. Gestures should look natural and be natural. One way to achieve this is to use general arm and hand movements during rehearsal. This is likely to loosen you up and lead to similar natural arm and hand gestures during the speech.

Gestures also include movements of the head and face. While speaking, try to move your head frequently to look from one part of your audience to another. You should also vary your facial expression to correspond with the thought patterns of your speech. Again, your movements should be natural.

Eye Contact Remember that your eyes may be your most effective means of body-motion communication. Many students ask, "Do I have to look right into the eyes of my listeners.?" Eye contact is very desirable because of the feeling it gives each audience member that you are speaking to him or her personally. However, if you find in your first few speeches that you get less confused and nervous by simply looking at your audience as a whole and not directly into individuals' eyes, then do so. However, you should make it your goal eventually to look directly into the eyes of several of your listeners.

● ACTIVITY

Controlling Stage Fright
Volunteer to stand in front of the class and tell them about the topic you have selected for an upcoming speech. Indicate what your topic will be, why you chose it, and how you feel it applies to them. To help control your stage fright while speaking, you might inject a bit of humor into your remarks. As you talk, try to make a few hand gestures, move a step or two away from the podium, and, if it is not likely to increase your nervousness, look directly at several of your listeners. Before you sit down, ask your audience if they have any reactions to, or suggestions about, your upcoming speech topic. (You will want to do this Activity in conjunction with the Activity on page 175.)

Handle Specific Symptoms of Nervousness

Some symptoms of stage fright may bother you more than others. The chart on page 173 shows several of the more obvious ones with suggestions for handling each. Successfully handling symptoms that you find particularly annoying will help build your confidence.

● SKILL DEVELOPMENT

Gestures
Ask students to demonstrate the use of gestures. Students could role-play a situation in which they are teaching a younger child how to perform a household task, such as washing dishes or vacuuming the floor. Students should use gestures as a way of making their instructions clearer.

● LEARNING STYLES

Kinesic Learning
Students could demonstrate the value of eye contact. Ask students to prepare a short speech in which they express words of sympathy to a friend. Have them work with a partner and express their sympathy in two ways—by simply saying the words and by using eye contact in addition to the words.

● ACTIVITY

You could videotape the speeches and play them back to the class. Ask students to evaluate each in terms of the three communicative body movements discussed on pages 169-170 and in terms of the use of humor. The evaluations could be written or oral.

TEACH

● **ENRICHMENT**

Many metropolitan areas have toastmasters' clubs whose members meet to give speeches. If there is a chapter in your community, invite a representative to your class to speak about stage fright and successful ways of handling symptoms.

AMAZING FACTS!

When making eye contact, it is important to make the contact for about three to five seconds. Glancing at a person for less time gives a speaker a shifty look. The Nixon-Kennedy debate is an example of the negative effect of darting eye glances. People who heard the debate on the radio gave the win to Nixon. However, those who watched the debate gave Kennedy the victory. Analysts believe that Nixon's shifting eye movements resulted in people having less confidence in what he had to say.

● **LEARNING STYLES**

❊ **Cooperative Learning**
Have small groups of students make lists of places in which people have opportunities to deliver speeches. Compile a class list and have students include the list in their portfolios.

---

172   CHAPTER 6 Building Confidence

Speak As Often As You Can

Confidence in public speaking is built more by the experience of giving speeches than by anything else. This class will provide you with several opportunities to deliver speeches, but it may not provide enough experience to make you truly confident of your abilities on the platform. If you genuinely want to feel at ease about public speaking, look for speaking opportunities outside the classroom. Many organizations that you are eligible to join sponsor speech contests each year. The Future Business Leaders of America (FBLA) is one such organization, as is the Future Farmers of America (FFA). Most local Optimist Clubs have speech contests for high school students. Scout organizations give merit badges for public speaking. In addition, your school may have a debating team or a speech club which sponsors tournaments with nearby schools. By getting involved in these kinds of activities you can gain valuable experience in public speaking as well as develop a much greater sense of confidence.

Use Speech Critiques to Your Advantage

Many speech students find both giving and receiving critiques of their classroom speeches awkward. You may be one of those who tolerates a critique of your speech by your teacher, but dislikes your classmates commenting on your presentation. Perhaps you feel even worse about having to critique someone else's speech, thinking that you may hurt or anger that person.

Speech critiques are one of the best ways of teaching you to become a confident and effective public speaker. You learn from your mistakes in giving speeches just as you did when you first took swimming lessons or were on your first softball team. Had your instructor or coach never told you what you were doing right and wrong, you might never have learned to swim or play ball very well. As a matter of fact, you might only have succeeded in deepening your bad habits. What makes a speech class different from a swimming lesson, though, is that your classmates are your real audience for your classroom speeches. Learning to adapt to a live audience is a major part of what giving speeches is all about. If your classmates are not allowed to tell what they feel are strong points and not-so-strong points in your speech, you will have a hard time discovering the best ways to relate to other audiences later on.

If what you dislike most about speech critiques is giving them rather than receiving them, remember that you are in a speech class to learn to *listen* as well as to speak. Preparing either a written or an oral critique

TEACH

● **LINKS TO PAST LEARNING**

Ask students to recall times when an instructor or coach criticized their performance. Discuss with students what type of criticism it was and why it was offered. Ask them how they reacted to the criticism and how it affected their future performances.

SUBSTITUTE TEACHER TIP

Ask students to prepare a short speech suggesting an action that their student council take. Have each student choose one of the symptoms of stage fright listed that he or she has experienced. Students should demonstrate a solution to the symptom that they could employ while presenting their speech.

● **LEARNING STYLES**

Visual Learning
Small groups or individuals could develop an illustrated poster or flyer suitable for duplication for the class. The symptoms and solutions for stage fright can be treated humorously.

Controlling Your Nervousness

Common symptoms of stage fright have practical solutions.

Symptoms	Solutions
trembling hands and a rattling manuscript	Use 3 x 5 cards. Place them on the lectern and slide each card to one side after it has been used.
stumbling over words—getting "tongue twisted"	Deliberately slow down your speaking rate until the problem disappears.
the feeling that you cannot get enough breath	Speak slowly. Take longer pauses between sentences. Breathe from your diaphragm through your nose.
unwillingness to look at the audience	In the beginning, do not look directly at individuals. Instead look just above their heads or slightly to one side of their faces. Later, pick the friendliest face in the audience and look first at that person.
excessive perspiration	Ignore it. Do not call attention to it by wiping your hands or forehead.
cold hands and feet	Make some platform movement and gestures.
hoarse or squeaky voice	Before a speech, tape record your rehearsal sessions and concentrate on eliminating vocal problems. If this problem occurs during a speech, ignore it.
dry mouth	Speak slowly to avoid getting tongue tied. Do not lick your lips in front of the audience.
tense muscles	Use platform movement and gestures.
cramps, butterflies, or stomach noises	Remember that the audience is ordinarily not aware of such symptoms. Ignore them as much as possible.
wanting to return to your seat	Resist this feeling at all costs. The best way to control stage fright is by having experience in public speaking.
feeling inferior	Try dressing for the speech in the outfit that makes you look your best. Naturally, it must be appropriate to the audience and occasion.

TEACH

● **LEARNING STYLES**

Limited English Proficiency
Students with limited proficiency in English could be paired with other students to develop a list of positive words and expressions that could be used in a critique. Students could then write sentences using these positive terms.

● **SKILL DEVELOPMENT**

Main Idea
Ask students to create a form that could be used in giving speech critiques. Ask students to think about what elements they would want an evaluator to focus on when developing a critique for a speech they are giving. Tell students to use these elements in developing their own forms.

15-Second Skill Opportunity
Ask students to think about their favorite television advertisement. In 15 seconds, have them describe this advertisement and explain why it is their favorite. As each student presents his or her speech, have the other students write one sentence bringing out a positive aspect of the speech. Call on volunteers to read their sentence.

---

174 CHAPTER 6 Building Confidence

of one of your classmates' speeches gives you an excellent opportunity to pay close attention to all the details of her or his presentation. You learn listening skills, and at the same time you discover techniques you may want to adopt or avoid in your own speeches.

Of course students just learning public speaking are not yet experts on the art of giving speeches. At times your critiques may include some bad advice. After a fellow student has critiqued your speech, listen carefully for any parts of that critique with which your teacher may disagree. It is your teacher who is the real expert on the subject in your speech class. He or she will be able to balance your classmate's critique with an assessment based on extensive training and experience.

Once you get involved in contest speaking, you also need to consider carefully the critiques of contest judges. Many of their comments will be valid, but judges differ in their approaches to, and perceptions of, how speeches should be given. Here again, go over judges' comments carefully with your speech teacher, looking for similar comments from a number of judges. This careful study is the best method for determining the validity of comments.

Finally, remember that everyone who hears your speeches is there to help you improve—your teacher, your fellow students, and contest judges. There is no place in a speech classroom for mean-spirited criticism. When you are asked to give a critique, begin by mentioning the strong points you noticed. Be specific and detailed. Then, in a kind, constructive tone, mention one or two areas where the speaker can improve. When you are on the receiving end of a critique, remember that your critic is trying to help you learn. Such a sharing and caring atmosphere in speech classrooms can help build speaker confidence as much as anything can.

How to Be a Good Speech Critic

- Begin with the positive points. Tell the speaker you found the speech well organized and easy to follow before you say he or she looked nervous.

- Be specific, especially with positive comments. It is much more helpful to say "Your use of humor was very good. The two stories about the giant and the clown really got our attention" than to simply comment "Your humor was good."

- Criticize the speech, not the speaker. Say "The point about the existence of witches needed more proof" rather than "You failed to prove that witches really exist."

RETEACHING

Have students use the concepts presented in this section to give a speech titled "How I Control My Nervousness When I Give a Speech." Students' speeches should include such elements as preparation, knowing the audience, injecting humor, and including eye contact.

EXTENSION

Analyze the critiques given by students in the activity on page 175. After each student presents his or her oral critique, have a class discussion to see how many of the points on pages 174-175 were used in the critique.

ASSESSMENT STRATEGY

Have students make a checklist of the things they need to improve in giving critiques of their classmates' speeches. Have students keep this checklist in their portfolios and record progress regularly

---

Controlling Your Nervousness

- State your reactions as your opinion. Avoid being dogmatic; don't say such things as "You needed to look more toward the right side of the room." Instead, state how you saw it and how effective it seemed to you: "I felt you needed to look toward the right side of the room more. I felt left out because I didn't notice you looking at me."

- Focus on improvement. Suggest how the speaker might improve a specific part of his or her performance the next time. Say "In your next speech, you might want to move a few steps to either side of the podium occasionally" rather than "You didn't move around enough."

- Don't debate your critique with the speaker. Remember, you're not the speech expert. Neither is the speaker. Offer your perceptions and suggestions, then let your teacher clear up any misunderstandings.

- Keep your critique brief. Usually it is best to mention only one or two positive, then one or two negative points. Don't give a speech of your own when you mention each point. State the point concisely, then move on.

- Show empathy for the speaker. Let the speaker know you understand how he or she felt during the speech. A comment such as "I get so nervous I usually talk too fast too" can help build a positive atmosphere about classroom critiques.

ACTIVITY

Critiquing Classmates' "Talks"

Before beginning the talks on upcoming speech topics (p. 171), each speaker should be assigned a partner who will prepare a brief oral critique and present it immediately after the speaker sits down. Read over the suggestions under "How to Be a Good Speech Critic" (pp. 174–175) as preparation for serving as critic for your partner. Since these "talks" are to be brief, you should also keep your critique brief.

ASSESS

● **STUDENT PERFORMANCE COMPETENCIES**

- Defines terms
- Explains how to control stage fright in order to speak effectively
- Describes specific methods for gaining confidence
- Understands the importance of humor and body movements in gaining confidence for speaking
- Understands the importance of critiques in becoming a more confident speaker

● **sca GUIDELINES**

- Understands suggestions to control stage fright
- Uses nonverbal signs in speeches to help overcome stage fright
- Expresses ideas clearly and concisely when giving speech critiques

PORTFOLIO ASSESSMENT

Standard
- Lack of Confidence Thoughts
- Use of Humor Checklist
- Critique Skills Checklist

Enrichment
- Humorous Remarks List
- List of Places for Speaking Opportunities

Challenge
- Stage Fright Symptoms and Solutions Guidelines

CHAPTER 6 REVIEW

● **SUMMARY**

Understanding the true nature of stage fright and learning how to control it are two of the most important things you can do as a beginning public speaker.

Understanding Stage Fright Stage fright is a problem that affects the great majority of public speakers, as well as the majority of other people who perform in public. While both experienced and inexperienced speakers suffer from it, those with experience generally handle it more effectively.

Stage fright starts in your mind. A strong psychological tension urges you to do well and at the same time reminds you that you might not do very well at all. This tension triggers physical reactions such as sweaty palms, a queasy stomach, a dry mouth, and shaking limbs. Such symptoms of stage fright can prevent a successful speech if allowed to get out of control. At a controlled level, however, it can be helpful and can actually promote a successful speech by "supercharging" your body and sharpening your thinking.

Controlling Your Nervousness One of the best methods for dealing with stage fright is thorough preparation. Knowing that you are completely ready for a speech can greatly reduce most nervousness. Practicing various relaxation techniques while waiting your turn to speak is helpful in relieving the physical symptoms of nervous tension. If you remember that audiences are sympathetic and that a little tension is good, you will be developing the right mental attitude for public speaking. Concentrating on your topic and the audience rather than on yourself is particularly useful in controlling excess tension. A speaker who is making sure that the audience is "getting the message" has little time to worry about the impression his or her performance is making.

In addition, injecting humor into your speech helps both you and your audience to relax, and using communicative body movements during your delivery dissipates a lot of your physical tension. In the process of learning to handle the specific symptoms of stage fright you will build your confidence. In addition, there is no substitute for actual speaking experience as a cure for stage fright.

Speech critiques can be a useful tool if they are used to benefit the speaker. Be attentive to the critiques of others, using their helpful suggestions. When you are the critic, always be as positive as possible. Be sure that your remarks are kind.

ASSESS

● **ASSESSMENT STRATEGIES**

Individual Assessment
- Participates in practice activities daily or weekly
- Completes classwork
- Demonstrates knowledge of content discussion, quizzes, and Chapter 6 test
- Displays improved speech skills in this chapter

Group Assessment
- Sets and achieves goals
- Demonstrates cooperative learning activities
- Supports efforts of team and class members
- Provides encouragement and feedback to members

VOCABULARY

Define each term in a complete sentence.

stage fright
tension
controlled stage fright
runaway stage fright
lack of confidence
overconfidence
platform movement

CHECKLIST

Confidence-Building Skills

1. Use the realization that most people experience stage fright to build self-confidence.
2. Understand why you experience stage fright, and control it by applying the knowledge you have gained in this chapter.
3. Use controlled stage fright as a positive impetus for becoming a good public speaker.
4. Be aware that uncontrolled stage fright can be harmful, and take steps to turn it into controlled stage fright.
5. Control nervousness by preparing your speeches thoroughly and by practicing relaxation before you speak.
6. Make use of audience sympathy to control stage fright.
7. Use humor in your speeches to help you build confidence.
8. Use body movements to help you release tension and become a polished speaker.
9. Speak as often as you can.
10. Learn to use speech critiques as a way to build confidence.

REVIEW QUESTIONS

1. Identify two emotions that cause the tension leading to stage fright.
2. Describe how controlled stage fright can help a speaker.
3. Name two causes of uncontrolled stage fright.
4. Name several ways in which stage fright can show itself during a speech.
5. Describe the role of an audience when a speaker experiences stage fright.

● **ANSWERS**

See the Answer Key for more complete answers.

REVIEW QUESTIONS
1. Two emotions are in conflict: (a) desperately wanting to do well and make a good impression and (b) knowing that something may cause us to be unsuccessful.
2. Controlling stage fright produces energy that increases mental and physical sharpness.
3. The two causes of uncontrolled stage fright are lack of confidence and overconfidence
4. Nervousness manifests itself through trembling, a feeling of breathlessness, an unwillingness to look at the audience, sweaty palms, and excessive perspiration.
5. As a rule, audiences are sympathetic to the person who is experiencing stage fright and usually react in a supportive manner.

ASSESS

6. Preparation reduces fear of the unexpected by increasing the speaker's control..
7. Yawn widely and take deep breaths. Rotate the head to relax neck muscles. Relax the body totally, slumping in a chair like a rag doll.
8. To control stage fright acknowledge it, recognize that it is a normal reaction, and understand that the energy of the increased tension can result in better performance.
9. Physical movements help the body get rid of tension that builds up prior to speaking.
10. A 3 × 5 note card reduces the chances that the audience will notice trembling hands or a rustling manuscript. Slowing down the rate of speech lessens the likelihood of stumbling over words.

DISCUSSION QUESTIONS

The following code is used to designate discussion questions and activities as suitable for students of varying ability levels:
- ▼ = below average to average
- ◆ = average to above average
- ■ = all students

1. ■ Invite others to discuss stage fright symptoms they experience and remedies they employ in their jobs.
2. ▼ Each group might be assigned a famous person, living or dead, who suffered or suffers from stage fright (e.g., Sir Lawrence Olivier, Abraham Lincoln, Adlai Stevenson, Sir Winston Churchill, Willard Scott).
3. ■ Provide examples of proper and improper use of humor.
4. ■ Perhaps students can provide examples from fiction or movies.
5. ▼ Criticism, whether well-intentioned or unwelcome, is a part of every phase of daily life, and students should discuss ways of dealing with or accepting it graciously, while not allowing negativity to damage self-esteem.

CHAPTER 6 REVIEW

6. Describe how thorough preparation for a public speech can reduce nervousness.
7. Describe several methods a speaker can use to relax before giving a speech.
8. Name several attitudes toward stage fright that can help a speaker control it.
9. Describe how physical movements can help to reduce stage fright.
10. Name a way to control each symptom of stage fright.

? DISCUSSION QUESTIONS

1. Discuss experiences you have had with stage fright in non-speech situations, such as sports events, musical performances, or fashion shows. How did those situations compare to delivering a public speech?
2. With the class, discuss your ideas about what causes stage fright in public speaking situations. If you know of any famous performers who have stage fright, identify them and include their remarks in your discussion. Identify factors that seem to increase tension and self-consciousness. Share your findings and try to identify some common themes.
3. Discuss ways that humor can be used to relax the speaker and to make positive contact with the audience. What precautions should be taken when humor is included in speeches? Make a class list of do's and don'ts for humor in public speaking.
4. Discuss with your classmates any experiences you can recall that involved overconfidence. Do athletic teams sometimes lose the "easiest" game of the season? Have you ever failed a test because of overconfidence? What causes overconfidence? What often results from overconfidence?
5. Discuss your feelings about giving and receiving criticism. Do you object to receiving criticism more from peers than from adults? Do you view all critics in the same way? Do you see value in criticism? Why or why not? What are your thoughts on self-evaluation? When you critique others, do you feel self-conscious? What can be done to deliver a critique in an objective manner?

ASSESS

⚠ CRITICAL THINKING

1. Analysis Imagine that you have chosen a topic for a speech that you are really interested in. Moreover, you have spent a number of hours researching your topic and have assembled a large amount of evidence to support the points you will make in your speech. Analyze the effects that this type of preparation is likely to have on stage fright. Have your chances of suffering from stage fright increased or lessened?

2. Evaluation A critique of a speech can benefit both the speaker and the person who offers the critique. How does a critique benefit a speaker? How does a critique benefit the one who gives it? In what ways is the giving of a critique similar to the giving of a speech?

ACTIVITIES

In-Class

1. Design a poster promoting a campaign to control stage fright. Think of a slogan and promote the idea that this mental monster can be brought under control. Include all of the steps outlined in the text for controlling your nervousness. If someone in your group is artistic, create a character that represents "fear." Choose the best poster and display it in your classroom as a constant reminder.

2. Invite a well-known local person who is frequently in the public eye or someone who is used to public performances to your class as a guest speaker. Try to find someone from the field of sports, from television, or from politics. Prepare a list of questions you will ask to find out (a) whether he or she experiences stage fright prior to or during speeches or performances, and (b) what techniques he or she uses to control stage fright.

3. Since most students report that the greatest problem with stage fright is in the opening moments of a speech, practice getting started by doing the following: (a) Rise from your seat and go to the front of the room. (b) Take a few seconds to observe your audience. (c) Give an introduction for a speech on a topic of your choice. (d) Receive

---

CRITICAL THINKING
1. **Analysis** Preparation is key to controlling
■   stage fright.
2. **Evaluation** Critiques, although often beneficial to both recipient and giver, are a difficult task for students.

ACTIVITIES
In-Class
1. Encourage creativity. Students might create
▼   a superhero (self-confidence) or parody a popular public-service campaign such as "Stage Fright—Just Say NO!" Display posters in the classroom.
2. Prepare students for the event by giving
◆   background information on the speaker and helping them write interview questions.
3. This process by itself can result in a lessen-
■   ing of student fears. Just standing in front of an audience for the first time often defuses stage fright and begins a confidence-building process.

ASSESS

4. Use the critique sheets and make copies available to students.

Out-of-Class
1. This activity is a valuable one for the student who is dedicated to improvement in speaking skills.
2. The student should use care to choose a silent partner who will devote time to reviewing the text material and who will be frank and constructive in providing sensitive criticism.
3. Assign an essay in conjunction with this assignment. Ask students to explain the effectiveness of the partnership between actions and attitudes. Ask them to cite other examples of occasions where this tactic might be helpful (interviews, recitals, meetings, etc.).

CHAPTER 6 REVIEW

audience reaction. (e) Return to your seat. This "practice" introduction will help you to feel that you have been in front of the audience, at least briefly, before you make a formal presentation. Write your response to the experience in your speech notebook.

4. Review a number of different types of critique sheets for various speech activities. Make certain that you understand the criteria listed. Determine the best critique sheet for public-speaking assignments for this class.

Out-of-Class

1. Read the symptoms of stage fright listed in this chapter. Which of these symptoms do you experience most often? Compose a list for your speech notebook. Put at the top of the list those symptoms that you feel most frequently, and put at the bottom of the list the symptoms that you seldom, if ever, experience. Concentrate on the symptom that causes you the most discomfort and write the suggested solution next to the symptom. Practice the solution. Then move down the list and deal with the next most discomforting symptom. Follow the same process until you have dealt with all of the symptoms on your list.

2. Identify a friend or relative who will be your "silent partner" for this semester in preparing for speeches. Choose someone who will listen to your speeches in rehearsal and will give you both positive feedback and constructive suggestions for improvement. Share your feelings about making a speech and explain the specific ways that you are working to overcome stage fright. Ask him or her to identify verbal or nonverbal signals that you are sending that may be distracting or that may be signs of nervousness. These signals may be unconsciously sent, and you will not be aware of them unless someone points them out to you. Keep track of your progress in your speech notebook.

3. Learn ways to "psyche yourself up" for the next speaking assignment. Choose a topic that you are really interested in. Get excited about your speech. Tell other people about your enthusiasm. Walk briskly to the front of the room. Send out positive nonverbal signals throughout the speech. Make yourself and others believe that it was a thoroughly enjoyable experience. Keep a record in your speech notebook of the effects of your enthusiasm. Did it help you make a better speech? Did you feel better about yourself and your performance? Did your enthusiasm reach your audience?

ASSESS

💡 CHAPTER PROJECT

Put together a videotape or audio-tape presentation on the subject of stage fright. Create a documentary or a docudrama and include

1. an analysis of the nature and causes of stage fright
2. a consideration of positive and negative aspects
3. general suggestions for overcoming nervousness
4. instructions for dealing with specific symptoms
5. testimony on the subject by well-known individuals
6. an evaluation of criticism as a tool for growth

Compose an outline or script for the program. Involve as many members of your class as possible. Rehearse it several times before taping it.

When the tape is complete, make it available to other groups and individuals in your school who participate in public performance. It should be especially welcomed by vocational clubs and special-interest organizations that feature public-speaking contests as a part of their annual activities.

CHAPTER PROJECT
- Students should use group discussion skills from Chapter 5 to make decisions about scripting, casting, scheduling, and the like. Encourage responsible participation in individual assignments and rehearsal. Have students critique the final product and decide by consensus which parts need to be rewritten or refilmed.

PREPARE

● CHAPTER PLANNER

Day 1	Day 2	Day 3	Day 4	Day 5
Prepare	Prepare	Prepare	Prepare	Prepare
Teach	Teach	Teach	Teach	Teach
Assess	Assess	Assess	Assess	Assess
Sub. Teacher Tip *p. 187*	Sub. Teacher Tip *p. 190*	Sub. Teacher Tip *p. 206*	Sub. Teacher Tip *p. 207*	Sub. Teacher Tip *p. 209*

● CHAPTER OVERVIEW

This chapter examines the following topics:
- Focusing on Your Topic *p. 184*
- Researching Your Topic *p. 191*
- Organizing and Outlining Your Speech *p. 205*
- Rehearsing *p. 214*

▼ PORTFOLIO PRODUCTS

Individual Projects
- Knowledge, Interests, and Opinion Inventory
- School Issues Survey
- Information Note Cards
- Chapter 7 Portfolio Products

Group Projects
- General Purpose Categories List
- Newspaper and Newsmagazine Articles

● sca GUIDELINES

- Distinguishes facts from opinions
- Distinguishes between informative and persuasive messages
- Expresses ideas clearly and concisely
- Expresses and defends point of view with evidence
- Organizes messages so that others can understand them
- Gives concise and accurate directions
- Summarizes messages
- Performs social rituals

182

CHAPTER 7

Preparing Your Speech

When you have completed this chapter you should be able to:

- Identify ways to choose a speech topic that appeals to an audience.
- Understand and put into practice research skills.
- Prepare a speech outline.
- Recognize the importance of rehearsal in preparation for a speech.

TEACH

● **LINKS TO PAST LEARNING**

Ask students to think back to a time as children when they needed to draft a plan before building something. Have them recall what they were building and what they needed to consider in their plan. Call on volunteers to share how having a plan helped in constructing their creation. Ask them why preparation would be important in giving a speech.

AMAZING FACTS!

Cicero, the Roman orator, stated five steps in preparing a speech: *invention* (in which a situation and audience are analyzed and materials selected); *disposition* (arranging materials into an introduction, discussion, and conclusion); *style* (use of words); *memory* (ways of memorizing); and *delivery* (the oral presentation).

> ❝In Maine we have a saying that there's no point in speaking unless you can improve on silence.❞
> —Edmund Muskie

● **ACTIVITY**

Four Cornerstones of Speech Preparation

Divide your class into four groups and have each group go to a corner of the classroom. Each group should hold a brief discussion about the importance of one of the four cornerstones of thorough speech preparation: Choosing an appealing topic. Doing in-depth research. Preparing a clear outline. Rehearsing carefully. When all four groups have discovered reasons why their particular cornerstone is important to successful speech preparation, each group should select a spokesperson to report the reasons agreed upon in that group to the class.

● **ACTIVITY**

Combine the groups' suggestions for each cornerstone of speech preparation into an informational poster, with four corners labeled and reasons each cornerstone is important listed under the appropriate label. Display the poster for later reference.

Preparing Your Speech

In order to construct a solid and functional house, builders must start with a set of plans. The process of drawing up the plans is, in some ways, as important as the actual construction process itself. Many critical questions must be answered in the plans: "Will the foundation be adequate to support the weight of the house? Are the rooms arranged properly for maximum convenience? Is the structure placed in the best possible position on the lot?" By first building the house in their minds and on paper, the builders can save great amounts of time and money. A mistake at this early stage is easily fixed; mistakes made after construction has started are generally very expensive to correct.

A well-prepared speaker goes into a speech confident of the outcome.

TEACH

● **MOTIVATION**

Ask students to imagine that they could hear a speech about any topic they wanted to. Have each student come up with a speech topic that he or she would like to hear about. Make a list of students' topics on the board. Ask volunteers to explain why they chose their particular topic.

● **SKILL DEVELOPMENT**

Main Idea
To help students learn how to focus on a topic, provide them with an inventory sheet with the following general categories: Knowledge, Interests, and Opinions. Under the "Knowledge" category have students list topics that they are exceptionally knowledgeable about. Under "Interests" have them include topics that they are interested in and would like to know more about. Under "Opinions" have students write opinions that they would be willing to support in a persuasive speech. Have students add the inventory to their portfolio products to be used in developing speech topics throughout the course.

Creative Thinking
Students could work in pairs to choose topics that they think would be interesting for a whole school assembly. Discuss the topics with the rest of the class to determine whether they would be interesting for a school assembly.

15-Second Skill Opportunity
Have students think of a strong opinion they have about something. Have them think about what they would say in their first sentence to identify their opinion and get the attention of the audience.

184

CHAPTER 7 Preparing Your Speech

Wise speakers will build their speeches in much the same manner that builders construct houses—first in their minds and on paper. Each speaker's preparation, like the builder's, should answer many critical questions: "What topic fits the occasion and is of interest both to me and to my audience? What strategy best suits the particular audience I will be addressing? Where can I locate the best sources of information and supporting evidence? In what order should I present my ideas?" Without ample time to answer these questions beforehand, a speaker runs a great risk of having the speech crumble into a disorganized jumble of words. On the other hand, a well-prepared speaker goes into a speech confident of the outcome. This chapter will deal with the four cornerstones of speech preparation mentioned in the opening Activity. Selecting your topic, doing careful research, preparing the outline, and rehearsing thoroughly.

● **FOCUSING ON YOUR TOPIC**

The first part of speech preparation involves focusing on your topic. This process starts with your selecting a general subject, then deciding on your general speech purpose. Once this has been done, you focus your topic by narrowing it to fit the particular interests of your audience and the time limit available to you.

Find a Subject That Fascinates You

Begin by searching your mind for a general subject that you find interesting. You should make this decision carefully because the choice of topic can make or break your speech. Write down a list of single words or short phrases naming subjects you find fascinating. At this point you are looking for broad subjects only. Here is a brief sample list:

Airplanes	TV	Equality
Camping	Disease	Space
Nuclear power	College choice	Holidays
The media	Teachers	Vacations
Stereotyping	Cooking	Economics
Health care	Summer jobs	Latin America
Farming	School grades	Computers
Music	Hobbies	Automobiles
Sports	War	Legislation

● **LINKS TO PAST LEARNING**

Ask students to recall speeches they have heard in which it was apparent that the speaker was passionate or enthusiastic about the topic he or she was speaking about. Call on volunteers to identify and describe these speakers to the class.

TEACH

AMAZING FACTS!

The repetition of phrases such as "Ich bin ein Berliner" and "I have a dream" is called anaphora. It can be a very effective element in stirring speeches.

● **LEARNING STYLES**

Cooperative Learning
Have students decide what kinds of things would be important for speakers to know about their audience. Small groups of students could design questions that speakers could ask themselves to find out about their audience.

Sometimes speech students think they must come up with a brand new or highly unusual topic if they want their speeches to succeed. Not at all. As long as you are enthusiastic about your topic, you will be able to generate enthusiasm among your listeners. Throughout history the speeches that have made the greatest impact have been given by speakers totally wrapped up in their topics. Martin Luther King, Jr.'s "I Have a Dream" speech was given by a man whose life was dedicated to attaining civil rights for all citizens of the United States. President John F. Kennedy's "Ich bin ein Berliner" speech was given by a man who had a deep love of freedom and great admiration for the brave citizens of West Berlin. Similarly, most student speakers who have won national speech contests have been those who chose a topic that genuinely concerned them and not those who simply latched onto any topic just to enter a contest.

Analyze Your Audience

Not every subject that is interesting to you will automatically be of interest to your audience. Classmates who do not sew may be difficult to reach in a speech about dressmaking. You may have problems convincing those with no interest in football that your speech about your favorite football player is electrifying. However, with enough enthusiasm you should be able to make most topics interesting to anyone. As you choose your subject, ask yourself "How can I make this topic interesting and acceptable to all the members of my audience?" Answering this question involves analysis, one of the most important steps in speech preparation.

When you are just beginning to select your speech topic, **audience analysis** consists of asking yourself a series of questions about any topic you are considering for your speech. Ask yourself questions such as the following:

- Do my audience members already know much about this topic?
- What can I tell them about this topic that they do not already know?
- Will this topic interest some audience members more than others?
- If I take a stand on this issue, will my audience agree with me?
- If they do not agree, what interest or needs do they have through which I might change their minds?

Asking and answering questions such as these about your audience will help you organize your topic presentation to a specific group of people. Just as in one-to-one conversation, an audience tends to be

TEACH

> *"Probably the strongest, most flexible, most humanizing device to bridge the space between speaker and audience."*
> —Bob Orben, speaking about humor

● LEARNING STYLES

Audio Learning
Have students review Susan B. Anthony's speech "Woman's Right to Suffrage" in the Appendix on page 576. Ask them to identify the kind of audience Ms. Anthony was probably addressing. Have students explain what clues in the speech led them to their conclusions.

● SKILL DEVELOPMENT

Main Idea
Have students choose an academic topic, such as "The Importance of Taking a Foreign Language in High School." Students could plan to present a speech on the topic to two or three different student groups in school. For example, one group might be a freshman English class, the second, an advanced senior English class, the third, a business, accounting, or typing class. While preparing their speeches for each class, students should ask themselves the series of audience analysis questions found on page 185. Ask students to compare their answers as they apply to different audiences, and, then, to decide on strategies.

● ACTIVITY

So that groups do not produce identical or similar topics, you could assign categories to each group. Possible categories are contemporary personalities (actors, musicians, etc.), travel, recreation and entertainment, and social issues.

CHAPTER 7 Preparing Your Speech

As a result of analysis of the audience, this speaker is able to take into consideration the knowledge, needs, interests, and attitudes of a specific group.

responsive when members perceive that a speaker has taken their knowledge, interests, needs, and attitudes into consideration.

Audience analysis for a classroom speech is relatively easy. After a few weeks in speech class you will become acquainted with most of the class members who will form the audience for your speeches. You can readily guess what their interest and attitudes are. Whenever you are unsure, you will have frequent opportunities to ask them directly. You may also find it helpful to discuss your possible speech topics with one or two friends from your speech class. Two or three of you can probably share insights about class members' interests that will prove helpful to each of you in selecting your speech topics.

Once you have chosen your topic, you will need to do more audience analysis than what has been mentioned thus far, especially for persuasive speeches. This further audience is treated in Chapter 11.

● ACTIVITY

Choosing Topics for a Class Speech
The class will divide into several small groups of from five to seven members each. Each group will discuss speech topics that the class would be interested in hearing about. Five topics will be chosen by each group and presented to the class for general discussion. A master list of all accepted suggestions will be prepared and distributed to each student. Keep this list in your speech notebook and refer to it for ideas when selecting a speech topic.

Select Your General Speech Purpose

The general purposes for which speeches are given fall into a fairly small number of categories:

Speeches to Inform   Here your general purpose is to teach your listeners new information. You want them to know more about your topic after your speech than they did before.

Speeches to Persuade   Persuasive speeches are designed to intensify or change listeners' attitudes, beliefs, or behavior patterns.

Speeches to Entertain   Speeches to entertain are given simply for the enjoyment and relaxation of the listeners. They are frequently delivered as after-dinner speeches.

Speeches of Introduction   These are usually brief speeches for the purpose of giving an audience background information on a main speaker they are about to hear.

Speeches of Welcome   These are given when a new person joins a company, a club, or a fraternity, or when a dignitary visits a city or town for the first time. Their purpose is to make the newcomer feel part of the group he or she is joining.

Speeches of Presentation and Acceptance   Here the purpose is to highlight the presentation or acceptance of an award or gift to a deserving individual or organization.

In addition, speeches are given to dedicate buildings, to honor graduates from school, to eulogize those who have died, to say farewell when someone is moving, to demonstrate a product, to motivate groups to perform and achieve, and to inspire an audience.

The two primary speech purposes are to inform and to persuade. Chapter 10 treats the informative speech in detail, and Chapter 11 deals with speeches to persuade. Many of the other types of speeches are covered in Chapter 12. You may want to look ahead to these chapters as you decide on your general purpose for your first speech.

As you look back at the list of general topics on page 184, notice that you can give several types of speeches on the same topic. The topic of "space" for example could become a speech whose purpose would be to persuade or to inform. You could design persuasive speeches on the Challenger disaster, on the costs of the United States space program, or on what parts of space we should explore next. Informative speeches on the "space" topic could include a comparison

TEACH

● **LINKS TO PAST LEARNING**

Knowing the difference between informative messages and persuasive messages is an important skill. Ask students to recall ads for nonprescription drugs that they have heard on the radio or seen on television. Discuss with them how they were able to tell which ad informed them about the particular drug and which ad tried to persuade them to purchase the drug.

● **ASSESSMENT STRATEGY**

You could tape the speeches from the 15-Second Skill Opportunity about drug testing and play them back to the class. Ask students to evaluate each in terms of how effectively it persuaded the audience.

● **LEARNING STYLES**

Cooperative Learning
Assign small groups one of the following general-purpose categories: informing, persuading, entertaining. Then assign three broad topics from the list on page 184. Have each group organize each broad topic into specific topics. Compile a class list for each of the three categories. Students could place their class list in their portfolios and use it as a general reference list.

● **SKILL DEVELOPMENT**

15-Second Skill Opportunity
Ask students to think of how they would respond to the following: Drug testing should never be allowed in the workplace. Have them state their opinion about the statement in 15 seconds.

---

of the United States' and the former Soviet Union's space technologies, how solid rocket fuel works, or how a black hole is formed. If you want to teach your listeners more than they already know about some aspect of space, you choose the general purpose of informing. If you want to have your audience adopt certain attitudes, or take some action connected with some space topic, you choose a persuasive purpose. The topic of "vacations" can also be used with more than one speech purpose. If you wish to convince your audience to choose a certain country for their next vacation, your purpose is one of persuading. If you simply want to give them helpful hints about how to pack efficiently for a vacation trip, your purpose is to inform. If you hope to amuse them with the story of your vacation on which everything went wrong, your purpose is to entertain. Most topics lend themselves to at least the three general purposes of informing, persuading, or entertaining.

Frequently in speech class, your teacher will assign a general speech purpose and leave the choice of speech topic up to you. When that happens, you move right from selecting your general topic to focusing on your specific purpose.

Focus on Your Specific Purpose

Once you know your general topic and general speech purpose, you are ready to focus on the specific purpose for your speech. The **specific purpose** is precisely what you want your listeners to know, think, believe, or do as a result of hearing your speech. Imagine that you have selected the general topic of "Airplanes," and your general purpose is to inform. Now ask yourself, "About what specific aspect of airplanes do I want to inform my audience?" Write your answer in a single sentence (called your **purpose sentence**). Here are several possibilities:

- The purpose of this speech is to inform the listeners about the safety of commercial airline travel.
- The purpose of this speech is to inform the audience about the history of commercial aviation.
- The purpose of this speech is to tell the listeners about my most memorable airplane ride.
- The purpose of this speech is to compare and contrast six different styles of commercial aircraft.

Notice that each of these purpose sentences states a specific idea about which a person might wish to speak. A purpose sentence such as "To inform my audience about airplanes" is useless. It is not a sentence. But more important, it shows that the speaker does not have a specific purpose in mind—only a general topic area.

TEACH

● **CURRICULAR CONNECTIONS**

History
Students could collect newspaper and newsmagazines articles with historical background. Students could evaluate each article to determine whether it is specific enough for use in a classroom speech. Students could compile their articles in a classroom folder for future use.

● **SKILL DEVELOPMENT**

Main Idea
Ask each student to choose a topic, select a general purpose for the speech, and write a statement of purpose.

● **LEARNING STYLES**

Limited English Proficiency
Students with limited proficiency in English could be paired with other students to work on developing purpose sentences. They might work with the following topics: music, sports, holidays, television. While working with a partner, the students with limited proficiency in English could create one purpose sentence for each of the four topics.

This ranger's specific purpose is to inform the tour group about a park or preserve.

As you go about focusing on a specific purpose, keep in mind the time available for your speech. Some topics are too broad for a short speech. For example, you could not do justice to a topic such as "The World's Major Customs" in a five-minute speech, since you would have time for only a few sentences about each custom. Without time to include more interesting details you would not be informing your listeners of anything they did not already know. Sometimes one part of a broad topic fits better within the allotted time. For example, a subject such as "Major Customs of the Japanese Farmer" could be better covered in five minutes than the topic dealing with all the world's major customs. As you attempt to focus on and narrow your speech topics, you will find it helpful to browse through magazines and newspapers for current subjects that could fit within your time limits. Here is a sample of current topics that might prove narrow enough for a short classroom speech:

The Problems of Commercial Airlines

How to Enjoy the Outdoors

Different Views of Music: Pop, Rock, Western, Jazz

How My Part-time Job Has Helped Me

Are High School Sports Too Competitive?

How to Do Découpage

How High School Students Can Become Politically Involved

TEACH

SUBSTITUTE TEACHER TIP

Have students use one of their purpose sentences and prepare a one-minute speech on that topic. Students should use the guidelines for setting time limits that are discussed on this page. Call on students to present their speeches to the class.

● **SKILL DEVELOPMENT**

Main Idea
Have students choose topics from the list on this page and write purpose sentences for both informative and persuasive speeches on these topics. Discuss students' purpose sentences.

● **RETEACHING**

Students could work in small groups to create an informative poster for speech class titled "Focusing on Your Topic." The posters should focus on the main ideas covered in this section: the process involved in focusing on a topic, analyzing the audience, and knowing the time frame. Posters should be illustrated and could have a cartoon-look to them.

---

190   CHAPTER 7   Preparing Your Speech

What It Means to Be the Principal's Daughter
The Thrill of Water Skiing
Learning How to Cross-country Ski
Solar Energy Versus Atomic Power
Should the United States Institute Socialized Medicine?
The Confidentiality of News Reporters' Sources Must Be Assured
Do Americans Watch Too Much TV?
The Horror of War: Can Our Generation Avoid It?
How It Feels to Be Stereotyped
All Hail to the Free Enterprise System!
The Day-to-day Life of a Bank Teller
Is There a Cure for Cancer?
Why I Hope to Become an Airline Flight Attendant
Playing the Stock Market: Legalized Gambling?
What Will the Space Program Cost in the Future?

In class, your teacher will usually set the limits for your speeches. Outside of the classroom, you should always inquire of anyone inviting you to speak: "How long do you wish me to talk?" Once you know the time limit, you can narrow your topic to fit within that limit. Some speakers make the mistake of deciding first how much they want to say, then trying to cram it all, somehow, into a very limited amount of time. This backwards process is much like trying to put toothpaste back into the tube—it's a very frustrating experience. If the time you have available is not sufficient for you to cover a complete topic, choose the most fascinating portion of that topic, which you can cover nicely in the allotted time. In addition, your audience will not come away feeling overloaded with information.

● **ACTIVITY**

Narrowing Your Topic
Choose three topics from the list of speeches on pages 189 to 190. Study each carefully to be certain that it is narrow enough for a two- or three-minute speech on the topic. If a topic is not narrow enough, narrow it further. For each topic, write a specific purpose statement that could be used to introduce a speech on the topic.

TEACH

● **MOTIVATION**

Ask students what they would do to find out about the following: the leading home run hitter in major league baseball, the coldest day on record in their community, the date of birth of the President of the United States. Record students' responses on the board. Point out to students that to find this information they had to research.

> *Knowledge is of two kinds. We know a subject ourselves, or we know where we can find information upon it.*
> —Samuel Johnson

● RESEARCHING YOUR TOPIC

Once you have settled on a topic that is right for you, for your audience, and for the occasion, you need to begin your research. You begin by taking stock of what you already know about your topic, then move to the library and other outside sources of information to complete your research.

Start with What You Already Know

The best way to begin organizing your thoughts is to take stock of what you already know about your topic. For a few speeches—"My Exciting Vacation Last Summer," for example—you will find you already have 90 percent of the information you need to interest and inform your audience. For more meaningful speeches, taking stock of what you already know will only scratch the surface of the total amount of information needed. If you find your topic demands a minimum of research, you may want to outline your speech before doing your research (see pages 205–214 on outlining). However, if you know very little about your topic, you must usually do some preliminary research before you can even begin an outline. Then the research and outlining can be completed together.

At least some research is necessary for nearly every topic to assure the listeners that the speaker has studied the topic. No one is credited with being the only authority on a given topic; even noted scientists and Presidents of the United States regularly use examples, statistics, and the opinions of the other people to support their own ideas in their speeches. For example, such a personalized speech as "My Exciting Vacation Last Summer" can be spiced up with statistics noting how many visitors passed through the area you saw or a reference to the time the Queen of England visited the same place. Adding details such as these also helps establish a vivid context for your topic.

Know What You Are Researching

Whether the purpose of your speech is to provide information or to persuade your audience to adopt new views, what you are looking for in your research is **support** for the various statements you will be making in your speech. Support is needed mainly to prove the accuracy of your statements, but it can also be used to illustrate points and make them more interesting. Audiences are accustomed to listening for distinct kinds of support. Among the most common types are facts, statistics, testimony, narrative, examples, and comparisons.

TEACH

● **CURRICULAR CONNECTIONS**

Language Arts
Ask students to determine what sources they would use to substantiate the three facts listed on this page.

● **SKILL DEVELOPMENT**

Critical Thinking
Have students listen to a newscast on the radio or on television. Have them determine which items in the newscast were facts and which were opinions. Ask students to describe the difference between facts and opinions. Students should explain why facts offer the strongest form of support.

Main Idea
Have students select an informative speech from the magazine *Vital Speeches* or from other sources. Have them analyze how well the speaker uses support for the various statements made in the speech.

---

192   CHAPTER 7 Preparing Your Speech

Facts, statistics, and testimony are among the forms of support that enhance a speaker's credibility.

For backing up the accuracy of your statements, facts offer the strongest form of support. A **fact** is an event or a truth that is known to exist or has been observed. A fact is very difficult to contradict or refute, especially if it has been witnessed by a large number of people. Here are examples of facts:

Beethoven's Ninth Symphony was written when the composer was totally deaf.
The population of the U.S. is over 250 million.
Gertrude Ederle was the first woman to swim the English Channel.

Notice that a fact is always something that has occurred in the past or is presently occurring. No future event can be used as a fact, since something could happen to cancel or alter it.

Statistics are a second useful form of support for accuracy of statements. **Statistics** are collections of facts stated in numerical terms. They can be used to present facts in percentages, rank order, and averages.

TEACH

● **ASSESSMENT STRATEGY**

You could tape the informative speeches and play them back to the class. Ask students to evaluate each in terms of how effectively the support materials were used.

● **EXTENSION**

Ask students to find a speech in which statistics are used. Have them evaluate the statistics in terms of their accuracy and fairness. If appropriate, students could suggest ways in which the use of statistics in the speech could have been improved.

● **SKILL DEVELOPMENT**

Main Idea
Have students support the following statements with facts, examples, or statistics. Have them list the support materials, with sources, on note cards: (a) Scientists are taking enormous strides in combating cancer. (b) Genetic engineering is an increasingly important science. (c) The population of the United States has grown considerably in the past 50 years.

● **SKILL APPLICATION**

Citizens Speak Out
Students could choose a topic and write an informative speech. They should use each of the following support materials: facts, statistics, and testimony. Call on students to present their speech to the class.

The following are examples of statistics:

Roughly 52 percent of the world's population is female, and 48 percent is male.

Americans spend $360 billion a year, or 10.6 percent of our gross national product, for health care. This is more than $1,500 for every man, woman, and child in the country. According to some experts, we may be spending 14 percent of the G.N.P. by the year 2000.

Another form of support, **testimony,** is the quoting or restating of another person's opinion to support a point. Often the person quoted is a recognized expert in the field. Here is an example of testimony:

As Helen Keller once wrote, "No barrier of the sense shuts me out from the sweet, gracious discourse of my book friends. They talk to me without embarrassment or awkwardness."

Naturally, testimony can consist of quotations of various lengths. In one of his own speeches, Senator Edward Kennedy used a longer example of testimony by quoting from a speech that had been given at an earlier time by his brother Robert:

A speech he made to the young people of South Africa...sums it up best..."Some believe there is nothing one man or one woman can do against the enormous array of the world's ills. Yet, many of the world's great movements, of thought and action, have flowed from the work of a single man. A young monk began the Protestant Reformation, a young general extended an empire from Macedonia to the borders of the earth, and a young woman reclaimed the territory of France. It was a young Italian explorer who discovered the New World, and the 32-year-old Thomas Jefferson who proclaimed that all men are created equal.

"These men moved the world, and so can we all. Few will have the greatness to bend history itself, but each of us can work to change a small portion of events, and in the total of all those acts will be written the history of this generation..."

Testimony is not as strong a form of support for accuracy as facts are since testimony is merely opinion. Even when a quoted source is considered an expert, that expert can make a mistake. However, testimony is frequently very useful, especially if you think your audience is likely to respect the views of the person quoted.

Narrative is supporting material in the form of a story, either real or imaginary. Besides being enjoyable and interesting, narratives are often used in a speech to help make a point that has already been or will soon be supported by facts or statistics. Here is an example of a brief

TEACH

● **EXTENSION**

Have students watch a world news television program in which a commentary is usually included. Students should analyze the commentary and the types of supports used for substantiation purposes. Ask students to count the number of times each of the following categories of supports is used: facts, statistics, testimony, narrative, examples, and comparisons. Students should cite specific examples of each type of support.

● **ASSESSMENT STRATEGY**

Hold a class discussion to determine the importance of the supports in the television broadcast that were cited in the Extension suggestion.

● **SKILL DEVELOPMENT**

Main Idea
Ask students to go to the library and find an example of a narrative, anecdote, fact, or quotation that they would find interesting in a speech. Each student should explain how he or she would use the item in a speech.

CHAPTER 7 Preparing Your Speech

story that might be told by a speaker who wishes to talk about dissatisfaction:

> A story is told of Ali Hafed who sold his farm and set out in search of a diamond mine. He searched over the entire world without success and finally died in despair. Meantime the man who had purchased his farm spotted a glittering object in his creekbed one day and soon became the owner of one of the world's richest diamond mines.

Examples are specific instances or occurrences of a situation or principle you are attempting to describe. Examples may be stated in the form of facts, statistics, testimony, or narrative. Thus, examples are general kinds of support that may include any one of several other forms. Three examples are used to support the following sentence:

> Some of this century's most noted speakers have been American presidents. Woodrow Wilson, Franklin D. Roosevelt, and John F. Kennedy are generally considered to have been excellent public speakers.

Examples may sometimes be used effectively to intensify or personalize your ideas. Notice how you are touched by this example of Ralph: "There are many hungry families in our community who could benefit from food donations. Let me tell you about Ralph. Ralph is four years old. He has big brown eyes and a mop of black hair and an empty belly. In all his four years on this earth, Ralph has never once enjoyed three square meals in a single day."

Comparisons involve the equating of essentially unlike ideas or phrases. They highlight the similarities that exist between basically dissimilar situations. Like examples, comparisons may take different forms. They may include facts, statistics, testimony, or narrative. They may also include the speaker's own opinions if the opinions seem to offer a useful means of illustrating the views being presented. The following is an example of a comparison based on opinion:

> The way some people shop at a sale reminds me of a swarm of bees clustered around a hive, each seemingly unaware of all the others crowded about.

After preliminary research, you can begin to build an outline. As you develop main heads and subheads (see page 209 for a discussion of outlining) you will begin to recognize what forms of support you need. This will help you as you proceed with more detailed research. For example, in a speech on "Land Pollution: Desecrating Our Landscape," a main head might read "How Efficient Have We Become at Littering?"

● CURRICULAR CONNECTIONS

Language Arts
Ask students to work in pairs and choose one of the topics on pages 189-190. Have them work together to develop main heads and subheads for the topic. Discuss the heads with the students.

● LEARNING STYLES

Beyond the Classroom
Ask the school librarian to speak to the students about how to use library resources. The librarian might suggest approaches students could use in starting their research and sources that would be the most helpful to them. Encourage students to ask questions of the librarian.

Obviously you will need to find an example or some statistics to answer this question. The answer might be:

> Fifty years ago the average American threw away every day a little over two-and-one-half pounds of garbage. Today each of us will create six pounds of trash....

Get to Know Your Library

When a teacher tells a class to "go to the library," many students feel like rats dropped in a maze. They wander around aimlessly, hoping to stumble over a piece of information they are looking for, but with little or no idea how to find the trail that will lead them to it. Once you know the key starting points, however, you can make the library work for you, instead of feeling lost in it.

The computerized location finder holds the master key to locating library information. Typically it is located in the library's entry lobby and consists of a computer screen and a keyboard with which you can determine whether the library houses the particular book you want. Larger libraries will often have several location finders available, either in the lobby or, in some cases, scattered throughout the library. If you are not familiar with using the location finder, ask a librarian to give you a brief lesson on how it is used.

Once you know the key starting points, the library can be a rich source of information.

TEACH

● **SKILL DEVELOPMENT**

Main Idea
Reinforce library skills through assignments that involve library searches to locate specific information. Possible topics for searches include nuclear energy, earthquake predictions, and business mergers and takeovers.

● **LEARNING STYLES**

Technology Tools
Provide students with opportunities to learn, or to review, the use of electronic terminals in finding books.

Technology Tools
Many students are familiar with encyclopedias on CD ROM. If possible, give students the opportunity to use this tool in their research.

CHAPTER 7 Preparing Your Speech

Generally, you begin by looking for the last name of the author or the first significant word in the title of a work. Sometimes, however, you may be interested in a subject but are not familiar with specific authors or titles. In that case, you scroll the listings by subject instead of by author or title. Once you have found what you are looking for, write down the catalogue number with which you can then determine whether the work you want is currently in the library.

Periodicals may also be displayed on the location finder. If you are looking for a recent issue of a periodical, you can usually find it displayed on open shelves in the library's periodicals room. In certain libraries, if you want an issue from a past year, the call number on the screen will direct you to the shelves where bound copies of older periodicals are kept.

But suppose you are researching for a speech dealing with American TV viewing habits. You need very specific information such as the number of TV sets purchased each year in the United States, or the kinds of programs most commonly watched. Perhaps your library's location finder contains few book or periodical titles that can help you. Or maybe you need to know how many colleges there are in the United States, or when the next total eclipse of the sun is going to occur. You might spend hours searching through individual books and periodicals and still not find such specific information. Now is the time to discover the wealth of information that is available to you through the library's **reference section.** The reference section contains encyclopedias, yearbooks, atlases, indexes, dictionaries, and biographical aids. Here are a few examples of the kind of information you can obtain from them:

Encyclopedias You may have one of the general encyclopedias in your home, such as the *Encyclopedia Americana* or the *Encyclopaedia Britannica*. Many libraries have these as well as several other general encyclopedias which cover all branches of knowledge. In addition, many libraries contain specialized encyclopedias dealing with certain fields, such as the *McGraw-Hill Encyclopedia of Science and Technology,* the *Encyclopedia of Psychology,* the *Encyclopedia of Education,* the *Encyclopedia of Religion and Ethics,* and *Grzimek's Animal Life Encyclopedia,* among others.

Yearbooks These are published annually and contain a tremendous amount of very detailed and concise information on a wide range of subjects. The *Facts on File Yearbook,* for instance, digests all the major national and international news events that occurred in a given year. The *World Almanac and Book of Facts* lists everything from the names of Nobel Prize winners since 1901 to sports records of college and pro teams. If you are interested in statistical information about the social, economic, and political aspects of life in the United States, you can discover such facts as the United States birth and death rates and median family income, broken down by state.

APPLY

● **LINKS TO PAST LEARNING**

Discuss with students the companies that they consider to be "good." Ask students to identify television commercials or advertisements in print media that project images of companies that are caring, patriotic, reliable, or honest. Discuss ways in which a public relations specialist might advance a positive image for a company.

● **LEARNING STYLES**

Beyond the Classroom
Invite a public relations specialist to speak to your class. Encourage students to ask questions of the specialist after the presentation. Students might have some questions prepared in advance.

CAREER CLOSE-UP

Public Relations Specialist

Many companies and public agencies employ public relations specialists to project a positive image of their organizations. To achieve this goal, "PR" specialists inform the public by means of speeches, interviews, and press releases. A PR person from a manufacturing company might write a press release on a new product the company has invented. An oil company PR person might give a talk on the importance of oil in industry. A candidate for a public relations position needs a college degree in liberal arts, public relations, or business administration.

Many of a PR specialist's responsibilities involve public speaking. Most public relations specialists agree that the key to a successful talk lies in its careful preparation. To begin their planning, specialists research the background of each speech and collect the evidence that will support their conclusions. They then select the pattern of speech organization that will best suit their need to convey information and be interesting to their audience. Once the speech has been organized, specialists repeatedly rehearse their talk so that their delivery will be smooth and powerful.

Public relations specialists perform an essential role by providing the connecting link between organizations and the public. Because their highly developed speaking skills enable them to portray how an organization is helping people, they serve not only the concerns they represent, but also the public welfare. In addition, PR specialists help ensure that their companies and agencies remain responsive by keeping them informed about the public's needs and interests.

The PR specialist projects a positive image of an organization through public speaking, interviews, and press releases.

TEACH

AMAZING FACTS!
The first school library in America was established in 1638 at Harvard University.

● **EXTENSION**

Ask students to compare finding books in the library by using card-catalogue cards with finding them by using an electronic terminal. Discuss with students the advantages and disadvantages of each.

● **SKILL DEVELOPMENT**

Research
Have students choose a topic. Then have them use the library card catalogue or the electronic terminal to find a list of books that could be appropriate to that topic.

CHAPTER 7 Preparing Your Speech

In beginning library research, you look up the last name of the author, a key word in the title, or a specific subject.

Biographical Aids The reference section also contains collections of biographical sketches of noted persons, both living and dead. *Who's Who in America, Who's Who of American Women, International Who's Who,* and the *Dictionary of American Biography* are several of the leading sources of biographical information about famous individuals. *Biography Index,* published four times each year, indexes biographical material that has appeared in certain books and periodicals. It is especially helpful if you need information about important living people.

Atlases Whenever geography is an important aspect of your speech topic, you will want to check an atlas. In addition to the usual maps of the world and each state in the United States, atlases provide you with important information about such matters as the population, politics, climate, energy, and food resources of the various parts of our world and even treat the universe beyond. Two of the best known atlases are *Times Atlas of the World, Comprehensive Edition,* and the *Rand McNally Cosmopolitan World Atlas.*

Periodical Indexes Once you have a general notion of the direction in which you wish to go with your topic, you will find more detailed discussions of it in periodicals, newspapers, and books. Several handy reference works list articles in periodicals under general subject headings. The *Readers' Guide to Periodical Literature* lists articles in current magazines, such as *Newsweek, Reader's Digest, Time,* and *U.S*

● CURRICULAR CONNECTIONS

Language Arts
Ask that each student write a note card paraphrasing a central idea from an article in a national magazine. Then have each student exchange cards with a classmate and identify the other student's main point.

● LEARNING STYLES

Cooperative Learning
Organize the class into research teams and give them a list of questions asking for specific facts to be found in a library "scavenger hunt." Develop the list from references such as encyclopedias, almanacs, and dictionaries. The hunt should involve a wide range of topics covered in a number of sources. The team that returns with the most answers in the shortest time will be declared winner.

● SKILL DEVELOPMENT

Research
Take students to the classroom or community library. To assist students with the use of biographical aids, ask them to choose a personality that they admire. Have them look through reference books such as *Who's Who in America, Current Biography,* and *Dictionary of American Biography* to find information about the person they chose. Ask volunteers to present the information they found to the class.

Researching Your Topic 199

News & World Report. If your topic deals with education, *Education Digest* lists articles that have appeared in education journals. The *International Directory of Little Magazines and Small Presses* lists lesser-known publications, such as literary magazines and scholarly journals that cover a wide variety of topics.

Feel free to browse in the periodical section of your library. Looking at pictures in magazines can stimulate your interest in topics you might not have considered otherwise. Regular reading, especially of magazines dealing with current events and issues, can provide you with a constant source of information on numerous topics. Though you can't be expected to read a dozen magazines every month, becoming familiar with one or two of them and reading them regularly will keep you abreast of current events and serve as a storehouse of support information whenever you need to deliver a speech. Any of the magazines in the list below could be used for this purpose:

Atlantic Monthly	*National Geographic*
Business Week	*National Wildlife*
Byte	*Natural History*
Commonweal	*Negro History Bulletin*
Creative Computing	*New Republic*
Discover	*Newsweek*
Ebony	*Popular Photography*
Field and Stream	*Popular Science*
Fortune	*Scientific American*
Harper's Magazine	*Smithsonian*
Motor Trend	*Time*
The Nation	*U.S. News & World Report*

Stories in newspapers are additional sources of information. Most major news stories are indexed in *The New York Times Index.* Even if your library does not store back copies of *The New York Times,* the stories in that newspaper were probably carried in other major metropolitan newspapers on the same dates as those indicated in *The New York Times Index.*

Computerized Databases In addition to the card catalogue and the reference section, many libraries have several other special resources to help you find information for your speeches. One of these is known as **computerized research services.** This service allows you to find

TEACH

AMAZING FACTS!
As of 1994, the total number of daily newspapers published in the United States was 1,556.

● **EXTENSION**

Have students bring in magazines that they or their households get or read on a regular basis. Students might combine these magazines in a table display. Ask students to determine which of the magazines would be useful in providing support information for speeches. Organize a file to collect activities by topic.

● **SKILL DEVELOPMENT**

Research
Have students find major news stories in *The New York Times Index* for a given date. Have them find out how many of those stories appeared in the metropolitan newspaper that they read.

CHAPTER 7 Preparing Your Speech

obscure or highly specialized information rapidly through the use of computers. What might take hours to find by searching through a number of periodical indexes, for example, can be located in minutes by using computerized indexes known as **databases.** If your library has computerized research services available, you may want to make use of such databases as *Magazine Index, National Newspaper Index, ERIC* (Educational Resources Information Center), *Social Science Citation Index,* and *ASI* (American Statistics Index).

Another special library resource is the documents section. This section contains bulletins and pamphlets published by state and national governments, religious institutions, business organizations, and universities. You may want to check this section of the library for information on certain topics.

Speakers can also find quotations to support their ideas in sources such as *Bartlett's Familiar Quotations, Brewer's Dictionary of Phrase and Fable, Granger's Index to Poetry,* and the *Oxford Dictionary of Quotations.*

Finally, do not forget about reference librarians. Their job is to help you locate materials you need. If you have difficulty, do not be embarrassed to ask for help.

Find Other Sources of Support

Although the library will often provide you with much of the information you need for a speech, do not overlook other valuable sources of information. Interviews with people knowledgeable about your topic can prove very helpful. If your topic concerns business, why not interview a teacher in the business department of your school or a local business leader? If your speech deals with anatomy, talk to a biologist or a physician. You may want to reread the section on interviewing on pages 104–111 in Chapter 4.

Other frequently overlooked sources of support for speeches are television and radio—particularly news programs. Since the main purpose of local and network news teams is to gather and sort out facts and testimony, their reports are a gold mine of current information with which to support your ideas. Keep up with world and local news and jot down the date of the program as well as the source of the information whenever you hear an item that might prove useful. Since newspapers are available for reading at any time, they possess an advantage over television and radio as sources of supporting materials. If you happen to miss a particular news broadcast, you often fail to obtain the information later. A newspaper can be retrieved and read months after the event has occurred.

APPLY

● **EXTENSION**

Have students choose a topic in which they are very interested. Students should research the topic keeping in mind the six basic types of supports for statements they might be making. For each statement of opinion to be included in their speech, have students try to provide as many supports as possible. Then, students should list these supports next to relevant statements during research.

● **SKILL DEVELOPMENT**

Research
Ask students to write note cards containing direct quotations. Explain that the quotation must be verbatim, punctuated as in the original, and that the source must be clearly identified by title, author, call number, and page number.

● **SKILL APPLICATION**

Interviews
Ask students to think of a topic for which they could interview an expert. Have students identify the person and his or her background. Then ask students to prepare a list of questions that they could ask the expert in a five-minute interview. After students interview the expert, evaluate the interviews in a class discussion.

Speaking IN ACTION

Researching through Interviews

Situation
For your next speech, plan to interview someone who has expert knowledge about your topic. If your speech will deal with medicine, you might interview a physician or a nurse; if your subject is crime, interview a detective or patrolman at the local police department; if it's education reform, talk with your school principal. By obtaining relevant information face-to-face from a knowledgeable person, you add greatly to your speech's impact.

Preparation
You need to decide which expert is most likely to give you the information you're looking for. Then call an individual in that field to arrange for the interview appointment. Whether you talk directly to the person, or a receptionist, explain that you are fulfilling an assignment for your speech class and that you need only five minutes' time. Be sure to leave yourself enough space before the interview for ample preparation.

Next you will want to write down just two to four questions that will give you the essential information to support an important part of your speech. Remember, you had asked for only five minutes, and you will want your interviewee to do most of the talking, so keep your questions to a minimum. Arrange the questions in the order most likely to provide the clearest pattern of information. Often, for example, you may want to open with a question about your interviewee's background and experience with your speech topic.

You also need to plan exactly how you intend to record the information your source provides. In every case you will want to take notes, and perhaps also use a tape recorder. If you decide not to record, then your notes will need to be more complete to assure that you can recall all the pertinent information. The obvious *advantage* of using a tape recorder is that you will have one hundred percent of the interview available for later recall. The biggest *problem* with taping is its tendency to make many interviewees nervous. If you wish to record, be certain you ask the interviewee's permission in advance.

Directing the Interview
Arrive early for the interview, in businesslike dress. Introduce yourself with a firm handshake, then open the interview promptly. Remind your interviewee of the purpose of the interview, and, if you are familiar with and respect the person's accomplishments, say so. A genuine compliment can get the interview off to a smooth and relaxed start. Throughout, use your prepared questions as your main agenda, but if the interviewee brings up an interesting point that had not occurred to you, be willing to pursue it briefly. Be alert to ask short follow-up questions if you do not understand an answer, but be careful not to go over your five-minute time limit. Of course, if the interviewee initiates a longer discussion than you had planned, listen politely and carefully. Be sure to express your thanks before leaving.

In your speech, be certain to mention the name, position, and any special knowledge, experience, or skills your source possesses before relating the information from the interview.

TEACH

PORTFOLIO PRODUCT

Ask students to choose a topic and find nonlibrary sources of support for it. These sources might include correspondence with experts, notes from radio or television broadcasts, interviews, or informal surveys. Students might include these sources in their portfolios.

● LEARNING STYLES

Cooperative Learning

Have students form small groups to develop an informal survey that they will use with friends and other classmates. Students should develop the survey about a school issue that they find interesting or important. Ask each group to develop questions for the survey and then conduct the survey. Have students present their survey and results to the class. Students might include their surveys in their portfolios.

● SKILL DEVELOPMENT

Research

For one week, have students collect information from television broadcasts and newspapers that could be used as support for a variety of speech topics. Students might include this information in their portfolios.

CHAPTER 7 Preparing Your Speech

By interviewing a professional, this student is able to incorporate into his speech the most current information available about a particular field.

Taking your own informal survey of public opinion among friends or neighbors can prove an effective type of support for a speech, particularly when you speak on local issues. Audiences are impressed when a speaker is sufficiently enthusiastic about the issues to conduct such a survey; they enjoy hearing what people living in their own town think about a topic.

When you are speaking on a controversial topic, you can frequently write to special interest groups to obtain information to support one side of an issue. Of course, you need to realize that information sent you by such special interest groups is bound to be biased in favor of the particular position on the issue involved. You can also obtain a great deal of information from government agencies on a wide variety of topics ranging from farming to space. If you do not know where to write to obtain materials, contact your congressional representative's office. Writing away for such information naturally means that you have to start your speech preparation well in advance to allow time for the information to reach you.

Record Your Evidence

As you discover facts, statistics, testimony, and other forms of support for your speech, be sure to write them down. Even though you are not certain you will use a particular piece of evidence in your speech, record it and the source where you discovered it while it is before you

ETHICALLY SPEAKING

Crediting Your Sources

In spoken communication, as in written communication, you will sometimes express your own ideas and sometimes express the ideas of others. When you write a short story or describe a vacation, for example, you are creating a tale or communicating your observations and feelings about your own experience. When you give a report or gather evidence to help others make a decision, however, you usually need to rely on the ideas and information of other people. In these situations it is necessary to credit the people and sources you have used.

No doubt you have learned to prepare footnotes for direct quotations in your English papers. Is the same level of attention also necessary when you are *speaking* rather than *writing*? After all, what you say in a conversation or a meeting is not graded like your English paper. Ethically speaking, though, it is important to credit the people whose information and ideas contribute to your communication.

If you are talking with a group of friends about a movie you saw over the weekend, you may freely exchange your own views about what you liked or disliked, what you thought was convincing or contrived, and whether you would recommend the movie to others. But suppose you are speaking about a particular movie in a discussion group or reporting on it to your class. If you base what you say on newspaper or TV reviews of the movie, you need to mention the reviewers' names in connection with their opinions.

You owe it to your listeners, to your sources, and to your own integrity as an ethical communicator to clearly identify ideas you take from others.

As you do research, it is important to credit the sources whose ideas contribute to your communication.

APPLY

● **MOTIVATION**

Invite students to share stories they have heard about plagiarism. Or encourage discussion by relating how China and other nations have been accused of making unlicensed copies of protected software and video programs. Encourage students to think of the similarities between the plagiarism of ideas or content in written or spoken material and the piracy of technological material in the global marketplace.

● **SKILL DEVELOPMENT**

Creative Thinking
Ask students to remember the FBI warning that usually accompanies a video they rent. Discuss the need to protect the ownership of this property just as a homeowner or car owner would want to protect the property of home or car. Have students identify the penalties for theft of property. Have students think of creative and effective methods for protecting intellectual and technical property.

Research
Have students study and imitate the correct form for the citation of written sources as presented in text bibliographies. Students could write the proper source citation using this textbook as a reference. Pairs of students could exchange source citations and make corrections as required. Then have pairs of students credit the source of an idea or opinion while commenting about a recent movie or television program.

TEACH

● **RETEACHING**

Ask students to prepare a persuasive speech about whether books, compact discs, and movies should be censored. Students should research their topic, and their speeches should include support material. Ask students to present their speeches. Have the rest of the class evaluate how well each speech used support materials.

● **SKILL DEVELOPMENT**

Research
Students could choose an interest that they have. For example, they might be interested in rock music, baseball, rollerblading, or mystery novels. Students could gather information and develop a file about their particular interest. They might record the information on note cards, such as the one on this page. Encourage students to record the source of the information on their cards. They could include the cards in their portfolios.

---

204 CHAPTER 7 Preparing Your Speech

Always take down more than you plan to use to avoid making ext trips to the library or rescheduling an interview.

It is best to establish a consistent system for recording speech ev dence. Most speakers prefer to take their notes on 3 × 5 index card recording only one item of information on each card. These can b arranged later in the best order for presentation and are easy to hand on the platform. When you discover an item of information you fe might be useful, first record a general heading for it at the top left-han corner of the card. In the center of the card place the quotation, exar ple, statistic, or fact. Sometimes the evidence may spill over to the bac of the card, or even to a second card. Finally, below the evidence, wri the source from which you obtained it. Take a moment to study th example of a note card, above.

Typing the cards you decide to use during delivery is useful, sinc it makes them easy to read on the platform. However, if your han writing is clear and legible, typing is not necessary.

Even when not preparing for a specific speech, you may find helpful to keep a general file of favorite topics for future use. You ca build a storehouse of information to support these topics by gatherin quotations, statistics, and other forms of evidence from books, mag zines, newspapers, television, or conversation. A student interested current events can usually spot information that may prove useful th next time a speech is needed.

A note card should contain a general heading for easy reference, the evidence itself, and the original source of this evidence.

Civil Rights

"Let us not seek to satisfy our thirst for freedom by drinking from the cup of bitterness and hatred. We must forever conduct our struggle on the high plane of dignity and discipline...."

Martin Luther King, Jr., from "I Have a Dream." (Speech given Aug. 28, 1963, Washington, D.C.)

TEACH

● **MOTIVATION**

Write the word *pattern* on the board. Ask students what that word means to them. Have them draw a pattern, and display the patterns on a bulletin board. Tell students that a pattern is a kind of arrangement. Tell them that this section will discuss patterns used in speeches.

● **ACTIVITY**

To complete the Activity on this page, have students work with the school librarian to learn how to use the *Reader's Guide to Periodical Literature*, specialized indexes, and vertical files. Work with students to provide suggestions and to check on their note taking.

● **LEARNING STYLES**

Audio Learning
Ask students to use the Speech Library and identify the chronological sequence of the speeches. Ask them to present these speeches to the class.

ACTIVITY

Using Reference Materials

Select a topic from any of the lists compiled earlier or choose a topic of your own that you believe listeners would be interested in hearing about. In your library, find at least five different sources of information that would provide you with supporting evidence for some aspect of your topic. Perform your research and collect information on 3 × 5 cards. Record your research information carefully and accurately. Be sure to ask your librarian for assistance in locating needed sources. Be prepared to submit your file cards to your teacher for checking.

● ORGANIZING AND OUTLINING YOUR SPEECH

As you go about researching your speech topic, you will also be deciding on an organizational pattern for your presentation. Though you are free to arrange your speech materials in any manner you choose, over the years certain methods of arrangement have proved effective for particular occasions and audiences. Your specific purpose will also have a great deal to do with the type of organizational pattern you select. Once your overall pattern has been selected, you are ready to write an outline on your topic.

Select a Pattern of Speech Organization

One common pattern for speeches is the **chronological pattern.** This arrangement proceeds from past to present to future; in other words, the speech develops in the same order that the events developed in time. One of the best known speeches using a chronological pattern is Abraham Lincoln's "Gettysburg Address." Notice how the first portion of the speech is about events that occurred in the past, the middle portion is about events of the present, and the last few sentences express Lincoln's hope for the future:

> Fourscore and seven years ago our fathers brought forth on this continent a new nation, conceived in liberty, and dedicated to the proposition that all men are created equal.
>
> Now we are engaged in a great civil war, testing whether that nation, or any nation so conceived and so dedicated, can long endure. We are met on a great battlefield of that war. We have come to dedi-

TEACH

> **SUBSTITUTE TEACHER TIP**
>
> Ask students to recall a recent vacation. Have them present a speech to the class in which they tell about the vacation, using a spatial organizational pattern.

● **SKILL DEVELOPMENT**

Outlining
Write the following outlines of speeches on the board and have students identify the organizational pattern used in each.

The Space Program
- Trial and error in the early years
- The golden sixties—a push for the moon
- The shuttle age
- The high frontier of tomorrow

Safety at Home
- Bathroom
    - Electrical shock
    - Falls
- Kitchen
    - Preventing burns
    - Electrical hazards

Arizona
- The cities
- The desert
- The mountains

15-Second Skill Opportunity
Ask students to explain their political orientation toward large or small government, using a topical organizational pattern. Have students present the first 15 seconds of their speech.

---

206 CHAPTER 7 Preparing Your Speech

cate a portion of that field as a final resting place for those who here gave their lives that that nation might live. It is altogether fitting and proper that we should do this.

But, in a larger sense, we cannot dedicate—we cannot consecrate—we cannot hallow—this ground. The brave men, living and dead, who struggled here, have consecrated it far above our poor power to add or detract. The world will little note nor long remember what we say here, but it can never forget what they did here. It is for us, the living, rather, to be dedicated here to the unfinished work which they who have fought here have thus far so nobly advanced. It is rather for us to be here dedicated to the great task remaining before us—that from these honored dead we take increased devotion to that cause for which they gave the last full measure of devotion; that we here highly resolve that these dead shall not have died in vain; that this nation, under God, shall have a new birth of freedom; and that government of the people, by the people, for the people, shall not perish from the earth.

Of course a speech in chronological order need not always contain all three time periods: past, present, and future. The essential feature of this pattern is that the ideas or events in the speech move forward according to a time sequence.

When the parts of a speech are tied together by space arrangements rather than by time sequence, the organizational pattern is called **spatial.** It is useful in speeches in which the speaker describes a place for the audience. If you wish to give a speech on "My Vacation Trip to Disney World," you might choose a spatial pattern of organization in which the four major sections of the speech would be about *Frontierland, Tomorrowland, Fantasyland,* and *Adventureland.* You would pinpoint the location of each "land" in the overall Disney World layout and describe the features of each section of the park.

A third organizational pattern, called **topical,** is also frequently used. This is a broadly defined pattern in which the subject is broken down into its natural parts. An example would be a speech about "The United States Congress" divided into Senate and House, then subdivided into Democrats and Republicans. A speech on "Modern Modes of Travel" might contain three divisions: monorail, wide-bodied jet, and space shuttle. A speech on "My High School Career" could be divided into sections about the naive freshman, the know-it-all sophomore, the know-nothing junior, and the mature senior. A speech topic may often be divided topically in several different ways. As long as the divisions represent natural parts of the whole topic, the organizational pattern is called topical.

The **problem-solution pattern** is still another pattern used in speeches. Here the speaker devotes roughly the first half of the speech to describing a problem that exists, or is about to occur, and the second

ENRICHMENT

Have students create an advertising campaign for imaginary products using Monroe's Motivated Sequence. Students will judge the effectiveness of the campaigns by "buying" only 25 percent of the products offered. For example, if 20 class members speak, at the end of all the presentations each student in the audience may "purchase" only 5 items. Students could tally the results to determine the most popular items.

ASSESSMENT STRATEGY

Ask students to discuss possible reasons for the popularity of the products in Enrichment. Have them discuss the effectiveness of Monroe's Motivated Sequence and how variables (such as the product itself) might affect the outcome of this strategy.

TEACH

SUBSTITUTE TEACHER TIP

Ask students to choose an organizational pattern and a topic and to write a brief outline for a speech using that pattern. As a class, compare and discuss the outlines.

---

half developing one or more solutions. Presidential addresses on national television generally follow this format. If, for instance, the issue is the drug problem in our country, the President might spend the first half of the time proving how serious the problem is and the second half calling on the American people to help him to find solutions. Sometimes speakers misuse this organizational pattern by spending nearly the entire time discussing the problem and then barely mentioning the solution in the final sentences. It is best to devote approximately equal time to the problem and the solution.

Another pattern used especially by salespersons is called **Monroe's Motivated Sequence.** This pattern was originally suggested by Alan H. Monroe for use in persuasive speeches. It consists of five separate steps (see p. 208):

1. The Attention Step
2. The Need Step
3. The Satisfaction Step
4. The Visualization Step
5. The Action Step

The first step is an obvious one. Gaining the audience's attention is always the first task of any speaker. It is a step necessary in every type of speech situation. Once the listeners are paying close attention, the second step for the speaker is to show them that they have needs not being met the way things are at present. The third step for a speaker using Monroe's Motivated Sequence is to present the opinion or solution that will satisfy these unmet needs of the audience. In the fourth, or visualization, step, the speaker must help the listeners actually see the change that will occur if they adopt his or her views. The final step involves telling the listeners what action they must take to bring about the improvement the speaker has promised. Salespersons, as well as speakers trying to persuade an audience, often use the five steps of Monroe's Motivated Sequence to organize their presentations.

Another organizational pattern, used mainly for after-dinner speeches or entertaining, is called the **string-of-beads pattern.** This pattern consists of a series of stories, jokes, or anecdotes strung out like beads on a string and tied loosely to some weak central theme. The jokes or anecdotes themselves usually carry the main impact in this kind of speech, and the topic or theme is less important. The famous comedian Will Rogers often used the string-of-beads pattern when addressing his audiences. An advantage of this pattern for an after-dinner speaker is its flexibility. Should a speech run overtime, the speaker can easily dispense with several anecdotes without the audience's feeling the speech is unfinished. This pattern does not ordinarily work well, however, for other types of speaking.

TEACH

● **CURRICULAR CONNECTIONS**

Art
Ask students to make a cartoon that illustrates the five steps of Monroe's Motivated Sequence. Have them include their cartoons in their portfolios.

---

208 CHAPTER 7 Preparing Your Speech

Monroe's Motivated Sequence

Attention Step

Need Step

Satisfaction Step

Visualization Step

Action Step

208

Start Your Outline with a Purpose Sentence

A good outline is like a tree without its leaves. All the basics are present in the tree—the overall direction, the necessary support, the division into branches. Only springtime is needed to fill it out with leaves. Your speech outline also needs a basic purpose or direction, supporting materials, and appropriate subdivisions. When time for delivering the speech arrives, you will be ready to fill it out with the necessary words.

If your speech outline is to have any order about it, you must know clearly what your purpose is in making the speech. The best way to begin a clear speech outline is by writing at the top of your outline the purpose sentence you selected earlier. The purpose sentence, remember, states exactly what you hope to accomplish by giving the speech: what you hope your listeners will know, think, believe, or do as a result of hearing your speech. Imagine you wish to tell your listeners something about prisons. You could have a number of different general speech purposes in mind, resulting in some very different specific purpose sentences:

- The purpose of this speech is to inform my listeners about overcrowding in today's prisons.

- The purpose of this speech is to convince my listeners that certain kinds of criminals should serve their sentences at home.

- The purpose of this speech is to entertain my listeners by describing my "queasiness" the first day on my new paper route in the local prison.

Notice that each of these purpose sentences states a specific idea about which a person might wish to speak. A purpose sentence such as "To inform my audience about prisons" is useless. It is not a sentence. But more important, it shows that the speaker does not have a *specific purpose* in mind—only a general topic area. By the time you begin outlining, you must have a specific purpose in mind. The purpose sentence serves to guide you as you complete this outline.

Sometimes speech students think a purpose sentence is a key sentence phrased for use at the beginning of the speech. Though you may often express the same general idea at the start of your speech, the purpose sentence itself is a *written* sentence only meant to guide your outlining process. When a speaker states the purpose aloud to the listeners, it is usually reworded in a much more conversational style.

TEACH

● **SKILL APPLICATION**

Interviews
Ask students to use the qualifications for a job that they listed in Skill Application suggestion on page 209. Tell them to support each qualification with examples. Point out to students that the examples of qualifications serve as subheads.

● **LEARNING STYLES**

Limited English Proficiency
Have students with limited proficiency in English work with partners to develop main heads and subheads for a speech. Have the students choose a topic and then write two general items they want to say about the topic. Point out to them that the general items constitute the main heads of the speech. Then have them write two support statements for each of the main heads. Tell them that the support statements constitute the subheads of the speech.

● **SKILL DEVELOPMENT**

15-Second Skill Opportunity
Have students use the main head and the subheads in this section to prepare a short speech. Have them present it in 15 seconds.

210

CHAPTER 7 Preparing Your Speech

As you begin an effective speech outline, you will utilize first a purpose sentence, then main heads and subheads stated as complete sentences.

Develop Main Heads and Subheads

The major divisions of a speech outline are referred to as **main heads**. Ordinarily the fewer main divisions you make of your topic the better. Most speeches should only have two or three main heads, though there are exceptions. A topic with eight or nine main divisions, however, becomes too difficult for the audience to follow or remember and hard for the speaker to fit into the time limit. If it seems impossible to avoid dividing your topic into a large number of main heads, you should consider narrowing the scope of your topic or combining several heads into one.

Suppose you are outlining a speech on "School Vacations." Your purpose sentence could read: "The purpose of this speech is to persuade the audience that our school calendar should include another week of vacation." If this is the case, your main heads might be:

I. Vacations help us become better students.
II. Our school has one week less vacation time than schools in neighboring towns.
III. Our vacations should be the same as those of our friends in neighboring towns.

As shown in the example above, each main head should directly support the purpose sentence and be approximately equal in importance.

Subheads relate to main heads in the same manner that main heads relate to the purpose sentence. They subdivide the main head into parallel parts. Notice how the following subheads A, B, and C support the first main head in a speech titled "Skydiving":

I. Skydiving is safer than most people imagine.
   A. Only highly qualified personnel may serve as trainers.
   B. Extensive training is mandatory before a "live" jump.
   C. Chutes must be checked and rechecked before a jump.

All subheads under a given main head must be of approximately equal importance.

While it is possible to subdivide further the ideas of the outline under sub-subheads, this is not ordinarily done. Most of the subdivisions below the subheads are reserved for supporting details rather than concepts or ideas. Notice in the example on pages 212 and 213 how the level below the subheads consists primarily of supporting details (examples, statistics, narratives, comparisons).

Use Complete Sentences for Main Heads and Subheads

Main heads and subheads in speech outlines should be stated as complete sentences. Although experienced speaker sometimes use word or phrase outlines, full sentence outlines are best for beginning speakers. Writing down the basic ideas in complete thoughts forces you to think through the ideas and also helps set them in your memory. This does not mean, however, that the sentences should be long. Actually, you should strive to keep them as brief and simple as possible, as long as they are grammatically complete.

Once you get below the level of subheads, words or short phrases may be all you need in order to remember most of your supporting details. A simple reminder, such as "Narrative about dog" or "Statistics on population," will often be sufficient to remind you of the complete piece of evidence you wish to use.

Notice how the sentences and phrases in the sample outline on pages 212-214 show the relative importance of levels of ideas by the way they are arranged on the paper. As you can see, this is done in two ways. First, different letter and number designations are attached to different levels of ideas. Main heads have Roman numerals (I, II, III), subheads have capital letters (A, B, C), supporting details have Arabic numerals (1, 2, 3). Second, the outline shows you at a glance which ideas are more important and which are less important through the use of indentation. Main heads start near the left margin, with the various

TEACH

● **ASSESSMENT STRATEGY**

You might tape students' speeches about what to do in case of emergency as suggested in the Visual Learning activity. Play them back to the class. Ask students to evaluate each in terms of clearly including the three main sections of a speech.

● **SKILL DEVELOPMENT**

Main Idea
Have students choose a speech from the Speech Library or from *Vital Speeches* and identify the following elements of the speech: purpose sentence, introduction, body, and conclusion.

● **LEARNING STYLES**

Visual Learning
Students could prepare a speech in which they teach a younger child what to do in case of emergency. Have them identify the nature of the emergency and prepare an outline. Students should include a purpose sentence and the three main sections of a speech. Students should develop visual aids like a poster to help the younger children remember what to do in the emergency.

CHAPTER 7 Preparing Your Speech

subheads indented in step fashion to show that each level is less important than the one above. The whole outline becomes a picture of the way in which each idea relates to each of the other ideas.

A Sample Outline

Now that you have considered each part of a speech outline separately, let's put them all together in a complete sample outline. A speech contains three main sections—an introduction, a body, and a conclusion—each of which should always be reflected in corresponding sections of your outline. Suppose, for example, that you have chosen "Playing Tennis" as your speech topic. Your purpose sentence and completed outline might look something like this:

Purpose Sentence The purpose of this speech is to inform my listeners about the basic techniques used when playing tennis.

Introduction
I. Answer the following multiple-choice question. According to last week's television special, what is the fastest-growing participation sport in this country today? (a) polo, (b) soccer, (c) tennis.
   A. If you answered "tennis" you were correct.
   B. If you don't yet play, you're a member of a rapidly shrinking group.

II. My "vast" experience of three years on the court only qualifies me to speak to you about the basics.

Body
I. Holding the racket correctly is crucial.
   A. Grasp it as if you were shaking hands with the handle for forehand shots.
      1. Most tennis instructors recommend this technique.
      2. This grip will help keep your shots level.
   B. Use this same grip for serving, except for special types of services.
   C. Turn your hand slightly counter-clockwise from this position for backhand shots if you are righthanded (clockwise if you are lefthanded).
      1. You should be able to lay your thumb flat along the back of the grip.
      2. Many players like to support their backhand grip with their other hand.

RETEACHING

Have students choose a topic. (They might use the topics they have gathered in their portfolios.) Have them write an outline for the speech and identify the three main sections. Have them transfer the outline to note cards and use the cards when delivering the speech.

SKILL DEVELOPMENT

Outlining
Ask students to transfer the information in the sample outline on pages 212–214 to note cards. Encourage students to include the major ideas of the outline and support statements on the cards.

II. Stance is also very important.
   A. Most beginners face the net directly when hitting the ball.
      1. I did it this way for four months before someone "clued me in."
      2. My shots showed me something was wrong.
   B. The better method is to stand with your side facing the net for forehand and backhand shots.
   C. When serving, you should face the net not directly but on a 45-degree angle.
      1. Notice the pros on television.
      2. Television camera angles sometimes make it difficult to see serving stances clearly.
   D. Sometimes when running for a ball, it is impossible to get in the correct position in time.
      1. I find this especially difficult.
      2. Steffi Graf doesn't seem to find it so difficult, however—her strength and agility enable her to make excellent return shots even from "incorrect" positions.

III. The swing is extremely important.
   A. You should begin with a wide backswing that fully engages your back and shoulder muscles.
      1. Using a short backswing will rob your shots of power.
      2. Andre Agassi's backswing.
   B. Try to contact the ball when it is waist high and slightly in front of you.
      1. Keep the ball level.
      2. Avoid "scoop" shots.
   C. Keep the racket level as you continue with your follow through.
      1. Pete Sampras's form.
      2. Michael Chang's form.
   D. Except for special shots and serving, the swing should be horizontal, not vertical.
      1. The overhead smash is a special shot for which you use a vertical swing.
      2. The lob, a high and lofting shot, is another special example—it requires a very controlled underhand swing.

TEACH

MOTIVATION

Ask students how they prepare for a sports event or how they learned skills such as riding a bicycle or swimming. Point out to students that just as they needed to practice to become skillful in these activities, they will need to practice delivering their speeches.

LEARNING STYLES

Audio/Visual Learning
Show a tape of a major presidential speech. Ask students to analyze the content and delivery of the speech.

SKILL DEVELOPMENT

Critical Thinking
Ask students to watch speakers on television. They should write descriptions of both a successful and unsuccessful delivery style. Students should explain what made one speaker more effective—his or her movement, voice quality, the way he or she adapted to the audience.

ACTIVITY

Have students incorporate the elements of the sample outline and the shortened statements to deliver the speech. Call on volunteers to present the speech to the class.

CHAPTER 7 Preparing Your Speech

Conclusion

I. You probably won't become an overnight Martina Navratilova or Andre Agassi with what I've told you today.

II. What you can do is start enjoying the fastest-growing sport in America as a participant and not merely as a spectator.

When the time for delivering your speech arrives, your teacher may allow you to take your outline to the podium. If not, you will want to transfer the major ideas from the outline to note cards. Using 3 × 5 cards makes it easy to insert the same-sized evidence cards you prepared earlier into the deck of outline cards at appropriate places. You then will have only a small stack of cards to handle on the platform. These will include the major ideas of your speech as well as statistics, examples, quotations, and other forms of evidence.

ACTIVITY

Making a "Delivery" Outline

As a class, look at the "Body" of the sample outline dealing with the basic techniques of tennis on pages 212–213. Each student will be asked to translate aloud how a particular main or subhead on the outline would appear once it were printed on a 3 × 5 notecard for use during delivery. Go down the rows of the class with the first person shortening roman numeral I, "Holding the racket correctly is crucial." Then the next person in the row states how he or she would shorten I. A, and so on until the class has completed the entire body of the outline. Remember, each statement should be changed into the fewest number of words possible in order to capture the essence of that statement.

REHEARSING

Rehearsal is the crowning point of speech preparation. Without rehearsal a speaker is like a beginning golfer entering the U.S. Open after having read all the golfing manuals but never having actually played. Nothing can take the place of thorough practice, and if well done, rehearsal can put you in top form for a successful speech.

TEACH

> **AMAZING FACTS!**
>
> On one occasion, Winston Churchill's valet heard Churchill speaking as he was taking a bath. When the valet asked Churchill if he was speaking to him, Churchill replied, "I was addressing the House of Commons."

Recognize the Importance of Thorough Rehearsal

One or two brief run-throughs does not constitute thorough rehearsal. Start preparing your speech well before the speaking date. Allow time for several rehearsal sessions. Rehearsal that is crammed into one evening is ineffective compared to three or four rehearsal sessions on successive nights.

In order to prepare yourself thoroughly for a speech, you must progress through several rehearsal stages, developing gradually from the stage in which ideas are simply listed on your outline or note cards to the point where they are firmly implanted in your mind. Since people's brains work subconsciously on such ideas between rehearsal sessions, you need time for well-spaced rehearsals if you are to have total command of the speech material.

Find a Place for Rehearsal

Since the actual speech will be spoken aloud, you need a place for rehearsal where you can speak aloud. Simply saying the speech to yourself, or whispering it quietly, only allows you to practice the mental parts of the speech—the ideas. But public speaking demands a number

Thorough preparation for a speech involves several rehearsal stages in which ideas grow from lists on note cards to being firmly implanted in your mind.

TEACH

> **AMAZING FACTS!**
> Abraham Lincoln's speech at Gettysburg was much shorter than anyone expected. However, the Gettysburg Address is a model of oratory.

● **LEARNING STYLES**

Limited English Proficiency
Help these students by summarizing the steps in speech rehearsals. Students might write these and include them in their portfolios.
(a) Allow ten practice sessions before a speech.
(b) Practice alone in a quiet, private place.
(c) Visualize the audience and imagine the occasion.
(d) Read your outline silently and then aloud to plant the ideas firmly in your mind.
(e) Deliver the speech all the way through with notes. Do this five to ten times.
(f) Deliver the speech all the way through without notes. Repeat until you are comfortable.
(g) Time rehearsals to make sure you are within time limit.

● **SKILL APPLICATION**

Citizens Speak Out
Have students practice and role-play coordination of delivery style with content. For example, students could use a chronological order to explain a complaint to an elected official. Have students present their speeches to the class.

CHAPTER 7 Preparing Your Speech

of physical skills as well. You need to rehearse proper breathing and voice projection, clear articulation, good timing, and correct synchronization of words with body movements. The ancient Greek orator Demosthenes is reported to have rehearsed his speeches on the seashore where he had to speak over the roar of the surf. It is also said that he practiced with pebbles in his mouth to make himself conscious of the need for clear articulation. Don't risk choking by using pebbles, but do consider practicing outdoors. It offers a very good place for speech rehearsal since you are forced to speak above the noise of wind and traffic. If you cannot find a suitable place outdoors, the next best place is a room similar in size and acoustics to the one in which you will give the actual speech.

Plant the Pattern of Ideas in Your Mind

Begin by reading your outline over silently to yourself several times, trying to set the **pattern of ideas** in your mind. Often the major segments of the outline will already be fixed in your mind since you are the one who wrote the outline. Your teacher may or may not allow you to use the outline during the actual speech, and even if you are permitted to use it you will want to depend on it as little as possible.

Once you feel you have the ideas firmly planted in your mind, stand up and say the ideas aloud to an imaginary audience. Speak the ideas in whatever words come to you as you are rehearsing. Try to go completely through, filling in details of the outline without starting over. Your speech will be halting at first with long pauses in places, but it will begin to smooth out with repeated practice. The second, third, and fourth times, do not try to say the ideas in exactly the same words you used the first time. Remember, what you are doing is planting the pattern of ideas in your mind, not a memorized pattern of words.

Have your outline or note cards handy (whichever you plan to use during the actual speech), and refer to them if you forget an idea. Run through the entire speech five to ten times or until you are certain you can go from beginning to end without hesitation. This will help establish your pattern of ideas securely in your mind.

Rehearse Alone and with Friends

Most people prefer to rehearse a speech alone, at least until they have it pretty well smoothed out. Once you feel you have the speech under control, however, rehearsing with a friend or two as your audience can improve your preparation. Having a dress rehearsal of this type can give you ideas about possible audience reactions you cannot obtain through a solo rehearsal: Are you speaking loudly enough to be heard in all parts of the room? Do the listeners react in an unexpected way to a particular portion of your speech? Do they follow the organization of your speech? Do they understand all of the message? Do they agree or disagree with all or part of your message? Knowing the answers to these kinds of questions beforehand can allow you time to make changes and produce a better effect on your real audience.

Time Rehearsals

Time yourself as you practice. Using a kitchen timer that shows how much time has been spent and how much is left can be helpful. The timing will probably not be too precise the first few run-throughs, but by your final practice session you should be able to conclude your speech within 30 seconds of your time limit.

For most brief classroom speeches your timing will need to be precise. Later, when you give 20- or 30-minute speeches to groups outside the classroom, timing will still be important, but two or three minutes leeway will probably be permissible. Any speaking you do on radio or television, of course, must be timed very closely and usually demands a manuscript for rehearsal rather than an outline.

● **ACTIVITY**

Rehearsing with a Friend

Pair up with another student in your speech class and arrange to rehearse an upcoming speech in front of one another. Both of you should have already done enough individual rehearsal to feel comfortable and prepared. Holding this "dress rehearsal" with an audience of one will give both of you the opportunity to make suggestions that will allow you to put a final polish on your speeches.

TEACH

● **RETEACHING**

After students have finished their speeches, have them evaluate themselves on the following criteria: place in which they rehearsed, audibility, body movements, pattern of ideas, and timing.

● **SKILL DEVELOPMENT**

Feedback
Encourage students to offer positive and constructive remarks to others giving speeches. For every negative comment about inappropriate gestures, pronunciation problems, overly long sentences, mumbling, monotonous voice patterns, and breathing difficulties, have them also make a positive remark.

● **LEARNING STYLES**

Cooperative Learning
Ask small groups to review the rehearsal tips discussed in this section. Encourage groups to give each member constructive feedback.

ASSESS

● STUDENT PERFORMANCE COMPETENCIES

- Defines terms
- Identifies ways to choose a speech topic that will appeal to an audience
- Understands research skills and puts them into practice
- Prepares a speech outline
- Recognizes the importance of rehearsal in preparation for a speech

● sca GUIDELINES

- Distinguishes facts from opinions
- Distinguishes between informative and persuasive messages
- Expresses ideas clearly and concisely
- Expresses and defends point of view with evidence
- Organizes messages so that others can understand them
- Gives concise and accurate directions
- Summarizes messages
- Performs social rituals

▼ PORTFOLIO ASSESSMENT

Standard
- Knowledge, Interests, and Opinion Inventory
- Information Note Cards
- General Purpose Categories List

Enrichment
- School Issues Survey
- Newspaper and Newsmagazine Articles

Challenge
- Monroe's Motivated Sequence Cartoons

CHAPTER 7 REVIEW

● SUMMARY

Speech preparation is the process of building your speech in your mind. Planning it in every detail beforehand can help you avoid embarrassing mistakes during the actual delivery.

Focusing on Your Topic Both your speech preparation and the speech itself will be easier if you choose a subject that fascinates you. Then analyze the background, attitudes, and interest of your audience to determine exactly how to approach your chosen subject. This may call for formal or informal polls, surveys, and perhaps a questioning of the person who invited you to speak. Selecting your general speech purpose means deciding whether you wish to inform, persuade, entertain, or fulfill some other purpose. Once you have done this, put your topic and general purpose into a specific purpose sentence.

Researching Your Topic Thorough research is necessary to discover support for the ideas you will present in your speech. Support takes a variety of forms, the most common of which are facts, statistics, testimony, narratives, examples, and comparisons. Getting to know how to use a library is critical to proper speech research. This means learning how to use the card catalogue and the reference section, as well as seeking help from computerized research services, the reference librarians, and special holdings of your library. Record all your evidence and the sources from which you obtain it on 3 × 5 index cards.

Organizing and Outlining Your Speech Certain general patterns of speech organization have proven effective for speeches with various purposes. Informative speeches are often organized according to the chronological, spatial, and topical patterns. Persuasive speeches more often follow a problem-solving pattern or Monroe's Motivated Sequence. The string-of-beads pattern is often used for speeches to entertain. Your speech outline should always be guided by a purpose sentence. Every main head in the outline should be a major subdivision of your topic. Subheads give supporting details for each main head.

Rehearsing All the earlier parts of the speech preparation process are brought together and perfected during rehearsal. Find a place for rehearsal that forces you to project your voice. Use your outline to plan the pattern of ideas in your mind, then speak the ideas aloud to an

ASSESSMENT STRATEGIES

Individual Assessment
- Participates in practice activities daily or weekly
- Completes classwork
- Demonstrates knowledge of content through questions, discussion, quizzes, and tests
- Displays improved speech skills as targeted in this chapter

Group Assessment
- Sets and achieves goals
- Demonstrates cooperative learning activities
- Supports efforts of team and class members
- Provides encouragement and feedback to members

---

maginary audience. Force yourself to speak completely through the outline without backtracking. Repeat your practice at least five to ten times to smooth out rough sections of the speech and to keep it within your time limit. Once you feel confident about solo rehearsal, hold a dress rehearsal with a friend or two.

VOCABULARY

Define at least fifteen of the following terms in a complete sentence.

audience analysis
specific purpose
purpose sentence
support
fact
statistic
testimony
narrative
example
comparison
card catalogue
title card
author card
call number
subject card
reference section
computerized research services
databases
chronological pattern
spatial pattern
topical pattern
problem-solution pattern
Monroe's Motivated Sequence
string-of-beads pattern
main heads
subheads
pattern of ideas

CHECKLIST

Speech: Preparation Skills

1. Analyze various topics before choosing one for a speech.
2. Organize and plan your speech carefully ahead of time.
3. Recognize the importance of appealing to your audience.
4. Be aware of the need to research your topic thoroughly.
5. Use the library to advantage as a valuable resource.
6. Outline your speech as part of your preparation.
7. Rehearse your speech, taking care to project your voice.
8. Time your speech as part of your rehearsal.

ASSESS

● **ANSWERS**

See the Answer Key for more complete answers.

REVIEW QUESTIONS
1. Identify a general subject area; analyze the audience, define the purpose, and formulate a specific purpose for the speech.
2. It is necessary to ask yourself how much the audience already knows about the topic, and how interested they are.
3. A topic must be limited so that it fits into the assigned time period.
4. Research supplies the speaker with appropriate support material.
5. Answers will vary. Periodicals, encyclopedias, yearbooks, biographical aids, and government documents are all popular sources of supporting material.
6. Patterns of organization include: chronological, spatial, problem–solution, Monroe's Motivated Sequence, and the string-of-beads approach.
7. A purpose sentence answers the question, "What do I want my listeners to know, think, believe, or do as a result of hearing my speech?"
8. The best place to rehearse is any place where you can give the speech out loud, free from distractions or limitations.
9. It is necessary to go over the speech several times in order to establish a pattern of ideas in your mind.
10. You should make sure that you are speaking loudly enough, that your speech fits into the time period, that you have included some physical movement and eye contact with your audience.

DISCUSSION QUESTIONS
The following code is used to designate discussion questions and activities as suitable for students of varying ability levels:
▼ = below average to average
◆ = average to above average
■ = all students

1. ■ Discuss any patterns in topics. Are topics narrow? Could they be broadened enough to appeal to other audience compositions? Rewrite several topics to appeal to other audiences.
2. ▼ List the pros and cons of memorizing and outlining speeches.
3. ◆ Students might role-play a politician who speaks beautifully but has nothing to say, or a mumbler who has something important to say but is not heard because of poor delivery. Discuss the results as a class.

220

CHAPTER 7 REVIEW

📋 REVIEW QUESTIONS

1. Explain the process involved in focusing on your topic.
2. Explain what you should know about your audience before you begin to prepare your speech.
3. Explain how the time available for your speech affects the topic you choose.
4. Explain the basic purposes of doing research in preparation for a speech.
5. Name some of the sources of supporting material.
6. Explain some typical patterns of organization used in developing a speech.
7. Explain the function of a purpose sentence.
8. Name the best place to rehearse a speech.
9. Explain why it is important to rehearse a speech several times.
10. Name some physical skills you should work on during rehearsals for speeches.

❓ DISCUSSION QUESTIONS

1. Hold a brainstorm session in which you identify at least twenty topics that have strong audience appeal to the members of your class. You might examine any list of topics previously developed or begin a new list. Choose someone to list the topics on the chalkboard as they are proposed. Each topic should be thoroughly discussed in terms of audience interest. For a topic to make the list of twenty, the class must agree that it is of obvious interest. Resolve differences of opinion by consensus, comprise, or majority vote. Record the final list in your speech notebook and save it for the future.
2. Conduct a class discussion about whether or not it is preferable to write a speech and then memorize it, or simply to fix a pattern of ideas in your mind and then speak from an outline. What kinds of problems could a speaker with a memorized speech encounter? Does an outlined speech encourage a smoother delivery?
3. Participate in a class discussion on the relative importance of speech content and speech delivery. Is one more important than the other? How effective is sound content without good delivery? Can you think of examples from your own experience when a speaker used effective delivery techniques but had very little to say? How effective was such a speech? How does one establish a proper balance between content and delivery?

220

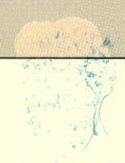

4. Imagine that you have been asked by a local civic group to give a five-minute speech at a luncheon meeting on an important historic building in your town. The only thing you know about this group is that they have an interest in local history. You know absolutely nothing about the building. You have one month to prepare for your speech. Discuss with your classmates the things you would do to prepare for your speech. What would you do before you gather information? What methods would you use to locate information? How would you structure your speech to gain the attention of your audience?

CRITICAL THINKING

1. **Synthesis** Think about the many commercials you see on television and listen to on the radio. Think about all of the advertisements you see and read in newspapers and magazines. Then identify a product that you believe is worthwhile. It can be something you invent, yourself, or it can be a product you have heard or read about. What would persuade you to buy this product? Would these same things persuade others as well? Use Monroe's Motivated Sequence to develop a commercial or advertisement for this product. Make sure that it contains each of the five separate steps.

2. **Evaluation** Think of a speech that you have listened to, either in class or somewhere else, which the speaker simply did not rehearse sufficiently. What are the signs of inadequate rehearsal? In what ways does inadequate rehearsal affect content and delivery? Develop a set of standards that you can use to help determine whether or not you or a partner have adequately rehearsed a speech.

ACTIVITIES

In-Class

1. Form small groups of from five to seven. Choose one of the following broad topics: Pets, Hobbies, Summer Jobs, Vacation Sites, Careers, Sports Greats. For each broad topic, identify narrower topics that could be used for five-minute speeches. See how many narrow topics you can identify in thirty minutes. Share your topics with those identified by other groups.

---

4. Student discussion should demonstrate an understanding of the necessary preparation a speaker would make for such an event.

CRITICAL THINKING
1. **Synthesis** These commercials can be audio- or videotaped for a more realistic presentation.
2. **Evaluation** Take care not to embarrass individual students. Use speeches from television or role-play incorrect methods.

ACTIVITIES
In-Class
1. Remind students that a five-minute speech allows little time for development and that a topic for such a speech must be very specific in nature.

ASSESS

2. Ask students to describe the steps they would go through to perform an audience analysis.
3. To expedite this activity, distribute a copy of a speech from the Speech Library. Have students meet in groups of five to seven to address the other activity questions.

Out-of-Class
1. Students learn that knowledge of the topic makes outlining easier. Research will help the outlining process.
2. This activity requires critical reading skills and may need some supervision. Consider analyzing an editorial on the board to give students an idea how the activity should progress.
3. Students should submit note cards containing evidence. Check note cards for an understanding of how evidence is collected.

CHAPTER 7 REVIEW

2. Discuss each of the following audiences. What kind of speech topic would probably be best for each? What kinds of topics would best be avoided?
   (a) a fourth grade class
   (b) a senior citizens' lunch
   (c) a meeting at a convention of chemists
   (d) a garden-club meeting
   (e) a bored student group that is being forced to attend the speech
   (f) an evening meeting of parents interested in learning about the curriculum
   (g) a meeting of people looking for new hobbies

3. Select a speech either from the Appendix of this text or from one of the standard collections of speeches. You should find a speech that can be read in five minutes or less. Identify the original audience for the speech and explain to your classmates whatever other information is needed to understand why the speech was given. Read the speech in class. After you have read the speech, conduct a class discussion about it. What was the purpose statement? Was the introduction effective? How was the speech organized? What kinds of evidence did the speaker use to support his or her main points? Did the conclusion tie all of the main points together?

Out-of-Class

1. Using the list of broad topics on page 184, choose one that you know well and write three possible topics for the subject in your speech notebook. Choose one of these three topics and write a skeletal outline for a speech on that topic. Your outline should include a sketchy introduction, three main heads, and a brief conclusion. Be prepared to discuss your topics and outline.

2. Locate an editorial or a column of opinion in a newspaper that you receive in your home. Paste it on a page in your speech notebook. Divide the page opposite it into two columns. In the first column, write all statements from the example that are opinions. In the second column, write all statements that are facts. In view of the number of facts that your example contains, how persuasive is it? If you were giving a speech on the topic of the editorial or column, would you have enough evidence to support your argument, or would you have to search for more?

3. Identify a topic that you have wanted to find out more about but have not had the time to research. Write the topic in your speech notebook and then write questions about it that you would like to have answered. Research the topic at the library by finding answers to your questions. Once you have conducted your research, use it as a topic for a future speech. Keep all your information about the topic in your speech notebook.

ASSESS

CHAPTER PROJECT

Working in pairs, choose a topic for an informative speech. Then you and your partner prepare to give five-minute speeches on two different aspects of that topic. Research the topic thoroughly in the library, keeping bibliographic notes of all sources that you investigate.

Write an outline for your speech based on the information you locate through your research. Write pertinent information on note cards. Make certain that your ideas are supported with evidence and coordinate with your partner to ensure that your speeches will complement, not duplicate, one another.

Prepare a folder-packet that includes your outline, note cards, and bibliography. Determine with your partner who should speak first and then deliver your speeches in class. Did the speeches work well together? Submit the packet to your teacher.

CHAPTER PROJECT

- The packet or portfolio should contain indicators of mastery for all steps in the preparation process: topic selection, research, organizational pattern, and outline. There should be research items such as copies of articles or handwritten notes, bibliographic indicators, an outline of the speech, note cards used during the speech, and any other material used in the course of the preparation. Because the chapter on delivery follows, you may choose to have the student put together the packet now, and deliver the speech later. In this case, the packet can serve as a research project that receives a grade during each section or a major grade as a total unit.

PREPARE

● CHAPTER PLANNER

Day 1	Day 2	Day 3	Day 4	Day 5
Prepare	Prepare	Prepare	Prepare	Prepare
Teach	Teach	Teach	Teach	Teach
Assess	Assess	Assess	Assess	Assess
Sub. Teacher Tip *p. 226*	Sub. Teacher Tip *p. 232*			

● CHAPTER OVERVIEW

This chapter examines the following topics:
- Differences Between Written and Spoken Language *p. 227*
- Making Spoken Language Clear *p. 228*
- Creating Levels of Emphasis *p. 233*
- Using Figures of Speech *p. 240*
- Avoiding Common Problems *p. 244*

▼ PORTFOLIO PRODUCTS

Individual Projects
- Simplification of Pretentious Terms
- Contrast Usage
- Pamphlet of Devices for Creating Emphasis
- Similes and Metaphors in Collection
- Chapter 8 Portfolio Products

Group Project
- Simile and Metaphor Cartoons

● sca GUIDELINES

- Expresses ideas clearly and concisely
- Gives concise and accurate directions
- Summarizes messages
- Describes differences in opinion
- Expresses feelings to others

CHAPTER

8

Choosing Effective Language

When you have completed this chapter you should be able to:

● Explain the difference between written and spoken language.

● Describe the characteristics of clear spoken language.

● Define the terms *concrete words* and *abstract words*, and give several examples of each.

● Define the term *economy of language,* and explain how to use such language in your speeches.

● Define and give examples of figures of speech that you can use to make your speeches interesting.

TEACH

● **LINKS TO PAST LEARNING**

Ask students to recall and compare speeches that were obviously memorized with those that were extemporaneous. Have them evaluate the effectiveness of both. Ask them to indicate which were more interesting to listen to and to explain why.

"Nothing surely is more alive than a word."
—J. Donald Adams

● **ACTIVITY**

You might record the differences between written language and spoken language that students cite on the board. Ask students to make a general statement about the differences. For more practice, students could choose passages in their social studies texts and rewrite them in simpler language, then read them aloud to the class. Students could evaluate the differences between written language and spoken language in these passages.

● **LEARNING STYLES**

Audio Learning
Ask a volunteer to read John Kennedy's words regarding Churchill's speeches. Ask students to rewrite the words, stating the main idea but deleting the eloquence.

Choosing Effective Language   225

● **ACTIVITY**

Written versus Spoken Language

The following is in "written language," the kind of expression that is clear to a reader (at least eventually):

> Many individuals will regularly proclaim that whenever that which has the most infinitesimal opportunity to go awry actually does derail, the derailment was caused by some perverse law of existence that predestines such misfortunes.

Write this paragraph in "spoken language," the kind that would be more immediately understood by an audience member listening to a public speaker. When everyone has rewritten the sentence in simpler language, each student should read his or her version aloud to the class. Then hold a class discussion about the differences between "written language" and "spoken language."

As the opening Activity suggests, this chapter is about learning to adopt a speaking style that is aimed at *listeners* rather than at *readers*. Since you have had many English classes in your life, but few if any speech classes, this chapter will introduce you to some simpler, more concrete, and oftener easier-to-understand ways of using language than perhaps you are used to. Words are the garments with which speakers clothe their ideas. Choosing effective language for a speech is like choosing the right clothes for a special occasion. Words can be courageous or timid, commanding or pleading, persuasive or entertaining, hurtful or kind. Their effect on the listeners can be enormous or microscopic, depending on how well the words clothe the ideas. Once when referring to Winston Churchill's speeches to the English people during World War II, John F. Kennedy stated: "He mobilized the English language and sent it into battle." Churchill's words may well have done more for the Allied cause than fifty planes or a dozen ships.

Speeches are made of ideas, but unless those ideas are expressed in carefully selected language, they may be overlooked. In this chapter you will find a number of suggestions that can help you choose the kind of language that will best express your ideas to audiences.

You may ask, "Does this mean I should write out my speeches word for word, then read or memorize them?" No, not usually. Most speech teachers today believe you should learn to give most of your

TEACH

SUBSTITUTE TEACHER TIP

Students could prepare short speeches on a topic of their choice. Call on them to present their speeches in two ways: speaking from a manuscript and speaking without one, directly to the audience. Ask students to discuss the differences between the two ways.

● SKILL APPLICATION

Citizens Speak Out

Illustrate the difference between written and spoken language by writing on the board the following sentence: "Citizens who want to know what advantages their government can offer them are better advised to determine instead what contributions they themselves might make to their homeland." Tell students that this awkward statement can be reworded into a famous spoken quotation. Ask the class to identify the quotation. ("Ask not what your country can do for you; ask what you can do for your country.")

Media Literacy

Ask students to tape and transcribe the text of a television or radio advertisement and to try to find a print media ad for the same product or service. Ask students to compare the language used in the two ads by using the five qualities listed on page 228.

● SKILL DEVELOPMENT

Research

Ask students to think of quotations they know by heart or to find them in books of quotations. Have them rewrite these quotations into statements, such as the example in Skill Application above. Put several examples on the board and have students try to guess the quotations.

● MOTIVATION

Students could record spoken language such as a club meeting, or a class discussion (with the permission of the participants). Ask them to transcribe the language for examination. Have them analyze the characteristics of spoken language. Ask them to compare how it is different from written language. After students have studied the next section, have them compare their observations with those in the text.

---

226   CHAPTER 8   Choosing Effective Language

Careful selection of the language for a speech can affect its impact dramatically.

speeches extemporaneously—outlining the ideas, but choosing the precise wording during the speech itself. Linda and Dick Heun, authors of a college speech text, put it this way:

> The main reason for not writing out a speech and reading (or memorizing) it is that your focus then would be on your wording rather than your audience's reactions. One unique advantage of oral communication is that you have direct eye contact with your audience and can watch, interpret, and adapt to its reactions.
>
> A second reason for not writing out your speech is that oral style is quite different from written style. In fact, Charles Fox, noted British politician and orator of the nineteenth century, once said, "Does it read well? Then it's not a good speech."

On some occasions, of course, you may need to speak from a manuscript. Your teacher may even assign one or more manuscript speeches in this class. But for the most part this chapter's immediate benefit to you will be showing you how to select effective language for those sections of your speech where you want to make the greatest impression—the introduction, the conclusion, and some occasional high points you may wish to read or memorize. In working on the language of these special parts of your speeches, you will also be gaining the skill to put words together effectively when speaking extemporaneously.

TEACH

● RETEACHING

After students have studied this section, have them compare their observations as suggested in the Motivation exercise on page 226 with those in the text.

● MOTIVATION

Ask students to choose a task that they are familiar with, such as playing a certain game or repairing a flat tire on a bicycle. Have them imagine that they need to explain the particular task to a friend who is unfamiliar with it. Call on volunteers to present their explanation. Have the class evaluate each presentation in terms of how clear the directions were and suggest ways for improvement. Tell students that in this section they will learn how to make spoken language clear.

● SKILL DEVELOPMENT

Creative Thinking
On the board write the following examples to illustrate how pretentious terms should be eliminated from speaking by simplifying and streamlining: He proffered the currency to the appropriate employee. (He gave the money to the salesclerk.) She sauntered to her domicile in the precipitation. (She walked home in the rain.) Ask students to provide ten other examples. Students might include their examples in their portfolios.

Differences Between Written and Spoken Language **227**

You will explore five qualities of spoken language that make if different from written language. Being aware of these differences will help you state your message clearly. Then the chapter will show you ways to emphasize important points in your speech. Speakers must know how to highlight important ideas so listeners will remember them. Finally, you will find a list of certain problems to avoid. The use of effective language involves four points—clarity, emphasis, interest, and caution. By following the suggestions in this chapter, you should find it easier to get your message across to your audience.

● DIFFERENCES BETWEEN WRITTEN AND SPOKEN LANGUAGE

The first step in choosing effective language for public speaking is to realize that language that is appropriate for writing is not always appropriate for speaking. In part, this is because the tasks of reading and listening are so different. Readers can set their own pace, stopping and reviewing anything that is hard to understand. Listeners, on the other hand, must try to keep up with the speaker. If they miss an idea, it is often gone for good. Effective language for speaking must therefore be immediately clear to the listener.

As with spoken language, effective signing must be immediately clear to the listener.

227

TEACH

● **CURRICULAR CONNECTIONS**

Language Arts
Ask students to find simpler spoken language substitutes for the following words: *morose, emaciated, encounter, termination, audacity, erroneous, undertake, proximity.*

● **SKILL DEVELOPMENT**

15-Second Skill Opportunity
Have students choose a topic for a short speech. Students might refer to the lists in their portfolios for their topics. Have them focus on using short, simple sentences and simple words in their speech. Ask students to present the first 15 seconds of their speech to the class.

Feedback
Ask students to evaluate the speeches, using the criteria discussed above. Have students provide examples of ways to improve the speeches.

● **LEARNING STYLES**

Multicultural Learning
Ask students to think of regional or cultural groups that a speaker might address, such as people from the Midwest or Hispanic people. List students' suggestions on the board and have them think of language and references that speakers might use when speaking to these particular audiences.

---

228   CHAPTER 8   Choosing Effective Language

In conversation, most people recognize this need to make spoken language immediately clear. In general, spoken language possesses five specific qualities that make it very different from written language.

1. Spoken language makes greater use of short and simple words.
2. Spoken language tends to be more concrete, less abstract.
3. Spoken language is usually specific.
4. Spoken language makes greater use of restatement.
5. Spoken language generally includes fewer unnecessary words.

The next part of this chapter will focus on these five qualities of spoken language. Although they are a natural part of spoken language, they are too often forgotten when it comes to giving public speeches.

● **MAKING SPOKEN LANGUAGE CLEAR**

A listener runs a much greater risk of missing ideas that are poorly stated than a reader does. If an audience fails to understand even a small part of a speaker's language, that part of the message will be lost to them. The world's great speeches have always been characterized by the clarity of their language. Language for public speaking must be simple, brief, and clear enough that listeners can easily understand it.

Keep Wording Short and Simple

Spoken sentences need to be shorter and simpler than written ones. A great number of long sentences make a speech difficult for listeners to follow. They also make it harder for an audience to pay attention for any length of time. Spoken language calls for short, simple sentences.

Say each of these sentences aloud, then decide which would be easier for a listening audience to grasp quickly:

Lengthy: We have gathered here today in order to explain and detail for you the reasons why one of our very own classmates deserves to be this school's next student council president.

Short: We're here to tell you why our classmate, Sheila Cox, should be our next student council president.

Similarly, spoken language calls for simple words. The use of simple words has long been considered a sign of clear language. Simple words are not always short words, though many are short. Rather, they are those that are among the ordinary vocabulary of your particular audience on any given occasion.

TEACH

● **CURRICULAR CONNECTIONS**

Writing
You might provide students with the following proverbs for use in writing anecdotes: "All that glitters is not gold." "Look before you leap." "Curiosity killed the cat." "The grass always looks greener on the other side." "Beauty is only skin deep." Encourage students to use clear spoken language and concrete and specific words.

● **SKILL DEVELOPMENT**

Creative Thinking
Stress to students that concrete, vivid language makes it possible for listeners to visualize ideas. Ask students to rewrite vague sentences using concrete words, as follows: Mary appeared happy and looked lovely. *Mary was aglow with smiles, a vision in pink satin.* Andy was frightened and looked ill. *Andy's teeth were chattering with terror, and he was as pale as a ghost.*

Feedback
You might tape students' anecdotes and play them back to the class. Have the class give feedback for each anecdote in terms of positive and constructive remarks.

● **LEARNING STYLES**

Cooperative Learning
Copy and distribute the following directions to each small group: "You go a couple of blocks or so down Maple until you see a gas station. The road sort of winds off to the right there and you go down there until you pass a school. Then soon you'll come to a rock wall and you turn left again. You can't miss the place; it's painted sort of a brown color." Ask each group to use concrete language to improve the directions. Call on a representative from each group to read their directions to the class. Have the class evaluate them, based on the concrete language used.

Making Spoken Language Clear

When speaking to your peers, people in your own age group with a similar level of education, your selection of language is relatively easy. Simply choose words you would typically use in conversation. When speaking to a much younger group or a less-educated audience adjust your language level downward appropriately. Watch the listeners' feedback carefully for signs of lack of understanding.

Decide which wording would be better understood by a group of fourth graders to whom you were speaking about computers:

Complex: The type of communications protocol existing between your systems unit and printer may present you with a critical consideration for the proper operation of your computer.
Simple: How your computer talks to your printer may be important to know if you wish to operate your computer well.

If you address a special group with a vocabulary of its own—a sports group, a religious group—it is permissible to use the special words of that group as long as the entire audience will understand the language used. The same is true when addressing groups composed of audience members from a specific region or cultural group. As long as you are a member of that group and nearly all your listeners understand the special regional or cultural terms, you should feel free to use them. Actually, you compliment such an audience by using language that is special to you and them. Do not, however, try to use the regional or cultural language of a special group if you are not a member of the group, or if there are many nonmembers in your audience.

Use Concrete Language

Language for public speaking must not only be simple, it must also be concrete. **Concrete words** and phrases are the kind that let the listener "see" the idea as well as understand it. A word such as *girl* is concrete since it stands for something that can be perceived by the senses. A word such as *beautiful* is **abstract** (the opposite of concrete), since you cannot see, touch, feel, smell, or taste *beautiful*. Compare the two following sentences and decide which one gives you a clearer mental picture of the ideas expressed.

Abstract: John seemed nervous, yet determined.
Concrete: John was shaking, but his jaw was tightly set.

The two sentences express essentially the same ideas, but the second sentence allows you to "see" those ideas. You can't see *nervous*.

TEACH

> *"The difference between the right word and the almost right word is the difference between lightning and the lightning bug."*
>
> —Mark Twain

● SKILL DEVELOPMENT

Active Listening
Point out to students that using specific words is very important in giving directions. Have students work in pairs, explaining to each other how to perform simple tasks such as lighting a stove, braiding hair, setting an alarm, or outlining a paragraph. Instructions should be carried out to the letter. Have students listen carefully to the directions and ask at least two questions to clarify the process.

● LEARNING STYLES

Limited English Proficiency
Work with students to understand the progression from general to specific. Ask students to generate a list of words that proceed from general to specific. Students might give examples such as:
- some–several–three
- army–soldiers–infantry
- trees–evergreens–Douglas firs.

CHAPTER 8 Choosing Effective Language

Now compare these two sentences and decide for yourself which is more concrete and which more abstract.

> The taste in Katie's mouth was like frozen strawberries, slowly melting on her tongue.
>
> The taste in Katie's mouth was cold and tantalizing.

● ACTIVITY

Using Simple Language

In a two-minute presentation to the class, relate an amusing or interesting story or anecdote. The story or anecdote may be about a real incident that happened to you, or it may be something you heard from someone else. Use language that is clear, concrete, and specific, so that your listeners will listen carefully. After you have finished, discuss your use of language with your classmates. Ask them to identify any parts of your story that might have been unclear.

Use Specific Words

A public speaker also needs to use specific words. **Specific words** are words that refer to a limited class of objects. For example, the word "hobo" is a more specific word than "traveler" since there are many travelers in the world who are not hobos. The class "traveler" is larger than the class "hobo" since hobos are just one form of traveler. A given word cannot be labeled general or specific. It will merely be more general or more specific than some other word. We just said that "hobo" is more specific than "traveler." But "traveler" is more specific than "person," which includes the class "traveler." Notice the progression from general to specific in this list:

galaxies

solar systems

planets

Mars

The trick when preparing a speech is to pick the most specific word you can find to tell your audience just what you have in mind.

TEACH

● **CURRICULAR CONNECTIONS**

History
Refer students to Frank Knox's speech, quoted here. Ask them to find out the issues involved regarding the entry of the United States into World War II.

● **SKILL DEVELOPMENT**

Main Idea
Read aloud a technical passage from *Scientific American, Discovery* magazine, or some other publication. Quiz students on the content. Scores will likely be low. Then read another technical passage, restating during your reading the main points about which you will be asking quiz questions. Have students compare the scores in both readings. Ask them how restatement helps listeners to remember the main ideas of a speech.

Making Spoken Language Clear 231

Restate Main Ideas

Restatement is a natural speaking device. It assures you that the listener does not miss or forget a part of your message. Writers have less need to restate, since the reader can carry out any necessary review by simply rereading a phrase or sentence. Since listeners do not have this opportunity, public speakers typically restate their main ideas a good deal, using somewhat different terms each time to make sure everyone gets the idea.

Notice how Frank Knox, Secretary of the Navy under President Franklin D. Roosevelt from 1940 to 1944, used restatement in a speech in order to make clear his belief that a nation must be willing to fight to preserve liberty and peace:

> The only peace in which the world can put any confidence, for at least one hundred years to come, is the kind of peace that can be enforced by the peace-loving nations of the world....
>
> You cannot preserve liberties such as we enjoy, save by willingness to fight for them if need be.
>
> The currency with which you pay for peace is made up of manly courage, fearless virility, readiness to serve justice and honor at any cost, and a mind and a heart attuned to sacrifice.
>
> We must also remember that it is only the strong who can promote and preserve a righteous peace....
>
> A powerful national defense, especially on the high seas, is a prerequisite of a peace-promoting, justice-loving America....

sing somewhat different rms each time, public peakers restate key points ensure that they "connect" with listeners.

231

TEACH

SUBSTITUTE TEACHER TIP

Students could practice removing unnecessary words from their speeches. Ask students to work in pairs and write a paragraph about what they would say to a sales clerk about an unsatisfactory product. Have them exchange paragraphs and rework them by removing unnecessary words.

AMAZING FACTS!

Edward Everett was considered one of the most famous speakers of the time. His remarks at the Gettysburg dedication ceremony were given front-page coverage in the contemporary newspapers, whereas Lincoln's remarks were covered in the inside pages. Everett himself, however, was quite moved by Lincoln's words. He wrote to Lincoln and said, "I wish that I could flatter myself that I had come as near to the central idea of the occasion in two hours as you did in two minutes."

● SKILL DEVELOPMENT

Feedback
Ask the class to evaluate the speeches suggested in Reteaching, basing their evaluation on the elements discussed in this section.

● EXTENSION

Ask students to find examples of speeches that reflect both economical and uneconomical use of language. Have them present their examples and discuss the use of language in them.

● RETEACHING

Ask students to prepare a 2-minute speech in which they present differences of opinion about responsibility for household chores to their parents. Ask students to use the elements discussed in this section: concrete words, specific words, and economical language.

---

232   CHAPTER 8 Choosing Effective Language

Remove Unnecessary Words

In daily life, being economical means not wasting money or other resources. In public speaking, being economical means not wasting words. Part of clear speaking consists of using only as many words as necessary to get the message across. Once you have accomplished that —stop! Did you know that on the same day that Abraham Lincoln delivered the Gettysburg Address, another speaker, Edward Everett, gave a speech that lasted nearly two hours? Lincoln's speech, only ten sentences in length, took about two minutes to deliver. Probably you have never heard of Edward Everett or his speech, but Lincoln's Gettysburg Address is known around the world. Part of the reason for the lasting effect of Lincoln's speech was undoubtedly his economy of language. Afterwards, Everett wrote Lincoln a letter in which he declared that he wished he could have done as much justice to the occasion with his two-hour speech as Lincoln had with his two-minute one.

One of the best ways of achieving **economy of language** is by chopping needless words from individual sentences. The speaker who says: "We must take into consideration the fact that this property comes under certain zoning restrictions" could save words (and energy) by shortening the wording: "We must consider certain zoning restrictions on this property." Let's look at several other examples:

Uneconomical: Regarding the situation in the flooded area, we must make a concerted effort to aid the local residents.
Economical: We must try to aid the residents in the flooded area.
Uneconomical: A period of sunny weather set in and remained for a whole week.
Economical: We had sunshine for a whole week.

In each of these examples many of the words in the uneconomical version are not needed. They do not add anything to the meaning of the sentence. They are unnecessary and should be left out.

● ACTIVITY

Economy of Language

Prepare a brief written description of a process that you are very familiar with. It could be a description of how to throw a curve ball or how to service a lawn mower. After you have finished it, reread it carefully, removing all unnecessary words. Now present your description from memory in the form of a short speech. After you have finished, discuss your speech with your classmates. Did they understand the process that you described? Were they aware of any words you used that were unnecessary?

TEACH

● **CURRICULAR CONNECTIONS**

Language Arts
To add variety to their speeches, have students check them for sentence structure. If too many sentences follow the subject-verb-object pattern, suggest they change the pattern to add variety. You might work with the language arts teacher to develop this skill.

> *Variety is the mother of enjoyment.*
> —Benjamin Disraeli

CREATING LEVELS OF EMPHASIS

So far we have considered the importance of using clear language when speaking in public. Language must also help make a speech memorable. Listeners will be more likely to remember your message if you choose language that emphasizes its important points.

Several language devices can be used to create levels of emphasis. Their purpose is to highlight certain parts of your speech and thereby downplay the other parts where they are not used. Among the most common of the devices used to create emphasis are contrast, rhetorical questions, repetition, and climax. Before you consider these devices, however, consider the most basic way of creating different levels of emphasis—the use of variety.

Variety Sets the Stage

Without variety in words and types of sentences, a speech quickly forms a repetitious language pattern. Any kind of regularly recurring pattern quickly distracts an audience, causing them to pay less attention to the speaker's message. But when there is variety in word usage and sentence length, certain points will stand out; others will recede into the background. Thus, language variety can be of great use in creating levels of emphasis.

Varying one's vocabulary, sentence length, and sentence structure can also help maintain listener interest. It can enliven your speech. Speeches which repeatedly use the same words to refer to a given idea

Keeping listeners' attention is achieved, in part, through variety in the use of words, length of sentences, and sentence structure.

● **LEARNING STYLES**

Cooperative Learning
You might provide small groups of students with a list of topics to develop speeches about processes. You could include the following: performing a dance, listening to classical music, making a telephone call, putting out a fire, learning sign language. Encourage students to select topics that reflect specific skills in areas that will interest others. If students have trouble editing their own work, have them exchange descriptions and edit one another's work.

Visual Learning
Ask students to find examples of paintings they like. Have them bring examples of these paintings to the class and indicate how the artist used variety in the particular painting.

● **SKILL DEVELOPMENT**

Vocabulary
Write the word *emphasis* on the board. Ask students what the word means. Have them give example of ways that they emphasize things they say. Ask them why they need to emphasize certain things they say. Hold a class discussion about which ways are the most effective. Tell them that they'll learn about how using emphasis can help make their speeches more effective.

Critical Thinking
Students could find speeches in the Speech Library or in *Vital Speeches* to illustrate ways in which variety was or was not used.

TEACH

● **LINKS TO PAST LEARNING**

Ask students to give examples of contrast in the arts that they have heard or seen. You could suggest the contrast between rock and classical music, for example.

● **ENRICHMENT**

Ask students to listen to or read a speech by a president or another government official. Have them pay attention to the use of contrast in the speech and record these uses. They might include these examples in their portfolios.

● **SKILL APPLICATION**

Citizens Speak Out
Ask students to find out about a community issue that is controversial. Then have them prepare a short speech in which they present their arguments either for or against the issue. Ask students to use contrast in their speech. Have students present their speeches to the class, and have the class evaluate them in terms of the use of contrast. Students might include their speeches in their portfolios.

CHAPTER 8 Choosing Effective Language

soon become monotonous. Speakers who use all short, simple sentences begin to sound like machine-guns clattering. Those who use only long sentences quickly lose the attention and interest of their listeners. A basic key to successful speaking is variety.

Contrast Sticks in the Listener's Mind

The language device called contrast has long been used to make important statements stick in listeners' minds. The following examples come from three speeches by the same person. Do you know who spoke them?

"Let us never negotiate out of fear. But let us never fear to negotiate."

"In the election of 1860 the great issue was whether this country would remain half slave and half free; in the election of 1960...the great issue is whether the *world* will remain half slave and half free."

"Ask not what your country can do for you—ask what you can do for your country."

Each of these uses of contrast by President John F. Kennedy became widely repeated statements. **Contrast,** a language device Kennedy used frequently, begins with two balanced phrases, clauses, or sentences. The words containing the ideas the speaker wishes to emphasize are the only words changed or rearranged in the second part of the statement. Notice how, in the second example above, Kennedy changed only three things: the date *1860* to the date *1960,* the word *country* to *world,* and the verb *would* to *will*. Thus he highlighted what he considered one of the most important issues in the 1960 election year. Had he stated only "The great issue in 1960 is whether the world will remain half slave and half free," his statement would not have carried as much emphasis, nor been remembered as long. Contrast is a language device that seems to stick in the listener's mind. The better your audience remember some of your key statements, the greater the overall impact your speech is likely to have.

Contrast is not an easy device to create. Ordinarily, speakers do not spout forth well-balanced statements of contrast on the spur of the moment. Such statements usually grow from extended thought and careful planning. Therefore, contrast is usually found when a speaker has had ample time to plan precise language. If you plan to use contrast, you will need to think it out before the speech and then use a manuscript or note cards showing the statements of contrast you wish to make. The time spent is not likely to be wasted. Well-planned use of contrast can prove effective in most speeches.

APPLY

● **LINKS TO PAST LEARNING**

Ask students to share images or words they recall when they thought a speaker or advertising campaign went "too far." List these examples on the chalkboard. Encourage the class to arrive at a consensus about those examples that did go "too far" or seemed to be an irresponsible and unethical use of language and images.

● **LEARNING STYLES**

Visual Learning
Ask students to bring to class examples of advertising that relies on strong visual images to create interest in a product or service. These images could become part of a poster, collage, or bulletin board.

● **SKILL APPLICATION**

Making Conversation
Students can relate examples of certain styles of dress that have created shocking images. Encourage them to discuss what the author refers to as "your standards of good taste and fair play." Small groups of students might explore both how such standards of good taste are developed and strategies for those who deviate from accepted standards. Discuss how a school or place of business could communicate those standards effectively.

ETHICALLY SPEAKING

Intensity of Language and Image

The success of your message often depends on the strength of your evidence—verbal evidence and visual evidence. Knowing this, it is tempting to assemble the most powerful arguments you can muster and to complement them with the strongest possible visual aids. Ethically speaking, is there a point at which language is too strong and visuals too graphic?

Suppose you are giving a speech in support of a "Stop Smoking" campaign. Among the arguments you plan are statistics about smokers' risk of respiratory disease (verbally and also in charts and graphs), the dangers of second-hand smoke, and the unpleasant odors and general messiness that smoking causes. Would it be going too far to describe the agonizing death of a victim of emphysema? or to show photos of lungs blackened by cigarette smoke? Would your listeners find these things convincing? Would they become so fearful and anxious that they needed a smoke? Or would they be so offended or sickened that they would tune out the message? (Some research suggests that such negative messages that are too strong fail to persuade.)

Suppose you are speaking out against U.S. trade policy with countries that condone child labor. In addition to presenting evidence about the young age and low wages of laborers in these countries, you also label anyone who purchases goods from these countries as a *murderer* and a *child molester*. And you show a photograph of a child whose growth has been terribly stunted by working in cramped quarters. If strong language and gruesome photography are used for a worthy goal, does the end justify the means?

There are no easy answers for ethical questions such as these. Generally, however, you should be guided by your knowledge of your audience, your standards of good taste and fair play, and your own integrity as a citizen and a communicator.

In presenting visual evidence to support your position, you should be guided by standards of good taste and your own integrity.

TEACH

CURRICULAR CONNECTIONS

History
Write the following quotation from Patrick Henry's Address to the Delegates of the Second Virginia Convention: "The gentlemen may cry Peace, peace!—but there is no peace. The war has actually begun! The next gale that sweeps from the north will bring to our ears the clash of resounding arms! Our brethren are already in the field! Why stand we here idle? What is it that the gentlemen wish? What would they have? Is life so dear or peace so sweet as to be purchased at the price of chains and slavery? Forbid it, Almighty God! I know not what course others may take, but as for me, give me liberty, or give me death!" Have students read the quotation and identify the rhetorical questions. Then ask them to provide examples of other rhetorical questions.

● ACTIVITY

Ask students to use the examples of contrast, rhetorical questions, and repetition that they found to create an illustrated pamphlet in which they explain these devices to a younger child. Students could include the pamphlets in their portfolios.

CHAPTER 8 Choosing Effective Language

● ACTIVITY

Finding Language Devices

Divide the class into three groups. Each group's task is to search through the "Appendix of Speeches," beginning on page 572, to discover examples of one of three types of language devices: Group 1 will look for as many examples of Contrast as the group can identify within five minutes; Group 2 will search for Rhetorical Questions during the same time period; and Group 3 will be searching for instances of Repetition. Afterwards, a group leader will read aloud the title of each speech containing one or more language devices, and read aloud the sentence containing the devices discovered by the group.

Contrast, however, is a device that can be easily overused. Since is generally saved to emphasize one of the major points in a speec overusing it can stress too many points. The audience may becom confused and forget all of them. One or perhaps two well-placed stat ments of contrast are ample, even in a lengthy speech.

Rhetorical Questions Demand Attention

Ideas in a speech can also be emphasized by putting them in the for of rhetorical questions. **Rhetorical questions** are questions that a not meant to be answered out loud. It is difficult, however, for mo people to ignore a question put to them. Thus, they will generally try answer it in their minds. A speaker can sometimes capitalize on th fact by occasionally asking rhetorical questions of the audience. Noti how Dr. Martin Luther King, Jr., used rhetorical questions in his speec "I've Been to the Mountaintop," delivered in Memphis, Tennessee, ju before his assassination. He was urging the members of the clergy wh were his listeners to join with striking sanitation workers:

> That's the question before you tonight. Not, "If I stop to help the sanitation workers, what will happen to all of the hours that I usually spend in my office every day and every week as a pastor?" The question is not, "If I stop to help this man in need, what will happen to me?" "If I do not stop to help the sanitation workers, what will happen to them?" That's the question.

Dr. King did not expect out-loud responses from his listeners t these questions. Rhetorical questions demand an answer in the mind each individual listener. They are difficult to ignore.

Repetition Highlights Important Points

Repetition is another effective device for highlighting important points. Listening to TV commercials, you might wonder whether modern television advertising ever makes use of any device other than repetition. Public speakers also make great use of repetition. Sometimes their basic purpose in using it is to persuade, to create an emotional reaction, or to aid listener recall. In many cases, however, the basic purpose is to emphasize important points. When used in this way its effect is like holding up a large sign stating: "Don't miss this! It's one of the most important points of my speech."

Repetition is different from restatement. Restatement (stating the same idea several times using *different* words) aids listener recall, but ordinarily does not drive a point home to the same extent that repetition does. **Repetition** (stating the same idea several times using the *same* words) is much more effective in signaling the important point for the audience. It sounds an emphatic note of insistence that is nearly impossible to ignore. Use repetition sparingly, however. Its overuse is very annoying.

Franklin D. Roosevelt used parallelism, a variation of repetition, with great effect in his radio speeches during the Great Depression and World War II.

TEACH

● **SKILL DEVELOPMENT**

15-Second Skill Opportunity
Ask students to prepare a "commercial" for a product they like or use. Have them use repetition to encourage the use of the product. Ask students to present their commercials to the class.

Feedback
You might tape the commercials and play them back to the class. Have students evaluate the effectiveness of repetition in each commercial.

● **LEARNING STYLES**

Cooperative Learning
Students could work in groups to give examples of climax ordering that they could use in a speech to encourage a change in a school policy. Call on groups to present their speeches and discuss their use of climax ordering.

TEACH

● EXTENSION

Refer students to the excerpt of MacArthur's speech on this page. Students could reword the sentences that use climax ordering by writing them in simple form. For example, the sentence in the second paragraph might be rewritten "On many occasions, I have witnessed . . . ." Point out to students how using climax ordering can improve a speech.

● RETEACHING

Ask students to view televised legislative proceedings, presidential addresses, presentations on community access channels, and editorial commentaries. Have students record in their notebooks the uses of variety, contrast, rhetorical questions, repetition, and climax ordering.

● LEARNING STYLES

Limited English Proficiency
Work with students who have limited proficiency in English to help them understand climax ordering. Have them develop a series of three items in which they describe someone's achievement. Help them to order the three items from least important to most important.

CHAPTER 8 Choosing Effective Language

A variation of repetition consists of beginning or ending sentences with the same single word or short phrase. This device, called **parallelism,** was used by President Franklin D. Roosevelt in a fighting speech during World War II:

> From Berlin, Rome, and Tokyo we have been described as a nation of weaklings—"playboys"—who would hire British soldiers, or Russian soldiers, or Chinese soldiers to do our fighting for us.
> Let them repeat that now!
> Let them tell that to General MacArthur and his men.
> Let them tell that to the sailors who today are hitting hard in the far waters of the Pacific.
> Let them tell that to the boys in the Flying Fortresses.
> Let them tell that to the marines!

But repetition should be used sparingly: It serves as a highly effective means of achieving emphasis only as long as it is not overused.

Climax Emphasizes the Last Item in a Series

When a speaker lists three or four items in a series, the item spoken of last carries the greatest emphasis. Suppose you wished, for example, to emphasize how seriously wrong you consider someone's behavior to be. The expected order would look like this: "His behavior is wrong, is immoral, it is actually criminal." This is called **climax ordering**—moving from less significant to more significant, and ending the series with whichever item is most important. If, in the example above, the speaker were to arrange the items in any other order, the audience would most likely become confused. Since audiences usually expect to hear climax ordering whenever items spoken in a series differ in importance, speakers can emphasize the last item by using it. General Douglas MacArthur, in a speech to the cadets at West Point, used climax ordering two times to describe the "American man-at-arms." They appear in italics in the following excerpt from his speech.

> But when I think *of his patience under adversity, of his courage under fire, and of his modesty in victory,* I am filled with an emotion of admiration I cannot put into words. He belongs to history as furnishing one of the greatest examples of successful patriotism. He belongs to posterity as the instructor of future generations in the principles of liberty and freedom. He belongs to the present—to us—by his virtues and by his achievements.
> *In 20 campaigns, on 100 battlefields, around 1,000 campfires,* I have witnessed that enduring fortitude, that patriotic self-abnegation, and that invincible determination which has carved his statue in the hearts of his people.

APPLY

● **LINKS TO PAST LEARNING**

Point out to students that the ability to persuade is very important for a lobbyist. Ask students to make a list of ways that they persuade others or attempt to persuade others every day. List these ways on the board. Ask volunteers what they say to be persuasive.

● **CURRICULAR CONNECTIONS**

History
Ask students to find out about the significance of lobbying in our government. Ask students to discuss whether the process is beneficial or detrimental.

AMAZING FACTS!
Many of the larger interest groups have lobbyists in Washington, D.C. There are more than 6,000 lobbyists serving clients in the country's capital.

CAREER CLOSE-UP

Lobbyist

Lobbyists represent special interest groups by influencing government policy and legislation at both the national and state levels. Because lobbyists participate at every stage of the lawmaking process, they must have a comprehensive knowledge and experience of how the legislature works. They meet with legislators and their assistants, testify at hearings on bills relating to their group's interests, and work to ensure an important bill's passage.

Because legislators are inundated with requests from interest groups, effective lobbyists must convey clear, concise, and emphatic messages to persuade others to follow their interest group's point of view. Choosing their words carefully, lobbyists rely on powerful, yet simple language to communicate their opinions. They select colorful word images to create unforgettably vivid pictures in the minds of their listeners.

Lobbyists often have only fifteen minutes to testify at hearings or to speak with legislators. Before each appointment, they prepare by streamlining their well-researched position so it can be presented simply. To make each idea memorable, key concepts are illustrated with specific examples, facts, or statistics. Lobbyists also reinforce their presentation by emphatically restating the main ideas.

A lobbyist must deliver a clear and vigorous message to be heard by busy legislators. When lobbyists combine their forceful public speaking with the ability to create vibrant words and images, they wield a powerful tool that leaves lasting impressions on the minds of others.

With a limited amount of time in which to testify at hearings or speak with legislators, lobbyists prepare by sharpening the focus of their well-researched positions. Then they illustrate key concepts with specific facts and statistics and reinforce through restatement of main ideas.

239

239

TEACH

● **MOTIVATION**

Ask students what the expression "It's just a figure of speech" means. On the board, list students' examples of figures of speech. Point out that figures of speech can help make speeches more colorful and interesting.

● **SKILL DEVELOPMENT**

Vocabulary
Ask students to identify three examples of similes and metaphors from a speech in the Appendix. Students could include their examples in their portfolios.

● **LEARNING STYLES**

Limited English Proficiency
Have students with limited proficiency in English work with partners to understand the difference between similes and metaphors. The partner might provide metaphors, such as "She's an angel," and the student with limited proficiency in English might provide similes for the metaphor, such as "She's like an angel."

CHAPTER 8 Choosing Effective Language

As is the case with most language devices used for creating levels of emphasis, climax must be used sparingly. Well-placed usage of such devices, however, can make the difference between a poor speech and an excellent one.

● **USING FIGURES OF SPEECH**

Language in a speech must sometimes be rich and imaginative; at other times plain and straightforward. The plainer parts help emphasize the richer ones. Few speakers can produce clever, imaginative language constantly, and even if they could the listeners would soon sicken of it. It would be much like eating steak every day, without the faintest hope of some ordinary hamburger now and then. The careful use of imaginative language can, however, add a great deal to your speeches. Knowing ways of creating rich language can help you make your meaning clear to your listeners.

In this section we'll look at several methods of making speech more imaginative, methods that are called figures of speech. **Figures of speech** are phrases and sentences that make a point by stating something that is not literally or exactly true. They rely on such things as comparison, contrast, and exaggeration to make meanings clear.

Similes and Metaphors

Two special forms of comparison, the simile and the metaphor, are frequently used to make ideas memorable for the listeners. A **simile** is a brief comparison of two basically unlike things, using the word *like* or *as*. When Adlai Stevenson lost the presidential election in 1956, he used a simile to express his feelings: "I feel like a little boy who has just stubbed his toe. I'm too big to cry, but it hurts too much to laugh." Very likely, few people would have remembered Stevenson's remark had he simply said, "Well, I'm too old to cry, but I certainly don't feel like laughing either." Instead, Stevenson's simile created a vivid picture that has endured in the public's mind.

A **metaphor** is a more direct comparison of two things than a simile, because it omits the word *like* or *as*. A student speaker used this metaphor:

> The Philippine islands are pieces of emerald that were dropped into the South China Sea by some beneficent giant.

The beauty of the Philippines is clearly evoked because the student used metaphor to link the very identity of these shimmering green islands with emeralds. The impact is immediate and powerful. Had the

CURRICULAR CONNECTIONS

Language Arts
Students could find examples of similes and metaphors in their favorite novels. They could compile a list of these and include them in their portfolios for future reference.

SKILL DEVELOPMENT

Vocabulary
Ask students to work in small groups and write several similes and metaphors. Then have them create or use cartoons illustrating these figures of speech. Students could share the cartoons with other groups and have them identify the simile or metaphor in the cartoon. Students might include their cartoons in their portfolios.

15-Second Skill Opportunity
Ask students to choose a vacation spot that they've enjoyed. Have them describe the spot in 15 seconds, using metaphors and similes.

---

speaker said "The Philippine islands seem like pieces of emerald…", the comparison would have been a simile.

Similes and metaphors usually are only one sentence in length. The often-heard retort of a jokester whose joke has fallen flat is a one-sentence simile: "Well, that went over like a lead balloon!" At other times a simile or metaphor may consist of several sentences. Hubert Farbes won a national high-school speech contest with a speech containing this combination of metaphor-simile:

> For there is a parasite in the minds of men today. It grows like a leech, taking its morbid existence from the strength of its host, warping his mind and character.

If a comparison grows beyond two or three sentences, however, it is ordinarily labeled an extended comparison, or an **analogy.** Similes and metaphors gain part of their impact from being short and pithy.

Similes and metaphors may be used quite frequently in a speech. This does no harm, as long as the speaker does not stuff the listener with such devices. Keep in mind that a substantial portion of your speech must consist of plain food, so that the special treat may be appreciated.

Personification

Personification is a figure of speech by which a speaker gives human qualities to inanimate objects, ideas, or nonhuman creatures. An effective use of personification was contained in a speech by President Franklin D. Roosevelt. When his political enemies accused him of wasting taxpayers' money by sending a naval destroyer to pick up his dog Fala on an Aleutian Island, Roosevelt gave human emotions to the dog in his reply. Notice how he gradually builds up to the personification:

> These Republican leaders have not been content with attacks on me, or my wife, or on my sons. No, not content with that, they now include my little dog, Fala. Well, of course, I don't resent attacks, and my family doesn't resent attacks, but Fala *does* resent them. You know, Fala is Scotch, and being a Scottie, as soon as he learned that the Republican fiction writers in Congress and out had concocted a story that I had left him behind on the Aleutian Islands and had sent a destroyer back to find him—at a cost to the taxpayers of two or three, or eight or twenty million dollars—his Scotch soul was furious. He has not been the same dog since. I am accustomed to hearing malicious falsehoods about myself—such as that old, worm-eaten chestnut that I have represented myself as indispensable. But I think I have a right to resent, to object to libelous statements about my dog.

TEACH

● SKILL DEVELOPMENT

Vocabulary
Point out to students how casually we personify objects: "That car is so temperamental." "My stereo set died last week." Ask students to write a sentence that includes a personification of each of the following subjects:
1. a movie theater after closing
2. a campfire trying to ignite in wet wood
3. a cat trying to avoid a young child

● ACTIVITY

After students have completed this Activity, have them compile the figures of speech. Students could prepare a bulletin board display that illustrates the six figures of speech discussed in this section.

CHAPTER 8 Choosing Effective Language

By focusing attention on the dog's feelings, Roosevelt was able to express some of his own feelings about the charges that had been made, but in a humorous way.

Personification may also be used to set a general mood. Consider the effect of an opening narrative that begins with these words: "It was a dark and gloomy winter's day, with stubborn clouds threatening us every moment...." You might expect suspense, mystery, or intrigue of some sort to follow. Part of the mood is created by the words "stubborn" and "threatening." Since these are qualities of human beings, and not of clouds, attributing them to clouds gives greater liveliness to a speech.

Hyperbole

Hyperbole is perhaps the most commonly used figure of speech in everyday conversation. It consists of intentionally exaggerating in order to emphasize a point. Because most of us engage in hyperbole so regularly, much of our everyday use of it has become subconscious. Ordinarily we are exaggerating subconsciously when using common expressions such as:

> She's the greatest!
> I'm completely exhausted.
> I'm dead!
> I jogged a thousand miles today.

Such statements are rarely true, of course, but the listener understands that the exaggeration is only intended to underscore the speaker's feelings.

In public speaking, hyperbole must be used sparingly, since in emphasizing too many points, a speaker winds up emphasizing none.

● ACTIVITY

Finding Figures of Speech

As you did in the last Activity on page 236, divide into three groups, this time looking for figures of speech in the "Appendix of Speeches" beginning on page 572. Group 1 will search for Similes and Irony; group 2 will look for Personification and Understatement; and group 3 will be after instances of Hyperbole and Metaphors. As before, after five minutes of searching, each group will elect a leader who will report that group's findings to the class.

APPLY

● **ENRICHMENT**

Ask students to examine television and radio advertising for figures of speech. If possible, record commercial spots for students to analyze. Discuss with the class the effects that figures of speech have on the persuasiveness of the message.

● **RETEACHING**

Call on students to give examples of similes, metaphors, personification, hyperbole, understatement, and irony.

● **LEARNING STYLES**

Cooperative Learning
You could organize the class into small groups to work on Speaking in Action. Members of each group could work together to help one another prepare their speeches. Students could evaluate the speeches at each step through delivery, providing suggestions for improvement.

Speaking IN ACTION

Student Speech

Situation

In preparation for your next in-class speech, write out both the speech introduction and the conclusion word for word. The object is not to read the opening and closing of the speech from a manuscript during actual delivery, but to demonstrate the power and elegance of carefully chosen language in these two critically important parts of a public speech.

Preparation

Before you can begin writing your introduction and conclusion, you will need to complete several other preliminary steps in the speech preparation process: You will need to select and focus your topic, write out a purpose statement, complete your research, and finish your preparation outline of the entire speech.

Before beginning to write your speech introduction, look ahead to Chapter 10 (pp. 288–345) to discover the major purposes that a good introduction should accomplish: gaining audience attention, building interest in your topic, previewing your topic, applying the message to your specific audience, and establishing your ethos. Also note the techniques mentioned in Chapter 10 for accomplishing those purposes—techniques such as anecdote, humor, common ground, shock technique, and suspense. Before beginning to write your conclusion, you should similarly review the purposes and techniques that make for a good conclusion (pp. 312–316). In other words, decide first upon the content, *what* you intend to write, before you begin to write it.

Next review the differences between written and spoken language. Especially remember that you want a high percentage of short, simple words that are concrete and specific and that describe things the listeners could see, hear, touch, taste, and feel. Now you are ready to begin writing.

Delivery

As you write, look for opportunities to use language devices: contrast that sticks in the listener's mind, rhetorical questions that demand listener attention, repetition which highlights important points, and climax that emphasizes the last item in a series. In addition, include some figures of speech, keeping in mind that a few can add luster but too many can deaden the message. One or two well-placed figures, such as metaphors, similes, personification, or hyperbole, would ordinarily be plenty for a brief introduction or conclusion.

Be wary of several common problems as you write. Avoid using words that may have negative connotations for your listeners. Use euphemisms sparingly, do not stereotype, use limited slang, and beware of grammatical problems. When you have completed writing the introduction and conclusion, proofread them several times, not only to catch any problems, but also to edit what you have written until it carries the maximum meaning and "punch" you can provide.

You should not *read* your introduction and conclusion to your audience on the day you deliver your speech. Instead, have them memorized so that you can maintain constant eye contact with your audience while getting the most benefit from your well-crafted language! Deliver the body of the speech using extemporaneous delivery.

TEACH

● **MOTIVATION**

Write the following terms on the board. Ask students to name the possible unfortunate interpretations that could be given to each:

evil	agitator
Communist	tacky
skinny	politician
cheap	tough

Tell students that this section will discuss ways to avoid problems in the language they use in their speeches.

● **SKILL DEVELOPMENT**

Vocabulary
Write the following sentences, containing words or phrases with inappropriate connotations: The slaughter of Abraham Lincoln left the nation in a real mess. The young violinist dreamed of playing a gig with the Chicago Symphony. Have them rewrite these sentences, substituting appropriate words or phrases.

CHAPTER 8 Choosing Effective Language

Understatement

Understatement is the opposite of hyperbole. Its purpose is to highlight something by playing down its importance or making what is significant sound insignificant. If a multi-millionaire is asked about the extent of her wealth, she might use understatement in her reply: "Let just say I'm not terribly worried about where my next meal is coming from."

Irony

Irony is a figure of speech in which the literal meaning expressed by person's words is the opposite of the meaning intended. If you wished to show your dislike and lack of respect for another person, you might exclaim "Oh, she's a fine person!" with a sarcastic tone in your voice that indicates you mean to convey the opposite of *fine*.

● **AVOIDING COMMON PROBLEMS**

Language can be a public speaker's greatest asset. Unfortunately, sometimes traps a speaker into saying what is not meant or meaning what is not said. Following are several problems encountered in choosing effective language. A couple of these should always be avoided Others may prove helpful or harmful, depending on how you use them

Avoid Unintentional Connotations

All words have a standard, dictionary meaning. This is a generally accepted, objective meaning known as a word's denotation. Words may also have connotations—special meanings for different people or different groups of people. If, for instance, a speaker were to use the word *gold*, the denotation would be "a heavy, yellow metal." The connotation, for some audience members, might include ideas of wealth or beauty. Speakers must be aware of the possible connotations the words they use are likely to carry for the bulk of their audiences. If the connotations are likely to cause strong negative reactions, it is wiser to choose other language.

Avoiding Common Problems 245

In editing a speech, you should be concerned with inadvertent connotations and the use of euphemisms, clichés, stereotypes, slang, and incorrect grammar.

Use Euphemisms Carefully

Euphemisms are gentle or softened expressions for harsh or unpleasant realities. People often say "He passed on" for "He died." Euphemisms are often helpful, since they allow a speaker to be tactful and avoid insulting an audience. Avoid using them so frequently that your message becomes clouded with soft terms, however.

Avoid Clichés

Clichés are expressions that at one time expressed a truth or idea clearly and briefly, but have become so overused as to be almost meaningless. Examples of clichés are "A stitch in time saves nine, " "Where there's smoke there's fire," "Green with envy," and "As pretty as a picture." The use of clichés generally bores an audience. It also causes listeners to lose a certain degree of respect for the speaker, since using clichés makes it appear that the speaker lacks originality.

TEACH

● **LEARNING STYLES**

Audio Learning
Have students listen to commentaries during news broadcasts on television or on the radio. Have them identify examples of euphemisms and clichés. Discuss with students the effect on the commentaries of using these expressions.

Multicultural Learning
Have students discuss ways that men and women are stereotyped. For example, women are sometimes portrayed as being ineffective in solving mechanical problems and men are sometimes portrayed as being ineffective in performing domestic chores. Discuss whether students have experienced stereotyping because of their gender. Ask students how this kind of stereotyping can be detrimental to a person.

TEACH

● **CURRICULAR CONNECTIONS**

Language Arts
Discuss with students why good grammar is so crucial to a speaker. Ask them what grammatical errors do to a speaker's credibility. Have students listen for examples of grammatical errors on television or on the radio.

● **SKILL APPLICATION**

Media Literacy
Ask students to discuss how television can contribute to stereotyping and to identify stereotyping in three programs of a similar type (family sitcom, soap, detective show, etc.).

● **LEARNING STYLES**

Cooperative Learning
Have students work in small groups and develop a list of slang terms that would be inappropriate in speeches given to adult audiences.

---

246   CHAPTER 8 Choosing Effective Language

Don't Stereotype

Stereotyping means assigning qualities to people or objects becaus they are part of a general group, without considering their individual di ferences. Stereotypes may be based on a person's appearance, type employment, nationality, religion, race, or age. "All bus drivers are rude and "Young people are lazy" are examples of stereotyping. Using word or phrases which stereotype greatly harms a speaker's image. The should always be avoided.

Use Slang Sparingly

Slang consists of contemporary words and phrases that come in and g out of style very rapidly. Because the majority of slang expressions hav a short life, using them in your speeches will confuse listeners wh have never had a chance to become familiar with them. Some years ag *cool* and *groovy* were "in" words. Today the person who uses ther sounds neither "cool" nor "groovy." You should also remember tha many slang expressions, current among young people, never get picke up by older people at all.

Be very thrifty in your use of slang even when talking to your class mates. You may wish to use it once in a while to produce an informa atmosphere, for novelty or humor, but beware of using it often in pub lic speaking. As you gain more and more exposure to various types speeches, notice how little slang good speakers use even in speeche delivered at very informal occasions. Slang dates your speech, and overused, shows a limited vocabulary.

Shun Incorrect Grammar

Remember, words are the garments with which speakers clothe the ideas. If you use *incorrect grammar,* it is a lot like appearing in publi with your shirt on backwards or wearing socks that don't match. It true that spoken language is often less formal than written language, bu that does not mean it can be incorrect. The speaker heard saying "All us in this room has a stake in this problem," stands out like a perso with shoes on the wrong feet. When the voice from the podiur announces "He laid down for a nap," listeners feel as they would whe looking at someone with green hair. We all make grammatical slip from time to time. It is the speaker who habitually does so who lose the respect of his or her listeners. Here is a chart showing some of th common problem areas in grammatical usage:

TEACH

● **RETEACHING**

Ask students to choose a topic for a speech. They might use the list of topics that they have saved in their portfolios. Then have the rest of the class evaluate the speeches, focusing on the following criteria:
1. Variety and types of sentence lengths
2. Appropriate choice of language (avoiding use of slang, overuse of euphemisms and clichés, etc.)
3. Rhetorical devices, figures of speech (use of contrast, rhetorical questions, climax ordering, similes, metaphors, etc.), and correct grammar

AMAZING FACTS!

Embolalia is the word for speech fillers, such as "He was like fifteen years old" and "Y'know what I mean?"

● **SKILL DEVELOPMENT**

Critical Thinking
You might ask students to give an example for several of the problem areas identified in the table on this page.

Errors in grammar may be repeated so often that they sound correct even when they are not. Practice proper usage until it sounds right to you.

Avoiding Common Problems 247

Common Problem Areas in Grammatical Usage

Problem area	Grammatical explanation	Correct usage
affect/effect	*affect* is usually a verb; *effect* is generally a noun	That mistake may significantly affect your career. The movie had quite an effect on me.
beside/besides	*beside* means "next to"; *besides* means "in addition"	John, stand beside Mary, I don't like him; besides, he squints.
between you and I	the object of the preposition *between* is *me*	between you and me
can/may	*can* means "is able to"; *may* means "is allowed to"	He can win the race. She may go to the head of the line.
could care less	should be "couldn't care less" to state that someone was unconcerned	John couldn't care less about Paul's illness.
farther/further	use *farther* for real physical distance; use *further* for other kinds of distance	Cincinnati is farther than Louisville. Nothing could be further from her mind.
irregardless/regardless	always use *regardless*	Regardless of the consequences, I am going ahead.
like	should not be used as a filler word, as in "He was like fifteen years old."	He was fifteen years old.
like/as if	do not use *like* in place of *as if*	You look as if (not like) you are thirsty.
that/which/who	*who* refers to people; *which* and *that* refer to things that are not people	I am the one who called. My car, which is ancient, won't start. I have a parrot that talks.

247

ASSESS

● STUDENT PERFORMANCE COMPETENCIES

- Explains the difference between written and spoken language
- Describes the characteristics of clear spoken language
- Defines the terms *concrete words* and *abstract words* and gives several examples of each
- Defines the term *economy of language* and explains how to use such language in speeches
- Understands five methods of creating emphasis in spoken language
- Defines and gives examples of figures of speech that can be used to make speeches interesting
- Describes several problems that often arise in choosing language for speeches and discusses how these problems can be avoided

● sca GUIDELINES

- Expresses ideas clearly and concisely
- Gives concise and accurate directions
- Summarizes messages
- Describes differences in opinion
- Expresses feelings to others

▼ PORTFOLIO ASSESSMENT

Standard
- Similes and Metaphors in Speeches
- Using Contrast

Enrichment
- Similes and Metaphors in Literature

Challenge
- Pamphlet of Devices for Creating Emphasis
- Simile and Metaphor Cartoons

CHAPTER 8 REVIEW

● SUMMARY

Words are the garments with which speakers clothe their ideas. Wise speakers choose their language very carefully in order to display their ideas effectively.

Differences Between Written and Spoken Language Language used in writing is different from language spoken aloud. Spoken language contains more short, simple sentences than does written language. It also uses simpler words, is more concrete and specific, has more restatement, and contains fewer unnecessary words.

Making Spoken Language Clear Clarity ranks as the most important quality of spoken language. Clarity means using reasonably short sentences and simple words. It means using concrete and specific language that paints pictures in the listeners' imaginations. It also calls for the restatement of the main ideas in a speech. Finally, it requires the removal of unnecessary words. Language that is simple and direct makes the best impact on an audience.

Creating Levels of Emphasis Language may also be used to emphasize certain points. Varying vocabulary, sentence length, and sentence structure is one way of achieving this. Other devices are contrast—the use of balanced phrases; rhetorical questions—questions that need no answer; repetition—repeating the same words or phrases; and climax—saving the most important item in a series until last.

Using Figures of Speech Figures of speech can help get your meaning across vividly. Comparison, contrast, and exaggeration can highlight ideas and make them memorable. Similes and metaphors compare two essentially unlike things. Personification is a way of giving human qualities to nonhuman things. Hyperbole emphasizes through intentional exaggeration. Its opposite, understatement, highlights a matter by downplaying its importance. Irony makes the literal meaning of the spoken word the opposite of the intended meaning.

Avoiding Common Problems Language problems to be avoided, or approached cautiously, include unintentional connotations, euphemisms, clichés, stereotypes, slang, and incorrect grammar. Some of these should always be avoided; others can be helpful if used sparingly.

ASSESS

● **ASSESSMENT STRATEGIES**

Individual Assessment
- Participates in practice activities daily or weekly
- Completes classwork
- Demonstrates knowledge of content through questions, discussion, quizzes, and tests
- Displays improved speech skills as targeted in this chapter

Group Assessment
- Sets and achieves goals
- Demonstrates cooperative learning activities
- Supports efforts of team and class members
- Provides encouragement and feedback to members

VOCABULARY

Define each word in a complete sentence.

concrete words
abstract words
specific words
restatement
economy of language
contrast
rhetorical questions
repetition
parallelism
climax ordering
figures of speech
simile
metaphor
analogy
personification
hyperbole
understatement
irony
euphemism
clichés
stereotyping
slang

CHECKLIST

Skills of Effective Language Choice

1. Speak in short and simple sentences whenever possible.
2. Use language that your audience will understand.
3. Use concrete language and specific words.
4. Use restatement to help your audience understand your message.
5. Remember that variety in words and types of sentences is essential if your message is to appeal to your audience.
6. Use contrast to help your audience remember what you say.
7. Use rhetorical questions and repetition to gain the attention of your audience.
8. Use figures of speech to help make your speech both imaginative and memorable.
9. Be certain that you use words correctly.
10. Take care to avoid clichés and stereotypes. Use slang sparingly in speeches.

REVIEW QUESTIONS

1. Identify five ways in which spoken language differs from written language.
2. Name four characteristics of clear language.

● **ANSWERS**

See the Answer Key for more complete answers.

REVIEW QUESTIONS
1. Spoken language uses short and simple words, is more concrete, is usually more specific, makes greater use of restatement, and includes fewer unnecessary words.
2. Clear language uses short and simple wording, concrete language, specific words, and restatement.

ASSESS

3. Because a listener does not have the opportunity to reread material as a reader does, restatement is used to ensure communication of the message.
4. To achieve economy of language, eliminate unnecessary words from sentences.
5. Vocabulary, sentence length, and sentence structure all should be varied in order to achieve lively speech.
6. Contrast is the device of noting differences. A *rhetorical question* is not meant to be answered out loud. *Repetition* is the practice of stating the same idea again using the same words. *Parallelism* is the practice of repeating part but not all of a grammatical structure or of the words in a phrase or sentence. *Climax ordering* is the device of presenting statements in order of increased significance.
7. (a) simile; (b) metaphor; (c) personification.
8. A euphemism is a gentle or softened expression used to discuss a harsh reality.
9. Avoid unintentional connotations, clichés, stereotypes, slang, and incorrect grammar.
10. Slang may be used occasionally to produce an informal atmosphere or for novelty or humor.

DISCUSSION QUESTIONS

The following code is used to designate discussion questions and activities as suitable for students of varying ability levels:
- ▼ = below average to average
- ◆ = average to above average
- ■ = all students

1. ◆ Many libraries contain recordings of Churchill's speeches. You may wish to find one of these recordings and play it for your class.
2. ◆ Students doing this activity should refer to the first section of the chapter, which discusses differences between written and spoken language.
3. ◆ You might wish to have students compare speeches of each type. For example, through research students might compare

250

CHAPTER 8 REVIEW

3. Explain the importance of restating main ideas when you are speaking.
4. Explain the best way to achieve economy of language.
5. Name several aspects of language that you should vary to keep your speech lively.
6. Define and give examples of contrast, rhetorical question, repetition, parallelism, and climax ordering.
7. Identify the figure of speech used in each of the following: (a) "I feel like a little boy who has just stubbed his toe." (b) "He is a prince." (c) "Even the stars cry out for justice."
8. Define and give an example of euphemism.
9. Identify five problems to avoid in spoken language.
10. Describe the circumstances in which slang can be used effectively in a speech.

? DISCUSSION QUESTIONS

1. As a class, discuss each of the following quotations of Winston Churchill:
(On becoming Prime Minister of Great Britain) "I have nothing to offer but blood, toil, tears, and sweat."
(On June 4, 1940, speech to House of Commons) "…we shall not flag or fail. We shall go to the end…we shall fight in the seas and oceans…we shall fight on the beaches, we shall fight on the landing-grounds, we shall fight in the fields and in the streets, we shall fight in the hills; we shall never surrender."
(When the RAF defeated the German Luftwaffe) "Never in the field of human conflict was so much owed by so many to so few."
Discuss Churchill's use of language. Do you agree with John F. Kennedy that Churchill "mobilized the English language and sent it into battle"? Discuss what President Kennedy meant by those words.

2. Think about a time when you heard a manuscript speech on television. Such speeches are often given by government officials. Even if the speaker uses a teleprompter and looks toward the audience, listeners can still tell that the speech is being read. Discuss why a listener can tell the difference between an extemporaneous speech and a read speech. Does the difference have something to do with word choice or with the way sentences are put together? Why may it be necessary for government officials to read speeches?

3. Eloquence is speaking that is marked by force and persuasiveness. The great speeches of the past are remembered today because they were eloquent statements of the speaker's position. Discuss what eloquence is. In what ways does each of the characteristics

of effective language mentioned in this chapter contribute to a speech that is eloquent and memorable?

4. The terms *justice, freedom,* and *education* are abstract terms. But what do these terms really mean? Discuss what each means to you. Compare your definitions with those offered by your classmates. Discuss what you really must do before others have a clear idea of what abstract terms like these mean to a speaker.

CRITICAL THINKING

1. Analysis Concrete words communicate exact meanings more readily than abstract words, and specific words communicate more precisely than general words. Explain how general words are different from abstract words. Explain how specific words differ from concrete words.

2. Evaluation When language is used effectively, listeners pay close attention and more easily remember a speaker's message. In which of the three main types of speeches—speeches to inform, persuade, and entertain—is effective language of critical importance? Why?

ACTIVITIES

In-Class

1. Look through magazines that you find in your home and locate some advertisements that you think portray the products they are selling most attractively. Find three very effective ads. Study the language that accompanies each ad. What is it about the language that makes it effective? Analyze the language in each effective ad and share your analysis with your classmates.

2. Work in small groups of from five to seven. Prepare a humorous skit that concentrates on one of the following language features. Rehearse and present your skit in class.
   (a) a skit filled with clichés
   (b) a skit involving hyperbole and understatement
   (c) a skit depicting various stereotypes
   (d) a skit featuring slang
   (e) a skit illustrating incorrect grammar or usage
   (f) a skit using euphemisms

ASSESS

Bryan's "Cross of Gold" speech and Henry's "Speech to the Virginia Convention" to Lincoln's "Farewell Address at Springfield" and Chief Joseph's "Speech of Surrender."
4. Discuss the necessity of defining abstract terms clearly by using restatements, examples, synonyms, antonyms, or dictionary definitions.

CRITICAL THINKING

1. Analysis Remind students of the meanings of the words *general, specific, abstract,* and *concrete* by writing the following on the board:
general refers to a *group of things*
specific refers to *one thing*
abstract refers to a *thing not directly sensed*
concrete refers to a *thing that can be directly sensed*
Point out that the word *men* is both general and concrete but neither abstract nor specific.

2. Evaluation This question is a bit tricky because it implies that effective language is less important in some types of speeches than in others. However, having students debate the question can lead them to realize how vital effective language is in all types of speeches.

ACTIVITIES
In-Class
1. In addition to having students bring magazines from home, plan to provide copies.
2. Limit skits to three minutes. Follow each skit with a discussion allowing the students to discuss the various language problems and how to avoid them.

ASSESS

3. Have students develop a checklist to analyze the speeches that they choose.

Out-of-Class

1. Before conducting this activity, have students define and give examples of each device.

2. In assigning this activity, provide three or four current examples that you know students will recognize. Also provide examples of dated slang expressions such as *hip* (1950s and 1960s) and the *bee's knees* (1920s).

3. Students will enjoy hearing the best of these compositions read aloud. Consider a duet reading in which one student reads the translation into contemporary English. If paragraphs are long, have students read them sentence-by-sentence. You may wish to share with students George Orwell's famous and instructive contemporary English translation of a passage from Ecclesiastes, given in his essay "Politics and the English Language."

4. Brainstorm clichés on the board. Divide the class into small groups and assign each group several clichés. After groups have developed substitutes, discuss them as a class. Were concrete and specific words used? Are the substitutes, like the clichés, metaphorical?

252

CHAPTER 8 REVIEW

3. Locate a speech either in the Appendix of Speeches in the back of this book, in an anthology of speeches, or in the publication *Vital Speeches of the Day*. Examine the speech carefully from the standpoint of effective use of language. Try to find as many of the effective language features mentioned in this chapter as possible. Report your findings in class.

Out-of-Class

1. In your speech notebook, compose sentences or short paragraphs to illustrate each of the following. Present your work in class and ask for feedback.

(a) literary contrast
(b) rhetorical question
(c) restatement
(d) repetition
(e) parallelism
(f) climax ordering
(g) simile
(h) metaphor

2. In your speech notebook, compile a list of current slang terms. Write a brief definition of each. Then consult a person who is from 15 to 20 years older than you. Ask that person to check your list and to tell you how many of the current terms he or she is familiar with. Then ask that person to identify and define as many slang terms as he or she can remember that were popular when he or she was your age. Write these terms and their definitions in your speech notebook. Report the results in class and discuss what you have learned about the nature of slang terms.

3. Locate a speech in a library source that was given before 1850. Find one paragraph in the speech that is representative of the language used throughout the speech. In your speech notebook, rewrite the paragraph so that it would be understandable to today's audiences. What changes did you make in word choice? Did you make any changes in sentence structure? Be prepared to explain your findings in class.

4. In your speech notebook, write your own fresher expressions for the following clichés. Then write as many other clichés as you can think of. Be prepared to share them with your classmates and to participate in the search for fresher substitutes.

(a) sink or swim
(b) the bottom line
(c) a clean break
(d) dog-tired
(e) last but not least
(f) a whole new ball game
(g) over the hill
(h) the bitter end
(i) pretty as a picture
(j) cold as blue blazes

ASSESS

CHAPTER PROJECT

You learned in Chapter 1 that our nation's history has frequently been shaped by the great public speakers who spoke on the vital issues of the day. It is altogether appropriate that students look at important historical speeches to analyze their content and determine what features of the speeches caused them to have political impact. Two such speeches appear in your Appendix: Abraham Lincoln's "Gettysburg Address" and Susan B. Anthony's speech delivered in 1872 on "Woman's Right to Suffrage."

Working in small groups, consider these two speeches very carefully. Apply all principles of rhetorical analysis that you have learned in this chapter. Determine which features of effective language are present in the speeches and collect examples of each.

When your group's analysis is complete, write it in the form of an oral report and select someone to deliver it to the class.

CHAPTER PROJECT

■ The analysis of both speeches should cover all the stylistic devices in the chapter:

concrete terminology	parallelism
abstract words	climax ordering
simile	analogy
metaphor	personification
restatement	hyperbole
economy of language	understatement
contrast	irony
rhetorical question	euphemism
repetition	specific words

The oral report should identify examples of these devices, as well as similarities and differences between the two speeches. It might also describe the rhetorical qualities that make a speech timeless.

PREPARE

● CHAPTER PLANNER

Day 1	Day 2	Day 3	Day 4	Day 5
Prepare	Prepare	Prepare	Prepare	Prepare
Teach	Teach	Teach	Teach	Teach
Assess	Assess	Assess	Assess	Assess
Sub. Teacher Tip *p. 257*	Sub. Teacher Tip *p. 263*	Sub. Teacher Tip *p. 267*	Sub. Teacher Tip *p. 273*	

● CHAPTER OVERVIEW

This chapter examines the following topics:
- Using Different Methods of Delivery *p. 255*
- Recognizing Nonverbal Aspects of Delivering a Speech *p. 260*
- Using Your Voice Effectively *p. 267*
- Special Problems of Delivering a Speech *p. 273*
- Analyzing and Evaluating Speeches *p. 278*

▼ PORTFOLIO PRODUCTS

Individual Projects
- Cartoons of Gestures
- Do's and Don'ts for Speech Conclusions
- Comic Strips of Uses for Lecterns
- Strategies for Dealing with Interruptions
- Chapter 9 Portfolio Products

Group Projects
- Situations for Four Kinds of Speech Deliveries
- Guidelines for Appropriate Dress
- Transition Words in Speeches

● sca GUIDELINES

- Uses words, pronunciation, and grammar appropriate for situation
- Uses nonverbal signs appropriate for situation
- Uses voice effectively
- Expresses ideas clearly and concisely
- Expresses and defends a point of view with evidence
- Gives concise and accurate directions
- Performs social rituals

254

CHAPTER

9

Delivering Your Speech

When you have completed this chapter you should be able to:

● Compare various methods of speech delivery.

● Identify the nonverbal aspects of delivering a speech.

● Explain how to use notes effectively when making a speech.

● Describe the importance of proper articulation and pronunciation.

● Explain ways of dealing with distractions and interruptions when giving a speech.

TEACH

● **MOTIVATION**

Write the following statement on the board for students to complete: "Delivering a speech is like…." Call on students to read their statements. Then ask students to write the advantages and disadvantages of the four methods of delivering a speech on the board. Discuss the items with the class. Come up with a class consensus about which method of delivery would be most effective.

● **LEARNING STYLES**

Kinesic Learning
Ask three students to explain how to make a sandwich. Have the first student do so by using verbal symbols only, but no gestures or body language. Have the second student do so by using mime but no verbal symbols. Finally, have the third student do so by using both verbal and nonverbal symbols. Afterward, discuss the necessity of using both verbal and nonverbal communication to deliver a message to an audience.

Audio/Visual Learning
Organize the class into groups of three. Have each group prepare a demonstration speech using both verbal and nonverbal symbols. One student in the group could prepare a script, another could deliver the speech, and another could videotape it. Then, play the speech for the class, first playing only the audio portion, then playing only the video portion, and finally playing both portions together. Discuss with students the effectiveness of each of the three methods.

Using Different Methods of Delivery 255

● **ACTIVITY**

Pros and Cons of Speech Delivery Methods

Before you can engage in this Activity, you need to read the opening paragraphs of this Chapter. Read only to "Comparing Methods of Delivery" near the top of page 256. *Do not read anything beyond that point.* Now hold a class discussion in which you identify as many advantages and disadvantages of each of the four methods of delivery, defined for you at the bottom of this page. You may want to refer back to these definitions occasionally as you hold your discussion. You should be able to come up with at least one advantage and one disadvantage for each of the four methods, and *several* advantages for two of them. Also discuss whether there may be ways of combining two or more of the methods effectively.

Delivering a speech is not the same as delivering the mail or a loaf of bread. Generally, the mail and the bread are neither improved nor harmed during the process of being delivered to their destination. On the other hand, a speech can be made much better or much worse by the manner in which it is delivered. Although delivery is not the most essential part of giving a speech, it is very important. Good delivery can make a weak speech seem a bit better. Poor delivery can ruin an otherwise excellent speech. This chapter begins by examining several different methods of speech delivery.

● **USING DIFFERENT METHODS OF DELIVERY**

Over the years, four basic methods for delivering public speeches have developed. One might be called the **manuscript method.** Using this method, speakers write down everything they plan to say to their listeners, then bring their manuscripts to the podium and read them to the audience. A second method, called the **memorization method,** also begins with a written manuscript but differs in that the manuscript is memorized word-for-word and not used during the delivery. Using a third method, the **extemporaneous method,** speakers prepare outlines of the *ideas* of their speeches beforehand, but do not memorize an exact pattern of *words*. They choose the words with which to clothe their ideas as they are speaking. Outlines or note cards may or may not be used. The fourth method, called the **impromptu method,** is used on occasions when people must speak "off the cuff," with no chance for previous preparation. This method demands that the speakers both organize their ideas and choose their words as they proceed through their speeches.

TEACH

● **MOTIVATION**

Demonstrate to your students each of the four methods of speech delivery by presenting *very brief* speeches that you have prepared using each of these methods, but do not identify the methods. Discuss with students the effectiveness of each method.

● **LEARNING STYLES**

Cooperative Learning
Organize the class into small groups. After students study the four methods of speech delivery presented in this section, have each group complete a chart using Type of Delivery, Definition, Advantages, and Disadvantages as column headings and the four methods of delivery as row headings.

● **SKILL DEVELOPMENT**

15-Second Skill Opportunity
Students could prepare a 15-second extemporaneous introduction in which they describe where they came from, hobbies, and plans for the future.

The manuscript method of delivery has the advantage of preventing "slips of the tongue," but it is important to avoid the impression that the speech is being read.

Comparing Methods of Delivery

The chapter opening Activity asked you to hold a discussion comparing the four methods of speech delivery, as well as considering possible ways of combining some of the methods. As you read this section of the chapter and the next on combining the four methods, check to see to what extent your classroom discussion was on target.

Each of the four methods has advantages and disadvantages. Let's take a moment to compare them. The manuscript method has an advantage in that there is no danger of forgetting a part of your speech. Unless a sudden wind blows away your manuscript, about the worst thing that can happen is momentarily losing your place while reading. The manuscript method also allows you plenty of time to choose the most effective language for your speech beforehand. Presidents of the United States and other heads of state often read from manuscripts when making major policy statements. This helps assure that they do not make any "slips of the tongue" that could result in embarrassment for their countries or in an international incident. Speeches read from manuscript often sound smoother than those delivered extemporaneously. The use of a manuscript also assures precise timing of a speech, a factor of great importance for televised speeches. Unfortunately, many speeches read from manuscript *sound* as if they are being read. The audience is aware of the manuscript, and it prevents the speech from sounding natural. How many times have you had to listen to a speaker read from manuscript and felt like screaming at the speaker: "Stop reading *at* us and start talking *to* us"?

Memorized delivery has some of the same advantages as manuscript delivery. You may choose the most effective language beforehand, and your speech may be timed precisely. Memorized delivery often sounds prepackaged, however, as indeed it is. Word-for-word

● LINKS TO PAST LEARNING

Ask students to recall speakers they have heard who have used each of the four methods of delivery. Have them describe how the speakers came across to the audience.

● EXTENSION

Explain to students that the optimal way to deliver a speech is to combine methods in such a way as to capitalize on the advantages of each method. Discuss the following possible combinations: breaking from a prepared manuscript to deliver extemporaneous asides; memorizing certain critical passages, such as the introduction; following a speech with a question-and-answer period.

TEACH

SUBSTITUTE TEACHER TIP

Ask students to choose one of the speeches in the Appendix. Ask volunteers to deliver the speech by the manuscript method. Ask others to deliver the speeches through the memorization method. Discuss with students which deliveries were most effective.

Using Different Methods of Delivery **257**

memorization also puts a tremendous burden on your memory for any speech longer than four or five minutes. This method of delivery is used rarely nowadays.

The major advantage of the extemporaneous method is that it sounds natural—much like ordinary conversation. Imagine for a moment that you and a close friend are planning to attend a big basketball game. At the last minute your friend is prevented from going, so she asks you to tell her all about the game later. How would you go about preparing your "speech" for your friend? You could make a strong effort to remember all the important plays, the score, the poor calls by the referees (you might even make a few notes to help you remember), but you definitely wouldn't write out your description of the game word-for-word and later read it to your friend. She would get bored listening to your "reading" about the game instead of "telling" her about it. To an audience, extemporaneous speaking sounds more like "telling" your speech than like "reading" it. No audience likes a speaker to read a message that can be told. They will usually become bored and lose interest, even if the reader reads well. However, they are very tolerant of a speaker who looks them in the eye and addresses them directly, even if the flow of words is a bit halting.

The extemporaneous method also gives you, the speaker, the best opportunity to make use of positive and negative feedback from your audience. By constantly monitoring the listeners' reactions and making necessary adjustments, you will improve your chances of maintaining a high level of audience interest and enthusiasm. Since the manuscript and memorization methods prevent this, they fall far short of the extemporaneous method of speaking.

temporaneous speaking characterized by "telling," and it enables you to ake use of positive and gative feedback from the dience.

● SKILL DEVELOPMENT

Creative Thinking

Have students work in small groups to generate a list of five to ten real-life situations or jobs that call for each of the methods of speech delivery. For example, manuscript method might include newscast, memorization method might include initiation ritual, extemporaneous method might include an on-the-scene reporter, impromptu might include an on-the-spot interview, and combination method might include an awards presentation. Students could include their lists in their portfolios for future reference.

● LEARNING STYLES

✳ Cooperative Learning

Organize the class into four groups. Assign each group a topic and one of the four methods of delivering a speech, but do not assign a topic to the impromptu group until you are ready to call on someone to deliver the speech. Call on students from each group to deliver their speeches to the class. Hold a class discussion to evaluate the four kinds of deliveries.

Audio Learning

Have students listen to a speech of President Franklin Roosevelt's. Have them describe his speech delivery and decide what type of delivery he used.

257

TEACH

● RETEACHING

Assign speaking parts based on the nursery rhyme "Jack and Jill." For example: a reporter interviewing an eyewitness to the accident; a friend calling Jack's family about Jack's accident; a doctor reporting on Jack's condition; a reporter sensationalizing the event; a police lieutenant questioning Jill; a priest or minister delivering a eulogy for Jack. Students should decide on the type of delivery to use and discuss it after each presentation.

● SKILL DEVELOPMENT

Feedback
Videotape the quiz show suggested in the Enrichment activity and play it back to the class. Ask students to assess their presentations.

● ENRICHMENT

Organize the class into small groups to prepare a quiz show, with class members participating as contestants. Speakers could include: an announcer, who would make a *memorized* introduction; an emcee who would speak *extemporaneously* and *impromptu* throughout the game; an announcer who uses *manuscript* speaking to introduce contestants and to present game rules; and prize contestants who would speak *impromptu*. Groups should consider the name of the show, rules, scorekeeping, props, and script. The game show could use course content from this or another course as quiz material.

CHAPTER 9 Delivering Your Speech

The only advantage of impromptu delivery is that it sounds natural—much like ordinary conversation. Its major drawback, of course,␣ its tendency to sound unprepared. Unless a speaker has had consider␣ able experience at impromptu speaking, this kind of delivery is likely t␣ sound jumbled and awkward.

Combining Methods of Delivery

In Chapter 7, you prepared an outline or a set of note cards to use fo␣ reference when delivering a speech. You concentrated on planting ␣ pattern of ideas in your mind, rather than on preparing a speech man␣ uscript to read or memorize. Thus you were really preparing to delive␣ an extemporaneous speech.

Of the four methods you have been comparing (manuscript, mem␣ orization, extemporaneous, and impromptu), extemporaneous deliver␣ appears to have the greatest number of advantages. Many of the be␣ speakers, however, find they are most effective when they combin␣ methods. One of America's greatest public speakers, President Frankli␣ D. Roosevelt, often prepared manuscripts for his major addresses, an␣ then regularly departed from them during delivery, speaking extempo␣ raneously instead. Although this practice annoyed newspaper owner␣ who had sometimes already printed the advance text in their papers, ␣ was extremely effective with Roosevelt's audiences. By combining th␣ methods in this way, he was able to gain the advantages of each, whil␣ avoiding their pitfalls.

Combining methods of delivery in this way requires a certain degre␣ of skill and experience. The listeners should not be able to detect whic␣ parts are being read from manuscript, which are memorized, and whic␣ are being spoken extemporaneously. Combining methods effectivel␣ also requires skill in the use of the extemporaneous method, since th␣ extemporaneous parts must sound as fluent and well prepared as th␣ manuscript sections. However, you can begin to use a combination ␣ methods in small ways.

You will probably find it helpful, at this point, to memorize you␣ introductory remarks and your conclusions. Memorizing the introductio␣ gets you off to a smooth start, sounds impressive, and helps build you␣ confidence for the body of the speech. A carefully worded, memorize␣ conclusion can make a lasting impression on the audience and en␣ your speech effectively. Major transition sentences within the body ␣ the speech may also be memorized. Most of the body of the speech ca␣ then be prepared using the extemporaneous method. The manuscri␣ method may be used for brief sections of the body where you wish ␣ insert a direct quotation in the original author's language or present a s␣ of statistics too complex to memorize. These kinds of material can ␣

TEACH

● **MOTIVATION**

Ask students if they've ever heard the expression "I can tell by the look on your face that ...." Ask them to discuss what that means. Ask them to give examples of things you can tell by the look on someone's face.

AMAZING FACTS!
People respond 8 percent to what other people actually say, 37 percent to their vocal inflection, and 55 percent to their body language and expression.

Using Different Methods of Delivery 259

Using note cards is an effective way of combining manuscript, memorization, and extemporaneous methods of speech delivery.

written out fully on 3 × 5 note cards or a manuscript page and read at appropriate points in your speech. Beware of preparing lengthy sections of the speeches you are now giving by the manuscript or memorization methods, however. Your main concentration should be on learning the extemporaneous method, since it will serve as the backbone for any combination of methods you may later wish to use.

● **ACTIVITY**

Extemporaneous Speech
Think about a book or a movie that you like and that you feel a friend would also enjoy. Prepare to speak extemporaneously to your friend about it. Jot down some notes and plan the opening and the ending of your talk. Then speak about the book or movie in an informal and conversational tone. When you are finished, ask whether your friend would like to read the book or see the movie. Also, ask if your presentation captured your friend's attention and whether or not it was clear and natural. Jot down useful feedback in your speech notebook.

● **SKILL DEVELOPMENT**

15-Second Skill Opportunity
Stress to students that a speech begins as soon as a speaker is acknowledged. Explain that a speaker is carefully observed from that point on. Call on students to demonstrate the following for beginning a speech: rising from the seat and walking with confidence to the platform; arranging notes on the lectern in proper order; taking a few seconds to look at the entire audience, acknowledging the presence of the audience, and signaling that the speech is about to begin.

● **ACTIVITY**

After students have completed the Activity, have them prepare a short extemporaneous speech to deliver to the class. The topic might involve defending a point of view about a school policy with which they agree or disagree. Have other students critique the use of the extemporaneous method.

259

TEACH

AMAZING FACTS!
According to research, much of our learning takes place through sight. The average person obtains 87 percent of his or her knowledge visually and 7 percent through hearing. For this reason, speakers have to give their audience something to see as well as to hear.

"The eyes have one language everywhere."
—George Herbert

LEARNING STYLES

Visual Learning
Ask students to explain what messages a speaker communicates when he or she does not look at an audience. Demonstrate poor eye contact by giving a brief lecture in which you look only at your notes, at the ceiling, or at the back of the room.

Cooperative Learning
Have students work in groups to come up with several examples of each of the four types of gestures. Then have each group present its examples to the class.

CHAPTER 9 Delivering Your Speech

RECOGNIZING NONVERBAL ASPECTS OF DELIVERING A SPEECH

People often think of a speech as a set of words spoken aloud. Actually, you communicate with an audience as much through nonverbal means as through words. Eye contact, gestures, platform movements, appearance, and the motions you make as you begin and end a speech will "say" a great deal about you and your message to the listeners.

Beginning Your Speech

You may think that your speech begins when you speak the first word. The audience, however, makes judgments about you from the moment you rise from your seat to approach the speaking platform. You nonverbally communicate self-confidence, poise, and leadership, or nervousness, disorganization, and timidity simply by the manner in which you approach the platform and take command of it.

Walk to the platform vigorously, but not hastily. Arrange any notes on the lectern. Turn your face up toward your listeners, and look about at various sides of the audience for several seconds before beginning to speak. This unhurried beginning assures those present of your confidence and command of the situation.

Making Eye Contact

As you speak, establish eye contact with your listeners. Look directly into the eyes of various audience members. This causes most listeners to feel as if you are devoting your attention to them personally in the same way you would if you were conversing with just one person. The greater the proportion of your speaking time you devote to eye contact, the deeper and more positive this impression becomes.

Looking at your listeners also performs a second important function. It makes it possible for you to monitor the feedback. Feedback is simply the total of all the visible and audible reactions of the audience to the speaker. It can consist of yawns, smiles, boos, nodding heads, hisses, questioning looks, and even fidgeting in the seats. When you use extemporaneous delivery, you are largely free to read your listeners' feedback and then adjust your approach to maintain positive feedback.

When making eye contact, look at one audience member for several seconds as you speak, then turn your head slightly to look at another. Don't forget the people at the sides of the room near the front. Because speakers must turn their heads farther to look at them, these listeners are often cheated out of eye contact.

Recognizing Nonverbal Aspects of Delivering a Speech

Some beginning speakers report that looking directly at their listeners makes them nervous and confused. If this happens to you, let your teacher know, and he or she will probably suggest that you look at your audience in general for awhile, rather than directly into individuals' eyes. Beware of getting into a habit of doing this, however. Eye contact is so important for both speaker and audience that its lack can sometimes ruin an otherwise good speech. Once you have gained some experience and have learned to relax on the platform, your should be able to maintain real eye contact without difficulty.

Using Gestures

Communicating nonverbally through gestures is a natural part of human communication, yet many beginning speakers freeze up when giving a public speech. Nevertheless, because we all gesture naturally, the urge to gesture will ordinarily return once a speaker has gained platform experience.

Most arm and hand gestures fall into one of four types. **Emphatic gestures** help the speaker stress what he or she is saying. These include making a fist, raising one hand with the palm up, and pointing with the index finger at your audience when saying something such as "It's your responsibility...." **Transitional gestures** show that you are moving from one part of your speech to another. They include using your fingers to enumerate points, placing both palms on the podium, and moving both hands, with palms facing each other, from one side to the other in front of you. When a speaker uses **descriptive gestures,** he or she moves the hands and arms to draw pictures in the air. These may indicate the size of an object, such as the "fish that got away," or the

Gestures accompanying speeches should be natural, appropriate, and not forced.

TEACH

● **SKILL DEVELOPMENT**

Gestures
Call on students to demonstrate the three hand and arm positions described on this page.

15-Second Skill Opportunity
Ask students to imagine that they are campaigning for a political candidate. Have them use eye contact and gestures when presenting the first 15 seconds of a campaign speech for the candidate.

Feedback
You could videotape the campaign speeches to play them back to the class. Ask the class to observe the use of eye contact and gestures in the speeches and provide constructive remarks.

● **SKILL APPLICATION**

Media Literacy
Students could observe speakers on television, such as talk-show hosts and news broadcasters. Have students focus on the way these personalities use gestures when they speak. Have them identify the type of gestures used and the effectiveness of these gestures.

TEACH

● **EXTENSION**

Have students view press conferences given by President Kennedy. Have them observe Kennedy's eye contact, facial expressions, and gestures during the press conferences. Ask them how these contributed to his reputation as a first-rate speaker.

● **CURRICULAR CONNECTIONS**

Art
Students could create amusing cartoons that show speakers using inappropriate expressions or gestures for the topic of their speeches. For example, they could use the example on the next page and show a somber person speaking about the topic "How to Shoot Rapids in a Canoe." Students could include their cartoons in their portfolios.

● **SKILL DEVELOPMENT**

Gestures
Point out that facial gestures can help a speaker to feel what he or she is saying more deeply and that audiences will respond in kind to such feeling. Ask students to demonstrate facial expressions used to communicate various messages.

CHAPTER 9 Delivering Your Speech

general shape of something. Finally, **locative gestures** direct the listeners' attention to some place, object, or person. They are usually made with the index finger or with the entire hand.

Books on public speaking used to include long lists and extensive illustrations of gestures, showing in detail how they should be made. The problem with that approach was that it was like telling a speaker which words to use. Each person has his or her own style of nonverbal communication, just as each chooses his or her own words. When you gesture during a speech, it should be because it feels natural at that point. If, for instance, you are describing a far distant place, and it seems appropriate to extend your arm to indicate how far away it is, extend your arm. If you refer to that same distant place later in the same speech, and this time it does not seem appropriate to extend your arm, you should not do so. It is basically a matter of what feels appropriate at the moment without any lengthy thought about it. While it is helpful for beginning speakers to make some gestures while speaking, it is no good to force gestures. Certainly it is not wise to decide during rehearsal that you are definitely going to make a certain gesture at a particular place in your speech. It would probably look rehearsed if made during the live speech.

Student speakers sometimes ask: "What should I do with my arms and hands when I am not using them to gesture?" Unfortunately, no single answer can be given. As with gestures, basic hand and arm positions must be both natural to you and well suited to the audience and the total speaking situation. Here are some commonly used positions that you may want to consider:

- One or both arms hanging naturally at your side.
- One or both hands resting on (not grasping) the speaker's stand.
- One or both hands held several inches in front of you.

These positions will look quite natural for some speakers but not for others. You can learn from the reactions of your teacher and classmates which suit you best.

Audience members ordinarily pay more attention to a speaker's head and facial gestures than they do to arm or hand movements. Smiles, frowns, nods, and any other movements of the head, eyebrows, chin, lips, or brow can create an impression of a dynamic and enthusiastic speaker, as long as they are appropriate to the spoken message. As with any gestures, head and facial movements must be natural. They must come from your inner enthusiasm about your message and not be practiced or tacked on for show.

Many beginning speakers show too somber a face to their audiences. Of course, some topics demand a serious countenance, but many

TEACH

● **EXTENSION**

Have students role-play, in mime, the following scenarios:
- a teacher responding to a student who is asking for a fourth extension of an assignment due a week earlier
- a hard-sell salesman pitching a vacuum cleaner

Suggest that the presentations be twenty to thirty seconds long and that they incorporate a minimum of three arm or hand movements and three head or facial gestures.

SUBSTITUTE TEACHER TIP

Ask students to prepare a speech about a favorite hobby or a favorite activity. Tell them to use facial expressions and gestures that really indicate their involvement with the topic and that will create enthusiasm in their audience.

Placement of the arms and hands during a speech should be comfortable for the speaker and natural-looking to the audience.

do not. A speaker describing "How to Shoot Rapids in a Canoe" need not look overly solemn to the listeners. A generally pleasant look, alternating with some facial expressions showing the adventure and thrill of canoeing, will make a better impression on the listeners.

Variety is the spice of public speaking, just as it is of life. Like all other parts of a speech, gestures (whether arm-hand or head-face) must be varied regularly to maintain audience attention and interest. A speaker who makes the same gesture repeatedly distracts the audience with that gesture. Pretty soon many listeners are wondering when the gesture will occur again and are paying little attention to the message. Although he was a first-rate speaker, President John F. Kennedy occasionally overused a gesture with his right arm during his campaign speeches. It became so characteristic of his speaking style that mimics began imitating the movement. But because Kennedy possessed so many outstanding qualities as a speaker, it was easy for listeners to excuse this overworked gesture. Unknown speakers, however, must be doubly careful of any gesture that becomes a regular pattern in their speech. While taking care not to overuse any one gesture, remember that using no gestures at all is just as deadly. In addition, a speaker's face should be expressive. Facial gestures such as raising the eyebrows, smiling, frowning, and widening the eyes, indicate your involvement with your topic and generate interest and enthusiasm in your audience.

TEACH

● **RETEACHING**

Ask students to review the material on platform movement in Chapter 6. Have students demonstrate proper and improper platform movement.

● **CURRICULAR CONNECTIONS**

Language Arts
Work with the language arts teacher to reinforce students' note-taking skills. The language arts teacher might review techniques for taking notes and might provide more opportunities for students to take notes.

● **SKILL APPLICATION**

Citizens Speak Out
Ask students to prepare a speech in which they give directions to their classmates about procedures necessary in order to vote. Have them research the information they will need for the speech. Then have them use the tips on page 265 to prepare and use their notes.

● **SKILL DEVELOPMENT**

Feedback
You might videotape the speeches suggested above and play them back to the class. Ask students to comment on how effectively each speaker used note cards.

---

264   CHAPTER 9 Delivering Your Speech

Using Platform Movement

The way in which a speaker uses platform movement (movement involving the entire body) can also project a certain image to the audience. In Chapter 6 you read about the basic forms of platform movement and the dangers of falling into distracting forms. (Remember the Ping-Pong Pacer, for instance?) The question here is, how can one make the best use of positive forms of movement? Like gestures, platform movement should look and feel natural. The best way to achieve this is to move when there is a reason to move and to remain still at other times. Legitimate reasons to move during a speech are similar to reasons for moving during a one-to-one conversation. Ask yourself: "When do I ordinarily move about if I'm having a conversation with a friend?" Your answers are likely to include at least two or three of the following reasons:

- To whisper something confidential or intimate to the other person.
- To compensate when the listener shifts his or her position.
- To change to a new topic or to change the mood.
- To provide variety.

Reasons for platform movement during a public speech fall into the very same categories. You may want to get closer to the audience to show greater confidentiality or intimacy, to compensate for audience members' fidgeting in their seats, to emphasize change to a new topic or section of your speech at major transition points, or to create a bit of visual variety.

Reasons for moving about while speaking are similar to those for moving during a one-to-one conversation.

264

Using Notes Effectively

Speaking extemporaneously means having your pattern of ideas clearly in mind as you begin your speech, but selecting your words spontaneously. Many extemporaneous speakers use **note cards** to ensure that they do not forget a major point, or to read an occasional direct quote or set of statistics. You have probably seen speakers who used note cards so effectively you were barely aware the speakers had them. You have also probably suffered through speeches in which the note cards were fumbled, dropped, or even lost. Observing a few tips on the preparation and use of note cards can make all the difference:

- Cards containing your outline should be very brief, containing only a word or short phrase to remind you of each point in your speech.
- Cards containing direct quotes or sets of statistics should contain only one item of information each, and should be arranged in the proper order before the speech begins.
- Be certain to write your source of information at the bottom of cards containing quotations or statistics. Write or type in large, bold characters so that each card can be easily read when resting on the podium.
- Place the cards near the top edge of the podium so the audience doesn't think you're looking at your feet when you're glancing at your cards.
- Feel free to hold one or more cards in your hand if you move away from the podium. (Use only 3 × 5 cards to do this.)
- Plan not to look at your outline card at all during your presentation. It should be there only as a comforting refuge should you forget a point.

Making the Most of Your Appearance

Much of the appeal of glamorous stars comes from their appearance—the carefully styled hair, the beautiful gowns, the glittering jewels. Speakers, too are often judged as much by how they look as by what they have to say. A speaker's appearance should be suited to his or her personality, the audience being addressed, and the occasion for which the speech is being given. The way speakers dress says a great deal about their attitudes toward their listeners and how much importance they attach to the speech itself. Speakers who radically violate the audience's expectations concerning clothing and general appearance have two

---

TEACH

● **SKILL DEVELOPMENT**

Creative Thinking
Ask students to work in small groups to develop a list of factors to consider in choosing dress for a particular audience. Factors might include the formality of the occasion, the ages of the people in the audience, the temperature in the place where the speech is to be delivered, style, comfort, and neatness. Students might include their lists in their portfolios.

● **LEARNING STYLES**

Visual Learning
Ask students to describe what a speaker should wear to each of the following speaking situations:
- a pep rally for your classmates
- a luncheon for senior citizens
- a school assembly for first graders
- an awards banquet for an athletic team

TEACH

> *"The voice that is difficult to hear doesn't show confidence, indicate enthusiasm or demonstrate leadership qualities."*
> —Edward J. Hegarty

▼ PORTFOLIO PRODUCTS

Have students make up a list of *do's* and *don'ts* for concluding a speech. Have students include their lists in their portfolios.

● CURRICULAR CONNECTIONS

History
Distribute a copy of Lincoln's Gettysburg Address (see Appendix, p.584). Have students read small sections of the speech and discuss these to make sure that they understand the vocabulary and the intent. Then have students practice saying these sections with various gestures.

● ACTIVITY

After students complete this Activity, have them review the type of gestures their classmates have recorded. Discuss whether the gestures were natural or forced and if they were effective.

---

266 CHAPTER 9 Delivering Your Speech

A speaker's appearance says a great deal about her attitude toward the audience as well as how much importance she attaches to the speech itself.

strikes against them before they say their first sentence. You can improve your chances of creating a good impression by asking yourself, "What is the most appropriate thing to wear for this particular audience and set of circumstances?"

A speaker's appearance is more than appropriate clothing, however. No matter what your personality, the audience, or the occasion, *neatness* is always necessary when giving a public speech. Even when the most informal mode of dress is called for, neat and clean clothes—together with clean hair, nails, face, and hands—are a must. A sloppy appearance automatically communicates to your audience: "I'm not very interested in giving this speech, so I didn't spend much time getting ready to meet you." Clearly, there is no benefit or advantage to be gained from sending this kind of message to an audience. However, by making the most of your appearance, you demonstrate respect for yourself and esteem for your audience.

● ACTIVITY

Gesturing
Think of an idea that you can communicate to the class in no more than four or five sentences. Once you know what you want to say, volunteer to step in front of the class and say it, with the intent of making two or three gestures of some kind while you're speaking. *Don't preplan a specific gesture for a particular spot in your statement.* Just be determined that before you sit down, you'll have made two or three gestures of some kind. Afterwards, ask your classmates to identify each of your gestures as to type: emphatic, transitional, descriptive, or locative.

TEACH

● **MOTIVATION**

Review diaphragmatic breathing with the students. Refer to Chapter 2 to review this process and ask volunteers to demonstrate it.

SUBSTITUTE TEACHER TIP

Copy and distribute the speech of Susan B. Anthony (p. 576) or the Gettysburg Address (p. 584). Have students study the passage and mark appropriate places in which to take breaths. Discuss students' choices. Then have students read the passages using proper diaphragmatic breathing.

● **LEARNING STYLES**

Kinesic Learning
Have students practice the following breathing exercise:
(a) Inhale deeply, through your nose, with your mouth shut. Use your diaphragm to fill your lungs completely. (If students do this properly, their stomachs should become extended as they inhale.)
(b) Exhale, through your mouth, again using your diaphragm. Make the exhalation slow and steady. (If students do this properly, their stomachs should become depressed as they exhale.) You might have students repeat this exercise, this time vocalizing as they exhale, perhaps saying "Ahhhhhh."

Audio Learning
Have students choose a passage from a speech that can be emphasized effectively by using changes in volume. Have them consider ways in which to use volume to achieve emphasis, such as the following:
(a) Speak at a moderate volume. Then make the emphatic point by using a significantly louder volume.
(b) Steadily increase the volume until the emphatic point is made. Then, go back to a moderate volume.

Recognizing Nonverbal Aspects of Delivering a Speech   **267**

Concluding Your Speech

Just as the speech begins at the moment you rise from your seat, it cannot be said to have concluded until you have regained your seat. You do not want to create the impression that you wish to leave the platform as quickly as possible. An unhurried departure is essential. Once you have spoken your final word, pause momentarily while still facing the audience to let the impact of your conclusion sink in. Then walk to your seat in a manner appropriate to your topic.

If your speech was serious in nature, a grave and solemn return is indicated. If the topic was light or entertaining, a more cheerful mode is appropriate. Above all, do not ruin the effect of a good presentation by showing you felt it was a poor job as you depart from the platform. Let the audience be the judge of that. You will learn more about concluding a speech in Chapter 10.

Using Your Voice Effectively

A good deal of emphasis is placed on the visual aspects of speech delivery—what an audience *sees*. A large part of the message of a speech, however, is carried by the voice—what an audience *hears*. How you control and use your voice can make the difference between a well received and a poorly received speech. Before you read this section, review "Vocalizing" in Chapter 2 (page 44), to recall the way in which vocal sounds are produced. Then you can proceed to consider a number of different factors involved when using your voice for public speaking.

Speak with the Right Volume

No matter how well organized, researched, and practiced a speech may be, if the listeners cannot hear what is being said, the speech cannot possibly succeed. Although it is possible to speak too loudly for a given room or audience, most beginning speakers have the opposite problem. They speak too softly and cannot be heard in the rear of the room. This may be due to nervousness; more often, inexperienced speakers simply do not realize they are not using sufficient volume.

Volume is controlled primarily by the amount of air a person forces through the vocal cords. By inhaling you obtain a supply of air in your lungs that can then be used to produce vocal tones (sounds) as you exhale, forcing the air across your vocal cords. If you are going to speak very loudly, you must have a considerable supply of air in your lungs. If you need to speak loudly for an extended period of time (as in a pub-

TEACH

> **AMAZING FACTS!**
> Experiments have shown that speaking at a faster than usual rate made the speaker seem more persuasive, more trustworthy, and more knowledgeable. It also improved recall among the listeners. On the whole, a 25 percent increase in a speaker's rate of speaking was preferred.

● **SKILL DEVELOPMENT**

Active Listening
Demonstrate reading to the class using speaking rates that are too rapid and too slow. Stress that a speaker must use a rate that will ensure audience comprehension. Also, the rate should be varied to keep a speech from becoming boring.

● **LEARNING STYLES**

Audio Learning
Have students listen to radio and television interviews. Ask them to focus on the vocalized pause. Ask them to indicate the effect of this pause on the listeners.

CHAPTER 9 Delivering Your Speech

lic speech), you need a constant, large supply of air. Research has found that people use sixty-six times as much energy addressing a large audience in a large room as they do in ordinary conversation. So the manner in which you inhale while speaking becomes very important. Inhale deeply through your nose, sucking in air by expanding your diaphragm. Upper chest breathing does not provide enough air for an extended sentence in a large auditorium. Diaphragmatic breathing, however, provides plenty. Besides, filling the lower lungs with air does not really take much longer than shallow inhalation.

How you exhale is also important in sustaining sufficient volume. If you let all the air out as you say your first few words, one of two problems will occur. Either the ends of your longer sentences will be too soft to be heard, or you will need to inhale so often you will begin to sound like an air compressor at work. As you gain experience in public speaking, you will learn to pace your exhalation, saving enough air for emphasizing important ideas with extra force.

Variety in volume is important too. A speaker who is constantly loud makes everything sound important. Eventually, nothing sounds important. One who is constantly soft is difficult to hear. Listeners eventually give up straining to hear such a speaker. Important or key ideas must always be spoken with sufficient force so that those in the back row can hear them easily. Transitions to new sections of a speech, the start of the conclusion, and the parts where you wish to be dramatic with a kind of "stage whisper" may be spoken more softly, but should still be audible for listeners in the rear of the room.

Vary Your Pitch

Pitch refers to the tone of the voice on the musical scale. Words or syllables to be emphasized are usually spoken in a higher key. Strong emotion is generally indicated by great differences in pitch among words or syllables that are used together. Think, for example, of the way in which you might pronounce the following sentence: "I certainly don't think that!"

Changing pitch as you speak comes naturally to you in conversation, but beginning public speakers often fail to maintain their pitch variety when speaking from a public platform. Speaking in a **monotone**, with no ups and downs in pitch, can quickly give an audience the impression that the speaker is not enthusiastic or sincere about the topic. Of course, pitch changes should not be affected. The enthusiasm must first be present. Then pitch variety will naturally follow.

Each of you has a general pitch—that portion of your range in which your voice usually hovers when you speak. For public speaking, each person needs to discover his or her optimum pitch, that pitch

TEACH

PORTFOLIO PRODUCTS

Have students make a list of transition words to use between sentences. Compile individual lists into one class list that students can include in their portfolios for future reference.

AMAZING FACTS!

Howard Hawks once denied Lauren Bacall a role because of her high-pitched, nasal voice. Bacall returned about three weeks later, sounding like a different person. "I had to admire her," Hawks remembered. "She wanted to work and she had to have put forth much time and effort to accomplish this."

● SKILL DEVELOPMENT

15-Second Skill Opportunity
Have students practice avoiding the vocalized pause. Ask them to give a speech in which they describe an accident to a police officer. Ask students to deliver the first 15 seconds of their description to the class.

Feedback
Tape record students' descriptions and play them back to the class. Have students evaluate how effectively they were at avoiding the vocalized pause.

Adapting your pitch when speaking from a public platform will follow naturally from the enthusiasm in your presentation.

which can be used most comfortably without strain for extended periods of time. The most comfortable tones are found most often in the lower half of a person's range.

Watch Your Speaking Rate

Normal speaking rate varies from 120 to 150 words per minute. Some people regularly speak more rapidly or more slowly than others, and nearly everyone varies his or her speaking rate for different situations. Barry Goldwater once said of the late Hubert Humphrey, former vice president and senator from Minnesota: "Hubert has been clocked at 280 words per minute with gusts up to 340."

Many times inexperienced speakers speak too rapidly due to nervousness. If your teacher says you are speaking too quickly, force yourself to slow down by concentrating on the problem. Changes in rate are brought about in two ways: by varying the number and length of pauses between words or by varying the length of time it takes to pronounce each syllable. If you are told that you are speaking too rapidly, the best place to start correction is with your pauses. Some speakers feel they must emit some kind of sound every second they are before their audience. However, a well-timed pause, supported by appropriate gestures, movement, and eye contact can often say much more than several sentences. Pause especially for several seconds between major segments of your speech and more briefly between sentences.

A specific problem, common to many speakers, is called the **vocalized pause.** This is the habit of filling in pause time with "uh," "er,"

TEACH

> *Except ye utter by the tongue words easy to be understood, how shall it be known what is spoken? For ye shall speak into the air.*
>
> —Bible, I Cor. 9:14

● **EXTENSION**

Students could collect tongue-twisters and practice these to develop better articulation habits.

● **LEARNING STYLES**

Audio Learning
Write the following sloppily articulated sentences on the board and have students translate them, aloud, into well-articulated sentences:
(a) Cheat yet? (Have you eaten yet?)
(b) Whazza madder? (What's the matter?)
(c) I'm gonna go; arn chew? (I'm going to go; aren't you?)

CHAPTER 9 Delivering Your Speech

"like," "you-know," or similar nonmeaningful sounds. If these sounds become numerous they can be very distracting to the listeners. Here are two methods for handling the vocalized pause.

1. Make a list of transition words to use between sentences and vary them regularly during your speech.
2. Rehearse your speeches with a tape recorder and listen to yourself.

Hearing a great number of vocalized pauses in one's own speech can often motivate a person to concentrate seriously on solving the problem.

Use Crisp Articulation and Correct Pronunciation

As you know, you are capable of producing vocal sounds that are not words. You can use your vocal cords to make sounds like those of a dog or cat, an airplane, automobile, or nearly any sound you choose to imitate. Crisp articulation and correct pronunciation are needed to turn these vocal sounds into recognizable words and verbal symbols.

"Watcha doin ta-day, Sam?" "I dunno. Wudder you?" This kind of talk may communicate very well during informal conversation with your friends, but clearer articulation is definitely called for in a public speech. **Articulation** refers to the way in which the tongue, teeth, palate, and lips are moved and used to produce the crisp, clear sounds of good speech. Most people are capable of producing vowel and consonant sounds clearly, but fall into lazy habits. They become unwilling to exert that extra bit of effort needed to produce clear speech. Unfortunately, when such bad habits are carried over into public speaking, an audience may show little respect for the speaker who sounds sloppy or mushy. When practicing your speeches, therefore, concentrate on moving your tongue, lips, and lower jaw vigorously enough to produce crisp, clear sounds. Be especially careful with consonants that are easily slurred or dropped altogether. Don't use "madder" when you mean "matter," "pacific" for "specific," or "gonna" for "going to."

Pronunciation can also play a role in determining the degree of respect given a speaker by the audience. **Pronunciation** means selecting the correct sounds and the proper syllable stresses. What makes certain pronunciation correct and another incorrect is usage. Once enough people agree to pronounce a word in a certain way, that becomes the correct way. But you cannot assume that your friends, or even all the people in your school, have cornered the market on correct pronunciation. The two best sources of the accepted pronunciation of words are (1) the dictionary and (2) the prominent speakers of the day such as national news commentators and noted government officials.

APPLY

● **LINKS TO PAST LEARNING**

Ask students to recall if they have ever seen interpreters on television. Students might recall interpreters serving in international conferences or in situations in which a foreign dignitary speaks to a U.S. reporter. Discuss with students what qualities a person would need to have to be an interpreter.

● **LEARNING STYLES**

Multicultural Learning
You may choose to demonstrate interpretation by having a student who speaks a foreign language speak before the class, pausing frequently to allow oral translation by a second student who speaks the same language.

Beyond the Classroom
If possible, invite a professional interpreter to speak to your class about his or her job.

CAREER CLOSE-UP

Interpreter

Interpreters translate spoken passages from one language to another. They listen carefully to what one speaker is saying and then quickly translate it into the language of the other speaker. Employed by many government agencies, hospitals, and corporations, interpreters are needed wherever people speaking different languages communicate. Although educational requirements in this field vary, applicants often are required to have a bachelor's degree in foreign languages.

These specialists use their voices skillfully to communicate well. They articulate distinctly so that they will be understood and maintain enough volume to be heard by everyone. Skilled interpreters develop the ability to adjust their speaking rates faster or slower according to the speed of those needing translation. Even when there is pressure to translate more quickly, interpreters must be wary of speaking so fast that they cannot be understood. To help with delivery in these situations, an experienced interpreter inhales deeply into the diaphragm so that there is enough air to complete a thought without losing articulation or volume.

Interpreters must be efficient nonverbal communicators to interpret the facial expressions, gestures, and other body motions of those from different cultures. They also must use nonverbal communication to help convey translated information. As interpreters apply both forms of communication to the delivery of their translations, they fulfill a vital role by enabling people to communicate who otherwise would be prevented from doing so.

Among the skills applied by the interpreter are distinct articulation, the ability to adjust speaking rate rapidly, and highly developed nonverbal communication.

271

271

TEACH

> **"Talking is like playing the harp. There is as much in laying the hands on the strings to stop their vibration as in twanging them to bring out their music."**
>
> —Oliver Wendell Holmes

CURRICULAR CONNECTIONS

Language Arts
Give students a list of often mispronounced words. Have students practice saying these words. Quiz them orally after a few days. The list might include the following:

accept	fifth	height	recognize
Arctic	creek	irreparable	significance
February	government	library	suppose
		literature	temperature
		mischievous	usually
		poem	vegetable
		preferable	Wednesday
		probably	

SKILL APPLICATION

Interviews
Have students work in pairs to role-play an employment interview. Ask them to imagine that they are interviewing for a job. One student should take the role of the interviewer and one the interviewee. Ask students to focus on using appropriate language and correct grammar as interviewees. Call on students to present their interviews to the class.

SKILL DEVELOPMENT

Critical Thinking
Discuss with students the effect that improper pronunciation has on a speaker's credibility.

Feedback
Have the class comment on the interviews. Have them focus on the use of accurate pronunciation and grammar.

---

272   CHAPTER 9 Delivering Your Speech

If you need to use proper names or technical terms in a speech, be certain you know the accepted pronunciation before beginning your rehearsal. Using the correct sounds and stresses during rehearsal will usually assure correct pronunciation during the live performance. When you pronounce unusual words with authority and without hesitation, your audience is likely to be impressed by the thoroughness of your speech preparation and to feel you have genuinely earned the right to speak to them.

Pause Effectively

Beginning speakers often have difficulty with pausing. Some rush ahead like a speeding train with no pauses at all; others fill their pauses with meaningless sounds, those vocalized pauses mentioned under speaking rate; still others pause in the middle of thoughts rather than at the end. Your teacher will work with you in correcting any such pausing problems you might have.

As you correct pausing problems, you will also want to discover ways to make pausing work for you to improve your speech. The well-known American writer, Mark Twain, who gave many speeches during his life, once said: "The right word may be effective, but no word wa

Mark Twain was a master of the precise pause.

272

- **RETEACHING**

Give students a copy of the following passages (or you might provide them with other passages):

"One of the most striking differences between a cat and a lie is that a cat has only nine lives."

—Mark Twain

"The gentlemen may cry, Peace, peace! but there is no peace. The war has actually begun! … I know not what course others may take; but, as for me, give me liberty, or give me death!"

—Patrick Henry

Have students prepare to deliver passages by focusing on proper articulation, pronunciation, volume, pitch, rate, and pauses.

TEACH

SUBSTITUTE TEACHER TIP

Help students to practice effective pausing in speaking. Have them choose speeches and mark them for pauses. Students may use a slash mark, or solidus, for a short pause (/) and two slash marks, or a caesura, for a long pause (//).

AMAZING FACTS!

George Jessel said that he learned how to use pauses by taking advice from George M. Cohan who "taught me how to pause while talking to an audience so as to make them believe that I was thinking of something important, or some new line that had just come to mind—when it was actually something tried and true that I knew would get a laugh."

Special Problems of Delivering a Speech **273**

ever as effective as a rightly timed pause." Especially in speeches to entertain, a pause of just the right length in just the right place can result in more thunderous laughter than a lengthy story.

There is no quick way to learn how to pause effectively in public speaking. It is mostly a matter of timing and comes primarily from experience. When listening to experienced speakers, notice when they pause and for how long. Pay attention to their audiences' reactions. Practice pausing when rehearsing your own speeches. Use pauses when you wish to create a dramatic effect, when you want to signal your listeners you are changing thoughts, or when you wish to create laughter. Be aware that what usually seems like a three-minute pause to a beginning speaker is actually about three seconds in length. When pausing for laughter from your audience, do not continue with your speech until the laughter has subsided. On the other hand, do not wait until several seconds after the laughter has died down to continue, lest you lose momentum or create the impression that you wanted more laughter than you received.

ACTIVITY

Discovering Your Best Average Volume

Prior to delivering your next speech, you may find it helpful to know in advance whether your average voice volume for public speaking in your classroom is too soft, too loud, or about right. Volunteer to stand behind your classroom lectern and begin counting aloud while your teacher, seated in the rear, signals "louder" with a thumbs up sign, "softer" with a thumbs down sign, and "about right" with a level palm. Continue counting for about a minute so that you get a sense of your best average volume. Keep in mind, of course, that in a real speech, you'll be aiming for that level as an *average*—you also need some variety in volume level throughout a speech.

ACTIVITY

Have students complete the Activity. Then have students prepare a speech in which they are soliciting funds for a charity. Have them deliver their speeches and have the class evaluate each speech on how effectively the speaker used volume.

SPECIAL PROBLEMS OF DELIVERING A SPEECH

Delivering a speech frequently involves dealing with special problems and situations. Among these are the use of a speaker's stand and microphone and coping with distractions and interruptions. Practice at handling these matters can aid you when you encounter them as a speaker.

TEACH

AMAZING FACTS!
The word *lectern* comes from the Latin word *lector*, which means "reader."

● **CURRICULAR CONNECTIONS**

Art
Have students illustrate the ways not to use a lectern discussed on this page. Students might make comic strips showing a speaker not using a lectern correctly. Have them include the comic strips in their portfolios.

● **SKILL DEVELOPMENT**

15-Second Skill Opportunity
After students have read about using the lectern, have them read one paragraph from this chapter using it and one not using it. Comment on the differences.

---

274   CHAPTER 9 Delivering Your Speech

Using the Speaker's Stand

In the majority of places where speeches are given a **lectern** (speaker's stand) is available. One can probably be found in your school's speech classroom. On occasion, however, you may encounter a situation in which a lectern is not available. Therefore, you need to know both how to use a speaker's stand effectively and how to get along without one.

The basic purpose of a lectern is to hold a speaker's notes or manuscript. It was never intended to serve as a support for speakers with weak backs or as a hiding place for those with wobbly knees. A person who uses the speaker's stand to lounge upon or to hide behind immediately reveals apathy or extreme nervousness to the audience. Allowing one or both hands to rest on the stand occasionally is acceptable, as long as one does not *grasp* the stand so desperately that the knuckles turn white. You should never place your foot on the base of the stand either. Your foot should be flat on the floor behind the stand. In general, the less the lectern is grasped, leaned on, caressed, or tapped on, the better the overall impression will be.

Usually the top surface of a lectern is tilted at an angle to allow a speaker to read note cards or manuscript pages with ease, but at the same time keep them out of sight. The best way to handle papers, when using a lectern, is to lay them on the stand at the start and *leave them there throughout the speech*. The audience should be as unaware of your notes as possible, so you must avoid picking them up and putting them down or carrying them in your hands. In addition, cards or manuscript pages should be brought to the lectern in a prearranged order. Try to avoid using paper clips or staples that will require removal or the flipping of pages. When the top card or page has been used, you want to be able to slide it gently and quietly to one side, exposing the next card or page. Picking up a stack of cards in order to place the used one on the bottom of the stack can be very distracting to the listeners, as is the flapping of stapled manuscript pages over the front of a speaker's stand.

Your teacher may ask you to give at least one of your classroom speeches without using the lectern. This can help prepare you for later occasions when no lectern is available. If you want to use note cards but know you will have no stand on which to place them, remember that the easiest size to hold is a 3 × 5 card. As each one is used, you can quietly slip it to the back of the deck, making the next card ready for reference. A full-sized manuscript is more difficult to handle without a speaker's stand. Thus, if you intend to read from manuscript, you should always find out whether or not a stand will be available.

One advantage of having no lectern when you are using note cards is the additional freedom you have to move about on the platform. Not

Special Problems of Delivering a Speech

feeling tied to the stand allows you to walk a few steps more often, reducing your tension and generating greater audience attention.

Adjusting the Microphone

When you are speaking to more than 80 people, or are in a room where the acoustics are poor, you will find a microphone helpful. A microphone must be properly used, however, if it is going to enhance the communication rather than harm it. The first step in its proper use comes before the speech begins. Test the microphone if at all possible! Probably more speeches have gotten off to weak starts because of untested, faulty microphones than because of any other single cause. It only takes a moment to make certain (1) the microphone is turned on, (2) there is no electronic feedback, and (3) it is set at the proper distance and height.

Students often ask: "How far should the microphone be from my mouth?" Microphones vary somewhat, but an average of 10 to 12 inches (25 to 30 centimeters) works well for most microphones. Of course you must keep this "mouth-to-mike" distance fairly constant while speaking. You cannot weave or move your head very much, or your voice will begin to fade in and out like a siren. One advantage of a **lavalier microphone,** the kind that hangs around your neck, is greater freedom to move about on the platform.

Occasionally a speaker will look at the microphone rather than at the audience. This can create a comical effect, since it appears to the audience that the speaker is addressing remarks to the microphone rather than to them.

Certain consonant sounds are easily distorted if spoken with too much force into a microphone. some of the worst offenders are *t, p, b, s, sh, z, g, k,* and *d*. You will want to avoid blasting your listeners or using too much force when uttering these sounds.

Microphones vary, but keeping a distance of between 10 and 12 inches from mouth to mike generally works well. It is wise to rehearse before your first live microphone speech.

TEACH

● SKILL DEVELOPMENT

Research
Give students practice using note cards when delivering a speech. Have them use note cards they've prepared for previous speeches. Ask them to demonstrate the use of note cards both when using a lectern and when not using one.

● LEARNING STYLES

Technology Tools
Make a microphone available in order for students to gain additional practice. Have them focus on the following rules when using the microphone:
(a) if the microphone is unidirectional, be very careful not to go off microphone.
(b) hold your head an even distance from the microphone.
(c) avoid saying the consonants *p, b, t, s, sh, z, g, k,* and *d* too loudly. Turn slightly off microphone when saying them.
(d) always check to make sure the microphone is working properly before beginning to speak.

TEACH

● **MOTIVATION**

Ask students to list situations that might occur during a speech delivery that might cause problems for the speaker. Ask them which of the items listed they have seen happen to a speaker to whom they were listening. Ask them what situations have happened to them. Discuss how the speakers dealt with each situation.

● **SKILL DEVELOPMENT**

15-Second Skill Opportunity
Have students choose a topic and deliver their remarks by using a microphone.

Active Listening
Ask for volunteers to prepare or read short speeches. Have the students present the speeches to the class. Other students could be given a distraction activity card with suggestions such as cough, sneeze, stand, drop a book. At random intervals you could point to a student who would then implement the designated distraction. Discuss how effectively the speakers dealt with the interruptions.

CHAPTER 9 Delivering Your Speech

Since the presence of a microphone makes certain demands upon a speaker, it is wise to rehearse with a live microphone, particularly before your *first* microphone speech. If at all possible, secure the room or auditorium in which the microphone will be used for a practice session. Run through your speech several times with the microphone on and have another person stand or sit at various locations. Even an untrained listener can tell you whether you are coming across clearly or not. Your speech teacher may be the ideal person to help you during such a practice session if his or her schedule permits.

Dealing with Distractions and Interruptions

During the delivery of a speech unexpected events sometimes occur that cannot be planned for beforehand. Although the list of such potential distractions and interruptions is large, it is a rare speech in which more than one such problem arises. Speakers, therefore, should not fear that a string of major disasters is likely to occur every time a speech is to be delivered. On the other hand, being aware of the problems that may arise can prepare you to deal with one confidently if it does occur.

Some interruptions distract the audience's attention only briefly. Noisy jets may fly over the building. A latecomer may interrupt to find a seat. You may lose your place or stumble over words, or people may cough or shuffle their feet. These do little harm to the listeners' basic interest in you and your topic. The best way to handle such noises and distractions is to pause briefly until the room is quiet, then proceed as i

Being aware of possible distractions or interruptions can prepare you to deal with them with confidence should they occur.

● **LINKS TO PAST LEARNING**

Have students describe ways that the President or other politicians have handled hecklers during a speech delivery. Ask students if the method used was effective. If not, ask what other course of action the politician might have taken.

● **LEARNING STYLES**

Beyond the Classroom
Arrange for students to listen to a speaker during a community function, such as a city council meeting. Have them observe the speakers and critique the speakers' ways of using the lectern and microphone, and in dealing with distractions and interruptions.

---

nothing had happened. Making a comment about this kind of interruption simply increases the distraction and usually does more harm than good.

Other interruptions—the kind that create a major breakdown in the audience's concentration on your speech—need to be handled differently from minor distractions. If a group of people arrives late, for instance, and their attempts to find seats distract a good portion of the audience, the speaker should fall silent and remain quiet until the entire group is settled. The speaker may even aid people in finding seats by pointing out empty chairs, thereby shortening the length of the disturbance. Should a loud noise begin and appear likely to continue for the remainder of the speech, the speaker should first attempt to be heard over the noise, or ask the audience to move closer to the speaker's stand, if possible. If it proves impossible to overcome, the speaker may have to abandon the attempt to deliver the speech.

If a heckler should begin to yell at you from the audience, handle the situation with dignity and poise. First, remember that the audience came to hear *you* speak, not the heckler, and their sympathy is basically with you. For a time it is usually best to ignore a heckler, attempting to be heard in between the interruptions. If the heckler's comments are too frequent or too loud to permit the audience to hear you, members of the audience may attempt to quiet the heckler themselves. As the speaker you should provide sufficient time for this to occur, since a heckler soon loses heart when it becomes obvious the audience does not support the disturbance. Only when all this has failed should you address the heckler directly, with a calm and dignified comment, such as: "Sir (or Madam), I will be happy to try to field any questions or comments from the audience as soon as I have finished my prepared remarks." Under no circumstances should you ever engage in a shouting match with a heckler, since this gives the intruder precisely what was hoped for—a major share of your audience's attention.

● **ACTIVITY**

Dealing with Distractions
Discuss with your classmates ways in which a speaker might handle embarrassing or unexpected distractions such as dropping notes, forgetting an important part of the speech, being interrupted by unruly audience members, being interrupted by a fire drill, and hitting the microphone by mistake. Then select students to role-play each situation and the strategy you have developed to deal with it. Make appropriate notes in your speech notebook for future reference.

● **ACTIVITY**

After students have completed this Activity, have them refer to their notes to compile a class list of strategies to deal with various interruptions and distractions. Students could include this list in their portfolios for future reference.

TEACH

● **LEARNING STYLES**

Cooperative Learning
Ask students to work in small groups to convert the questions asked in the Analysis First section into an evaluation form. Students could include these forms in their portfolios as a handy reference for evaluation in the future.

CHAPTER 9 Delivering Your Speech

● **ANALYZING AND EVALUATING SPEECHES**

Now that your have delivered a speech in class, and have heard several given by your classmates, you are ready to begin analyzing and evaluating their quality. By listening and watching carefully when others are speaking, and providing helpful suggestions to improve their next performance, you discover ways to better your own speechmaking. In addition, by honestly assessing your *own* performance following the speeches *you* give, you can find ways to enliven your next speech. Constructive speech criticism, of both your own and your classmates' presentations, always results in an improved level of speechmaking in later rounds. Let's look first at how you should go about analyzing and evaluating your own speeches.

Analysis First

Before you can accurately answer the question "How well did I do?" you need to recall precisely *what* you did in your last speech. In other words, you must analyze your speaking behavior objectively before you can judge its merits. You will want to review your speaking techniques in six broad categories, asking yourself questions in each, and writing your answers to the questions on a sheet of paper:

1. How did I go about selecting my speech topic?
   - Did I utilize brainstorming to select a topic that would prove exciting to both me and my audience?
   - Did I strive to narrow my topic to fit within the time limits, then later rehearse my speech with a watch to fine-tune its length?

2. How did I organize, research, and rehearse my speech?
   - After selecting my topic, did I begin by clarifying my general speech purpose?
   - Did I follow that step by writing a specific purpose sentence?
   - Did I select a pattern of speech organization appropriate for my topic?
   - Did I draft my outline and begin my research early enough to allow for several days of rehearsal?
   - Did I use complete sentences when writing both main and subheads in my outline?
   - Did I make use of the sources of supporting materials mentioned in Chapter 7?

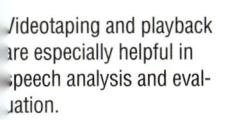

Videotaping and playback are especially helpful in speech analysis and evaluation.

- How many times did I rehearse and over how many days?
- Did I concentrate on remembering the pattern of ideas during rehearsal, or a precise pattern of words?
- Did I rehearse both alone and with friends?
- Was my research sufficiently thorough that I was the class member most knowledgeable about my topic on the day I delivered my speech?

3. What techniques did I utilize to control my stage fright?
   - Did I recall that a controlled level of stage fright is actually a positive sign that will enable me to give a better speech?
   - Did I remind myself that audiences tend to be quite sympathetic towards nervous speakers?
   - Did I use the methods of physical relaxation mentioned in Chapter 6, such as yawning, and the rag doll exercise in which one tenses, then relaxes various muscles?
   - Did I maintain my focus on my topic and audience, rather than on my own performance?
   - Had I prepared thoroughly, including extensive rehearsal prior to my delivery date?
   - Did I remember to make some gestures and platform movement during the speech to siphon off some of my nervous energy?

4. Was my speech prepared and presented using the extemporaneous method?
   - Did I begin with an outline, or by writing my speech out word for word?
   - During its presentation, was I concentrating on an exact pattern of words, or on a pattern of ideas?

TEACH

● SKILL DEVELOPMENT

Critical Thinking
Have students choose a speech from the Appendix or Speech Library for applying the questions in analysis. Have them work individually in analyzing the speech, based on the six broad categories. Work with students who are having difficulty analyzing their speaking techniques.

TEACH

● **SKILL DEVELOPMENT**

Feedback
Have students look back at the answers to their analysis questions. Ask them to choose the questions for which the answers showed that the criteria were not met successfully. Have them come up with ways to use the criteria more successfully in the future.

CHAPTER 9 Delivering Your Speech

- Was I watching the faces of my audience, ready to restate a point if they seemed not to understand or agree?
- Did I have only a phrase outline of my ideas on three or four note cards, or complete sentences on full-sized paper?
- Did my fluency approach that used in ordinary conversation? Did I have about the same number of vocalized pauses as when I converse? Did I have more?
- How frequently, and for how long, did I glance down at my notes?
- In general, was I working from my notes while delivering the speech, or from my head?
- Did it seem as though I were "talking with" my listeners, or "reading at" them?

5. What characterized my language usage and style during my speech?
   - Did my speech contain slang words? Incorrect grammar? Any acronyms or technical terms which I did not define or identify for my audience?
   - Did I frequently use words that painted pictures for my audience, or mainly abstract terms?
   - Were my words and phrases usually short, simple, and specific?
   - Did I use repetition and restatement regularly?
   - Were rhetorical questions and contrast used occasionally?
   - How often were figures of speech such as similes, metaphors, personification, and irony employed?
   - Did I avoid stereotyping, and the use of clichés?

6. What delivery techniques did I employ during the speech?
   - Did I establish eye contact with my listeners? How much? Did I look at all sections of my audience?
   - What were my arms and hands doing during my speech? Did I keep them in the same position throughout most of my presentation? Did I use them to gesture occasionally? Were my gestures natural, or pre-planned, forced movements? Did I vary the at-rest positions of my arms regularly?
   - Could my vocal volume be easily heard in the back row at all times? Did I find my tongue getting twisted more than once or twice? Was I speaking rapidly or slowly? Were the speech sounds clear and distinct, or slurred and mushy?

Evaluation Next

If you have been honest with yourself when answering the above questions about what actually occurred during the preparation and presentation of your speech, the evaluation step is easy. Actually, without realizing it, you have nearly completed it. The final task is that of judging the merits of your performance. You already have discovered *what* you did—now it's time decide *how well*. Your analysis gave you the facts about your performance. Now you are ready to determine its quality.

In order to complete your self-evaluation, you need only look back at the answers you wrote to your analysis questions, this time with an eye toward the *quality* of your speech techniques. Let's look at a few of the questions as examples:

> **Analysis question:** "Did I use complete sentences when writing both main and subheads in my outline?"
>
> If your answer is "no," do you now understand how that could have diminished the clarity of your ideas for your audience? If your answer was "yes," give yourself points for having done a good job during this phase of your speech preparation.
>
> **Analysis question:** "Did I draft my outline and begin my research early enough to allow for several days of rehearsal?"
>
> If you realize you didn't, you may recognize this as a cause of some hesitation and lack of fluency during your speech. If you realized you *did* start early enough, congratulate yourself!
>
> **Analysis question:** "Did I begin with an outline, or by writing my speech out word for word?"
>
> If you remember the benefits of using the extemporaneous method of speech preparation and delivery, you will quickly recall which is the better approach.

By glancing over your list of answers to the analysis questions, you can quickly pick out those areas in which you excelled, and those still needing work. You may wish to target two or three of your weaker points for strengthening in your next speech. If you have doubts about how to correct a problem, talk with your speech teacher.

Analyzing Classmates' Speeches

For some students, being asked to evaluate their classmates' speeches seems more difficult that judging one's own—or if not more difficult, then more distasteful. But once you recognize that, outside of your teachers' critiques, your feedback provides classmates with their best learning experiences, you become more willing to comment on their performances. Student critiques are covered at the end of Chapter 6 in connection with stage fright. You may wish to review them at this point in the course.

TEACH

● **SKILL DEVELOPMENT**

Feedback
Ask students to use the evaluation forms to comment on their own speeches. Ask each speaker to complete the evaluation form for his or her own speech. When students have completed the evaluations, have them form small groups to compare evaluations and to get feedback for ways of improving specific aspects of the speech.

ASSESS

● STUDENT PERFORMANCE COMPETENCIES

- Compares various methods of speech delivery
- Identifies the nonverbal aspects of delivering a speech
- Explains how to use notes effectively when making a speech
- Explains the importance of proper articulation and pronunciation
- Explains ways of dealing with distractions and interruptions

● sca GUIDELINES

- Uses words, pronunciation, and grammar appropriate for situation
- Uses nonverbal signs appropriate for situation
- Uses voice effectively
- Expresses ideas clearly and concisely
- Expresses and defends a point of view with evidence
- Gives concise and accurate directions
- Performs social rituals

PORTFOLIO ASSESSMENT

Standard
- Do's and Don'ts for Speech Conclusions
- List of Appropriate Dress
- Transition Words in Speeches
- Completed Assignments, Quizzes, Projects, and Chapter 9 Test

Enrichment
- Strategies for Dealing with Interruptions
- Situations for Four Kinds of Speech Deliveries

Challenge
- Cartoons of Gestures
- Comic Strips of Uses of Lecterns

CHAPTER 9 REVIEW

● SUMMARY

The way a speech is delivered is quite important. Good delivery will improve almost any speech, while poor delivery will ruin an otherwise excellent one.

Using Different Methods of Delivery A speaker may choose from four different methods for delivering speeches—manuscript, memorization, extemporaneous, and impromptu. While each has certain advantages and disadvantages, the most helpful one for a beginning speaker to master is the extemporaneous method, where the pattern of ideas is prepared beforehand, but the exact wording is chosen during delivery. Once speakers have gained some experience with this method, they can begin experimenting with various combinations of the methods until each speaker discovers his or her own most effective style.

Recognizing Nonverbal Aspects of Delivering a Speech
Remember that your speech begins when you rise from your chair and approach the speaker's platform. Move vigorously, but not hastily; arrange any notes you may have; and look at your audience for several seconds before speaking. Other nonverbal aspects of speech delivery include eye contact, gestures, platform movement, and appearance. Finally, you should remember that your speech is not truly over until you have regained your seat. When you have concluded your speech, look around your audience, then leave the platform in a confident, unhurried manner, and return to your seat.

Using Your Voice Effectively Since being heard is basic to giving a speech, learn to breathe deeply and maintain enough volume to be heard easily in all parts of the room. Vary your volume, pitch, and rate to create interest or change a mood. Articulation and pronunciation both play an important part in forming sounds into recognizable words and verbal symbols. Avoid "lazy-lips" and know the correct pronunciation of each word and name in your speech. Use pauses effectively as well.

Special Problems of Delivering a Speech As a speaker, you must know how to deal with a number of special situations. First, you must know how to handle a lectern, as well as how to get along without one. A speaker's stand is a convenient place to lay notes or a manuscript. When one is not available, notes must be held inconspicuously in the hands. You must also be able to handle a microphone. You should rehearse with it and test it shortly before the

ASSESS

● **ASSESSMENT STRATEGIES**

Individual Assessment
- Participates in practice activities daily or weekly
- Completes classwork
- Demonstrates knowledge of content through questions, discussion, quizzes, and tests
- Displays improved speech skills as targeted in this chapter

Group Assessment
- Sets and achieves goals
- Demonstrates cooperative learning activities
- Supports efforts of team and class members
- Provides encouragement and feedback to members

---

speech. If distractions or interruptions occur during a speech, they must be handled calmly and with poise. If the interruption is minor, it is usually wise to ignore it; if it creates a major disturbance, you must handle it decisively.

VOCABULARY

Define each term in a complete sentence.

manuscript method
memorization method
extemporaneous method
impromptu method
emphatic gestures
transitional gestures
descriptive gestures
locative gestures

note cards
monotone
vocalized pause
articulation
pronunciation
lectern
lavalier microphone

CHECKLIST

Speech-Delivery Skills

1. Be aware of the best methods of speech delivery and employ them when you give a speech.
2. Combine methods of delivery for greater effectiveness.
3. Be aware of the nonverbal aspects of speech delivery and use them effectively.
4. Use note cards efficiently and unobtrusively.
5. Be poised, confident, and well-groomed when speaking.
6. Speak with proper volume and pitch. Be sure not to speak too rapidly or too slowly.
7. Use clear articulation and correct pronunciation.
8. Use pauses effectively in your speeches.
9. Learn to use a lectern and a microphone properly.
10. Develop effective ways of dealing with distractions and interruptions when giving a speech.

REVIEW QUESTIONS

1. Name the four different ways to deliver a speech.
2. Identify the method that requires planting a pattern of ideas in your mind.

● **ANSWERS**

See the Answer Key for more complete answers.

REVIEW QUESTIONS
1. One can deliver a speech using the *manuscript method*, the *memorization method*, the *extemporaneous method*, or the *impromptu method*.
2. The *extemporaneous method* involves planning a pattern of ideas but not the exact wording.

ASSESS

3. The following should be memorized: the introduction to enable the speaker to begin with confidence; the conclusion to ensure an effective ending; and the major transitions.
4. Manuscript delivery is used by people who want a carefully prepared text—such as politicians or others giving televised addresses that require precise timing.
5. Eye contact is valuable for audience and feedback.
6. Variety in facial expressions helps maintain audience interest.
7. Speakers use platform movement to compensate for audience members' fidgeting, to emphasize transitions, and to provide visual variety.
8. General rules for ending a speech are as follows: Pause at the end of the last word, look at the audience for a few seconds, acknowledge any audience feedback, and then return to your seat.
9. *Volume* is the loudness or softness of the voice. *Pitch* is the tone of voice on a musical scale. *Rate* is the amount of time it takes to pronounce each syllable and to pause between words and sentences. *Articulation* is the clarity of sounds provided by the lips, tongue, teeth, and palate.
10. The lectern is provided to hold a speaker's notes or manuscript.

DISCUSSION QUESTIONS
The following code is used to designate discussion questions and activities as suitable for students of varying ability levels:
▼ = below average to average
◆ = average to above average
■ = all students

1. Responses will vary. ■
2. An audience tends to notice gesturing for emphasis. ▼
3. Proper use of a lectern provides a sense of security but can also be a barrier. ▼
4. Pausing is used primarily for four purposes: to breathe, to create dramatic effects, to signal changes of thought, and to allow time for audience response. ▼
5. The distractions discussed in this activity should be real ones that your students have to cope with. ▼

CRITICAL THINKING
1. **Analysis** Of course, students' answers to these questions will vary. One excellent feature of this exercise is that it requires students to make lists of the principles of good delivery before ranking these principles. ◆

284

CHAPTER 9 REVIEW

3. Describe the parts of a speech that should be memorized.
4. Describe the use of manuscript in speech delivery.
5. Name the most important reasons for keeping eye contact with an audience.
6. Explain the value of variety in a speaker's facial expressions.
7. List several reasons for using platform movement.
8. Describe several ways to end a speech.
9. Name and define four aspects of vocal delivery.
10. Describe the proper way in which to use a lectern.

? DISCUSSION QUESTIONS

1. As a class, discuss which of the four methods of speech delivery would be most appropriate for the following situations. Note: A combination of methods might also recommend itself. (a) The mayor of a city talks at a press conference about an agreement just reached with the city's sanitation workers. (b) A candidate accepts a political party's nomination for the office of governor. (c) A sales manager analyzes last year's performance at a sales meeting. (d) A woman is asked by a television reporter on the street for her assessment of a new housing law.
2. Discuss the role of gesture in speaking—from the audience's point of view. What kinds of gestures would distract an audience? What kinds of gestures would the audience find natural and barely noticeable? What role does variety play in gesture?
3. Discuss the use of a lectern during a speech. What benefits does the speaker receive from using a lectern? What are the disadvantages? Would you prefer to speak with or without a lectern?
4. Discuss the importance of learning to pause effectively while speaking. What effect can a well-timed pause have upon an audience? What happens to an audience when a speaker delivers a speech at a rate that never varies?
5. Discuss the distractions that are likely to occur in a classroom during a speech. What kinds of distractions can a speaker learn to live with? What kinds of distractions are truly troublesome? What can a speaker do when faced with major distractions?

▲ CRITICAL THINKING

1. **Analysis** Of all of the principles of good delivery, which are the most difficult to master? Which come more naturally to the beginning speaker? Arrange a list in the order of difficulty from most difficult to least difficult.

2. Synthesis Imagine that you have only one side of a 3 × 5 index card on which to list the most important delivery advice to speakers. The card will be attached to the speaker's lectern. What advice would you list? Make maximum use of this very small space. Put your most important piece of advice first.

ACTIVITIES

In-Class

1. Prepare a brief introduction and conclusion of a speech. Memorize both. Then perform the following activity in class: (1) Walk from your seat to the front of the room and stand behind the lectern or at the place from which you will speak. (2) Establish eye contact with your audience. (3) Deliver the prepared introduction to your speech. (4) Pause briefly. (5) Deliver the prepared conclusion of your speech. (6) Return to your seat. Your classmates will react and provide feedback on your delivery.

2. Select a descriptive passage from your literature anthology or from some other source which can be read in approximately one minute. Read the passage aloud several times. Then read the passage and make a tape recording of your reading. Listen to the tape three times. Each time you listen to it, focus on one aspect of vocal delivery. First, listen for rate and pausing. Then listen for variety in pitch. Finally, listen for articulation and pronunciation. Write a brief evaluation of each aspect of your vocal delivery. Then play the recording in class. Ask your classmates for their reactions and suggestions.

3. Select a speech in the Appendix of Speeches and study it carefully. Jot down the main ideas in the speech on note cards. Make certain that you arrange the cards in the proper order. Then practice using the cards to summarize the speech to a group of from five to seven classmates. Do not attempt to give the speech word for word. Simply provide the basic information that is in the speech in your own words. As you summarize the speech, the other students in the group will compare your information with the actual speech. Discuss the quality of your performance with the other members of the group.

4. Choose a small group of students who will work together to devise a variety of interruptions that could arise during a speech. Each individual in the class will then deliver a part of a speech that was developed or given earlier and attempt to deal with the variety of interruptions offered. The class will then discuss and evaluate each individual speaker's response to the interruptions.

ASSESS

2. Synthesis You might want to limit the card to three or five reminders, or you might actually give students 3 × 5 cards to use for the activity.

ACTIVITIES
In-Class
1. The memorized speech will take more time to prepare than would an impromptu or extemporaneous speech.
2. Copy and distribute evaluation forms. Ask students to use this sheet for their self-evaluations.
3. This activity will help students break their dependence on manuscripts and force them to think on their feet.
4. Check the students' proposals before subjecting speakers to the interruptions, and maintain strong control of student behavior during the speeches.

ASSESS

Out-of-Class

1. You can achieve greater consistency in this activity by having all students watch the same speech or by videotaping a speech by a political leader and showing it in class. In any case, make certain that the students consider the differences between spoken and written language explained in Chapter 8 of the text. Make certain, too, that they consider such nonverbal signals as facial gestures and eye movement.
2. Breath control exercises are vital for serious students who want to alter breathing habits and develop better speaking abilities. To give credit to students who engage in this activity, require logs in which notes are made of days and time spent doing breathing exercises.
3. Tongue twisters are enjoyable and valuable for people of all ages. Dr. Seuss includes them in his writings for children. They also appear in many college textbooks for refinement of articulation in adults. Group reading of these tongue twisters in class will likely increase interest in doing them at home.

CHAPTER 9 REVIEW

Out-of-Class

1. Attend a public speech. Carefully observe the speaker's eye contact with the audience, and answer the following questions in your speech notebook. (a) What approximate percentage of time did the speaker look at the audience rather than at notes? (b) Did the speaker use a pattern of eye contact that started at some point in the audience and then moved to another point? (c) Did the speaker ignore any part of the audience? (d) Did the speaker respond in any way to audience feedback? How did the speaker respond?
2. Develop breath control by doing the following two exercises every evening before going to bed or upon rising in the morning. (a) Inhale slowly and steadily, filling your lungs with air as much as you can. Now begin counting from 1 to 25 while exhaling slowly, controlling your breath with each number that you say. Repeat this activity until you can count from 1 to 25 on a single breath of air. (b) Lie flat on the floor and place a relatively heavy book on your stomach, just below your rib cage. Inhale and exhale, causing the book to rise and fall with your breathing.
3. As rapidly as you can, say each of the following tongue twisters three times in succession. Go only as fast as accuracy will allow. Time yourself on each tongue twister to see if your articulation improves. Return to this activity from time to time. Remember that you must articulate accurately for a time to count. Keep a record of your progress in your speech notebook. (a) Sally Sunshine sews her socks. When Sally Sunshine sews her socks, the seams she sews seem sealed like stocks. (b) Peter and Paul play paddle ball. Peter plays perfectly as does Paul. A perfect pair, playing paddle ball. (c) Mary Macer makes many messy meals. Since most of Mary Macer's meals are messy, Mary Macer's mother makes Mary make her meals less messy. (d) Brother Brather bothers mother. Mother bothers brother Brather. Brother Brather's brother, Baffer, baffles Brather and his mother.

ASSESS

CHAPTER PROJECT

Deliver a three- to five-minute speech on the topic "A Person Worth Knowing." The person might be someone you actually know, a person who is known for some accomplishment, or a historical figure. Gather whatever information you need about the person, write and memorize an introduction and conclusion for your speech, prepare notes and an outline for an extemporaneous delivery, and rehearse your speech carefully before delivering it in class.

While you are speaking, your fellow students in the audience will complete a critique sheet on your speech. Your verbal and nonverbal performance will be rated. The critique sheets will be given to you. Check them carefully to determine what aspects of speaking you can work on in the future. Take note in your speech notebook of those areas that need improvement.

CHAPTER PROJECT

- Some students will find a topic for this assignment immediately. They will have personal collections of articles and pictures at home about a particular celebrity who intrigues them. Others will need to explore the library, looking in magazines, encyclopedias, and special reference works for articles that trigger their interest.

To ensure adequate preparation and appropriate notes, have the students turn in their note cards to you at the end of the speech. Give a separate grade for the note cards in addition to the performance grade.

PREPARE

● PERFORMANCE OBJECTIVES

- Participates in daily 15-second drills when asked
- Demonstrates improved skills in various public speaking occasions
- Analyzes and evaluates message and delivery of various types of public speeches
- Participates in group research and learning activities

● sca GUIDELINES

- Listens effectively to various types of speeches
- Identifies the main idea in public speeches
- Distinguishes between informative and persuasive speech strategies
- Expresses ideas clearly and concisely
- Supports main ideas with evidence and logic
- Performs social rituals

● UNIT FOCUS

Unit 4 concentrates on the various types of speeches for public occasions. The importance of relating speeches to the type of audience and the purpose of the occasion is emphasized.

● CONTENTS

10 Speaking to Inform *pp. 290–345*
11 Speaking to Persuade *pp. 346–379*
12 Other Kinds of Speaking *pp. 380–411*

▽ UNIT PORTFOLIOS

Individual Portfolios
- Analysis and Evaluation Checklists for Various Speeches
- Tapes of Informative, Persuasive, and Other Speeches
- Graphic Organizers to Aid in Speech Presentations
- Certificates of Recognition

Group Portfolios
- Team Research for Informative Speeches
- Feedback Checklists for Student Speech Performance
- Videos of Best Speech Performances

Class Portfolios
- Commencement Address Program
- "Roast" of Designated Students or Teachers
- Banquet Program and Arrangements

UNIT 4

TYPES OF PUBLIC SPEAKING

PREPARE

● UNIT PLANNER ● ANCILLARY RESOURCES

Chapters	Time Management	📁	📄	📘	📼	🎴
10 Speaking to Inform *pp. 290–345*	Week 1	✔	✔	✔	✔	✔
11 Speaking to Persuade *pp. 346–379*	Week 2	✔	✔	✔	✔	
12 Other Kinds of Speaking *pp. 380–411*	Week 3	✔	✔	✔	✔	✔

● PROFESSIONAL RESOURCES

Print

Gudykunst, William, and Young Yun Kim. *Communicating with Strangers: An Approach to Intercultural Communication.* 2nd ed. New York: McGraw-Hill, 1992.

Littlejohn, Stephen W., and David M. Jabusch. *Persuasive Transactions.* Glenview, IL: Scott, Foresman, 1992.

Osborn, M. and S. Osborn. *Public Speaking,* 2nd ed., Boston: Houghton Mifflin Co., 1991.

Thomas D., and M. Fryar. *Business Communication Today.* 2nd ed. Lincolnwood, IL: National Textbook Co., 1988.

Film

Speech: Planning Your Talk (McGraw-Hill/Young America Films, 1221 Avenue of the Americas, NY, NY 10036).

Using Visuals in Your Speech, (McGraw-Hill, 1221 Avenue of the Americas, NY, NY 10036).

10
Speaking to Inform

11
Speaking to Persuade

12
Other Kinds of Speaking

Ancillary Resource Key

- 📁 = Portfolio Product Activities
- 📄 = Tests/Answer Key
- 📘 = Speech Library
- 📼 = Self-Help Videos
- 🎴 = Audiotape

289

PREPARE

CHAPTER PLANNER

Day 1	Day 2	Day 3	Day 4	Day 5
Prepare	Prepare	Prepare	Prepare	Prepare
Teach	Teach	Teach	Teach	Teach
Assess	Assess	Assess	Assess	Assess
Sub. Teacher Tips *pp. 293, 297*	Sub. Teacher Tips *pp. 301, 302, 308*	Sub. Teacher Tips *pp. 311, 315, 321*	Sub. Teacher Tips *pp. 322, 325*	Sub. Teacher Tips *pp. 327, 328, 336*

CHAPTER OVERVIEW

This chapter examines the following topics:
- Types of Informative Speeches *p. 292*
- Beginning an Informative Speech *p. 295*
- Imparting the Message of an Informative Speech *p. 305*
- Concluding an Informative Speech *p. 312*
- Conducting a Question and Answer Period *p. 317*
- Using Visual Aids *p. 319*
- Analyzing and Evaluating Informative Speeches *p. 331*

PORTFOLIO PRODUCTS

Individual Projects
- Glossary of Speech Terms
- Tape of Informative Speech
- Graphic Visual Aid
- Chapter 10 Portfolio Products

Group Projects
- Research Notes for Informative Speech
- Video of Informative Speech
- Evaluations of Historical Informative Speeches

sca GUIDELINES

- Listens effectively to informative speeches
- Identifies main ideas in informative speeches
- Distinguishes between informative and persuasive messages
- Asks questions to obtain information

CHAPTER 10

Speaking to Inform

When you have completed this chapter you should be able to:

- Identify the main characteristics of a speech that is meant to inform.
- Explain how to gain audience attention and build interest in your topic during the introduction of a speech.
- Describe how to maintain attention, react to feedback, and execute smooth transitions during the body of an informative speech.
- Identify the types of visual aids that are available.

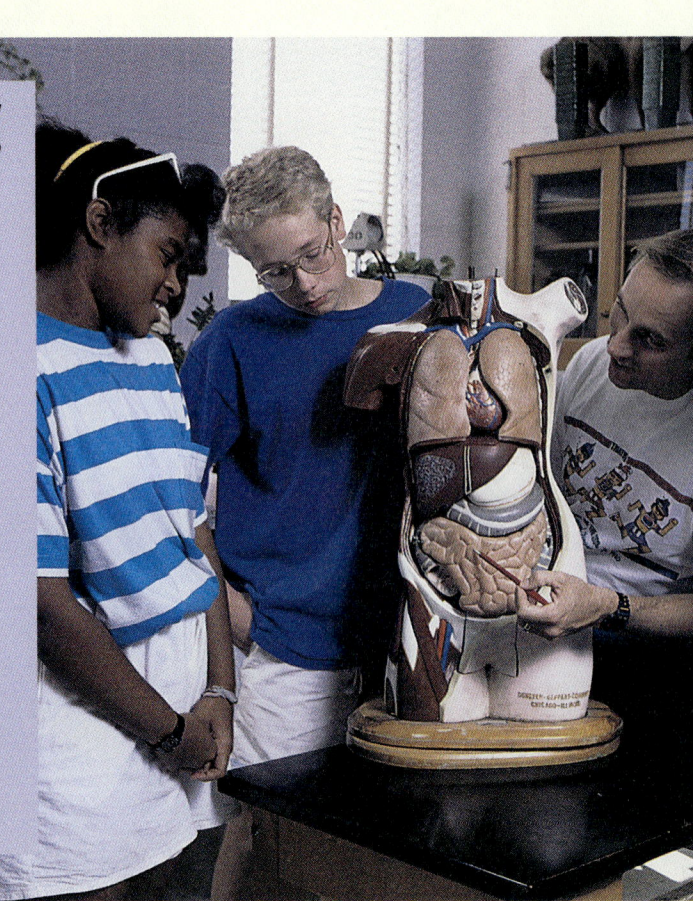

TEACH

● **LINKS TO PAST LEARNING**

Ask students to think of how they get information they need about schedules and activities in school. Suggest comparisons between P.A. announcements and more formal speeches.

● **MOTIVATION**

Ask students to think of the times they have heard or seen references to the "Information Highway." Discuss their participation in it now and in the future. Discuss how their knowledge and use of the Information Highway will impact on their earning capacity and quality of life as adults.

● **ACTIVITY**

Based on the discussion of the everyday situations involving information, the class could make an illustrated collage to illustrate some of the information exchanges commonly used. Students could find a picture or headline in a newspaper or magazine that would exemplify speaking for information purposes.

Speaking to Inform 291

● **ACTIVITY**

Defining Informative Speaking

Hold a class discussion in which you define and describe informative speaking. What makes it different from other types of speaking? What are some situations in everyday life where informative speaking is used regularly? Is it possible for a speaker to have a mixed purpose for a speech, such as to inform and persuade, or to inform and entertain? Can you think of examples?

Occasionally a speech may be given to inspire, to entertain, to introduce someone else, to accept an honor given, or to eulogize a person. The Appendix of Speeches at the back of the book presents models of some of these different types of speeches for you to study. Most speeches, however, are given for one of two basic reasons: to inform or to persuade. This chapter discusses informative speaking. Chapter 11 is about persuasive speaking, and Chapter 12 covers other kinds of speaking.

As you no doubt discussed in the opening Activity, when you give a speech to inform, your basic purpose is to provide the listeners with information they do not already have. Even though the audience may have some general knowledge of your topic before you begin, an **informative speech** will impart new knowledge or more in-depth information on that topic.

Speeches given to inform serve many useful functions in everyday life. Reports at business meetings, classroom lessons and demonstrations, reports to labor unions, tours through state and national parks, speeches given at civic clubs—all are examples of informative speeches.

The informative speech will impart new knowledge or more in-depth information on a particular topic.

291

TEACH

> *"All want to know, but none want to pay the fee."*
>
> —Juvenal

● **LEARNING STYLES**

Cooperative Learning
Ask small groups to discuss the differences between "boring" information and "interesting" information. Encourage groups to provide examples of each. Discuss which is boring—the information or merely the manner in which information is presented. Discuss what makes some information interesting to one person and what makes it seem boring to another.

● **SKILL DEVELOPMENT**

15-Second Skill Opportunity
Give students time to think about what they think they need to know to succeed in life. Ask volunteers to complete the sentence, "The information I need to succeed in life is…."

CHAPTER 10 Speaking to Inform

Notice that a speech is considered informative whenever the speaker's *primary* purpose is to impart new knowledge. In some cases a speaker may have a mixed motive. Along with imparting new information the speaker may also wish to persuade listeners by influencing their beliefs, attitudes, or behavior. Teachers, for example, often speak with such mixed motives. Along with showing you how to work with decimals, a math teacher might wish to persuade you of the importance of knowing how to work with decimals. Since the teacher's main purpose in speaking is to impart new knowledge, however, you would call this math lesson an example of informative rather than persuasive speaking.

If you are like most people you will give many speeches to inform during your life. Let's take a look at four types of informative speeches.

● **TYPES OF INFORMATIVE SPEECHES**

There are a number of ways to classify types of informative speeches. Your teacher may choose to use different names for these types or a different number of types. He or she may assign only one or two kinds for in-class speeches. Those presented here, however, will include most of the specific informative topics you and your classmates choose.

Speeches About Objects

Speeches about objects deal with anything you can see, feel, hear, taste, or smell. These speeches deal with particular items in our physical world. As used here, the term "objects" includes persons living or dead

A presentation on the topic of fine art entails a speech about objects.

TEACH

● **CURRICULAR CONNECTIONS**

Writing
For each of the speech topics identified, you could ask students to think of an application in another area of the curriculum. For instance, you might ask students to think of speeches about objects that would be appropriate to math, science, or history.

SUBSTITUTE TEACHER TIP
Clip and bring to class magazine and newspaper articles that inform readers about some topic. Ask students to compile a list of topics for informative speeches taken from these articles.

● **SKILL DEVELOPMENT**

Research
From the list of general topics provided here or from the Substitute Teacher Tip list, ask students to select one area and write a sentence that would define the purpose of an informative speech about that topic.

Main Idea
From the list of general topics provided here, ask students to select one area and write a sentence that would define the purpose or main idea of an informative speech about that topic.

Types of Informative Speeches   **293**

animals, places, plants, and structures. Here are several *general* topics you could use for a speech about objects:

space travel	Albert Einstein
Statue of Liberty	computers
dinosaurs	*Hamlet*
the human brain	Bill Clinton
Venus' flytrap	guitars
chestnut trees	Monticello

In order to focus on your *specific* informative purpose, you next need to select a particular aspect of your topic and state it in a purpose sentence. Here are a few examples:

- My purpose is to inform my audience what to look for when buying a home computer.
- My purpose is to inform my audience of the major accomplishments of the Clinton presidency.
- My purpose is to inform my audience about the architectural style of Thomas Jefferson's home, Monticello.
- My purpose is to inform my audience about the anatomy of the human brain.

Speeches about objects may be given in chronological, spatial, or topical order. The organizational pattern you choose will depend upon you specific purpose for giving the speech. If your purpose is to trace the background or history of an object, you will choose chronological order:

> My purpose is to inform my audience about the development of the computer industry in the United States.

If you wish to deal with your topic primarily from a geographical viewpoint, you will use spatial order:

> My purpose is to inform my audience about the layout of Thomas Jefferson's estate, Monticello.

Often speeches about objects lend themselves more readily to the topical pattern of organization:

> My purpose is to inform my audience about the major functions of the human brain.

TEACH

> *Time is a great teacher, but unfortunately it kills all its pupils.*
> —Hector Berlioz

● **TEACHING**

You could write labels for basic types of speech organization on the chalkboard. These include Chronological, Spatial, and Topical forms of organization. Be sure that students understand these forms of organization and ask for examples of each. Discuss whether chronological order is appropriate for history topics only.

● **SKILL DEVELOPMENT**

On the Job
Discuss various ways that information is shared and communicated on the job. Ask students if they prefer to get information in person, electronically, or in print.

CHAPTER 10 Speaking to Inform

Speeches About Events

An informative speech about an event may be about anything that either has happened or is happening, or that is regarded as happening. Here are some examples of general topics:

Mardi Gras	architecture
football	the Boston Massacre
the Great Depression	fads
acid rain	gold mining
tornadoes	earthquakes in Mexico
famine in Africa	child psychology

As with informative speeches about objects, you need to focus on some specific aspect of your topic:

- My purpose is to inform my listeners about the devastating earthquakes in Mexico during the past century.
- My purpose is to inform my audience about famine currently ravaging parts of Africa.

Speeches about events often fall into the chronological pattern of organization, as in the above cases. When your purpose is to focus upon the causes of events rather than upon their history, a causal pattern of organization may be called for. Such a pattern would be appropriate when your purpose sentence reads like these:

- My purpose is to inform my listeners why Mexico has experienced such devastating earthquakes during the past century.
- My purpose is to inform my audience about the causes of the current famine in parts of Africa.

Speeches About Processes

A process is a related series of events that lead to a specific result or product. The following process speech topics have already been focused into specific purpose statements:

- My purpose is to inform my audience about how to make the basic shots in tennis.

- My purpose is to inform my listeners about the basic steps in the process of making bread.
- My purpose is to show my audience how to make high-quality photographs with a simple camera.
- My purpose is to teach my audience how to perform several basic moves in karate.

Note that with some speeches about processes, the purpose is only to have the audience understand the process. In others, it is to enable the listeners to perform the process themselves. Many speeches about processes require the use of visual aids. Selecting and properly handling visual aids is discussed later in this chapter.

Usually, informative speeches about processes are arranged in chronological order. Occasionally, when you want to focus on the principles or techniques involved in the process rather than on the steps, you may want to use topical order.

Speeches About Concepts

Speeches about concepts are more abstract than those about objects, events, or processes. Concept speeches include those dealing with beliefs, theories, ideas, and principles. Here are three examples of purpose sentences for speeches dealing with concepts:

- My purpose is to inform my listeners about the basic tenets of democracy.
- My purpose is to inform my audience about the major principles of mathematics.
- My purpose is to inform my audience about the guiding principles of nonviolent resistance.

Speeches about objects are usually arranged in topical order. A less frequent approach is that of comparing and contrasting competing schools of thought on the topic.

BEGINNING AN INFORMATIVE SPEECH

Many speech authorities consider the introduction the most important part of any speech. Listeners quite often base their opinions about a speech on their first impressions. Thus, the quality of the introduction

TEACH

> **"Nothing is more dangerous than an idea, when you have only one idea."**
> —Alain

TEACHING

Emphasize the notion that speeches about ideas are sometimes organized in a compare-contrast format.

SKILL DEVELOPMENT

15-Second Skill Opportunity
Invite volunteers to read the excerpt on this page about airline safety. Discuss techniques that could be used to emphasize the humor.

---

may determine the effect of an entire speech. Because of the importance of an introduction, a large portion of this chapter is devoted to ways you can make your introductions most effective. There are five important things to remember when introducing an informative speech.

Gain the Audience's Attention

Perhaps the first and most important way you can use an introduction is to attract the audience's attention. If a speaker fails to gain the listener's attention at the beginning of a speech, it is highly unlikely that the speech will ever fulfill its purpose. Audience members will mentally test a speaker for the first few moments of a speech. If the material sounds dull or uninteresting, their attention will quickly turn to other matters—a homework assignment or what will be served for supper. So one of the speaker's first tasks is to demand the listener's attention by using special material as an **attention device.** Over centuries of speech making, certain types of material have proven effective and become widely accepted for this purpose.

One of the most widely used attention devices is **humor.** Nearly everyone enjoys a good joke, so most audiences will automatically pay attention to a speaker who uses humor. Humor that is closely related to one's speech topic, the occasion, or the audience is usually more effective, however, than just a standard joke. The speaker who relates a funny incident that serves as a smooth transition into the main body of the speech will not lose the listener's attention as soon as the joke is over. This was the approach used at the start of a speech on the safety of commercial airline travel:

> Last week, shortly after the takeoff of a Boeing 767 at Chicago's O'Hare Field, the passengers heard a voice over the intercom: "Ladies and gentlemen, you are privileged to be the first passengers on an historic flight. There is no pilot or co-pilot in this aircraft. Your entire flight today, from takeoff to landing is being controlled by a system of electronic tapes from the ground. You need not worry in the least. These tapes have been thoroughly tested, and have been found to be completely foolproof…foolproof…foolproof…foolproof…"

This lighthearted opening to his subject gave the speaker a natural opportunity to turn his audience's attention to the more serious issues involved in airline safety.

Some people are more effective at being funny than others. Before attempting to use humor in a public speech, ask yourself whether you are an effective humorist. If you are able to make friends laugh in private conversation or at a party, you have probably developed an ability

● **TEACHING**

Make a list of the five important things to remember in introducing an informative speech. These are presented in the text as (1) gain the audience's attention, (2) build interest in the topic, (3) preview the topic, (4) apply the message to the audience, and (5) establish ethos. This material is presented over many pages in the text. It is helpful to show the students where each of these headings appears.

TEACH

SUBSTITUTE TEACHER TIP

Have a list of at least five top comedians ready on the chalkboard. Tell students that each have one vote to select the best comedian of all time. If they would like to nominate others than those you listed on the board, they may do so if they can give a good reason to include the additional name.

>*Everything is funny as long as it is happening to someone else.*
>
>—Will Rogers

● **LEARNING STYLES**

Cooperative Learning
Small groups could investigate the various types of humor and report on each. Each group should include a definition and some examples of this type of humor. Students should also include information about when each type of humor is appropriate as well as some indication of when that type of humor would not be appropriate.

Audio/Visual Learning
You might ask students to bring a video or taped segments of classic comedy routines. Discuss some examples of visual humor. After hearing a joke, ask for a volunteer to repeat the joke or story. Begin to talk about why some people are better than others at using humor effectively. Discuss whether students think the use of humor is a skill that can be improved.

● **SKILL DEVELOPMENT**

15-Second Skill Opportunity
Invite the humorists in class to pretend there is an "open mike" in a comedy club. They have 15 seconds to tell a great joke or a funny story suitable for family entertainment. Some students might want to devise some kind of applause meter to judge the appeal of the story or joke.

Beginning an Informative Speech   297

The use of tasteful humor that is related to the speech topic is an excellent way of focusing the audience's attention.

to be humorous. If you seldom get a laugh when you wish to, it is wiser to wait until you have had a chance to develop this technique before using it in a speech introduction. Attempting humor in a public speech, and then having it fall flat, can deflate the speaker's confidence and often does more harm than good.

If you are one of those people who is an effective humorist, you may be strongly tempted to overuse humor in your public speeches. Do not give in to this temptation. Humor acts as a spice in public speaking—a little bit is helpful; too much can destroy the "flavor" of your speech. Audiences respect a speaker who can be both humorous and serious, but if the purpose of the speech is to inform, the listeners expect to be informed, not merely entertained. Use humor sparingly as an attention device.

Finally, make sure any humor you use is in good taste. Though some members of your audience may laugh at offensive humor, their respect for you will decrease. Since a speaker's character in the listener's eye has always been considered one of his or her most potent means of influence, a joke that is offensive will be harmful rather than helpful. It will diminish you in the minds of your audience and make it that much harder for you to gain their serious attention.

An attention device similar to humor is the **anecdote.** A story does not need to be funny in order to be fascinating and to secure the attention of an audience. Speakers who use anecdotes in their introduction are almost sure to capture their listeners' attention. As with humor, a story that has a natural connection with the speech topic is far better than one without any connection.

297

TEACH

> **People will confess to treason, murder, arson, false teeth, or a wig. How many of them will own up to a lack of humor?**
>
> —Frank Moore Colby

● **TEACHING**

Try to arrive at a common understanding of the term "in good taste." Humor is sometimes used to mask negative feelings. Ask students when they have witnessed or heard this kind of humor. Discuss whether the opening to the airline safety speech on page 296 would have been considered "in good taste" if there had been a major airline crash with many fatalities the day before the speech. Discuss how circumstances of time and place influence the acceptability of humor.

● **LEARNING STYLES**

Multicultural Learning

Various cultures have different notions of humor. Some people are sensitive to humor involving specific topics. Ask students if they think there is much use of humor in speeches given at the United Nations and discuss reasons for their opinions. Invite members of the class to share examples of topics that might be taboo as subjects for humor with various cultures.

---

298   CHAPTER 10 Speaking to Inform

Notice the effective way in which one speaker gained audience attention by starting with the following anecdote in a speech on cardiopulmonary resuscitation:

> You may have read the story, in last Wednesday's paper, about Joe Bowers and Susan Atkins. Joe was swimming at the Northside Swim Club, doing laps for exercise. Susan, an eighteen-year-old lifeguard at Northside, had just taken her seat in one of the guard chairs as Joe Bowers started his laps.
>
> No one saw it happen. Maybe Joe was daydreaming, or maybe he just misjudged the end of the pool. When Susan spotted him, he was lying on the bottom in the deep end, after ramming his head into the wall. With a blast of her whistle, warning the other guard, Susan tore to the end of the pool and pulled Joe to the surface. Once they hauled him out, Susan started CPR while the paramedics were on their way. The newspaper called Joe Bowers very lucky; it called Susan Atkins a hero.

Avoid the temptation to make the story too detailed or too lengthy. Many stories need to be shortened and adapted to a particular speech, especially if the entire speech is rather short. A five-minute story as an attention device in a ten-minute speech is too long. Keep in mind the general rule that introductions should usually account for only about ten percent of the total speech.

The **common ground technique** is another widely used means of gaining listener attention. When using this device, speakers begin by identifying hobbies, interests, careers, experiences, or preferences that they share in common with their listener. They might note similarities in political or religious background, ethnic heritage, or interest in certain sports. The common ground technique includes anything that highlights the fact that speaker and listener share common interests. When Princess Margaret of the United Kingdom visited the Kentucky Derby and was asked to present a cup to the owner of the winning horse, she began her presentation speech by noting the similarity between the Kentucky Derby and the English Derby.

The common ground technique gains listener attention most effectively when the similarities between the speaker and listeners are greatest. If there are few real likenesses between you and your listeners on a given occasion, you would be better off choosing another attention device. Do not try to force weak similarities.

The attention device called **shock technique** is used to demand quick, almost instantaneous attention from an audience. Shock technique consists of mentioning an unusual, frightening, or hard-to-believe fact, statement, or statistic. It usually is used at the very beginning of a speech. The purpose is to blow away any mental "cobwebs" in your listeners' heads and startle them into instant mental alertness. Thom Mayer, a student speaker, made excellent use of the shock technique in a speech on "The Population Bomb":

> If I were to tell you that there are 3.6 billion people on the earth, with more arriving at the rate of 132 per minute, these figures would probably do nothing more than bore you. If, on the other hand, I were to say "There's a bomb in this room and it could explode at any second!" it is likely that I would have your attention, and you would realize the urgency in what I had said. The cold facts, however, are that the bomb I warned you about and the figures I cited are actually one and the same thing. That bomb is known as the Population Bomb, and it is ticking right now in this room and all over the world.

Not only did Thom Mayer assure listener attention from the first words of his speech, but the statistics led naturally into the main body of his speech on overpopulation. As with humor and narrative, the shock technique works best when it is closely tied to the main message of the speech. Speakers using the shock technique must always have evidence to prove the shocking statements they make.

Suspense is another device useful for developing rapid listener attention in an introduction. Usually suspense is developed by withholding one's theme or topic from the audience for several moments and by hinting at its importance or uniqueness. A speaker who is building suspense talks "around" the topic for several moments, teasing the audience into trying to guess what the topic will be. Marie Ransley, a student speaker, used suspense in the following manner at the beginning of a classroom speech:

> "Warning: the green slime is here." It sounds like a creature out of a grade-B horror movie. But unfortunately it's more real than that. The *New York Times Magazine* warns: "…a monster has been loosed among us. In…countless incidents around the world, one can almost hear the sloshing of the algae as they grow and expand like the mucid mutations of the late-night horror movies, crawling everywhere and smothering life beneath the slime of cells gone berserk."
>
> Yes, algae is the monster and the immediate victims are the country's lakes.

When used as an attention device in an introduction, suspense must be built quickly. A brief amount of suspense makes an audience curious and expectant, but suspense drawn out beyond several moments rapidly loses its effect. The listeners begin to resent the speaker for not "letting them in on" the speech topic.

TEACH

● **TEACHING**

Emphasize the point that an introduction to a speech should be about 10% of the total speech. Then have students figure out how long the introduction should be for speeches of various lengths.

> ❝ *The making of an American begins at that point where he himself rejects all other ties, any other history, and himself adopts the vesture of his promised land.* ❞
>
> —James Baldwin

● **SKILL DEVELOPMENT**

15-Second Skill Opportunity
To give students practice in telling contemporary anecdotes, ask them to bring in a local newspaper or national magazine. Ask them to select an article and present an anecdote based on the article.

● **LEARNING STYLES**

Mulicultural Learning
You could ask pairs of students of different backgrounds to team up and develop a common-ground reference that could be used as a bridge in an introductory remark. To get this activity started you might use the James Baldwin quotation above and ask students what the author might consider common ground for Americans.

TEACH

AMAZING FACTS!

Michel Lotito (b. 1950) of Grenoble, France, has been eating metal and glass since he was nine. His diet has included 10 bicycles, 7 TV sets, a Cessna plane, and a computer.

● TEACHING

Ask students to use the Amazing Fact as part of an introduction to a speech to be given at an annual meeting of dieters anonymous. If they prefer, students could think of other examples to use to illustrate the shock technique.

● CURRICULAR CONNECTIONS

Writing

Students could target an area studied in a world cultures or history class and write a list of several common-ground topics that could be shared if they had to address people from that different time and place.

● ACTIVITY

You might want to present Certificates of Merit to those students who have delivered the best examples for using suspense, shock or common-ground techniques. These certificate forms are available at supply stores and can be duplicated for several uses. You might consider making the presentation of certificates similar to the "Academy Awards" format.

● SKILL DEVELOPMENT

15-Second Skill Opportunity

Ask students to find and share a "believe it or not" type statement that could be suitable for including in introductory remarks.

● ACTIVITY

Sample Attention Devices

As a class, recall aloud examples of various attention devices used by your classmates in earlier speech rounds. For example, someone might begin with "Well during the last round, I think it was Doug that began with a combination of shock technique and suspense. Remember, he started by telling us that there's a disease lurking in this country, one that strikes one teenager every 30 seconds. He also told us that this disease will affect 40 percent of today's fourteen-year-olds before they reach 20. After giving us several more facts about this disease, he told us what it is—teenage pregnancy."

Other class members could follow up by recalling instances of other attention devices from earlier speeches—humor, anecdote, or common ground technique. If some people cannot remember a classmate's attention device, they might mention one that they themselves used.

Build Interest in the Topic

Besides gaining the listeners' attention, a speaker should build the interest in the speech topic during the introduction. Some topics a naturally more fascinating to certain audiences than others are. speaker who has analyzed the audience beforehand will know wheth she or he must build audience interest in the topic.

Building interest in one's topic is not the same as gaining attentio but many of the same devices may be used to accomplish it. Earlier this chapter it was mentioned that humor as an attention device wor best if it is easily tied to the speaker's topic. Telling a humorous incide unrelated to your topic may gain your listeners' attention, but it do nothing toward building their interest in your topic. A topic-related jok however, can fulfill both these important functions at once. The sam principle holds true for the anecdote and for the common groun shock, and suspense techniques.

There are other methods of building interest in the speech top which have also been found effective. One is the practice of starting th speech with questions related to the topic. A speech dealing with fu niture-making, for instance, might begin with a series of questions: "D you know which is the hardest wood in existence? Do you know whic is the most expensive hardwood still used for making furniture? Whic is the most commonly used wood for furniture construction?" You rea in Chapter 8 that these are called rhetorical questions. The speaker do

- **RETEACHING**

List the various techniques for introducing an informative speech and ask students which examples they enjoyed the most. Discuss which of the techniques they feel most comfortable using. Suggest that these techniques become tools that they have available to them as they prepare formal and informal speeches. Suggest that these techniques could also be useful to them in preparing written reports in school or in writing business letters when they pursue a career.

SUBSTITUTE TEACHER TIP

Demonstrate the appeal of suspense to the class using "Trivial Pursuit" type questions. Ask a question and pause one second before giving the answer. Repeat the procedure but wait 5 seconds before giving the answer. Ask students at what point someone would lose interest in learning the "answer" to an interesting question.

AMAZING FACTS!

The world's top-selling mystery writer is Dame Agatha Christie. Her 78 mystery novels have sold an estimated 2 billion copies in 44 languages.

- **SKILL DEVELOPMENT**

15-Second Skill Opportunity
Ask all students to think of a second sentence to follow the old saw, "It was a dark and stormy night." They should suggest what happens next. Ask volunteers to deliver their two-sentence speech.

---

not expect an "out-loud" answer from the listeners. Rather, it is intended that the listeners will mentally try to answer the questions. The speaker thereby generates attention and builds interest in the speech topic. Occasionally, speakers will ask *real* (not rhetorical) questions, which they expect audience members to answer aloud. This can sometimes be done by a show of hands or by inviting specific listeners to answer aloud. This technique can build topic interest as well as arouse attention, but it is a bit risky. Since the speaker may not receive the expected answer, he or she may be caught off guard and become confused. If you plan to use real questions, prepare to react to various kinds of responses.

Another interest-building technique consists of beginning a speech with a quotation that highlights an important aspect of your topic. Audiences are usually interested in the thoughts of others, particularly if quoted from some well-known or well-beloved person. One way to build listener interest in a patriotic speech, for example, would be to introduce your topic with John Kennedy's famous quotation "Ask not what your country can do for you; ask what you can do for your country." The use of a quotation from the Bible or another religious work in introductions has long been a favorite interest-building device of members of the clergy. The quotation identifies the general topic area for the listeners and creates a mild suspense about how the speaker will develop the particular topic within the area.

Directly challenging your audience is still another means of building topic interest. When you ask rhetorical questions that challenge your audience to formulate answers, for example, you generate interest in your own answers as well. You build interest by directing a real challenge to your listeners—by including them.

Preview the Topic

On the covers of many paperback books you will find intriguing hints about the contents of the book. These are meant to help sell the book. A speech introduction serves a similar function prior to the main body of the speech. Audiences have learned to expect the speaker to "clue them in" on the speech topic, its purpose, and often the main points that will be covered. Thus, previewing the topic is a significant function of most speech introductions.

The most obvious and straightforward method of previewing the topic consists of simply stating your speech purpose to the audience during the introduction. Sometimes, however, this type of introduction may fail to fulfill the other important functions of an introduction at the same time. An introduction that merely previews the topic, without at the same time generating attention and building interest in the topic,

TEACH

SUBSTITUTE TEACHER TIP

Bring in several paperback books and ask students to read the blurb that describes the story. Based on these previews, ask students to vote on the book they would most like to read.

● TEACHING

Discuss with students how they get "clues" about what their classes will cover every day. Ask if they would like more or fewer clues about the content and expectations for their classes. List suggestions for clues about content on the chalkboard.

● SKILL DEVELOPMENT

15-Second Skill Opportunity

Give students the opportunity to practice asking a rhetorical question to create interest in an assigned topic. Perhaps you could suggest the topic, "Weather Forecasting," and ask students to think of a rhetorical question to build interest in that topic. Ask volunteers to stand and introduce that topic using a rhetorical question.

● LEARNING STYLES

Multicultural Learning

Ask small groups of students to look into sayings, proverbs, or quotations from other cultures that might be appropriate for use as part of a speaker's introductory remarks for a speech. Students could also indicate topics and occasions for the use of these quotations.

Cooperative Learning

Small groups of students could collect and analyze a variety of speeches and notice how the various elements mentioned in this section are used in the speeches they have. They could develop an evaluation sheet that would help them judge the effectiveness of a speech.

---

302 CHAPTER 10 Speaking to Inform

might be labeled a clear but dull introduction. Notice how this introduction to a speech on modern laboratories begins by focusing the listener's attention, builds their interest in the speaker's subject, and finishes by previewing the topic for the audience:

> If you are like me, you hate going to the dentist. Even the remote chance that he might find a cavity, followed in rapid-fire order by the pain of the novocaine needle, the siren-like whine of the dreaded drill, and later by the leathery lip which won't allow you to eat with dignity—all this sends shudders through most of us. If you have ever done really serious time in the dentist's chair, say for a root canal or to have a full crown fitted, you probably look upon dental science as a science barely emerging from the Neanderthal Period. Even some of the tools the dentist waves before your eyes remind you of prehistoric instruments, looking about as subtle as stone-headed axes as they are forced inside your gaping mouth.
>
> The truth is, though, that dentistry is a very modern, high-tech science in which measurements must be made in tens of thousandths of a millimeter. Every day, researchers and technicians in dental labs deal in minute expansions and contractions of plasters, wax, gold, and plastic to assure that dental patients will enjoy perfectly fitting dental products. Today I want to share with you some of the fascinating "high-tech" insights I gained while working in such a dental lab last summer.

Again, as you can see, the previewing of the topic is a very important function of the introduction in speeches given to inform. Because the principal purpose of the speech is to teach, the speaker must make sure the message is received. To ensure audience understanding, good public speakers use several opportunities to restate their message. Previewing the topic in the introduction is the first opportunity to give the listener the basic message in a brief form. If the members of the audience hear the topic previewed in the introduction, are told the complete message in the body of the speech, and then hear the message summarized in the conclusion, most of them are likely to receive the message.

Apply the Message to the Audience

A fourth function of the introduction is a natural follow-up to previewing the topic. As soon as you tell your listeners what you propose to talk about, show them how that topic applies to them. Applying the message to the listeners means showing them what they stand to gain from hearing the message, why the topic should be of particular interest to them, and why it has significance for them.

TEACH

● **TEACHING**

Explain that practical application of knowledge is often the hardest part of teaching, or giving a speech. Discuss whether it is the primary job of the teacher or of the student to apply information to real life.

● **CURRICULAR CONNECTIONS**

Writing
Students could think about their having to give a speech to older Americans on the topic of older Americans. Read the excerpt from Louis Housman's speech. Ask students to write a similar introduction using any of the techniques presented in this section.

AMAZING FACTS!
An estimated record audience of 800,000 attended a free concert in Central Park, New York City, conducted by Zubin Mehta on July 5, 1986, to celebrate the Statue of Liberty Weekend.

● **SKILL DEVELOPMENT**

On the Job
Discuss the kind of "speeches" workers expect to encounter on the job. Ask how skilled and technical and professional workers stay informed after they have received their formal training.

It is important to demonstrate how your topic relates to and has significance for the audience.

Louis Housman applied his message in a speech on "Older Americans" by showing that the speech dealt with a significant topic and by implying that his listeners stood to gain from hearing about this topic:

> There are 31 million Americans 60 years and older. They constitute the single largest minority in the nation.
> This minority, since 1900, is growing at twice the rate of our total population.
> The way in which these older Americans are viewed by society as a whole, by younger persons, and by themselves, has important implications for all of you concerned with the well-being of older persons.

Establish Ethos

The Ancient Greek rhetorician Aristotle claimed that three forces influenced an audience—the speaker's logic, appeals to the listeners' emotions, and the character of the speaker. He wrote that the speaker's character, which he called **ethos,** was the most powerful of the three. Although Aristotle was writing about persuasive speaking, and though some modern speech authorities would disagree with his ranking of the three elements, no one would claim that the speaker's character and credibility are unimportant, even in informative speeches. You have undoubtedly noticed how you accept what some people tell you much more readily than you accept the words of others. Ethos is also the basis for the old adage among salespersons: "You have to sell yourself first."

Since listeners more readily accept information from a source they believe and have confidence in, establishing one's ethos is an important task for a public speaker to accomplish during the introduction of an

TEACH

> *Character is what a man is in the dark.*
> — Dwight L. Moody

● TEACHING

Establish the importance of credibility in conveying a message. Provide examples of notable frauds or deceptions. Or you could talk about the reputation of used-car salespersons or lawyers. Students could brainstorm suggestions as to how people in these occupations could improve their reputations.

● CURRICULAR CONNECTIONS

Language Arts
Ask students to think of several alternate terms to the expression "ethos." Then ask them to think of several historical and contemporary examples of people with this trait. You might suggest various categories of people. It might be easier for students to think of sports figures, for example.

---

304 CHAPTER 10 Speaking to Inform

Character, or ethos, is established through the speaker's credibility, expertise, and sincerity.

informative speech. Of course, not all speakers need to begin by establishing their expertise and sincerity. Well-known personalities or speakers fortunate enough to be introduced to their audience by someone else are usually wiser to accept their reputation in modest silence. Most speakers, however, must themselves fulfill the job of convincing the listeners of their knowledge, sincerity, and likability. When this job is left up to you, as it will be in most of your speeches, you should establish your ethos early, preferably during the introduction.

Ethos exists in the minds of your listeners. It consists of their inward answers to three unspoken questions: "Is this speaker thoroughly familiar with the subject?" "Is this speaker being completely open and honest with me?" "Do I enjoy listening to this speaker?" Many of the techniques useful for gaining audience attention and building interest in the speech topic may also aid in building speaker ethos. Humor, for instance, usually increases an audience's enjoyment when listening to a speaker. Devices such as anecdote and the shock technique can show listeners the speaker has done research and is informed about the topic.

Several specific techniques for building ethos can be used on occasions when you feel a special need to "sell your credentials" to your audience. One of these is straightforwardly mentioning some of the research and preparation you did for the speech. This can be worked into your introduction not in a bragging way but simply to show the listeners you have earned the right to speak to them. A similar technique of ethos-building consists of mentioning some experience you have had that qualifies you as an "expert" on your topic. Here is an example of such as ethos-builder:

> "Perhaps the process by which soft drinks are bottled sounds like an awfully dry and humdrum topic for a classroom speech. Last year I probably would have considered it boring too, but my job last summer in a bottling plant showed me that, far from being humdrum, it's exciting and sometimes even dangerous. This afternoon I'd like to share with you some of the experiences...."

Such an introduction, besides building interest in the speaker's topic, shows the listeners they are listening to an eyewitness—someone who has earned the right to speak to them on this particular topic.

On occasions when you are introduced to the audience prior to your speech, you ordinarily will not want to attempt much, if any, ethos building of your own at the start of your speech. Usually a simple "Thank you, Bob" or "Thank you for that kind introduction" is all that is needed. If the introducer has been extremely flattering, you may want to insert a humorous comment to show modesty, such as "My generous introducer got so carried away, I found myself sitting here trying to imagine who was going to give this marvelous speech!" If, on the other hand, your introducer should fail to give you enough credit, you should modestly supply some of the missing facts yourself during the speech introduction. This should be done very matter-of-factly, as an attempt to fill in some information the introducer overlooked. Here is an example:

> Thank you, Sharon, for that introduction. Something Sharon did not mention was my two years as a Little League umpire. I bring this up because that experience gave birth to many of the ideas I will be expressing in my speech tonight.

IMPARTING THE MESSAGE OF AN INFORMATIVE SPEECH

The central part of an informative speech, sandwiched between the introduction and conclusion, is called the body of the speech. The body contains the essential message of the speech, completely developed. The speech outline, of course, plots the speaker's individual approach to the topic, and the way in which the subject unfolds during delivery is unique to each individual speaker and speech occasion. Still, certain general rules must be followed while imparting the message if the informative speech is to have its maximum impact.

Maintain Attention

A basic function of the introduction is to gain the initial attention of the audience. Gaining attention at the start, however, does not automatically give the speaker a guarantee of unbroken attention for the rest of the speech. Since people's attention usually focuses on one person or idea only briefly and shifts constantly from one object to another, a public speaker must make a constant effort to keep the listeners focused on the message.

TEACH

● **TEACHING**

To help students get an overview of this section, use the major headings to list the techniques for developing the body of an informative speech. These headings are: (a) Maintain Attention, (b) React to Feedback, (c) Make Smooth Transitions, (d) Avoid Becoming Too Technical, and (e) Personalize Your Speech.

● **TIME MANAGEMENT**

You may want to compress this part of the chapter and spend more time developing practice in the introduction and conclusion portions of informative speeches.

● **LINKS TO PAST LEARNING**

Ask students to remember occasions at worship or other assemblies where the speaker asked members to move closer to the front. Discuss how people feel when they are asked to move to the front of a classroom or assembly.

● **LEARNING STYLES**

Kinesic Learning
Ask students to think about the size of the school auditorium. If there were 100 people who came to hear a speech delivered there, ask about the best seating arrangement for the speaker and the audience. Discuss how the speaker could ask members of the audience to move.

CHAPTER 10 Speaking to Inform

Most of the attention devices that are useful during the introduction of an informative speech may also be sprinkled throughout the speech to maintain listener attention. A humorous anecdote, an occasional story, a set of shocking statistics, or a bit of suspense during the body of the speech can regain flagging attention and renew audience interest.

Careful preparation regarding nonverbal attention-factors can also help to capture audience attention effectively. The way your audience is seated is one of these nonverbal attention-factors. Speakers have found that audience attention generally remains at a higher level the closer the audience members are to one another. Audience members generate attention among themselves, thus relieving the speaker of part of the task of keeping their attention. Whenever you find yourself facing a sparse or scattered audience, with numerous empty chairs between your listeners, invite the audience to sit more closely together in front rows. Maintaining their attention throughout your speech will prove considerably easier.

A second nonverbal attention-factor relates to listening conditions. The more you, the speaker, can assure comfortable conditions for effective listening, the more likely you will be to have the continuous attention of your audience. Whenever possible, arrive at the speaking location before your audience to arrange for proper listening conditions.

React to Feedback

As you proceed through your speech, be alert to audience reactions and respond to them whenever necessary. Reacting to audience feedback is not a technique a beginning speaker can acquire all at once during a first or second speech. It is an important skill to develop, however, since a public speech involves two-way communication just as a conversation does. Not to show any reaction to audience feedback may cause some listeners to feel you are ignoring them. Many audiences may find this lack of response insulting.

In order to respond to feedback, you must first learn to interpret it. As you begin giving speeches you will notice that some listeners react more vigorously than others do. Some people will appear more interested, more alert, and more intense in their reactions. Pay closer attention to these individuals as you speak, and look for signs of understanding, puzzlement, agreement, or disagreement in their faces, in their posture, and in their eyes. Once you have developed the ability to recognize positive and negative reactions, you can begin to adjust your message, language, and delivery techniques a bit to lessen negative reactions and increase positive forms of feedback.

Adjust especially to an audience reaction if it comes from a sizable proportion of your listeners. If only one or two listeners frown, fo

TEACH

● TEACHING

Emphasize that audience reaction is manifested in many ways. Some of the ways are obvious. You could list some of those reactions, such as clapping, yawning, and laughing, on the chalkboard. Encourage students to add to the list.

● CURRICULAR CONNECTIONS

Math/Science
Some students may be interested in researching various scientific experiments or studies that have been conducted on animals to condition their response to certain stimuli. A notable example is Pavlov's dog. Make comparisons to human behavior. Discuss how people usually react to a smile.

> *"It is greed to want to do all the talking but not to want to listen at all."*
> —Democritus

● LEARNING STYLES

Multicultural Learning
Ask students to find out about the kind of reactions to speeches that are common in a variety of cultures. They could try to find out if clapping, for instance, is a form of feedback given in all cultures.

Imparting the Message of an Informative Speech   307

Learning to interpret and respond to feedback is a valuable speaking skill.

instance, their action may only mean that they did not understand or did not agree with something you just said. However, if thirty or forty percent of your listeners frown, whatever you just said probably needs repeating or clarifying

Make Smooth Transitions

A **transition** is like a switch on a railroad line. It allows a speaker to change from one aspect of the topic to another. Well-planned transitions go unnoticed by the listeners but give them an impression of a smoothly flowing speech. Not planning one's transitions results in jerky shifts from one main point to another, making the speech sound like a series of disconnected mini-speeches.

Transitions between major points (the main heads of your outline) may consist of only a sentence or two that relates what you have just finished saying to what you will say next. Transitions between minor points (subheads) can often be made with just a word or phrase, such as "First…," "Second.…" In either case they all must be thoroughly planned and rehearsed, not left to chance. Word-for-word memorization may be useful when rehearsing transitions to assure they will tie the parts of the speech together clearly.

Speakers commonly plan major transitions (those between main heads) by selecting a key word or phrase to make one point and then using it again to make the next point. Notice how President John F. Kennedy, in his inaugural address, linked the past to the present by

TEACH

SUBSTITUTE TEACHER TIP

Have students look at the speeches in the Appendix and locate transition devices.

TEACHING

Provide several examples of transition words or phrases for students. Keep a list of these on the chalkboard. To emphasize the three purposes of using transitions, write the words "summary, preview, relationship" on the chalkboard. Provide examples of each.

CURRICULAR CONNECTIONS

Writing
As the text suggests, you may ask students to write out a transition statement for a speech and suggest they memorize it. Then give them practice in delivering that transition statement to the class.

SKILL DEVELOPMENT

15-Second Skill Opportunity
Ask students to write a transition sentence that could link one major point of a speech to the second major point of the speech. The text suggests that memorization may be a useful technique when rehearsing transitions. Ask students to memorize their transition sentence and then ask for volunteers to speak that sentence.

15-Second Skill Opportunity
Ask volunteers to read one of the transition examples provided in the text. Then ask others to stand and give their own versions of transition statements.

The transitions that characterized President John F. Kennedy's inaugural address helped to create a sense of momentum in the presentation.

focusing on the past and present tenses of the verb *summons* in a transition:

> Since this country was founded, each generation of Americans has been summoned to give testimony to its national loyalty. The graves of young Americans who answered the call to service surround the globe.
>
> Now the trumpet summons us again—not as a call to bear arms, though arms we need—not as a call to battle, though embattled we are—but a call to bear the burden of a long twilight struggle, year in and year out, "rejoicing in hope, patient in tribulation"—a struggle against the common enemies of man: tyranny, poverty, disease and war itself.

A typical transition accomplishes three purposes: first, it summarizes the point you have just finished; second, it tells the listeners what you will cover next; finally, it shows the relationship between the two. Usually a good transition does all of this in one or two sentences. For example, if you were giving a speech telling your classmates about your summer job as a hospital volunteer, a transition between your first and second main points might state: "In addition to helping people in need as a hospital volunteer, I also gained valuable job experience." Here are several other examples:

- Increasing the amount of money spent on education is only one part of the solution. The other part is to ensure that the money is spent wisely.

- Now that we have explored the ancient origins of astrology, let us turn to its modern popularity.

TEACH

● **TEACHING**

Ask students to read the excerpt on autism in the text and make a list of the technical words used in that speech. Compare the first with the second version. Suggest that some students rewrite the speech using their own examples and words.

> *"An expert is one who knows more and more about less and less."*
> —Nicholas Murray Butler

● **LEARNING STYLES**

Technology Tools
Students can provide examples of increased use of technology in the workplace. Ask them to imagine how the use of technology will probably increase throughout their adult years. Invite them to think of technology-related words that are commonly used today that did not exist five or ten years ago.

Visual Learning
Using the topic of autism, ask students to prepare visual aids that could be part of this speech. The visual or graphic information should aim to make the topic more personal and less technical for listeners. These visual aids could be used as a portfolio product as well.

Imparting the Message of an Informative Speech

- So much for the present; what about the future?
- We've seen what high protein diets can do for you. What about high carbohydrate diets?

Your teacher may ask you to write your transitions out word-for-word in your speech outline and memorize them. Clearly stated transitions give listeners one of their best means of keeping track of your speech.

Avoid Becoming Too Technical

Imagine you are listening to one of your classmates giving a speech explaining the disorder known as "autism" in children. Your hear him say:

> Autism is a severe communication and behavioral disorder occurring in infants and characterized by ritualistic response to environmental stimuli. Symptoms include an inability to utilize language meaningfully and an inability to process information about the environment. Half of all autistic children are totally mute; those who have limited capacity for verbalization tend to repeat mechanically any aural stimuli to which they are exposed. Other common symptoms are a vacant, withdrawn facial expression, fascination with mechanical objects, and resistance to environmental alteration.

Chances are you wouldn't pay attention to the speech very long. Even if you tried to pay attention, you might wind up with a severe headache within five minutes! What is wrong with such a speech? The speaker is using too much **technical language.** His information is quite accurate, but he is expressing it in language understood by trained psychiatrists. If our student speaker were willing to tackle such a technical subject for his informative speech, he needed to understand it thoroughly first, then put it into simple language that his audience could understand. He might have done it this way:

> Imagine this: You are the parent of a beautiful little boy. He may not speak at all, ever; half of all autistic children don't. If he does speak, he may just croon the same word over and over in a singsong voice, perhaps a word you've said to him a minute or so earlier. Much of his time is spent rocking his body, back and forth, back and forth, endlessly. He lives almost entirely in his own world, inside his own head. But that doesn't mean he's not aware of what's going on around him. Beware of changing something in his room or moving his toys around! He may become frantic and fly into a tantrum.

APPLY

AMAZING FACTS!
Eloise and Charles Shields visited 331 national parks between 1991–1993.

● ENRICHMENT
If possible, a park ranger could be invited to speak to the class, or students could write for information from any of the national parks.

● CURRICULAR CONNECTIONS

History
Some students might find out about the national historic parks and sites in the United States. Students could compile a list of these and identify them in terms of location and characteristics.

● SKILL DEVELOPMENT

Research
Ask students to imagine they are conducting a tour of a historical site or national park of their choice. They need to tell the visitors on the tour an interesting story or anecdote about the place they have selected. They could research information to develop a story. Give them an opportunity to practice telling their stories.

CAREER CLOSE-UP

Park Ranger

The National Park service was established in 1916 to conserve certain areas in the United States for the enjoyment of future generations. Park rangers serve as guides and answer questions for visitors to the various National Parks. Although park rangers primarily conduct tours (up to ten per day), they also give talks and slide presentations for schools, senior citizens, and other organizations. To qualify for a position with the National Park Service, a park ranger needs at least two years of a college program with a history major, including courses in English composition and speech.

Park rangers are knowledgeable about their site and can speak about its history in a way that will be intriguing. This information must be updated with material researched in libraries or the site's archives. Regardless of their experience, rangers regularly rehearse their talks to ensure that they will flow smoothly, even as new information is added.

Effective park rangers do more than merely recite facts, however. They include colorful details in each talk to maintain their listeners' interest. Because each audience is so varied, rangers begin with anecdotes that everyone can relate to. This helps focus the group's attention. To express enthusiasm, rangers vary the pitch of their voices and maintain eye contact with listeners.

The park ranger's ability to speak spontaneously to meet the interests of different audiences results from superior speaking skills and the careful preparation of talks, which rangers prepare themselves. Because of this expertise, rangers successfully immerse visitors in the drama of our nation's past, thus fulfilling the goal of the National Park Service.

One of the responsibilities of the park ranger is to speak spontaneously in response to the questions posed by audiences with a wide variety of interests.

● **TEACHING**

Emphasize the fact that most people are interested in the stories of other people. To illustrate that fact, invite students to share stories about complicated issues like medical research that have a personal dimension. The issue becomes interesting when people know of another person's involvement.

● **RETEACHING**

Students could make a list of all the techniques presented in this section for the body of a speech. Ask them to evaluate their performance in each area. Identify their best and their worst areas and suggest ways that they can improve in a targeted area.

TEACH

SUBSTITUTE TEACHER TIP

Bring to class copies of current magazines or newspapers. Ask students to read the opening paragraphs and note the number of times articles introduce a topic in a personalized way.

Imparting the Message of an Informative Speech

In listening to this second version, you would be able to understand it easily. The only technical word was "autistic," the word the speaker was defining.

In addition to avoiding language that is too technical, you will want to watch out for selecting informative speech topics that are too technical. Remember what you studied about your audience on pages 295–305 in this chapter. You can probably make almost any topic understandable to any audience to a certain degree, but highly technical topics demand first that you be an expert in the area, then that you take great pains in simplifying your language to ensure audience understanding. Usually it is not possible to simplify a very technical topic for a five-minute classroom speech. This doesn't mean, of course, that you should never choose a classroom topic more technical than "How to Bake a Cake." At the same time, be wary of trying to give a five-minute speech on "The Theory of Quantum Mechanics."

Personalize Your Speech

People are interested in people. Probably nothing maintains the attention and interest of an audience as well as having a number of stories, examples, and humor involving people. The speaker who frequently brings people into his or her speeches is **personalizing** the speech.

Suppose you are speaking about the effects of radiation—the kind of radiation emitted by such ordinary items as microwave ovens and video display terminals. You could give your listeners tons of statistics showing how many people are affected by such radiation each year, and how many additional health care dollars it takes to treat them. *Some* statistics of that sort would be very helpful. But if you want to be certain of regaining your listeners' wavering attention following a string of numbers, give them an example with a person in it:

> Becky Krimson worked for the Citizens National Bank of Chicago. Throughout her three-year period of employment there, Becky often complained of headaches, dizziness, fatigue, and loss of hair. Her boss said she occasionally suffered partial memory loss, while her co-workers frequently complained about Becky's emotional instability. Upon a visit to her doctor she was given some pills, told to take a few days' rest, and sent home. At the time Becky did not know that the video display terminal she worked with at the bank was zapping her with radiation, and that rest and pills could not cure her symptoms.

Personalizing your speech does not mean you must always use real people as examples. You might create a fictional person who is meant to stand for the "average" individual in certain circumstances. In so

> 66 *I am proud of the fact that I never invented weapons to kill.* 99
> —Thomas Alva Edison

● **SKILL DEVELOPMENT**

15-Second Skill Opportunity
Ask students to use the paper or a magazine to find an interesting anecdote. Give them practice time to tell the story and relate the anecdote to a specific topic.

● **LEARNING STYLES**

Cooperative Learning
Ask small groups of students to identify interesting characters from real life (historical or contemporary) and from fiction. Discuss which type of character they find most interesting.

TEACH

> *Better is the end of a thing than the beginning thereof.*
> —Bible, Ecclesiastes

● **TEACHING**

To give students an overview of this section list the major headings with their page numbers on the chalkboard. Ask students to anticipate the area they think will be the most difficult for them to practice.

● **LINKS TO PAST LEARNING**

Ask students to describe how they recognize when a class, or a dinner, or a movie will end. Are conclusions easy to recognize? Discuss their impressions of concluding techniques.

● **LEARNING STYLES**

Audio Learning
Ask students to reflect on the author's comment that the tone of voice changes in the conclusion of a speech. Ask students to describe those changes. Some may want to tape concluding comments of speeches.

● **ACTIVITY**

You could invite students to develop a chart or checklist that they could use to identify the types of things they should be aware of in reacting to feedback. Not all the things listed will be relevant in every speech.

● **SKILL DEVELOPMENT**

15-Second Skill Opportunity
Ask students to make a list of the signal words included in the text and add their own. Suggest that these terms and expressions can increase the tools they have available to use in their speeches. Give students the opportunity to practice a signal conclusion sentence.

---

312   CHAPTER 10 Speaking to Inform

doing, you are able to present your information in story form rather than as a string of statistics. One student speaker created Vladimir, a typical Russian child, for a speech on life in the former Soviet Union. He was able to show his listeners how the Russian school system differs from ours by tracing Vladimir's progress through his years of schooling.

● **ACTIVITY**

Reacting to Feedback

Following the speeches in an upcoming round, plan for one student to critique how well each speaker reacted to audience feedback. As you watch your assigned speaker, ask yourself questions such as "Is the speaker watching his audience while speaking in an effort to read their feedback?" "Does the speaker appear to glance most frequently at audience members who are more alert and intense in their reactions?" "If the speaker seems aware of audience feedback, does she or he make any adjustments in content or delivery to respond to the feedback?" As you critique, remember that responding regularly to audience feedback is not a technique inexperienced speakers learn overnight.

● **CONCLUDING AN INFORMATIVE SPEECH**

Speech conclusions are typically brief, accounting for only about five percent of the total speech. However, the conclusion may represent the most important part of many speeches. Since the audience hears the conclusion last, they are likely to remember it the longest. You should use as much care preparing your conclusion as you did your introduction. Like introductions, speech conclusions accomplish several key purposes in speeches.

Signal Your Conclusion

Audiences typically expect speakers to do certain things for them during speech conclusions—summarize the main points, reinforce the central idea, and psychologically close the speech. Before listeners are able to pick out these guideposts, however, they must know when the conclusion of the speech begins. Therefore your first job in concluding a speech is that of giving your audience a clear signal that you are about to conclude.

TEACH

● **TEACHING**

Ask students to use the excerpts of speech conclusions found on pages 313–316 to identify the major points made in the body of each speech.

> ❝*A word is dead
> When it is said,
> Some say.
> I say it just
> Begins to live
> That day.*❞
> —Emily Dickinson

● **SKILL DEVELOPMENT**

🕐 **15-Second Skill Opportunity**
Students could select one of the excerpts on pages 313–316 and practice reading it to use voice and tone to signal the end of a speech. Students could work in pairs to gain practice reading a speech conclusion. Then ask volunteers to read the conclusion for the entire class.

Concluding an Informative Speech

Because it is last and is likely to be remembered the longest, use as much care in preparing the conclusion as you did the introduction.

How do you send this signal? One of the simplest ways is by beginning your conclusion with signal words, such as "In conclusion," "In closing," "My purpose has been," "Let me end by saying," "Let me leave you with," or "Finally." A second way is through subtle changes in your wording and your manner of delivery. By an extra long pause prior to your conclusion, by changes in vocal tone, volume, and pacing, or by moving a few steps as you start your conclusion, you can signal the end of your speech. Your wording, too, becomes "larger," more grand in tone as you return to the general theme with which you began the speech. Without actually saying "in conclusion," you signal your audience that you are about to close. Notice how effective Kathy Weisensel, a student speaker, concluded her speech dealing with misconceptions about the victims of mental retardation:

> While misconceptions are slow to pass away, they must surely die. Out nation's retarded are not mentally ill, totally ineducable, or incapable of happy and productive lives.
> I know, in a deeply personal way, the pain that these misconceptions inspire. But I also know that the world is changing. I have a deep faith that you and others of our generation will reject the senseless and destructive stereotypes of the past. As Bernard Posner has said: "The young people of the world seem to be forging a new set of values. It appears to be a value system of recognizing the intrinsic worth of all humans, retarded or not,…a value system of acceptance: of accepting life as it is, and people as they are."
> Thank you for your acceptance.

TEACH

> *Anybody who graduates from college never having taken a speech course should be classified as a bum.*
> —Mari Pat Varga

● **TEACHING**

Help students identify sources for good concluding quotations. You might work with the librarian to identify sources that are available in your school library or local bookstore.

● **ENRICHMENT**

Students might request copies of student speeches given in class, select the best ones, and consider publishing a digest of them.

● **SKILL DEVELOPMENT**

15-Second Skill Opportunity
Students could select any of the examples of concluding remarks and prepare a delivery of those remarks to the class. Give them time to practice and critique their own conclusions.

● **LEARNING STYLES**

Cooperative Learning
Ask students to note the collection of excerpts from student speeches in this text and in this chapter in particular. Have students evaluate these excerpts and compare the performance of the students quoted in the text with student performance in your class.

Summarize the Main Ideas

The **summary** is the main part of a speech conclusion. Though a conclusion may have other functions as well, its principal function is summarizing the major ideas, especially in an informative speech. Summarizing means presenting the basic message again in very brief form. This is generally accomplished by using the device called restatement—repeating the same ideas, but in different words. Observe how Mary Nielsen summarized an informative speech on bats.

> This, then, is the bat. This ugly creature whose appearance makes it very easy to hate. This creature that belongs to the same biological class as people. A much maligned creature who has been used by storytellers and entertainers to inspire fear and horror in their audiences for centuries. A creature that has been the victim of half-truths and exaggerations. Now, however, scientists are beginning to understand the worth of this creature—its place in nature and in the laboratory. Perhaps nobody will put a bumper sticker on a car stating, "Have you hugged a bat today?" but maybe now we can learn to understand them.

In this student's summary, the main ideas of the entire speech were again presented in brief form. Even without reading the entire speech, you were able to know the topic of the speech and its main points.

Reinforce the Central Idea

Since your conclusion is your last chance to impress the central message of your speech upon your listeners, you will often try to do this in several ways. A summary, of course, typically restates the central idea, but often simply restating it fails to "brand" it into the listeners' minds.

Ending with a **quotation** is an additional means of ensuring that the audience will remember your speech. Here, for instance, is how Randy Larsen concluded a speech on the growing use of lasers in surgery:

> But even with these problems, the laser's future seems bright. We hear so much about military "Star Wars" technology; it's encouraging to know the laser has life-saving capacities as well. Dr. Janos Voros believes, "The laser will revolutionize surgery." In some areas, it already has.

Closing quotations are especially effective when they relate closely to the central message of the speech, and are brief.

A **dramatic statement** that you yourself make up is another way of impressing your basic message upon the listeners as you conclude. In a speech on suicide prevention, a student made striking use of this technique when she concluded:

> My friend is back in school, participating in activities she never did before—and enjoying life. I'm happy and proud to say she's still fighting for her life and even happier she failed to kill herself. Otherwise, I wouldn't be here today trying to help you. You see, I am my 'friend,' and I'm more than glad to say, I've made it.

Naturally, her audience was stunned by this dramatic conclusion. Probably none of them soon forgot the basic message of her speech.

Another method by which to reinforce your speech's central idea in the conclusion is by referring back to your introduction. Since the introduction nearly always contains a preview of the speech's purpose, a reference back to it in the conclusion serves to implant that purpose firmly in the listeners' minds. A speaker who opened her speech by stating that "Disney World in Florida is really not a Mickey Mouse organization; it is truly big business!" concluded her speech in the following way:

> I hope I have given you a sense of the scope and complexity involved in running the Magic Kingdom. Were you allowed to see behind the scenes—behind the fairyland to the maze of computers, behind Donald Duck and Goofy to the army of interviewers screening job applicants, behind Cinderella's Castle and the Monorail to the planners and risk takers who constantly pour millions of dollars into this fantasy world—you would recognize that Disney World is by no means a Mickey Mouse operation. It is truly big business!

Psychologically Close the Speech

Audiences not only want to *know* a speech is over; they want to *feel* it is complete too. Did you ever have to leave an exciting basketball game shortly before it ended? You were probably left with a feeling of incompleteness that was not erased by later reading the final score in the newspaper. Speech audiences expect speakers to tidy up any loose ends during their conclusions. In addition to restating the main points and refocusing on the central idea, speakers frequently should finish by involving their listeners in the topic one more time.

One way of doing this is by issuing a *challenge* to your audience. Gale Klappa, vice president of Southern Company Services, Inc., closed a speech on attitudes toward the media by asking for his listeners' help:

> I hope you'll join me in that effort. I hope you, too, are concerned—that you want to turn public anger and outrage toward the media into admiration and respect.

TEACH

● **RETEACHING**

Ask students to name several TV programs they have watched recently and to describe how each program ended. Compare those endings with the conclusion techniques mentioned in this section. Ask students to point out similarities and differences.

● **ACTIVITY**

You could assign topics for this activity from the following list: "The New Season on TV," "How to Fill Out a Job Application," or "Writing an Essay for a College Application."

CHAPTER 10 Speaking to Inform

A second way is to ask a **rhetorical question.** Rhetorical questions can involve the audience at least as effectively when used in your conclusion as in the introduction. When used at the end of a speech, they often linger in the listener's mind because no answer was provided. They can cause individual listeners to keep trying to provide themselves satisfactory answers well after the speech has ended. If you are a person who is always late, would you later re-think this student speaker's closing rhetorical question?:

> So remember, people who are always late aren't just disorganized. There are three possible reasons for repeated lateness: first, they could be trying to defy authority; second, they could be trying to gain power over the other person; and finally, they could be trying to live up to stereotypes about groups of people. Could any of these reasons describe you?

A final method of psychologically closing a speech is by repeating a **theme** or **slogan,** first mentioned in the introduction. This technique is much like that of referring back to your central purpose, except here you are trying to plant a brief statement in the listener's memory—a theme or slogan that will vividly recall your speech to mind. Preachers frequently use this approach when they begin a sermon with a Bible verse, then close by repeating it word-for-word.

Whichever techniques you use to close your speeches, remember every informative speech needs some form of conclusion. Never end with your last main point. The audience expects you to "put it all together" before you sit down. Conclusions need not be lengthy—as a matter of fact, they should almost always be brief—but they must always be there!

● **ACTIVITY**

Making Conclusions Work

Working in groups of four or five, decide on a speech topic and purpose. Discuss at least four possible conclusions for the speech and then write them down. Be prepared to explain the type and purpose of each conclusion. Take turns reading each one aloud, pausing in the most effective places and stressing the most important sections. Discuss with the group how well each conclusion fulfilled its purpose.

● **MOTIVATION**

Ask students to read the reasons for gaining practice in question-and-answer sessions. Award "bonus points" to the student who can think of the most (or best) benefits.

> *It is better to ask some of the questions than to know all the answers.*
> —James Thurber

● **LEARNING STYLES**

Cooperative Learning
Give each small group a limited amount of time to generate at least five questions about a topic that has been discussed in class. Then ask a volunteer from another group to stand and try to answer the question raised by the first group.

● **SKILL DEVELOPMENT**

15-Second Skill Opportunity
Suggest to students that questions can generally be asked around the basics of who, what, where, when, and why. Ask them to select one of those trusty standbyes and develop a question based on a topic recently discussed in class. Ask volunteers to share their question with the class.

● CONDUCTING A QUESTION-AND-ANSWER PERIOD

At the conclusion of your in-class informative speeches, your teacher may ask you to remain at the lectern for a brief question-and-answer period with the class. This gives class members an opportunity to ask about points in your speech that are unclear to them. They can ask for additional information or simply delve more fully into your topic. Question-and-answer periods are also helpful for you in several ways. For one thing, they provide an opportunity for you to learn to think on your feet by forcing you to form answers without preparation beforehand. This should not alarm you if you know your subject thoroughly. A second reason for practicing question-and-answer periods stems from their frequent use following speeches given outside of the classroom. A large number of informative speeches given to civic clubs, religious groups, or business groups call for the speaker to respond to questions from the audience about the speech topic.

Invite Questions

You will generally know whether or not a question-and-answer period is likely to follow a speech. Some clubs and organizations consider such a session traditional. Or you may anticipate your topic arousing enough interest to cause a number of audience members to ask questions. Whenever you expect a question-and-answer period to follow a speech, it is a good idea to invite such a session when you begin your speech. Mentioning at the start that you will be happy to respond to any questions when you have finished gives the listeners a chance to develop questions during your talk. When a speaker ends the speech with "Now, are there any questions?" without giving any prior warning, the audience is caught off guard and often cannot form any significant questions quickly.

Once a question-and-answer session has begun, the speaker must be as impartial as possible in recognizing listeners who have questions. Naturally, preference should be given to the first hands raised over the later ones and to those who have not yet asked a question over those who have already had a turn. If there is a pre-arranged time limit for questions or if you feel that the audience is getting bored or that the questions are becoming repetitive, you can provide a warning that you are about to close the session. For example, you might make a comment such as "I believe we have time for only two more questions. I'll recognize the woman in the second row, then the man in the rear."

TEACH

> *"It is not every question that deserves an answer."*
>
> —Publilius Syrus

● TEACHING

Suggest to students the situation in which they have been asked to speak at a conference session that lasts 50 minutes and is to include questions and answers. Their speech lasts 30 minutes. Brainstorm ways to encourage the audience to ask questions about their topic.

● LEARNING STYLES

Visual Learning
You could show an excerpt from a film that shows a question-answer situation such as in the Steve Martin film, *A Leap of Faith*. Discuss how the speaker handles an unexpected, or difficult question such as "When will it rain?" in *A Leap of Faith*.

● SKILL DEVELOPMENT

15-Second Skill Opportunity
Give students practice in answering questions concisely by following the suggestions in the text. Pairs of students could work together, one asking and the other answering questions about speech topics.

---

318   CHAPTER 10 Speaking to Inform

If you expect a question-and-answer period to follow a speech, it is a good idea to mention it at the start. This will give listeners a chance to develop questions as you talk.

Answer Questions

If you are thoroughly prepared and knowledgeable about your speech topic, you will be able to answer most questions easily. Occasionally, of course, a question will be raised to which you do not know the answer. When this occurs, simply respond "I'm sorry, I can't answer that question." For informative speeches you will not appear to be avoiding the question, but merely indicating a lack of knowledge on your part. Audiences do not expect speakers to be all-knowing on any topic, so using this response occasionally causes no one embarrassment.

In the next section you will learn about using visual aids during your speeches. If you have used one or more of these visual aids during an informative speech and someone asks a question related to a visual, be certain it is again brought into full view of the audience before responding to the question. This allows listeners to perceive your answer through two channels, verbal and visual. You may also wish to point to a particular part of a visual while responding, if the question relates specifically to that part.

When you are asked a question requiring both a direct answer plus some explanation, provide the direct answer first, then the explanation. Usually the questioner is more interested in the factual answer than in a list of reasons or causes, and making the person wait for the core of the answer can irk the questioner. Occasionally, you may feel there is strong justification for reversing this order, but ordinarily give the direct answer first followed by the explanation.

Finally, be complete and concise in answering questions. Avoid, on the one hand, single word answers such as "Yes" or "No." On the other hand, once you have answered the question, stop. Do not be tempted to ramble on with fascinating information that strays too far

● **TEACHING**

You might bring to class a collection of visual aids that includes an overhead with a transparency, handouts, a graphic image, an advertisement, a poster, a globe, etc. Ask students when they recall each of these props being used.

● **LINK TO PAST LEARNING**

Ask students to think about their days in kindergarten when they had a "show and tell" opportunity regularly. Discuss their enjoyment and memories of those situations.

> *"By speaking in front of the class every week, you learn how to make what you say more interesting, colorful, believable, and understandable."*
>
> —Mari Pat Varga

TEACH

● **SKILL DEVELOPMENT**

15-Second Skill Opportunity
Ask students to bring or use an assigned visual aid and make a short presentation using the visual aid.

---

from the topic and which may only bore your listeners. If the matter is fairly technical in nature and requires some explanation for a complete answer, by all means give the explanation, then stop. Often there may be several others anxiously waiting to ask a question that is very special to them.

● USING VISUAL AIDS

Dr. Ray Birdwhistell, one of the foremost scholars in nonverbal communication, claimed that words account for only thirty-five percent of what we communicate; the remainder is largely accomplished by body motion. Though the figure may be exaggerated, it emphasizes an important concept for public speakers. As a public speaker, you can accomplish communication through what the audience *sees,* as well as through what the audience *hears*.

Visual aids have been found very helpful for both the speaker and the listeners, especially during informative speaking. For the speaker they provide a natural excuse to move about on the platform, to gesture, and to point. They can also help the speaker to remember details of the presentation. If the speaker is giving a demonstration, they may be an essential part of it. Members of the audience find that visual aids deepen their perception and understanding of the speaker' message and help them remember the details of the speech.

While visual aids, well used, can better a speech in a number of ways, they can also turn a speech into a disaster if a speaker attempts to use them without thorough preparation and practice. Because speaking with visual aids involves doing two things at once—maintaining the verbal flow and handling physical objects—it is never easy. So more careful preparation is called for than for a speech without visual aids.

Deciding When to Use Visuals

One of the first questions that will arise is "How do I know when to include visual aids in an informative speech?" During this course, your teacher may answer that question for you by saying "Your next speech should include visual aids." This is especially likely to happen if you are asked to give a demonstration. On other occasions, however, you will have to decide for yourself whether one or more visual aids should be used. Ask yourself these two questions: "If I use a certain visual, will its presence make it easier for me to get my point across? Will using a certain visual make the point more meaningful for my audience?" If the answer to either question seems to be "Yes," then you should include

TEACH

● **TEACHING**

Try to model for the class the use of an overhead projector or a slide carousel in a presentation. Emphasize the need to coordinate content with the visual aid and the importance of timing.

● **SKILL DEVELOPMENT**

Visual Aids
Ask students to develop a brief speech about a family vacation. They could use maps, photos, slides, or postcards to illustrate some of the places visited. Their speech should be brief, no more than five minutes.

CHAPTER 10 Speaking to Inform

the visual. Suppose, for example, that you are asked to give a speech o "How to Thread a Motion Picture Projector." Using a sideview drawin that shows the working parts of a projector, or even better, an actua projector to thread with film as you talk, will save you an enormou number of words and much time. If you are giving a speech on "M Trip to the Grand Canyon," using several color slides will surely deepe the impression on your audience.

Once you have decided to use visual aids in a speech, beware o the temptation to overuse them. Visual aids in public speaking shoul always remain in the role their name implies—aids. Once they becom the main center of audience interest and attention they have ceased be aids and have turned a speech into a presentation of the visua themselves. Using five or six of your best slides as visual aids in speech on "My Trip to the Grand Canyon" greatly enhances you speech, but showing twenty-five or thirty slides during a six- to eigh minute presentation means you are no longer giving a speech wi visual aids; you are giving a slide show with a brief commentary.

Types of Visual Aids

At times you will want to use a series of visual aids, at other times on one will be necessary. It all depends on your speech topic and the rel tionship of the visual aids to it. Following are brief descriptions, wi examples, of visual aids that are available to a speaker.

Charts A drawing showing the relationships among the parts of whole is a **chart.** The drawing usually includes lines and words and ca deal with almost any subject. One commonly used type of chart is th *line-staff* chart showing the relationships among members of an org nization. An example appears on the next page.

Graphs A second common type of visual aid is the **graph.** Grap picture large amounts of information (usually quantitative or numerica at a single glance. They consist primarily of lines with occasional wor and numbers. One frequently used type is the line graph on page 32 When the area under the peaks and valleys in a line graph is darkene to provide greater visual contrast, the graph is called a profile graph.

The bar graph, shown at the bottom of page 322, is another form line graph, often used to show the same kind of information.

A circle graph, or pie graph as it is sometimes called, is used indicate parts of a whole. A typical circle graph is shown on page 32

Picture graphs are similar to bar graphs in basic design, but inclu pictorial materials to heighten visual appeal. Since they demand mo artistic ability, they are more difficult and time-consuming to prepare. the top of page 324 is a picture graph.

TEACH

● **TEACHING**

Make a list of all the terms defining visual aids in this section. Be sure that students understand the differences and similarities that characterize visual aids.

SUBSTITUTE TEACHER TIP

Bring a copy of a newspaper like *USA Today* to class and identify the number of visual aids on each page.

● **LEARNING STYLES**

Visual Learning
Ask students to find examples of all the visual aids mentioned in this section and display them in a poster or on a bulletin board.

Using Visual Aids   321

A sample line-staff chart

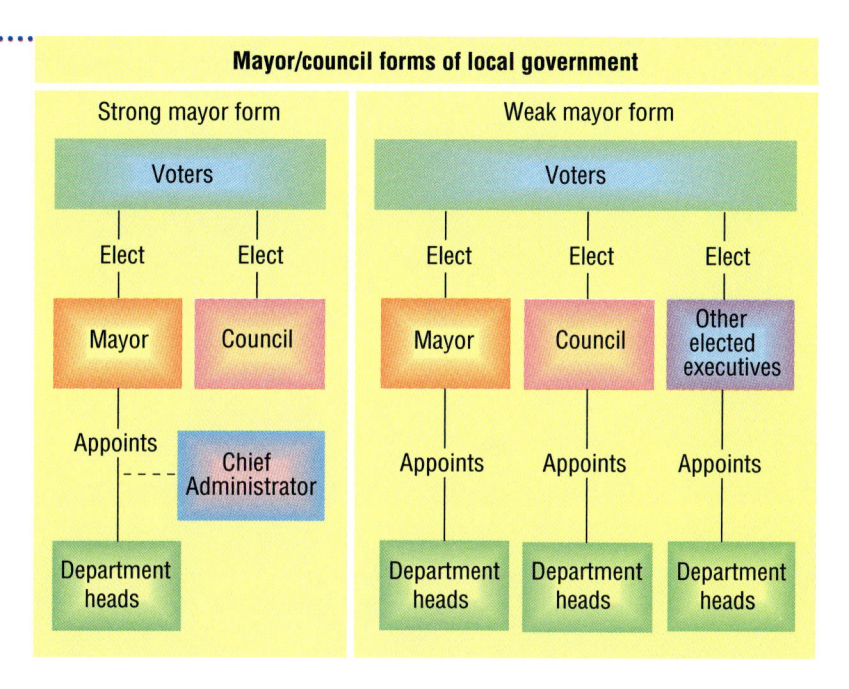

Mayor/council forms of local government

(Strong mayor form: Voters elect Mayor and Council; Mayor appoints Chief Administrator and Department heads.)

(Weak mayor form: Voters elect Mayor, Council, and Other elected executives; each appoints Department heads.)

Diagrams   Like a chart and a graph, a **diagram** is used to show the relationship of a part to a whole. Diagrams, however, generally rely more on drawing and less on words and numbers than charts and graphs do. Diagrams may range from very simple line drawings to very complex pictures with shading and perspective. The figure at the bottom of page 324 is an example of a diagram.

Maps   A **map** shows information that is geographical in nature. Some maps are used simply to indicate location, whereas others show location as it relates to elevation, weather at a given time, agricultural production, or any number of other items. The figure at the top of page 325 is a map showing land use in China.

Posters   A relatively easy type of visual aid to prepare is one consisting of print or lettering on a **poster.** Lists of important points in your speech, key phrases, slogans, and humorous sayings can all be visually presented through print. Simply printing the main ideas of a speech on a large sheet of paper and showing it to the audience does not make an effective visual aid, however. Printed visual aids should be genuinely attention-getting or essential memory aids. The lettering must be imaginative, with attention given to spacing, color, size of letters, and their type style. (See the guidelines at the bottom of page 325.)

TEACH

SUBSTITUTE TEACHER TIP

Ask students to write a caption for each of the visual aids presented in this section.

CURRICULAR CONNECTIONS

Math/Science

Some students could calculate the size the various visual aids would have to be if they were to be used effectively in your school auditorium.

A sample line graph

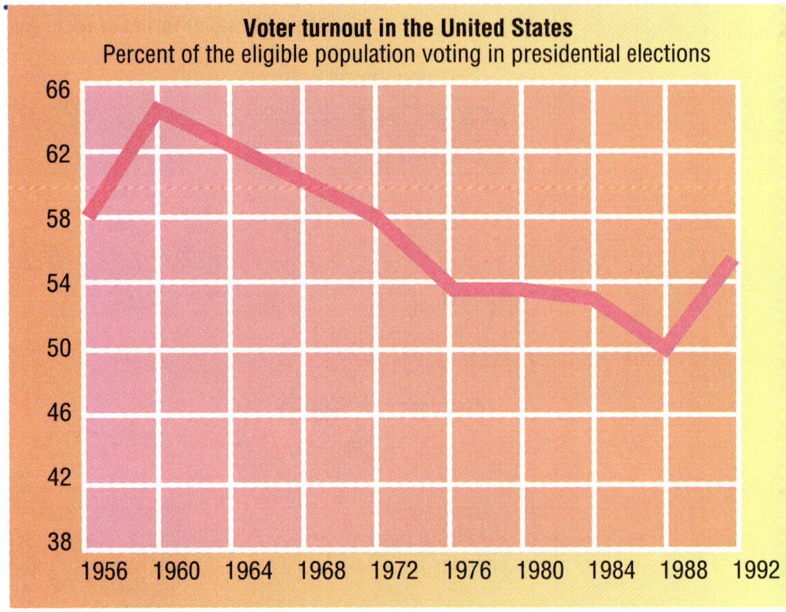
Voter turnout in the United States
Percent of the eligible population voting in presidential elections
66
62
58
54
50
46
42
38
1956 1960 1964 1968 1972 1976 1980 1984 1988 1992

A sample bar graph

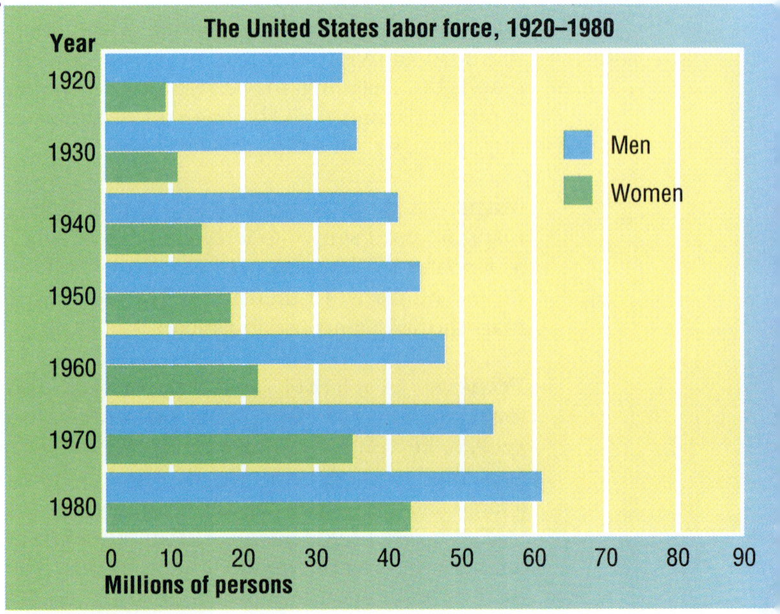
The United States labor force, 1920–1980
Year
1920
1930
1940
1950
1960
1970
1980
Men
Women
0 10 20 30 40 50 60 70 80 90
Millions of persons

● **TEACHING**

Bring in a weather map from the daily newspaper and ask students to think about the amount of time that is spent reporting the weather on TV news each day. Discuss the kind of visual aids meteorologists use during televised broadcasts.

AMAZING FACTS!

The first known "map of the world" is a Babylonian clay tablet that dates about 600 years before Christ. This is a disk—about three by five inches—and depicts the world as a circle with two lines running down the center representing the Tigris and Euphrates rivers.

● **SKILL DEVELOPMENT**

15-Second Skill Opportunity
Ask volunteers to use the weather map as a visual aid to report on the local weather for the day.

Using Visual Aids 323

sample circle or pie graph

Sample expense budget for school newspaper
Total budget $2,800

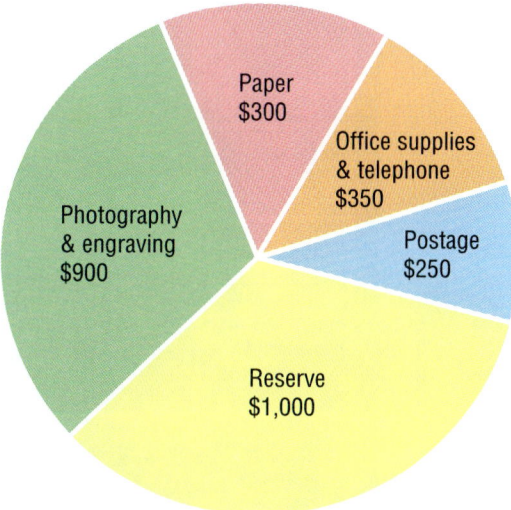

- Paper $300
- Office supplies & telephone $350
- Postage $250
- Reserve $1,000
- Photography & engraving $900

Cartoons Cartoons turn humor into a visual aid. A **cartoon** is simply a funny or satirical drawing used to make a point. Though cartoons demand a certain artistic ability to be effective, their impact on an audience can be great when they are well prepared.

Pictures Whether simply printed or in the form of a photograph, slide, filmstrip, or film, a **picture** can be a very effective visual aid. Two cautions, however, must be observed when using pictures. First, they must be large enough to be easily seen by the whole audience. If necessary, they must be enlarged through projection. Second, the pictures themselves can easily become the center of attention and distract the audience from the speaker and the message. They must, therefore, be used sparingly. When these cautions are observed a picture can, indeed, be worth a thousand words.

Objects The visual aids discussed thus far are two-dimensional. A three-dimensional **object**, however, will make a deeper impression than a picture or representation. One of the great sales advantages of an auctioneer is being able to present the object being sold as he or she talks. Thus using a collection of Indian arrowheads, rather than drawings of them, as visual aids in a speech will gain greater audience attention and interest. At times if may be possible for audience members to handle as well as to see actual objects.

323

TEACH

● **SKILL DEVELOPMENT**

15-Second Skill Opportunity
Ask students to think of a comment that could be made about either of the graphics on this page and use the visual as part of a statement.

CHAPTER 10 Speaking to Inform

A sample picture graph

Top five breeds of dogs registered with the American Kennel Club in 1981
(Each picture represents 20,000 dogs)

Poodles	
Cocker Spaniels	
Doberman Pinschers	
German Shepherds	
Labrador Retrievers	

A sample diagram

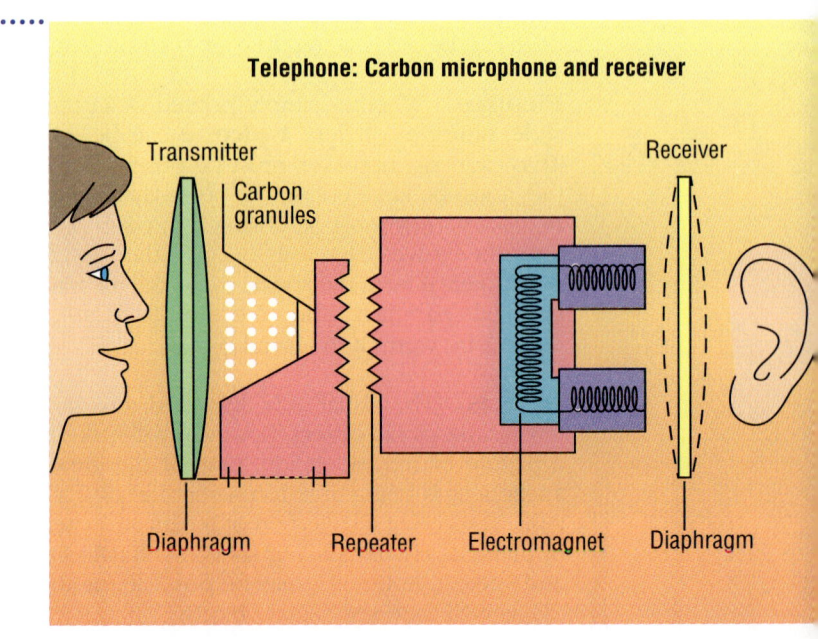

Telephone: Carbon microphone and receiver

Transmitter — Carbon granules — Receiver
Diaphragm — Repeater — Electromagnet — Diaphragm

TEACH

SUBSTITUTE TEACHER TIP
Bring in the opinion page of the newspaper and display the political cartoon(s) appearing there. Ask students to explain their meaning.

● LEARNING STYLES

Visual Learning
A group of students interested in photography might bring in examples of award-winning photos and make a bulletin board for the class.

Using Visual Aids 325

A sample map

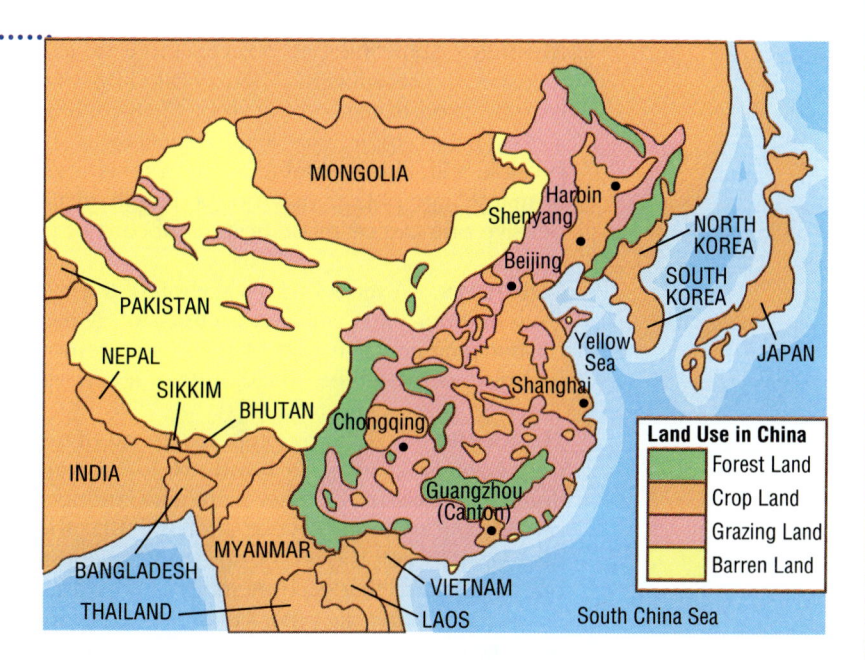

Land Use in China
- Forest Land
- Crop Land
- Grazing Land
- Barren Land

Following these guidelines will help you produce an effective visual aid.

Lettering visual aids: problems and solutions

STYLES	SIZES	COLORS
Styles that are too fine are difficult to see.	Lettering that is too small to be seen by your audience will not help get your message across.	Light colors on a light background cannot be seen easily.
𝔖𝔱𝔶𝔩𝔢𝔰 that are too fancy are difficult to read.	½″ letters (12.7 millimeters) cannot be seen from more than about ten feet (3 meters) by people with normal eyesight.	Dark colors on a dark background cannot be seen easily.
SIMPLE block styles are best.	1″ letters (25.4 millimeters) can be seen from about 30 feet (9.1 meters) by people with normal eyesight.	Use colors that contrast with your background colors.

325

TEACH

● **LEARNING STYLES**

※ **Cooperative Learning**
Small groups of students could be asked to construct a model they could use in a speech. Some American businesses sponsor school competitions that invite high school students to design model cars, build bridges, or work as a team on a stock portfolio. Discuss the process of teamwork in the construction of a model.

CHAPTER 10 Speaking to Inform

Models Sometimes, an object is too large to be conveniently brough to a speech presentation. Then a scaled-down version, called a **model** may be used instead. A two-foot (58.8-centimeter) plastic model of a rocket, for example, enables the speaker to show parts and views no possible with either a real rocket or a two-dimensional drawing. Model of many large objects may not be readily available, but often an inex pensive one can be made from cardboard or paper-maché.

Cutaways A model with a section of the outer covering removed to show interior parts is called a **cutaway.** A model of an internal com bustion engine, with part of the casing removed to show the valve and pistons, would be an example of a cutaway.

Handouts Something prepared ahead of time to give to each mem ber of your audience is a **handout.** It can contain explanations, direc tions, maps, charts, or other material. Handouts are especially useful to present information to your audience that they will want to refer to after your speech is over. Be sure to have enough copies of your hand out available so that each member of your audience can have one.

Handouts and the other visual aids mentioned here are not the onl types of visual aids available; they are simply the ones most commonl used. Anything that can visually support the speech and is appropriate for the speaker, audience, and occasion may be used as a visual aid.

Preparing Speeches Using Visual Aids

Because speeches containing one or more visual aids are more difficul to deliver than speeches without visual aids, precise preparation and practice is called for when aids are to be used. Speakers usually prepar their own visual aids, but even in cases where the visual is readily avail able (objects, for example) careful rehearsal of the speech with th visual is essential to achieve perfect timing and handling.

A first principle regarding the selection and preparation of any visua aid you plan to display is that it must be capable of being seen easil from all parts of the room. Elementary as this may seem, it is one of th most frequently violated rules regarding the use of visual aids. Fo graphic visuals such as charts, graphs, diagrams, maps, cartoons, an posters, this means that letters, numbers, and lines should be large an heavy and have sufficient contrast with the background on which the are mounted to be easily seen by all audience members in the bac rows. The best way to ensure this is by stepping to the back of th room in which the speech will be given and checking the visual durin its construction. Pictures cut from newspapers or magazines are rarel large enough for even a classroom audience of thirty people to se

● **CURRICULAR CONNECTIONS**

Math/Science
Ask students to look through other textbooks and find examples of cutaway models. Encourage students to share these examples with the class.

SUBSTITUTE TEACHER TIP

Prepare a handout with a copy of a lesson plan or a speech and distribute to students. Ask them to indicate the time they think will be devoted to each topic in one margin and the actual time spent in the other margin. If it is a speech, ask students to annotate it with possible visual aids that the speaker could use to enhance the presentation.

Using Visual Aids 327

details without projection. Snapshots almost always require projection. Occasionally actual objects or models are too small for easy viewing of details. Remember, however, that it is necessary for the audience to see only whatever degree of detail you consider important. If minute details of the visual are not essential to your speech, then it is not essential that they be large.

A second necessary element in a visual aid is that it be neat and attractive. It need not be a work of art, but it should never be sloppy. One of the major problems with drawing a visual on a blackboard or easel while you are speaking is that most people who are not artists cannot produce a visual in a neat and attractive way under pressure. Preparing well-proportioned visuals ahead of time, on the other hand, can greatly enhance your prestige with your audience. It gives listeners the impression that you were concerned enough about the reception of your speech to take pains to create attractive visual aids. When preparing them, the stress should be on neatness, but don't overlook the opportunity to highlight important items through the use of various colors and varied media. Felt tip pens, crayons, pre-made lettering ink, and many other elements can be combined to produce a visual that is both informative and appealing.

You will also need to plan prior to the speech how to display the visual aid. Small objects, models, and cutaways can be held in the hands and shown to the audience with relative ease. Most good graphic and pictorial aids, however, will be so large that holding them while speaking will appear clumsy and awkward to the audience. If an easel is available, it can be very useful in displaying this type of visual, as long as you make sure that it is placed at the proper angle to be seen from all parts of the room. When an easel is not available, you may want to bring masking tape to help you properly display the visual. When displaying it by attaching it to the wall, be certain it is placed high enough so that the audience can see it. You should also make sure it is far enough from the lectern so your body will not block the listeners' views. Finally, if you decide to lean the visual against something—an easel, the lectern, or a blackboard—you must use cardboard that is heavy enough to remain in place without being held.

Naturally you will need to point to various details on your visual at certain points in your speech. Pointing with your hand often means your arm blocks part of your audience's view of the visual. Thus you should use a pointer if at all possible. When using a pointer, hold it in whichever hand is closer to the visual so you do not have to reach across your body to point. Look at the visual only long enough to locate the spot to which you wish to point. Then, with your pointer held on that spot, turn your eyes immediately back to your audience. If your visual is such that you will be pointing to it repeatedly, continue holding the pointer in your hands during that portion of the speech in which

TEACH

SUBSTITUTE TEACHER TIP

You could ask students to identify the number of type styles that are available on their personal computers or the school computer system. Discuss how type styles and sizes influence the meaning and impression created by words.

● TEACHING

Survey with the students the guidelines presented in the text for the use of visual aids in a speech. These guidelines could be represented in a poster or handout that the students could retain for their continued use. Ask students to develop a checklist based on these guidelines.

● SKILL DEVELOPMENT

15-Second Skill Opportunity

Write a list of key words on the chalkboard. Give students a pointer and give them time to practice using the pointer to refer to the words or terms of the board. Students should note the guidelines for using a pointer in the text.

CHAPTER 10 Speaking to Inform

you are making frequent reference to the visual. If, on the other hand, you plan to refer to the visual at only a few widely separated times during the speech, lay the pointer aside and pick it up again the next time it is needed.

Two other important matters to consider are the point at which you first wish to display a visual and the length of time you will want to continue to display it. If the aid will be referred to off and on throughout most of the speech, you want to show it to the audience when you first make reference to it and then let it remain in view until the speech is completed. If the visual is to be referred to only once, or for the final time long before the speech is completed, you should put it aside or cover it immediately after your last reference to it. Otherwise, it will distract the listeners by remaining in view. Visuals mounted on cardboard may be turned face down on a desk or table. Objects, models, and cutaways can be covered with a piece of cloth.

In order for a speech involving visual aids to look smooth and professional, you must practice coordinating the verbal and the visual elements. Practice when to first display the visuals, how to display them, for what length of time, and when and how to remove them from view. Be sure that your body does not block the audience's view of visual aids.

Some visuals are used to make a single point in a speech. If you plan to use one or more visual aids of this type, be certain to give the audience sufficient time to view them. Inexperienced speakers often work hard to produce a neat, attractive visual, then lose its effectiveness by displaying it for only two to three seconds. If the audience is going to have just one opportunity to see a visual, they will ordinarily need about ten to twelve seconds to familiarize themselves with its content. It is perfectly acceptable to display an aid in silence for several seconds after explaining it to the audience.

Demonstration Speeches and Visual Aids

A common purpose for giving an informative speech is to demonstrate a process or procedure to an audience. If your speech purpose is to show your listeners how to do something, how to make something, or how something works, it may be labeled a **demonstration speech**. Many demonstration speeches demand the use of visual aids.

To teach your listeners to *perform* a process themselves, arrange the steps in the process sequentially, demonstrating each step in order. For this form of demonstration speech, aids such as objects, models, and mock-ups usually prove more effective than graphs, charts, and diagrams. Don't overlook your own body as an effective visual aid. A talk on how to do aerobic dance, for example, demands no other aid than your demonstrating some of the steps during the speech.

APPLY

● **MOTIVATION**

You might bring to class a copy of one of the tabloid newspapers and examine the photographs, visuals, and headlines on the front page. Invite students with skills in photography to discuss the current technologies that enable substantial manipulation of images. Discuss student opinions about the tabloid's use of visuals in a responsible manner.

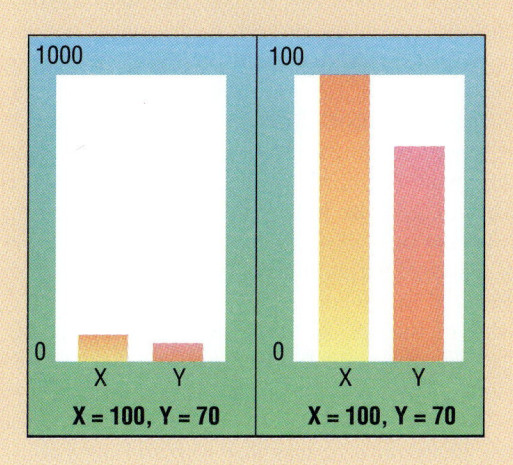

● **LEARNING STYLES**

Cooperative Learning
Ask small groups of students to work with a similar set of statistical data. You could provide your school's scores on state or national tests. Ask each group to think of a responsible and an irresponsible way to represent that information graphically or visually.

● **SKILL APPLICATION**

Media Literacy
Ask students to select a photo or other visual image from a recent magazine, a newspaper, or this textbook and write an appropriate legend or caption to accompany it.

ETHICALLY SPEAKING

Using Visual Aids Responsibly

's no secret—and no lie—that "a picture is worth a thousand words." The same is true of map or a chart or a graph. Supporting your message with appropriate visual aids can significantly improve their impact on an audience. But ethically speaking, what is appropriate? re there visual aids that are irresponsible either in substance or in presentation? Pictures on't lie, do they?

Use a photograph in the same way you would use any other piece of evidence. Be sure ou are not using it in a way contrary to its purpose. Do not use only part of the photo, if e part you cut out would change its meaning. For example, if you show a photograph of a olitical candidate at a rally and you fail to show that large segments of the audience were ooing and heckling the candidate, you may be misrepresenting the intent of the photoaph. Moreover, certain electronic techniques make it possible to manipulate pictures, bstituting one person for another or rearranging the people or the details of the picture. eck to be sure you are not using photos or other kinds of pictures in such irresponsible ays.

Likewise, graphs and charts can be made to present statistical information in misleadg ways. Suppose you are trying to show the difference in calories between two different ands of crackers. The difference may be only 30%, but you can show that difference in a r graph on a 1000-point scale that minimizes the difference, or you can show it on a 100- int scale that maximizes the difference. Be sure your representation of facts and figures straightforward and does not shade the truth in order to strengthen a particular position.

1000	100
X Y	X Y
X = 100, Y = 70	X = 100, Y = 70

329

329

TEACH

> **"Appearances often are deceiving."**
> —Aesop

● LINKS TO PAST LEARNING

Ask students to share memories of times when equipment did not work as planned. How did the teacher or presenter react? Ask students to describe the audience reaction. You might also extend the discussion to situations when equipment did not work in the home or work environment.

● LEARNING STYLES

Visual Learning
Demonstrate for the class the proper use of the overhead projector and the technique of exposing only the part of the overhead that is currently being discussed. After you have modeled the technique, ask volunteers to come to the front of the class to repeat the procedure.

---

330 CHAPTER 10 Speaking to Inform

When teaching listeners how to do something, keep the number of separate steps in the process to a minimum. If the process has more than five separate steps, try to group the steps into stages. This will aid the listeners' memories. Likewise, avoid handling too many separate aids. Use one, two, or three key aids to demonstrate the process.

When the purpose of your demonstration speech is to have your audience *understand* a process, you have greater choice in how you arrange the steps. Arrangements such as easy-to-difficult, order-of-importance, known-to-unknown, and chronological order may be used. To demonstrate three methods of thawing a frozen pipe, for example, you might use an order of most-preferred to least-preferred:

1. Heat the pipe with a torch.
2. Pour boiling water over cloth wrapped around the pipe.
3. Wrap the pipe with electrical heat tape.

Graphs, charts, and pictures may often be just as useful as objects and models when you wish your listeners to understand a process. A picture or drawing of a torch heating a frozen pipe, for instance, should prove just as effective as, and easier to handle than, an actual torch.

When giving demonstration speeches, student speakers sometimes fall into the trap of allowing the "demonstration" part to steal the show. That is not a speech supported by a visual demonstration; it has become a demonstration, supported by a few remarks.

Using Equipment with Visual Aids

Some visual aids can best be presented through the use of some form of equipment—an overhead projector, an opaque projector, a videotape unit, a movie projector, or a slide projector. When equipment is to be used, rehearsing with the equipment is as crucial as rehearsing with the visual aids themselves. Most projectors require a darkened or semi-darkened room, so you must be certain this can be arranged before choosing a visual requiring projection. Many times it is best to arrange for a friend or classmate to run the equipment during your speech and to turn the lights on and off at the proper times to relieve you of having too many responsibilities all at once. Naturally, such preparations must all be rehearsed in advance.

The day of the speech itself, carefully set up the equipment and check it prior to the speech. Don't assume that the projector bulb is all right or that the videotape player is working properly. More good speeches have probably been ruined by burned-out bulbs than by any other single cause. Finally, it is wise to plan how you will handle the situation if a piece of equipment malfunctions during your presentation.

An overhead projector is an effective means of presenting many visual aids.

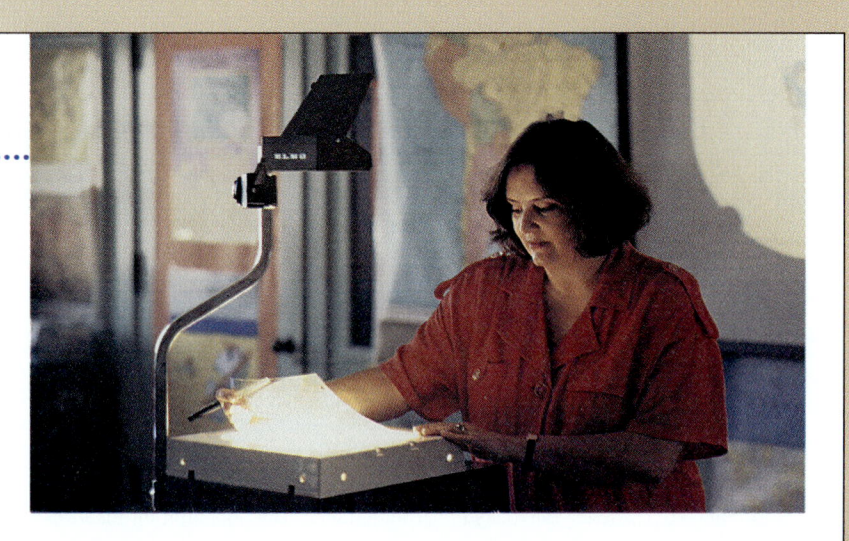

Perhaps you can prepare handouts in advance to use in case other materials cannot be used. It may be possible for you to explain verbally the material you had planned to display. Remember that audiences are usually sympathetic, so don't panic.

● **ACTIVITY**

Judging Visual Aids

During the round of in-class visual aid or demonstration speeches, keep all the aids presented by the class members until the round is complete. When everyone has given a speech, discuss, then vote on the best visual aids. Criteria you should consider are appropriateness to the topic, neatness, ease of viewing, clarity, deftness of handling, length of time displayed, and smoothness with which multiple aids are presented. Your teacher may wish to add other criteria.

● **ANALYZING AND EVALUATING INFORMATIVE SPEECHES**

In Chapter 9 we suggested ways of analyzing and evaluating speeches—*all* kinds of speeches. Now we're going to focus on analyzing and evaluating *informative* speeches, both your own and those of your classmates. When analyzing informative speeches, you will want to continue to ask all of the same questions you asked in Chapter 9. Now, however, you will need to add additional questions pertaining more to the *content* of the speeches you give, and those you hear. As before, force yourself to analyze first, then go back and evaluate. We'll begin with the informative speeches *you* have delivered.

TEACH

● **LEARNING STYLES**

Cooperative Learning
Ask small groups of students to think of the process of driving a car. Encourage them to reduce this complex process to three steps. Share the steps each group has identified. Discuss how the process could best be demonstrated.

● **SKILL DEVELOPMENT**

15-Second Skill Opportunity
Ask students to think of how they would demonstrate to the class the process of tying a shoe. Suggest that they limit the demonstration to three steps. Ask volunteers to demonstrate using a three-step process.

331

APPLY

> **"Speech is civilization itself. The word, even the most contradictious word, preserves contact —it is silence which isolates."**
> —Thomas Mann

● ENRICHMENT

You could ask students to submit transcripts of the speeches they give. These speeches could also be taped for reviewing and evaluation. The tape might be submitted to the local civic club.

● LEARNING STYLES

Cooperative Learning
Small groups of students could develop checklists or evaluation guidelines to help judge the speeches given by students. After sharing these guidelines the class may choose to use a single evaluation form or pursue separate checklists.

Speaking IN ACTION

Speech to a Civic Club

Situation
Hold a round of informative speeches using visual aids in which every student will speak on the topic "What my speech course means to me." When the round is completed, vote for the best speech, which will then be delivered by the winner to a local civic club—Rotary, Lions, Kiwanis, Optimist, Civitan, or another in your community. Your teacher will make the arrangements. The time limit for the in-class speeches could be about 5–7 minutes, though the winner may wish to lengthen it to about 15 minutes for the civic club.

Preparation
This speech is one about an event—your speech course. Your purpose is to inform your listeners about the benefits from taking this class. As you prepare this speech, you will want to review this chapter step-by-step in an effort to turn in your best performance yet. After completing your outline, begin by deciding which attention device or devices you will choose to create a powerful and interesting introduction. Consider how you will preview your topic for your listeners, apply it to them, and how you will build their interest in that topic. Know exactly how you plan to establish your ethos during your opening remarks.

Review your speech outline for ways and places to maintain listener attention, make smooth, clear transitions, and personalize your speech. Also plan reaction to audience feedback, and watch for technical language that you may need to define or explain to your listeners.

Planning your conclusion is equally important. Signal that it is approaching, and summarize your main points. You will also want to reinforce the central idea and psychologically close your speech.

Many civic clubs expect their speakers to answer a few questions after their conclusions. The suggestions on pages 317–319 will help you during a question-and-answer session. (Your teacher may ask everyone to respond to questions after each classroom presentation.)

Finally, check your options for the most appropriate visual aids, and techniques for handling them (see pages 319–331). Well-presented visual aids can add considerable "class" to a solid informative speech.

Delivery
Your teacher may be able to accompany the winner (or winners) on the day you deliver your speech to the civic club. Be sure to arrive on time, dressed professionally. If a meal is being served, and you are too nervous to eat, simply tell your hosts so—they will understand. Many experienced speakers decline to eat before giving speeches. Also realize that your audience does not expect to hear a perfect or highly polished speech. They will certainly empathize with your anxiety, and will admire your courage. Realize too, that by giving this speech you are both telling them *and* demonstrating that you see the importance of acquiring public speaking skills—skills many of your listeners may never have acquired.

TEACH

● **TEACHING**

Ask students to use the questions suggested for analysis to make a checklist for themselves. Discuss words or phrases students would prefer to use to analyze their performance.

> ❝Everyone complains of his memory, and no one complains of his judgment.❞
> —La Rochefoucauld

● **LEARNING STYLES**

Cooperative Learning
If students feel comfortable with each other and sharing their assessment of performance, you might suggest that they work in pairs or small groups to share their impressions of their speeches. Some students will find that they are harder on themselves than others are.

Analyzing and Evaluating Informative Speeches

Analyzing Your Introduction

Since the introduction conveys that all-important set of "first impressions" to your audience, you will want to recall the opening techniques you used to achieve a well-crafted opening. Here are some of the questions you should ask yourself:

1. What devices did I use to gain initial audience attention?
   - Did I begin with a joke or humorous incident? Am I generally a humorous person, able to make people laugh easily? Were my opening jokes long or short? How many did I use?
   - Did I use a story or anecdote to begin? Did its content have a natural connection with the subject matter of my speech? How detailed did I make the story in relation to the overall length of my speech?
   - If I used the common ground technique, were the similarities between myself and my audience significant and real, or minor and forced?
   - Did I use shock technique to startle the audience to quick attention? Was it used at the very beginning of my speech? Had I thoroughly checked out the accuracy of my unusual, frightening, or hard-to-believe fact, statement, or statistic?
   - Was the use of suspense an appropriate attention device for my speech? How long did I talk "around" my topic in my effort to fascinate my listeners? Did my audience appear tantalized by the suspense?

2. What techniques did I employ to build my audiences' interest in my topic?
   - Was I able to analyze my audience in advance to gauge my listeners' initial level of interest?
   - Did most of my interest-building devices allow for a smooth transition to my speech topic?
   - Did I begin with a question (rhetorical or real), with the aim of igniting rapid audience interest in my subject?
   - Was I able to use a quotation in my introduction to highlight an important facet of my topic?
   - Did I issue a challenge to my audience?

3. Did I preview my topic, and apply me message to my audience?
   - Did I remember that previewing the speech topic is nearly always necessary during the introduction of an informative speech?

TEACH

● **RETEACHING**

These questions could be used to summarize the material in this chapter. Ask students to add page references to the text material that explains each of the techniques mentioned.

CHAPTER 10 Speaking to Inform

- Before the close of my introduction, did I "clue my audience in" on my topic, its purpose, and perhaps the main points was about to discuss?
- Was I able to incorporate some attention-getting and interest building devices while previewing my topic?
- As an immediate follow-up to previewing my topic, did I show my audience what they stand to gain from listening to my speech, why it should prove of particular interest to them, why my topic is important?

4. Did I use my introduction to establish my ethos with my listeners
   - During my speech preparation, did I recall that audiences are always vitally interested in a speaker's competence, honesty and her or his likeability?
   - If I had had direct experience with the subject area of my speech, did I refer to that experience during my introduction
   - If I had not had direct, personal experience of my topic, did allude to my research and preparation for my speech?
   - Was I able to use some of my attention- and interest-building techniques to help build my ethos—techniques such as humor common ground, and relating personal anecdotes?
   - On occasions when I was given a speech of introduction, did I remember not to build my own ethos, unless my introduction was overly flattering or omitted one of my important credentials?

Analyzing the Body of Your Speech

The body of your speech contains the primary message you've prepared for your audience. As with the speech introduction, you will want to recall what techniques you used to maintain audience attention, react to listener feedback, provide smooth transitions, avoid too-technical language, and personalize your speech. Let's look first at how you maintained your audience's attention.

1. How did I go about maintaining audience attention?
   - After planning one or more devices to gain the initial attention of my listeners, did I remember the importance of maintaining it throughout my speech?
   - Did I continue to use attention-getting techniques, such as humor, stories, and suspense during the body of my speech

TEACH

● **ASSESSMENT STRATEGY**

Students could be encouraged to think of a portfolio product that would best reflect the quality and content of the body of their informative speech. This could be an outline of the major points or a tape of this portion of the speech.

> ❝The advantage of doing one's praising to oneself is that one can lay it on so thick and exactly in the right places.❞
> —Samuel Butler

● **LEARNING STYLES**

Cooperative Learning
Ask small groups of students to assign a numeric value to each of the points suggested in this analysis. The total number of points should equal 100. Emphasize the need to prioritize and weigh each of the points. Discuss which items are more important and those that seem less important.

Analyzing and Evaluating Informative Speeches   335

Your teacher can help you evaluate your informative speech and the techniques you used.

- When facing a sparse or scattered audience, did I remember to invite my listeners to sit more closely together near the front to improve group attentiveness?
- On occasions when I could control certain comfort conditions in the speech setting, did I arrive early enough to assure that factors such as room temperature, microphone location, and seating arrangements were conducive to good listening?

2. Did I react to audience feedback during my presentation?
   - As I was speaking, did I observe audience reactions, particularly in the faces, posture, and eyes of my listeners?
   - Did I remember to look most often at those audience members who appeared most alert and interested?
   - Was I especially sensitive to listener feedback when it came from a sizable proportion of my audience simultaneously? Did I adjust my approach when this occurred?

3. Were my transitions between main points in my speech smooth and easy to follow?
   - Did I carefully plan (perhaps even memorize) my transitions when preparing my speech?

335

TEACH

> **SUBSTITUTE TEACHER TIP**
>
> Ask students to give copies of the conclusions to their speeches to a partner. Based on the conclusion, ask the partner to develop an outline of the major points made in the conclusion.

336 CHAPTER 10 Speaking to Inform

- Did my transitions frequently summarize the point just completed, preview what was coming next, and show the relationship between the two?
- Were most of my transitions no longer than one or two sentences?

4. Did I avoid becoming too technical?
   - Did I select a speech topic that was not too highly technical to explain in simple language within the time limits of my speech?
   - Were my words concrete and clear, given a limited understanding among my audience?
   - Was I able to select language that painted pictures in the imaginations of my listeners?
   - Were my words the kind that were likely to give my audience a quick headache, or the type that were easy to follow?

5. Did I remember to personalize my speech?
   - Did I regularly mention people in my speech through humor, stories, and examples?
   - Did I favor such stories over the frequent use of statistics?
   - Did I remember that I can use fictional as well as real persons to enliven my speech?

Analyzing Your Conclusion

Since the conclusion of your speech is most often remembered longest, analyzing its impact is equal in importance to analyzing your introduction. You will want to determine whether you signaled your conclusion, summarized the main points of you speech, reinforced your central idea, and psychologically closed your speech.

1. Did I signal my conclusion for my audience?
   - Did I use phrases such as "in conclusion," "in closing," "let me end by saying," or "let me leave you with" to signal my listeners that I was about to conclude?
   - Did I use nonverbal signs, such as subtle changes in voice tones, an extra long pause, or moving a few steps to signal the beginning of my conclusion?
   - Did my words echo the larger, grander theme with which I began my speech as another method of signaling the start of my conclusion?

2. Did I summarize the main points of my speech in my conclusion?
   - Did I recall that summarizing is the primary function of the speech conclusion, particularly in informative speeches?
   - Did I use the device called restatement (repeating the main ideas of the speech in brief form) to summarize?
   - Would audience members have been able to understand my speech purpose and main ideas from my summary, even if they had heard only my conclusion?
3. Did my conclusion reinforce my central idea?
   - Was I able to discover and use a brief quotation with which to conclude my speech?
   - Did I use a dramatic statement to reinforce my central idea?
   - Did I repeat, or rephrase, a central statement announced in my introduction as a closing remark?
4. Did I psychologically close my speech?
   - Did my conclusion cause my listeners not only to understand that my speech was over, but to feel it was as well?
   - Did I issue a challenge to my audience to accomplish this?
   - Did I conclude with a rhetorical question?
   - Did I repeat a theme or slogan, first mentioned in my introduction?

Now that you have recalled *what* you did during your informative speech, review the answers to each of the questions you have just asked yourself, and allow those answers to indicate *how well you did*. As was suggested at the end of Chapter 9, use this evaluation as a springboard for improvement in your next informative speech.

Analyzing Classmates' Informative Speeches

Chapter 6 included a list of suggestions about critiquing speeches in a positive, constructive way. There, the emphasis was on facets of the speaker's delivery. Now it's time to focus on the content of the speech—matters such as supporting materials, use of sources, and the preparation and handling of visual aids.

As your classmates present their informative speeches, listen closely for supporting materials. In informative speaking, supporting materials are the speech's vitamins that provide the energy to make a speech go. Examples, statistics, expert opinion, stories, and illustration—all give life to the skeleton of ideas listed in the speech outline. Without these

---

TEACH

● **LEARNING STYLES**

Audio Learning
Encourage students to analyze the content and organization of speeches given by classmates. Ask them to listen for clues to the organization of the speech and to take notes while the speech is given. At the end of the speech, ask student to identify what they think the main points of the speech were. Then invite the speaker to comment on the correlation between what students in the audience identified and the outline from which they spoke.

TEACH

> **"It is a good thing for an uneducated man to read books of quotations."**
> —Winston Churchill

● **TEACHING**

Ask students to cite the sources of information they use in their speeches, based on the school style for bibliographic sources. You might want to work with the librarian or English Department to emphasize uniformity of style.

CHAPTER 10 Speaking to Inform

As you listen to your classmates' speeches, be alert for supporting materials and references to outside sources.

invigorating details, a speech will inevitably sound dull and lifeless. Listen for a variety of source materials—several examples, some statistics, an opinion or two. As a speech critic, demand such diversity as the best way to enliven speechmaking.

Once you hear your classmates providing a healthy blend of support for the ideas contained in their speeches, next insist that they tell you the sources from which they obtained that support—not just occasionally, but *every time* they relate a story, use an illustration, or give a statistic. Of course, a speaker's own experience with the topic being presented is one very valid source of information, but it should never be the *only* source a speaker relies on. If certain of your classmates rarely cite a source outside themselves, your critique should gently suggest that they could increase their credibility as speakers if they would refer regularly to outside sources. After all, even well-known experts typically identify outside sources for their information when speaking.

> **PORTFOLIO PRODUCTS**
>
> Students could develop a "report card" or "progress report" to help analyze speeches. These report cards should contain the kind of information and comments and suggestions that students would personally find helpful.

TEACH

● **SKILL DEVELOPMENT**

Feedback
Ask students to prepare a brief written statement that would give the student speaker positive feedback and suggestions for improvement.

Finally, since informative speeches can frequently be improved by including some visual materials, you should also be prepared to comment on your classmates' preparation and handling of visual aids. As you watch as well as listen to classmates' presentations, ask yourself questions such as these:

- Was the aid easily seen in the back of the room?
- Was the aid prepared in a neat and professional manner?
- Was the aid's content well organized and easy to understand upon first reading?
- If the speaker used a graphic aid, such as a graph, chart, or diagram, was it headed properly and accurately?
- Were there any parts of an aid which communicated information irrelevant to the speech topic, and served as a distraction to the audience?
- Did the speaker always point to the aid with whichever hand was closer to it?
- Did the speaker look at the aid extensively during the speech, or only momentarily to draw the audience's attention to it?
- Did the speaker give the audience sufficient time to see and absorb the content of the aid?
- Did the speaker remove the aid from the audience's view once it had served its purpose in the speech?
- If the speaker used some form of equipment to show an aid, had the equipment been used during rehearsal, then checked for workability just prior to the performance?

When you have completed analyzing and evaluating your classmates' informative speeches according to all these criteria *plus* those more generic questions asked in Chapter 9, you should have learned a great deal about the ingredients that go into constructing an effective informative speech.

ASSESS

STUDENT PERFORMANCE COMPETENCIES

- Understands and uses various types of informative speeches
- Uses techniques to gain audience attention and build interest in an informative speech
- Reacts to audience feedback and executes smooth transitions in the delivery of an informative speech
- Uses visual aids effectively in an informative speech

sca GUIDELINES

- Listens effectively to informative speeches
- Identifies main ideas in informative speeches
- Distinguishes between informative and persuasive messages
- Asks questions to obtain information

PORTFOLIO ASSESSMENT

Standard
- Glossary of Speech Terms
- Identification of Visual Aids for Speech Use
- Written Segments of Introduction, Transitions, or Conclusion to Informative Speech

Enrichment
- Tape of Informative Speech
- Quotations for Use in Informative Speeches
- Certificate of Merit for Outstanding Performance

Challenge
- Evaluation of Introduction as "Best in Class"
- Evaluation of Body of Speech as "Best in Class"
- Evaluation of Conclusion as "Best in Class"
- Compilation of Best Student Speeches

CHAPTER 10 REVIEW

SUMMARY

The main purpose of speeches given to inform is to impart new knowledge to the listeners.

Types of Informative Speeches Informative speeches may be classified into four types. Speeches about objects deal with anything you can see, feel, hear, taste, or smell. Speeches about events tell about anything that has happened, or is happening, or is regarded as happening. Speeches about processes treat related series of events that lead to specific results or products. Speeches about concepts deal with beliefs, theories, ideas, and principles.

Beginning an Informative Speech The introduction to an informative speech should gain audience attention, build interest in the topic, preview the topic and apply it to the audience, and establish the ethos of the speaker. The speaker should draw upon several attention devices to carry out these functions.

Imparting the Message of an Informative Speech Several functions must be fulfilled during the main part of a speech. A speaker should maintain audience attention by using attention devices and by checking seating arrangements and listening conditions. A speaker must also react to audience feedback and make smooth transitions during the speech. Finally, it is important to avoid becoming too technical. Personalize the speech regularly.

Concluding an Informative Speech The conclusion of an informative speech should summarize the major points made during the body of the speech. It should also signal the conclusion for the audience, reinforce the central idea of the speech, and psychologically close the speech.

Conducting a Question-and-Answer Period Be prepared for a question-and-answer period and promise to answer audience questions. Be impartial in recognizing questioners and aware of any time limit for the session. If you do not know the answer to a question, say so. If a question relates to a visual aid, display it while answering. Answer questions directly, completely, and briefly.

ASSESS

● **ASSESSMENT STRATEGIES**

Individual Assessment
- Participates in practice activities daily or weekly
- Demonstrates knowledge of content through questions, discussion, quizzes, and Chapter 10 test
- Displays improved skills in delivery of informative speeches

Group Assessment
- Sets and achieves goals
- Analyzes and evaluates student skills in introducing, delivering, and concluding an informative speech
- Delivers feedback to team members in a constructive and positive manner
- Organizes topics for coordinated group research

Using Visual Aids Use visual aids only to clarify a point or make it more meaningful. Choose the most appropriate types of visual aids and be sure that they can be seen easily from all parts of the room and are neat and attractive. Rehearse with each visual to find the best method for using it.

VOCABULARY

Define each term in a complete sentence.

informative speech	rhetorical question
attention device	theme
humor	slogan
anecdote	chart
common ground technique	graph
shock technique	diagram
suspense	map
ethos	poster
transition	cartoon
technical language	object
personalizing	model
summary	cutaway
quotation	handout
dramatic statement	

CHECKLIST

Skills for Speaking to Inform

1. Be aware of your basic purpose in speaking to inform.
2. Use a purpose sentence.
3. Learn to focus on a specific aspect of your topic.
4. Formulate a good introduction.
5. Use attention devices to gain audience attention.
6. Apply your message to your audience.
7. Attend to audience feedback.
8. Use smooth transitions.
9. Use language that your audience will understand.
10. Prepare properly if you plan to use visual aids.

ASSESS

● **ANSWERS**

See the Answer Key for more complete answers.

REVIEW QUESTIONS
1. The purpose is to impart knowledge.
2. Introductions gain attention, build interest, apply the message to the audience, and build ethos.
3. Attention devices include: humor, quotations, shock techniques, and suspense.
4. The body conveys the message of the speech.
5. Audiences listen better if they are seated in close proximity in comfortable surroundings.
6. Audiences remember the conclusion longer than any other part.
7. A summary reviews the main ideas.
8. Visual aids include diagrams, maps, and models.
9. Visual aids should usually be used.
10. The aid should be displayed as the answer is given.

DISCUSSION QUESTIONS
The following code is used to designate discussion questions and activities as suitable for students of varying ability levels:
   ▼ = below average to average
   ◆ = average to above average
   ■ = all students
1. Have students brainstorm new lists.
   ▼
2. Students could work in small groups.
   ■
3. Each group should write a paragraph to exemplify an abstract idea that is made personal.
   ▼
4. Students could list the types of visual aids mentioned.
   ■

342

CHAPTER 10 REVIEW

REVIEW QUESTIONS

1. Identify the primary purpose of an informative speech.
2. Name several functions that an introduction fulfills.
3. Describe several devices you can use to capture the audience's attention during your introduction.
4. Describe the main purpose of the body of an informative speech.
5. Identify the nonverbal factors that can affect the audience's attention to a speaker.
6. Describe the importance of the conclusion of a speech.
7. Name the different parts of a summary.
8. Identify some two-dimensional and three-dimensional visual aids.
9. Describe when visual aids should be used.
10. Describe the use of visual aids during the question-and-answer period after a speech.

? DISCUSSION QUESTIONS

1. As a class, discuss possible topics for each of the four categories of informative speeches. Focus upon topics that would be of interest to your age group at the present time. Try to identify at least ten topics in each category that are of interest to the class.
2. Discuss possible openings for a speech that explains how in the future the sea will be a greater source of human food than it is now. How might you gain the audience's attention in such a speech? What devices might you use to build interest during the introduction?
3. Discuss how you might personalize a speech on any of the topics that you have identified earlier. What kinds of experiences would you turn to in order to introduce a real person into your speech?
4. As a class, pick an informative speech topic about a process. Discuss the kinds of visual aids you might use in a 10-minute speech on this topic. What kinds of aids would help both the speaker and the audience? How could you use visual aids to develop and maintain audience interest?

ASSESS

CRITICAL THINKING

1. Analysis Under what circumstances would it be appropriate to invite questions from the audience after an informative speech? How knowledgeable about the topic should the speaker be? What procedure should the speaker follow if asked a question that she or he cannot answer?

2. Evaluation Imagine that you are giving a speech on the longest rivers of the world. Each time you introduce a river, you use a beautiful slide of the capital city of the country through which the river flows. How necessary and effective are these visual aids? What aids might help an audience during a speech on this topic?

ACTIVITIES

In-Class

1 Work in groups of from five to seven. Select a topic from either the sample speech topics in Chapter 7 that are suitable for informative speeches or the topics that you identified during the discussion questions. Suggest as many effective attention-getting devices as you can to introduce the topic. Try to include examples of each of the techniques studied in this chapter. Select someone to compile the list and present it to the class as a whole for reaction and feedback from classmates.

2. Work in groups of from five to seven. Each group will design a critique sheet that allows for rating the use of visual aids. The sheet should rate the selection, the construction, and the use of visual materials. Assign one group member to explain the form to the class. The class will then select the best features from each group's sheet. A usable critique sheet for visual aids can then be developed and used to evaluate future speakers and speeches.

3. Work in groups of from five to seven. Each member of each group will tell an anecdote based upon personal experience or upon a story from someone else. Each group will then select the most interesting anecdote and present it to the class as a whole. Discuss how

---

CRITICAL THINKING
1. **Analysis** With a list of topics, ask students to decide which are appropriate for question and answers.
2. **Evaluation** The examples of inappropriate visual aids should help students understand the need to use visuals that directly relate to their topics.

ACTIVITIES
In-Class
1. Brainstorm ideas to use as attention-getting devices.
2. Have students follow the format using evaluation sheets.
3. Give students time to come up with an interesting anecdote to share.

343

ASSESS

Out-of-Class
1. Essays should reflect an understanding of introductions and the importance of attention-getting devices.
2. Check for an understanding of conclusions in a speech.
3. Review the text on visual aids. Students should explain why they would use one over another.
4. Have students develop a checklist for questioning strategies.

344

CHAPTER 10 REVIEW

each anecdote might be used to build interest in a speech. Be sure to identify the topic of an informative speech that the anecdote could be used with.

Out-of-Class

1. Examine the speeches in the Appendix of Speeches at the back of this book or in one of the standard speech collections in your library. Find a speech introduction that you believe is striking and engages the attention of the audience. Copy the introduction in your speech notebook. With an understanding of the speech's original audience in mind, write an analysis of the introduction, pointing out why it would immediately get the audience's attention. Be prepared to present your findings in class.

2. Using the Appendix of Speeches at the back of the book, a standard anthology of speeches, or *Vital Speeches of the Day,* examine the conclusions of at least four speeches. Then answer the following questions in your speech notebook. (a) How do the various speakers introduce their conclusions? (b) Which of the speeches examined contains the best summary of the points made in the speech? Copy the summary. (c) Do any of the speeches end with a quotation, a dramatic statement, or a rhetorical question? Give examples. (d) What percentage of the speeches refer back to the introduction in the conclusion? Be prepared to present your findings in class.

3. Assume that you will give an informative speech on one of the following topics: "Alligators and Crocodiles," "Breeds of Cats," or "Living Costs in Major American Cities." Think about the visual aids that will help your audience learn more about the topic. List and describe the visual aids you would use in your speech notebook. Be prepared to present your list in class and to add other aids suggested by your classmates.

4. Choose a topic for an informative speech that was presented in the text or identified in one of the various activities devoted to topic selection. Find a topic that you know little or nothing about. In your speech notebook, write a series of questions that audience members are likely to ask about the topic before they hear the speech. Be prepared to discuss with your classmates how this question-writing technique might be usable in speech preparation.

344

ASSESS

💡 CHAPTER PROJECT

Prepare an eight- to ten-minute demonstration speech in which you explain either how to do something or how something works. Choose a topic that you already know something about and that lends itself to the use of visual aids. Follow these steps: (a) Organize the body of the speech into an outline. (b) Write an introduction that gets the attention of your audience. (c) Carefully consider the structuring of the body of your speech. (d) Compose a carefully thought-out conclusion. (e) Memorize the introduction, important transitions, and the conclusion. (f) Prepare your visual aids, referring to the checklist in this chapter as you do so. (g) Be prepared to participate in a two- to five-minute question-and-answer period following your speech.

CHAPTER PROJECT
- This could also be used as a unit project. Review the use of all visual aids before the speech delivery.

PREPARE

● CHAPTER PLANNER

Day 1	Day 2	Day 3	Day 4	Day 5
Prepare	Prepare	Prepare	Prepare	Prepare
Teach	Teach	Teach	Teach	Teach
Assess	Assess	Assess	Assess	Assess
Sub. Teacher Tip *p. 349*	Sub. Teacher Tip *p. 353*	Sub. Teacher Tip *p. 361*	Sub. Teacher Tip *p. 369*	

● CHAPTER OVERVIEW

This chapter examines the following topics:
- Types of Persuasive Speeches *p. 347*
- Three Sources of Persuasion *p. 350*
- Pathos: Analyzing the Needs of Your Listeners *p. 350*
- Ethos: Establishing Your Prestige *p. 356*
- Logos: Being Logical *p. 362*
- Being Responsible *p. 367*
- Analyzing and Evaluating Persuasive Speeches *p. 369*

▽ PORTFOLIO PRODUCTS

Individual Projects
- Glossary of Speech Terms
- Tape of Persuasive Speech
- Graphic Visual Aid
- Research Notes
- Chapter 11 Portfolio Products

Group Projects
- Video of Persuasive Speech
- Group Action Plan
- Research Notes
- Evaluation of Persuasive Speeches

● sca GUIDELINES

- Listens effectively to persuasive speeches
- Identifies persuasive techniques used in speeches
- Distinguishes between informative and persuasive messages
- Asks questions to obtain information

CHAPTER 11

Speaking to Persuade

When you have completed this chapter you should be able to:

- Describe the difference between informative and persuasive speaking.
- List characteristics of positive, neutral, disinterested, and opposed audiences.
- Explain how evidence and reasoning work together to create logical persuasion.
- Define and explain what is meant by responsible persuasion.

TEACH

● **LINKS TO PAST LEARNING**

Ask students to recall any recent election. Identify the major candidates and ask students to describe the speaking style of each. Discuss the message the candidates used to try to persuade voters to vote for them.

● **MOTIVATION**

Ask students to think about the thing they would most like to convince their parents to do. Short of a miracle, encourage students to think of what words or circumstances might persuade them. You might turn this activity around and ask students to imagine how parents might possibly persuade their children to clean their rooms.

● **ACTIVITY**

To help organize this Activity you might list some possible topics for the persuasive mini-speech. The list could include: "Why I need a car for Christmas" or "Let's go to Antarctica for vacation this year." Give students some preparation time in class. Each student could keep the speech to one minute or less in order to complete the activity within the class period.

● **ACTIVITY**

Persuasive Mini-Speech

As a means of introducing persuasive speaking, each class member should prepare, then deliver a speech not to exceed one minute in length. Its purpose should be to express your opinion on any topic that is important to you. This is not a speech for which you are expected to do research. You are not expected to provide evidence and sources for this speech. Actually, your preparation could be completed within fifteen minutes of class time, then the speeches could begin. The purpose is for the class to become familiar with some of the types, purposes, and techniques of persuasive speaking. Following each speech, listeners might answer these questions: "Did the speaker's topic present us with a question of fact, of value, or of policy?" "Were the speaker's appeals mainly to our needs, our reasoning, or based upon the prestige and competence of the speaker?"

Much of public speaking has as its primary purpose providing information of listeners—informing them about subjects the speaker knows more about than they do. But another purpose which accounts for a great number of speeches is that of persuasion. A speech given to persuade has as its primary goal the influencing of the attitudes, beliefs, or behavior of the listeners. Political figures try to secure votes through persuasive speaking. Lawyers use persuasion to secure a jury's decision. Legislators speak persuasively for or against a pending bill. All citizens have numerous opportunities for persuasive speaking. You might want to convince members of your PTA to take a certain stand on the school budget, tell your city council why you believe they should vote for an ordinance you favor, or explain to other members of your investment club why you feel a certain stock should be bought. All would be exercises in persuasion.

The opening Activity asked you to discover several types and techniques of persuasive speaking. Of course, this more difficult kind of speaking has all the principles of good public speaking covered in earlier chapters as its foundation. This chapter will build upon that foundation by discussing the specific types and techniques of persuasion.

● **TYPES OF PERSUASIVE SPEECHES**

Persuasive speeches are given in situations in which two or more points of view about a topic are in conflict. The speaker tries to convince

TEACH

> *If you would convince others, seem open to conviction yourself.*
> —Lord Chesterfield

● **TEACHING**

You could present an overview of this section by listing the headings: Questions of Fact, Questions of Value, and Questions of Policy. Provide an example of each type and then invite students to add to the examples in each category.

● **SKILL DEVELOPMENT**

15-Second Skill Opportunity
Students should examine the examples of questions of fact given in the text. Give them time to develop their own statement of purpose based on a question of fact. Suggest that they could use the daily newspaper or content from a course they are taking to develop their question. Ask volunteers to state their question of fact for the class.

● **LEARNING STYLES**

Cooperative Learning
Ask small groups of students to choose a question of medical ethics or political behavior. Let the group discuss and finally define the issue of value linked to the question. Encourage each person in the group to make a statement for or against the question as the group defined the issue.

CHAPTER 11 Speaking to Persuade

those who disagree that his or her point of view is the correct one. Another way of saying this is that persuasive speeches are given when there is some *question* about which view is correct. Three types of questions give rise to persuasive speech situations: questions of fact; questions of value; and questions of policy.

Questions of fact deal with occurrences and the reasons that they have happened, are happening, or will happen in the future. Here are several examples of purpose sentences for persuasive speeches dealing with questions of fact:

- My purpose is to persuade my audience that a major earthquake will hit California within the next fifteen years.
- My purpose is to convince my audience that there should be increased security in airports.
- My purpose is to persuade my audience that gun control measures will reduce violent crime.
- My purpose is to convince my listeners that the existence of nuclear weapons continues to threaten world peace.

Notice that each speech purpose deals with occurrences about which there is some element of doubt. If it were now a solidly proven fact that Oswald acted alone in the Kennedy assassination, there would be no reason for anyone to give a persuasive speech on the subject. The

This voter registration drive utilizes persuasive speeches relating to questions of policy.

same is true of the topics that relate to the present, such as political terrorism, and of course to those dealing with the future, such as a California earthquake, since nothing in the future can yet be considered an established fact.

Is DNA research morally justifiable? What are the ethical responsibilities of journalists? These are **questions of value.** Though such questions involve matters of fact, they go further. They also call for judgments about right and wrong, ethical and unethical, good and bad, proper and improper. "How many journalists are there in Washington, D.C.?" is purely a question of fact since it involves statistics. However, a question such as "What are the ethical responsibilities of journalists regarding more medical care for the elderly?" goes much further since it demands a moral judgment. A person's answer to this second question depends not only on his or her knowledge about medical care for the elderly, but also on his or her moral values. Notice how the following purpose sentences for speeches of value also require this kind of judgment:

- My purpose is to persuade my audience that the original *Star Wars* is a classic movie.
- My purpose is to persuade my listeners that the state should have a better food-stamp program.
- My purpose is to persuade my audience that in the long run it still pays to buy American-made cars.

Questions of policy deal with whether certain courses of action should be taken. They include matters of both fact and value within themselves, but go beyond them to consider what should or should not be done. A question such as "What steps should be taken to control the problem of car theft?" demands both that the audience know certain facts about car theft, and that they consider it wrong. Once this is established, the speaker can go further to advocate that one or more solutions be carried out. Here are some examples of purpose sentences for speeches dealing with questions of policy. Notice that most such sentences contain the word "should":

- My purpose is to show my audience that a permanent site should be established for the Olympic Games.
- My purpose is to persuade my listeners that stricter controls should be placed on genetic research.
- My purpose is to convince my audience that the U.S. government should adopt a tougher policy to deal with terrorism that affects American citizens traveling abroad.

TEACH

> *Some of mankind's most terrible misdeeds have been committed under the spell of certain magic words or phrases.*
>
> —Robert Burchfield

● **TEACHING**

You might bring a copy of Aristotle's *Rhetoric* to class. Explain the meaning of the words in boldface, *pathos, ethos,* and *logos.* Discuss which type of argument seems to be most influential for high school students.

● **CURRICULAR CONNECTIONS**

Language Arts
Encourage students to make lists of words that are related to the Greek words mentioned in this section. Students could provide definitions and derivations of these Greek words.

● **LEARNING STYLES**

Visual Learning
Ask students to collect print advertising samples and develop a poster or collage using these samples. Students should offer an explanation of the type of persuasion each sample uses.

● **ACTIVITY**

If students have difficulty selecting a topic for this activity, they might use one of the topics suggested in the text on pages 348–349.

350 CHAPTER 11 Speaking to Persuade

● THREE SOURCES OF PERSUASION

Before people will believe, think, or do something, they must *want* to do it. **Persuasion** is simply a means by which one person can cause another to *want* to believe, to think, or to do. You adopt new beliefs, attitudes, and actions constantly. Think for a moment why you might decide to see a certain film, admire a certain singer, or learn to drive a car. Basically, each decision is made only when you *want* to make it. Whenever someone else tries to convince you to decide a certain way, that person is using the process of persuasion.

Over 2500 years ago, the Ancient Greek, Aristotle, wrote a book on persuasion called the *Rhetoric*. The *Rhetoric* is still considered by most speech scholars to be the most influential book written on the subject. In it, Aristotle stated that there are three primary sources by which people can be persuaded: **pathos,** which means the listeners' own personal drives, needs, and desires; **ethos,** by which he meant the way in which an audience perceives the character and personality of the speaker; and **logos,** meaning the listeners' own thinking processes. Persuaders must concentrate on each of these factors. They must know their listeners' needs, establish their own prestige when attempting to influence an audience, and build logical arguments that their listeners can follow. A knowledgeable, sincere, logical speaker stands a good chance of successfully persuading others.

● **ACTIVITY**

Types of Persuasive Speeches

Divide the class into three groups. Each group will choose five topics that are suitable for a persuasive speech. For each topic, develop a purpose sentence that deals with a question of fact, a question of policy, and a question of value. You should be able to develop all three sentences for each topic. If you have difficulty, explain your problem when the groups come together to discuss the topics and purpose statements as a class. Keep these purpose statements in your speech notebook for future persuasive speeches.

● PATHOS: ANALYZING THE NEEDS OF YOUR LISTENERS

Most people like to consider themselves very logical creatures. They prefer to think they make decisions and behave in certain ways based

350

TEACH

● TEACHING

Provide students with an overview of the types of audience attitudes presented in this section. Encourage students to think of alternative descriptions to identify the spectrum of support for an issue by an audience.

> *Logic is one thing, the human animal another. You can quite easily propose a logical solution to something and at the same time hope in your heart of hearts it won't work out.*
> —Luigi Pirandello

● LEARNING STYLES

Cooperative Learning

Have the following list of audiences on the chalkboard. Ask each group to select several and discuss what they perceive to be the needs of each group. Then the group should try to predict the degree of support each audience would have for (1) raising the minimum wage; (2) restricting immigration; (3) zero tolerance for underage drinking. The audience list includes: students, parents, teachers, medical doctors, farmers, brewers, diplomats, stock brokers, and computer programmers.

Pathos: Analyzing the Needs of Your Listeners **351**

solely on logic. But if they were to make an honest analysis of the reasons for much of their behavior and many of their decisions, they would probably be forced to admit that they are sometimes not logical at all. People frequently believe, decide, or act in particular ways simply because they want to or need to, rather than because reason or logic points to these choices.

If you plan to persuade people, you must appeal to the needs and desires of your listeners as well as to their brains. Some people consider this beneath the dignity of a persuader. This is not the case at all, as long as the needs and desires to which you appeal are legitimate, and you honestly believe in the cause you are promoting.

Discover the Needs of Your Audience

The effective persuader seeks out the special needs and attitudes of each audience prior to a speech in order to plan the strategy most suited to that group of listeners. Remember the section on audience analysis in Chapter 7? Knowing the particular needs and attitudes of an audience is especially important when you are speaking to persuade. In a persuasive speech the success or failure of your entire speech can depend on how well you know your audience beforehand.

Audiences may have hundreds of special needs and attitudes depending on the subject of a given speech and the listeners' pervious experiences with the topic. These many different needs can be grouped according to how they affect the audiences' reception of you and your topic. An audience's attitude toward you and your topic will fall somewhere on a scale between "very positive" and "very negative." Essentially, audiences fall into four basic categories: the positive audience, the

In order to deliver the most effective speech, you will want to identify your audience's attitudes as carefully as possible on a scale from "positive" to "opposed."

TEACH

> **"The best way I know of to win an argument is to start by being in the right."**
>
> —Quintin McGarel Hogg

● **LINKS TO PAST LEARNING**

Ask students to recall public opinion polls that identified the range of public opinion about specific topics. Discuss where they thought they fit into the categories. Did they think the poll reflected popular opinion accurately?

● **CURRICULAR CONNECTIONS**

Math/Science
Take a school-wide survey about an issue that has a wide range of opinions. The class could work to formulate the issue as a question of value. Encourage the class to develop an attitude rating scale. The results can be tabulated and the measure of statistical variation calculated. Post the results for the entire school to view.

● **LEARNING STYLES**

Visual Learning
Some groups of students could represent the results of the school survey as suggested in the Math/Science Curricular Connections to show the variety and percentages of responses.

---

neutral audience, the disinterested audience, and the opposed audience. Each has a different set of needs and must be approached differently by the speaker. You will want to try to place your audience's pre-speech attitudes as carefully as possible on this scale.

The **positive audience** is one that already agrees with your basic persuasive purpose. If you are speaking to librarians about the need to raise money for the local library, most of your listeners are likely to be in favor of your idea before you begin. If you are speaking to students about the need to oppose a curfew for young people in your community, most of your audience will again be likely to support your idea. Of course, this is the easiest type of audience to persuade. Your only persuasive task is to deepen their feelings about the topic. Their basic need is simply for a "recharging."

The **neutral audience** has a different need. They are neither for nor against your topic—they simply do not know very much about it. Their basic need is for information that will make it possible for them to form an opinion. Suppose you are trying to sell a brand new dishwashing detergent, and the people in your audience have never heard of it before. If you are going to persuade them to buy it, you must first give them some information about it. You might, for example, tell them that it washes more dishes per bottle than brand X, is smells better than brand Y, it cleans better than brand Z, and it is easier on the hands than all three!

The **disinterested audience** knows about the topic but couldn't care less. They consider it a dull issue or an unimportant one, not particularly relevant to them or their needs. This kind of audience needs to be "electrified." They need to be shown the seriousness of the problem, the closeness of the danger, or the way in which they will be affected. Before they can be persuaded to do anything, they must be motivated to care.

The **opposed audience** is the most difficult kind of audience for a persuasive speaker to face. It is composed of people who disagree with your stand on the topic. They feel as strongly about the issues as you do, but they have opposing opinions. Sometimes they may distrust you simply because you hold a viewpoint different from theirs. Their need is first for open-mindedness, then for conviction. You must first succeed in getting a fair hearing for your side, then attempt to convince them of your viewpoint.

How do you discover whether you will be facing a positive, neutral, disinterested, or opposed audience? Usually by the same methods mentioned under "Audience Analysis" in Chapter 7 starting on page 185. Ask the person who invites you to speak about the attitudes and needs of the listeners. Ask friends and acquaintances who know your future audience members. Talk to other speakers who have addressed the same group in the past. In each case, ask questions designed to te

In order to persuade a neutral audience, the speaker must provide new information that will encourage individuals to form an opinion.

you about the attitudes of the audience toward your topic and about their needs in relationship to the topic.

If you are planning a speech that strongly advocates greater freedom for editors and reporters on your school newspaper, appropriate questions to ask about members of your future audience might include the following:

- How many of my audience members will be fellow students?
- How many will be teachers and school administrators?
- What is the attitude of our organization of parents and teachers towards the school paper?
- Are there certain opinion leaders among the group? If so, what are their views on freedom of the press?
- Have any of the audience members been bothered in the past by insistent school reporters?
- Do some of the school administrators feel our school press is too liberal in its editorial views?

Questions of this kind should enable you to make an educated estimate of the attitudes and needs of the particular audience you will be facing. Once you know those attitudes and needs you can begin planning your persuasive strategy. Strategies differ, depending on the type of audience.

353

TEACH

AMAZING FACTS!
The median age for males at the time of their first marriage is 26.5; the median age for females is 24.4.

• TEACHING

You could ask volunteers to read the excerpt from Beth Simmons' speech, "It's Hard to Be Human." Discuss the techniques she uses to persuade her audience to her point of view. Ask students to speculate about the nature of the audience to whom she gave this speech. Ask the class to identify the conclusion Beth wanted her audience to come to.

• SKILL DEVELOPMENT

15-Second Skill Opportunity
Ask students to complete the sentence "It is hard to be human because. . . ."

• SKILL APPLICATION

Citizens Speak Out
You could write the statistic about the median age for first marriages on the chalkboard. Then encourage students to think about how they could use such information as a parent, as an employer, as a politician, as an insurance salesperson. Ask each student to assume one of those roles and make a persuasive statement to a young man or woman.

---

354   CHAPTER 11   Speaking to Persuade

Use Different Approaches for Different Audiences

For the positive audience, your job is a relatively easy one—keep them happy or make them even happier! Since the positive audience already is in basic agreement with you, you have probably been invited to speak either to rededicate or remotivate them or talk about means rather than ends. A common example of a speaker facing a positive audience is that of a coach giving a pep talk to a team before the big game. The team members form a positive audience in the sense that they share the same goal as the coach—they all want to win. The coach's job as a speaker, then, is not to convince them that they should win, but to "psych them up" and to convince them that certain tactics will work better than others. Speeches of this kind, given to positive audiences, are sometimes referred to as **inspirational speeches.**

The neutral audience needs information. Certain kinds of information, especially factual information, can be convincing in themselves, particularly when fact is piled upon fact. The strategy for handling a neutral audience, then, is one of presenting the listeners with information from which they can reach only one conclusion—the conclusion you want them to reach. Beth Simmons, a high school student, shows how to apply this strategy in her speech called "It's Hard to Be Human."

> From early America's melting pot to today's claim that "Everybody Needs Milk" our differences have been homogenized to produce an era of paper people. Now you take a society, fold it into convenient sizes, cut carefully, unfold, and PRESTO! Nameless, faceless, expressionless silhouettes meaninglessly holding hands.
>
> Whoever your are, the message in any fortune cookie is universally didactic. If you need a friend, phone dial-a-smile to hear continuous laughing for three minutes, only interrupted by a voice reminding you that it is just a recording. It's easy to become satisfied with having things done for us by our computers and tape recorders. And, just as easy, to slip into the efficiency of automatic communication.

Notice how Beth Simmons used specific examples and experiences common to most of her listeners. In this manner, she increased her chances of persuading her audience to agree that it is difficult to be an individual in an increasingly impersonal world.

Facing a disinterested audience is harder than facing a neutral one. When an audience is aware of an issue, but considers it unworthy of any mental strain on their part or too dull to bother getting excited about, the speaker's main persuasive task is somehow to light a fire under those listeners. Often this can be done by showing the audience how the topic will affect them directly. President Ronald Reagan used

TEACH

● **TEACHING**

Ask students to use the speeches in the Appendix to find examples of techniques speakers used to involve disinterested listeners.

> *"A word is not a crystal, transparent and unchanging, it is the skin of a living thought and may vary greatly in color and content according to the circumstances and time in which it is used."*
> —Oliver Wendell Holmes

● **SKILL DEVELOPMENT**

15-Second Skill Opportunity
Give students a moment to think about the dullest topic they can imagine. Ask them to identify that topic for the class. Challenge others to think of a tactic a speaker might use to create interest in the dull topic that the student identifies.

---

this technique when appealing to his listeners' basic need for survival in a speech calling for a stronger U.S. defense capability:

> For 20 years the Soviet Union has been accumulating enormous military might. They didn't stop when their forces exceeded all requirements of a legitimate defensive capability. And they haven't stopped now....
>
> As an example, the United States introduced its last new intercontinental ballistic missile, the Minuteman III, in 1969 and we are now dismantling our even older Titan missiles. But what has the Soviet Union done in those intervening years? Well, since 1969 the Soviet Union has built five new classes of ICBM's, and upgraded these eight times....

Dealing with the opposed audience requires a double strategy. First, the listeners must be "softened up" to the point where they will really listen to your arguments and consider them fairly. Second, you must present sound evidence to back your position. Imagine that you have discovered some "shady dealings" during your school's most recent election for class officers. You plan to expose these practices in your next classroom speech, to be titled "Whatever Happened to Integrity?" You know you will face an opposed audience, since most of the members of your speech class were very active and involved in the election process either as candidates or campaign workers. Starting your speech with a direct attack on the issue would be an almost certain way to lose that kind of audience right at the beginning:

> Student politics and student government in this school are riddled with graft and corruption. The recent election showed me quite clearly that we cannot trust either the winners or the losers. In an election where vote buying occurred and campaign workers tampered with ballot boxes....

Such an opening will only deepen the negative feelings of an opposed audience. Even with facts to back up your claims, it is unlikely that you would achieve a fair hearing for your case. A better approach for this kind of audience would be:

> This school has always had good student leadership. I think you will agree that since our first year here we have been fortunate in the people we have elected as our class officers. I know many of you are dedicated to good student government here, as I am. I was very surprised and shocked, therefore, to discover some irregularities in our recent election process. Please listen as I recount some facts that have come to my attention....

TEACH

> *Nothing in education is so astonishing as the amount of ignorance it accumulates in the form of inert facts.*
>
> —Henry Adams

● TEACHING

Explain to students that human beings tend to be motivated according to five categories of basic needs: physiology, safety, belonging, esteem, and self-fulfillment. Use the excerpts in this section to identify the basic need that is used to try to motivate the listener.

▽ PORTFOLIO PRODUCTS

Students could be encouraged to make a chart that would list the various types of audiences speakers might encounter and, next to each type, to identify the styles of strategies a speaker might use to persuade or influence each audience.

● LEARNING STYLES

Cooperative Learning

Ask students to imagine giving a speech before an audience of 100 on the topic of curfews in your local community. Have the group try to guess the spectrum of attitudes in the audience and the number of people in each category. Based on their projections, ask the group to identify the best strategy for persuading this audience to their point of view.

● SKILL DEVELOPMENT

15-Second Skill Opportunity

Ask students to answer the question raised in the classroom speech titled, "Whatever Happened to Integrity?"

● ACTIVITY

After students have voiced their opinion about a controversial topic, discuss whether it is easy or hard for them to talk about controversial subjects. Identify reasons for their answers. Talk about strategies they learned in this section that might make it easier to address controversial topics.

This approach may not persuade your listeners to believe you ar[e] more than they would have with the first approach, but at least, in th[e] second case, your audience is likely to listen to your arguments an[d] consider them. If the arguments you then present in the body of th[e] speech are strong enough, the listeners may actually be persuaded.

Of course, positive, neutral, disinterested, and opposed audience[s] do not always occur in pure form. Many times an audience is com[-]posed of people who disagree among themselves. When an audience [is] made up of positive listeners and neutral listeners, the speaker's task [is] not too difficult. Giving persuasive information to such a group satisfie[s] the neutral listeners and recharges those who already agree. The sam[e] approach can also be used effectively with an audience of neutral an[d] opposed listeners but should be preceded in this case by some "min[d] opening" tactics before presenting the factual information. For a disi[n]terested and opposed group, the approach suggested for oppose[d] listeners alone may prove effective. Perhaps the worst combination [to] face is an audience of positive and opposed listeners. Here, too, th[e] safest approach might be to use the strategy of opposed listeners. [By] appealing mainly to them, you may gain some converts from you[r] opposed listeners and are unlikely to lose any of the positive ones. Th[e] next section will present specific kinds of evidence that can be useful [in] dealing with these different types of audiences.

● ACTIVITY

Audience Analysis

Hold a series of brief class discussions on such topics as abortion, the AIDS virus, capital punishment, gun control, the ozone layer, or similar subjects. Encourage everyone to make at least one statement about her or his opinion on each topic brought up. As you listen to the discussion of each topic, take some notes about the division of class opinion on that subject. Later, your notes can form a solid basis for analyzing your classmates' positions when you wish to give a speech on one of the topics discussed.

● ETHOS: ESTABLISHING YOUR PRESTIGE

In Chapter 10 you read that the ancient Greek rhetorician Aristotle use[d] the term *ethos* to describe a speaker's prestige. He felt it was the mo[st] powerful form of proof a speaker could possess. No matter how logic[al] a speaker, no matter how well that speaker appeals to the needs of th[e]

TEACH

● **RETEACHING**

On the chalkboard, list the audience categories as positive, neutral, disinterested, and opposing. Have students make a chart using these headings and ask them to list the characteristics of each type of audience. Have them identify the type of evidence that would most appeal to each group. This chart could become a portfolio product for individual assessment.

AMAZING FACTS!

Students at St. Andrews Presbyterian College in Laurinburg, NC, together with staff and friends, debated the motion "There's no place like home" for over 517 hours in April, 1992. The purpose of the debate was to increase awareness of the problems of being homeless.

Ethos: Establishing Your Prestige

listeners, if those listeners do not respect the speaker's character, there is little chance of successful persuasion. Thus, as a speaker, you must establish ethos, especially when attempting to persuade an opposed audience. This is done by showing listeners you are well prepared and competent, by being sincere in what you say, and by appearing genuinely interested in your audience.

Competence: Let Your Preparation Show

If a persuader ever hopes to convince listeners of anything, that speaker must show a high degree of **competence** and **confidence.** Audiences do not follow frightened or hesitant speakers. Only speakers who know their topic thoroughly and feel confident in their preparation are likely to succeed at persuasion. If your preparation has been shallow or haphazard, you will find it almost impossible to convince your audience of anything. Abraham Lincoln's well-known saying applies aptly to persuasive speaking: "You can fool some of the people all of the time, and all of the people some of the time, but you cannot fool all of the people all of the time." Incompetence and lack of confidence will usually become obvious to most audiences after a very short period of time.

While audiences seldom fail to notice incompetence, they may occasionally fail to recognize a truly competent speaker. If no one points out a speaker's knowledge, preparation, and ability to the listeners, they can misjudge the true qualities of that speaker. Sometimes a speaker's competence is mentioned when someone introduces him or her to the audience before the speech begins. In such introductions the audience is informed about the speaker's qualifications to speak on the topic. When a speaker has already established a national reputation in a given field or is well known to a local audience, it is unnecessary to remind listeners of the speaker's competence. Unfortunately the speakers most needing this kind of "prestige-boosting," the unknown or inexperienced speakers, are the ones who least often receive it. This leaves them with the task of building their own ethos during their speeches.

One of the most effective methods of assuring your audience of your competence is to let your speech preparation show during the speech. This can be accomplished in several ways. One way is by frequent use of evidence and supporting materials. The use of facts, survey results, statistics, and quotations from known authorities in the field says several important things about your knowledge and preparation. First it assures the audience that you are not simply "putting your mouth in motion." Listeners who hear sufficient amounts of evidence will recognize that you have backing for what you are saying and are not merely expressing your own unsupported opinions. Second, referring to

TEACH

● **TEACHING**

You might have names on the chalkboard of notable people that most individuals respect. Or, conduct a brief poll in the class to ask students to name the man or woman they most respect. Then discuss the characteristics that the people named seem to share.

● **LEARNING STYLES**

Visual Learning
Some students might prepare a bulletin board using photos of famous people, contemporary or historical, who have enjoyed widespread respect. Encourage them to identify each person and provide a brief quotation about or from each.

CHAPTER 11 Speaking to Persuade

outside sources of evidence shows the audience you have taken the time and effort to discover that evidence. Even though they may be an opposed audience, they will admire you for doing thorough research to support your point of view. They will realize you have earned the right to speak to them about your topic.

A second way of showing your competence is by referring to your own experience with your topic, particularly during the introduction of your speech. Audiences have learned to expect this kind of self competence building from unknown speakers and do not consider it bragging, as long as it is done in a subtle and sophisticated manner. Notice how this student speaker established his competence by referring to direct family experience at the end of his introduction:

> Have you ever attended a Special Olympics competition? Do you know what the Special Olympic Games are? They are modeled on the International Olympic Games, but competition is limited to people with some form of developmental disability. Their purpose is to give these people their day in the sun, as they compete against one another in 100-yard dashes, the long jump, discus throwing, and many other track and field events. Their motto is "Let me win, but if I cannot win, let me be brave in the attempt." Why do I know so much about the Special Olympics? Because my little brother has competed in them for the last four years.

In addition to focusing his audience's attention on his topic by the use of two rhetorical questions, the speaker established his competence by relating his personal connection with the Special Olympics.

You can also show experience or preparation by mentioning a part time job you have had, by describing an informal survey you have taken, or simply by saying, "While researching for this speech, I noticed..." So long as you do not overdo this kind of reference, your ethos will grow in the minds of your listeners.

Sincerity: Don't Fake It!

Sincerity is the second part of a speaker's prestige. Like competence, it must be genuine to make a lasting positive impression. Insincere speakers can impress audiences for a time, but eventually most are exposed as "fakes." What is meant by **sincerity** in persuasive speaking? Basically it means that the speaker's motives for advocating a particular attitude belief, or behavior must originate from a genuine concern for the best interests of the audience rather than from self-interest.

● **ENRICHMENT**

Students could find out the number of social workers that serve your local community and the agencies that employ them. You might ask the school guidance counselor to identify schools that train social workers and provide a list of such for interested students.

● **CURRICULAR CONNECTIONS**

Math/Science
Some students could find out statistics about the number of social workers in the U.S. Data might include years of training, regional employment of social workers, median wages, and union or professional memberships.

> *Were our knowledge of human relationships a hundredfold more reliable than it is now, it would still be foolish to seek ready-made solutions for problems of living in the index of a book.*
> —Mirra Komarovsky

● **SKILL DEVELOPMENT**

On the Job
Many businesses offer employee assistance programs to help workers deal with problems related to family, alcohol, abuse, absenteeism, and drugs. Ask students to develop several interview questions they would like to ask a social worker.

APPLY

CAREER CLOSE-UP

Social Worker

Social workers are employed by public government agencies, private agencies, or hospitals. They are often assigned to families. Welfare workers visit homes, interview family members, and make decisions for promoting the family's welfare. Educational requirements for social workers include a bachelor's degree followed by a Master's in Social Work (MSW) program.

Interviews are among the most important form of contact with clients. Each interview is prepared carefully, with questions planned in advance. Experienced social workers report that when they are sufficiently prepared they feel more confident and can listen more attentively to their clients. To gain the family's trust and respect, they begin the first interview with positive comments. This technique allows clients to feel more at ease.

While a sincere desire to help people is essential, a social worker cannot be successful without the ability to listen carefully and communicate convincingly with clients. Social workers must possess a repertoire of persuasive strategies so that they may select the technique most likely to convince clients that the prescribed course of action is best for them.

Social work can extend well beyond securing such basics as food and shelter for clients. To serve clients fully, social workers must often intervene persuasively on their behalf with groups and agencies that provide education, job training and placement, counseling, medical care, or other services. Such advocacy is effective only when social workers gather and present relevant information in a clear, well-reasoned manner.

For the social worker, carefully prepared interviews, with questions planned in advance, are among the most important forms of contact with clients.

TEACH

> *Self-respect—The secure feeling that no one, as yet, is suspicious.*
>
> —H.L. Mencken

● **TEACHING**

Have students list the techniques identified in this section for assuring your audience of your competence.

● **SKILL DEVELOPMENT**

Creative Thinking
Ask students to brainstorm other techniques or strategies for establishing ethos with an audience. Encourage volunteers to try these techniques out in class. Ask members of the class to comment on the relative effectiveness of each strategy.

15-Second Skill Opportunity
Volunteers could provide a brief introduction in which ethos is established about a specific topic.

● **LEARNING STYLES**

Cooperative Learning
In small groups ask each student to prepare a written one-sentence introduction of another student in the group. Each student should give the written statement to the other and then the student who is being introduced should add another sentence to the introduction that would enhance ethos.

● **SKILL APPLICATION**

Citizens Speak Out
You might debate the issue of qualifications for politicians and ask the class how they would identify insincere politicians. Suggest ways that citizens could limit the influence of insincere politicians.

360

---

360   CHAPTER 11   Speaking to Persuade

The speaker's motives for advocating a particular attitude, belief, or behavior must originate from a genuine concern for the best interests of the audience.

If a politician speaks to the people about a solution to a problem during an election year, the listeners sometimes find it hard to believe that the politician is attacking the problem unselfishly. A natural question in their minds is "Is the purpose of this speech to help solve the problem or to assure election?" A politician speaking under such circumstances needs to make a special effort to convince the audience of her or his sincerity. Audiences will more readily accept a speaker they consider somewhat incompetent than a speaker they consider insincere. The slightest hint of insincerity will turn many listeners against a speaker instantly.

A few public speakers are gifted with *charisma*. Charisma is difficult to define, but it often enables speakers who have it to influence and dominate their listeners in a way that ordinary speakers cannot. Charismatic speakers seem to be taken almost at face value as sincere and possessing great credibility. They are highly captivating and can often carry their audiences away with their words. Because they wield such power over their listeners, speakers who possess this gift have a special responsibility to use it wisely. To use it for wrong purposes not only harms the particular audiences that hear such a speaker; it also breaks down the trust that must exist between speakers and listeners everywhere if persuasion is to continue to be a means by which decisions are made in a democratic society.

● **ENRICHMENT**

Ask students to look up the words "ethos", "competence", "sincerity", and "good will" in various dictionaries and thesauruses. Develop synonyms or alternate expressions for each of these terms.

SUBSTITUTE TEACHER TIP

Try to use one or more of the techniques for establishing good will that are identified in this section. These tips include: (1) showing appreciation, (2) complimenting the class, (3) speaking directly to individuals in the class, (4) identifying common interests, (5) using humor.

Good Will: Show a Genuine Interest in Your Audience

Audiences will be more open and receptive to a speaker who shows an interest in them or good will toward them. Particularly with opposed audiences, persuaders need first to open the minds of their listeners to assure a fair hearing for their side of the issue. Getting an audience to like you as a person can lead to its members liking and accepting your arguments.

One commonly used method of showing an interest in one's audience is the practice of expressing appreciation for the invitation to speak to the group. The first thing ordinarily done by many speakers is to voice an appreciation for the privilege of addressing the audience.

Closely related to thanking one's audience is complimenting them. If you genuinely believe "This club represents the leaders in our community," then do not hesitate to tell the club. If you consider your audience to be a fair-minded group of people of sound judgment, tell them that, especially if your topic is likely to demand that they be fair as they listen: "This group has a reputation for being open-minded and fair in its decisions. I feel confident you will listen to what I have to say today in that same spirit." An opening such as this compliments the listeners and challenges them to be fair-minded as they listen to your speech.

Another way to show interest in your audience is to speak directly to various individuals in the group. If you are well acquainted with members of your audience, you may want to call them by name during your introductory remarks: "I see my friend Charles Stevens here today. I'm glad you could be here, Charlie." This sort of public recognition flatters Charles and probably puts him in a more receptive frame of mind toward you and your message. But calling audience members by name can be risky. If you call one friend's name, you'd better call all of your friends by name; otherwise, those left out may feel slighted. If you see twenty-eight of your friends in the audience, however, you'd better avoid such a roll call! Take care also not to identify someone as a friend if that person is only a nodding acquaintance. This comes across as false and insincere.

To show interest in your audience in another way, you might identify interests and experiences you and your listeners have in common. The use of the common-ground technique (see page 298) is a good method for demonstrating a genuine interest in your listeners as people. Audiences appreciate this. Effective use of humor (see page 296) also makes the speaker seem a likable person. If you can make your listeners laugh with you, they are more likely to listen receptively to your serious, persuasive message.

> ❝ *Civility is not a sign of weakness, and sincerity is always subject to proof.* ❞
> —John F. Kennedy

● **SKILL DEVELOPMENT**

15-Second Skill Opportunity
Ask students to select one of the techniques for establishing good will or rapport with the audience and make an introductory remark that uses one of those strategies.

● **LEARNING STYLES**

Visual Learning
If possible show film or taped excerpts of several charismatic speakers. You might include John F. Kennedy, Martin Luther King, Jr., and Ronald Reagan. Discuss the appeal of these speakers. Ask students if the appeal of charismatic speakers is lost if their speeches are merely read.

TEACH

● ACTIVITY

Students might be asked to develop a checklist that they could use to identify the various characteristics of establishing ethos. You might suggest that the class vote by secret ballot to identify the student with the best skills in developing ethos. You might award that student with a Certificate of Recognition.

● SKILL DEVELOPMENT

15-Second Skill Opportunity

Ask students to think of the biggest fakes and phoniest people they know or have seen on TV or in movies. Encourage volunteers to share their impressions of the biggest fakes they know. Discuss with the class how people spot insincerity.

Feedback

Learning how to give feedback is sometimes difficult and takes practice to improve. For each student speech, ask other students to write down at least one strength and one area that could be improved. Give students the opportunity to praise specific elements of other student work in class. Encourage them to be specific in their comments.

CHAPTER 11 Speaking to Persuade

● ACTIVITY

Critiquing Ethos

When asked to critique a classmate's persuasive speech, plan to include specific suggestions about the speaker's ethos. Note in what ways the speaker conveyed a sense of competence, how her sincerity came through, and how good will (a genuine interest in the audience's welfare) was projected. You might also note any techniques which the speaker might have overlooked for building any of the three parts of ethos.

● LOGOS: BEING LOGICAL

Have you ever been in an argument with someone and found yourse saying, "You're not being logical!" If you have, you probably still remer ber how frustrated you felt because the other person wouldn't argu according to the rules of logic. People frequently make decisions base on their needs and desires, but they like to feel they have decide logically. A persuasive speaker's job is to show listeners through log how to fulfill their needs and desires. Logic, then, is a powerful tool persuasion.

Use Valid Evidence and Correct Reasoning

Being logical in persuasive speaking means using valid evidence ar correct reasoning. **Evidence** is the raw material with which you mu begin. **Reasoning** is the process of putting this raw material togeth into a logical argument, which in turn may be used to reach a logic conclusion. The process of building a logical argument to use in a pe suasive speech can be compared to the way in which mighty rivers a formed. Rivers begin in the mountains and hills in tiny rivulets ar creeks (evidence), which then flow together (the reasoning process) form larger streams. Finally, these larger streams run together in a migh river (the conclusion). Imagine that you wish to persuade your fello townspeople that your city desperately needs a new hospital. In th diagram on page 363, the creeks represent your evidence, the path taken to form streams represent the reasoning process, and the enti process results in a river—your conclusion.

TEACH

▼ **PORTFOLIO PRODUCTS**

Students may generate another type of graphic that could be used to present evidence that supports the conclusion of their argument that the city needs a new hospital.

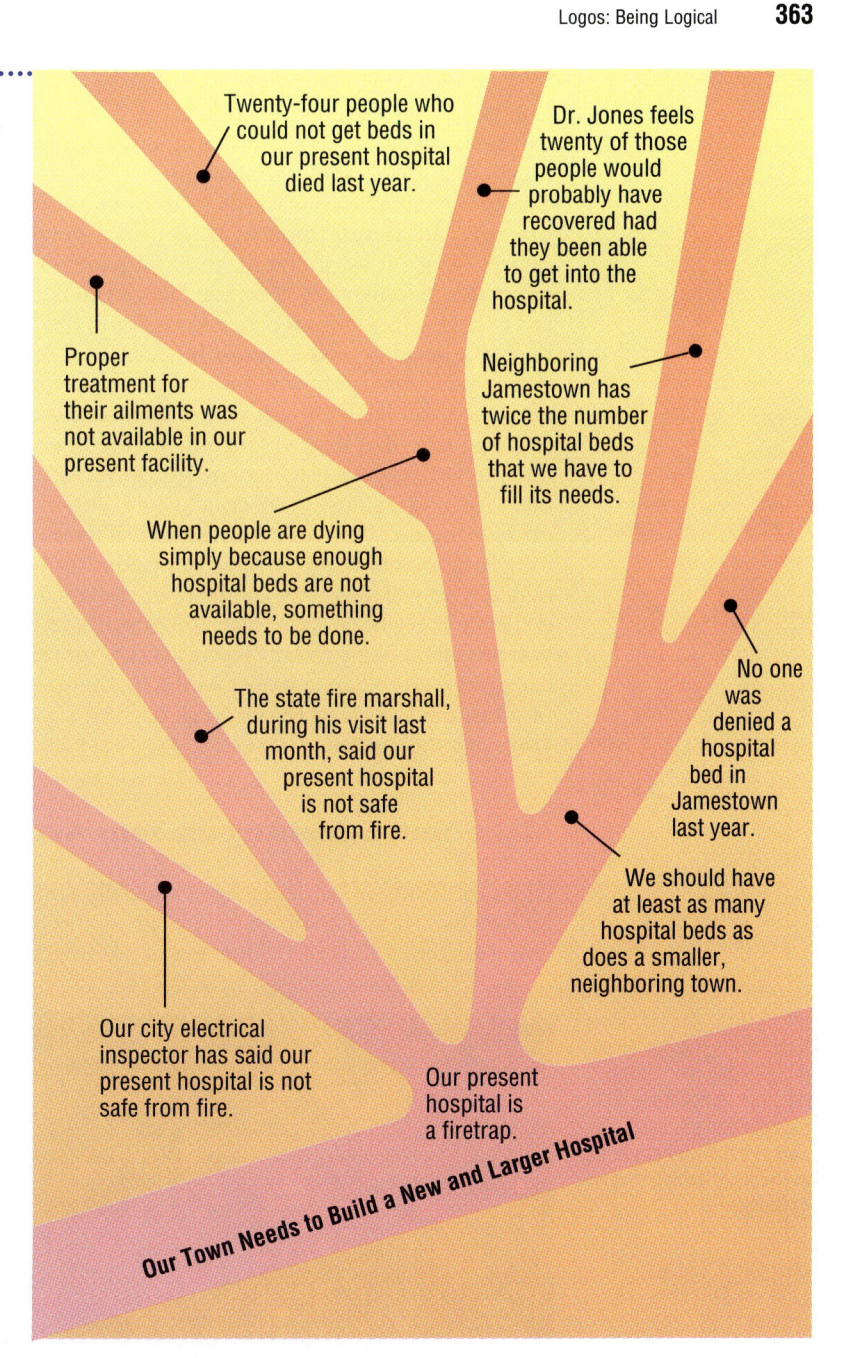

● **LEARNING STYLES**

Visual Learning
Ask students to use the graphic to identify the argument used to support the conclusion that the city needs a new hospital. Have them identify the strongest argument presented in the graphic. Discuss whether students would prefer to read a graphic or a paragraph of text to get the same information.

Logos: Being Logical **363**

...hese streams of evidence
...d reasoning flow logically
...ward the conclusion: Our
...wn needs to build a new
...d larger hospital.

Twenty-four people who could not get beds in our present hospital died last year.

Dr. Jones feels twenty of those people would probably have recovered had they been able to get into the hospital.

Proper treatment for their ailments was not available in our present facility.

Neighboring Jamestown has twice the number of hospital beds that we have to fill its needs.

When people are dying simply because enough hospital beds are not available, something needs to be done.

The state fire marshall, during his visit last month, said our present hospital is not safe from fire.

No one was denied a hospital bed in Jamestown last year.

We should have at least as many hospital beds as does a smaller, neighboring town.

Our city electrical inspector has said our present hospital is not safe from fire.

Our present hospital is a firetrap.

Our Town Needs to Build a New and Larger Hospital

363

TEACH

AMAZING FACTS!

A jury in Sturgeon, MO, listened to testimony for 657 days and deliberated for two more months in the longest civil case heard by a jury in the United States. The case involved an alleged toxic chemical spill.

● LINKS TO PAST LEARNING

Ask students to remember TV programs that showed evidence being presented in a courtroom. Discuss their impressions of the scene. Discuss differences between TV portrayal and real judicial proceedings.

● ENRICHMENT

You might arrange to have a trial lawyer visit the class and talk about the importance of evidence and reasoning in persuading a judge and jury.

● SKILL DEVELOPMENT

Research

Students can work as individuals, in pairs, or in a cooperative learning group to research information and obtain evidence they could use to present an argument for more or better city services. If students cannot think of an example, they could use the case presented in this section calling for a new hospital.

---

364 CHAPTER 11 Speaking to Persuade

To reach this conclusion, you must begin with good evidence. I Chapter 7, you studied a number of different types of evidence th can be used to support your arguments: facts, statistics, testimony, na rative, examples, and comparisons. The most persuasive evidence yo can use generally consists of facts or statistics. Testimony, when th opinions are based upon facts, is also a very persuasive type of ev dence. Notice how, in the diagram on page 363, the pieces of evidenc are either statements of provable fact or opinions that can be backed b facts. Since support for a conclusion almost always begins with such ev dence, a good persuader must be certain of the correctness of the ev dence which is used throughout the argument.

Once you have chosen your evidence, use the process of reasonir to make sure that the evidence flows together logically to produce th conclusion you wish to reach. If you have given equally persuasiv facts for and against your conclusion, you cannot expect your aud ence to agree with your conclusion. If your conclusion is based o three arguments but you have supported only one of them with ev dence, you will also have difficulty in convincing your audience. If you evidence is weak or contrary to the practical experience of the audienc you are again likely to fail. To succeed, your reasoning must show ho each piece of evidence works with the other pieces of evidence, how a of them together lead to one very definite conclusion—the conclusic you wish the audience to reach.

Make Your Evidence Suit Your Audience

Different forms of evidence are especially suitable for certain kinds c audiences. The chart on page 365 gives the four basic types of aud ences and the kinds of evidence that are effective with each.

To persuade your audience successfully, your reasoning must demonstrate that each piece of evidence works with the other pieces of evidence, leading to one conclusion.

364

Logos: Being Logical

ntify the audience before
hering your persuasive
dence.

Type of Audience	Kinds of Evidence
Positive	Narrative, Examples, Comparisons
Neutral	Facts, Statistics, Testimony, Examples
Disinterested	Facts, Statistics
Opposed	Narrative, Facts, Statistics, Examples, Comparisons

The positive audience needs recharging, not convincing. Anecdotes, examples, and comparisons seem most effective with such listeners. The neutral audience lacks information. They find examples helpful, but are likely to be more impressed with facts, statistics, and testimony. The disinterested audience must be given facts and statistics. They must be shown that a serious problem exists or is about to become critical and that it affects them. The opposed audience needs all the tools at the speaker's command. A speaker is wise to start with humor, common-ground devices, or compliments. An anecdote can also work well at the beginning. Once the listeners have decided to give the speaker a fair hearing, these can be followed with the harder forms of evidence (facts, statistics, examples, and comparisons). Mixed audiences react best when the speaker analyzes their needs correctly, then applies the various kinds of evidence in the best proportions. Correct reasoning is important no matter what type of audience you face. Logical reasoning is especially important, however, when facing an opposed audience.

● ACTIVITY

Presenting Evidence

Using one of the topics the class discussed during the Activity on page 356, find three pieces of evidence that help substantiate your own reasoning about that topic. Whenever possible, try to find one example, one piece of statistical evidence, and one quotation or paraphrase from an expert. Come prepared to identify your topic, then read aloud the three pieces of evidence you have found which argue for your position on that topic.

TEACH

● LEARNING STYLES

Audio Learning
Ask students which of the three types of evidence they most like to hear. Tally the results of the survey, and some students might make a bar graph to represent the results. Ask if they think their results are typical for most Americans.

● ACTIVITY

Students could use the newspaper or a current magazine to find the three types of evidence identified in the Activity. To emphasize the types of evidence, you could write the labels, examples, statistics, and quotes on the chalkboard.

APPLY

> *[Competition] stems from the desire of the individual somehow to prove his own worth, his own potential.*
>
> —Walter H. Wheeler

● LINKS TO PAST LEARNING

Encourage students to share their experiences with other contests. Ask them for examples of successful contests and those that failed. Encourage them to analyze factors in the successes and failures. Try to develop guidelines for a successful speech contest.

● MOTIVATION

To encourage participation in the speech contest, you might work with other teachers and the school administration to think of a prize or reward that would represent prestige and visibility for the winner and other participants. Such recognition could be the presentation of a plaque or trophy during a school assembly, Certificates of Recognition given to all participants, a media opportunity, and discount coupons for use at supporting community businesses.

● LEARNING STYLES

✳ Cooperative Learning

Students might find it helpful to work in small study groups to conduct the research phase of preparing their persuasive speeches. Study groups are often used in the college context and this could give students valuable experience.

Speaking IN ACTION

Speech Contest

Situation

As a class project, your speech class will sponsor a contest to be held with the entire school as the audience near the end of your speech course. Any student may enter, whether a member of the speech class or not. Only persuasive speeches may be given, with the length of each speech being 8–10 minutes. Speakers may select their own topics and will be expected to do their own preparation, though the speech teacher may listen and react to entrants' speeches beforehand as time permits. Three teachers, not including the speech teacher, will serve as a panel of judges, each of whom will complete an individual score sheet provided by the speech teacher. Once all speakers have spoken, the scores from all three judges for a given speaker will be combined to form that speaker's total score. First-, second-, and third-place winners will be selected and will receive appropriately engraved trophies. In cases of tied scores, the judges will confer and break the tie.

Preparation

You may plan to deliver your speech using the extemporaneous delivery method as outlined in Chapter 7, or you may decide to deliver it using manuscript method. Some speakers find it helpful to write out, and largely memorize, their introduction and conclusion, while delivering the body of the speech extemporaneously. To the extent that you read from manuscript, you should plan to make eye contact with your listeners a high percentage of the time. Some speakers both write out the entire speech beforehand, *and* make a preparation outline. During delivery this gives them the flexibility of switching from one method to another, though this is often difficult for inexperienced speakers.

Analyzing your audience beforehand will be central to your success as a persuader. Talk to fellow students about your topic during the days while you are preparing your speech to assess their attitudes towards your topic—do they agree with you, disagree, or are they somewhere in between? Knowing this can have a strong impact on what approach you select, and on the overall effectiveness of your presentation.

Delivery

Very likely, you may never have faced an audience the size of your school's entire student body. Remember, however, that talking to your speech class is really no different than speaking to this larger group (with the possible exception that you will likely need a microphone in this case). Keep your mind focused on convincing your listeners of whatever your persuasive purpose is. If you have researched your topic thoroughly, outlined your ideas clearly, and rehearsed repeatedly, your speech will make a positive impression on your audience. You may even walk off with a trophy! Good luck!

ENRICHMENT

Some students might volunteer to conduct a publicity campaign for the persuasive speech contest. The campaign could include both audio and visual strategies for reaching the school population. The campaign could also include notifying parents and the local community.

CURRICULAR CONNECTIONS

Math/Science
Compare and contrast how conclusions are reached and how evidence is used in the scientific and legal methods. Discuss how people usually arrive at conclusions.

> *"The trouble with lawyers is that they convince themselves that their clients are right."*
> —Charles W. Ainley

LEARNING STYLES

Cooperative Learning
Ask each group to review the types of audiences there are and select one for the focus of this activity. Each group should identify the type of evidence with examples that would probably work best with the type of audience they selected.

Use a Logical Framework

Two of the speech patterns discussed in Chapter 7 provide an especially logical framework for persuasive speeches. These are the problem-solution pattern and Monroe's Motivated Sequence. You may want to review that section of Chapter 7, giving particular attention to these two patterns. Both offer certain ideas that may be useful in developing a logical strategy for your own persuasive speeches.

Whatever pattern you use, your persuasive speeches must have an introduction, a body, and a conclusion. These three basic parts of a speech, which were discussed in Chapter 10, serve similar functions in almost every speech. However, a special emphasis should be given to several specific functions in persuasive speeches. In the introduction, building your ethos becomes particularly important. In the body, it is essential to use valid evidence and correct reasoning. In the conclusion, you must reestablish your ethos and clearly indicate the response you desire from your audience. As you can see, building ethos, or establishing **prestige,** is especially important in persuasive speaking.

● BEING RESPONSIBLE

Persuasive speaking is, in many ways, more difficult than speaking to inform. It demands detailed audience analysis, considerable research, and a well-planned strategy for building your prestige, particularly in the face of an opposed audience. For these reasons and others, persuasion has long been considered the highest level of public speaking. A speaker who can effectively persuade wields great influence over the minds of others. With this influence comes heavy responsibility as well.

Persuasive speaking is one of the major ways in which decisions are reached in a free society. The President of the United States attempts to persuade the American public to adopt a plan for fighting inflation. Members of Congress attempt to persuade one another to vote for or against the passage of an important bill. Business leaders work constantly to persuade customers to buy. Citizens have the opportunity to persuade each other to vote for particular candidates in each election. Responsible persuasive speaking is necessary if such a society is to function well.

Centuries ago, the Roman rhetorician, Quintilian, defined the ideal orator as "a good man skilled in speaking." In doing so, he placed major focus on good character as the primary requirement for effective persuasive speaking. Being a responsible persuader does not guarantee you will always be right in what you advocate to an audience, but it does mean you honestly *believe* you are right. If you try to convince

APPLY

● MOTIVATION

Ask students to consider the oath that witnesses take when they testify at a trial. They promise to tell "the whole truth." Ask students to think of examples when they do not think the whole truth was told about a news story or historical event.

● LEARNING STYLES

Cooperative Learning
Have small groups of students select a topic or product and ask half the group to obtain information that would support its advantages or benefits and the other half to learn about its liabilities. Ask the entire group to decide if the evidence is stronger in support of assets or liabilities. Have them discuss the responsibilities of a marketing department to represent the faults of its product.

● SKILL DEVELOPMENT

On the Job
Ask students to select a company that makes environmental products. Have them imagine that they are in either the marketing or public relations department. They need to write a 50-word statement suitable for media release to describe a new product.

368

ETHICALLY SPEAKING

Telling the Whole Story

One of the most challenging types of communication is a speech intended to persuade an audience to a particular point of view. When you prepare such a message, you are putting yourself in a *win-lose* situation. Because of this, you may be inclined to "go all out" to get your point across to your listeners. Whatever it takes to gain the agreement of your audience you will want to consider, and your preparation will be involved mostly with finding evidence to support your position or opinion. But what if your research turns up evidence that weakens your argument or refutes it? What if you discover that the position you are advocating might actually be harmful? What is your ethical responsibility in these circumstances?

Suppose, for example, that you are planning a speech to persuade your listeners to join the armed forces after high school. When you research the topic, you will learn that military training is patriotic, that it builds discipline and character, and that it provides an opportunity to gain useful career skills. These will be important points to emphasize in your speech to build your case for joining the armed forces. But suppose you also learn that there is another side to the story. You may discover, for example, that military training is not for everyone, that it can be life-threatening, and that a certain percentage of those who enlist are hurt not helped by the experience. It is not your responsibility to give equal attention to evidence such as this that weakens your argument. However, as an ethical communicator, you will want to suggest that some people are better suited than others to army life and that those who are considering a military career need to figure out whether they can be happy and productive in the service.

Similarly, suppose your speech is to persuade listeners that Dobermans make good family pets. Perhaps you own a Doberman and appreciate the qualities of that breed of dog. However, if you also know that Dobermans need strict obedience training and an inordinate amount of attention, and that at times they can be aggressive, you need to tailor your remarks so that your listeners understand how to interpret and use your message in their own circumstances.

Ethically speaking, remember to be as responsible to your listeners as you are to your particular point of view.

In addition to patriotism, discipline, and character-building, military service can also bring the experience of being a prisoner of war, to whom this speaker pays tribute.

368

> ● **RETEACHING**
>
> Refer to the speech patterns (the problem-solution and Monroe's Motivated Sequence) in Chapter 7. Discuss why these patterns are particularly useful when giving a persuasive speech.

> **SUBSTITUTE TEACHER TIP**
>
> Sometimes the comic section of your newspaper can be an occasion for teaching about logic. Bring to class, some of your favorite cartoon strips. Ask students to explain the logic in particular cartoons. Discuss what is wrong, or missing, from the argument. It is often the missing logic that makes the cartoon funny.

your neighbors to vote against a property tax increase, for example, you should sincerely believe that a tax increase in unwise at the moment, and not just wish to avoid paying higher taxes. If you are asking a group of people to vote for you, you should believe honestly that you are the best-qualified candidate, and not wish simply to increase your own personal power.

Responsible persuasion can mean different things to different people. For centuries, however, most persuaders have agreed on certain ethical standards, without which the process of persuasion loses much of its value. At the top of the list is the belief that any form of deception is wrong. You should be honest. Don't present false evidence. Don't present the ideas of others as if they were your own. Don't appeal to the emotions of your listeners without any basis in fact. Don't pose as an authority if you are not. These forms of deception are considered both irresponsible and unethical. Responsible persuasion means telling the truth as you have discovered it.

> ❝There are two kinds of statistics, the kind you look up and the kind you make up.❞
>
> —Rex Stout

> ● **SKILL DEVELOPMENT**
>
> **Outlining**
> Ask students to develop a short outline for a topic. They should identify Part I as the Introduction, Part II as the Body, and Part III as the Conclusion. They should indicate the main point(s) made in each part and support each point with one of the types of evidence identified in this section.

● ANALYZING AND EVALUATING PERSUASIVE SPEECHES

The kinds of questions you need to ask when analyzing and evaluating *persuasive* speeches are mainly questions that explore how well you used the three main sources of persuasion—pathos, ethos, and logos—and how responsibly you acted as a persuader. By now you are familiar with the approach that calls for you to first analyze objectively what you did, then evaluate how well you did. You have also come to expect that we will discuss analyzing your own speeches before those of your classmates.

Analyzing Your Use of Pathos—The Needs of Your Listeners

Since your use of pathos deals with how well you understand and speak to the attitudes and needs of your audience, we will look first at your audience analysis, then how accurately you selected the persuasive approach best suited to that audience.

- During my preparation for my persuasive speech, did I recall that audience analysis is even more critical in persuasive speaking than in other types?
- Am I comfortable with the notion that "appealing to the attitudes and needs of a particular audience" does not mean I am being false

TEACH

> *"What is politics but persuading the public to vote for this and support that and endure these for the promise of those?"*
>
> —Gilbert Highet

● LINKS TO PAST LEARNING

Ask students to identify what they found helpful in the analysis and evaluation of informative speeches. If they can identify additional suggestions to make the process more constructive, try to incorporate those comments and suggestions into this process.

▼ PORTFOLIO PRODUCTS

Students can review the content here and develop a form or chart that will identify the areas they should be considering in the analysis and evaluation of their speeches. This form or chart can be used as a portfolio product.

---

to my own convictions, but that I use my listeners' needs and attitudes as a filter through which to persuade them?

- Did I determine, in general, where along a line from "positive" to "opposed" the pre-speech attitudes of my audience fell regarding my topic?
- Did I do this by asking friends and acquaintances who would be in my audience, or who knew those who would form my audience what my listeners' attitudes and needs were likely to be with respect to my topic?
- If my audience was likely to be positive towards my topic, was my planned approach one of rededicating or remotivating them?
- If I perceived my audience would likely be neutral about my topic did I plan to provide them with lots of information in order to aid them in forming an opinion on my subject?
- If I were about to face a disinterested audience, did I decide to show them the seriousness of the problem, the closeness of the danger, or how they will be affected?
- If I found my audience would be initially opposed to my point of view, did I plan to start by developing an atmosphere of mutual trust and open-mindedness, *then* work on convincing them by using logic and evidence?
- Did I remember that audiences do not always come pre-packaged as simply "positive," "neutral," "disinterested," or "opposed"—that sometimes a given audience must be approached as a mixture of two or more of these?

Analyzing Your Ethos—Your Personal Credibility

Perhaps more than either of the other two factors of persuasion, ethos—your audience's overall perception of you—will determine your success as a persuader. When analyzing your ethos, remember that your listeners listen and look for competence, sincerity, and good will. In analyzing how you used this persuasive tool, you will need to be especially objective when judging how effectively you portrayed your credibility to your listeners.

- Had I thoroughly researched my speech, and did I display my competence to my audience by regularly citing sources during my speech?
- Had I rehearsed my speech to the point that my self-confidence was evident to my listeners?

- Did I frequently include surveys, facts, statistics, and quotations from recognized authorities to show my audience I had "earned the right to speak to them" on my topic?

- Did I refer (usually in my speech introduction) to any direct, personal experience I'd had with my topic?

- Did I show sincerity towards my audience by being honest with them through not falsifying evidence, using it out of context, or failing to mention a strong counterargument?

- Did I remember to express my appreciation for the opportunity to speak to them on my topic?

- Were my motives for advocating a particular attitude, belief, or behavior primarily motives of self-interest, or a concern for the best interests of my listeners?

- Did I make use of techniques such as humor and common ground as additional means of showing my interest in my audience?

Analyzing Your Logos—Your Reasoning and Evidence

Your ability to reason correctly and convincingly, and to support your reasoning with sound evidence provides you with a third powerful tool of persuasion. In analyzing your logos, you will want to assess both the soundness of your reasoning, and the strength of your proofs (evidence). Here are some questions to ask:

- Did I begin my preparation for my persuasive speech with a clear understanding of the relationship between evidence and reasoning?

- Did I thoroughly check the correctness of my evidence when I was gathering it?

- Once I had gathered my evidence, did I make certain it all flowed together smoothly to form a logical argument?

- During my preparation, did I eliminate any pieces of evidence that were weak, or did not fit in clearly with other evidence?

- If facing a positive audience, did my evidence consist primarily of anecdotes, examples, and comparisons?

- If I spoke to a neutral audience, did I mainly use facts, statistics, and testimony?

- Did I usually use facts and statistics when speaking to a disinterested audience?

● **LEARNING STYLES**

Cooperative Learning
Small groups of students can work together to analyze sections of their speeches using the major points identified in this section. These points can be used as a checklist for every student.

These groups could also assign numeric value to each of the points in their checklists. They could prioritize and weigh the points so that speech performance would reflect weighted priorities.

TEACH

> **To be a critic, you have to have maybe three percent education, five percent intelligence, two percent style, and ninety percent gall and egomania in equal parts.**
> —Judith Crist

● **TEACHING**

Review with the class the strategies suggested in this section for evaluation of other students' persuasive speeches. Emphasize the two different approaches described here. Ask students to provide examples of the questions or impressions they would focus on for both approaches.

● **SKILL DEVELOPMENT**

Feedback

Encourage students to take notes as they listen to their classmates deliver their speeches. Their notes should include identification of strong points in organization and delivery as well as areas they think could be improved. Students can be given the opportunity to say something positive about each speech. They should also be given the opportunity to identify an area for improvement. These comments should be constructive and as specific as possible.

CHAPTER 11 Speaking to Persuade

- With an opposed audience, did I begin by using such tools as humor, common ground, and complimenting my audience as ways of getting a fair hearing? *Then* did I later argue using facts, statistics, examples, and comparisons?

Now that you've analyzed your persuasive speech, back up as you have done in Chapters 9 and 10 and evaluate your use of pathos, ethos, and logos.

Analyzing Classmates' Persuasive Speeches

There are several vantage points from which you can analyze and evaluate persuasive speeches you hear. One approach is by asking yourself the question "What impact did the speaker have on *my* attitudes, beliefs, or behavior patterns?" In other words, to what extent was *I* persuaded? A second approach is to look at the speech itself, objectively, as though you were not a true member of the audience, but present only to evaluate the presentation as a speech critic. Here you are asking the question "How effective *should* this speech be?" (whether or not it had the desired effect upon me).

By using both of these approaches in tandem, you can often come to a more valid judgment about a persuasive speech than by applying only one of the two approaches. Let's look at a few examples of how this two-pronged approach might be applied following one of your classmates' persuasive speeches.

Imagine Jennifer has just give a persuasive speech whose purpose statement read: "To convince my listeners that capital punishment should be abolished in the United States." Your teacher asks you to write a speech critique of Jennifer's speech. Here are some of the kinds of questions you might ask yourself (using both approaches together):

As a listener, what was my attitude towards capital punishment before hearing Jennifer's speech? (Suppose you were in favor of retaining capital punishment—an opposed position.) Your next question then might be: Can I estimate what percentage of the class members shared her view as contrasted with my view about capital punishment? In other words, do I think Jennifer analyzed the class as basically a positive audience, or primarily an opposed audience? If you think most class members were actually opposed, but Jennifer used an approach more suitable for a positive audience, then you would judge her speech more negatively, *not* simply because she failed to convince *you*, but because she chose a poor persuasive strategy for an opposed audience. But, you might argue, at the moment Jennifer finished her speech, I probably didn't have many clues *which* way the majority of her listeners leaned on capital punishment. At that point I was largely guessing about

● ASSESSMENT STRATEGY

Students could be encouraged to think of a portfolio product that would best reflect the quality and content of their persuasive speech. This could be an outline of the major points, or a tape of all or some of the speech.

● SKILL DEVELOPMENT

On the Job
Ask students to think about the opportunities they have in work situations to persuade management or their supervisors that they are good workers, deserving of more responsibility, more training, or a raise. Discuss strategies for persuading a supervisor to send an employee to a workshop to get additional technical training that could be useful in negotiating a raise.

What impact did the speaker have on *my* attitudes? How effective should this speech be?

who among the class were "for" and "against" capital punishment. So, how *do* you find out before sitting down to write your critique of Jennifer's speech? By listening to the tone of the questions during the question-and-answer period that follows the speech. If nearly everyone who speaks up seems in agreement with Jennifer's position, and she had used the strategy for a positive audience, then your critique can hardly accuse her of a weak speech. Although she failed to convince you, an opposed listener, she had both analyzed her audience appropriately as a positive one beforehand, and approached them correctly during her speech. On the other hand, if most of the discussion following Jennifer's speech seems to indicate a high level of disagreement with her position, than you might conclude her speech did have a flaw. It was flawed not simply because it failed to convince you (and most of the class too), but because she had misanalyzed her audience and had chosen the wrong persuasive approach.

Another example of how to critique a classmate's persuasive speech, both as an individual audience member *and* as a speech critic, may be seen in evaluating the speaker's organization. Suppose Brad gives a persuasive speech dealing with drug use in America's schools. As an individual listener, you find his speech strangely organized—you strain while listening to keep track of even the central idea, let alone Brad's four main points. Yet when classmates begin questioning Brad about the topic, you realize that you were apparently one of the few who found it disorganized. Others of your classmates seem to have clearly identified main points, and discuss them with clear recollection and understanding. Here too, as when analyzing Jennifer's speech, you need to ask yourself not only how did the speech impact *me*, but how was it perceived by the *whole* audience?

This same dual method of analyzing persuasive speeches may be applied to other areas of the speechmaking process. Language usage, speaker charisma, the perceived enthusiasm, dynamism, and sincerity of the performer, and the speaker's level of command of the ideas presented—all lend themselves to this type of thorough evaluation and critique.

ASSESS

● STUDENT PERFORMANCE COMPETENCIES

- Understands and uses various types of persuasive speeches
- Uses techniques to gain audience attention and build interest in a persuasive speech
- Reacts to audience feedback and executes smooth transitions in the delivery of a persuasive speech.
- Uses ethos effectively in the introduction and conclusion of a persuasive speech
- Demonstrates strong use of evidence and logical reasoning in a persuasive speech

● sca GUIDELINES

- Listens effectively to persuasive speeches
- Identifies persuasive techniques used in speeches
- Distinguishes between informative and persuasive speeches
- Asks questions to obtain information

▼ PORTFOLIO ASSESSMENT

Standard
- Glossary of Speech Terms
- Outline of Various Segments of a Persuasive Speech
- Analysis and Evaluation Checklist

Enrichment
- Tape of Persuasive Speech
- Examples, Statistics, and Quotes for Inclusion in Persuasive Speech
- Certificate of Recognition for Outstanding Performance
- Bar Graph Showing Class Preferences for Type of Evidence Used to Persuade

Challenge
- Award for Best Persuasive Speech
- Media or Publicity Campaign Participation to Promote School Contest
- Interview of Trial Attorney for Tips on Presentation of Evidence

---

CHAPTER 11 REVIEW

● SUMMARY

The primary goal of persuasive speaking is to influence the attitudes, beliefs, or behavior of the listeners. To do this, a speaker must combine the skills needed to give an informative speech with a number of additional skills that are special to persuasive speaking.

Three Sources of Persuasion Persuasive speaking involves making an audience want to think, believe, or do something they might not have done otherwise. The three major factors that are most likely to influence people are their own needs, their own thinking processes, and the character and personality of the speaker. Thus, a persuasive speaker must appeal to personal needs and logic, while stressing his or her own prestige.

Pathos: Analyzing the Needs of Your Listeners To appeal to listener needs, you must first discover what those needs are. Knowing whether you face a positive, neutral, disinterested, or opposed audience—or some combination of these four—can help you determine what strategy to use.

Ethos: Establishing Your Prestige The speaker's prestige (ethos) has long been accepted as a powerful, persuasive influence. In order to achieve this kind of prestige a speaker must be seen as competent and sincere and must clearly act with good will toward the audience. Methods of building speaker prestige include making frequent references to evidence, noting your experience in the topic area, being convinced of the truth of your viewpoint, using the common-ground technique, and showing sincere appreciation of your audience.

Logos: Being Logical Logical appeals consist of the proper use of evidence and reasoning. Evidence is the raw material upon which arguments are based. Reasoning is the process of putting evidence together into larger conclusions which in turn prove the main points of your speech. Certain forms of evidence may prove more effective with different kinds of audiences. Anecdotes, examples, and comparisons work well with positive audiences. A neutral audience is generally most impressed by statistics, facts, and testimony. Disinterested listeners also need facts and statistics. The opposed listener usually requires all forms of evidence at the speaker's command.

ASSESS

● **ASSESSMENT STRATEGIES**

Individual Assessment
- Participates in practice activities daily or weekly
- Demonstrates knowledge of content through questions, discussion, quizzes, and Chapter 11 test
- Displays improved skills in delivery of persuasive speeches

Group Assessment
- Sets and achieves goals
- Analyzes and evaluates student skills in introducing, delivering, and concluding a persuasive speech
- Delivers feedback to classmates in a constructive, positive, and specific manner
- Organizes topics for coordinated group research

Being Responsible The ability to persuade others is a powerful tool and carries with it a heavy responsibility. Decisions in a free society are regularly reached through persuasive speaking. Therefore, those who wish to persuade not only must know the best techniques but must practice them ethically. Any form of deceit in persuasion will be discovered and does harm to the democratic decision-making process.

VOCABULARY

Define each term in a complete sentence.

questions of fact
questions of value
questions of policy
persuasion
pathos
ethos
logos
positive audience
neutral audience
disinterested audience
opposed audience
competence
confidence
sincerity
good will
evidence
reasoning
prestige

CHECKLIST

Skills of Persuasive Speaking

1. Realize the primary goal of a persuasive speech.
2. Know when to use a particular type of persuasive speech.
3. Understand the three primary sources of persuasion.
4. Show your audience that you are competent and confident.
5. Be sincere and show good will toward your audience.
6. Use valid evidence and correct reasoning.
7. Use evidence that suits your audience.
8. Be responsible when speaking to persuade.

ASSESS

● **ANSWERS**

See the Answer Key for more complete answers.

REVIEW QUESTIONS
1. The primary goal of a persuasive speech is to influence the listeners' beliefs.
2. Pathos, ethos, and logos are the three primary factors that cause people to change attitudes, beliefs, or behavior patterns.
3. Audience analysis is especially important for the persuasive speaker because, in order to persuade people, the speaker must appeal to the needs and desires of the audience.
4. Positive audiences agree; neutral audiences do not have an opinion; disinterested audiences do not care; opposed audiences disagree.
5. Refer to the Answer Key for a detailed explanation.
6. The two components are evidence and reasoning.
7. Evidence supports the argument; logic/reasoning advances the argument.
8. See the Answer Key for a detailed answer.
9. Establish prestige by reflecting competence and being sincere.
10. The speaker should be informed, honest, and convinced.

DISCUSSION QUESTIONS
The following code is used to designate discussion questions and activities as suitable for students of varying ability levels:
   ▼ = below average to average
   ◆ = average to above average
   ■ = all students
1. ▼ Students should have an understanding of persuasion in a free society.
2. ◆ Refer to the section on responsibilities.
3. ◆ Discuss situations where persuasion goes wrong due to the prestige or charisma of the speaker.
4. ■ Have students come up with a checklist to evaluate persuasive speeches.
5. ▼ Students should refer to audience analysis materials.

376

CHAPTER 11 REVIEW

📝 REVIEW QUESTIONS

1. Name the primary goal of a persuasive speech.
2. Name the factors that cause people to adopt attitudes, beliefs, or behavior patterns.
3. State why audience analysis is especially important for a persuasive speaker.
4. Describe the chief characteristics of each kind of audience: positive, neutral, disinterested, opposed.
5. Name the approach a speaker should use to persuade each kind of audience.
6. Name and define the two components of logic.
7. Describe the differences between evidence and reasoning.
8. Describe the types of evidence that are especially suited to each type of audience.
9. Describe three ways in which you can establish your prestige as a persuasive speaker.
10. Name the characteristics of a responsible speaker.

❓ DISCUSSION QUESTIONS

1. Discuss the role that persuasion plays in a free society. In what sense is the right to persuade at the heart of the democratic process? What is the connection between persuasion and the right to speak out? Under what circumstances could persuasion be used for harmful purposes?
2. Discuss the responsibilities that accompany the right to persuade. Why is responsibility a key factor in evaluating a persuasive speaker? In what ways must the persuasive speaker be responsible? Why did the Roman orator Quintilian say that the persuasive speaker is "a *good* man skilled in speaking?"
3. Discuss the importance of evidence and reasoning in the persuasive process. How does the prestige of the speaker affect evidence and reasoning? Can the prestige of the speaker ever be a substitute for evidence and reasoning?
4. Discuss the role of the listener in the persuasive process. What should the listener concentrate upon? Does the listener have responsibilities as a target of persuasion? What might they be?
5. Discuss the challenges that the persuasive speaker faces when the audience is disinterested. What techniques can the speaker use to interest such an audience?

ASSESS

CRITICAL THINKING

1. Comprehension Can a speech be both informative and persuasive? How? Can it be persuasive without being informative? How? Can a persuasive speech be informative without being persuasive? How?

2. Analysis Think of the many commercials that you have seen on television. How do ethos, pathos, and logos operate in these commercials? At which of these sources of persuasion do many commercials seem to be aimed?

ACTIVITIES

In-Class

1. After a brief period of preparation, present a two-minute persuasive speech in which you advance one argument to support your position. Choose a topic that you have already thought about a great deal. Support your argument with at least three types of evidence. Your speech should also present sound reasoning and strong emotional appeal. Present your speech first to a group of from five to seven. Receive feedback and make any necessary adjustments. Then present your speech to the entire class.

2. Conduct a class discussion about credibility. Agree on a list of at least five public figures who possess credibility. Then determine what it is about the people that makes them credible. What characteristics do these people have that cause you to think well of them and to believe them? What role does appearance play in your feelings? What role does their status or position play? What role does past performance play? Try to assemble a list of characteristics that credible people possess.

3. As a class, decide upon a persuasive topic that everyone is knowledgeable about and can support. The class might agree, for example, that recreational programs should be offered in the schools on Friday evenings. Then divide the class into three groups. One group should prepare an introduction for the speech as if it were to be given to a friendly audience. The next group should prepare an introduction for a disinterested audience. Finally, the third group should prepare one for an opposed audience. Present the introductions to the class as a whole. Discuss the merits of each introduction that is presented.

CRITICAL THINKING
1. **Comprehension** Evidence consists of facts, statistics, and narratives.
2. **Analysis** Assign small groups the task of identifying a commercial for each of the persuasion categories.

ACTIVITIES
In-Class
1. Students could videotape their presentations, review the tape to make adjustments, and deliver the speech to the class.
2. Have students brainstorm a list of public figures.
3. Review the discussion of introductions in Chapter 10.

ASSESS

4. After the skit, have students evaluate the performance in small groups. Perceptions of benefits will vary.
5. Divide the class into three groups. Each group should work with relevant newspaper articles about their topic.

Out-of-Class
1. Follow the activity with a discussion to summarize observations.
2. Have small groups exchange accounts and discuss the means of persuasion that brought about the change of opinion.
3. List students' choices on the chalkboard. Identify the qualities the people have in common.

CHAPTER 11 REVIEW

4. Select two members of the class to improvise a skit in which one of them plays the customer and the other the sales representative in an automobile dealership. They should act out a scene in which the sales representative tries to persuade the customer to purchase the car. After the skit, discuss the message that it contains for persuasive speakers. Pay particular attention to how the salesperson tried to make the product appealing to the customer. As you analyze the exchange that took place, keep the following question in mind: "Whose benefit appeared to be most important during the exchange?"

5. As a class, identify at least three issues that are being discussed in your community at this time. For each issue, develop a question of fact, a question of value, and a question of policy that could give rise to persuasive speeches about the issue. Then compare the questions developed with the written arguments and speeches that have already been made about each issue.

Out-of-Class

1. Visit at least three stores to examine and request information about a product that has to be explained (a VCR, for example, or a home computer or camera). Listen closely to the sales presentation that each salesperson makes. What level of credibility did each salesperson possess? Did the salesperson use logical appeals, or emotional appeals, or both? Did the salesperson let it be known that the product would benefit you? How was this done? Write a report about your experience in your speech notebook.

2. Identify an attitude or conviction that you once had that is now changed dramatically. For example, you might have once thought that summer jobs were to be avoided, but you now feel that a useful summer job would be most desirable. What was your original attitude? What is your current attitude? Who caused you to change your thinking, or what facts and arguments altered your belief? Write an account of this change in attitude in your speech notebook. Be sure to identify its causes as fully as possible.

3. Certain contemporary speakers are widely acknowledged to possess the magical quality of "charisma." Identify one speaker who possesses that quality, in your opinion. Identify the things the person says and the way the person says them that suggest charisma. What kinds of actions and statements do you expect that person to make? Do you have high expectations about that individual? Briefly summarize your impressions and observations in your speech notebook.

4. In your speech notebook, keep a log of the times you personally use the process of persuasion during a single day. Log both one-to-one exchanges and group presentations. Do not overlook minor efforts to persuade parents, brothers and sisters, friends, and teachers. Also, keep a log of the times that other people attempt to persuade you during an ordinary day. Be prepared to bring both logs to class to compare with those of your classmates.

CHAPTER PROJECT

Prepare a five- to seven-minute persuasive speech that will be delivered in class extemporaneously. Choose a topic on an issue that you feel strongly about and that you believe will interest the student audience. Research your topic thoroughly, gathering as many types of support as possible. Keep your evidence on note cards and outline your speech, perhaps using Monroe's Motivated Sequence as an organizing principle. Write an introduction and a conclusion and memorize them. Rehearse the speech at least five times and deliver it in class.

ASSESS

4. Compare student logs.

CHAPTER PROJECT
- Give students time to research and prepare notecards. Students might work in pairs to prepare and clarify their thoughts. They could also rehearse with a partner and benefit from that partner's feedback before they deliver speeches to the class.

PREPARE

CHAPTER PLANNER

Day 1	Day 2	Day 3	Day 4	Day 5
Prepare	Prepare	Prepare	Prepare	Prepare
Teach	Teach	Teach	Teach	Teach
Assess	Assess	Assess	Assess	Assess
Sub. Teacher Tips *pp. 383, 387*	Sub. Teacher Tips *pp. 391, 397*	Sub. Teacher Tip *p. 399*	Sub. Teacher Tip *p. 400*	Sub. Teacher Tip *p. 402*

CHAPTER OVERVIEW

This chapter examines the following topics:
- Speeches Focused on Persons *p. 382*
- Speeches for Special Occasions *p. 393*
- Sales Presentations *p. 400*
- Impromptu Speaking *p. 404*

PORTFOLIO PRODUCTS

Individual Projects
- Glossary of Speech Terms
- Tape of Special Occasion Speech
- Visual Aid or Compilation of Quotes for Special Occasions
- Chapter 12 Portfolio Products

Group Projects
- Feedback Checklist for Speech Analysis and Evaluation
- Video Collection of the Best Special Occasion Speeches

sca GUIDELINES

- Uses words appropriate for special situations
- Expresses ideas clearly and concisely
- Expresses feelings to others
- Performs social rituals

CHAPTER

12

Other Kinds of Speaking

When you have completed this chapter you should be able to:

- Explain the general purposes of speeches for special situations.
- Define the specific purposes of several kinds of speeches focused on persons.
- Define the purposes of several kinds of speeches for special occasions.
- Describe the essential difference between impromptu speaking and other kinds of speeches covered in this chapter.
- Deliver an impromptu speech in class.

TEACH

● **LINKS TO PAST LEARNING**

Ask students to recall a special "toast" at a family dinner, or an invocation at graduation, or a special birthday, or get-well wish. Encourage them to identify special occasions that call for special words. Discuss what makes such occasions memorable.

● **MOTIVATION**

You might bring to class a collection of greeting cards for special occasions such as birthdays, sympathy, engagements, etc. Display these in class and invite students to add to the collection. Point out that the appeal of these cards is related to the succinct and meaningful use of words in an attractive format. Ask students to try expressing their own "greeting card" words for a special occasion.

● **ACTIVITY**

The text asks students to brainstorm special occasions that might be featured in this chapter. After students have compiled their predictions on the chalkboard, guide them through the chapter to identify the types of special occasion speeches covered here. Indicate a match between text and student list with a checkmark or some other symbol.

Other Kinds of Speaking   **381**

● **ACTIVITY**

Identifying "Other" Kinds of Speaking

As a class, begin this chapter by listing aloud how many "other" kinds of speaking there are in addition to speeches to inform and to persuade. Speaking to entertain is one type. Now, how many others can you suggest aloud as your teacher lists them on the board? This chapter will discuss eight more. Probably your class will be able to name at least that many, perhaps more. As you think about these "other" types of speeches, you will best discover them by reflecting on their *purposes*.

"Ladies and gentlemen, it is my great pleasure and distinct honor to introduce..." "How do I find the words to thank you adequately, my friends for so many years...?" "Today is a sad day for those of us who knew and loved her, but for Betty it is a day of glory and unending joy..." "So, as you leave these halls of learning and step into the wider world of danger and opportunity..." Each of these lines comes from speeches given every day—speeches of introduction, speeches of acceptance, commemorative speeches, commencement speeches. Though informing and persuading are the two primary purposes for which public speeches are given, you will be faced with many occasions on which you are expected to introduce a speaker, honor a fellow worker who is leaving, express a public "thank you" for a gift, deliver a keynote speech at school, or give an impromptu speech without advance warning. This chapter will give you some suggestions about these special kinds of speech situations under two categories—speeches focused on persons; and speeches for special occasions. Although you will find elements of informing and persuading in nearly all of these special situation speeches, that is not their primary purpose. Typically their chief purpose is to inspire, to challenge, to honor, to entertain. They are given to make us feel good about ourselves and those around us. Now, have you thought of additional types of special speeches not identified in the opening Activity?

Because the purpose of such speeches differs from that of informative and persuasive speeches, you must focus on different speaking skills when giving special situation speeches. All of the skills of researching, finding supporting materials, organizing your speech, building ethos, and the like, certainly remain important. However, in most speeches for special situations, you will want to put more focus on

TEACH

AMAZING FACTS!
Over 1.1 million Americans graduated from college in 1992. Think of the number of commencement speeches given!

● TEACHING

List the following types of speeches on the chalkboard: Introduction, Presentation, Acceptance, Commemorative, Testimonial, Eulogy, Keynote Address, Commencement, Dedication, Public Relations, Entertainment, and Sales Presentation. Ask students to predict which of these they will probably have to make as adults.

● TIME MANAGEMENT

Based on the adjoining list, you might choose to concentrate on only some of the types of speeches presented in this chapter. Or you may want to let students choose three or four examples and share with the entire class.

In honoring a particular individual, it is important to use vivid language and to make the speech occasion a celebration.

your speech skills of language usage, memory, and delivery. Vivid language is important to inspire the audience and to make the speech occasion a celebration. Well-chosen words help you to highlight the formality and seriousness of most special situation speeches. Memorizing brief, but key portions of these speeches also adds impact to the speaker's delivery. Reading even short portions from manuscript detracts greatly from the listeners' feelings about the speaker's sincerity.

● SPEECHES FOCUSED ON PERSONS

Has it ever occurred to you to ask yourself, as you sat through what seemed an unending funeral oration or a tedious commencement speech, "Why do we bother with such speeches at all"? They can seem endless and boring to those not directly involved with the person or people being honored, but when it is your grandfather being honored, or your own graduation ceremony, it usually means a great deal more. We honor those who have achieved great things because we value what they have accomplished. We could privately hand a terrific swimming coach who is leaving our school a watch or a plaque without saying a word. That would honor the coach to some extent, but a public speech accompanying the plaque makes it an occasion. The coach is more fittingly thanked with the gift *and* the speech, and those who hear the speech are again reminded of the importance of those qualities the coach showed—kindness, patience, leadership, and concern for her swimmers.

TEACH

> **SUBSTITUTE TEACHER TIP**
>
> Begin a Compare and Contrast chart on the chalkboard to help students identify, in terms of audience, purpose and appropriate techniques, the similarities and differences between informative and persuasive speeches, and those that are given for a variety of special occasions.

● **LEARNING STYLES**

Cooperative Learning
Each small group could target one of the types of speeches that focus on people. The text identifies speeches of introductions, speeches of presentation, speeches of acceptance, and commemorative or testimonial speeches. The group could find an example of the type of speech they selected and practice giving that same speech for other members of their group.

● **SKILL DEVELOPMENT**

Creative Thinking
Ask students to use the anecdote about Lord Balfour and think of alternative retorts to the overlong introduction.

Though there are several additional types of speeches that focus on persons, probably those given most frequently are speeches of introduction, speeches of presentation, speeches of acceptance, and commemorative speeches honoring persons. You should know the purpose of each of these kinds of speeches and some guidelines for delivering them.

Speeches of Introduction

Speeches of introduction are intended to say to the audience "You will benefit from listening to this speaker." They should also tell the speaker "This audience is anxious to hear your speech." The two major purposes facing someone who introduces a guest speaker, however, are:

- To build enthusiasm for the guest speaker by establishing his or her credibility.
- To build audience interest in the guest speaker's topic.

Too often those giving speeches of introduction make little or no preparation and simply read a few lines from a speaker's résumé to the audience. Such an approach does little to fulfill either of the basic purposes, and cheats both the guest speaker and the audience. Following a few guidelines when preparing a speech of introduction can make a tremendous difference.

First, keep speeches of introduction brief. They typically last from thirty seconds to three minutes. If the speaker is already well-known to the audience, thirty seconds is enough. An extreme example of a too-long introduction occurred during World War I. When Lord Balfour, Britain's Foreign Secretary, was to give a major speech at a rally in the United States, the speaker who introduced him gave a 45-minute oration on the causes of the war. When Lord Balfour finally got the opportunity to speak, he said: "I'm supposed to give my address in the brief time remaining. Here it is: 10 Carleton Gardens, London, England." Imagine the embarrassment of his introducer!

Second, be absolutely accurate. Start with your pronunciation of the speaker's name. Nothing can more surely destroy the impact of an otherwise superb speech of introduction than to mispronounce the main speaker's name. If you think you might forget it, have it in front of you in writing. If it is a difficult name to pronounce, be certain to learn the correct pronunciation beforehand, then practice it. Be certain that you know the basic facts about the speaker's background. Since speeches of introduction are brief, you should have no problems with

TEACH

> *In terms of graciousness, dignity, propriety, and the kind of modest eloquence that makes guests comfortable and the guests of honor glow, Nixon acting as host or master of ceremonies was the best in the business.*
>
> —William Safire

LEARNING STYLES

Cooperative Learning
Give small groups of students a copy of the school or local newspaper. Ask them to list all the special events reported in the paper that will probably have speakers. Have them identify the type of special-situation speech that might be used at each of those events.

SKILL DEVELOPMENT

15-Second Skill Opportunity
Based on the information provided in the index card activity suggested in Teaching, ask students to prepare an introduction for another student.

On the Job
Ask students to imagine that they are working at a restaurant supply company and their supervisor has just hired a new employee and asked them to take the new person around and introduce him or her to the rest of the people on the team. There are five people on this team. Have students prepare their introduction of their new co-worker.

TEACHING

You could give the students index cards and ask them to write down their names and three pieces of information they would like a speaker to use in an introductory speech. Give students time to write the information, exchange cards, and prepare introductory remarks based on the information provided.

384

A speech of introduction should be brief, accurate, suited to the appropriate level of formality, and supportive of the speaker. It should also set the stage and generate a sense of expectation among the audience.

memory. However, if you think there is any chance you may forget an important fact, or reverse the order of some facts, bring a brief outline on a note card with you to the podium.

Next, suit your level of formality to the occasion. Obviously, you would be more formal and restrained were you selected to introduce one of your teachers as the main speaker for a PTA meeting, than you would when introducing him or her to lead a roast for a departing school principal. Your language would undoubtedly be more formal and serious in the first case, as would the whole tone of your introduction. For the roast, a more informal approach would be appropriate.

Make the speaker you are introducing feel good. Not only are you trying to generate enthusiasm in the audience, you also want your introduction to serve as a springboard from which the speaker can launch an inspiring speech. Be factual about his or her accomplishments and show how the speaker's background and experience have prepared him or her to speak with authority on this topic. Be wary of overdoing it. Don't embarrass the speaker with excessive praise. Be especially careful not to praise his or her speaking skills. Telling the audience that they are about to hear one of the greatest speakers of the last decade starts the poor speaker off with little or no chance of succeeding. Finally, don't reveal personal incidents of the speaker's life that could be embarrassing. Sometimes this is done in an attempt to get a laugh: "Why, I've known Seth Mobley since he was the dumbest kid in the fifth grade. How he ever managed to become a lawyer is still a mystery to me!" The audience may laugh, but Seth won't come to the podium feeling good about himself and his speech.

The introducer should also show the listeners the relationship among the speaker's background, the chosen topic, and the audience's interests. This is the basic job description of an introducer. An introduction that simply lists the accomplishments of the speaker and stops, fails to fulfill its basic purpose. What each audience member wants to know from an introducer is "Why will this speaker, speaking on this topic, b

TEACH

● **ENRICHMENT**

Ask students to imagine that they must introduce Julie Harris (or another award-winning performer) the night she received her last Tony. They should obtain biographical information about her and research what the critics wrote of her performances. Suggest that they incorporate some of this information into their introduction.

● **ASSESSMENT STRATEGY**

After students have given their speeches of introduction, ask the class to select the five "best" introductions and compile these introductions on tape or in print. Certificates of Recognition could be awarded to the students making the best introductions.

Speeches Focused on Persons **385**

interesting to me?" A competent introducer shows why the speaker's background qualifies him or her to speak on this particular topic, and why it will prove interesting to this particular audience. Too often, an introducer fails to discover in advance what topic the speaker plans to talk about. This makes it difficult to tie the speaker's topic and the audience's interests together. The wise introducer will always check with the main speaker several days before the speech occasion to learn not only what the topic will be, but what approach the speaker plans to take.

Finally, work to build a feeling of expectation and drama among the members of the audience. Speeches of introduction are similar to an appetizer before a meal. Both tease the taste buds in anticipation of the main course to come. Probably the most common technique for doing this in speeches of introduction is that of saving the name of the main speaker until the end of the introduction. This works best, of course, when the speaker is not already well-known to most members of the audience. At any rate, introducers use this strategy to make the speaker's name the high point of the introduction. In those cases in which most of the audience already knows the speaker, it is best to concentrate on discovering little-known facts about the speaker's background and to focus on the topic. It is also effective to mention lesser-known facts about the speaker's background that relate to his or her knowledge and expertise on the topic.

Generating a sense of expectation and drama requires a well-rehearsed speech of introduction. Many introducers neglect to rehearse a single time because they are "just" the introducer. The brevity of speeches of introduction seems to lull many people into a false sense of preparedness. Though there is little chance of forgetting, remember that the effectiveness of such speeches relies on language usage, memory, and delivery factors. Each of these requires thorough rehearsal.

● **ACTIVITY**

Speeches of Introduction

Plan and deliver a speech of introduction for one of the following occasions:

1. a sports superstar speaking at a high-school assembly
2. a representative from a major university addressing your class about planning for college
3. a recruitment officer speaking at a career day about opportunities in the military
4. a magician performing at an elementary-school assembly
5. a police-department safety officer speaking to a driver-education class

---

● **LEARNING STYLES**

Audio Learning
Students could plan to tape record their speeches of introduction. Then ask them to replay the tape and analyze and evaluate these introductions. Encourage them to identify the strong points of their own introductions. List what they did well. Then have them identify areas for improvement. Based on their own analysis of performance, encourage students to repeat the introduction and include the second introduction as a portfolio product.

Multicultural Learning
Since the U.S. has so many cultures represented in its population, the correct pronunciation of names is sometimes difficult. You could use your local phone book and ask students to identify various ethnic names. Write these names on the chalkboard and give students practice in saying each name correctly.

● **ACTIVITY**

Encourage students to select a subject for a speech of introduction from the list provided. Before they prepare their remarks, students should review the guidelines presented in this section.

385

TEACH

AMAZING FACTS!

Walt Disney won more Oscars, awards of the Academy of Motion Picture Arts and Sciences, than any other person. He received 20 statuettes and 12 other plaques and certificates.

● **TEACHING**

Use the text to help students identify the typical purpose, audience, length, and organization of a speech of presentation. Emphasize the three-point pattern of organization.

● **SKILL DEVELOPMENT**

Presentations
Students can silently read the speech of presentation given by Gregory Peck. Ask for volunteers to read the speech aloud for the class. Appoint a student to time the length of the speech. Discuss its organization in terms of the points identified in the text.

CHAPTER 12 Other Kinds of Speaking

Speeches of Presentation

Frequently, when people receive gifts or awards, there is need for a **speech of presentation.** Typical examples include awards ceremonies at the end of a school year; the Tony, Emmy, and Oscar awards; and those countless occasions when gifts are presented to friends who are moving, retiring, or completing a term of office. The primary purpose of a speech of presentation is, of course, to honor the recipient. Secondary purposes (when necessary) include explaining the intent for which an award is being given and praising the losers in cases where there has been competition for an award.

Speeches of presentation are short, usually lasting no more than four or five minutes. In delivering very brief speeches, for example, when presenting a gift, the presenter typically asks the recipient to stand near the podium during the presentation speech. Then the award is presented. During longer speeches of presentation, ranging up to four or five minutes, the recipient remains seated until the speech is completed. As in the case of speeches of introduction, the presenter should take care not to overpraise and risk embarrassing the recipient. It is usually best to restrict your remarks primarily to the actions or qualities of the recipient for which the award is being given.

An often-used pattern of organization for a speech of presentation consists of three parts. The speaker 1) describes the award and reads any engraved message with which the audience is not familiar; 2) indicates the values the award attempts to honor; and 3) shows how the actions and character of the recipient reflect those values. The order of the three parts may vary. Often a presenter will intertwine a description of the values with a recounting of the actions and character of the recipient. The description of the award may come first or last. No matter what pattern of organization is used, the chief purpose of a speech of presentation is to honor the recipient. Notice how effectively actor Gregory Peck honored entertainer Danny Kaye for his service to others:

> It's a long trip from Brooklyn to Buckingham Palace, and it's a far piece from Beverly Hills to an obscure village in Bangladesh. Danny Kaye has made both journeys, sustained by his remarkable gifts, his grace, and his intelligence. He has been a star of the first magnitude since his remarkable talent exploded on the Broadway stage in *Lady in the Dark* in 1941, and one who has had a high sense of priority: His wife, Sylvia, and daughter, Dena, have always come first in his life—and then, in no special order, his work, the world's children, and great music.
>
> For UNICEF (United Nations International Children's Emergency Fund), he continues to travel the world, bringing joy and hope to children on all the continents, and initiating programs to save them

TEACH

● **ENRICHMENT**

Ask students to watch or review Academy Award presentations. Students should evaluate presenters and recipients and nominate the best in each category. Students should identify the criteria they use to select the best presenter and the best recipient.

SUBSTITUTE TEACHER TIP

Ask students to imagine that they get to select the recipients of awards given at the school-wide assembly at the end of the year. Students can suggest the five best award categories and nominate students to receive those awards using the organization of the speech of presentation.

● **SKILL DEVELOPMENT**

15-Second Skill Opportunity
Ask students to think of all the awards that are presented and identify an award they would most like to receive as an adult. Ask volunteers to complete the sentence, "The award I would be most honored to receive is…."

Speeches Focused on Persons 387

from hunger and give them a better chance in life. He has been doing this for years, with no pay and without fanfare. No trumpets. No headlines. His reward, the laughter of children.

As forbearing and skillful as he is with children, so he is with symphony orchestras, groups of seventy or eighty highly disciplined artists. He cannot read music, yet he has conducted major orchestras all over the world with musicianship that is sensitive, completely serious, and, at times, likely to veer off alarmingly into the hilarious. Danny's irrepressible *joie de vivre* makes his concerts joyous occasions for musicians and audiences alike. Bach and Mozart have no better friend. Nor have the orchestras and their pension funds. Nor have we.

And thus, for his prodigious labors for the children of the world, for the wondrous people who make music, the Board of Governors proudly gives the Jean Hersholt Humanitarian Award to a "Citizen of the World" who does honor to our profession—Mr. Danny Kaye.

Speeches of Acceptance

If you have watched such ceremonies as the Academy Awards, the Emmys, or the Tonys on television, you know that acceptance speeches can take many forms and can vary in length from a simple "thank you" to a lengthy monologue. **Speeches of acceptance,** in their ideal form, however, have the simple purpose of thanking both those bestowing the award and those who helped the recipient gain it. If you have any doubt whether or not you are expected to give a speech when accepting an award, ask the presenter for advice. Most audiences respond favorably to a speech of acceptance, as long as it is *brief*. Unless it is clear that the award is expected to serve as the introduction for a major

Remember that an acceptance speech should be brief and that it is for the benefit of the audience.

387

TEACH

AMAZING FACTS!

The Nobel prizes are awarded under the terms of the will of a Swedish chemist and engineer, Alfred Nobel, who died in 1896. Awards are given every year in the fields of physics, chemistry, medicine, literature, and world peace.

● LEARNING STYLES

Cooperative Learning

Ask small groups to read together the acceptance speech of Danny Kaye presented in the text. The group could develop an outline of the major points made in the speech. Then have them identify the elements of the speech that they liked the most. Compare group preferences with the entire class. Ask students to identify the elements of humor in the speech.

● SKILL DEVELOPMENT

Acceptance Speeches

Ask a representative of each of the cooperative learning groups to prepare a reading of Danny Kaye's speech. Compare presentations in terms of voice, gesture, and style.

● CURRICULAR CONNECTIONS

Math/Science

Some students might research who the recipients of the Nobel prizes in physics, chemistry, and medicine have been in their lifetime. They could prepare a presentation speech for one of the awards.

---

388   CHAPTER 12 Other Kinds of Speaking

speech, keep acceptance speeches to no more than two or three minutes. Also bear in mind that an acceptance speech is given for the audience's benefit. It is an acknowledgment that the award has been accepted and appreciated.

Sometimes you will be taken by surprise by the presentation of an award. When that happens, you have no choice but to speak impromptu (see "Impromptu Speaking," on page 404). Whenever you think there is a reasonable chance that you might receive a gift or award, prepare a brief speech of acceptance in advance. Be certain to thank everyone involved in both presenting and helping you attain the award. You may also modestly mention your commitment, and that of others, to the values and actions for which the award is given, but place the focus on the values and actions, not on yourself. The speech that follows is Danny Kaye's acceptance speech given after the presentation speech, quoted on pages 386–387, by Gregory Peck. Notice that Mr. Kaye's speech is brief, humble, and gracious.

> I am terribly excited to be given this great honor. And I'm so delighted that I find myself, as we say, trembling. If I were any more delighted, I think I'd be in an institution.
>
> However, I feel a little bit guilty about all the praise that Greg lavished on me. It was really no hardship at all. Really. I am crazy about children. I am crazy about conducting, and I am crazy about flying.
>
> I am definitely not crazy about disease or famine or neglect. But, then, neither are any of you. And we, all of us in our profession, share a long and wonderful tradition of doing something about it—of giving of our time and our talent wherever and whenever needed—without prejudice, without stint. That's one of the reasons that I am so very proud of our profession and so proud to be one of you.
>
> I share this award with you, with all of you, and I give thanks to the memory of Dag Hammarskjold and Maurice Pate, with whom I started to work for UNICEF about twenty-eight years ago. And to Gene Ormandy, who put a baton in my hand, my little nervous hand, and made me an offer I couldn't refuse—to stand in front of a symphony orchestra and conduct. Wow! That's the greatest feeling of neurotic power in the world. You ought to try it!
>
> My special thanks to the Board of Governors. I love this and I love you. Thank you.

Commemorative Speeches

Commemorative speeches remain among the most inspiring and best remembered in our country's history. Abraham Lincoln's Gettysburg Address, Edward Kennedy's speech at his brother Robert's funeral, an

TEACH

● **ENRICHMENT**

If you can secure a copy of the Kennedy Memorial Album, bring it to class and share it with students. If you are unable to locate a copy, you could convert this into a research project and ask students to see if they can locate a copy. Award a Certificate of Accomplishment to the student(s) who locate the record.

AMAZING FACTS!

The record, *John Fitzgerald Kennedy — A Memorial Album*, was recorded on the day of his assassination, November 22, 1963, and sold 4 million copies at 99 cents in six days!

● **LEARNING STYLES**

Cooperative Learning
Small teams of students could work together to plan a "roast" of a highly respected student, coach, or teacher. Ask students to review the guidelines presented in the text about the purpose, length, and characteristics of testimonial speeches. Each member of the group should prepare a testimonial suitable for the roast and practice delivering those remarks to the small group.

Ronald Reagan's speech following the Challenger disaster served to implant the memory of brave people in our minds and to inspire us to reach for the ideals for which they stood. Though commemorative speeches sometimes recall events rather than persons, here we will look at those that are focused exclusively on persons—testimonial speeches and eulogies.

Testimonial speeches are given to honor living persons. Their purpose is to praise someone or to celebrate an occasion focused around persons. You may hear testimonial speeches given in the form of toasts at weddings and retirement dinners, as speeches of farewell and appreciation when a boss or co-worker is moving away, or as roasts for those successful and well-liked in their careers. They may range in length from a toast of a few seconds to a roast with a dozen or more speakers taking five to ten minutes each to honor an individual with tongue-in-cheek humor. Most often they are given in connection with a dinner, or at least when food is being served—for example, at a wedding reception.

The testimonial speaker deals in feelings, not facts. He or she tries to stir emotions, not thoughts. Though the speaker may narrate some scenes from the life of the person being honored, the purpose is to generate respect, admiration, appreciation, and best wishes for the future. The speaker will evoke joy, laughter, celebration, and sentiment from the audience while honoring the special person. Testimonial speakers depend heavily on the creative use of language. If an informative speaker can be compared to an essayist, the testimonial speaker is like a poet. A good testimonial speaker chooses language rich in connotation and steeped in emotion to create a warm and positive mood fitting the occasion.

When humor is used, as is the case at roasts, its purpose should always be to honor the individual for whom the roast is given. Occasionally speakers at roasts, keen on getting laughs from the audience, will relate a funny incident that is truly embarrassing. Such an approach does not honor the person, and usually harms the speaker's image in the audience's eyes, even though the listeners will laugh at the joke. If you are asked to speak at a roast, pick humor that you know will genuinely amuse the roastee as well as the audience. If you have any doubt, either ask the roastee privately beforehand, or skip that particular story.

Eulogies are commemorative speeches, given usually to honor those who have died. Though they are most often delivered at a funeral service, they may be given weeks, months, or even years later. As with testimonial speeches, their purpose is to honor and praise an individual. An equally important purpose of eulogies is to comfort and uplift the listeners who feel the loss of a loved one or a great person. The eulogist has a difficult task since emotions of sorrow and loss are usually high in

TEACH

> **"A man's dying is more the survivors' affair than his own."**
>
> —Thomas Mann

● LINKS TO PAST LEARNING

Ask students how many of them have attended a wake or funeral where a eulogy was given. Encourage them to share their reactions to the eulogy and help them define the characteristics of a well-delivered eulogy.

● SKILL DEVELOPMENT

15-Second Skill Opportunity

Ask students to read to themselves the remarks that Adlai Stevenson made at a memorial service for Winston Churchill. Have students identify the elements mentioned in the text that Stevenson employed in his remarks. Ask volunteers to read the excerpt as if they were delivering the eulogy. Discuss how students use voice, tone, gestures, and timing differently when giving a eulogy.

CHAPTER 12 Other Kinds of Speaking

the audience. The eulogist must respect those feelings while attempting to inspire those present by recounting the virtues of the deceased.

The eulogist typically picks out several of the most noble and praiseworthy attributes of the deceased and extols them with examples from the person's life. The eulogist may also call upon the listeners to remember and imitate those virtues. However, the essence of a eulogy is to honor the person who has died. As with testimonial speeches honoring the living, the most important tool for the eulogist is lofty language. Great care must be taken to select words and phrases that are noble, dignified, and moving. Notice how Adlai Stevenson, one of this country's most eloquent speakers, used such language at a memorial service for Sir Winston Churchill.

> Today we meet in sadness to mourn one of the world's greatest citizens. Sir Winston Churchill is dead. The voice that led nations, raised armies, inspired victories and blew fresh courage into the hearts of men is silenced. We shall hear no longer the remembered eloquence and wit, the old courage and defiance, the robust serenity of indomitable faith. Our world is thus poorer, our political dialogue is diminished and the sources of public inspiration run more thinly for all of us. There is a lonesome place against the sky.

Because the eulogy depends so much on eloquent language, it is often written in advance, then delivered from manuscript or memory. Experienced speakers will occasionally use a combination of read, memorized, and extemporaneous delivery with excellent effect. The following example of a eulogy was given by a student in a public speaking class, honoring her grandfather. It exemplifies the best features of a dignified and moving eulogy:

My Grandfather

Kim Lacina

Every day people are born and people die. Human beings come into this world and leave it—most without their names being immortalized in any history books. Millions of people have lived and worked and loved and died without making any great claims to fame or fortune.

But they aren't forgotten—not by their friends, not by their families. And some of these people, some very special people, are not forgotten even by those who hardly knew them. My grandfather was one of these very special people.

What made him so special? Why is he remembered not only by friends and family but even by casual acquaintances? Very simply,

TEACH

● **TEACHING**

You might want to read aloud or have students read silently the eulogy that Kim Lacina gave in honor of her grandfather. Discuss the appeal of the words despite the fact that you did not know the person who died.

▽ **PORTFOLIO PRODUCTS**

Ask students to prepare a reading of Kim Lacina's eulogy and record it or an original one that they prepare. Tape the eulogy and invite students to include it as a portfolio assessment.

SUBSTITUTE TEACHER TIP

You might bring an obituary column to class and read or share an announcement with the class. Based on the information provided, ask students to write two sentences that would eulogize the person who died.

> *"To die will be an awfully big adventure."*
> —James M. Barrie

● **SKILL DEVELOPMENT**

Special Occasions
Have students think of a relative, friend, or pet that died. Ask them to write a brief eulogy to honor that memory.

Speeches Focused on Persons 391

because he was the essence of love. More than that, he was the essence of what I think of as "active" love. Just as his heart was not empty, his words were not empty.

He didn't just speak of compassion. During the Great Depression he took homeless people off the street into his home when they needed a place to sleep. He gave them food when they needed something to eat. And though he wasn't a rich man by any means, he gave them money when they had none. Those people off the street will remember the man who had enough love in his heart to share with them all that he had.

He didn't just speak of tolerance. During the 1960s, when his peers were condemning those "long-haired hippies," I can remember riding in the car with my grandfather, picking up dozens and dozens of those "long-haired hippies" who were hitchhiking, and going miles out of our way to give them a ride somewhere. Those men and women will remember the man who had enough love in his heart to bridge the gap between his world and theirs and to practice the spirit of brotherhood.

And he didn't just speak of courage. He proved his courage time and time again. He proved it to a little girl who was trapped in the basement of a burning building. He pulled her out of the flames and gave her back her life. And that little girl, now a grown woman, will remember the man who had enough love in his heart to risk his life for a person he didn't even know.

He also proved his courage, in a more personal way, to his family. In 1966 he was told he had leukemia and only a year to live. He immediately started chemotherapy treatment, and I don't know which is worse—the effects of the disease or the effects of those treatments. In the ensuing year we saw his hair fall out, we saw his skin turn a pasty shade of gray, and we saw him lose so much weight that he seemed to shrivel up into half the size he had been. We didn't want to see him go out that way.

And we didn't. He fought that disease with all his strength and all his courage. And despite the pain he endured, he never complained. I think about him when I catch myself complaining about my "tons of homework" or a "terrible headache," and suddenly that homework or that headache doesn't seem so terrible after all.

He lived through that first year, and he lived through eight more. And that disease never stopped him from working, and it never stopped him from caring. All through those years of suffering, he continued to show compassion and tolerance and courage.

He died in 1975. And though he left this world without ever making the pages of a history book, he still left the world a great deal. He left to the people who knew him a spirit to exemplify life—a spirit of unconditional, selfless, and truly inspiring love.

APPLY

> ❝ *I went to two high school all-star games recently where the kids had no affiliation or stake in the game. It was a chance for them to show how good they are.... Instead, the kids were like thugs. They needed to show their virility. I see that behavior in the colleges and pros. The gestures and put-downs of the opposition. It's come to symbolize excellence. I try to tell my kids that game is for fun, not humiliation.* ❞
>
> —Vic Gatto

● SKILL DEVELOPMENT

15-Second Skill Opportunity

Students who have played for the coach invited to speak to the class might prepare a testimonial remark. These should be rehearsed before the coach's appearance in class. The class might select some class or team representative to conclude the visit with a testimonial.

● ENRICHMENT

Invite one of the school coaches to class and have students prepare interview questions about the skills used to motivate the team. Perhaps the coach would consent to have the remarks taped.

● EXTENSION

Members of the class could interview team players and ask them what sayings or remarks they best remember a coach giving them or the team. Students might ask to tape these remarks so that they could compile and publish a list of favorite sayings.

CAREER CLOSE-UP

Coach

Coaches of sports teams at any level direct participants through the entire competitive experience. They must be experienced players of the sport they are coaching and must be familiar with its strategies and regulations. Above all, coaches need excellent communications skills, since they deal not only with the players on their teams, but with the public as well.

Often coaches must deliver speeches of acceptance or presentation. To prepare for these speeches, coaches list the topics they plan to discuss on a note card. When they deliver their speech, the note card helps to focus their thoughts. To convey their enthusiasm more powerfully, coaches memorize their introductory and concluding remarks to maintain direct eye contact with the audience. As part of their final preparation, they rehearse their speech using the note card as their only aid.

During speeches of presentation, coaches honor individual players and those inner qualities that contributed to the success of the individual and the team. By recognizing team members, coaches reinforce the characteristics and values they have been stressing all season.

Coaches who are successful public speakers add an invaluable dimension to their coaching abilities. By honoring athletes, coaches inspire others to emulate their admirable qualities. When rousing the team before a competition, the coach's choice of words and spirited delivery motivate players to greater achievement. In these ways, a coach's speaking ability enables him or her to help young athletes realize their potential.

Through superior communications skills, coaches are able to inspire players to superior achievement.

TEACH

● **TEACHING**

Have students preview the material presented in this section by listing the boldface headings on the chalkboard. The speeches for special occasions include: Keynote, Commencement, Dedication, Public Relations, and Entertainment.

● **ACTIVITY**

Ask students to refer to the models of commemorative speeches in the text, the Appendix, and the cassette tape. Have students rehearse their commemorative speeches with a partner. When both think they are ready, deliver the commemorative speech for the entire class.

● **SKILL DEVELOPMENT**

Creative Thinking
Have students think about the person they would like to make a keynote address for the annual convention of Students of America. Students could offer nominations with remarks prepared according to the guidelines presented here for speeches of introduction. When all the nominations are in, ask students to "vote."

On the Job
Explain that some corporations hold annual meetings and telebroadcast the keynote address of the chairperson of the Board of Directors. Have students get a copy of a stockholders annual or quarterly report. Most of these contain a letter or a copy of the address of the CEO or chairperson. Students can deliver these remarks and videotape their performances.

Speeches for Special Occasions 393

● **ACTIVITY**

Commemorative Speeches
Write and deliver a commemorative speech—either a testimonial or a eulogy. Your primary purpose will be to inspire, to challenge, or to honor. You may select as your subject a historical figure, a famous person, or someone known to you personally. Plan your speech to be from three to five minutes long. Focus on making your language and delivery appropriate to the purpose and person you have chosen.

● SPEECHES FOR SPECIAL OCCASIONS

Various kinds of public occasions are highlighted by speeches. Graduation ceremonies, large meetings and conventions, dedication ceremonies, and some public lectures employ a speech as a focal point of the event. Generally, the purpose of such speeches is to commemorate the meeting or ceremony that is taking place. We will look briefly at five kinds of special occasion speeches: keynote speeches, commencement speeches, dedication speeches, public relations speeches, and speeches to entertain. Finally, we will consider a special way of delivering speeches—impromptu speaking.

Keynote Speeches

Meetings or conventions of many large organizations begin with a **keynote speech.** Most Americans are familiar with the keynote addresses delivered near the opening of the Democratic and Republican conventions every four years. In addition to these political speeches, keynote addresses occur regularly at business and professional conventions ranging from those of the American Medical Association to those of the National Association of Teachers of English. Keynote speeches serve several purposes. First, they rally the members of the organization around its central goals and purposes. Since such large organizations typically meet only once a year, the keynote address opens each new convention by renewing the enthusiasm and

TEACH

AMAZING FACTS!
Almost 2.5 million high school students graduated in 1993. The dropout rate among high-school-aged students is almost 12%.

● **ENRICHMENT**

Students might get a list of commencement speakers who addressed your high school graduates for the past ten years. If possible, get a copy of their commencement remarks. Students could use these remarks and prepare commencement speeches based on these comments.

● **LEARNING STYLES**

Cooperative Learning
Ask small groups of students to imagine the best possible commencement address. They should identify the ideal length of time, the ideal speaker, and the ideal topic. Compare group requisites, especially the length of time.

● **SKILL DEVELOPMENT**

Active Listening
Ask a volunteer to read Barbara Bush's Commencement Address from the Appendix, page 577. Have students take notes as they listen to the speech. After the speech is read, ask students to identify the most memorable things said with a checkmark on their notes. Encourage students to share their impressions.

394

---

394   CHAPTER 12 Other Kinds of Speaking

commitment of the membership to its values and purposes. Second, provides a common theme or focus for the particular meeting tha year. The speaker will sometimes need to stress the specific goals an issues facing the organization in the upcoming year. On other occa sions the need may be to sound a call for unity if the organization threatening to splinter apart. Still other circumstances may deman that the keynote address focus on a crisis facing the organization an stress the importance of this year's convention in meeting it. Finall since a keynote speech usually provides the central focus for a cor vention, it also commemorates it. Such speeches later come to stan for the themes or highlights of past conventions.

The keynote speaker is usually either a well-respected member the organization, or some well-known person from the outside wh has great credibility with the members. The keynote speaker's job that of a cheerleader, molding the members into an enthusiastic an involved group.

Commencement Speeches

Commencement speakers often have a difficult time keeping the atter tion of their listeners. Graduation ceremonies are frequently held ou doors in late spring or in a sweltering gymnasium packed wit graduates, teachers, families, and friends. Nearly everyone in attendanc wants to be there, but not for long!

Commencement speeches both celebrate an occasion and hono the graduates. Their purposes are to applaud the accomplishments the students while in school, recognize the contributions of those wh helped them, and tell the graduates of the challenges ahead. Since th word "commencement" means a beginning, most commencemer speakers spend the bulk of their time inspiring the graduates to me their new challenges and responsibilities. Typically a commencemer speaker gives a great deal of advice about the future. However, to much stress on advice and the future can quickly wear the audience patience thin. A graduation ceremony is also a celebration and a time honor the graduates. When that part gets lost amid an undergrowth endless advice, especially in a hot and crowded gym, the speaker ca quickly lose the attention of the audience.

For several years, you are more likely to sit in the listener's chair commencement speeches than you are to stand behind the podiun However, you may find some real benefit from giving a commence ment speech in class. Try the following Activity.

TEACH

▼ PORTFOLIO PRODUCTS

Students might tape their commencement addresses and include them as a portfolio product for assessment.

> *"Education is to get where you start to learn."*
> —George Aiken

● ACTIVITY

This activity could be approached in three sections. Let students focus on preparing their notes or on writing an introduction to their commencement address and practice its delivery. Then proceed to the body, then to the conclusion.

● SKILL DEVELOPMENT

15-Second Skill Opportunity
As a warm-up to the commencement activity, you might ask students to remember what they were like when they were in kindergarten. Invite volunteers to share a favorite or memorable experience from those early school years.

Speeches for Special Occasions   **395**

● ACTIVITY

Giving a Commencement Speech

Imagine that you have been invited to give the commencement speech at the graduation of the elementary school that you attended. Prepare notes for a three- to five-minute speech in which you briefly congratulate the graduates and those who assisted them. Spend some of your time telling the students how to get the most out of the years ahead of them. Use your own experiences in junior and senior high school to provide helpful and useful anecdotes for the graduates. Be prepared to give your speech in class and to compare your advice with that given by your classmates.

Dedication Speeches

Several dictionary definitions of the word "dedicate" read: "To set apart for any special use, duty, or purpose; To commit (oneself) to a certain course of action or thought; To open or unveil (a bridge, statue, etc.) to the public." Thus cities dedicate new city halls, schools, libraries, and parks. Citizens dedicate the opening of the annual United Way fund drive. Clubs dedicate their founding.

The dedication speaker focuses the attention of the audience on the goals and values that a new endeavor represents.

395

TEACH

> ❝We cannot dedicate....❞
> —Abraham Lincoln

● **RETEACHING**

Use the last sentence in this section to emphasize the three key elements for the success of most special occasion speeches: use of clear and lofty language, memorization of key passages, and direct and dynamic delivery. You could write the key words on the chalkboard: Language, Memory, Delivery. Ask students to develop a report card using those three "subjects" for evaluation purposes as students give their speeches.

● **CURRICULAR CONNECTIONS**

Language Arts

Ask students to use dictionaries or a thesaurus for explanations of the term "dedication." They could share the etymology of the word with the class and provide examples of the proper use of the term.

● **SKILL DEVELOPMENT**

15-Second Skill Opportunity

Ask students to imagine that they are going to give a brief dedication speech to place their locker in the school hall of fame. Give them time to prepare their thoughts and ask volunteers to present their dedications.

---

396 CHAPTER 12 Other Kinds of Speaking

Public speeches make up the major part of dedication ceremonies. They serve to highlight the meaning of a new creation that is being dedicated, or a new endeavor that is being started. The dedication speaker focuses the listeners' attention on the goals and values that the new creation (building, bridge, piece of artwork) represents, or that the new endeavor (fund drive, new organization, Olympic Games) stands for. The length of **dedication speeches** may vary, depending mainly on the scope of the new creation or endeavor and on the expectations of the audience. Sometimes only one speaker will address those gathered for the ceremony; at other times there will be a series of briefer speeches.

When dedicating a new school gymnasium, for example, a speaker might briefly outline the history of the building project and mention the names of key school board members and administrators whose vision and planning resulted in the completed structure in which the audience is now seated. The speaker's main thrust, however, would be to stress what the new gym will mean to the school in the future. The speaker would note the importance of physical education in a school curriculum, then paint a picture of the stampede of eager students who can now begin to enjoy the new gym for generations. The speaker might recall the importance of "a sound mind in a sound body," then depict the pure fun that will now begin to come from basketball games, tennis, pep rallies, and dances. As with other speeches for special occasions, the speaker's success will depend largely on clear and lofty language, memorization of key passages, and a direct and dynamic delivery.

Public Relations Speeches

Do you remember any television commercials of several years ago? Certain restaurant chains were building their images as bigger and better than the competition. Today, business and industry spend a great amount of time and money on image building. They do it not only through television, but also by regularly sending their executives out on the lecture circuit. Carl Terzian, a consultant in executive speech training has noted that

> A growing number of executives not only are enthusiastically acknowledging lecture requests, but are actually seeking them out. Influencing others is very rewarding. Some employ the platform to champion the cause of industry; to create a healthier business climate; to generate sales; to proclaim ambitious corporate goals; to promote an image…

PORTFOLIO PRODUCTS

Students could write or tape a public relations statement for a targeted company and include it in their assessment portfolio.

SUBSTITUTE TEACHER TIP

Bring a newspaper to class and ask students to look for examples of companies promoting their product or service through public relations statements. Invite students to share "damage control" stories about companies that faced a major disaster and issued public relations statements to clarify issues.

SKILL DEVELOPMENT

On the Job
Suggest that students identify a company that has taken a beating in the stock market and ask them to imagine they worked in the public relations department of that company. Have them develop a public relations statement that would be suitable for a press release.

The public relations speech has a strong persuasive purpose: to promote an overall positive image of an organization.

In addition to corporations' increasing use of **public relations speeches,** or speeches that promote their companies, government service and educational institutions are also using this approach to maintain contact with the public and to promote a positive image.

Unlike the other special occasion speeches we have looked at, the public relations speech has a strong persuasive purpose. However, that purpose is not to sell a particular product or a specific service. Rather it is to promote an overall positive image of the organization. Such speeches often include a broad informative purpose as well, since promoting a positive image frequently demands giving the listeners facts about one's company.

A public relations speaker typically makes three general points. He or she outlines the goals and purposes of the organization; shows the audience how those goals tie in with their needs and values; and indicates how the organization can help people. At times, the public relations speaker may represent not only his or her own organization, but an entire group of similar organizations. For example, the speaker who works for a national retail chain may address the question "How can large retail chains recapture the spirit of the old country store?" Such a topic does not directly promote the company's products, or the products of other retailers, but it does help the consumer in the audience see giant chains as reaching for a more personal, down-home brand of service.

TEACH

> **"** Humor is one of God's most marvelous gifts.... Humor endows us with the capacity to clarify the obscure, to simplify the complex, to deflate the pompous, to chastise the arrogant, to point a moral, and to adorn a tale. **"**
>
> —Sam Ervin

● **LEARNING STYLES**

Audio/Visual Learning
Students would enjoy hearing or watching a comedy segment and then analyzing it in the light of the guidelines presented in the text.

● **ENRICHMENT**

Some students could tape a monologue segment of a late-night show and share it with the class. This could be reviewed in the light of the guidelines presented here. You might ask volunteers to try their hand at repeating some of the monologue for the class.

CHAPTER 12 Other Kinds of Speaking

Speeches to Entertain

Many speakers, when delivering informative or persuasive speeches, use humor effectively. Only when the primary *purpose* of a speech is to cause the audience to relax, smile, and enjoy the occasion, however, do we label it a **speech to entertain.** Speeches to entertain are frequently called "after-dinner speeches," since they often form a program of entertainment following a banquet or meal. The after-dinner speech should have a theme or focus. Though the focus need not be as sharp as that of an informative or persuasive speaker's, there should be a central theme that the audience can pick out.

A comedian giving a monologue, on the other hand, can hop rapidly from one subject to another. The entertaining speaker cannot. Joe Creason, the late writer for the Louisville *Courier Journal,* often gave a highly entertaining speech dealing with a brand of humor that he found to be special to Kentucky. Though the humorous stories he related dealt with widely different situations, the theme that glued the speech together was "There is a special brand of Kentucky humor that is unlike that in other states."

Originality should also mark a good speech to entertain. While speakers may insert material read or heard elsewhere, they should develop the general subject matter, the specific theme or focus, and much of the specific material of the speech themselves. Think for a moment of professional entertainers whose humor you especially enjoy. In most cases, each of them has developed his or her personalized approach to getting laughs. One tells funny stories on himself or herself; another focuses regularly on certain topics such as money problems or politics; a third always works with another person and uses dialogue to entertain the audience. An entertaining speaker, too, needs to develop an original, individual style and approach that suits his or her personality. Much of the speech material should also be developed by the speaker. The entertaining speaker who simply tells the audience a series of stock jokes will usually not entertain very well. Good sources for humorous topics often come from looking at a familiar subjects from an unusual vantage point. Many topics that are usually looked at seriously have a humorous side when you search for it. Could you develop an entertaining speech from these topics and speech titles?

Topic	Entertaining Theme
Summer jobs	"Summer jobs for high schoolers: The daily diary of the American nightmare."
Taking tests	"What tests *really* mean to teachers."
Camping out	"Petrified in a pup tent: The night the rattlesnake came in from the cold."

Like a professional entertainer, a speaker should develop an original, individual style and presentation suited to his or her own personality.

Of course some of your specific stories and examples will have to come from other sources. Audiences do not expect every sentence in a speech to entertain to originate from the speaker's personal experience. If you develop an overall approach and style that fits you, and use a great deal of original material, your listeners should enjoy the speech. Many entertaining speakers will take a humorous story they have heard or read and retell it as if it happened to them or to some member of their audience. If this does not embarrass anyone in the audience, it is an effective technique. Consult your library if you need some good sources of humorous material.

As with other special occasion speeches, language and delivery are important in speaking to entertain. In making language choices, aim for vividness—words and images that paint pictures in the listeners' imaginations. Of course, your language should also be light, and appropriate for a relaxing occasion. Memorize as much of your material as you can, especially punchlines. Reading a punchline to an audience is far less effective than maintaining eye contact while speaking it. In addition, an extemporaneous delivery contributes a feeling of relaxation.

Nonverbal communication is an important part of delivery in speeches to entertain. Timing is particularly important. Knowing when to pause, and where to emphasize a point often makes a difference in whether your audience "gets it" or not. When the listeners laugh, wait

TEACH

SUBSTITUTE TEACHER TIP

You could introduce the section on entertaining speeches by bringing a collection of jokes to class or writing the Max Adrian quote on the chalkboard. Ask students to tell a partner a joke or funny story. You might ask the class to nominate the student with the best sense of humor.

"There just isn't room for two doctors and two vampires in one small town."
—Max Adrian

● SKILL DEVELOPMENT

15-Second Skill Opportunity
Explain that some people tell stories and jokes easily and others feel awkward. This is a skill that improves with practice. Students could work in pairs to practice telling an entertaining story. Then one in each pair could tell an entertaining story to the entire class.

Active Listening
Discuss why it is easy for some to remember the punchline of a story and for others it is difficult. Draw on the experiences of the class. Ask students to identify their classmates who tell entertaining stories or jokes well. Invite those so designated to share their "secrets" for punchline delivery.

TEACH

SUBSTITUTE TEACHER TIP
Bring to class clipped articles from a newspaper or magazines. Put these in a box and ask each student to take one. Give them one minute to read the article (keep them short). Then call on various students and ask them to stand and talk for one minute about the topic suggested by the article.

SKILL DEVELOPMENT

On the Job
When students join the work force they will probably attend numerous meetings. They should be prepared to offer opinions in an informed and sometimes entertaining way. Students might question their parents about the meetings they attend on the job or the situations where they are called upon to express an opinion. These anecdotes could be shared with the entire class.

ACTIVITY

You might assign students certain tasks in organizing and planning the "banquet." Students should carry out their activities as if they were really going to have the banquet. They should plan the purpose, time, and place, and draw up a list of those to be invited. They should plan the food, the quantity, the price of tickets, and the publicity. Some students should be designated to prepare speeches of introduction, presentation, acceptance, and entertainment. Other students could actually design and print a program for the banquet. All of these efforts would produce products suitable for inclusion in students' portfolios.

LINKS TO PAST LEARNING

Ask if any students have been to an improv theater or play where the audience is invited to provide suggestions or lines for actors to use by which the audience determines the ending or influences the dialogue. Discuss the success of the improv strategy from the audience point of view. Then focus on the skills the actors require in order to feel comfortable with improvisation.

---

400   CHAPTER 12   Other Kinds of Speaking

until the laughter has subsided before you go on. Do not be discouraged if your audience does not laugh as often as you hoped or at the precise points you expected. Plan during rehearsal how you will react if several of your funniest lines should fall flat. Finally, remember that your job is basically to make your listeners relax and enjoy themselves. That does not always mean they have to be laughing nonstop.

ACTIVITY

Speeches to Entertain
As a class, plan an imaginary banquet that celebrates a specific event or occasion or honors a specific person. The banquet may mark the end of a sports season or a debate season, honor the birthday of a famous person, or acknowledge someone for a special contribution to your school or community. Prepare a list of speakers and assign students to introduce them. Simulate the banquet and have students introduce the speakers. If appropriate, awards may be given and accepted.

SALES PRESENTATIONS

Presentations whose basic purpose is to sell a product or a service are really a specialized kind of persuasive communication. When we think of selling, we typically think of a salesperson attempting to convince a client or customer to make a purchase. Often such speaking takes place on a one-to-one basis, with a single salesperson talking to just one or two customers. Some sales occasions, however, call for a full-blown public speech in which the speaker attempts to persuade an entire audience to buy a line of products or a brand of service.

Whether you are trying to sell to an audience of one or a hundred, you are likely to be most convincing if you follow the organizing pattern known as Monroe's Motivated Sequence, mentioned in Chapter 7. This organizational pattern, based upon the psychology of how people become convinced, has proven quite successful as a tool for sales presentations. Let's take a closer look at it.

TEACH

● **LINKS TO PAST LEARNING**

Ask students to recall an item they recently purchased. Discuss whether a salesperson was involved in the purchase. Talk about the process of buying. If possible, link the process to the five steps identified in Monroe's Motivated Sequence.

● **ENRICHMENT**

Many students have probably had some sales experience in stores over the summer or at the Christmas retail season. Invite them to talk about the sales training they received. Or, you might invite sales professionals from the local community to speak to the class about the communication skills needed for successful sales.

> *"He's a man way out there in the blue, riding on a smile and a shoestring.... A salesman is got to dream, boy. It comes with the territory."*
> —Arthur Miller

● **LEARNING STYLES**

Visual Learning
Some students could make a poster or bulletin board that would identify and illustrate the five steps of Monroe's Motivated Sequence. These posters could be displayed in the classroom and used as a portfolio product.

Sales Presentations **401**

The successful sales presentation begins by focusing the attention of the client on the product.

Monroe's Motivated Sequence

You recall that Monroe's Motivated Sequence contains five major steps:

1. The Attention Step
2. The Need Step
3. The Satisfaction Step
4. The Visualization Step
5. The Action Step

Suppose you have been hired as a salesperson for a major computer company. Whether you are about to call upon a single client (the principal of a high school who is thinking about changing brands of computers for classrooms), or a roomful of teachers from an entire school system (who will jointly decide on a new line of computers), you must begin by quickly focusing the attention and interest of your audience on your product (attention step). You do this by using the same methods you used to stimulate audience interest in other kinds of speeches: rhetorical questions, shock technique, humor, narrative, suspense, and examples. Since you are selling computers, displaying several of your

TEACH

SUBSTITUTE TEACHER TIP
Bring the classified ad section to class and ask students to select one of the sales jobs advertised. Students could write a job description, based on the ad, and a cover letter to apply for the job.

● LEARNING STYLES

Cooperative Learning
Small groups of students could practice making sales presentations to each other. If the group does not want to use the computer example, encourage them to use another one. Members of the group should limit their presentation time to no more than three minutes. Encourage them to determine the relative distribution of time within the five stages.

● SKILL DEVELOPMENT

On the Job
Most students will be familiar with the practice of selling a product or a service. Suggest that much of their career growth may be linked to their ability to sell an idea for a new product, or a new procedure to their manager. Encourage students to investigate how companies bought into new paradigms that transformed their organization.

CHAPTER 12 Other Kinds of Speaking

latest models may prove an especially compelling attention device, in combination with several of the other approaches.

Once you have aroused your listener's interest in your product, you move swiftly into the need step. Here you show your audience that they have needs no longer being met by their current line of computers. You might do this by asking them such questions as "Are your current computers still highly compatible with the latest lines of educational software available?" "Do you now need an integrated learning system set up in a computer lab arrangement?" "Do your computers have the kind of graphics capabilities necessary to teach graphic art, for example?" Once you have highlighted their need for a more contemporary, sophisticated line of computers, you are ready to move to the satisfaction step.

In the satisfaction step, you tell your listener or listeners that *your* brand of computers will best satisfy those unmet needs which their current computers are not fulfilling. You lay out for them the capabilities of your computer, stressing that it *will* accomplish what they need for it to accomplish.

This is followed immediately by the visualization step, in which you show your audience *how* your product will address their needs. Here you would demonstrate your product's capabilities, showing specifically how each feature of your computer would address a particular need not currently being met by their present brand. You would be demonstrating how the positive features of your product will offset the negative images the audience recalls from recent use of their outdated machines.

The final step is the action step. This usually calls for a brief, direct challenge or invitation to your listeners to take action. As a computer salesperson, your action step might be as simple as "If you have no more questions, may I order several of our computers for you today?" Or, less direct, "If you are interested in exploring our product further, we would be happy to set up a time when you could visit our showroom at 830 Broad Street where our regional sales manager would be glad to show you additional models in our line." The action step should include specific, detailed instructions showing the customer how to take action. Frequently this step demands that you talk about dates, times, locations where the transaction will be completed, and price. You might sometimes initiate the action step by mentioning such matters as warranties, service, or the reputation of your company or product.

When making a sales presentation, you will employ all that you have learned about persuasive public speaking in general, then use Monroe's Motivated Sequence as your organizing pattern. In many cases, it will serve as a fine finishing tool with which to give a special luster to your sales speech.

APPLY

● **TEACHING**

To prepare for a class field trip, secure the necessary permission from the administration and from parents.

● **ENRICHMENT**

Some students could research the reviews of specific computers in various computer magazines. They could develop a rating system so that they become familiar with the warranties and reputations of the computers they will look at.

▼ **PORTFOLIO PRODUCTS**

Students could make a chart to compare and contrast both the characteristics of computers as well as the sales presentations they observed on their field trip. These charts could become the basis for analysis and evaluation.

Speaking IN ACTION

Class Shopping Trip

Situation

Plan a class field trip in your community on which you go to two or three computer firms and listen to a sales presentation with the aim of making a recommendation to your principal about which brand of computers the school should purchase next. Even if your school has recently bought a new line of computers, your recommendation may provide valuable information for the *next* time computers must be purchased.

Preparation

Once your speech teacher or principal has selected the firms you will visit, each of you should do individual preparation to assure that you are thoroughly ready to listen carefully and ask intelligent questions about each company's product. You will need to secure, in advance, brochures about their products from each of the companies the class plans to visit.

You should also be particularly familiar with Monroe's Motivated Sequence (Chapter 7, p. 207, and this chapter, p. 401), and be ready to identify which of its five steps each sales representative uses in her or his presentation. The various salespeople making the presentations to you will probably not have heard of Monroe's Motivated Sequence, but if they are good at their trade, they should touch upon all, or at least most of the five steps in some way.

Plan also to watch for matters such as the salesperson's competence and self-confidence, clarity of answers to your questions, nonverbal communication style, language usage, how well visual aids are handled (the demonstration models), and, of course, the overall impression he or she makes upon you.

Delivery

When you return to class, hold a class discussion comparing and contrasting the presentations made by each of the computer salespersons. When your discussion is concluded, the class will vote on which brand of computer you will recommend the school should purchase the next time that becomes necessary. Your speech teacher will inform the principal of your recommendation.

AMAZING FACTS!
Between 30 and 35 million households in the U.S. have personal home computers!

● **LEARNING STYLES**

❋ **Cooperative Learning**
Small groups of students could conduct research about the computer market. They should find out what computers are currently being used in your school, what characteristics they have, how frequently they are used, by whom, and where they are located. This information could be compared with information about computers in other schools in your district. Groups could compare their research and identify the qualities that would be most useful to have in school computers.

403

TEACH

AMAZING FACTS!
Albert E. van Schmus watched 16,945 movies between 1949 and 1982 as a rater for the Motion Picture Association of America.

● **TEACHING**

Ask students to summarize the four guidelines presented here using one word for each point. Explain that impromptu speeches are sometimes stressful and if they have a short, easy way to remember a pattern for impromptu remarks, they will feel more confident. Give students time to think of their one-word cues. Share those cues with the entire class.

CHAPTER 12 Other Kinds of Speaking

● **IMPROMPTU SPEAKING**

The types of speeches for special occasions mentioned so far in th chapter (keynote, commencement, dedication, and public relatior speeches) are just that—types of *speeches*. **Impromptu speaking,** c the other hand, is a *method* of speaking—a way of delivering any kir of speech. In Chapter 11 we compared impromptu speaking with mar uscript, memorized, and extemporaneous delivery. We called it the kir of delivery one must use when called upon to speak with no advanc notice and with only a moment or two for immediate preparation. reality, you are giving an impromptu speech each time a teacher calls c you suddenly to "tell us what you think" in the midst of a class discu sion. After you graduate, you will occasionally be asked to make point or react to what someone has said in a public meeting or gathe ing. Ordinarily you will be asked to speak only about subjects wit which you are fairly familiar. Sometimes you can do so informally, fror your seat; at other times you will be expected to speak from a podiun Whatever the situation, the first rule to keep in mind is DON'T PANIC When you realize that you have actually given a number of imprompt speeches in the classroom without knowing it, you can have conf dence in your ability to speak off the cuff to other groups. Audience don't expect impromptu speeches to be polished orations. They jus want to hear your thoughts spoken in whatever language comes t you. They also do not expect to hear a lengthy impromptu speech. Lis teners are nearly always sympathetic with public speakers, no matte whether they have had time for preparation or not. They are especiall sympathetic with those speaking impromptu.

Though the flow of your words may not be as smooth as yo would prefer when speaking impromptu, you can manage to soun well-organized. Here is a simple four-step plan of organization that wi help you collect and present your thoughts, and that you can apply t most impromptu speaking situations:

1. State the point you are answering (if you have been asked t respond to a previous speaker).
2. State the main point you wish to make. You do not need to elab orate on your point.
3. Support the main point with appropriate examples, statistics, an testimony.
4. Summarize and restate you main point. (If your speech has beer less than a minute in length, you may want to omit this step.)

In cases in which you are not responding to a previous speaker, simpl eliminate step 1 and use only steps 2, 3, and 4.

When you realize that you have given a number of impromptu speeches in class, it will build your confidence in other off-the-cuff situations.

Many of the impromptu "speeches" you are asked to give are really brief "statements" during meetings or conversations with friends. When, in a meeting of your school's yearbook staff, someone asks you: "Jamie, what 'look' do you feel the overall layout should promote this year?" everyone else falls silent waiting for your answer. That answer, however brief, is an impromptu speech. More formal occasions may call for more formal delivery and perhaps a longer speech, but they are essentially no different from the answer to the question about layout. Use the many opportunities that arise to give brief impromptu responses, take advantage of using the organizational pattern suggested above. Then, when you are asked to give a "bigger" impromptu speech, you will be an old hand at the basic method.

TEACH

● **TEACHING**

Emphasize the distinction that impromptu speaking is a method of speaking not a type of speech.

● **ACTIVITY**

Impromptu Speeches

The "brave" students in your class may request an end-of-semester round of impromptu speeches. Your teacher will prepare a number of topics and place them in a box for drawing. When each speaker's turn comes, the student may pick three topics from the box, decide which one she or he wishes to present, then return the other two topics to the box. That speaker is then given one minute to organize her or his thoughts and give a brief speech on the topic (approximately one to two minutes). Your teacher may either have the entire class participate or ask for volunteers.

405

ASSESS

● STUDENT PERFORMANCE COMPETENCIES

- Understands and uses various speeches suitable for special occasions
- Describes the difference between impromptu speaking and the other speeches for special occasions
- Delivers examples of speeches focused on persons and speeches for special situations

● sca GUIDELINES

- Uses words appropriate for special situations
- Expresses ideas clearly and concisely
- Expresses feelings to others
- Performs social rituals

▽ PORTFOLIO PRODUCTS

Standard
- Glossary of Speech Terms
- Tape of Special-Occasion Speech
- Visual Aid or Compilation of Quotes for Special Occasions

Enrichment
- Feedback Checklist for Speech Analysis and Evaluation
- Video Collection of the Best Special-Occasion Speeches
- Testimonials for Coach Interview
- Consumer Research for Computer Field Trip
- Compilation of Best Stories and Jokes Presented in Class

Challenge
- Comparison and Contrast of Computer Products or Computer Sales Presentations
- Banquet Program and Speeches
- Entertainment Program for Class or School

406

CHAPTER 12 REVIEW

● SUMMARY

Public speeches are given daily to honor persons and to celebrate special occasions. The primary purpose of such speeches is neither to inform nor persuade, but to inspire, challenge, honor, or entertain.

Speeches Focused on Persons Speeches of introduction are intended to build both audience enthusiasm for the main speaker and interest in the topic. They should be thoroughly prepared—but brief—and they should relate the main speaker's topic to the audience.

Speeches of presentation honor the recipient of an award and may also serve to explain the reasons for making the presentation. Recipients often make a brief acceptance speech, but should ask the presenter whether this is appropriate. Humility, brevity, and graciousness should characterize speeches of acceptance.

Commemorative speeches fall into two major types: testimonial speeches and eulogies. Testimonial speeches praise living persons or celebrate occasions focused upon persons, and they evoke joy, laughter, celebration, and sentiment. Eulogies are given to honor the dead and to console the living. They are often written in advance and delivered from manuscript or memory.

Speeches for Special Occasions Speeches given to mark special occasions include keynote speeches, commencement speeches, dedication speeches, public relation speeches, and speeches to entertain.

Keynote speeches often open large conventions or meetings of government, business, and professional groups. They serve to rally the members around the organization and commit them again to its goals.

The purpose of commencement speeches is to honor graduating students by noting their accomplishments, recognizing the contributions of those who have aided them, and elaborating on the challenges ahead.

Dedication speeches depend on clear and lofty language to highlight the meaning of a recent creation or a new endeavor. The speaker's job is to focus attention on the goals and values of the event.

Unlike most special occasion speeches, the public relations speech has a strong persuasive purpose: to promote a positive image of an organization. Public relations speakers typically outline the goals and purposes of their organizations, show how these tie in with the needs and values of their listeners, and indicate how their organizations can help.

Speeches to entertain, often called "after-dinner speeches," serve to relax an audience with humorous stories and vivid language. They

ASSESS

● **ASSESSMENT STRATEGIES**

Individual Assessment
- Participates in practice activities daily or weekly
- Demonstrates knowledge of content through questions, discussion, quizzes, and Chapter 12 test
- Displays improved skills in the delivery of various speeches for special occasions
- Displays improved skills in telling humorous stories or jokes

Group Assessment
- Sets and achieves goals
- Analyzes and evaluates student skills in delivering various special occasion speeches
- Organizes topics for group research
- Participates in class field trip and in the planning of the class banquet project

---

differ from a comedian's monologue in that they have a theme or focus.

Impromptu speaking—speaking with no advance notice—is a method of speech delivery. In order to give an organized impromptu speech, speakers state the main point, give supporting evidence, and then summarize and restate the main point.

VOCABULARY

Define each term in a complete sentence.

speeches of introduction	keynote speeches
speeches of presentation	commencement speeches
speeches of acceptance	dedication speeches
commemorative speeches	public relations speeches
testimonial speeches	speeches to entertain
eulogies	impromptu speaking

✔ CHECKLIST

Skills for Other Kinds of Speaking

1. Know the different purposes of speeches that relate to persons.
2. Be prepared when giving even the briefest speech.
3. Be accurate in pronouncing names and giving facts when you introduce a speaker.
4. Remember to suit your level of formality to the occasion.
5. Build feelings of expectation and drama in your audience.
6. Be poised when giving an impromptu speech.
7. Realize the fact that the testimonial speaker must appeal to the emotions of the audience.
8. Know the value of public relations speeches in business.

REVIEW QUESTIONS

1. Describe the general purposes for which special situation speeches are usually given.
2. State why special situation speeches demand emphasis on the speech skills of language usage, memory, and delivery.
3. Name five types of special situation speeches that focus on persons.

● **ANSWERS**

See the Answer Key for more complete answers.

REVIEW QUESTIONS
1. Special situation speeches inspire, entertain, challenge, and honor.
2. Vivid language is more inspiring. See the Answer Key for details.
3. Speeches of introduction, presentation, acceptance, testimonial, and eulogy are examples.

ASSESS

4. For descriptions, see the Answer Key.
5. Introductions last up to three minutes; presentations no more than five minutes; acceptances are two minutes; testimonials could last up to ten minutes.
6. Keynote, commencement, dedication, public relations, and entertainment are examples.
7. See the Answer Key for descriptions.
8. They differ in purpose.
9. Impromptu speaking is a method of delivery.
10. The first rule is "Don't Panic."

DISCUSSION QUESTIONS

The following code is used to designate discussion questions and activities as suitable for students of varying ability levels:
- ▼ = below average to average
- ◆ = average to above average
- ■ = all students

1. ▼ Monitor the groups carefully to help them synthesize ideas.
2. ■ Students will have to research dates and events for this activity. Encourage creativity.
3. ■ When the class agrees about the nature of heroism, they will make better choices.
4. ▼ An effective eulogy can be uplifting for listeners by recounting happy memories.

CHAPTER 12 REVIEW

4. Describe the specific purpose of each of the five kinds of speeches focused on persons.
5. State the appropriate length for each of the following kinds of speeches: introduction, presentation, acceptance, and testimonial.
6. Name five kinds of speeches for special occasions.
7. Describe the specific purpose of each kind of speech for special occasions.
8. Describe how public relations speeches and speeches to entertain differ from keynote, commencement, and dedication speeches.
9. State how impromptu speaking differs from everything else covered in this chapter.
10. Identify the first rule to remember when you are asked to speak impromptu.

? DISCUSSION QUESTIONS

1. What qualities characterize an admirable person? Each person in the class will name someone whom he or she admires and then provide three reasons why that person deserves respect. The person named may be living or dead, someone who is well known, or someone who is a personal acquaintance. Discuss the characteristics that all of those named have in common. What kinds of speaking occasions could this information be used in? What would be the purpose of speeches made to mark what these individuals represent or have accomplished?

2. Commemorative speeches are often made to honor special occasions, such as Independence Day and Veteran's Day. What special occasion is overlooked and should be honored? Discuss historical events you think should be honored because of their importance.

3. People are often honored in speeches of presentation because they have done things that have great historical significance, or they have made a worthwhile and obvious contribution to society. Are there any individuals and groups that you know of who work quietly and without fanfare, but who accomplish things of real value? Discuss overlooked and silent heroes who would be excellent people to honor with awards.

4. Discuss the tone that should be maintained in a eulogy. Should it be consistently somber and remind listeners of the sadness of the loss? Or may it also celebrate and recall the actions of the person being eulogized?

ASSESS

CRITICAL THINKING

1. Analysis Compare and contrast the impromptu speech and the extemporaneous speech. In what ways are they alike? In what ways are they different? What do listeners have a right to expect of an extemporaneous speaker? What should they expect of an impromptu speaker?

2. Synthesis Imagine that you are in a position to give a public relations speech on behalf of an organization that you are connected with. It might be your school or a social, civic, or religious organization that you belong to. What three general points would you make in your speech? What kinds of things would you say in order to develop a positive image of the organization?

ACTIVITIES

In-Class

1. Work with a partner. Invent a special award that will be presented in class. The award may be given for a genuine achievement, or it may be given for humorous reasons. One of you will present the award. The other will play the part of the recipient. Decide which role each of you will play. The presenter will then plan a presentation speech and the recipient will prepare an acceptance speech. Present your speeches in class.

2. As you probably know, a "roast" is an event in honor of someone, during which humorous speeches are given that draw attention to the person's supposed faults. As a class, choose someone to roast. It might be a classmate, another student in your school, or a staff member. Be sure to choose someone whom everyone in the class is familiar with. Then work in groups of from five to seven. Each group must prepare a humorous speech that concentrates on some of the personal traits of the person being honored. Remember that the speeches are made in the spirit of good fun. Be sure that nothing is said to insult or embarrass the person being honored. Do whatever interviewing might be necessary to discover information about your subject. Choose someone from your group to give the speech in class.

3. As a class, develop a number of topics that are suitable for impromptu speeches. Some might deal with popular entertainment or sports figures. Others may be abstract concepts like "fairness" or "embarrassment" that the speaker will have to define. Still others may be drawn from recent newspaper headlines. Write each topic on a 3 × 5

CRITICAL THINKING
1. **Analysis** Neither the impromptu nor the extemporaneous speech requires extensive preparation time.
2. **Synthesis** Students can count the benefits of belonging to a club, and it gives others a chance to learn about other activities.

ACTIVITIES
In-Class
1. The students themselves can decide what the award can be.
2. Make sure that the "roast" has a positive approach to the person honored.
3. The impromptu speech helps the beginning speech student who relies too much on notes.

409

ASSESS

4. This could be done with Question 3 though the emphasis here is more local.

Out-of-Class
1. Commemorative speeches often convey a great rhetorical style.
2. Make every effort to find an audience for this activity outside the classroom.
3. This speech could also be delivered outside the classroom for the appropriate group.

CHAPTER 12 REVIEW

index card and put the cards in a bag or box. Each student will go to the front of the class, draw a card, read the topic to the class, and speak on the topic for no longer than two minutes. The class will provide feedback and may wish to vote to determine the best impromptu speaker.

4. As a class, identify someone in your school or local community who is worthy of an "Unsung Hero Award." Instead of an individual, you might choose to honor an occupational group that performs a community service. Individuals and groups should be thoroughly discussed when they are proposed. Reach a consensus about the individual or group to be honored. Then discuss in detail the reasons why the person or group deserves to be honored. Appoint a small group of from five to seven to prepare a testimonial or presentation speech. You may consider honoring the person or group in class or at a school assembly.

Out-of-Class

1. Check standard speech anthologies or *Vital Speeches of the Day* to locate a commemorative speech. In your speech notebook, analyze the speech in depth, pointing out how it meets the criteria presented in this chapter. Be prepared to read the speech in class and to present an oral report of your analysis.

2. Assume that you have an opportunity to deliver a public relations speech on the value of training in speech communication. Choose a specific audience for your speech, such as a group of students who are considering taking a course, a civic group made up of owners of small businesses, or a parent-teacher organization. In your speech notebook, outline and assemble notes for your speech. Be sure that your speech presents the goals and purposes of a speech course, shows how the goals cater to the needs of those who will take the course, and demonstrates how such training will pay dividends in the future. Be prepared to give your speech in class. Describe the makeup of your imaginary audience before you begin.

3. Choose a famous historical figure, one whom you have always been interested in and whom you always wanted to find out more about. In your speech notebook, write a eulogy for this individual. Gather whatever information you need from standard biographical sources. Choose your language carefully and arrange your content for maximum emotional impact. Be prepared to deliver your eulogy in class.

ASSESS

CHAPTER PROJECT

Choose a topic for a five- to seven-minute speech that is designed to entertain. Be sure to choose a topic that you personally find humorous. Outline your speech and gather whatever material you need to enhance the humorous content. Write and memorize the introduction, the conclusion, and the important transitions between sections. Rehearse the speech as frequently as you need in order to be at ease with it. Be prepared to deliver your speech in class.

CHAPTER PROJECT
- This requires much time. You might allow two weeks for the preparation, research, and rehearsal. Be prepared to help students find enjoyable topics for their speeches.

PREPARE

● PERFORMANCE OBJECTIVES

- Participates in daily and weekly skill drills
- Completes classwork
- Demonstrates knowledge of debate and parliamentary procedures
- Gathers and organizes research information to support and defend points of view
- Distinguishes facts from opinions

● sca GUIDELINES

- Uses voice effectively in debate and public meetings
- Identifies main ideas in debate arguments
- Distinguishes facts from opinions
- Supports debate position with evidence and logic
- Answers objections effectively
- Uses a variety of reasoning techniques to present arguments in a public meeting

● UNIT FOCUS

Unit 5 focuses on the procedures involved in debate and parliamentary systems. Emphasis is on understanding basic principles and applying them to real situations.

● CONTENTS

13 **Debate** *pp. 414–447*
14 **Parliamentary Procedure** *pp. 448–473*

▽ UNIT PORTFOLIOS

Individual Portfolios
- Agenda for Public Meeting
- Summary of Parliamentary Procedures
- Research for Debate Topic
- Chart Indicating Debate Formats

Group Portfolios
- Classroom Debate
- Agenda for Classroom Meeting
- Checklist for Debate Performance and Judging
- Best TV Cross-Examination Segments

Class Portfolios
- Video of Class Meeting Using Parliamentary Procedures
- Video of Debate Team
- Interview Questions for Attorney and/or Health Service Administrator

UNIT 5

DEBATE AND PARLIAMENTARY PROCEDURE

PREPARE

● UNIT PLANNER

Chapters	Time Management	📁	📄	📕	📼	🎴
13 Debate *pp. 414–447*	Week 1	✔	✔	✔	✔	✔
14 Parliamentary Procedure *pp. 448–473*	Week 2	✔	✔	✔	✔	

● ANCILLARY RESOURCES

● PROFESSIONAL RESOURCES

Print
Bartanen, Michael, and David Frank. *Lincoln-Douglas Debate.* Lincolnwood, IL: National Textbook Company, 1994.

Freely, Austin J. *Argumentation and Debate: Critical Thinking for Reasoned Decision Making.* 8th ed. Belmont, CA: Wadsworth Publishing Co., 1993.

Goodnight, Lynn. *Getting Started in Debate.* 2nd ed. Lincolnwood, IL: National Textbook Company, 1992.

Robert, III, Henry M. *Robert's Rules of Order.* Glenview, IL: Scott Foresman, 1985.

Thomas, David A., and Jack Hart, eds. *Advanced Debate: Readings in Theory, Practice & Teaching.* 4th ed. Lincolnwood, IL: National Textbook Co. 1993.

Film
Critical Thinking—Making Sure of the Facts (Coronet Films, 65 East South Water St., Chicago, IL 60601).

13
Debate

14
Parliamentary Procedure

Ancillary Resource Key

📁 = Portfolio Product Activities
📄 = Tests/Answer Key
📕 = Speech Library
📼 = Self-Help Videos
🎴 = Audiotape

413

PREPARE

● CHAPTER PLANNER

Day 1	Day 2	Day 3	Day 4	Day 5
Prepare	Prepare	Prepare	Prepare	Prepare
Teach	Teach	Teach	Teach	Teach
Assess	Assess	Assess	Assess	Assess
Sub. Teacher Tip p. 417	Sub. Teacher Tip p. 424	Sub. Teacher Tip pp. 428, 432	Sub. Teacher Tip pp. 437, 438	Sub. Teacher Tip p. 441

● CHAPTER OVERVIEW

This chapter examines the following topics:
- The Nature of Debate *p. 415*
- Preparing to Debate *p. 418*
- Using Different Strategies *p. 426*
- Meeting the Opposition *p. 435*

▽ PORTFOLIO PRODUCTS

Individual Projects
- Glossary of Speech Terms
- Research on Debate Topic
- Tape of Debate Segment
- Chapter 13 Portfolio Products

Group Projects
- Checklist for Debate Strategies
- Evaluation Guidelines
- Team Research for Debate Topic
- Video of Best Debate Speeches

● sca GUIDELINES

- Uses voice effectively
- Identifies main ideas in debate arguments
- Distinguishes facts from opinions
- Expresses ideas clearly and concisely
- Supports debate position with evidence and logic
- Answers objections effectively

CHAPTER 13

Debate

When you have completed this chapter you should be able to:

- Explain the major differences between debate and discussion.
- Analyze a debate proposition.
- Find evidence to support logical reasoning when building a debate case.
- Describe different stages that can be used by each side in a debate.

TEACH

● LINKS TO PAST LEARNING

Ask students to recall a situation or meeting where a plan of action was put to a vote. If they were on the side of the majority, how did they feel? Discuss the alternative— being on the losing side. Suggest that knowing debate strategies might have influenced the outcome of the proposition.

● MOTIVATION

Distribute an index card to every student. Suggest that what they put on this card could be equivalent to the winning lottery card. Ask each to write a definition of "debate" on the card. They should sign their cards and these could be collected. During the study of the chapter, the student with the definition that matches the definition in the text most closely could win a prize. Prizes might include a Certificate of Recognition, a discount at the cafeteria or bookstore, a night free from homework, etc.

● ACTIVITY

The differences between debate, discussion, and arguments could be role-played by several students. The topic for the debate, discussion, and argument could be related to the topic of whether to go to bowling or to a movie on Saturday night.

● ACTIVITY

Debate versus Discussion

Before you begin reading this chapter, hold a brief class discussion in which you identify the major differences between debate and discussion as decision-making processes. As you contrast the two, think both about formal debates held in schools and colleges, and about everyday forms of debate, such as between opposing attorneys in our law courts. Then, as you read the opening pages of this chapter, be watching for the answers!

The ancient Greeks were among the first to recognize the value of placing ideas in open competition in order to arrive at decisions about important matters. This same practice is followed today in legislatures and law courts. Debating is perhaps the most challenging form of oral communication in which you can engage.

The benefits you gain from participating in debate are many. Among the most important are the stimulation of your interest in current issues, the development of your critical thinking ability, the sharpening of your communication skills, and improvement in research abilities. In addition, you learn how thoughtful, positive, and orderly change may be brought about in a democratic society. Without the opportunity to decide matters and reduce conflict among ourselves through the clash of ideas, we would often be left with little choice but the clash of arms.

This chapter will introduce you to debate as a decision-making process and as a means of persuasive argument. Although this chapter will focus on **formal debate**—the kind used in school contests—you should be aware that any time you argue the strengths of two political candidates with your neighbor, speak for or against increasing the school budget, or take a stand on the energy issue, you are debating informally.

● THE NATURE OF DEBATE

The formal debates held in schools and colleges throughout the country are contests. Each can, in fact, be seen as a mental tug-of-war. There is an issue to be decided with two sides holding opposite views. At the end a judge will usually decide who is the winner. The purpose of formal debate is to determine the set of arguments which seem more

TEACH

> **"Quarrels would not last long if the fault were only on one side."**
> —La Rochefoucauld

● **TEACHING**

This chapter focuses on the formal debate format used in school contests and is a proving ground for the skills of logic and decision-making that can be used in a wide variety of situations, including the work place.

● **SKILL DEVELOPMENT**

Critical Thinking
Encourage students to begin a sheet that will help them compare and contrast the format and purpose of debates and discussions. Emphasize the key point that a debate is a contest and the decision is arrived at through a judge or jury. In a discussion, a decision is usually reached through consensus.

● **LEARNING STYLES**

Cooperative Learning
Debate contests emphasize teamwork and collaboration. Students could choose, or be assigned, to work with debate partners. Guidelines about the format and nature of debate could be distributed.

● **SKILL APPLICATION**

Debate
Have students individually, or in their cooperative learning group, study the examples of debate propositions in the text. The six characteristics of a debate proposition should be noted. Discuss the relative importance of each characteristic.

Debate pits one side against another in order to discover the best answer through mental and verbal battle.

convincing by testing both sides under pressure. No other form of oral communication discussed in this book has these characteristics. Conversation is certainly not a contest. It is built on a basis of cooperation. Group discussion is also built on cooperation. It is not a contest but a cooperative search for the truth about a matter. Nor is public speaking a contest. Instead the speaker informs or persuades the listening audience. Only debate pits one side against another in order to discover the best answer through mental and verbal battle. By bringing the best evidence on each side out in the open, debate enables those listening to judge wisely as to the best solution, the best candidate, or the best course of action.

Did you notice one of the answers to the opening Activity regarding the differences between debate and discussion in the preceding paragraph? Debate is a *contest* between two opposing points of view; discussion uses an atmosphere of *cooperation* to arrive at decisions. A second important difference relates to who makes the decision at the conclusion of a debate or discussion. In debate, some neutral third party, such as a judge or jury, renders the final decision; in discussion, often the members of the discussion group themselves make the decision, either by consensus, compromise, or majority vote.

The Clash of Ideas

Not every issue is debatable. Debate is restricted to issues that have only two sides. Thus a question such as "What should be done about inflation?" is not debatable. There may be numerous answers. In order to assure only two sides in a debate, and a direct clash of ideas between the two, debate issues are stated in the form of a **proposition.** A formal debate proposition is a statement that can be answered by yes and no.

TEACH

TEACHING

Students tend to confuse the affirmative and negative sides of a debate. Emphasize that the affirmative side proposes a change in the *status quo*. The negative side opposes the change.

CURRICULAR CONNECTIONS

Language Arts
Have students list and define all the words and terms used in this chapter. Vocabulary for debate is very specific and needs definition or explanation. Students could keep cards for each term. Encourage them to clip examples from the paper when they see any of these terms used in print.

SUBSTITUTE TEACHER TIP

To facilitate the students' participation in the activity that has them writing debate propositions, bring in copies of recent newspapers. Groups of students could use the papers to generate ideas for debate topics.

LEARNING STYLES

Visual Learning
Invite students to make a poster or flier that lists the characteristics of debate propositions as presented in the text. This list could be displayed prominently in the classroom and/or distributed to each student.

SKILL APPLICATION

Debate
Designate half the students to represent the affirmative side and the other half, the negative. Have students read the section on the responsibilities of the affirmative and the negative sides in a debate. Let the affirmative students summarize their responsibilities and the negative side do the same. Some students could list the points made by both sides on the chalkboard.

ACTIVITY

Give cooperative learning groups time to write three debate propositions. Before they submit their propositions, ask them to apply the guidelines presented on this page. Then give them time to revise their propositions so that the characteristics are met.

The Nature of Debate 417

It also generally demands that some specific action be taken or not taken. Here are two examples of debate propositions:

> Resolved, that the United States should adopt a system of national health insurance.

> Resolved, that more on-site job experience be incorporated into the high-school curriculum.

A well-worded formal debate proposition has several features:

1. It is worded as a statement, not a question.
2. It is worded to permit only a *for* and *against* response.
3. It is worded so that each side has an equal opportunity to argue its position successfully. In other words, the proposition is not slanted to favor one side.
4. It is worded to address a current, controversial issue.
5. It is worded to call for a change from present policy.
6. It is worded using specific, concrete language that does not make judgments about the topic.

Using these guidelines to write a debate proposition will help define an issue, which then may be supported or opposed.

ACTIVITY

Writing Debate Propositions
The class will divide into four groups. Using the guidelines presented in this chapter, each group will write three debate propositions. The class as a whole will then select the five propositions that are judged best. These will be used later in the chapter

The Opposing Sides

The two sides in a formal debate are called the **affirmative** and the **negative.** Each side may be represented by any number of speakers, but usually either one or two people argue each side. The affirmative has two basic tasks: attacking the way things are at present (the **status quo**) and arguing that a specific change should occur. Suppose the debate proposition reads "Resolved, that compulsory education should end after the eighth grade." The affirmative side must show that there

TEACH

● **TEACHING**

To help students learn the important steps in preparing for a debate, have them find the major headings in this section and list these on the chalkboard. The steps are: (1) Analyze the Proposition, (2) Build a Case, (3) Work with Your Partner, and (4) Support Your Case.

● **RETEACHING**

Give students time to prepare to "teach" what a debate is and how it works to another group of "students." They should review the section and identify the major points. Ask them to make a "lesson plan" they would use if they were to teach a junior high class about debate.

● **SKILL DEVELOPMENT**

Main Idea
Students could work in pairs and select one of the debate propositions that was written earlier. Each pair should define unfamiliar words or terms, identify several main issues raised by the proposition, and brainstorm opinions about the proposition. Encourage them to use the questions raised on the next page to analyze the proposition they have.

---

418 CHAPTER 13 Debate

are serious problems with the present requirement that young people stay in school until age 16 or older. They must also argue that many of these problems could be solved by allowing people to leave school after the eighth grade. The basic structure of an affirmative argument might go like this:

> There is a serious problem (or series of problems) caused by the present situation.
> The affirmative proposes an alternate plan of action that will solve the serious problems of the *status quo* and will be in and of itself beneficial.

The affirmative side in a debate is the side proposing a change from present policies. Thus, it has the responsibility of proving that a problem exists and that the solution stated in the proposition would work better than the present system. This affirmative responsibility is called the **burden of proof.** Just as in court trials, where defendants are presumed innocent until the prosecution proves them guilty, so in debate the *status quo* is presumed the best way of continuing until the affirmative proves another plan better.

The basic task of the negative side in a debate is to disprove, or **refute,** the attacks on the *status quo* made by the affirmative side. The negative side must prove the *status quo* is satisfactory or that the plan for change proposed by the affirmative side will not work.

The opposing sides take turns presenting their arguments. Because the affirmative side is the one proposing a change from present conditions, it always presents the first and the last arguments. In some debates both sides are also given the chance to **cross-examine,** or question, the other side about their statements. Various debate formats permit different arrangements of affirmative and negative speakers. These formats are explained in detail later in the chapter; however, three such arrangements are shown on page 420.

● **PREPARING TO DEBATE**

Formal debate, with a set order of speakers and usually an audience, demands careful preparation. This means you must carefully analyze the debate proposition. You must prepare sound evidence and reasoning to build an organized case. Then you must plan with your debate partner so that you will work well together. All of this takes time. Political candidates will tell you that they never prepare for a debate overnight. You, too, must prepare carefully in advance.

Analyze the Proposition

Your first step in preparing for any formal debate is to begin with the proposition. It is the written source that dictates the direction the debate must take. Analyze it carefully. Decide upon the words or phrases which need to be defined, and write down the definitions you consider fair. The first affirmative speaker will begin the debate by defining the terms. If the negative considers certain definitions to be unfair, it should provide its own definitions in its first speech.

Discover the background that has caused the proposition to become a debatable issue. Find out as much as you can about the opinions on both sides of the question. It doesn't matter whether you will be taking the affirmative or negative side of the debate. You will need to know the possible arguments of the opposition as thoroughly as you do your own in order to plan how to handle them.

Focus on the **issues.** The issues in a debate are the major points of disagreement. They are the key arguments on which acceptance or rejection of the debate proposition hangs. In most debates there will be only three or four main issues. Often you can discover major issues by asking questions such as these about the topic:

- Are serious problems being created by the present system? Can these problems be better solved by some other approach?
- What other approach, if any, would better solve the problems? Is such an approach feasible? Practical? Too expensive?
- Is the proposed solution the best solution?
- Will another solution to the problems have certain disadvantages? Will these disadvantages be as serious as those of the proposed solution or the present system?

Once you have located the main issues of the proposition, you are ready to begin to build a case. Then you must work with your partner, and support your case.

Build a Case

In debate, the term **case** refers to a team's total argument on any given proposition, set down in writing. There are at least two methods for outlining a debate case, either of which can be effective, depending on the side you will be debating and on your own personal preference.

A **brief** is a full outline of your case, written in complete sentences. It contains, as main heads, what you consider the major issues in the

TEACH

AMAZING FACTS!

In the U.S. there are over 826,000 lawyers, or one for every 312 people. It is estimated that the U.S. has more than 50% of the world's supply of lawyers.

● **TEACHING**

Explain the two methods for outlining a debate case. Demonstrate the brief format that uses the main issues as organization headings. Point out the advantages for the affirmative team. Demonstrate the use of evidence cards and the advantages for the negative team.

CHAPTER 13 Debate

Three common arrangements for debate are the standard format, the cross-examination format, and the Lincoln-Douglas format.

Standard format	Speaking time
First affirmative constructive speech	10 minutes
First negative constructive speech	10 minutes
Second affirmative constructive speech	10 minutes
Second negative constructive speech	10 minutes
First negative speaker's rebuttal	5 minutes
First affirmative speaker's rebuttal	5 minutes
Second negative speaker's rebuttal	5 minutes
Second affirmative speaker's rebuttal	5 minutes

Cross-examination format	Speaking time
First affirmative constructive speech	8 minutes
First negative speaker cross-examines	3 minutes
First negative constructive speech	8 minutes
Second affirmative speaker cross-examines	3 minutes
Second affirmative constructive speech	8 minutes
Second negative speaker cross-examines	3 minutes
Second negative constructive speech	8 minutes
First affirmative speaker cross-examines	3 minutes
First negative speaker's rebuttal	4 minutes
First affirmative speaker's rebuttal	4 minutes
Second negative speaker's rebuttal	4 minutes
Second affirmative speaker's rebuttal	4 minutes

Lincoln-Douglas format	Speaking time
Affirmative constructive speech	6 minutes
Negative cross-examination	3 minutes
Negative constructive speech	7 minutes
Affirmative cross-examination	3 minutes
Affirmative speaker's rebuttal	4 minutes
Negative speaker's rebuttal	6 minutes
Affirmative speaker's rebuttal	3 minutes

ENRICHMENT

Invite an experienced member of the debate team to speak to the class about strategies for building a case for or against the debate proposition. A video of the school debate team could be shown to demonstrate the debate format and speaking styles.

SKILL APPLICATION

Debate
The selection of a debate partner, business partner, or marriage partner is a major decision. Encourage students to think about their own strengths and weaknesses. Have them identify the qualities they would want in an effective debate partner. Have them work with selected or assigned partners to choose the type of format they will use to research information to begin to build their case.

---

case. The subheads are the evidence and proof for those issues. Specific examples, quotations, and statistics are sometimes written out fully as sub-subheads. They may also be placed on individual evidence cards and then referred to by number in the brief. Affirmative teams usually find it easier to prepare a case in the form of a brief than negative teams do. Since the negative often does not know the specific plan the affirmative will use, preparing a complete brief is difficult. However, negative teams sometimes prepare several briefs. During the debate, the negative chooses the one that presents the case that works best against the issues raised by the affirmative team.

The second method of preparing a case is to outline it on evidence cards. This is often simpler for negative teams. Particular cards may be inserted into the case, deleted, or rearranged, depending on the approach taken by the affirmative. The method for building a case on evidence cards consists of numbering the individual pieces of evidence (one on each card) in the order in which they will be presented during the debate. Additional evidence cards must be handy for use whenever the opposition inserts an unexpected issue into the debate. Thus, evidence cards are more flexible and adaptable than a complete brief.

The brief includes all the debater's analysis and reasoning. Evidence cards contain only the evidence. Inexperienced debaters will probably find it helpful to prepare both. Preparing a brief like the model on page 423 firmly establishes the logic of the case in one's mind. The evidence cards are simpler and easier to handle during the actual debate.

Whether you prepare your own case on evidence cards or by writing a brief, it is important that you plan what your opponents are likely to say in response to your arguments as you proceed. As you build your case, be constantly alert to discover the best refutation to each of your points. Put yourself in the other side's position, and research their probable answers as you look for support for your own case. In this way you will be best prepared to meet their responses during the actual debate.

Work with Your Partner

Just as attorneys often work in teams to represent a client, so do most school debates involve two-person teams. Teamwork in preparation, and consistency in the team's presentations, are very important in debating. If you are going to debate with a partner, prepare for the debate with that partner. This does not mean that each of you cannot do research independently. However, the overall planning of your strategy, deciding on the major issues, writing the brief, and rehearsal must

TEACH

> **"The first thing we do, let's kill all the lawyers."**
> —Shakespeare

● **LEARNING STYLES**

❋ **Cooperative Learning**
Each group could organize the research they are pursuing for the debate proposition using the format presented in the outline on the next page. Discuss other uses or applications for this outline format. Students could think of other classes or opportunities to use the skill of outlining.

---

422   CHAPTER 13 Debate

If you are scheduled to debate with a partner, it is important that overall planning, deciding on the issues, writing the brief, and rehearsing be done as a team.

be done as a team. Each person must be certain which issues the othe will deal with. Each must know how the team will handle unexpecte points brought up by the opposition. Thorough rehearsal also gets yo used to your partner's speaking style and ensures that all parts of th case mesh properly. Nothing can hurt a team's chances of winning debate as much as a contradiction or disagreement between member

During the actual debate, listen carefully as your partner is speaking Everything you say should agree with your partner's presentation. An disagreement between team members must be resolved either before hand or privately during the debate. You will need to recognize one c your team members as leader. When a disagreement arises during debate about the team's strategy, the matter must be settled quickly There is not time for extended discussion. After a brief private exchang of views on the matter, the recognized team leader should decide.

Support Your Case

The kinds of evidence and reasoning that you use to support a debat case are the same as those used for support in a public speech. Begi by reviewing "Know What You Are Researching" on page 191 and "Ge to Know Your Library" on page 195 in Chapter 7. Then review "Logo Being Logical" on page 362 in Chapter 11. These will remind you c places to look for evidence. They will also show you how to put tha evidence together to form a convincing argument.

This model brief shows the basic order and structure to use when outlining a case or debate.

INTRODUCTION

"Resolved: that (state the proposition) _____."

I. The justification for the debate (cause for discussion)
   A.
   B.
   C. (And so on)
II. The history of the question
   A.
   B.
   C. (And so on)
III. Definition of potentially controversial terms
   A.
   B.
   C. (And so on)
IV. Waived issues
V. Conceded matters
VI. The main issues of the debate
   A. To be established by the affirmative
      1.
         a.
         b.
      2. (And so on)
   B. To be established by the negative
      (developed in the manner just shown)

DISCUSSION

I. First main contention _____ for
   A. First subcontention _____ for
      1. Evidence _____ and
         a. _____ and
         b. _____ for
            (1) _____ for
               (a) _____
   B. (And so on)
II. Second main contention (developed in the manner just shown)
III. (And so on)

CONCLUSION

I. Since _____ , and
II. Since (include as many points in summary as there are main contentions)_____
Therefore, (repeat proposition by affirming or denying it).

● **SKILL DEVELOPMENT**

Outlining
Students could use the editorial page of the paper and select an article or editorial to outline. Have them complete an outline based on the article they selected and share the argument with the class.

TEACH

SUBSTITUTE TEACHER TIP
Bring to class some "Trivial Pursuit" type questions. Explain that knowing how to get answers is often more valuable than actually knowing an answer. Read a question to the class and ask students where they might find the answer. Repeat this several times.

> ❝I'll not listen to reason.... Reason always means what someone else has got to say.❞
>
> —Elizabeth Gaskell

● **LEARNING STYLES**

✻ Cooperative Learning
The groups should try to set goals for the pursuit of research that will support the team's debate position. Each person's responsibilities should be clarified. Discuss sources for quotes, statistics, and examples that each team will find useful.

Technology Tools
Ask students familiar with computers and various on-line services to share information with the class about sources of information commonly available through computers. Discuss how access to the information highway has changed the nature of research.

● **SKILL DEVELOPMENT**

Research
Assign library search activities such as information scavenger hunts. With a partner, students can consult references to develop bibliographies and other sources for gathering information.

---

424   CHAPTER 13 Debate

Working with Evidence How much evidence is sufficient? There is no magic answer to this question. It would be nice if you could be sure that a combination of three direct quotes, four sets of statistics, and two individual examples would always beat an opponent. But since, in debate, the team with the greater amount of sound evidence usually wins, the wise team will gather as much evidence as possible.

The methods of recording evidence for use in debate are slightly different from those of recording evidence for a public speech. For one thing, a public speaker will ordinarily not record much evidence beyond what will actually be used during the speech. A good debater, however, should have on hand about three times the number of evidence cards expected to be used in the debate. This is always necessary because neither team knows beforehand what kind of approach to the topic the other side will take.

Quotations, statistics, and examples are recorded on 3 × 5 cards, as for a public speech. For debate, each card heading should list the issue to which the card relates and which position that piece of evidence supports. Underneath the heading, note the source from which you obtained the information, including the author's name and qualifications, the title and date of the work you are quoting, and the page number where the evidence can be found. Below that, record the quotation, statistic, example, or other evidence. Note these elements on the evidence card shown on page 426.

Because, in debate, the team with the greater amount of sound evidence usually wins, you should have about three times as much information as you expect to use.

LINKS TO PAST LEARNING

Review students' experiences with bibliographies and term papers. If there is a school manual of style for research papers, take this opportunity to review what the school considers "correct" format.

CURRICULAR CONNECTIONS

Writing
Ask students to demonstrate proper citations for quotations and references used to gather information and statistics.

SKILL DEVELOPMENT

Research
Have students practice using index cards to record quotations, statistics, and examples with proper source citations. Peer editing might be useful to help partners work with each other to ensure consistent reference treatment.

Using Reasoning Reasoning is the mental process of forming logical conclusions from one's evidence. Through reasoning, a debater builds an affirmative or a negative case. Reasoning enables a debater to refute arguments of the opposition during a debate. For centuries, several forms of reasoning have been considered valid. Among these are induction, deduction, cause to effect, effect to cause, and analogy.

Induction is reasoning from specific facts or cases to general principles. Here a person begins by stating a number of facts that are similar. If these similarities are consistent enough, the reasoner concludes that they represent a general principle. For example, if you wish to prove that having smoke alarms in homes can save lives, you could give statistics for the last five years comparing the number of deaths caused by fires in homes with smoke alarms versus the number in homes without smoke alarms. From these statistics you could conclude that having smoke alarms in homes can save lives.

In **deduction** you reason from general principles to specific cases. In using deduction, a debater attempts to prove a specific case is true because it falls under a general principle or law. Thus, if you wished to show that an affirmative team's plan should be rejected because it could lead to greater inflation, you would start with the general principle, "Any plan that causes greater inflation is undesirable." Next you would give evidence to show that the plan of the affirmative side would cause higher prices. Your conclusion, then, is "this plan will very likely lead to more inflation. Therefore, it should be rejected."

Reasoning from what began something to its result is reasoning from **cause to effect.** If you show that one event will take place as a result of another event, you are using cause-to-effect reasoning. In attempting to prove that jury trials should be done away with, one of your arguments could be that serving on juries causes hardship on the jurors. The cause would be serving on juries. The effect would be hardship on the jurors.

Reasoning from a result back to what started it is reasoning from **effect to cause.** In arguing the other side of the jury system topic, you would be using effect-to-cause reasoning if you showed that the excellent record of court decisions in this country is largely due to the jury system.

An **analogy** is a comparison. When using analogy, you prove the truth of something by showing its similarity to something else. For example, in debating the safety of nuclear power plants you might argue: "Building and operating a nuclear power plant today is about as safe as lighting one's campfire within three feet of a wooden keg of gunpowder. As long as you exercise extraordinary caution, everything is fine. But take your eyes off that fire for just a few minutes, and the results can be unbelievable!"

TEACH

● TEACHING

Explain to students that there are at least five forms of reasoning they can use to build or refute an argument. List these on the chalkboard and provide examples of each. The five are (1) induction, (2) deduction, (3) cause to effect, (4) effect to cause, and (5) analogy.

● LEARNING STYLES

✳ Cooperative Learning
Students can discuss each of the five forms of reasoning and find examples of each that are used in advertising, TV, and newspapers every day. Groups should evaluate the relative strength of each form of reasoning. Encourage individual students to identify the form of reasoning that seems most effective for them to use. Discuss why variety is a useful tool in developing an argument for or against a proposition.

Visual Learning
Use the illustration of the model evidence card to point out the important elements that should be on each card.
Have students make their own cards based on the model.

● ACTIVITY

Help students prepare a brief for one of the issues involved in the debate proposition they are working on. Again, the peer editing strategy could be effective in helping students arrive at consistency of format and useful information.

CHAPTER 13 Debate

This model evidence card shows how to record information.

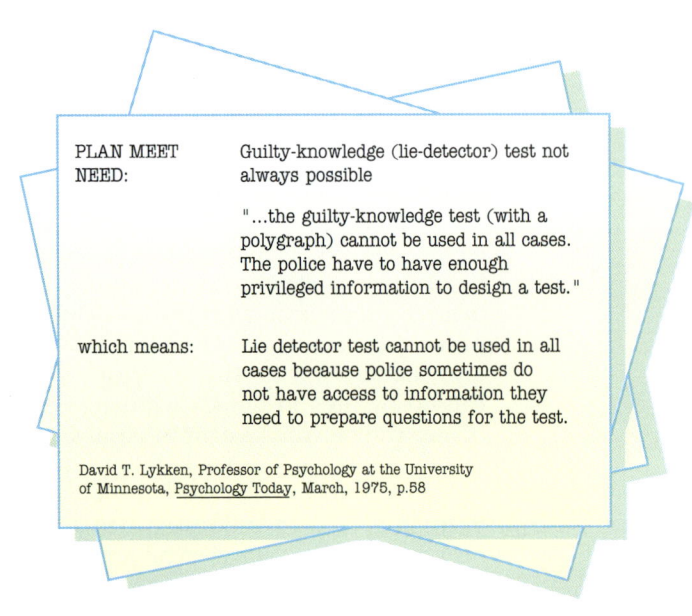

PLAN MEET NEED:	Guilty-knowledge (lie-detector) test not always possible
	"...the guilty-knowledge test (with a polygraph) cannot be used in all cases. The police have to have enough privileged information to design a test."
which means:	Lie detector test cannot be used in all cases because police sometimes do not have access to information they need to prepare questions for the test.

David T. Lykken, Professor of Psychology at the University of Minnesota, <u>Psychology Today</u>, March, 1975, p.58

For reasoning to be successful, of course, it must be supported by sound evidence. If you think of reasoning as a steel bridge that can carry an argument from start to finish, evidence can be seen as the individual girders that support the bridge itself. Without the support of examples, statistics, and quotations, the structure of reasoning collapses. Beware of going into a debate armed with reasoning, but without having researched enough evidence to support that reasoning.

● ACTIVITY

Using Evidence and Reasoning
Analyze one of the debate propositions selected in the previous Activity. Discover one major issue of the proposition, gather at least four pieces of evidence for it, and write each piece of evidence on a separate index card. Then prepare a brief, or outline, for a well-supported argument on this issue.

● USING DIFFERENT STRATEGIES

Each side in a debate is responsible for certain tasks. You read about these tasks on pages 417 and 418. How each side goes about fulfilling their responsibilities depends on the strategy each chooses to use, as well as the format of the debate.

ETHICALLY SPEAKING

Using Quotations Responsibly

When you use a direct quotation from someone to support your communication, or even when you paraphrase someone's ideas in your own words, it is similar to using someone's personal property. The quote does not belong to you, so you need to take every precaution to use it carefully and properly. Ethically speaking, here are some guidelines for using quotations:

Be sure to identify the person you are quoting or paraphrasing, so that there is no confusion among your listeners about the ideas in your message that you originated, and those that are borrowed.

Use the quotation or paraphrase in its proper context. If you are quoting from an essay that is generally negative, for example, it is not fair to quote the one positive comment that the essay may contain, unless you explain that is what you are doing.

If you edit the quotation, be sure your edited version remains true to the original intent. If the person you are quoting uses qualifying words such as *perhaps, probably, often, presumably, frequently,* etc., it would be irresponsible to eliminate these words to make a stronger statement. Editing of this nature would misrepresent the intent of the person who made the statement.

In using other people's words and thoughts, be as careful as you would be if you were using their books or clothes or apartment. The owners are not present to explain or defend themselves, so it is your responsibility to do so.

With the use of another person's work comes the responsibility of accurate quotation and correct attribution to the source.

427

APPLY

● **CURRICULAR CONNECTIONS**

Language Arts
Ask students to use one of the quotations provided in this teacher's edition, if you have shared them with the class, or to find a favorite quotation. In addition to naming the source of the quotation, ask students what additional information they would be interested in having when they use, or hear, a quotation.

● **LEARNING STYLES**

Cooperative Learning
Have small groups of students read a review of a movie, play, or television program. Ask the group to select the one sentence, word, or phrase they would want to use if they were in charge of its publicity. The group could develop a newspaper ad using that quotation. Groups could compare their ad with movie or theater ads that use quotes.

● **SKILL DEVELOPMENT**

Main Idea
Have students select one of the speeches printed in the Appendix. Ask them to edit the speech so that they have a quotation that does not exceed 50 words. Invite volunteers to read their quotation to the class while members of the class open their books to the complete document. Comment on the speaker's success in remaining true to the original intent and style.

427

TEACH

SUBSTITUTE TEACHER TIP

You could bring a humorous book to class that compiles famous, stupid, or silly sayings. Share some of them with the class and invite them to identify the gaps in logic or reasoning.

● **CURRICULAR CONNECTIONS**

Language Arts
Students might enjoy reading parts of *Alice in Wonderland* for examples of crazy, mixed-up logic. Invite them to share examples with the class.

● **SKILL APPLICATION**

Debate
Emphasize the nature of a *prima facie* case and ask students to find examples of this kind of argument in current mass media literature.

CHAPTER 13 Debate

Fulfilling Responsibilities of the Affirmative Side

The first task of the affirmative in carrying its burden of proof is that presenting a **prima facie case.** A *prima facie* case means an over argument that would convince any reasonable judge who has not y heard the response of the other side. Say the proposition being debate is "Resolved, that the federal government should provide a guarantee annual income for all U.S. citizens." If the affirmative fails to show th harm comes from U.S. citizens not being guaranteed an income, ar merely claims it would be helpful for everyone to have the money, has failed to present a *prima facie* case. The argument is too weak deserve a response. In such an instance, a judge could decide in fav of the other side even before hearing any of its arguments.

The affirmative side always opens a debate. If you are the fir speaker for the affirmative, you should begin by stating the deba proposition. You should also define any terms in the proposition th need definition. Then you must present your proposal for change l proving that there are serious weaknesses in the *status quo*. These a often needs that are not being met (or cannot be met) by the prese approach to the problem. If the debate proposition calls for changir the jury system, for example, you might argue that the present jury sy tem causes undue hardship through lengthy delays. You might al: argue that the present jury system is terribly expensive. Once a speak from the other side has had a chance to respond, the second affirmati speaker generally presents the team's plan for change. This speak shows the advantages of the plan over the *status quo*. In this case, th second affirmative might argue for a team of six professional juro whose experience would enable them to decide cases much more ef ciently, thus hastening trial dates and saving money in the long run.

The responsibilities of the affirmative team are frequently divide along the following lines:

First affirmative	*Second affirmative*
States proposition	Presents affirmative plan
Defines terms	Shows advantage of plan
Attacks *status quo*	Summarizes entire affirmative case

If there is only one debater on each side, then all of the above tasks fa to the single affirmative speaker.

This form of affirmative argument based on need → plan → adva tages has long been the most common approach to building an aff mative case. It has usually been called the **needs case.**

In recent years, however, a slightly different type of affirmative re soning has often been used instead of the needs case. This other for

● **TEACHING**

You might suggest that each debate team make something similar to "cue" cards to identify the steps, time, and emphasis for each type of responsibility identified in this section. Compare the "Needs Case" argument with the "Comparative Advantages" argument. Have debate teams examine their debate proposition and determine which strategy would work best for their argument.

> *"I never dared be radical when young*
> *For fear it would make me conservative when old."*
> —Robert Frost

● **SKILL APPLICATION**

Debate
Ask some student partners to develop a comparative advantages–based argument and others, a needs case argument. Let students get practice presenting both types of arguments to each other. Let each pair identify their own suggestions to strengthen their arguments.

---

of affirmative case is called the **comparative advantages case.** Instead of the typical need → plan → advantages form of arguments, this affirmative case consists of agreed goals → plan → comparative advantages. With certain debate topics, it is sometimes more useful than a needs case. An example would be a debate proposition that reads, "Resolved, that the state's sales tax should be abolished." In using a comparative advantages case to debate this topic the affirmative would begin by calling upon the negative to agree that everyone should be allowed to keep as much of their personal income as possible to spend as they see fit. The negative can hardly disagree with that idea. It would be an **agreed goal.** The debate then revolves, not around the goal of personal economic freedom, but around a comparison of two means by which to achieve that goal. The affirmative would then argue that their plan—for example, to reduce certain state services—would prove better for citizens than paying the sales tax to get those services. A good affirmative debater will carefully analyze a debate proposition. Then the debater will decide which strategy—a needs case or a comparative advantages case—will work better for a given topic.

A comparative advantages case generally calls for a division of speaking responsibilities quite different from that used with a needs case:

First affirmative

States proposition

Defines terms

Presents goals negative will have to agree with

Presents plan for meeting goals

Outlines advantages of plan

Second affirmative

Responds to attacks of first negative speaker

Reinforces plan

Fulfilling Responsibilities of the Negative Side

The basic task of the negative side is to disprove the attacks on the *status quo* made by the affirmative. There are several ways the negative may do this. Any one of these may win the debate for the negative if done well enough. One way is by attacking the affirmative's arguments of need. The negative may claim that the *status quo* is completely satisfactory or that the affirmative has failed to prove it unsatisfactory. There is no need for a change.

Another possibility is for the negative to center its attacks on the affirmative plan. Here the negative argues that the affirmative plan

TEACH

● **LEARNING STYLES**

Cooperative Learning
Ask students who are taking the negative side of the debate proposition to identify the four approaches described in this section. These could be listed on the "cue" cards mentioned earlier or listed on the chalkboard.

● **SKILL APPLICATION**

Debate
Debate strategies include the need-plan wedge argument. Have partners develop a need-plan wedge argument and practice the delivery of it. Have them analyze the relative strength of the argument and develop modifications based on their own evaluations.

---

would create problems more serious than those currently being experienced under the *status quo*. This is usually the best strategy to use against an affirmative comparative advantages case.

A third option is the **need-plan wedge case.** When using this approach, the negative does not attack the affirmative's need or plan directly. Rather the negative attacks the logical link between the two. The negative argues "even if the need the affirmative claims did exist (which is doubtful), and even if their plan were a workable one (which is doubtful), their plan is incapable of satisfying the need they have outlined."

A fourth approach, and perhaps the most common one, is called the **running-refutation negative case.** Here the negative side attacks all parts of the affirmative case. It claims that the *status quo* is handling the situation satisfactorily and that the affirmative has failed to show a need for a change. It also argues that the affirmative plan is not workable, that the plan would not produce any significant advantages, and that it might produce some disadvantages.

Unlike the affirmative side, which begins the debate knowing its own strategy, the negative has the disadvantage of having to wait until the debate has begun to decide its specific plan of attack. However, this does not mean the negative cannot prepare beforehand. Thorough preparation for the negative consists of researching all of the major issues the affirmative might use. Then the negative must prepare a response to whatever kind of case the affirmative might choose. The affirmative team's strategy will become evident during their first speech. Then the negative side can insert its most appropriate proofs and its most appropriate case.

The duties of the first and second negative speakers differ according to how the affirmative case is presented as well as according to how they decide to disprove the affirmative case. If the affirmative uses a needs case, the first negative speaker will generally refute the affirmative needs. The second negative will generally attack the plan and its advantages. If the affirmative has chosen to use a comparative advantages case rather than a needs case, the negative response will be different. In that case, the first negative will generally attack the affirmative advantages. These will have been heard in the first affirmative speech. The negative will usually try to show that the affirmative plan cannot produce the advantages claimed, that the advantages are not significant, or that they can be gained without the affirmative plan. The second negative will generally refute the plan itself and try to show it to be unworkable. The argument will usually be that the plan will produce disadvantages that outweigh any advantages.

Having prepared to refute an array of possible affirmative arguments, the responsibilities of the negative speakers might be summarized as in the list on the following page.

If the affirmative uses a needs case;

First negative	**Second negative**
Agrees with or redefines affirmative's definitions	Attacks affirmative plan
Refutes affirmative's needs	Refutes advantages

If the affirmative uses a comparative advantages case:

First negative	**Second negative**
Agrees with or redefines affirmative's definitions	Attacks affirmative plan
Attacks advantages of affirmative plan	

Debate Formats

Many different formats can be used for conducting debates. The format that is used depends on the time available, the seriousness of the issue, and the number of debaters on each side. Here the discussion will focus on three formats widely used in high school debates.

In the **standard format** two different kinds of speeches are made by each of the two speakers on each team. Each speaker gives both a constructive speech and a rebuttal. The **constructive speeches** are lengthy, usually ranging from eight to ten minutes each. They are used to present and develop the major points of each team's case. **Rebuttals** typically last four to five minutes each. They are used to refute the opposition's arguments and to answer objections to one's own case.

In the standard format this is the order of speakers:

Speaker	**Number of minutes**
First affirmative constructive speech	10
First negative constructive speech	10
Second affirmative constructive speech	10
Second negative constructive speech	10
First negative rebuttal	5
First affirmative rebuttal	5
Second negative rebuttal	5
Second affirmative rebuttal	5
Total time	60

TEACH

SUBSTITUTE TEACHER TIP

You could make a large diagram of a clock and block out the minute segments for each of the phases of the debate schedule. Some students might want to serve as timekeeper for the various debate speakers.

• LINKS TO PAST LEARNING

Ask students to identify situations where every minute or second counted. There are many movie and TV scripts that depict such situations. Share examples and make the connection with the timing of debate speeches.

• ENRICHMENT

Some students might determine which of the current members of Congress were once members of their school debate team either in high school or college. The information could be presented in graphic form and shared with the class.

"Judge—a law student who marks his own examination papers."
—H.L. Mencken

• SKILL APPLICATION

Debate
Students could role-play a scene from a movie or TV program that involved a courtroom and the cross-examination of a key witness.

CHAPTER 13 Debate

Notice that the order of affirmative and negative speakers switches in the rebuttal period. This is done to assure that the affirmative team both opens and closes the debate.

The **cross-examination format** also has two speakers representing each side. In this format, cross-examinations follow immediately after each constructive speech. A member of the opposite team attempts to expose weaknesses in each speaker's arguments by asking questions for the speaker to answer. High school cross-examination periods usually last about three minutes. The order of speakers in the cross-examination format is shown in the list below. Note that debates following the cross-examination format differ from debates following the standard format in only one respect: Each constructive speech is followed by a cross-examination period.

Speaker	*Number of minutes*
First affirmative constructive speech	8
First negative speaker cross-examines	3
First negative constructive speech	8
Second affirmative speaker cross-examines	3
Second affirmative constructive speech	8
Second negative speaker cross-examines	3
Second negative constructive speech	8
First affirmative speaker cross-examines	3
First negative speaker's rebuttal	4
First affirmative speaker's rebuttal	4
Second negative speaker's rebuttal	4
Second affirmative speaker's rebuttal	4
Total time	60

The times for each presentation in both the standard and the cross-examination format may be shortened to insure that a debate will fit within a class period. In tournament competition, however, the times indicated should be strictly observed.

Another debate format that is often used in competitions is called the **Lincoln-Douglas format.** It gets its name from the famous debates between senatorial candidates Abraham Lincoln and Stephen A. Douglas in 1858. In Lincoln Douglas style debates, each side is represented by only one speaker. This style of debate, as it is usually practiced, is little more than a modification of the standard cross-examination format.

● LINKS TO PAST LEARNING

Take a poll of students' favorite TV trial lawyers. Students could nominate their choices in a brief speech. Votes could be tallied and the winner announced. Discuss the traits of great trial lawyers.

● ENRICHMENT

Students could write to the local trial lawyer association to obtain information about the requirements for this profession and the number of practicing trial lawyers in your area. A trial lawyer could be invited to speak to the class and share stories about the training and communication skills required in the court room.

APPLY

"The public regards lawyers with great distrust. They think lawyers are smarter than the average guy but use their intelligence deviously. Well, they're wrong; usually they are not smarter."

—F. Lee Bailey

● SKILL DEVELOPMENT

15-Second Skill Opportunity
Ask each student to prepare an interview question they might ask a trial lawyer.

● SKILL APPLICATION

Debate
Students could ask the career counselor at school about the requirements for entry into law school. The costs and time involved should be identified and compared. A copy of LSAT preparation books could be available for interested students.

CAREER CLOSE-UP

Trial Lawyer

Lawyers interpret our increasingly complex body of laws. To accomplish this task, they must have a firm knowledge of the law and the legal system. Attorneys also need to communicate effectively with all types of people, and understand the process of debate. Law candidates must obtain a bachelor's degree followed by a law degree. Graduates then must pass the bar examination in the state in which they plan to practice.

As trial lawyers, attorneys must collect and carefully prepare the evidence needed to present a convincing case. They confer with the opposing lawyer to compare facts and to detect the other's strategy. Trial lawyers often rehearse their presentation to ensure that their delivery will be as sound as their preparation. In the courtroom, trial lawyers engage in debates as they represent their clients.

In such cases, lawyers must know how to search for weaknesses in the opposing lawyer's case. These flaws can be used to reveal an opponent's faulty reasoning, thus strengthening their own case. When both sides present their final argument, effective lawyers select only the most convincing facts, testimonies, and conclusions from the trial so that the judge or jury will be persuaded to decide in their client's favor.

Trial lawyers who master the art of debate are better able to champion the legal rights of their clients. Even more than that, when lawyers add a persuasive, well-documented presentation to their conscientious interpretation of the law, the rights of everyone in our society are better protected.

Inasmuch as debate is the medium for trial lawyers, those who master the art are better able to champion the legal rights of their clients.

433

TEACH

● **CURRICULAR CONNECTIONS**

History
Let some students research the circumstances and arguments of the Lincoln-Douglas debates. Individuals might want to impersonate the two historical figures and present one of their speeches.

● **SKILL DEVELOPMENT**

Critical Thinking
Ask students to use the explanations in the text to compare and contrast the three debate formats identified. Discuss which of the three versions would be easiest for most people to follow. Refer to the table on p. 420 for review.

Creative Thinking
Ask students to imagine that they are directing the campaign of a political candidate who has been challenged to a debate. Encourage them to plan a debate format that would best present the candidate's stand on the issues. Present their debate format to the class.

---

434   CHAPTER 13 Debate

The 1858 Lincoln-Douglas debates centered on the issue of slavery. Lincoln lost to Douglas in his run for the Senate but was elected president two years later.

    This exciting style of debate usually deals with a proposition of value rather than one of policy. The proposition "Resolved that the recently passed five-cent sales tax on gasoline should be revoked" would be inappropriate for Lincoln-Douglas debate because it is a proposition of policy. However, the proposition "Resolved, that the recently passed five-cent sales tax on gasoline will prove beneficial to our country" would fit this format well.

    Lincoln-Douglas debate is less formal and more philosophical than most other styles. It depends more on analysis and reasoning and less on evidence. Since it does not deal with a policy proposition, no plan is called for in the affirmative case.

    Lincoln-Douglas debate provides challenges and advantages to the individual debater that cannot exist when there are two people on a side. The challenges come from being alone and therefore totally responsible for arguing your side of the case. The advantages are that you do not have to coordinate your case with anyone, either during preparation or during the actual debate. You are forced to do your own research and preparation, two of the great benefits debate has to offer, and you alone can claim whatever credit your win-loss record shows.

    Participation in Lincoln-Douglas-style debate provides excellent preparation for the typical forms of informal debate that occur in everyday life. Most of the informal debates that you will engage in at home or on the job will have only one person advocating each side of a question. However, debates involving opposing teams do sometimes occur in everyday life, and therefore most people can benefit from gaining experience in both standard-format and Lincoln-Douglas-format debates

TEACH

● **TEACHING**

List the five topics that this section will concentrate on. These are (1) methods for testing the evidence of opponents, (2) faulty reasoning, (3) note-taking techniques during debate, (4) cross-examination techniques, and (5) persuasive delivery of debate speeches. Ask students to identify the area in which they think they need the most help.

● **LEARNING STYLES**

Cooperative Learning
Students could work in pairs to give and listen to an argument for or against an issue. The partner should respond to the argument. Together they should gain practice in identifying the strengths and weaknesses of their arguments.

● **SKILL APPLICATION**

Media Literacy
Have students look for examples of unsupported assertions in print advertising found in papers and magazines. You might also encourage students to find examples of ads that offer some support for their assertions. Discuss the strength or weakness of specific advertising assertions.

In debates following the Lincoln-Douglas format, the order of speakers is as follows:

Speaker	Number of minutes
Affirmative constructive speech	6
Negative cross-examination	3
Negative constructive speech	7
Affirmative cross-examination	3
Affirmative rebuttal	4
Negative rebuttal	6
Affirmative rebuttal	3
Total time	32

● **MEETING THE OPPOSITION**

Once a debate begins, your two primary tasks are to present your own case in the most favorable light possible and to refute the arguments of the opposition. This section will discuss methods of testing the evidence and reasoning presented by your opponents, the process of note-taking during a debate, cross-examination techniques, and delivery of debate speeches.

Look for Weaknesses in the Opposition's Evidence

The foundation on which any argument rests is its evidence. A good debate team will first be certain that its own evidence is both true and valid. Then, as the debate progresses, it will constantly look for weaknesses in the opponents' evidence.

Have your opponents presented sufficient evidence? Occasionally, debaters make statements they wish to have accepted as fact, but provide no supporting evidence. These statements are called **unsupported assertions.** Obviously, unsupported assertions represent the weakest form of argument. Suppose your opponents claim "Socialized medicine has worked effectively in other countries. There is no reason it cannot work effectively in the United States as well." They have made an unsupported assertion. Unless your opponents supply at least several examples of particular countries where socialized medicine has been effective, you should vigorously attack their argument as an unsupported assertion.

TEACH

> *Youk'n hide de fier, but w'at you gwine do wid de smoke?*
>
> —Joel Chandler Harris

● **SKILL DEVELOPMENT**

Creative Thinking
Challenge students to think of additional questions they might consider as they listen to the arguments of their opponents. Add these to the list they developed above.

● **TEACHING**

Have students read the questions they could use to test the quality of the opponent's evidence. Ask them to think of one-word summaries for each bullet and memorize the key words they selected. Suggest that these key words may help them respond to their opponents' comments.

CHAPTER 13 Debate

In meeting the opposition, you should look for weaknesses in the evidence and be alert to faulty reasoning.

It is obvious that without evidence it is impossible to win a case, but remember that the quality of a debater's evidence is just as important as the quantity. As you listen to an opponent's constructive speech, try to ascertain which pieces of evidence presented are questionable and open to attack during rebuttal. Here are several questions you can ask yourself to test the quality of your opponents' evidence:

- Is my opponent's source of evidence reliable? Is the person who is being quoted someone who is trustworthy? Knowledgeable in the field? Unprejudiced on the matter quoted?

- Are the statistics being presented sound? Have they been carefully gathered? Are they being reported accurately? Is the sample valid? Do the people questioned in the sample accurately represent the entire population?

- Are the proposition's examples appropriate? Has each individual case been reported by an eyewitness? Are there enough individual examples to support the debater's conclusion?

- Is the evidence being offered up-to-date? On certain debate topics where rapid change is not occurring, older evidence is acceptable. On a topic such as the energy crisis, however, statistics and examples from 1970 are no longer valid.

- Are there major pieces of evidence that contradict or invalidate the evidence presented by my opponents?

Watch Out for Faulty Reasoning

Sometimes debaters use sound evidence but still arrive at the wrong conclusion through faulty reasoning. Here are a few questions that can be used to test your opponents' reasoning:

- When reasoning by induction, has the opposition given enough examples? For instance, can a debater who cites three examples of dogs that have bitten children logically conclude "dogs make dangerous pets"? Obviously not.

- When arguing by deduction, have my opponents considered all reasonable alternatives? Consider this argument from a debate on socialized medicine: "To improve health care in this country we must institute a system of socialized medicine." The flaw in this argument is the failure of the debater to consider alternative solutions (other than socialized medicine) for improving health care, such as methods for easing the shortage of doctors in some areas of the country.

- When arguing by cause and effect, has the opposition shown that an event was actually *caused* by a preceding event or did it simply occur later? Suppose someone said, "We had baked apples for dessert last night and everyone in the family got sick. We'll never eat baked apples again." This person has blamed the baked apples when they may not have been the cause of the illness at all.

- When arguing by analogy, did my opponents overlook any essential differences in the two things being compared? A Russian once claimed to an American visitor that his system of government was as democratic as ours by arguing that they held elections, just as we do. The American found the flaw in the analogy and retorted that in the United States there is more than one party from which the voters may choose their candidates.

Take Notes and Keep a Flow Sheet

During a debate, you should take notes of your opponents' arguments. Be sure to include notes about any weaknesses you find in their evidence or reasoning. Include only those key points you want to respond to. In a typical debate, your opponents will bring up a much greater number of arguments than you will have time to answer. The approach of one high school debater was to begin a speech: "The negative team has asked us to answer a long list of questions. We are more than happy to do so, so here goes: yes, no, no, maybe, you've got us there, maybe, no, yes, yes...." Although this method may have secured a laugh from the judge, it probably did not win the debate for its user. A good debater will respond only to key arguments that apply directly to the case.

One useful method for selecting the key arguments to refute is to construct a flow sheet as the debate progresses. A **flow sheet** is your own summary outline written in a continuous manner to show how the arguments on each issue progress throughout the debate. It is written during the debate, usually in vertical columns on a large legal pad or art pad. Each column represents one speech that is given. If you record, in brief sentences or phrases, the essence of each argument—and the response to it in a subsequent column—you will have a picture of the debate at any point along the way.

TEACH

SUBSTITUTE TEACHER TIP
Make a generic three- or four-column table with room for topic identification and space to record information. This table could be duplicated and distributed to students to use as a flow sheet to record the organization and progress of a debate.

> ❝In the old days all you needed was a handshake. Nowadays you need forty lawyers.❞
> —Jimmy Hoffa

● **LEARNING STYLES**

Audio Learning
Ask students to tape a segment of a TV program. Using the tape, have students listen to the argument and summarize the action or statements of those taped. Ask students to discuss how viewers are encouraged to keep track of the characters or "arguments" of soap operas or other TV serials.

● **SKILL DEVELOPMENT**

Note Taking
Ask students to think of their own version of shorthand for words they commonly use or hear in debate. Have them make a list of at least ten words, and next to those words develop a symbol or shorthand abbreviation that they could use to make note taking easier.

438

---

438 CHAPTER 13 Debate

A partial flow chart from a debate on energy in the United States

1st. Aff. Con.	1st. Neg. Con.	2nd Aff. Con.
	Theme — Status quo can solve any problems.	
	Topicality — NO PLAN TO SOLVE	
	Sig. — NO QUANTIFICATION OF SOLVENCY	
	Harm — Economic harms are not pragmatic	→ reserves are not reliable
I. U.S. is dependent on oil (must import)	—SQ can decrease dependence Fossil Fuels	
A. Are dependent:	Oil demand is decreasing	→ Exxon evidence is biased
B. Imports will increase (36% needed)	We have enough Alaska's Oil } North Slope Oil }	→ Must compare to Arab reserves
	—Present System can Decrease Dependence	
II. Harms (personal)	→ No harm to Arab investment	→ Doesn't apply
A. Purchasing power decreasing ($45–$60 bill)	→ Doesn't hurt economy	→ Bad housing (deaths?)
B. Oil Crisis likely (only have enough reserve for 60 days)	→ OPEC can't afford embargo	
C. Problems will continue		Oil prices will increase
III. Harms (other)	→ A. No sig. impact	
A. Trade deficit is caused by oil.	B. Deficit must allow for investment	
B. Will get worse.	C. Deficit doesn't devalue dollar	PLAN I. National Coal Gasification Board
IV. Harms (economic)		II. Enforcement
A. The dollar devaluates.		III. Funding
B. Link–(Economy is tied to Energy.)		ADV–Less pollution
C. Inflation leads to higher oil prices		A. 65% sulfur and ash removed
D. Inf. will continue		B. Coal can't be undermind by OPEC

Meeting the Opposition

2nd. Neg. Con.	1st. Neg. Reb.	1st. Aff. Reb.
→X	No Sig?	
→X (plan in 2AC is unfair)	No Inh	
→X	No Impact to Harm	
→Energy demand is slower		
→Best (only) evidence given		→Aff. evidence is better
	→X	
	→goes both ways	
→Difficult link	→X	
	→X	
→X		
→X		
*Trade deficit not shown to be the same as devaluation of the dollar	→Extra topical	→can't deny the advantage.

SKILL DEVELOPMENT

Creative Thinking
Based on the notes presented in this flow sheet, ask students to identify which they consider to be the strongest team—the affirmative or negative. Then have them target the strongest or weakest argument and prepare a strategy for responding to the debate.

LEARNING STYLES

Technology Tools
Ask students to think of ways that a laptop computer might be useful to a debate team. Then brainstorm suggestions for other possible uses for laptops. Ask students to think of ways they would use one personally as well as in school or at work. Survey the number of students who think they will use them within the next five years.

TEACH

● **LINKS TO PAST LEARNING**

You might show an excerpt from a movie or TV program that illustrates the cross-examination process. *The Verdict* or *Twelve Angry Men* might be suitable for your class.

● **LEARNING STYLES**

Visual Learning
Ask students to prepare posters that would illustrate the guidelines for the cross-examination process described on this page. They might use cartoon figures to identify the roles of the questioner and the respondent.

---

440 CHAPTER 13 Debate

A flow sheet enables you to see the arguments you have not responded to thus far in the debate and helps you select arguments for refutation that seem to be key points. Another advantage of keeping a flow sheet is being able to see which of your own arguments your opponents have been able to refute. The part of a sample flow sheet illustrated on pages 438 and 439 will give you an idea of how yours can be constructed.

Make Effective Use of Cross-examination

The brief cross-examination periods included in many high-school debates can be the most exciting part of a debate. These questioning sessions, modeled on courtroom cross-examination, give each team a chance to expose weaknesses in the opposition's case through clever questioning. Though skill at cross-examination requires some experience, here are suggestions for both the questioner and the respondent to consider:

For the Questioner

Prepare general questions on each of the major issues before the debate. During the debate, try to tie your questions as closely as possible to the specific arguments actually used by your opponents.

Never ask a question for which you think the opponents might have a strong answer. If their response is strong, you only score points for the opposition by giving them a free chance to state it.

Keep questions brief and clear. Do not attempt to confuse your opponent with long or complicated questions. You will also confuse the judge.

Demand brief answers. You cannot demand a simple yes or no. If the respondent begins to give a little speech, however, you may cut it off.

Do not comment on the responses you receive during the cross-examination period. This should be done in your, or your partner's, later speeches. You may, however, use follow-up questions during the cross-examination period.

For the Respondent

Be constantly on guard. The purpose of the questioner is to make your case look weak and foolish.

Remember that you do not have to answer an unreasonable question. If you are asked, "Are all your examples as bad as that one?" you may point out that this is a loaded question and refuse to answer it.

Keep your answers brief, but complete. You cannot be forced into single word answers. Briefly giving a reason or qualification for your answer is always permissible.

Meeting the Opposition

If you do not know the answer to a question or are not familiar with the context of the question, say so immediately.

If you do not have a strong answer to a particular question, it is better to yield the point immediately rather than offer a weak response. A weak response gives the questioner a chance to make you look bad with a series of embarrassing, follow-up questions.

Speak Persuasively

All the rules for public speaking and persuasion explained in Unit 4 apply in debate. Since a debate is a special kind of speaking situation, a few special rules need to be mentioned.

You are trying to convince the judge, not your opponents. Direct your arguments and your eye contact to the judge.

Be thoroughly familiar with your evidence cards. This will enable you to maintain a large measure of eye contact with the judge while reading them.

Do not develop the tendency of many debaters to try setting a speed record. A good speaking rate for any kind of persuasive public speaking is also a good speaking rate for debate. The judge is not interested in how many arguments you can squeeze into eight or ten minutes, but in how effective your arguments are.

Do not forget the value of gestures, platform movement, and facial expressions. Be dynamic and forceful in your delivery.

Maintain variety in vocal expression. Changes in pitch, rate, and volume give persuasive impact to your message.

Never allow yourself to get angry with you opponents. No matter how outrageous they seem, stick to the issues. Do not attack the debaters.

● ACTIVITY

Keeping a Flow Sheet

Keep a flow sheet for a debate. You may actually attend the debate, listen to it on a recording, or hear it read by students in class. Note each major argument in the debate, and the opponent's response to it, in the proper column on your flow sheet. At the end of the debate, compare your flow sheet with those of your classmates. Did they interpret the arguments as you did? Take a class vote on which side won the debate. Briefly discuss the value of keeping a flow sheet. Discuss arguments that might have been made by either side in the debate but were not.

ASSESS

● STUDENT PERFORMANCE COMPETENCIES

- Explains the differences between debate and discussion
- Analyzes a debate proposition
- Gathers and uses evidence to support and build a debate case
- Describes and uses various debate strategies
- Demonstrates techniques to research and organize information quickly
- Applies debate skills to real situations

● sca GUIDELINES

- Uses voice effectively in debate and public meetings
- Identifies main ideas in debate arguments
- Distinguishes facts from opinions
- Expresses ideas clearly and concisely in public
- Supports debate position with evidence and logic
- Answers objections effectively

PORTFOLIO ASSESSMENT

Standard
- Glossary of Speech Terms
- Research Notes on Debate Topic
- Flow Sheet for Debate Summary
- Tape of Debate Segment
- Completed Assignments, Quizzes, Projects, and Chapter 13 Test

Enrichment
- Checklist for Debate Strategies
- Team Research of Evidence, Statistics, and Quotations
- Video of Best Debate Speeches
- Evaluation Guidelines
- Interview Questions for Debate Team

Challenge
- Winner of Class Debate
- Demonstration of Debate Procedures and Format
- Enactment of the Lincoln-Douglas Debate

CHAPTER 13 REVIEW

● SUMMARY

Debate is perhaps the most challenging form of oral communication. It is used daily in courts and legislatures as a means of arriving at decisions about important issues. It has also been used in schools for centuries as a means of training for responsible decision making.

The Nature of Debate A formal debate begins with a proposition—a statement that something should be considered or done—that is answerable by both yes and no. There are only two sides in a debate. The affirmative upholds the proposition by proving that a problem requiring change exists in the *status quo* and that its plan for a solution would work better than any other. The negative argues against such a change by refuting the affirmative's arguments. A judge decides the winner.

Preparing to Debate Preparing to participate in a debate demands careful analysis of the debate proposition, the writing of a fully outlined case, close work with your debate partner, gathering sound evidence, and the development of clear reasoning. Analyzing the proposition includes deciding what terms need definition, obtaining background information about the proposition, and focusing on its major issues.

Using Different Strategies The affirmative side always opens a debate by first presenting a *prima facie* case— an overall argument that would convince any reasonable person who has not also heard the negative side. The affirmative may use a needs-case strategy, present a plan to meet those needs, and then show the advantages of that plan. Another approach is the comparative advantages case, in which the affirmative presents goals on which both sides can agree, followed by a plan it attempts to show is better than the negative's approach.

The negative side must disprove the attacks of the affirmative. They may attack the affirmative's claims of need, its plan, or the logical link between the needs and plan. A fourth way is to attack all parts of the affirmative case. This is called the running-refutation negative case.

Meeting the Opposition When a debate begins, you must continually test your opponents' evidence and reasoning and also take careful notes on a flow sheet to determine how the arguments

ASSESS

● **ASSESSMENT STRATEGIES**

Individual Assessment
- Participates in practice activities daily or weekly
- Completes classwork
- Demonstrates knowledge of content through questions, discussion, quizzes, and Chapter 13 test
- Displays debate skills of research, argument, cross-examination, and rebuttal

Group Assessment
- Sets and achieves goals
- Works as effective member of the debate team
- Supports efforts of the team and class members
- Provides encouragement and feedback to members of the debate team

on each issue are progressing. Never ask a question during cross-examination if you know there is a strong answer. Keep questions brief and clear, and demand brief answers. Respondents should always be on guard. They should keep their answers brief and admit immediately if they do not know an answer.

VOCABULARY

Define each term in a complete sentence.

formal debate	analogy
proposition	*prima facie* case
affirmative	needs case
negative	comparative advantages case
status quo	agreed goal
burden of proof	need-plan wedge case
refute	running-refutation negative case
cross-examine	standard format
issue	constructive speech
case	rebuttal
brief	cross-examination format
induction	Lincoln-Douglas format
deduction	unsupported assertion
cause to effect	flow sheet
effect to cause	

✔ CHECKLIST

Debate Skills

1. Understand the kinds of issues that are debatable.
2. Be able to debate the affirmative and negative sides.
3. Prepare carefully for a debate by analyzing the proposition.
4. Focus on the issues—the major points of disagreement.
5. Learn to use two methods for outlining a debate case.
6. Learn to work with a partner in debate.
7. Learn several different formats for conducting debates.
8. Use correct reasoning and self-control in debates.

● **ANSWERS**

See the Answer Key for more complete answers.

REVIEW QUESTIONS
1. The purpose is to determine which argument is most persuasive.
2. Debate issues are stated in propositions.
3. See the Answer Key for all the characteristics.
4. Preparation requires analysis, evidence, logic, and briefs.
5. Five forms are induction, deduction, cause to effect, effect to cause, and analogy.
6. During a debate, look for weak arguments and faulty reasoning, and keep a flow sheet.
7. The affirmative side proves that a problem exists and the solution would work better.
8. The negative side shows that the proposed plan is undesirable.
9. Cross-examination allows for questions right after the speech.
10. The questioner keeps questions brief and clear and demands short answers.

DISCUSSION QUESTIONS
The following code is used to designate discussion questions and activities as suitable for students of varying ability levels:
  ▼ = below average to average
  ◆ = average to above average
  ■ = all students

1. ■ Emphasize the role of discussion and mass communications in decision-making.
2. ▼ Review arguments and discuss how they apply to the affirmative and negative positions.
3. ■ Discuss the importance of correctly worded propositions.
4. ▼ In a formal debate, the affirmative's task is to present a *prima facie* case.

444

CHAPTER 13 REVIEW

REVIEW QUESTIONS

1. State the purpose of formal debate.
2. Describe how debate issues are stated.
3. Identify the characteristics included in a well-worded debate proposition.
4. Identify the steps you should take in preparing to debate.
5. Name five forms of reasoning that may be used to support a case.
6. Name three things you should do during a debate to prepare yourself to meet the opposition during rebuttal or cross-examination.
7. Describe the responsibilities of the affirmative side in a debate.
8. Describe the responsibilities of the negative side in a debate.
9. State the differences among the standard format, the cross-examination format, and the Lincoln-Douglas format.
10. Describe how a questioner should proceed during a cross-examination.

? DISCUSSION QUESTIONS

1. Discuss the role of debate in American society. Where is debate used? How important is it in the political process? What impact has television had on the role of debate?
2. Select one of the debate propositions from an Activity. Discuss the various arguments that could be developed on both the affirmative and negative sides of the issue. Which side of the issue would you prefer to argue? Why?
3. Discuss the following statement: "Resolved, that the brutal game of football should be abolished." Is this a well-worded debate proposition? If not, how could it be reworded to become one?
4. Discuss the elements that must be present before a *prima facie* case can be made. Refer to one of the propositions developed in the Activities. Give an example of an argument that does not constitute a *prima facie* case. Then develop an example that does meet the standards of a *prima facie* case.

ASSESS

CRITICAL THINKING

1. Analysis Assume that you are asked to debate the following proposition: "Resolved, that an increase in the state sales tax would provide better services to the state's citizens." Develop an affirmative or a negative case for this proposition.

2. Evaluation Assume that you are serving as a judge for a debate. Make a short outline of the things a judge needs to be alert for during the arguments. How would you use what you have learned about debate to decide on a winner?

ACTIVITIES

In-Class

1. As a class, select a policy issue and develop a properly worded debate proposition for it. Then work with a partner to prepare a case for either the affirmative or the negative side of the proposition. Analyze the question, plan your arguments, and gather evidence to support your viewpoint. If you are to argue the affirmative side, check your case to be sure that it meets all basic requirements. If you are to argue the negative side, decide on the best strategy to refute the likely arguments of the affirmative. Debate the proposition in class with two-person teams on opposing sides, and with the class serving as judge. Which pro and con strategies worked best? Why?

2. Invite a local attorney to speak to the class on the role of debate in the legal profession. Ask this person to explain in detail how a trial is conducted and what kinds of arguments are admissible. Ask questions about rules and standards of evidence—including what they are, how they may differ according to the type of case being tried, and what criteria are used to determine whether or not any given piece of evidence meets their stated requirements. Ask your guest to explain how a court case can be lost even though the evidence presented is sound.

CRITICAL THINKING
1. **Analysis** Review the text, then have students write the cases or meet in groups to work on the assignment.
2. **Evaluation** Discuss the importance of the judge's impartiality and knowledge of the debate process.

ACTIVITIES
In-Class
1. Allow several class periods for preparation and research.
2. Ask students to prepare questions before the visit.

ASSESS

3. Review the various types of reasoning with students.

Out-of-Class

1. The political debate is influenced by the popularity, charisma, and style of the participants.
2. Students should develop a properly worded debate proposition, conduct research, and gather evidence to support their position.
3. Students could select their own programs to evaluate, or you could tape a program for the class to discuss.
4. You could do this as an optional activity and conduct it at night, serving refreshments to the group.
5. Prepare cross-examination questions for use with this activity.

446

CHAPTER 13 REVIEW

3. Work in groups of from five to seven to develop a debatable proposition. Decide whether to argue the affirmative or the negative side of the issue and then gather evidence to support your case. Use your evidence to support an inductive, deductive, cause to effect, or effect to cause argument, and an analogy. Decide as a group which argument best supports your side and share your best argument with other groups.

Out-of-Class

1. Conduct research on both the Lincoln-Douglas debate of 1858 and the Kennedy-Nixon debate in the 1960 presidential campaign. In what ways has debate been affected by the technology of television? What aspects of debate have remained constant? How do you feel about the role of personal style and appearance in the debate process?

2. Develop a debate proposition of your own and choose either the negative or affirmative side of the question to work on. Find as much evidence as you can and record each piece on a separate card. Identify each card for use in a debate round. Start an evidence file that you can use in a class debate. Add additional evidence to your file as you collect it.

3. Watch television programs that use a debate format. Note the types of topics chosen for discussion. In your speech notebook, evaluate the effectiveness of each program. Summarize each discussion and decide whether or not the format that was used allowed for adequate coverage of the topic or debate proposition. Be prepared to share your evaluations with classmates and to offer suggestions for how these television debates could be improved.

4. Attend a formal debate. In your speech notebook, keep a flow sheet that shows how the arguments progressed. If possible, speak to some of the participants and find out how they conducted their research and planned for the debate. Summarize this information in your speech notebook.

5. Prepare a set of cross-examination questions for use in one of your classroom debates. Develop questions that you think the opposition will find difficult to answer. Make certain that your questions are brief and clear, and touch upon major issues of the debate. Be ready to adapt your questions to meet the changing needs of the live debate situation.

CHAPTER PROJECT

As a class, choose a debatable proposition and conduct a mini debate tournament in either the standard debate format or the Lincoln-Douglas format. Students may debate either individually or in teams. Each student or team will debate two rounds, one affirmative and one negative. Arrange for a judge who will decide the winners of each round. Undefeated debaters will meet other undefeated debaters. Eliminations will continue until two debaters or teams remain. The debate between these two final individuals or teams will determine the winners of the class championship.

CHAPTER PROJECT
- Although debate does involve winning and losing, students should realize that their grade depends on the debate process and skill, not on their winning or losing the debate. Award Certificates of Recognition to those who participate.

PREPARE

● CHAPTER PLANNER

Day 1	Day 2	Day 3	Day 4	Day 5
Prepare	Prepare	Prepare	Prepare	Prepare
Teach	Teach	Teach	Teach	Teach
Assess	Assess	Assess	Assess	Assess
Sub. Teacher Tip *p. 451*	Sub. Teacher Tip *p. 453*	Sub. Teacher Tip *p. 463*	Sub. Teacher Tip *p. 465*	

● CHAPTER OVERVIEW

This chapter examines the following topics:
- Basic Principles *p. 450*
- Holding a Meeting *p. 451*
- Motions *p. 455*

▼ PORTFOLIO PRODUCTS

Individual Projects
- Glossary of Speech Terms
- Meeting Agenda
- Written Resolution
- Tape of Meeting
- Chapter 14 Portfolio Products

Group Projects
- Transcript of Meeting
- Tape of Meeting
- Media Report on Meeting

● sca GUIDELINES

- Identifies main idea in meetings
- Distinguishes fact from opinion in public meetings
- Expresses and defends position during a public meeting
- Uses variety of reasoning techniques to present arguments in a public meeting
- Answers questions to clarify information in a public meeting

448

CHAPTER 14

Parliamentary Procedure

When you have completed this chapter you should be able to:

- Explain the purposes of parliamentary procedure.
- Describe several of the basic principles of parliamentary procedure.
- Explain the duties of the chair.
- Describe the purposes of each of the types of motions.
- Explain the order in which motions may be made.

448

TEACH

● **LINKS TO PAST LEARNING**

You might display a photo of the House of Parliament Building in London and ask if any students have visited there. Explain how Parliament and other representative houses are organized and why there is a need for procedures that make discussion and decision making in a large group easier.

● **MOTIVATION**

Suggest to students that they have ten minutes to plan a class field trip. At the end of the allotted time, ask what decisions they made, how those decisions were made, and if all students voiced opinions and voted. Introduce the notion of following a set of rules for conducting decision-making meetings.

● **ACTIVITY**

Conduct the quiz on parliamentary procedure and tally the results. The answers to the quiz are:

1. When the motion comes from a committee or board.
2. To bring the assembly to an immediate vote on one or more pending questions.
3. Fifty percent plus one, of members present and voting.
4. Two-thirds.
5. No. Though similar, their rules are referred to as Rules of the House.

If any students answered all five questions correctly, perhaps those students could be excused from homework or given a Certificate of Recognition.

Parliamentary Procedure 449

● **ACTIVITY**

Challenge Quiz on Parliamentary Procedure

Before reading this chapter, which of you can tell the class the correct answer to these questions?

1. When does a main motion *not* require a second?
2. What is the purpose of the motion called "Previous Question"?
3. How is "majority" ordinarily defined in parliamentary procedure?
4. What vote is required on the motion called "Limit or Extend Debate?"
5. Is parliamentary procedure the form of procedure used in the United States House of Representatives?

Some, but not all of these questions are answered in this chapter. If no one knows the answer to all five questions, perhaps your teacher will give you the answers, or will ask you to find the answers in the library.

Have you ever attended a meeting with more than five people present? Have you been frustrated by everyone talking at once? Did it seem to take forever to arrive at a decision? **Parliamentary procedure** is a set of rules designed to reduce that kind of frustration. Probably you have attended meetings of clubs, student government organizations, or other groups that use these rules to conduct their business. Parliamentary procedure makes discussion at such meetings more efficient and productive. The rules are also designed to protect the rights of the individual. These include the right to be heard, the right to remain silent, and the right to full and free discussion of every issue presented. While parliamentary procedure provides for majority rule, it also protects the rights of the minority.

Parliamentary procedure did not suddenly spring into existence fully developed. Years ago a few basic rules were formed in the early English Parliament. They were gradually expanded and changed to fit the needs of that growing body and other democratic groups and societies where it came to be used. Today a number of standard codes of parliamentary procedure are in use. By far the most popular in the United States, however, is *Robert's Rules of Order Newly Revised,* on which this chapter is based. This chapter will not make you a **parliamentarian** (an expert on parliamentary procedure). It will, however, explain the fundamentals of parliamentary procedure. Copies of these codes are readily available for anyone who wants to learn more.

449

TEACH

> **"There never was a democracy yet that did not commit suicide."**
> —John Adams

● SKILL DEVELOPMENT

Critical Thinking
Students should examine the five basic principles that form the basis of parliamentary procedure. Based on these principles, discuss what the underlying assumptions about meetings and participants might be. Encourage students to think of several consequences that would result from the implementation of these principles.

15-Second Skill Opportunity
Ask students to write a question on a piece of paper. Collect all the questions. Discuss how each question could be asked and discussed to everybody's satisfaction.

● LEARNING STYLES

Multicultural Learning
Ask students to identify countries that do not practice parliamentary procedure in their government assemblies or public meetings. Students could identify these areas on a world map and display the information in the classroom.

CHAPTER 14 Parliamentary Procedure

● BASIC PRINCIPLES

Several fundamental principles form the basis of parliamentary procedure. Once you have these in mind, all of the lesser rules, regulations, and motions will seem logical.

One Question at a Time

Order can be maintained in a group by debating and voting on only one issue at a time. The members may not always vote on an issue before moving on to another one. But this principle dictates that they must dispose of a pending issue *in some way* before considering another.

Majority Rule

In bodies following parliamentary procedure, each member automatically agrees to abide by the decision of the majority. A **simple majority** is at least one more than half the people who voted. In special situations at least two-thirds of those voting must vote favorably in order for the issue to pass.

Protection of Minority Rights

Voting members of an organization who make up the minority group on an issue are not necessarily wrong. Voting with the **minority** means only that on that particular vote less than half the members agreed with

In parliamentary procedure, each member agrees to abide by the majority decision.

450

PORTFOLIO PRODUCTS

Students could get lists of the monthly meetings held at you local library. Note the topics and ask volunteers to attend some of these and report on the procedures. These meetings could be taped and included as a portfolio product.

ENRICHMENT

Ask students who belong to various school clubs to bring a copy of the club's bylaws to class. Have them note the quorum requirement in their bylaws. Share the information with the class and compare and contrast the various provisions.

TEACH

SUBSTITUTE TEACHER TIP

Bring in recent newspapers and professional magazines. Have students make a list of all the meetings, workshops, seminars, and training sessions that are mentioned and advertised. Ask students to fill in the dates and times in a monthly calendar for the meetings publicized. Discuss the number of meetings available to the public.

AMAZING FACTS!

The House of Lords in Great Britain has the smallest quorum of any legislature in the world—less than one third of one percent. To transact business, only three peers, including the lord chancellor or his deputy, must be present.

SKILL APPLICATION

Media Literacy
Ask students to write an announcement for a club or association meeting. The notice should include the basic who, what, when, and where information as well as topic, speaker, cost, and reservation information. Have students work with a partner to evaluate their announcements or read them to the entire class. Students should indicate what additional information they would like in order to make decisions about attending the meeting.

SKILL DEVELOPMENT

Decision by Committee
After reviewing the information about quorums, ask students about how they would fix a quorum number for a stockholders' meeting. Discuss what they would consider a fair representation of that group.

Holding a Meeting **451**

them. The rules of parliamentary procedure protect the rights of the minority. One of the rights protected is the right to continue to be heard and to try to change the minds of members in the majority group.

Equality of Rights and Responsibilities

In a body that follows parliamentary procedure, everyone is equal. Each has an equal right to speak or to remain silent, to vote or not to vote. At the same time each has the same responsibility to take an active part in discussion, to cast her or his vote, and to serve as an officer of the organization when called upon to do so. Though some members may be more active than others in exercising their rights and in fulfilling their responsibilities, all are equal in their possession of those rights and responsibilities.

Free Debate

Free debate is essential to enable members of an assembly to vote intelligently on issues. Parliamentary procedure attempts to guard open discussion of every issue, so long as a reasonable number of those present want it to continue. Motions to limit debate or to cut it off entirely require consent of two thirds of the members to pass. Free debate also means that ordinarily only one person may speak at a time, and only after having obtained the floor by recognized procedures.

● HOLDING A MEETING

Parliamentary procedure provides a number of very specific rules for holding meetings. These rules allow meetings to be efficient, productive, and democratic. They regulate the way meetings are announced and the number of members who must be present to conduct business. They also regulate the manner in which the business is conducted and the duties of the presiding officer.

Notice

When an organization plans to hold a meeting, notice must first be given to all of the members. **Notice** means that all of the members are told about the meeting far enough in advance so that they can plan to

451

TEACH

AMAZING FACTS!
The earliest known legislative assembly was a bicameral house meeting in Erech, Iraq, as early as 2800 B.C.

● **TEACHING**

Suggest that students use the typical agenda format of a meeting as enumerated on this page and develop an "agenda" for the class period. They should also provide approximate time designations for each category.

● **TIME MANAGEMENT**

Ask students to think of ways that participants and meeting chairs prevent meetings from accomplishing their stated goals within the specified length of the meeting. Discuss who has the most responsibility for productive meetings, the chair or the participants.

● **LEARNING STYLES**

Cooperative Learning
Have small groups of students think of the best and the worst time to have meetings. Discuss the relative advantages of morning, afternoon, and evening meetings. Encourage them to think about the optimum length of a meeting.

CHAPTER 14 Parliamentary Procedure

participate. Ten days' notice is normal. Failure of the officers to give adequate notice can invalidate decisions made at a meeting. If it can be proven that the officers conspired to hold a "secret meeting"—thereby preventing certain members from participating—they can be removed from office. Notice should ordinarily be given in writing. It is often routinely given for regularly scheduled meetings by mailing out to the membership beforehand the list of items to be discussed (the **agenda**) with the date, time, and place of meeting.

Quorum Requirements

Once the time for the meeting has arrived, the presiding officer must determine whether a quorum is present before calling the meeting to order. A **quorum** is the number of members that *must* be present before any meeting can be held or any official business conducted. Though each organization can set its own quorum requirements in its bylaws, the standard requirement for legislative bodies is a majority of all the members in good standing. For a nonlegislative body with, say, forty members, this would mean they would need twenty-one members present to conduct business. Therefore, ordinary bodies have the option of setting their own quorum requirements at less than a majority in their bylaws. This assures that business may be conducted when attendance is low. However, it is dangerous to set the quorum too low. This would make it possible for a very small minority to set policy and decide important matters for the entire organization. Setting quorum requirements too high should also be avoided. It might become difficult to secure enough attendance to conduct business.

Order of Business

The **order of business** for a meeting is an agenda. This is a listing of the various items of business in the order in which they will be taken up during the meeting. This is generally the agenda followed:

1. Call to order
2. Reading and approval of the minutes of previous meetings
3. Reports of officers, boards, and standing committees
4. Reports of special committees
5. Unfinished business
6. New business
7. Announcements
8. Adjournment

TEACH

● **RETEACHING**

The best way to learn parliamentary procedure is to use it. Conduct the class as a meeting following the basic parliamentary principles.

● **CURRICULAR CONNECTIONS**

Language Arts
You could take this opportunity to talk about the use of nonsexist language. Develop a list of sexist terms and their nonsexist alternatives. You might begin the list with the term "chairman" to "chair."

SUBSTITUTE TEACHER TIP

Suggest that students make a list of all the terms that appear in bold face in this chapter and make a crossword puzzle using as many as possible.

Holding a Meeting 453

After the call to order, minutes of the previous meeting are read and approved.

● **LEARNING STYLES**

Visual Learning
Students could present the six functions of the meeting chair in cartoon form in order to help summarize chair responsibilities. Display these posters or cartoons for the class.

Ordinarily, an organization will follow this regular order of business unless its bylaws call for a different order. Occasionally, though, if a special reason exists it is possible to shift around certain items.

● **ACTIVITY**

Basic Definitions
Without looking back at the text, tell the class in your own words what is meant by the following terms or phrases: One question at a time. Majority rule. Equality of rights and responsibilities. Free debate. Notice. Quorum requirements. Order of business.

Duties of the Chair

The **chair** is the name given to the person presiding over a meeting of an organization. Ordinarily this duty is exercised by the president of the organization. The vice-president usually presides if the president is absent. The chair has the same right to vote that any other member has. A number of other duties are also fulfilled by the person in this position.

● **ACTIVITY**

You might conduct the equivalent of a "spelling bee" to get students to give definitions of the many terms used in this chapter. Or you might ask volunteers to develop a computer-published manual on parliamentary procedure. This manual could be a portfolio product for an individual or a group.

453

TEACH

> **AMAZING FACTS!**
>
> The longest continuous speech in the history of the U.S. Senate was that of Senator Wayne Morse on April 24–25, 1953, when he spoke on the tidelands oil bill for 22 hours 26 minutes without taking his seat.

● **SKILL DEVELOPMENT**

15-Second Skill Opportunity
Ask students to practice recognizing a speaker in a meeting. Some may practice recognizing speakers wanting to speak for and those wanting to speak against a topic or motion.

● **LEARNING STYLES**

Cooperative Learning
Have each small group conduct a brief 20-minute meeting about a topic of their choice. The chair could rotate so that each member of the group serves as chair for five minutes. Encourage students to discuss the difficulties they experienced as chair.

Maintains Control The chair's main task is to maintain control over the meeting, continually making sure that each member's rights are protected. The chair is not the ruler of the assembly, however; she or he serves the organization.

Maintains Order The chair must maintain order at all times. He or she should prevent debate that takes the form of personal attack rather than a discussion of the issues. The chair must also guard against the railroading of matters through to a vote without time for sufficient thought and discussion. Sometimes members of a group try to prevent a vote on an issue by making long speeches to waste time. This is called **filibustering.** The chair should discourage such stalling tactics and must always restore order at the first sign of any form of disturbance.

Acts Impartially The chair should not take sides on issues being discussed. If, on rare occasions, the chair wishes to speak for or against a particular measure, another officer should be asked to preside for as long as the chair takes part in debate. If the chair possesses information about a matter that is unknown to the other members, he or she may state such information impartially without relinquishing the chair.

Recognizes Speakers Impartially The chair must be especially impartial in allowing members to speak. This process, which is called **recognizing** members, follows certain rules. When a particular member has made a motion, the chair should always give that member the right to speak first about the proposal. Then, the chair should alternate between those speaking against and for the topic. If there is uncertainty about who is in favor and who against, the chair should ask before permitting a member to have the floor. The chair should also recognize those who have not yet had a turn to speak on the subject before those who have already had an opportunity.

Assures Understanding The chair should be sure that every member understands each matter being discussed. All members should know what they are voting on and what effects their vote will have.

Keeps the Meeting Moving The chair must insure that the meeting moves along at a good pace. Members will then be more likely to pay attention and be enthusiastic. At the same time, the chair must not deny members their parliamentary right of full discussion.

As you can see, the chair must be constantly alert in exercising these duties. Much of the responsibility for a productive meeting rests squarely on the shoulders of the presiding officer.

● **ENRICHMENT**

Students could write or contact the National Association of Parliamentarians to find out about the qualifications for membership. Perhaps a video could be used in class to demonstrate certain procedures.

TEACH

"It shall be the duty of the parliamentarian to advise the presiding officer on points of parliamentary law, and also give similar advice to the society and the board of managers when they request it."
—Robert's Parliamentary Law

● **ACTIVITY**

Encourage students to identify as many of the functions of the meeting chair as they can remember. Then encourage them to identify "optional" functions that a person in charge of a meeting might undertake.

● **SKILL DEVELOPMENT**

15-Second Skill Opportunity
Ask every student to think of a motion and stand and make that motion in front of the class. Once the motion has been made, ask the class to decide which option they want to pursue as identified in this section.

● **ACTIVITY**

Duties of the Chair

Without looking back at the text, define aloud for the class six of the basic duties of the "chair" (presiding officer) in a parliamentary meeting. Class members who are not called on to define one of the six duties may be able to add to some of their classmates' definitions.

Methods of Voting

There are several ways in which members may show how they wish to vote on an issue. These methods of voting include voice votes, rising, raising hands, roll calls, and secret ballots.

The most common method of voting is a voice vote. The chair usually calls for a voice vote by saying "All those in favor say aye," and then "All those opposed say no." If the vote is a close one, or if the motion requires a two-thirds vote to pass, the chair may instead ask members to rise or to raise their hands. The wording is similar: "All those in favor please rise (or raise your hands)." "This is followed by a count of the votes in favor. Then the chair asks those opposed to rise or to raise their hands.

Roll-call votes are required in the bylaws of some organizations. A roll call may also be necessary if guests who don't have the right to vote are present at the meeting. A roll-call vote is announced by the chair in the following way: "Those in favor will answer aye as their names are called. Those opposed will answer no. The secretary will call the roll."

Voting by secret ballot is required in elections of officers and when voting on important issues. The chair should be sure that each member has a ballot and understands how aye and no votes are marked before the vote is taken.

● **MOTIONS**

When a meeting is being conducted according to parliamentary procedure, business is handled through the making of **motions**. A motion is a formal suggestion or proposal made by a member for consideration and action by the group. Before any new business can be discussed in

TEACH

> **"Too bad that all the people who know how to run the country are busy driving taxicabs and cutting hair."**
>
> —George Burns

● **SKILL DEVELOPMENT**

15-Second Skill Opportunity
Ask some students to read or make a motion and then invite other students to second the motion if they wish to discuss the matter.

● **LEARNING STYLES**

Cooperative Learning
Ask each group to specialize in one of the four main motions identified. The groups could define what the particular motion is and provide examples of its use. The groups should then try to explain their motion to the rest of the class. Encourage each group to use visual aids or video segments to demonstrate the type of motion they researched.

---

a parliamentary meeting, someone must make a motion. Without a motion on the floor the group cannot accomplish anything. It is as if they were all sitting in an automobile ready to start a trip and no one bothered to turn the ignition key.

Once a motion is made, the members must act on it in some way. They may vote for it or against it. They may postpone consideration of it. They may refer it to a committee or handle it in any of several other ways. But they may not simply forget about it.

How Motions Are Made

What should you do during a meeting when you wish to make a motion? First you must obtain recognition from the chair to speak. This may be done by holding your hand in the air until you are called upon by the chair, standing until recognized, or whatever the local custom demands. The chair will recognize you by calling your name or by pointing to you. Then you may state your motion. Always begin with the words "I move." Never begin with "I suggest" or "I recommend" or "I think that we should." The words "I move" are a signal that you are making a motion—a formal proposal that you wish the group to debate and act upon.

Formal motions require a **second,** which is an indication by one other member of the assembly that he or she wishes to see the matter debated and acted upon. This is accomplished by someone's saying "Second" or "I second the motion" immediately after it has been made. Though a second is usually made by a member who agrees with the intent of the motion, it is not necessary that the seconder agree. The second only indicates that she or he also wishes to have the matter considered and acted upon. The seconder may actually intend to vote against the motion.

Immediately following the second, the chair restates the motion by saying "It has been moved and seconded that we (do such and such)." Then, if it is a debatable motion, the chair says, "Is there any discussion?" This restatement by the chair officially puts the motion on the floor and makes it a **pending motion**—a motion that is under consideration.

Here is an example of a motion being made:

Liz, *a member:*	(*raises hand*)
Chair:	Liz.
Liz (*rises*):	I move that we hold a pancake breakfast to raise money for the scholarship fund. (*Liz sits down.*)
Nick, *a member:*	I second the motion.
Chair:	It has been moved and seconded that our club hold a pancake breakfast to raise money for the scholarship fund. Is there any discussion?

● **TEACHING**

To demonstrate the variable nature of a simple majority vote, divide the class into three groups with unequal members. Explain that each group will vote on a motion to extend farm subsidies to tree farmers. Ask each group to determine how many in that group will want to vote on that issue. Then conduct the vote and determine the number required to pass the motion based on those who voted.

● **ENRICHMENT**

You might discuss how an elected president of the U.S. could be a minority president even though elected by a majority vote.

> *It's not the voting that's democracy: it's the counting.*
> —Tom Stoppard

TEACH

Motions 457

Motions are divided into four types. These are main motions, subsidiary motions, privileged motions, and incidental motions. Let's look at each type of motion and some of the rules governing them.

Main Motions

Main motions are those which deal directly with the items of business being considered. They are directly concerned with the issues before the group. Here are a few examples of main motions:

"I move that this club donate $100 to our college scholarship fund."
"I move that we initiate a new membership drive immediately."
"I move that we raise our local dues by $1.00, starting May 1."
"I move that we accept Evan Lee as a new member of this board, to complete the unexpired term of Wanda Malik."

Main motions introduce items of new business to an assembly. They must ordinarily be made first, before any of the other classes of motions would make any sense. Main motions are the foundation of parliamentary business.

Main motions require a *second* before they may be debated. They are debatable motions, and they require a simple majority vote to pass. A simple majority means fifty percent plus one of those present and voting. Suppose thirty members are present for a meeting, and only twenty

Main motions introducing items of new business to an assembly must be seconded before debate and require a simple majority to pass.

TEACH

● **LEARNING STYLES**

Cooperative Learning
Organize seven groups and have each concentrate on one of the subsidiary motions described in the text. Each group should prepare to describe and provide examples of their topic. Encourage students to use visual aids in their explanation to the class. Each group might prepare several true or false questions based on the information they present and encourage students to answer their questions. Award students with correct answers.

● **SKILL DEVELOPMENT**

15-Second Skill Opportunity
Ask each student to prepare to make one of the seven subsidiary motions described in this section. Then ask all those who prepared motions to postpone indefinitely to stand and make their motions. Repeat this procedure with each category.

---

458 CHAPTER 14 Parliamentary Procedure

decide to vote on a particular motion. The majority required to pass that motion would be eleven. When the vote is taken, the chair must always ask for both the affirmative and the negative sides of the vote.

Subsidiary Motions

Subsidiary motions allow members to change the nature of main motions or to handle them in some way other than ordinary debate and a vote. They allow such things as postponements, amendments, and limitations on debate. Following are seven commonly used subsidiary motions in the order in which they may be made following a main motion. You will see the purpose of each, whether each is debatable and what size vote is required to pass each. Subsidiary motions are always proposed after the main motion to which they apply. They must be debated and voted on before the group returns to debate on the main motion.

Postpone Indefinitely The purpose of making the subsidiary motion to **postpone indefinitely** is to prevent any further discussion or voting on a pending main motion. By not allowing the main motion to come to a direct vote, you can assure that it will be defeated. Assume, for example, that the following main motion is pending: "I move that this club donate $100 to our local college's scholarship fund." A member who wishes to see this motion defeated might get recognition to speak and state, "I move that we postpone this motion indefinitely." If there is a second, this subsidiary motion may then be debated and voted upon. If a simple majority votes in favor of the motion to postpone indefinitely, the main motion to donate the $100 is defeated or killed. If the majority votes against postponing indefinitely, the assembly returns to the debate on the main motion.

Amend The purpose of a motion to **amend** is to change a main motion in some way. Again assume the pending main motion is to donate $100 to the college scholarship fund. Someone may propose an amendment such as "I move that we change $100 to $50 in the main motion" or "I move we add 'by this coming weekend' to the main motion." Although amendments may change a main motion, they must be **germane** to the main motion to which they apply. Being germane means they must be logically and directly connected with the subject of the main motion. Suppose someone tried to amend the main motion to donate $100 by adding "and raise the salaries of all our club officers." The chair would have to rule the amendment out of order since it is not germane. Raising the officers' salaries is not directly connected with the matter of donating $100 to a scholarship fund.

Motions

As is the case with all subsidiary motions, debate and voting on an amendment occur before returning to the main motion. A simple majority vote is required to pass an amendment. If an amendment passes, the assembly returns to debate on the amended version of the main motion. If the amendment fails, the group debates on the main motion in its original form.

Refer to Committee The motion to **refer to committee** is used when a group wants to save time by allowing a small sub-group to discuss a complicated matter. It is also used when the assembly wishes to insure privacy on a delicate matter. Referring to a committee can put off a decision until later, or it can defeat a matter if the committee is hostile. This motion may be made in the simple form: "I move that we refer this motion to a committee." When makers of this motion wish, they may include any pertinent details they desire in the motion. Details may include how many members should be on the committee, who the members should be, and when the committee should report back to the main assembly. Another detail could be whether the committee may only recommend action or whether it has the power to make a decision for the entire assembly. If a motion to refer to a committee passes, any such details not given in the motion are them decided by the chair of the assembly.

The motion to refer to a committee may be debated briefly. Debate is restricted to selection of the committee, instructions to it, its membership, and duties. A motion to refer to a committee requires a simple majority vote to pass.

Postpone Definitely Whenever it is desirable to put off consideration of a pending motion, with the intention of bringing it up again at a later time, a motion to **postpone definitely** should be used. Unlike the motion to postpone indefinitely, the motion to postpone definitely includes a specific time when the pending matter will again come up for consideration. Suppose the main motion to donate $100 is pending. Someone might move "to postpone consideration of this matter until after we have heard our annual budget report at the next regularly scheduled meeting." This motion to postpone definitely assures that the motion on the $100 donation will again be on the table following the budget report at the next meeting. Matters may also be postponed definitely until a time later in the same meeting in which the motion is made.

The motion to postpone definitely, as is the case with all formal motions, requires a second. It may be debated briefly. Debate is restricted to the reasons for and the time of postponement. It requires a simple majority vote for passage.

TEACH

● **ENRICHMENT**

Some students might enjoy collecting some of the many jokes that relate to decision making by committee. These could be compiled and shared with the class.

AMAZING FACTS!
The Senate of the U.S. relies on the work of 16 standing committees and 4 select and special committees to do the work of the Congress. The House has 22 standing committees.

● **LEARNING STYLES**

Cooperative Learning
Organize small groups of students and explain that they will function as a committee. Have them review the various ways a committee can function and ask them to develop their own rules for the way they would like their committee to work. Give them 15 minutes to determine the rules for their committee. Then have each group explain what their rules are and how they arrived at their plan.

● **SKILL DEVELOPMENT**

15-Second Skill Opportunity
Ask students to prepare a motion to refer a matter of their choice to a committee. Volunteers can demonstrate the procedure.

TEACH

> *"Democracy is the recurrent suspicion that more than half of the people are right more than half of the time."*
>
> —E.B. White

● **SKILL DEVELOPMENT**

15-Second Skill Opportunity
Ask volunteers to demonstrate how to postpone a motion definitely. Ask students to think of situations when this would be a useful strategy. You might list those suggestions on the chalkboard.

Critical Thinking
Ask students to note the circumstances when each of these strategies is useful. Compare and contrast when and how they are used. Make a chart that lists each strategy and identifies what it is, when it is used and why, and how it influences discussion and decisions.

Decision by Committee
Ask students to imagine that they are attending a sales meeting that began at 8:00 A.M. It is now 10:00 A.M. and only one item on the agenda of five topics has been discussed and the group is far from reaching a consensus. Ask students to think of various parliamentary procedures that might be used to complete the task of discussing and voting on all items and end the meeting at 11:00 A.M.

CHAPTER 14 Parliamentary Procedure

Limit or Extend Debate The motion **to limit or extend deba** either restricts the time to be devoted to debate on a pending motion removes any limitation placed upon it. Its more common use is to lim rather than to extend debate, however. There are a number of ways make such a motion:

"I move that we limit debate to a total of fifteen minutes."
"I move that we limit debate to one minute per speaker."
"I move that the debate on this motion cease at 2:30 P.M."

Since the very purpose of the motion to limit debate is to restrict fu ther discussion, the motion to limit debate itself may be debated on briefly. Debate must be restricted to the type and time of the limit tion. Because limiting debate violates a basic principle of parliame tary procedure—complete and free discussion of every issue—th motion requires a two-thirds majority to pass.

Previous Question This motion, if it passes, instantly cuts o debate on a pending motion and brings it to a vote. Assume that th main motion to donate $100 has been placed on the floor for debat Either right away, or after some discussion on it, a member gets reco nition and says: "I move the *Previous Question*." The purpose could t to prevent further discussion which the member feels would damag her or his side of the case. The purpose could also be simply to mov business along more speedily. In any case, if there is a second, th chair stops debate and immediately takes a vote on the motion to vo immediately. Since its purpose is to stop debate, it is not a debatab motion. Also, since, like the motion to limit debate, it cuts off further di cussion, it requires a two-thirds majority to pass. If it passes, the cha then takes an immediate vote on the pending motion. If it fails, th assembly returns to debate on the pending motion.

Lay on the Table The motion to *lay something on the table* se aside consideration of a pending matter until some unspecified tim later in the same meeting, or at the next regularly scheduled meeting. not taken from the table before the close of the following meeting, th question dies. It differs from the motion to postpone definitely in th laying something on the table does not specify a particular time which the matter will again be discussed.

One reason for making a motion to lay something on the table is secure more information about a pending matter before voting. Anoth reason is to set aside an unwelcome motion in the hope that it will n be brought up again. This motion is not debatable. It requires a simp majority vote to pass.

APPLY

● **ENRICHMENT**

You might invite a health care administrator from a local hospital or nursing home to speak to the class about the communication skills needed to relate to clients and their families, as well as to the numerous professionals on their staff.

● **LINKS TO PAST LEARNING**

You might ask students to share family experiences with health care providers. You might discuss how the reputation of health services has changed in the past five years.

> *In medicine, as in statecraft and propaganda, words are sometimes the most powerful drugs we can use.*
> —Sara Murray Jordan

● **LEARNING STYLES**

Cooperative Learning
Small groups of students could obtain information about the variety of health service professions that exist in your community. Groups might investigate pharmaceuticals, hospitals, geriatrics, etc. Students might use the Yellow Pages of your local phone directory to get an idea of the number and location of the health services provided in your area. Another group might investigate the health services provided through various government agencies.

● **SKILL DEVELOPMENT**

On the Job
Ask students to identify a health care issue that they believe will affect their lives or the lives of their parents. They could conduct a debate on the issue or role-play a meeting of a board of directors meeting to decide a matter of policy involving the issue.

CAREER CLOSE-UP

Health Services Administrator

Health services administrators supervise and coordinate a hospital's numerous departments. They are responsible for managing personnel, executing public relations activities, and preparing the hospital budget. A career in this profession requires a master's degree in one of these fields: hospital administration, public health, or business administration.

The hospital's board of directors, the most important group the administrator works with, determines the hospital's operating budget. The administrator must present the hospital's financial needs to the board to receive the necessary funding. Many hospital boards use parliamentary procedure to conduct their business. Effective administrators use this set of rules to their advantage in order to communicate the hospital's most pressing needs.

Because parliamentary procedure dictates that participants be notified of upcoming meetings, administrators can utilize this time to research and prepare any essential information. During meetings, their phrasing and timing of motions may be so exact that discussion is encouraged or discouraged according to their needs. When the administrator's position on an issue is opposed to the board's, parliamentary procedure guarantees him or her the opportunity to state the hospital's position completely without interruption.

By itself, a competent use of parliamentary procedure is not enough to achieve budgetary goals. However, when the administrator's ability to speak persuasively is combined with an expert use of parliamentary procedure, obtaining the funds necessary to maintain high standards of health care becomes more likely.

Under parliamentary procedure, participants must be notified of upcoming meetings; administrators can use this time for research and preparation.

TEACH

> **"All politics are based on the indifference of the majority."**
>
> —James Reston

● **ACTIVITY**

You could use this Activity as an opportunity to reteach the various subsidiary motions presented in the text. If the class, or students, developed charts or other visual aids to identify the various motions, these could be allowed in the review process.

Students could also work in pairs to review the various types of motions. When they both think the other has mastered the definitions, they can make a badge or other sign of accomplishment.

● **SKILL DEVELOPMENT**

15-Second Skill Opportunity
Ask students to think of a matter they would like to table and prepare to make a motion. Ask volunteers to demonstrate the procedure of tabling a motion.

Creative Thinking
Explain the urgent nature of the privileged motions described here. Then encourage students to think of situations in the classroom where they would like to invoke a question of privilege.

15-Second Skill Opportunity
Each student should prepare a motion for one of the three privileged motions.

CHAPTER 14 Parliamentary Procedure

● **ACTIVITY**

Defining Subsidiary Motions
Without looking back at the text, explain aloud to the class the purpose of each of the subsidiary motions. Also note in each case whether the motion you are describing is debatable, and what size vote is required to pass it.

Privileged Motions

Three motions are considered to be of such an urgent nature that they form a class called **privileged motions.** Unlike subsidiary motions, they do not relate to the items of business before the assembly. They refer instead to the organization and its members. Because of their urgent nature, they may be made and considered ahead of any of the other classes of motions. They are the motions calling for question of privilege, recess, and adjournment.

Question of Privilege Though sometimes a motion, the **question of privilege** is often a request made by a member and granted or denied by the chair. A question of privilege may be made to secure immediate action on some urgent matter that relates to the comfort, convenience, rights, or privileges of the assembly, or one of its members. It may also be made to secure permission to make an urgent motion while some other matter is pending. The following example shows how a question of privilege may be presented:

Member: Mr. Chairman, I rise to a question of privilege.
Chair: State your question of privilege.
Member: I ask that we send someone to check the public records in the courthouse before we vote on this current matter.

If the courthouse records are likely to have a direct bearing on the assembly's decision on the pending matter, the chair would probably grant such a request.

Recess If a motion to **recess** passes, it calls a halt to a meeting without ending it. A motion to recess must always include a time when the body will resume the meeting. Though recesses are usually brief, they can last for days. The time of the recess cannot extend beyond the time for the next regularly scheduled meeting of the group, however. The motion to recess requires a second. It may be debated briefly regarding the time or need for the recess. It needs a simple majority vote to pass.

Adjournment Passage of a motion to **adjourn** ends a meeting. Unlike the motion to recess, which only calls a halt in a meeting, the motion to adjourn legally concludes a meeting. When members of an assembly meet again following an adjournment, they do not take up at the point where they left off on their agenda (as in the case of a recess). Rather they begin a new meeting with a new agenda. Business that was interrupted or left unfinished by an adjournment comes up on the agenda of the next meeting under the heading "Unfinished Business." Since it would defeat the purpose to debate a motion to adjourn, it is not debatable. It requires a simple majority vote to pass.

Incidental Motions

The last type of motion relates to procedures having to do with the conduct of parliamentary business. Some of these are true motions, requiring a second and a vote. Others are simply requests, granted by the chair. Here are the names, purpose, and vote required (if any) of the eight most common **incidental motions:**

Appeal An **appeal** motion allows a member who disagrees with a ruling by the chair to put that ruling to a vote. This is a true motion requiring a second and a majority vote in the negative to overturn the chair's ruling.

Suspend the Rules A motion to **suspend the rules** is also a true motion. It allows the assembly to set aside some procedural rule so the members can do something not ordinarily allowed by that rule. Only procedural rules may be suspended. Suppose the bylaws of an organization call for a particular order of business, but the officer who should make the next report has not yet arrived. A member may make a motion to suspend the rules and allow that officer to report later so the group may proceed with other business in the meantime. Such a motion would require a second and a two-thirds majority vote.

Objection to Consideration This allows an assembly to avoid debate and a decision on a pending motion. The assembly may believe it to be embarrassing or unprofitable, or may have some other good reason for not wishing to consider it. Since it completely avoids consideration of an issue if it passes, **objection to consideration** is a motion requiring a second and a two-thirds majority to pass.

Point-of-Order This is a request used to call to the attention of the chair and the assembly that an error is being made. Perhaps a procedure is being violated. A member must gain attention by calling **"point of**

TEACH

> *It is better to ask some of the questions than to know all the answers.*
> —James Thurber

● LEARNING STYLES

Visual Learning
Encourage students to make a diagram or flow chart that will show the normal progress of a motion through the voting process.

● SKILL DEVELOPMENT

15-Second Skill Opportunity
Ask students to draft a motion to withdraw or a division of question. Ask volunteers to serve both as the chair and as group members and practice making and processing these motions.

● CURRICULAR CONNECTIONS

Language Arts
Some students could examine the *Congressional Quarterly* to identify some of the issues debated in Congress. References to parliamentary procedure should be noted as well as references to any of the terms or motions mentioned in this chapter. This information could be shared with the class.

---

464   CHAPTER 14 Parliamentary Procedure

order" immediately after the error has occurred. After stating what sh or he believes the error to be, an immediate ruling is given by the chai No vote is taken.

Parliamentary Inquiry   Parliamentary inquiry is a request tha gives a member an opportunity to ask the chair questions about parlia mentary procedure dealing with a motion under consideration at tha time. Because it is a request addressed to the chair and not a motion, does not require a second. The chair answers the inquiry, so no vote i necessary.

Withdraw a Motion   Withdraw a motion enables a member whe has made a motion to remove it from consideration before a vote i taken. Such a motion may be withdrawn by simple request of its make if (a) the chair has not yet restated the motion to the assembly or (b) th chair has restated it, but no one objects to its being withdrawn. If jus one member objects in the second case above, however, the request t withdraw becomes a motion requiring a simple majority to pass.

Division of Question   A division of question is used to separat a motion having two or more independent parts into separate motion for purposes of separate debate and voting. This is ordinarily a reques granted by the presiding officer, unless a member objects. Then, like th motion to withdraw a motion, it must be voted upon and requires a sim ple majority to pass.

Some incidental motions require a second and a vote.

464

Motions 465

Division of Assembly If a vote has been taken by voice, and anyone is unsure about which side has the majority, a member may request a **division of assembly.** This is simply a method of retaking such a vote by a show of hands or by having members rise in their places to be counted. Such a request is ordinarily granted by the chair as long as there is a reasonable question about the outcome of the voice vote.

Precedence of Motions

All of the motions discussed, except the incidental motions, must be dealt with in **order of precedence.** This is a ranking system that tells you the order in which you must vote on each of the motions. There are two rules that govern the order of precedence:

1. When a motion is pending, only motions above it in the order of precedence may be made.
2. When motions have already been made, they must be debated and acted upon in the opposite order from that in which they were made. In other words, the motion made most recently is acted upon first.

Earlier in this chapter when you read about the different kinds of motions, they were presented in the order in which they could be introduced. The order of precedence reverses that order and lists the motions in the order in which they would be acted upon. This reversal reflects the need to work back to the main motion. It guarantees that the main motion will be addressed only when all other motions that affect it have been dealt with. The order of precedence looks like this:

Privileged	1.	Adjourn
Motions	2.	Recess
	3.	Question of Privilege
Subsidiary	4.	Lay on the Table
Motions	5.	Previous Question
	6.	Limit or Extend Debate
	7.	Postpone Definitely
	8.	Refer to Committee
	9.	Amend
	10.	Postpone Indefinitely
Main Motion	11.	Any Main Motion

The first rule of precedence means that only motions of higher rank may be made while another motion is pending. Suppose, for example, that a member has made the main motion to donate $100 to a scholar-

TEACH

SUBSTITUTE TEACHER TIP

You could write on the chalkboard several examples of conflicting rights and discuss how precedence is determined. Your examples might include: (1) rights of individuals and majority rule; (2) private property and eminent domain, (3) baseball players, baseball owners, and fans.

● **LEARNING STYLES**

Cooperative Learning
Organize groups with 11 students each. Prepare beforehand a collection of index cards each with a number and label reflecting the numbered sequence of the order of precedence described in the text. Explain to the group that the student who drew the number 11 must try to get card number 1 and go through the entire 10 steps with or without the cooperation of the group. Give each group ten or fifteen minutes to accomplish the task. Then discuss the process with the entire class.

465

TEACH

> *The last function of reason is to recognize that there are an infinity of things which surpass it.*
> —Blaise Pascal

PORTFOLIO PRODUCTS

To demonstrate some of the important strategies of parliamentary procedure, encourage the class to develop a short (ten or fifteen minutes) video that they would write and produce. Such a video might become a commercial endeavor as well, since there are many clubs and associations that might welcome a simple, brief explanation of basic procedures.

CURRICULAR CONNECTIONS

Writing

Some students might take on the task of putting together a simplified, one-page summary "ALL YOU EVER NEED TO KNOW ABOUT PARLIAMENTARY PROCEDURE." These students might enlist the aid of the artistically and computer inclined to develop visuals and a format that makes it easy to access information.

LEARNING STYLES

Visual Learning

Some students could develop cartoon visuals to illustrate the chart presented on this page. Such a visual aid might be included in the "One-Page Guide" mentioned above.

CHAPTER 14 Parliamentary Procedure

ship fund. While this main motion is pending, someone else moves to amend the amount to $50. This motion to amend is permissible, or in order, since the motion to amend (9) is of higher rank than the main motion (11). During the debate on the amendment, however, someone attempts to make a motion to postpone indefinitely (10). The chair must rule this motion out of order. This means it cannot be made at that time. This is because the motion to postpone indefinitely (10) is of lower rank than the pending motion, amend (9).

The second rule of precedence means that members must always first dispose of the last motion made. Then they can proceed backwards to the first one proposed. Suppose, for instance, they start with a main motion. A member proposes an amendment to the main motion. Then someone moves to limit debate. The assembly must first decide on whether or not to limit debate before returning to debate on the amendment to the main motion.

The incidental motions have no order of precedence. They may be made at any time they are appropriate and must be acted upon

Rules governing motions with order of precedence

	Can Interrupt?	Requires Second?	Debatable?	Amendable?	Vote Required?
Privileged motions					
1. Adjourn	no	yes	no	no	majority
2. Recess	no	yes	yes	yes	majority
3. Question of privilege	yes	no	no	no	none
Subsidiary motions					
4. Lay on the table	no	yes	no	no	majority
5. Previous question	no	yes	no	no	two-thirds
6. Limit or extend debate	no	yes	no	yes[r]	two-thirds
7. Postpone definitely	no	yes	yes[r]	yes[r]	majority
8. Refer to committee	no	yes	yes[r]	yes[r]	majority
9. Amend	no	yes	yes	yes	majority
10. Postpone indefinitely	no	yes	yes	no	majority
Main motions					
11. The main motion	no	yes	yes	yes	majority

(r = restricted)

TEACH

● **ASSESSMENT STRATEGY**

Pairs or teams of students could prepare at least five true and false questions about the material in this chapter or section. The answers to the questions could be given with each. You could collect the questions and ask students to select partners for a type of "Trivial Pursuit" quiz about parliamentary procedure. The quiz could be conducted as an "open book" project or closed book contest.

> *In a hierarchy every employee tends to rise to his level of incompetence.*
> —Laurence J. Peter

● **LEARNING STYLES**

Visual Learning
This chart could also be supported with cartoon illustrations or other visual aids. It could become a portfolio product and used in the "One-Page Guide."

● **SKILL APPLICATION**

Citizens Speak Out
Ask students to imagine that the National Association of Parliamentarians has asked your class to nominate a candidate to become a member of the association. Students could nominate their classmates on the basis of knowledge and understanding of procedures and the ability to apply procedures to real situations.

Rules governing motions with no order of precedence					
Incidental motions	**Can Interrupt?**	**Requires Second?**	**Debatable?**	**Amendable?**	**Vote Required?**
Appeal	yes	yes	yes	no	majority
Suspend rules	no	yes	no	no	two-thirds
Objection to consideration	yes	no	no	no	two-thirds
Point of order	yes	no	no	no	none
Parliamentary inquiry	yes	no	no	no	none
Withdraw a motion	yes	no	no	no	majority
Division of question	no	yes	no	yes	none
Division of assembly	yes	no	no	no	none

immediately. The chart on page 466 and the chart above on this page summarize these and other motions. Used together, these charts should provide you with all the basic information you will need in order to deal with motions made during a typical meeting.

● **ACTIVITY**

Defining Privileged and Incidental Motions
If you hope to use parliamentary procedure effectively in meetings, you need to commit to memory details of the purposes and procedures relating to some of the commonly used motions. Without referring to the text describing privileged and incidental motions, or to the charts on these two pages, describe aloud to the class the purpose and procedures relating to one of these motions when called upon.

● **ACTIVITY**

This activity might be done with pairs of students who work together as a team to develop three questions that they could ask another team of students in order to quiz them about the various types of motions.

ASSESS

● **STUDENT PERFORMANCE COMPETENCIES**

- Explains the purpose of parliamentary procedure
- Describes and applies the basic principles of parliamentary procedure
- Explains the duties of the chair
- Describes the purpose of each type of motion and uses them in the proper sequence

● **sca GUIDELINES**

- Identifies main idea in meetings
- Distinguishes fact from opinion in public meetings
- Expresses and defends position during a public meeting
- Uses variety of reasoning techniques to present arguments in a public meeting
- Answers questions to clarify information in a public meeting

▼ PORTFOLIO ASSESSMENT

Standard
- Glossary of Speech Terms
- Meeting Agenda
- Written Resolution
- Tape of Meeting
- Chart Summarizing Responsibilities of Chair

Enrichment
- Visual Aid Illustrating Parliamentary Procedures
- Chart to Summarize Motion
- Nomination for Class Parliamentarian
- Trivial Pursuit Questions About Parliamentary Procedures
- Map of the World Showing Parliaments
- Jokes about Committee Decisions

Challenge
- Transcript of Meeting
- Tape of Meeting
- Media Report on Meeting
- One-Page Summary of Parliamentary Procedures
- Video Demonstration of Parliamentary Procedures
- *Congressional Quarterly* Summary

CHAPTER 14 REVIEW

● **SUMMARY**

Parliamentary procedure is a set of rules designed to streamline the conduct of business at meetings and at the same time protect the democratic rights of the participants. It began in the English Parliament and has developed over the years as a set of basic principles.

Basic Principles Parliamentary procedure is based on five principles: only one question may be considered at a time; the majority rules; the rights of the minority are protected; all members share equal rights and responsibilities; and every issue may be subjected to free debate.

Holding a Meeting Holding a meeting according to parliamentary procedure begins with giving notice. This means informing members about the meeting, usually about ten days in advance. When the time for the meeting arrives, the chair must determine whether a quorum is present before beginning. The usual order of business consists of the call to order, approval of the minutes, reports of officers, reports of standing and special committees, unfinished business, new business, announcements, and adjournment. During a meeting the chair's duties include keeping order, recognizing members to speak, insuring that all members understand the issues, and moving the meeting along. Methods of voting include voice votes, rising, raising hands, roll calls, or secret ballots.

Motions Business is handled during meetings by the making of motions. Motions are formal proposals made by members for consideration and action by the assembly. Motions fall into four major types. Main motions deal directly with the issues before the assembly. They are the foundation of a parliamentary meeting. Subsidiary motions allow members to change the nature of main motions, or to handle them in some other way than by ordinary debate and a vote. Privileged motions relate to urgent matters dealing with the organization and its members. Incidental motions have to do with procedural matters and the conduct of parliamentary business. Order of precedence determines the order in which each motion must be addressed.

ASSESS

● **ASSESSMENT STRATEGIES**

Individual Assessment
- Participates in practice activities daily or weekly
- Demonstrates knowledge of content through questions, discussion, quizzes, and Chapter 14 test
- Displays improved skills in parliamentary procedures

Group Assessment
- Sets and achieves goals for the group
- Develops and completes cooperative learning projects
- Supports efforts of team and class members
- Provides encouragement and feedback to members

VOCABULARY

Define at least 15 terms in complete sentences.

parliamentary procedure	refer to committee
parliamentarian	postpone definitely
simple majority	limit or extend debate
minority	previous question
notice	lay on the table
agenda	privileged motion
quorum	question of privilege
order of business	recess
chair	adjourn
filibustering	incidental motion
recognizing	appeal
motion	suspend the rules
second	object to consideration
pending motion	point of order
main motion	parliamentary inquiry
subsidiary motion	withdraw a motion
postpone indefinitely	division of question
amend	division of assembly
germane	order of precedence

CHECKLIST

Skills of Parliamentary Procedure

1. Be aware of the purpose of the rules that govern parliamentary procedure.
2. Make use of published codes of parliamentary procedure.
3. Apply the basic principles of parliamentary procedure at meetings whenever possible.
4. Learn the specific rules of parliamentary procedure.
5. Learn and apply the duties of the chair.
6. Know the various methods of voting by which members may show how they wish to vote on an issue.
7. Follow proper procedure for making motions.
8. Learn the differences among the various kinds of motions.

● **ANSWERS**

See the Answer Key for more complete answers.

REVIEW QUESTIONS
1. The principles are: one question at a time, majority rule, minority rights, equality, and free debate.
2. Refer to *Robert's Rules of Order* and *Sturgis Standard Code of Parliamentary Procedure*.
3. A simple majority is at last one more than half of the members present and voting.
4. Membership entails attendance, participation, listening carefully, observing rules, and acceptance of majority decisions.
5. A *quorum* is the minimum number of members required to hold a meeting and vote.
6. The order of business is explained in the Answer Key.
7. The chair maintains order, recognizes speakers, and keeps the meeting moving.
8. They are main, subsidiary, privileged, and incidental motions.
9. See the explanation in the Answer Key.
10. See the answer in the Answer Key.

DISCUSSION QUESTIONS
The following code is used to designate discussion questions and activities as suitable for students of varying ability levels:
- ▼ = below average to average
- ◆ = average to above average
- ■ = all students

1. ■ Encourage students to consider parliamentary procedures in other organizations.
2. ■ Students should comment on changed opinions about parliamentary procedures.
3. ■ Review the section in the text about the duties of the chair.
4. ◆ Use a sample main motion as an example and have students suggest reasons for tabling it.
5. ■ Review the text on duties of the group.

CHAPTER 14 REVIEW

REVIEW QUESTIONS

1. Name the five principles that form the basis for parliamentary procedure.
2. Name the most commonly used code of parliamentary procedure.
3. Define a simple majority.
4. List several guidelines for responsible membership in an organization.
5. Define the term *quorum*.
6. List the usual order of business for a meeting.
7. Name the duties of the chair.
8. Identify the four types of motions used in parliamentary procedure.
9. State the purpose of each of the four types of motions.
10. State the order of precedence for these motions.

DISCUSSION QUESTIONS

1. Discuss the contribution that parliamentary procedure can make to the functioning of a democracy. What fundamental democratic principles does parliamentary procedure help to safeguard? How might these be jeopardized if the principles of parliamentary procedure were not adhered to?
2. Discuss the use of parliamentary procedure in organizations to which you belong. Do most of them use parliamentary procedure? How can you encourage organizations to do a more efficient job of conducting business? What problems might occur regularly in organizations that do not use parliamentary procedure in their meetings? How would these problems be solved?
3. Discuss the duties of the chair or presiding officer. Why is this job so important? What personal qualities should a presiding officer possess in order to chair a meeting effectively?
4. Discuss the circumstances under which it is advisable to table a motion. What are the possible outcomes of tabled motions? How can this device be used by the minority to strengthen its position?
5. Discuss the responsibilities that members of a parliamentary group have. What must members do to ensure that the group operates effectively and efficiently?

CRITICAL THINKING

1. Analysis Assume that a legislative body sets its quorum requirements at ten percent of its elected members. Would such a requirement promote the serious consideration of issues? What effect would such a requirement have upon an established majority?

2. Evaluation Imagine that all debate has ended on an important issue in a legislative assembly. A vote is called for, and the chair decides upon a voice vote. It is very difficult to determine which side has a majority, but the chair rules that the motion is defeated. Comment on the chair's action. What should the chair have done, instead, under the circumstances?

ACTIVITIES

In-Class

1. Select members of the class to make brief reports on the following topics. Be prepared to add to the information supplied or to correct mistaken information.
   (a) which motions are not debatable, and why
   (b) why certain motions are classified as "privileged"
   (c) what a chair should do to ensure impartiality
   (d) the proper use of a motion to amend and the limitations of this type of motion
   (e) why some motions require a two-thirds majority to pass while others require a simple majority
   (f) the necessity of careful planning when formulating by-laws for an organization
   (g) the procedure for indicating that proper procedures have not been followed
   (h) the procedure for registering disagreement with the chair on the chair's rulings

2. Imagine that your class is a state legislative body. Decide on three laws that will be debated during a meeting. Establish an agenda for the meeting and elect a chair. During the meeting, attempt to use as many types of motions as possible. Remember to rise to a point of order if either the chair or a member violates a rule of procedure.

CRITICAL THINKING
1. **Analysis** Cite examples of specific organizations and the effect the quorum requirement would have.
2. **Evaluation** In parliamentary procedure there are checks and balances to allow the members to correct errors made by the chair.

ACTIVITIES
In-Class
1. Encourage students to provide feedback to those students who give reports.
2. Appoint a committee to write proposed laws and agendas.

ASSESS

3. Use several specific motions and have the class show how the minority would attempt to pass or defeat them.
4. Ask students if they feel comfortable in the role of chair.

Out-of-Class

1. Students who attend a meeting where parliamentary procedure is not used should write an account of the meeting to share with the class.
2. Students can summarize the agenda of the meeting and evaluate how effectively the business was conducted.
3. Students could conduct research in the library and ask for the help of the history teacher.
4. Ask each student to report on the outcome of the proposal.
5. The history of parliamentary procedure will focus on its importance and influence.

CHAPTER 14 REVIEW

3. As a class, discuss what the minority tries to accomplish at a meeting. What tactics does the minority use to accomplish its goals? If you were a member of the minority when an important proposal was being discussed, what rules of parliamentary procedure would you use to gain the most exposure for your cause?

4. During a mock meeting to determine how to spend surplus money in the student activities fund, take turns with various class members serving as chair. After the meeting, discuss the problems and successes each of you had while acting as chair.

Out-of-Class

1. At the next formal meeting of an organization to which you belong, practice the correct use of the motions explained in this chapter. If the organization does not currently use parliamentary procedure in its meetings, point out the benefits that such rules would bring to the organization.

2. Attend a meeting of a local government board, a town or city council, or a school board. Note the way in which parliamentary procedure is used during the meeting. Summarize what took place at the meeting in your speech notebook. Be prepared to report your findings to the class.

3. Find examples in U.S. legislative history where the filibuster rule was used effectively either to prevent, postpone, or draw attention to an issue. Why do you think the filibuster rule became a part of parliamentary procedure? Share your examples and conclusions with the class.

4. Decide upon a course of action that you would like to see taken by a real or imaginary organization. Describe in your speech notebook how you would gather support for your proposals. Draw up whatever motions might be necessary to get your proposals approved. If you belong to the organization, try to implement your plans according to the rules of parliamentary procedure.

5. Research the history of parliamentary procedure. Find out who Henry Robert was and examine a copy of *Robert's Rules of Order Newly Revised*. Prepare a brief oral report on parliamentary procedure, including the reasons for its development and eventual adoption, and deliver it to the class.

CHAPTER PROJECT

Select a group of students to develop a public-information program about parliamentary procedure. The program could be presented at a school assembly or at a meeting of an interested organization. The class as a whole should decide upon both a format and an outline for the demonstration, and should prepare charts or any other visual aids needed to enable the presenters to communicate clearly. The program could take one of any number of forms, such as a series of short lectures, a combination of lecture and demonstration, or a docudrama that reenacts the history and present-day use of parliamentary procedure. After everything is prepared, the group of presenters should give a performance for the class and then request reactions and feedback. Incorporate valuable suggestions for improvement into the program before presenting it to the public.

CHAPTER PROJECT
- This project could make school organizations more efficient and productive.

PREPARE

● PERFORMANCE OBJECTIVES

- Participates in daily 15-second skill drills when asked
- Explains the influence of radio and television
- Describes types of performances on radio and television
- Uses group research and discussion techniques effectively

● sca GUIDELINES

- Uses voice and gestures effectively for radio or TV communication
- Identifies main ideas in a TV or radio broadcast
- Distinguishes fact from opinion in radio and TV advertising
- Summarizes a public service message on radio or TV

● UNIT FOCUS

Unit 6 focuses on mass communication, particularly radio and television.

● CONTENTS

15 Radio and Television *pp. 476–499*

▼ UNIT PORTFOLIOS

Individual Portfolios
- Glossary of Speech Terms
- Comparison of Radio and TV Programs
- Classified Ads for Radio and TV Personnel
- Script for Radio or TV Commercial
- Emmy Nominations for Best Programs and Performers

Class Portfolios
- Video of TV Segment or Commercial
- Checklist for Radio or TV Productions
- Timeline for Inventions Related to Radio and Television
- Script and Production of Infomercial
- CD ROM List of the 100 Best Radio and Television Shows of All Time

School Portfolio
- Video Production of News Broadcast or School Sports Event

UNIT 6

MASS COMMUNICATION

PREPARE

● UNIT PLANNER

Chapter	Time Management					
15 Radio and Television *pp. 476–499*	Week 1	✔	✔	✔	✔	✔

● ANCILLARY RESOURCES

● PROFESSIONAL RESOURCES

Print

Beckert, C. *Getting Started in Mass Media*. Lincolnwood, IL: National Textbook Company, 1992.

Deming, C., and S. Becker. *Media in Society: Readings in Mass Communication*. Glenview, IL: Scott, Foresman, 1988.

Schrank, J. *Understanding Mass Media*, 4th ed., Lincolnwood, IL: National Textbook company, 1991.

Video

American Tongues (30 min, Center for New American Media, 455 W. Main Street, Wyckoff, NJ 07481).

Audiocassettes

Effective Communication, set of 4 audiocassettes developed by Jeffrey Schrank (The Learning Seed Company, 330 Telser Road, Lake Zurich, IL 60047).

15 Radio and Television

Ancillary Resource Key

- = Portfolio Product Activities
- = Tests/Answer Key
- = Speech Library
- = Self-Help Videos
- = Audiotape

475

PREPARE

● CHAPTER PLANNER

Day 1	Day 2	Day 3	Day 4	Day 5
Prepare	Prepare	Prepare	Prepare	Prepare
Teach	Teach	Teach	Teach	Teach
Assess	Assess	Assess	Assess	Assess
Sub. Teacher Tip *p. 480*	Sub. Teacher Tip *p. 484*	Sub. Teacher Tip *p. 491*		

● CHAPTER OVERVIEW

This chapter examines the following topics:
- The Nature of Radio and Television *p. 477*
- The Development of Electronic Media *p. 478*
- The Purposes of Radio and Television *p. 486*
- Performing on Radio and Television *p. 489*
- Producing for Radio and Television *p. 492*

▽ PORTFOLIO PRODUCTS

Individual Projects
- Glossary of Speech Terms
- Comparison of Radio and TV
- Classified Ads for Radio and TV Personnel
- Script for Radio or TV Commercial
- Chapter 15 Portfolio Products

Group Projects
- Tape of Radio or TV Segment
- Video of TV Segment or Commercial
- Checklist for Radio or TV Productions

● sca GUIDELINES

- Uses voice and gestures effectively for radio or TV communication
- Identifies main ideas in a TV or radio broadcast
- Distinguishes fact from opinion in radio and TV advertising
- Summarizes a public service message on radio or TV

CHAPTER 15

Radio and Television

When you have completed this chapter you should be able to:

- Explain how radio and television are different from other types of communication.
- Discuss the development of radio and television and their impact on people's lives.
- Discuss the verbal and nonverbal requirements for radio and television performers.
- Describe special communication skills necessary for different types of radio and television performers.
- Describe some of the jobs that are part of radio and television production.

● LINKS TO PAST LEARNING

Ask students to think about their favorite weekly TV program. Or you could ask students which night is the best night for TV programs. They may want to tally the results of student opinion. Then ask which is their favorite radio station. Tally the results and discuss the reasons for their choices.

● MOTIVATION

Ask students to name their favorite TV or radio personality and have them identify the characteristics that they think are important for a person on radio or TV to have to be the "best." Discuss whether all media personalities have these qualities in varying degree.

TEACH

> **"***Television is the first truly democratic culture—the first culture available to everyone and entirely governed by what the people want. The most terrifying thing is what people do want.***"**
>
> —Clive Barnes

Mass communication, whether in the form of newspapers, books, movies, radio, television, video, or CD-ROM, differs from all other types of communication. It is designed to reach large audiences who are not usually physically present and who can "turn off" the senders at will.

The importance of mass communication can be seen in the history of Lincoln's Gettysburg Address. When President Lincoln spoke his Gettysburg Address in 1863, the audience that heard his words was very small compared to the number of people who later read the speech in newspapers, magazines, books, and CD-ROM.

Mass communication in written forms has been available for hundreds of years. More recent technological advancements have not only improved the methods of producing written forms of mass communication but have also made possible the development of electronic forms of mass communication. Through the **electronic media** of radio, television, and video, large audiences can now not only hear and see something happening on the other side of the world, but can also witness it at the moment it occurs. Radio and television have become very effective means of mass communication.

● THE NATURE OF RADIO AND TELEVISION

One reason for the success of radio and television is their capacity to attract enormously large audiences. It is estimated that the average number of radio sets per household is 5.6. Over 93 million American households own a television set, and more than 59.5 million homes have multiple sets. The average household watches TV 7 hours and 40 minutes a day.

Continual developments in technology have produced rapid changes in the use of electronic media and the effect they have on people's lives.

TEACH

AMAZING FACTS!
It was reported in 1988 that the average child in the U.S. sees at least 26,000 murders on TV by his or her 18th birthday!

● **CURRICULAR CONNECTIONS**

History
Have students research the invention of radio, TV, or other electronic media. They could present their findings in the form of an illustrated timeline.

● **LEARNING STYLES**

Cooperative Learning
Have small groups of students make lists of all the electronic equipment they have at home and use at school. They should also record the quantities of each item that households have. The group could prepare a bar graph to identify and illustrate the electronic media students use regularly. Display the bar graphs produced by each group. Students could figure the average and the mean figures in each category.

Visual Learning
Ask students to name all the TV programs they watched last night. List these on the chalkboard. Encourage students to speculate about the total number of Americans watching each program. Invite them to begin to think about the number of people involved in the production of a single TV program.

CHAPTER 15 Radio and Television

Radio and television have also made it possible for countless numbers of people to share a single experience. In 1969, over 600 million people throughout the world heard men speak from the surface of the moon. The estimated global television audience for the 1990 Soccer World Cup finals played in Italy was 26.5 billion.

Another important characteristic of radio and television is their ability to communicate over long distances in very short amounts of time. Think about it. Radio and television have made it possible for someone to hear live music from New York City and to see a football game as it is being played in Dallas, Texas—all without ever leaving the confines of a living room in Boston, Massachusetts. Because radio waves travel at the speed of light, or about 186,282 miles (299,792 km) per second, it is even possible for people listening to the sounds of a live concert being broadcast from another state to hear the sounds a split second before the sounds reach the back of the room in which they are being made. Radio and television can bring you into direct and immediate contact with other people and places all over the world.

Perhaps the most significant aspect of radio and television is the amount of control the audience has over the media. With radio and TV, the listener is not part of a "captive" audience. If you do not like what is being communicated, you can simply push a button and change the message. Furthermore, if you do not wish to hear or see any message at all, you are equally free to remove yourself quickly and easily from what is being communicated, or simply to shut the medium off altogether.

● **THE DEVELOPMENT OF ELECTRONIC MEDIA**

The electronic media have developed within the last hundred and fifty years. Before the invention of radio and television, long distance communication of sound required the use of wires such as those used in telegraph and telephone service. The gradual development of the "wireless"—as the early radio was called—marked the beginnings of important changes in the way people could communicate. Continual developments in technology have produced rapid changes in the use of electronic media and the effect they have on people's lives.

A Brief History of Radio

No one person or country can be credited with the invention of the radio. In the late nineteenth and early twentieth centuries many scientists and inventors working in the fields of electricity and magnetism contributed to its development. In 1897 a British patent was obtained for

● **LINKS TO PAST LEARNING**

Students could interview their parents and grandparents about the radio programs they remember and what they liked about radio. Encourage students to think of the nonentertainment functions of radio.

● **ENRICHMENT**

You might play excerpts from radio "greats" for the class to enjoy. Ask students to nominate the ten best radio performers after they have researched or listened to radio personalities.

AMAZING FACTS!

The most durable radio program of all time was the Grand Ole Opry, which broadcast continuously from November 1925 to May 1992, a total of more than 66 years.

● **SKILL DEVELOPMENT**

15-Second Skill Opportunity
Have students prepare to read a paragraph for the class. The class should face the back of the room and not watch the reader. The speaker will have to rely solely on voice to convey meaning and personality. After several volunteers have read their material, ask students if they think it would be harder to be a radio or TV performer.

The Development of Electronic Media 479

Early radio broadcasts were the occasion for family gatherings to hear favorite shows.

"communication using electro-magnetic waves." In that same year, the first permanent radio installation was established in England.

At first, radio could only transmit coded sounds as the telegraph did. But, by the early twentieth century, radio operators were communicating with each other in words. One of the most important uses of early radio was providing a direct communication link from ship to shore and from ship to ship. In 1912 the survivors of the sunken Titanic were rescued because of their radio distress calls.

In the 1920s, radio began to capture the interest of the American public. By 1923 over five hundred separate radio stations were broadcasting on a regular basis. In the 1930s and 1940s, countless families gathered around household radios to hear voices being transmitted through the air and into their kitchens or living rooms.

Radio became "big business" as well as "show business" when individual companies bought time on radio stations to advertise their products and produced their own live comedy, variety, and musical programs to attract audiences. Soap manufacturers developed continuing drama programs for broadcast during the daytime that have been known ever since as *soap operas*. Situation comedies were also first developed through radio. News and sports programs were broadcast regularly. In the 1930s and 1940s, Joe Louis's championship boxing matches were so popular that movie theater operators would often stop the film in order to broadcast the program for their audiences. In the 1990s, over 11,000 authorized radio stations broadcast programs throughout the United States.

479

TEACH

SUBSTITUTE TEACHER TIP

Bring copies of TV program guides and ask groups of students to concentrate on a certain day of the week and note the type of programs offered. Share conclusions of each group. Encourage students to guess which day of the week has the most prime time viewers.

AMAZING FACTS!

Ninety-eight percent of American homes have a color TV set and watch TV an average of 7 hours 40 minutes a day.

● **SKILL DEVELOPMENT**

15-Second Skill Opportunity
Ask students to think of memorable TV lines and share them with the class. They should also provide background information with each example.

● **SKILL APPLICATION**

Media Literacy
Have students make a list of the TV advertisers they remember from watching TV last night. Encourage them to note the number of commercials presented during one commercial break. Compile a list and then have the class figure out how many sponsors a 30-minute TV program has, on the average.

480

---

480   CHAPTER 15 Radio and Television

A Brief History of Television

Almost as soon as people learned how to transmit sound through the air over long distances, experiments to do the same with pictures were begun. As with radio, no one person can take all the credit for the invention of television. Rather, a series of independent discoveries over a relatively short period of about thirty years made television possible. Although experiments with television began as early as 1884, progress was slight until the discoveries made between 1920 and 1950. In 1923 the first television camera suitable for broadcasting was introduced. By 1929 complete television systems were available, and by 1939 America was broadcasting television on a regular basis. The American public, however, did not respond very eagerly to this new invention. Few television sets were sold in the late 1930s and early 1940s because of the public's attachment to radio and the expense involved. After World War II ended in 1945, interest in television increased greatly. By 1950, the great television boom was in full swing. It wasn't long before the medium of television had completely overtaken radio in popularity.

One of the reasons television proved to be so popular was the way it was able to incorporate the best of both film and radio. Like a movie, TV was visual. Like a radio broadcast, TV was immediate. With television, people found that they could, for example, not only see an event but could do so almost as quickly as it happened. Today, viewers can watch more than one television program simultaneously with picture-in-picture (pip) capability.

Early television was almost always broadcast live. Live broadcasting can make programs more interesting, but the possibility of something going wrong always exists. Some people remember the time Betty Furness, while doing a live television commercial, found, to her horror, that the refrigerator she was demonstrating would not open when she pulled on the handle. Later, all TV commercials were put on film even if the rest of the broadcast was live.

Television programs and technology continue to evolve. Talk shows, prime time, and sports events compete for viewer attention. Sony developed a jumbo color TV screen for an international expo in 1985 that measured 80 by 150 feet. The smallest color TV was developed by Casio in 1992, with a screen size of 1.4 inches. Many households have already gone beyond simple television. Over 77 percent of American homes own videocassette recorders (VCRs), and more than 61 percent receive cable. Personal home computers hooked up to television offer the possibility of interactive programming and access to the "information highway."

The invention and increasing use of **videotape** in the mid-1950 permitted television stations to record not only commercials but also entertainment programs on tape for quick rebroadcast. This led to other

● **LINKS TO PAST LEARNING**

Ask students to identify electronic media that they take for granted but which their parents considered a novelty. Then have them try to anticipate the future and guess what their own children will take for granted that they do not currently have. Discuss how these changes have influenced the business, educational, and entertainment worlds.

> **AMAZING FACTS!**
> The first fully edited and packaged VHS video tape of the wedding between Prince Andrew and Sarah Ferguson was sold commercially only 5 hours 41 minutes after the departure of the royal couple for their honeymoon!

● **LEARNING STYLES**

Audio/Visual Learning
Suggest that groups of students concentrate on learning about radio while others concentrate on TV. Ask each group to prepare a report that would summarize their medium's history, major advances, prevalent uses, and prognosis for the future.

● **SKILL DEVELOPMENT**

15-Second Skill Opportunity
Have students imagine that they have 15 seconds to ask a radio or TV talk show host a question on the air. Have volunteers enact their call-in question.

---

recording techniques, including instant replay, slow motion, stop action, and split screen. Videocassette cameras and videocassette recorders have become very popular. In 1993, about 72 million homes in the United States had at least one videocassette recorder.

Even with the many technological advances, some talk shows and sporting events are still broadcast live. Newscasts often use a combination of videotape and live broadcasting. The vast majority of television programs today, however, are completely videotaped.

Another important invention, color, first appeared in television in 1954. Now, most of the homes in the United States have at least one color TV set, and almost all programs are produced in color.

The overseas transmission of television through the use of satellites began in 1962. This not only opened up new markets for American broadcasting but also made live television from other countries available to the American public. "What's next?" you may be asking. It is difficult to say exactly what technological changes will be made in television in the future.

Radio Today

Television's quick rise in popularity had a very negative effect on radio, and at one time even threatened to make it obsolete. Radio's survival has depended upon its ability to adapt. By concentrating on its strengths and making necessary programming changes, radio has been able to provide some services that television doesn't.

One advantage radio has is that receivers are often small, lightweight, and inexpensive. Portable radios, run by batteries, have made it possible for people to listen while shopping, sunbathing at the beach, or working outdoors. Most automobiles are equipped with radios. Many people prefer radio because they can listen while they do other things.

The largest regular radio audience listens to the British Broadcasting Corporation (BBC) World Service. In 1993, a worldwide survey indicated that 124 million listeners heard broadcasts in 39 languages.

Radio has also made important changes in its programming in recent years. Gone from most radio stations are the soap operas, situation comedies, and variety shows. In their place radio now offers more news, music, and talk shows. In fact, many radio stations attempt to attract listeners by specializing in specific types of programs. People who are interested, for example, in classical music can easily find radio stations that specialize in presenting classical music. Many radio stations have included more live talk shows in their programming. Studies have indicated that these programs attract large numbers of listeners. Experts speak on foreign affairs, or political or environmental issues. Guest speakers give self-help hints, and listeners telephone to discuss

TEACH

> *"Some television programs are so much chewing gum for the eyes."*
> —John Mason Brown

● **LEARNING STYLES**

Multicultural Learning
Ask students to examine a copy of the TV programming for a week and identify those programs that are supposed to appeal to ethnic audiences. Discuss the content of these programs and considerations concerning market share of the viewing public and advertising strategies.

● **SKILL DEVELOPMENT**

Creative Thinking
Have students write a 15-second commercial that would be suitable for radio or TV prime time viewing.

● **SKILL APPLICATION**

Debate
Students could gather information about the suggestion to cut federal funding for public television. You might encourage students to write a debate proposition on this topic and organize a debate team to argue for and against the proposal.

482

---

482 CHAPTER 15 Radio and Television

their opinions on various subjects. Many presidents of the United States have used radio to provide information and nurture popular support.

Television Today

Television, too, has adapted itself to changing times by the technological improvements already discussed and also by the types of television service available. Several different kinds of television have emerged in the last forty years. Each of these has been designed to fulfill specific audience needs.

Commercial TV The vast majority of available television programs are transmitted by commercial stations. **Commercial television** is paid for by companies who buy air time to advertise their products. The major criticism of this kind of television is that it has become more of a business than a service. Because producing commercial television programs is expensive, large fees are charged for advertising time. Stations and networks must be able to guarantee large audiences for sponsors paying these large fees. Only those types of programs that will attract the greatest number of people remain on the air. The different commercial stations and networks continually compete against each other for a larger share of the audience.

Television options today include commercial, educational, public, cable, and pay presentations, as well as the ability to "reprogram" through the use of the VCR.

TEACH

● **ENRICHMENT**

Students could write and produce a 15-minute segment suitable for public television. They should define their audience, format, and sponsors.

AMAZING FACTS!
The *Muppet Show* is the most widely watched TV program in the world, with an estimated audience of 235 million in 106 countries.

● **SKILL APPLICATION**

Media Literacy
Students could try to learn how much it costs to produce a 30-minute segment for public television. They could make a list of companies that sponsor or provide grants for public television programs.

● **LEARNING STYLES**

Beyond the Classroom
Have students prepare remarks that might be used on public television to seek donations or subscriptions from the viewers.

Educational TV The Federal Communications Commission has set aside television channels strictly for educational use. Many offer classes and instruction for credit to TV viewers. **Educational television** generally broadcasts instructional programs and programs of cultural enrichment, such as concerts, operas, and ballets. Educational TV has been dependent on government grants, and public debate sometimes questions issues of funding and influence.

Public TV **Public television,** which is funded mainly by company grants and donations from viewers, strives to produce a wide variety of television programs, especially those not provided by commercial stations. Programs include ones that are entertaining, informative, instructional, and culturally enriching. Public television's audiences are usually smaller than those of commercial television, but very dedicated. Programs produced by local public television stations are made available to other public stations throughout the country. Programs are also purchased from other countries and from independent television production companies. Some of public television's most popular shows are its children's programs including "Sesame Street." The "Muppet Show" is the most widely viewed program in the world, with an estimated audience of 235 million viewers in 106 countries. Public television depends upon company grants and donations from its viewing audience for support. Consequently, viewers have more direct control over programming than they have over commercial TV.

Cable TV Cable TV began in the 1950s. It was used originally by people who lived in areas with poor television reception, such as the mountains or large cities, to improve the quality of reception. These people would pay a monthly fee to a cable TV company to have their television sets connected by a cable to large antennas. Communities decided which cable TV company would be allowed to provide service in their areas. Cable TV also attracted a large number of people who wished to increase the number of television stations they could receive on their sets. Over 56 million homes, or 61 percent, have cable television. Some cable systems now produce their own local TV programs and televise local sports events. The growing use of satellite dishes expands access to TV channels and digital programming.

Pay TV or Toll TV It has taken a long time for **pay TV** to become popular in the United States. Early experiments with this kind of TV failed miserably. The American public has only fairly recently shown a willingness to pay for television viewing. For the most part, pay TV offers its viewers first-run movies and a wide variety of sporting events not available on other stations. Basically, there are two types of pay TV. Closed-circuit pay TV uses a cable to transmit is programs within a

TEACH

SUBSTITUTE TEACHER TIP
Bring to class the stock market section of a newspaper. Have students identify the companies that produce radio and television products. Discuss what company they would invest in if they had $10,000 to buy stock in a mass-communication company.

AMAZING FACTS!
The Nielsen Media Group estimates that 61.2 percent of American homes receive cable television.

● **SKILL APPLICATION**

Citizens Speak Out
Cable TV companies must secure permission from local governments to provide service in local areas. Have students prepare a statement that would support or oppose the introduction of a cable TV provider in your area.

● **ENRICHMENT**

Ask students to imagine that they are going to produce a CD ROM with 20 of the all-time favorite TV programs. Have them develop criteria to use to make the selection of the programs to be included.

CHAPTER 15 Radio and Television

closed system—from a boxing ring in Las Vegas to a movie theater in New York, for example. In this case, the viewers simply go to the theater and pay the price of admission. Broadcast pay TV uses special receivers that can be connected to regular household TV sets. These receivers are designed to decode signals sent through the air. Some of the receivers record the amount of viewing time so the viewers can be properly billed on a per-program basis later. In other cases the company running the service charges a regular monthly fee and subscribers may watch as often as they like. The Nielsen Media Research Group estimates that over 68 percent of households viewing TV watch pay cable during prime time.

Radio's and Television's Impact on the Public

Although both radio and television have changed greatly over the years, both have continued to have a strong impact on the public. Perhaps the best example of the potential impact such media can have is found in an account of a Halloween night radio broadcast in 1938. Orson Welles, then a well-known radio broadcaster, gave thousands of people the scare of their lives. In honor of the holiday, Orson Welles broadcast an adaptation of H. G. Wells' *War of the Worlds*—a radio drama made up of fictional news accounts describing a Martian invasion of earth. Many people listening panicked. They besieged police stations with telephone calls; some left their houses in search of safety; still others armed themselves and prepared to do battle with the alien invaders. Although this broadcast had a short-term effect on people, it illustrates the potential radio has to influence the behavior of millions.

Another example of radio's power is illustrated by this quotation from S. I. Hayakawa's *Language in Thought and Action:* "It is only a slight exaggeration to say that Hitler conquered Austria by radio."

In the 1930s and early 1940s, President Franklin D. Roosevelt was one of the first American public figures to understand the political potential of electronic mass communication. By using radio to broadcast his "Fireside Chats," Roosevelt was able to sway public opinion in support of his social reforms. Since then, radio and television have greatly affected political campaigns in America. Because candidates are now able to reach millions of people at a time, the public has become more politically aware. This has affected the outcome of many local and national elections.

Some people are very concerned about the long-term effects television has upon the public. TV has raised the hopes of many people for a higher standard of living, but it has also been a source of deep frustration for others who perceive a big difference between the way they have to live and the ideal world that television sometimes seems to portray.

APPLY

● **LINKS TO PAST LEARNING**

Have students compile a list of the radio shows that are broadcast during the commute time in the morning from 7 to 9 A.M. Discuss the assumptions about the needs and interests of the radio audience at that time.

● **ENRICHMENT**

Invite a local radio announcer to speak to your class about the communication skills required for a career in radio. If this is not practical, ask students to write a letter to a radio announcer offering views about the radio programming and format.

● **EXTENSION**

Have students examine the programming of the National Public Radio station. Make a list of available programs and have students guess which programs they think are most popular. Then have a student contact the station to inquire about the data the station has about the numbers of listeners for various programs. Compare the real data with students' guesses.

CAREER CLOSE-UP

Radio Announcer

Radio announcers entertain and inform their listening audiences. A career in radio broadcasting is best achieved by completing a college degree in liberal arts, broadcasting, journalism, or communications. Regardless of their major, prospective radio announcers should include courses in speech and English composition.

Radio announcers need exceptional verbal and nonverbal communication skills. Announcers also must be able to read script so that it sounds fresh and natural. They must be ready at any time to speak extemporaneously. The ability to sustain a sincere, enthusiastic tone of voice, whether reading from a script or ad-libbing, is a skill an announcer gains from experience.

Radio announcers perform for live audiences, but unlike many performers, they neither hear nor see their listeners. As a result, there is no immediate feedback to help them gauge their effectiveness as communicators during a broadcast. Feedback, when it exists, occurs much later in the form of letters or telephone calls from the listening audience. Because of this lack, announcers must be vigilant about articulating precisely, varying voice volume without speaking too loudly or softly, and altering pitch for emphasis.

Effective radio announcers contribute much more than entertainment to their listeners. Whether broadcasters are speaking informatively about the music they select or alerting listeners to a news update, their facility for expressive communication allows them to improve the quality of life for vast audiences.

This radio announcer's ability to sustain a sincere delivery—whether reading from a script or ad-libbing—is a skill gained through experience.

> ❝Radio was one unruffled day from Cheerios in the early morning through Music to Read By at midnight. Radio was fraught with politeness.❞
>
> —Fred Allen

● **LEARNING STYLES**

Audio Learning
If one is available, play a recording of an old radio program for the class. Compare the old radio programming with current programs.

● **SKILL DEVELOPMENT**

On the Job
Ask students to prepare a 30 to 60 second tape that might be used to audition for the job of a school DJ or radio announcer.

TEACH

> **AMAZING FACTS!**
> The winner of the most Emmys is television producer Dwight Arlington Hemion. He has won 16 and also holds the record for the most nominations, 37!

● **SKILL DEVELOPMENT**

Critical Thinking
Encourage students to analyze and evaluate the influence of television on their generation. Begin a chart to identify the positive and negative consequences of television.

Creative Thinking
Ask students to think of how they will manage or limit the amount of TV their own young children will be able to watch.

15-Second Skill Opportunity
Have students prepare a statement for or against censorship or rating of TV programs. Invite volunteers to give their brief statement. Spend time discussing the merits of the arguments for and against TV censorship.

CHAPTER 15 Radio and Television

Many parents worry about the effect of TV violence on their children. It is estimated that most American children, by the time they reach 18, have seen at least 26,000 murders on television. Many people believe seeing so much violence is harmful to children.

Television has also affected people's social lives. It has become the major leisure-time activity in America. In fact, next to sleeping and working, Americans spend the most time watching television, with household viewing averaging over seven hours a day.

Television has long been referred to as the "electronic babysitter." But now many parents are not sure that they approve of the amount of time their children are spending in front of "the tube." Studies show that children (or adults for that matter) who are always "tuned in" to television are often "tuned out" to other equally or more important activities, such as reading, participating in sports, or homework. Some parents have begun to take positive action. They have installed devices that prevent young children from turning on the television set themselves. A number of parents who have used these devices have reported positive changes in the behavior and habits of their children. Other parents try to guide their children toward what they consider the most worthwhile television programs.

● THE PURPOSES OF RADIO AND TELEVISION

Radio and television have three major purposes: to entertain you, to inform or educate you, and to sell you something.

For Entertainment

The number of ways radio and television have entertained their audiences in the past sixty years is practically limitless. Feature films and situation comedy capture the largest viewing audiences on a regular basis. Full-length movies are scheduled daily on major networks. These networks also offer new situation comedies every season in hopes of gaining audience interest and loyalty. Some comedy shows like *The Mary Tyler Moore Show* and *Cheers* enjoyed long runs. *The Mary Tyler Moore Show* won more Emmy awards (29) than any other. *Cheers*, though, was nominated for a whopping 109 awards.

Drama is another important form of radio and television entertainment. Westerns, police stories, science fiction, and soap operas are only a few of the kinds of drama that have been used by both radio and television at one time or another. Suspense and mystery drama programs

TEACH

● **TEACHING**

List the three major purposes of radio and TV on the chalkboard. Use *TV Guide* or a weekly program summary to estimate the relative amount of time presented on TV in each area.

● **ENRICHMENT**

Ask students to collect cartoons or quotes about radio and TV programs. These could be displayed or presented on the bulletin board. Some students might create their own cartoon to illustrate a reality of mass communications.

> *If the proverb is true that prison is college for crime, I believe for young disturbed adolescents, TV is a preparatory school for delinquency.*
> —Ralph S. Banay

● **LEARNING STYLES**

Visual Learning
Have students, as a class or in small groups, nominate their ten most favorite entertainment programs on TV. Categorize the programs in terms of comedy, drama, music, or sports. Encourage students to nominate the best program in each category.

● **SKILL DEVELOPMENT**

15-Second Skill Opportunity
Have students prepare and deliver a short nomination for best TV show in one of the categories mentioned in this section—comedy, drama, music, and sports.

The effect of mass media on interests, attitudes, and behavior is a source of continuing discussion and debate.

rank third in viewing popularity, while general drama ranks fourth. The six- to ten-hour "miniseries" drama is also very popular. This format has made possible the filming of material too long for regular-length drama.

A third form of entertainment that has always been available is music. Whether played or sung, music—rock, jazz, classical, country-western, or easy listening—has been an important part of radio's and television's past and present. Music Television (MTV) is a very popular form of cable television. The programming is centered around the dramatization of top pop-rock hits, and is especially popular with high-school and university audiences.

The type of entertainment that has attained the largest one-time radio and television audiences is the live broadcast of sporting events. Audiences have always enjoyed listening to and viewing events such as the Olympic Games and championship matches between professional sports teams—especially football, baseball, and basketball championships.

For Information

One of radio's and television's most useful functions is to inform and educate the public. The most common way to inform the public has been through frequent news broadcasts. Almost every radio station provides its listeners with some local and world news every hour. And the major TV networks schedule several newscasts every day. Almost 14 million Americans watch some news broadcast between 6 and 7 P.M.

The television **news magazine** is another way people have kept informed. Programs such as "60 Minutes" and "20/20" are news programs that encourage reporting in greater depth. And CNN has become a reliable source for continuous news coverage.

TEACH

AMAZING FACTS!
The estimated global audience for the 1990 Soccer World Cup finals played in Italy was 26.5 billion.

● ENRICHMENT
Ask students to think of a new commercial for a fast-food chain. They could be encouraged to sketch or draft the story board sequence and script. Have them estimate the cost of producing the commercial. Discuss the influence of commercials in affecting consumer choices.

◆ PORTFOLIO PRODUCT
The advertising rate for 30 seconds of TV time during Super Bowl XXV was $800,000 in 1991. Those commercials reached over 120,000,000 viewers. Ask students if they can remember any of those high-priced commercials. Have groups of students plan a 30-second commercial for the next Super Bowl.

● SKILL DEVELOPMENT

Critical Thinking
You might ask students to learn more about the various categories of music audiences. The categories of rock, jazz, country, and easy listening are mentioned in the text. Ask them to identify the kind of information they would prefer in order to make a choice about investing in or producing a music program.

◷ 15-Second Skill Opportunity
Have students prepare a statement that would support or oppose the opinion that TV is a part of the information highway.

● LEARNING STYLES

✱ Cooperative Learning
Have small groups of students prepare a short "infomercial" that would be suitable for production on your closed circuit school TV.

Technology Tools
Discuss interactive TV possibilities and what new uses students might expect for their televisions in the future.

● ACTIVITY
The data collected in this Activity could be used in a variety of ways. Ask students to think of at least three ways this information could be used to increase the profitability of their stations. Discuss the amount of research that is done to identify audiences.

CHAPTER 15 Radio and Television

The **documentary** is another important source of information. Both radio and television present documentary programs. They provide the public with in-depth reports on one important subject.

Finally, educational television and radio also play their part in transmitting important information. Because these special fields of broadcasting tend to deal mostly with academic subjects, the messages they send are more concerned with educational issues than with contemporary up-to-the-minute news.

For Profit

The third major purpose of radio and television broadcasting is to make a profit. Commercial radio and TV stations sell time to advertisers. In this business, time is money. If the stations are able to take in more money from their advertisers than they spend on programming, they make a profit. In turn, individual advertisers make money by using commercials to sell a product or a service. The problem with this system is that the public is caught in the middle. The money that first goes to the advertisers and later to the commercial radio and TV stations comes from the public. Yet because the public doesn't pay directly for any broadcast time, it has very little control over the quality of programs and commercials.

But commercials can also fulfill all three major purposes of radio and television by being entertaining, as well as by informing the American public about the existence of new products—thereby enabling people to judge for themselves the comparative advantages and disadvantages of competing ones. Finally, how much would you be willing to pay for television if advertisers were no longer willing to spend the money necessary to get most programs produced? Consider the record breaking costs of producing *The Winds of War*. The seven-part mini series cost $42 million to produce. Sponsors count on commercials to create sales and profits.

● ACTIVITY

Exploring the Influence of Radio and Television
Survey the class to determine how many radios and televisions are in each household and how many hours per week family members spend listening and watching. Discuss the effects of the mass media on your interests, attitudes, and behavior. What kinds of shows do you enjoy most? Do shows cater to a variety of tastes? How are you affected by commercials? Do commercials persuade you to buy a certain product? Is this good or bad?

PERFORMING ON RADIO AND TELEVISION

Radio and television performers are people who have learned important and valuable verbal and nonverbal communication skills. In addition, different types of performers have developed special skills in order to be successful at this type of work. This section will look at various types of performers and then at the particular communication skills they must develop.

Types of Radio and TV Performers

Many people immediately connect the word *performer* with the word *actor*. But actors are only one type of performer on radio and television. In fact, on radio today, actors rarely perform.

While actors do perform in television drama, actors and other entertainers often appear not as characters but as personalities on television programs called "specials." One of the most popular types of entertainer is the comedian. Other types of entertainers, including singers, dancers, and musicians, usually communicate by demonstrating a particular talent. These performers spend long hours practicing their skills in preparation for their appearances on television.

Another type of radio and television performer is the talk-show host. This job, common on both radio and TV, is very difficult. Above all else, the talk-show host must be able to communicate with all types of people.

A large number of television and radio performers can be grouped under the category of announcer. One type of announcer is the radio disc jockey, whose responsibility is to establish a warm, friendly relationship with the listening audience. Disc jockeys must be good speakers and have the talent to ad-lib between tapes and commercials.

Another type of announcer is the newscaster. Radio and television newscasters are sometimes responsible for writing and editing news stories as well as for reading them accurately. Newscasters have become very specialized, in recent years. Several newscasters may appear on the same program, each reporting on a particular specialty and handling different news topics, including world news, local news, sports, weather, the arts, and special reports.

Another type of announcer is the news commentator. Most news commentators have had many years of newscasting experience. Now, their job is to analyze the news and give their own informed opinion about important news stories.

The final group of radio and television performers can be called specialists. Former talk show host Johnny Carson is a legendary TV

TEACH

AMAZING FACTS!
Women over the age of 55 watch more television than any other group—more than 44 hours per week; teenage girls watch the least, at 21 hours per week, according to Nielsen Media Research.

LEARNING STYLES

Cooperative Learning
Each group of students could represent one of the categories of performers identified in this section. Have them imagine they represent a specific person in that category as agent. Let each group list the strengths of the person they select and plan a bargaining strategy.

SKILL DEVELOPMENT

Critical Thinking
Have students make a note of the credits that follow a TV news broadcast or other program. List the titles associated with the program. Discuss the numbers of people that work behind the scenes to support radio and TV performers.

On the Job
Have each group select a representative to negotiate the contract for the radio or TV personality they chose. The groups should work with the negotiator to identify the terms of the contract they would like.

SKILL APPLICATION

Media Literacy
Discuss why contracts are so important in the field of mass communication. Do students think there is a lot of job stability or turnover in the field of newscasting, for instance?

TEACH

> **"I don't know the key to success, but the key to failure is trying to please everybody."**
>
> —Bill Cosby

● SKILL DEVELOPMENT

Creative Thinking
Ask students to think of some of the more unusual talk show topics they have heard. Some of these topics have been criticized as bizarre. Encourage students to think of several talk show topics that they think would be entertaining, informative, and profitable all at the same time.

Gestures
Some comedians and political satirists exaggerate the gestures of those they imitate to create their humor. Ask students to identify gestures or idiosyncrasies of radio and television personalities. Ask volunteers to imitate those facial expressions or gestures.

● LEARNING STYLES

Visual Learning
You might show some segments of television shows to demonstrate the importance of nonverbal communication, especially gestures and facial expression.

CHAPTER 15 Radio and Television

In addition to reading specialized news stories, this newscaster may be responsible for researching, writing, and editing features on a variety of topics.

specialist. TV personality Hugh Downs has been on camera more than 10,000 hours in forty-plus years.

Special Skills Needed for Different Types of Performances

All performers on radio and television must develop their skills as communicators. Special skills are also needed for different types of performers.

If you plan to portray roles in dramatic productions on television as an actor, you must develop your abilities to analyze and develop characters, memorize lines, and relate to audiences. Chapter 17 presents a discussion of these aspects of acting. In addition, television performances require other skills. Viewers of television drama are usually watching and listening alone or in small groups. This makes it necessary for actors to adapt their voices and gestures to a small audience rather than to a larger one. Microphones and cameras are controlled by others, and the timing of performances must be carefully monitored. These aspects of television acting must be considered during rehearsals as well as during performances.

If you are interested in becoming a comedian, you should develop all of the skills required of other radio and television performers. Not only must your words be understood by the audience, but your voice should have a quality that catches and holds people's attention. Remember, it isn't only the joke that makes someone sound funny. It's also the way the joke is told. TV comedians must also have good nonverbal communication skills. Their facial expressions and the way they move communicate something to their audiences. This can be a positive feeling or a negative one, depending on how good the performer is

Television comedians must be able to think quickly on their feet, gauge audience reaction, and make slight adjustments in their performances. If a studio audience is present, these tasks are somewhat easier than they would be if a comedian were trying to judge what effect a performance was having on people in their homes. Timing lines so that audiences have time to laugh, without missing what comes next, is most important. This can be a difficult task for comedians when no studio audience is present. Becoming a successful comedian requires a great deal of practice and experience.

If you plan to perform as a singer, dancer, or musician on radio or television, concentrate on developing your skill in communicating your particular talent. Be sure to take advantage of every opportunity to perform in public.

A talk-show host on radio or television should have a wide range of interests, be well informed about current events, and be genuinely concerned about people and their problems. Good interviewing techniques (see Chapter 4) and listening skills (see Chapter 3) are essential. You may wish to review Chapter 4 for one-to-one communication skills used by hosts.

If you want to be an announcer, take as many speech classes as you can while you are still in school. Debate, drama, foreign languages, journalism, and English can also be helpful. Announcers must be able to communicate exceptionally well verbally. Their whole line of work centers around what and how they speak.

In studying to be an announcer, you should also develop your ability to read from a script. Make sure you don't rattle it while you read because it will sound to your listeners as if the furniture is being moved. This is because the microphone is designed to pick up the smallest bit of sound and amplify it. Practice using a microphone correctly. Review that section in Chapter 9 that discusses using a microphone. Have someone watch you to see if you have the habit of moving your head back and forth. Moving your head back and forth will do strange things to the volume and pitch of your voice as it is broadcast over the air. If you are interested in television announcing, practice reading from a script or cue cards while looking at an imaginary camera. Develop any special interests you have that could improve your skills in announcing in that field. Scientific subjects, sports, music, and political affairs are only a few of the specialties from which you might wish to choose.

You should be aware that even radio performers are in the public eye. They have a responsibility to be neat, clean, and well dressed when in public or at least to remember that they are creating an image, however unusual or exotic they may choose to be. Radio and television performers must also be dependable people. They always have to show up for work on time. Performers must also be willing to work odd hours of the day and night.

TEACH

SUBSTITUTE TEACHER TIP
Bring several index cards with short anecdotes, articles, or jokes taped to them. Distribute them to students and have each read the card as if they were radio announcers. Then have them repeat the exercise as if they were reading the card on a television prompter. Compare the two presentations.

AMAZING FACTS!
Compact discs were introduced in 1982 and are changing the recording and computer industries. The first recorded CD to sell a million copies worldwide was Dire Strait's *Brothers in Arms* in 1986.

● **SKILL DEVELOPMENT**

15-Second Skill Opportunity
If possible bring a microphone to class and have students gain additional practice speaking into the microphone. After several have practiced, discuss the techniques speakers should follow for the most effective use of a microphone.

● **LEARNING STYLES**

Visual Learning
Have students pretend that they can televise a school sports event as if it were a nationally televised event. Students could audition for the roles of announcer, statistician, "color" commentator. In addition, technical persons should present clips of their videography to qualify as camera operators. Others will be interested in sound, music, and film editing. Another group might pursue the visuals that would have to be developed for a "set" or for station breaks. Encourage another group to work on "advertising" and commercial sponsors as well as publicity for the televised event.

TEACH

AMAZING FACTS!

In 1992, BBC Radio received the George Foster Peabody Award "for the consistency, range, variety, intelligence, and humor provided to English-speaking audiences worldwide."

ENRICHMENT

You might invite the school career counselor to class and address the many careers available in mass communications. The counselor could identify the major qualifications for such careers and indicate where people receive the training for jobs in radio or television.

CURRICULUM CONNECTIONS

Math/Science

Students could learn about the sophisticated equipment used in recording studios, and in radio and TV productions. They could identify the inventions and discoveries that make modern mass communications possible.

SKILL DEVELOPMENT

Creative Thinking

You might share the information about the BBC Radio award and ask students to think of American institutions that might qualify for the same award. Encourage them to nominate institutions or individuals who reflect the same criteria.

LEARNING STYLES

Cooperative Learning

Organize teams of students around production functions such as sound, special effects, lighting, camera work, and editing. Each group could attempt to talk with a professional, or budding professional, in the field of production they have chosen. They could develop a list of guidelines, or a checklist of functions they would have to perform, if they were to work in that area of production for a radio or TV show.

CHAPTER 15 Radio and Television

PRODUCING FOR RADIO AND TELEVISION

The production of a radio or television broadcast requires the work many people you never hear on the air or see on camera. The "behind-the-scenes" people need a wide variety of creative and techcal skills to bring radio and television programs to the audience. Ma of these skills are similar to those found in producing theatrical even It should be mentioned that most of the jobs in production today a found in television. Radio programs require small production staffs. fact, radio performers often do most of the production work ther selves. Disc jockeys or newscasters will frequently ad-lib to fill ex seconds between recorded music or commercials. On television, eve second of time is carefully planned, and each taped segment of a sho or commercial must fit into its time slot exactly. This kind of progra ming requires professional production people.

Before any production work is started on a television program, programming committee meets to decide on the kind of progra needed. This committee develops what is called a **program conce** and then hires a producer to fulfill this concept. The producer is t executive in charge of all aspects of the production. He or she is respo sible for both the budget and the actual activities of the producti staff.

A producer's first step in transforming the program concept into performance is to hire a director and a scriptwriter. The scriptwri develops a detailed outline and script for the broadcast. Scripts can va in size from an outline of topics an interviewer will cover with a gue to a fully developed dramatic dialogue including stage directions. T script is usually revised in rehearsals as the director and performe help to develop their interpretations of it. The final result is called t working script.

In cooperation with the director, the producer must then auditi and hire any performers needed for the programs. Production speci ists, such as a costumer, a set designer, a stage manager, and a co poser, must also be hired.

Working very closely with the producer, the director is the one w must imagine the scenes and guide the performers into a unified p sentation. A director runs rehearsals. Rehearsals include coordinati all movement on the stage and working with the performers to he them understand the role each one plays in the program. The direc may also guide the composer in writing music suitable to the progra theme.

The technical side of directing involves careful planning of came shots, angles, and special photographic techniques needed for a p ticular program. Most performances are run with the assistance of ma

TEACH

● CURRICULUM CONNECTIONS

Writing
Have students develop a program concept for a new television program. The concept should identify the major audience, format, possible sponsors, and suggested actors or performers. The concept could be submitted for review by a group of judges or left to a majority vote by members of the class.

● RETEACHING

Suggest to students that they can audition for one of the jobs mentioned in this chapter. They must identify the job they think they are best suited for, write a job description, and develop a short audiotape or videotape that will explain or demonstrate their capabilities for the position.

> *"I hate television. I hate it as much as peanuts. But I can't stop eating peanuts."*
> —Orson Welles

Behind-the-scenes staff bring a variety of creative and technical skills to television production.

technical specialists under the supervision of a stage manager. Technicians and engineers who have special training and licenses are needed to mix the sounds and to combine background music with the show. Other technicians do the lighting changes, operate the microphones, and run the cameras. Program assistants and stagehands work with a stage manager to help the director. Making copies of the script, distributing them, notifying performers of rehearsal times, taking notes, getting copyright clearance for music, and typing script revisions may be included in a program assistant's tasks. Stagehands move furniture, sets, and props. They also handle cue cards or operate a TelePrompTer, which is used to help the performers remember their lines.

● SKILL DEVELOPMENT

Creative Thinking
Ask students to imagine they are part of a program committee for a major network and the task is to play the new fall lineup of programs. Various groups of students could try to come up with a schedule for prime time TV for each night of the week.

◐ 15-Second Skill Opportunity
Have students reflect on TV shows that did not last an entire season or that they considered really weird or dumb. Ask volunteers to stand and identify the dumbest television program they can remember.

● LEARNING STYLES

Technology Tools
If 30 seconds of commercial time during the Super Bowl can cost $800,000, students can appreciate the value of each second on radio and television. Have students watch a 30-minute program and keep careful track of how time is used during the program. Calculate the exact number of seconds given to each commercial. Discuss what happens when a news broadcast runs short or long.

● ACTIVITY

Students should be encouraged to list all the functions connected with the news broadcast. Encourage them to write a script and rehearse the production. Students could include news, weather, human interest stories, and sports.

● ACTIVITY

Creating a Newscast
Divide the class into groups of from five to seven members. Each group will decide on the roles of its members and then work together to produce a 15-minute newscast. Rehearse and time your newscast carefully and then stage the show for the class. Record the production on audiotape or videotape. Play each tape in class and evaluate the effectiveness of each newscast. Discuss what each segment of the newscast contributed to the overall production.

493

ASSESS

● STUDENT PERFORMANCE COMPETENCIES

- Explains how radio and television are different from other types of communication
- Identifies the major purposes of radio and television
- Describes the necessary communication skills of various radio and television performers
- Identifies some of the jobs connected to radio and television production

● sca GUIDELINES

- Uses voice and gestures effectively for radio or TV communication
- Identifies main ideas in a TV or radio broadcast
- Distinguishes fact from opinion in radio and TV advertising
- Summarizes a public service message on radio or TV

▼ PORTFOLIO ASSESSMENT

Standard
- Glossary of Speech Terms
- Comparison of Radio and TV Programs
- Classified Ads for Radio and TV Personnel
- Completed Assignments, Quizzes, Projects, and Chapter 15 Test

Enrichment
- Script for Radio or TV Commercial
- Emmy Nominations for Best Programs and Performers
- Video of TV Segment or Commercial
- Checklist for Radio or TV Productions
- Timeline for Inventions Related to Radio and Television

Challenge
- Script and Production of Infomercial
- CD ROM List of the 100 Best Radio and Television Shows of All Time
- Video Production of News Broadcast or School Sports Event

CHAPTER 15 REVIEW

● SUMMARY

Mass communication reaches vast audiences who can "turn off" the message at will. The electronic media of radio and television are available every day to almost every member of this society.

The Nature of Radio and Television Radio and television reach people over long distances quickly and bring them into immediate contact with the rest of the world and even with outer space. With radio and television, the audience has a great deal of control. If you dislike the message being sent, you can switch to another, turn it off, or leave.

The Development of Electronic Media Many scientists and inventors working with electricity and magnetism between 1880 and 1920 contributed to the development of radio, which caught on with the American public in the mid-1920s. Advertising helped radio become big business as companies funded comedy, variety, and musical programs between 1930 and 1950. A series of independent discoveries aided the development of television, and in the 1950s television overtook radio in popularity. Most successful radio programs were quickly adapted for television, which was almost always live. Now most television shows are videotaped. To compete with television, radio stations now specialize in music, news, and talk shows. Television programming has also changed. Five basic kinds of television—commercial, educational, public, cable, and pay—offer a variety of programs and services. Radio and television are powerful media whose effects on millions of adults and children have been both praised and condemned.

The Purposes of Radio and Television The three main purposes of radio and television are to entertain, to inform or educate, and to sell products and services. Educational radio and television often provide information in more depth than do commercial radio and television stations, which make a profit by selling broadcast time to advertisers.

Performing on Radio and Television The major types of television and radio performers include actors, entertainers (comedians, singers, dancers, musicians), talk-show hosts, announcers (disc jockeys, newscasters, news commentators), and specialists. Each type of performer must develop special skills, as well as those general communication skills necessary for all effective speakers.

ASSESS

● **ASSESSMENT STRATEGIES**

Individual Assessment
- Participates in practice activities daily or weekly
- Completes classwork
- Demonstrates knowledge of content through questions, discussion, quizzes, and Chapter 15 test
- Displays improved evaluation skills in analyzing radio and television programs

Group Assessment
- Sets and achieves goals
- Develops cooperative learning projects
- Supports efforts of team and class members
- Provides encouragement and feedback to members

Producing for Radio and Television Radio and television production involves people with a variety of creative and technical skills. The producer is in charge of all aspects of the production. The director helps hire performers and musicians, runs rehearsals, directs the action of the performers, and guides composers in writing suitable music. The scriptwriter develops an outline and later writes a script. Production specialists include technicians, engineers, program assistants, and stagehands, working under the supervision of a stage manager.

VOCABULARY

Define each term in a complete sentence.

mass communication
electronic media
videotape
commercial television
educational television
public television
cable TV
pay TV
news magazine
documentary
program concept

✓ CHECKLIST

Skills for Radio and Television

1. Study the history of radio and television to better understand mass communication.
2. Be aware of the differences between radio and TV.
3. Be aware of the purposes of radio and TV.
4. Be aware of the difference that exists between an actor and a performer.
5. Develop the appropriate acting skills if you wish to act on TV.
6. Take advantage of every opportunity to act, sing, or dance before an audience.
7. Be aware of the importance of speech courses for those who wish to be announcers.
8. Realize the importance of production jobs in radio and TV.

ASSESS

● **ANSWERS**

See the Answer Key for more complete answers.

REVIEW QUESTIONS
1. Mass communication has a large, impersonal audience.
2. Electronic media refers to radio, television, and other mass media.
3. Satellites permit instantaneous, global transmissions.
4. Radios are small and inexpensive and generally have better sound quality.
5. Radio focuses on news, music, and talk shows.
6. Commercial, educational, public, cable, and pay television are available.
7. Radio and television entertain, inform, and make money through advertising.
8. Performers include actors, announcers, newscasters, and talk show hosts.
9. Actors use movements and voice suitable for use on the microphone. Announcers read cues and use the microphone.
10. Producers, directors, script writers, set staff and stage hands work in television production.

DISCUSSION QUESTIONS
The following code is used to designate discussion questions and activities as suitable for students of varying ability levels:
- ▼ = below average to average
- ◆ = average to above average
- ■ = all students

1. The differences will be apparent; students
■ will need help with similarities.
2. Ask students to examine the rights and
◆ responsibilities of the news media.
3. Advertising has become more sophisticated
■ over time.
4. Discuss censorship in general and give specific examples of products considered too controversial to be advertised on television.

CHAPTER 15 REVIEW

REVIEW QUESTIONS

1. Define mass communication.
2. Define electronic media.
3. Explain how the use of satellites has affected television programming.
4. Name several advantages of radio over television.
5. State how radio programming has changed since the development of television.
6. Name several types of television service available today.
7. Name three purposes of radio and television.
8. State what types of performers work in radio and television.
9. Identify some of the special communication skills required for each type of radio and television performer you mentioned in your answer to question 8.
10. Name at least five jobs that must be performed in television production.

? DISCUSSION QUESTIONS

1. Compare a front-page newspaper story with radio and television coverage of the same story. Discuss the ways in which the treatments differ. What accounts for those differences? How would you present the newspaper story if it were a television or radio account?
2. Hold a class discussion on the question, "Does television newscasting merely report the news, or does it shape public attitudes toward events as well?" Try to reach a class consensus on the proper role of the news media in communicating information to the public.
3. Discuss radio and television commercials and their influence on the behavior of audiences. How large a role does emotional appeal play in commercials? Which commercials do you enjoy and why? Have you ever bought a product because of a commercial?
4. Discuss how public pressure is brought to bear upon the broadcasting networks. Is there any evidence of censorship? What are the dangers of censorship? Can you think of an instance where censorship might be necessary?

5. Compare the offerings of public television and radio stations with those of commercial networks. Discuss the types of programs that appear on each. How does the need to produce profits influence programming decisions on commercial networks? How might a lack of adequate funding influence programming at public radio and television stations?

CRITICAL THINKING

1. **Analysis:** Compare news commentary and news reporting. In what ways are they alike? In what ways are they different? Do you think that the public sometimes confuses the two? What effect might this confusion have on public opinion?

2. **Evaluation:** The Federal Communications Commission requires all licensed television and radio stations to devote part of their air time each week to public service programs. What kinds of programs are these and when are they broadcast? How do you think the system could be improved in order to serve the public more effectively?

ACTIVITIES

In-Class

1. Discuss the impact that pay TV is having on the television industry. Do people judge television differently if they have to pay to watch it? Survey the class to find out which current programs classmates would actually pay to watch. Survey classmates who have pay TV in their homes and determine how satisfied they are with the programming. Make a graph showing the kinds of programs classmates would be willing to pay for.

2. When television first became popular, some people predicted that radio would decline and disappear. Although radio has changed in some ways, it continues to be a popular form of entertainment. In

---

ASSESS

5. It is said that TV commercials are geared to a twelve-year-old mentality. Ask students to comment.

CRITICAL THINKING
1. **Analysis** If possible, play a recording of a news commentary and compare it to news reports on the same topic.
2. **Evaluation** Students might write scripts for their own public service program.

ACTIVITIES
In-Class
1. Students should meet in small groups to develop a survey form.
2. Programming choices should reflect an understanding of the radio's audiences.

ASSESS

3. In discussion, compare schedules and analyze similarities and differences in programming choices.

Out-of-Class
1. Review scripts and choose those that demonstrate effective radio reporting.
2. Encourage students to distribute surveys to a representative variety of people.
3. The report will show skills in library research and organization.

CHAPTER 15 REVIEW

groups of from five to seven people, develop five programming concepts for radio that might attract a large listening audience. These may be music, news, or talk-show programs, or they may be an altogether different format. As a class, discuss the concepts developed by each group.

3. Imagine that your class has been given the task of programming a television station for one weekday, from 6 A.M. to 12 midnight. Divide the class into six groups, with each group responsible for programming a different three-hour segment. Decide what programs will air. As you make each programming decision, explain why you would offer a particular program at a particular time. When the entire day has been planned, compare each group's programmed segment to a typical day of commercial television. Whom might your newly developed programs attract?

Out-of-Class

1. Examine the first few pages of your local newspaper carefully. Determine which stories appear to be most important. In your speech notebook, prepare a script for a ten-minute radio news broadcast. Be sure to include a sports summary and a weather forecast. After you have written and timed your script, make a tape recording of your broadcast to play in class.

2. Prepare a survey form that can be used to judge the listening and viewing habits of people in your community. It should include places for the following information and for any other appropriate information.
   (a) age and gender of survey respondents
   (b) hours per week spent watching television
   (c) hours per week spent listening to radio
   (d) best-liked personalities on television
   (e) best-liked personalities on radio
   (f) best-liked programs (by name)
   (g) best-liked types of radio and television programs

Prepare a rough draft of your survey form in your speech notebook. Then type it, copy it, and distribute it to your selected audience. Be prepared to report on the results of the survey in class.

3. Gather information from your local library about broadcasting laws developed by the Federal Communications Commission. Collect information about the licensing of stations as well. Write a brief report on your findings in your speech notebook. Be prepared to share your findings with your classmates.

4. Find out as much as you can about the early days of radio. Learn about the most popular programs and personalities. Prepare an oral report on the early days of radio. Try to give your audience a look into the past by playing recordings of news and popular programs during your report.

CHAPTER PROJECT

As a class, develop a topic that would be suitable for a thirty-minute television documentary. Write a script that also includes descriptions of the scenes and situations that would be filmed. Determine how many people would be needed to produce the program and decide when it would be shown. If you have access to a videocamera, it might be possible to tape parts of your documentary.

ASSESS

4. Students should use historical events or social conditions in the program they select.

CHAPTER PROJECT
- Select the topic as a class. Assign groups to do the writing, production, direction, and performance of technical tasks.

PREPARE

● PERFORMANCE OBJECTIVES

- Participates in daily 15-second skill drills when asked
- Explains the appropriate use of oral interpretation
- Analyzes literature for understanding and performance potential
- Uses voice and gestures effectively when delivering an oral interpretation or drama script
- Uses group research and discussion techniques effectively

● sca GUIDELINES

- Uses voice and gestures effectively for theatrical performance
- Expresses ideas and character clearly
- Expresses feelings to others in small and large groups
- Performs social rituals

● UNIT FOCUS

Unit 7 focuses on communication skills in the performing arts, particularly oral interpretation and drama.

● CONTENTS

16 Oral Interpretation *pp. 502–537*
17 Drama *pp. 538–571*

▽ UNIT PORTFOLIOS

Individual Portfolios
- Glossary of Speech Terms
- Audition Tape for Storytelling or Drama Casting
- Written Introduction for Oral Interpretation Selection
- Awards Lists in Various Performing Arts Categories

Class Portfolios
- Video or Recording of Best Oral Interpretations
- Publicity for Oral Interpretation or Theatrical Event
- History of Drama Project
- Display of Award-Winning Films and Actors

School Portfolio
- Production of Theatrical Event
- Oral Interpretation Contest

UNIT 7

PERFORMING ARTS

PREPARE

● UNIT PLANNER

Chapters	Time Management	📁	📄	📙	📼	🎞
16 Oral Interpretation *pp. 502–537*	Week 1	✔	✔	✔	✔	✔
17 Drama *pp. 538–571*	Week 2	✔	✔	✔	✔	✔

● PROFESSIONAL RESOURCES

Print
Cooper, Pamela, and Rives Collins. *Look What Happened to Frog: Storytelling in Education.* Scottsdale, AZ: Gorsuch Scarisbrick, 1992.

Heinig, Ruth Beall, and Lydia Stillwell. *Creative Dramatics for the Classroom Teacher.* 3rd edition. Englewood Cliffs, NJ: Prentice-Hall, 1988.

Pelias, Ronald. *Performance Studies*. New York: St. Martin's Press, 1992.

Film
Coronet/MTI Film and Video, 1108 Wilmot Road, Deerfield, IL 60015.

- *Destination: Communications* (part of the EPCOT Educational Media Collection, 20 min color).
- *Stage Fright* (13 min color).

Scripts
For reader's theater scripts, write Theodore Kundrat, 400 E. Randolph Street, #2208, Chicago, IL 60601

16 Oral Interpretation
17 Drama

Ancillary Resource Key
📁 = Portfolio Product Activities
📄 = Tests/Answer Key
📙 = Speech Library
📼 = Self-Help Videos
🎞 = Audiotape

501

PREPARE

● CHAPTER PLANNER

Day 1	Day 2	Day 3	Day 4	Day 5
Prepare	Prepare	Prepare	Prepare	Prepare
Teach	Teach	Teach	Teach	Teach
Assess	Assess	Assess	Assess	Assess
Sub. Teacher Tip *p. 505*	Sub. Teacher Tips *pp. 507, 508*	Sub. Teacher Tips *pp. 510, 513, 515*	Sub. Teacher Tip *p. 525*	Sub. Teacher Tip *p. 527*

● CHAPTER OVERVIEW

This chapter examines the following topics:
- A Brief History of Oral Interpretation *p. 504*
- Types of Material for Oral Interpretation *p. 506*
- Choosing Material for Oral Interpretation *p. 508*
- Interpreting Your Selection *p. 513*
- Two Final Steps: Introduction and Practice *p. 524*

▼ PORTFOLIO PRODUCTS

Individual Projects
- Glossary of Speech Terms
- Timeline of Oral Interpretation Materials
- Tape of Oral Interpretation
- Chapter 16 Portfolio Products

Group Projects
- Staged Interpretation of Selected Material
- Checklist for Analysis and Evaluation of Oral Interpretation Materials

● sca GUIDELINES

- Uses voice and gestures effectively for theatrical performance
- Represents another's viewpoint in oral interpretation
- Expresses feelings to others in small and large groups
- Performs social rituals

CHAPTER

16

Oral Interpretation

When you have completed this chapter you should be able to:

● Define oral interpretation.

● Identify occasions when oral interpretation is appropriate.

● List different types of literature available for oral interpretation.

● Analyze a piece of literature for understanding.

● Practice a selection, using your voice properly to reinforce your meaning.

TEACH

● **LINKS TO PAST LEARNING**

Ask students to share the names of some of their favorite stories from childhood. These were stories that were probably read over and over and enjoyed each time they were heard. You could also ask those students who baby-sit to describe the younger children they care for and the stories they enjoy hearing.

● **MOTIVATION**

You might prepare an oral interpretation of one of your favorite selections. Start with a good introduction that alerts students to the important features of your selection. Explain that oral interpretation is often considered an art form and that different artists can bring different skills and interpretation to the same selection.

● **TEACHING**

Use the introductory remarks here to provide an overview of the material presented in this section. You might write the organizing questions on the chalkboard.

In order for you to hear a piece of music someone must play it. It is a musician's job to transform what is written on a sheet of music into what is played on an instrument. But more than just playing notes, a good musician must interpret the music. What you hear is really a musician's understanding of *how* the music should be played. By interpreting a piece of music a musician is said to *perform* it. People attend concerts not only to hear the music but also to experience a particular musician's performance of that music. *How* the music is played is just as important as *what* music is played.

A good speaker can perform literature just as a good musician performs music. By transforming written words into spoken sounds the speaker can provide a way for you to hear literature. Just as a good musician does not simply play notes, a good speaker does not simply read words. To perform a piece of literature a speaker must interpret it orally. **Oral interpretation** is the process by which a speaker performs literature aloud for an audience.

In this chapter you will study some of the methods used to turn literature into a successful performance. These are the techniques of oral interpretation. First, however, some background information may be in order. How has oral interpretation been used in the past? When is it performed today? What is its value in daily life? What types of literature can be used? With the answers to these questions in mind, you will find it easier to choose selections and prepare to perform.

By transforming written words into spoken sounds, the speaker performs literature aloud for an audience.

TEACH

AMAZING FACTS!
The longest novel of note ever published was written by a French author, translated into English as *Men of Good Will,* and published in 14 volumes between 1933–1946.

● **TEACHING**

Explain to students that long before stories or information was written down, stories and information were communicated orally. You could provide numerous examples of this. Point out that much of the Old Testament existed as oral tradition before it was written down. The famous epics of Homer, the *Iliad* and the *Odyssey,* were recited for generations before being written down.

● **LEARNING STYLES**

Audio Learning
Ask pairs of students to read a segment from a poem, newspaper, or short story to each other. Once the selection is read to the other, ask the listener to identify what he or she will remember of the reading and why. Discuss the role of refrain in oral traditions.

● **SKILL DEVELOPMENT**

15-Second Skill Opportunity
Ask students to recite a short poem, nursery rhyme, or "saying" from memory. You might then discuss and list some of the elements of our American culture that most Americans could recite from memory. These might include the Pledge of Allegiance, the "Star Spangled Banner," certain nursery rhymes, and some political sayings

On the Job
Ask students to add to the list of those people who use oral interpretation skills in the workplace. Encourage them to think of situations where their own parents use skills of oral interpretation.

---

504   CHAPTER 16 Oral Interpretation

● **A BRIEF HISTORY OF ORAL INTERPRETATION**

Oral interpretation is one of the oldest of human social activities. Before writing, people communicated primarily by word-of-mouth. Because there were no newspapers, magazines, or books, ideas were handed down orally from one generation to the next. In this way, literature was preserved in memory rather than on paper. Some of the greatest literature survived for hundreds of years in oral form before it was finally written down. Professional storytellers, known as **minstrels** or **bards** traveled from village to village bringing news and entertaining people with their stories.

As writing became widespread and people learned to read, the oral tradition did not end. Great writers in the nineteenth century not only read their work to audiences, but expected their novels to be interpreted orally by others. In homes where their stories were popular, the best oral interpreter in the family would read aloud a chapter every evening. In the early twentieth century professional oral interpreters traveling through America on reading tours were a common source of entertainment. Young children today are first exposed to literature when their parents orally perform stories and poems for them. Thus the tradition has endured from earliest times to the present.

Before writing was widespread, professional storytellers, known as minstrels or bards, brought entertainment and news from village to village.

504

Occasions for Oral Interpretation

There will probably be many times when you will be able to interpret some type of literature orally. In school you may be called upon to read part of a story or to recite a poem. At home or while babysitting, you may read to younger children. Many professions also call for this ability. Teachers, lawyers, religious leaders, librarians, and broadcasters are only a few of the people whose jobs demand that they read aloud skillfully.

The Value of Oral Interpretation

You may ask: Why study oral interpretation? What value does it have? What are its benefits? In order to answer these questions you must consider two separate points of view—the speaker's and the listener's.

For the speaker, there is often a sense of personal pride associated with reading orally. Aside from the enjoyment of reading something well, it makes people feel good to share their experiences of literature with others. Sometimes people take on the characteristics of the material they orally interpret. It may not be just a joke that is amusing, but also the way it is told. Another person may become more interesting to others when reading an interesting newspaper article aloud.

Oral interpretation also provides a number of other benefits for the speaker. By carefully preparing for a performance, you can develop a better understanding of a piece of literature. The process of developing an oral interpretation encourages you to read carefully and think about the literature to be performed. This extra effort not only helps to improve your study skills, but can also help to clarify meanings and may often lead to new insights. You should see your English grades improve as you develop your skills in analyzing literature.

From the point of view of the listener, oral interpretation is primarily a source of entertainment. When literature is performed, it seems to come alive for the audience. As a listener you not only experience the reader's enthusiasm for the material being performed, but you also benefit from the speaker's understanding of that material. An oral performance may offer you new insights into what you have read before, or it may serve as an introduction to literature you have not previously experienced. Oral interpretation also helps you develop your listening skills. By listening to different interpretations, you become better able to judge a good performance from a bad one. Finally, by giving speakers your full attention, you will not only appreciate others for their skill in communicating literature, but will also discover new ways to improve your own performances.

TEACH

SUBSTITUTE TEACHER TIP

Students could choose to read a comic strip segment to the class. In addition to the words used in the comic strip, students should be encouraged to describe the setting and characters to the class so that other students can fill in the details of mood and meaning through their own imagination.

● **SKILL DEVELOPMENT**

Active Listening
Explain that the impact of strong oral interpretation is dependent, at least in part, on the skills of active listeners. To develop listening skills, ask each student to think of three things they want to remind their parents or siblings about before they plan to go on vacation. Have students role-play the reminder being received with both good and poor listening skills.

TEACH

> **"Literature is news that STAYS news."**
> —Ezra Pound

● **SKILL DEVELOPMENT**

Critical Thinking
For each of the categories of literature identified in this section, ask some students to find examples that would be suitable for oral interpretation. Have other students find examples of material that would not be suitable for oral interpretation. Encourage students to identify the reasons for their thinking a selection is suitable or not. Students could begin to develop guidelines for the selection of appropriate material based on this discussion.

15-Second Skill Opportunity
Have students prepare a brief reading around the question "Who am I?" Students should select an excerpt from an autobiography and, through words, gestures, voice, and prop(s), help students identify the original speaker.

506

CHAPTER 16 Oral Interpretation

● TYPES OF MATERIAL FOR ORAL INTERPRETATION

One of your responsibilities is to recognize what types of materials are available for interpretation. Just because something is written does not necessarily mean that it is suitable for reading aloud. You would, for example, have difficulty performing a grocery list, a set of directions, or the ingredients listed on the back of a soup can. Essentially, your task is to distinguish literature from other types of writing.

Literature says something of lasting value and says it well. The literature used for oral interpretation in this chapter falls into two very broad categories: prose and poetry.

Prose

Compared to poetry, **prose** is closer to the language of everyday use. When an author writes in prose, he or she generally tries to duplicate the way someone would speak aloud. Although it wasn't a popular literary form until the sixteenth century, prose is now by far the most common form of literature. Every time you read a book or a magazine article you are reading prose. Prose is used by authors to tell or describe something. The two types of prose are fiction and nonfiction.

Fiction **Fiction** is material created in the imagination. The author of fiction has complete freedom to add, subtract, or change any of what is being written. Fiction deals with imaginary characters and events. Novels and short stories are the two most common types of fiction. Do not be misled if an author includes some facts in a work of fiction. In order to make their stories more believable, many authors create their fiction around actual events or real people. These facts, in a sense, serve as a background for the author's imagination. They suggest what did, could, or would happen. For example, a story about the bombing of London during World War II would be based on actual events of history. But by introducing imaginary characters in imaginary situations, the author creates a work of fiction.

Nonfiction **Nonfiction,** on the other hand, is based entirely on truth as the author understands it, on real people, and on actual events. Nonfiction is written to inform the reader and is usually the result of an author's research. A biography, for example, is a work of nonfiction about someone's life. Its very nature demands accuracy and truth. An autobiography is simply a biography written by the person it is about. If you were to do an oral interpretation of an autobiography, you would try to speak and act like the person who wrote it. The quality of your

Types of Material for Oral Interpretation

performance would depend upon your ability to show what this person is really like. Another interesting type of nonfiction is the essay. Essays are used to state a position, to analyze, or to interpret something. In writing an essay, an author makes a statement and supports it with facts.

Poetry

Poetry, the oldest of the literary arts, can trace its roots directly to the very beginnings of the oral tradition. Most of the oldest literature in existence today, which includes such works as *Beowulf, The Odyssey,* and *The Iliad,* is poetry. The bards were really the first poets. Each of their stories had a specific rhythm and rhyme. The rhythm helped them to remember the number of syllables in a line; the rhyme gave them clues as to the actual words. The result was a kind of chanted story-poem.

Poetry can be described as communication of thought and feeling through the careful arrangement of words for their sound and rhythm as well as their meaning. Poetry has not only survived as literature for thousands of years; it is considered by many people to be the most noble form of literature. As an oral performer you will be concerned with two major types of poetry: the narrative poem and the lyric poem.

Narrative Poetry **Narrative poetry** is poetry that tells a story or describes something that has happened. Narrative poetry is not as popular as it used to be. Most modern writers use prose to tell stories.

Lyric Poetry While narrative poetry concerns events, **lyric poetry** deals with what happened or is happening inside the poet. Used mainly to express deep thoughts or feelings, lyric poetry frequently takes the form of a sonnet, ode, hymn, or elegy. Lyric poems are usually very musical. In fact, the word *lyric* means "song-like." If you stop to think about it, a song is really just a poem put to music.

● ACTIVITY

Working with Poetry

Choose a poem at the end of this chapter and identify its literary form. Read the selection several times to be certain that you understand the poet's message. Pay particular attention to any figures of speech in the poem, such as metaphor, simile, personification, hyperbole, and allusion. Come to class prepared to explain how an analysis of the poem can help you interpret it effectively.

TEACH

SUBSTITUTE TEACHER TIP

You might bring a collection of short contemporary poems to class. Demonstrate the reading of a short poem and ask for volunteers to read the same poem or others from the collection. You could also use any of the selections on pages 536–537.

> *"The tongue of man is a twisty thing, there are plenty of words there of every kind."*
> —Homer

● LEARNING STYLES

Cooperative Learning
Write a couple of short, three- or four-line poems on the chalkboard. Ask groups of students to memorize one of the poems. When each has a poem memorized, ask students to stand. Note the amount of time from shortest to longest for the memorization exercise. In small groups, discuss why it is easy for some and difficult for others to recite something from memory.

Multicultural Learning
Encourage students to bring examples of poetry from other cultures to class. Most cultures have a classic epic narrative poem in their tradition. Students could develop a chart that would identify various cultures and their classic epic poem.

TEACH

SUBSTITUTE TEACHER TIP

Bring to class copies of the words to songs that are probably familiar to the students. Ask the students what happens in their minds when they see the words to music they recognize. How does the process of mentally supplying music enhance the experience of reading or hearing the words to songs?

> **"Music is feeling, then, not sound."**
> —Wallace Stevens

● LEARNING STYLES

✳ Cooperative Learning

Have groups of students think of songs they consider to be good examples of poetry set to music. Have each group share their examples with the entire class.

● TEACHING

You could use the headings in the section about choosing material for oral interpretation to preview the topics involved in selecting good material. These headings could be written on the chalkboard.

● CURRICULUM CONNECTIONS

Language Arts

Students could make a list of words, like *lyric,* that derive their meaning from their Latin roots. Encourage students to find at least ten words in common use that are related to Latin or one of the romance languages.

---

508 CHAPTER 16 Oral Interpretation

● CHOOSING MATERIAL FOR ORAL INTERPRETATION

The first step in oral interpretation is to choose your material. If you are not assigned to perform a particular piece of literature, then your choices are practically limitless. It is always wise to approach the oral interpretation process with an open mind. You shouldn't be afraid to read something by an unfamiliar author or to consider a type of literature you have not read before. A good library may be your best source since it can provide you with anthologies of poems and prose passages from many different authors and types of literature. Do not hesitate to spend some time carefully examining a poem or a prose passage before making a choice. The range of literature is so wide that it is difficult to suggest specific methods for choosing literature for oral interpretation. However, it is wise to consider some of the basic characteristics of good literature.

Universal Appeal

As you examine a piece of literature keep your audience in mind. Ask yourself: Will this piece be interesting to others? Does it deal with feelings or ideas that are common to all people? Stories and poems that can be appreciated and enjoyed by many people at many different times are

A good library is an excellent source of material for oral interpretation because it provides a range of poetry and prose from a variety of authors and classes of literature.

TEACH

● **TEACHING**

In *The Book of Virtues*, compiled by William J. Bennett, the qualities of self-discipline, compassion, responsibility, friendship, work, courage, perseverance, honesty, loyalty, and faith are identified as "fundamental traits of character." Discuss if selections related to these qualities would satisfy the universal appeal requirement. Encourage students to draft their own list of universal human qualities that most cultures honor and respect.

> **"What is important—what lasts—in another language is not what is said but what is written. For the essence of an age, we look to its poetry and prose, not its talk shows."**
>
> —Peter Brodie

● **SKILL DEVELOPMENT**

15-Second Skill Opportunity
Ask volunteers to read the poem by Emily Dickinson on this page. Compare oral interpretations of various students. Encourage students to think of which reading had the greatest intellectual or emotional appeal and why.

● **LEARNING STYLES**

Cooperative Learning
You could ask small groups of students to think of at least five stories or books they have read that gave them some insight into the human condition. Encourage students to share those stories with the rest of the group.

Choosing Material for Oral Interpretation

said to have **universal appeal.** In other words, they deal with problems or experiences that everyone can easily recognize and identify with. Some of the more popular universal themes include growing up, loneliness, parent-child relationships, and love.

In choosing a selection for oral interpretation, it is usually best to choose a work with universal appeal, a work whose theme is likely to appeal to almost any audience. Consider Emily Dickinson's lyric poem "I'm Nobody! Who Are You?"

> I'm nobody! Who are you?
> Are you nobody, too?
> Then there's a pair of us—don't tell!
> They'd banish us, you know.
>
> How dreary to be somebody!
> How public, like a frog.
> To tell your name the livelong June
> To an admiring bog!

Dickinson's poem can be appreciated by many people because almost everyone has, at one time or another, had the desire to be "somebody." You need not belong to a certain group of people or possess a special kind of knowledge to appreciate the meaning of this poem.

Insight

Good literature also deals with important ideas. It provides a new way of viewing life by drawing your attention to everyday things and helping you to see them in a different light. In this manner, good literature increases your range of experience. As an oral interpreter, you will find it easier to get and maintain the interest of your audience if you choose a poem or a prose passage that offers this kind of experience, that goes beyond the obvious to suggest a new and exciting way of looking at something. Literature with this particular quality is said to offer insight. Having **insight** means that you have a particularly clear understanding of something. In the following prose story from *The Tarot of Cornelius Agrippa* by Frederick Morgan, the author gives the reader insight by having the main character come to a new understanding of something. What did the stonemason think he saw in the mirror? What do you think this experience taught the stonemason about death that he had not realized before? What do you think a reader might gain from this story?

> A stone mason who in the course of one winter lost his wife, his son and his best friend, put aside the tools of his trade and went out in search of DEATH, whom he conceived as a tall pale man dressed in

TEACH

SUBSTITUTE TEACHER TIP

Explain that most newspapers and TV news shows try to carry some "human interest" story to engage their readers or viewers. Encourage students to identify a human interest story in the current news that has elicited a strong emotional appeal and to identify the universal qualities reflected in the individual's story.

● LEARNING STYLES

Cooperative Learning

To emphasize how difficult it is to agree about what is beautiful ask each group to examine several pictures or photographs. Ask them to imagine they are a panel of judges and must award a first prize to the "most beautiful submission" in this photography contest. Give them time to discuss and evaluate each "submission." After they agree on the "first place" entry they should be prepared to explain the reasons for their choice.

As a variation on this activity, you might display works of student photography or art prints around the classroom. Small groups could serve as panels of judges. All groups could evaluate the selections and make a choice. Then compare each group's first choice and reasons for selection.

---

black, with a face like a skull. Setting forth from his house, he brought with him only the money he had saved through the years, and his old trusty musket, with which he intended to execute his enemy. "For," he said to himself, "if I find him and kill him, I shall not only have avenged myself—I shall have bestowed the greatest possible blessing on my fellow men and women."—And so he went traveling methodically through the land, searching for his victim in lonely farmsteads, in the streets of great cities, in the homes of rich and poor. But nowhere did he find Death, though he found many who had been marked by him.

Late one night in the tenth year of his quest, when he was staying over at a small inn in a country village, he was awakened suddenly from a dream in which he was being pursued by serpents. Coming slowly to himself, he got down from the bed, stood erect, and opened his eyes. The first faint light of dawn came palely in through the window—and by it he could see a figure that stood at the far side of the room, watching him. The body was that of a skeleton, the head was his own…He reached for his musket and was about to fire, when he realized that the person confronting him was his own reflection in a tall standing mirror. As he approached, it became more and more commonplace and recognizable. The sun was rising, he put down his gun.

It was only a mirror—yet he could not escape the conclusion that he had at last come face to face with his enemy. He gave up his search, went back home, and resumed his old ways. But for the remainder of his life he turned his thoughts more and more inward.

Beauty

Another quality to look for in good literature is **beauty**. These lines from Henry Thoreau's *Walden* offer a good example:

> If a man does not keep pace with his companions, perhaps it is because he hears a different drummer. Let him step to the music which he hears, however measured or far away.

In only a few words Thoreau suggests a way of understanding people who do not think and act like the majority. Keep in mind that the best writers are often able to explain difficult ideas in very simple terms. Their skill lends a sense of beauty to literature.

Of course, people disagree about what is, or is not, beautiful. The sounds you find pleasant may not be enjoyed by others. A description may seem well-stated to you but not to your listeners. There are no rules in such cases, but there are guidelines. Look for literature that has noble ideas presented in language that is pleasant to the ear. Avoid poetry that stresses sound too much and has few good ideas. Avoid

TEACH

> *"What's beautiful is all that counts, pal. That's all that counts."*
> —Jack Nicholson

prose that has many ideas but sentences that are unclear. Literature that achieves a harmony between words and ideas can be truly beautiful.

ACTIVITY

Finding Beauty in a Selection

Bring to class a poem or a prose selection that in your opinion is beautiful. Read your selection to the class, identifying and explaining the beauty that you find in it. The class will discuss each selection and will decide which are most suitable for oral interpretation. Make a list of the preferred selections and keep it for reference in your speech notebook.

Technical Quality

The way in which a piece of literature is put together by an author—its **technical quality**—is another thing you should consider when choosing material for oral interpretation. Are the author's ideas expressed clearly? Can they maintain a person's interests?

The way an author introduces an idea to a reader is one aspect of the technical quality of literature. When you read orally, be sure that you choose material that quickly provides your listeners with enough detail to get them involved.

The way an author approaches the high point of a story or poem is also important. Many passages in literature describe events leading up to and passing some critical stage. This is usually called a climax. The point at which the climax occurs is a measure of an author's ability to arrange events properly. Examine passages for climaxes and ask yourself: Does the climax occur in the middle or toward the end of the piece? If it occurs in the middle, does the second half of the material seem less interesting than the first? On the other hand, a selection that drags on and on, finally arriving at a climax that should have occurred earlier, is equally undesirable. Look for prose and poetry selections that will keep the attention of your listeners from beginning to end.

Your Preference and the Occasion

The most important thing to remember when selecting literature for oral interpretation is to choose something you truly like. If you do this, your audience will be more likely to share your enthusiasm for the selection and you will have more fun sharing it with them.

ACTIVITY

You might emphasize the beauty of poetry well read by playing a recording of a poet reading his or her own work. Hearing the poet's voice and inflection often suggests the meaning and conveys the emotion of the selection.

LEARNING STYLES

Multicultural Learning

Some cultures, like Haiti, have a rich tradition of oral storytelling. Bring a copy of Diane Wolkstein's *The Magic Orange Tree* to class. Share some of the selections. Encourage students to read a selection from this book or another of their own choosing.

SKILL DEVELOPMENT

Active Listening

Ask students to think of scary Halloween stories they have heard or told. Encourage them to share a "ghost story" with the class.

Choosing Material for Oral Interpretation 511

TEACH

● **CURRICULAR CONNECTIONS**

Language Arts
You might work with the English teacher to give students practice in adapting material to an appropriate length for an oral presentation of one, five, or ten minutes. Follow the guidelines presented in the text for cutting prose.

● **LEARNING STYLES**

Cooperative Learning
Suggest that each small group select one of Chaucer's *Canterbury Tales* suitable for classroom presentation. Adapt the story so that it would be suitable for a two-minute oral reading. Once the adaptation is done, students could practice the reading and record their best effort.

As an alternative, all groups could work on the adaptation of a single story and then groups could compare their adaptations and discuss reasons for their decisions.

CHAPTER 16 Oral Interpretation

The occasion for a performance, your purpose in performing, and the type of audience are all important considerations in choosing material for oral interpretation. If you were baby-sitting and you wanted to entertain a young child, your choice of material would be vastly different from the choice you would make if you were asked to give an oral interpretation of a literary work at your high school.

Finally, you should be very conscious of the amount of time that you have to interpret a work. Avoid selecting a short story, for example, that you suspect will require more time to perform than you are given. Your oral interpretation will be spoiled if you have to speed up halfway through in order to finish on time. Besides making you nervous, the need to quicken your speaking rate could annoy your audience. If you have a choice between a piece of literature that is too long and one that is too short, choose the shorter one, and do it well. Be aware that you don't always have to perform an entire piece of literature. In fact, most literature is much too long to be read in one performance. It is perfectly acceptable to cut a piece of literature down to a manageable size as long as you make your listeners aware that they are not hearing the whole piece, and as long as you do not change any of the words.

Adapting Material for the Occasion

Many times you must adapt or cut your chosen selection. As you read above, cuts are made if the selection is too long. You will sometimes need to cut because of inappropriate material. You may also need to cut if parts do not read will aloud.

If you must cut or adapt materials, your first consideration should be the preservation of the writer's intent. Just as a pianist would not change the notes of a Chopin polonaise, neither does an oral interpreter have the right to change an author's intent or rewrite creative material. Keeping this restriction in mind you can nevertheless cut prose in some of the following ways:

1. You can cut unnecessary tag lines such as "he said" and "she cried loudly" if you have established the identity of the character by other means, such as vocal changes or physical changes.
2. You can cut explanations of a character's state of mind or manner such as "John's tone was faltering." These indicate to the reader how to read the dialogue.
3. You may condense or eliminate some description.
4. You may omit minor characters.
5. You may omit anything that would offend the taste of your audience. Some language or material may not offend the silent reader but may offend an audience when it is read aloud.
6. You may cut repetitive material if it serves no purpose.

TEACH

SUBSTITUTE TEACHER TIP

You could refer students to the poetry selections at the end of this chapter on pages 536–537. Ask students to apply the guidelines for cutting poetry and adapt a longer poem to a length of 5 to 10 lines for class recitation.

Interpreting Your Selection — 513

If you need to cut poetry, follow these guidelines:

1. Preserve the rhyme and rhythm of the poem.
2. Cut only to shorten or to eliminate offensive parts.
3. Cut large segments, such as stanzas.
4. Narrative poetry may need more abridgment than other types of poetry.

When you must cut a difficult selection, share the process with your teacher.

● INTERPRETING YOUR SELECTION

There are many different ways to interpret orally any piece of literature. Just as two musicians who perform the same musical piece do not sound exactly alike, no two people who perform the same piece of literature interpret it in exactly the same way. A story about "Old Weird Harold" would sound different if Bill Cosby did not perform it. Young children learn that different people interpret the wolf in "Little Red Riding Hood" in different ways.

It is important to remember that there is never a single "correct" oral interpretation of a poem or story. Everyone experiences literature differently. Although a piece of literature can have many "correct" interpretations, some interpretations are better than others. It is therefore important that you carefully develop the skills necessary for good oral interpretation.

No two people will interpret a literature selection in the same way, just as there is never a single, "correct" oral interpretation.

> ❝*If the word has the potency to revive and make us free, it has also the power to bind, imprison and destroy.*❞
> —Ralph Ellison

● **SKILL DEVELOPMENT**

Active Listening
Have students prepare a reading of a well-known fairy tale or one of Aesop's fables for class. Emphasize that even though they have heard the story many times, the delight is always present because of the universal truth or beauty the story reveals. As they practice their oral interpretation, have students define and focus on the emphasis or emotion they want to convey to the audience.

TEACH

> **"To communicate, put your thoughts in order; give them a purpose; use them to persuade, to instruct, to discover, to seduce."**
> —William Safire

● **CURRICULAR CONNECTIONS**

Language Arts
Have students examine the poem of Marianne Moore, "To a Prize Bird," on page 536. Ask them to make a list of unfamiliar words and references. Ask them to use dictionaries and other references to learn the meaning and allusions to the following: chaff, rick, Samson's pride, colossal, brazen, staunch. Discuss why the poet compares the bird to Samson. Encourage students to read the Bible story of Samson again so that their oral interpretation of the poem will emphasize the words that link the poem to the Bible story.

● **SKILL DEVELOPMENT**

Vocabulary
After students have defined the words and researched the allusion in Marianne Moore's poem "To a Prize Bird" (p. 536) ask them to prepare an oral interpretation of the poem. They could either present the oral interpretation in person or tape it for presentation to the class.

---

514   CHAPTER 16 Oral Interpretation

In order to prepare a good oral interpretation you should know all you can about the literature you have chosen to perform. You must understand your selection thoroughly. You must also consider some of the elements within the literature that will affect your performance. These include the person speaking in the selection, the imaginary audience being spoken to, and the setting in which it occurs.

Understand Your Selection

When you choose a selection to perform, be sure you understand the meaning of every word it contains. A dictionary can help you with the meanings of unfamiliar words. Your selection may also contain references to real people or events from history or to imaginary characters from other pieces of literature. Look in encyclopedias, biographical dictionaries, or other reference books to see why these people and events have been mentioned in your selection.

While concentrating on meaning, remember the importance of pronunciation. Don't take a chance on pronouncing words incorrectly during your performance. Check and practice the pronunciation of any words you are unsure of. Feel free to mark accents in your manuscript (as long as you are not using a book).

You may also find it helpful to know something about the author of your selection and why he or she wrote it. Perhaps the piece has some particular meaning based on the time or place in which it was written. Knowing the background of your selection can make your interpretation of it more meaningful for your audience.

Know the Fictional Speaker

You should be aware of who is speaking in any piece of literature you perform. Sometimes the authors themselves speak directly to the reader. Sometimes, however, in order to provide a specific point of view, an author uses a **fictional speaker.** The voice you hear telling the story or poem when you read silently is the voice of the fictional speaker. Quite often, the fictional speaker is a main character in the story or poem.

Consider the speaker in the following passage from Mark Twain's *The Adventures of Huckleberry Finn*.

> You don't know about me without you have read a book by the name of *The Adventures of Tom Sawyer,* but that ain't no matter. That book was made by Mr. Mark Twain and he told the truth, mainly. There was things which he stretched, but mainly he told the truth. This is nothing. I never seen anybody but lied one time or another, without it was Aunt Polly or the widow, or maybe Mary. Aunt Polly—

Interpreting Your Selection **515**

For many in the audience, actor Hal Holbrook became the Missouri storyteller in *Mark Twain Tonight*.

Tom's Aunt Polly, she is— and Mary and the widow Douglas is all told about in that book, which is mostly a true book, with some stretchers as I said before.

The voice you hear in this passage is that of Huck Finn. The story is therefore told from his point of view. In this case, Mark Twain even used the fictional speaker to poke fun at himself. By carefully reading this passage you begin to understand the kind of person Huck Finn is.

If Mark Twain had chosen to make Huck a little older and more educated, *The Adventures of Huckleberry Finn* might have begun something like this:

> Unless you have perused the volume entitled *The Adventures of Tom Sawyer*, you can have little knowledge of me, but that is of small consequence…

The meaning is the same in both passages, but the characteristics of the fictional speaker have changed. Huck is a different type of person in the made-up version from what he is in the original.

Your experience of literature depends in part upon the author's characterization of the fictional speaker. By paying close attention to this characterization you will be better able to fulfill your role as an oral interpreter. In other words, you are expected to find out as much as you can about the fictional speaker so that you can communicate the story or the poem as if you *were* that speaker.

TEACH

SUBSTITUTE TEACHER TIP

You might show a portion of the *Mark Twain Tonight* performance by Hal Holbrook. Or, as an alternative, you might show a portion of Lily Tomlin's *The Search for Intelligent Life in the Universe*. Discuss the actor's ability to interpret a variety of characters

> ❝*All modern American literature comes from one book by Mark Twain called* Huckleberry Finn.❞
>
> —Ernest Hemingway

● **SKILL DEVELOPMENT**

Critical Thinking
You might write the two opening sentences from *Huckleberry Finn* on the chalkboard. Have students identify the words that Huck Finn would never have used. Discuss what the reader knows about the fictional speaker from that first sentence. Encourage students to rewrite that sentence retaining its meaning but changing the personality of the fictional character.

● **LEARNING STYLES**

Kinesic Learning
Invite each student to think of the characters of Huck Finn and Tom Sawyer. Ask them to think of a gesture or facial expression that would be a suitable "signature" for each of those characters. Invite volunteers to share the gestures with the class.

515

TEACH

> **"No tears in the writer; no tears in the reader."**
> —Robert Frost

● **SKILL DEVELOPMENT**

Critical Thinking
Have students work in pairs to read the poem by Robert Frost "Stopping by Woods on a Snowy Evening." Ask students to make a list of things they think they know about the fictional speaker of the poem. Then in front of each item, have them write "F" for fact and "S" for suggestion. Compare lists with the class.

● **LEARNING STYLES**

Cooperative Learning
Organize groups with four students in each group. Have them discuss the meaning and interpretation of Frost's poem. Each student should prepare an oral reading of one of the stanzas of the poem. The group could determine who reads which stanza.

Visual Learning
Some students might want to find illustrations that would be appropriate to set the scene for the reading of the Frost poem. These could be incorporated into the oral interpretation.

---

516   CHAPTER 16 Oral Interpretation

The text of the literature can help you identify the characteristics of the fictional speaker in two ways: (1) by directly stating facts or details about the speaker; (2) by suggesting details about the speaker.

You will find as you work on your interpretation that in most cases the suggestions far outnumber the facts. Look for a moment at "Stopping by Woods on a Snowy Evening," a poem by Robert Frost.

> Whose woods these are I think I know.
> His house is in the village though;
> He will not see me stopping here
> To watch his woods fill up with snow.
>
> My little horse must think it queer
> To stop without a farmhouse near
> Between the woods and frozen lake
> The darkest evening of the year.
>
> He gives his harness bells a shake
> To ask if there is some mistake.
> The only other sound's the sweep
> Of easy wind and downy flake.
>
> The woods are lovely, dark and deep,
> But I have promises to keep,
> And miles to go before I sleep,
> And miles to go before I sleep.

Notice that while the poem tells us a good deal about what the speaker is looking at, it makes almost no direct statement about the speaker. Perhaps only three facts can be stated as certainties:

1. The speaker is familiar with the scene or at least with the probable owner of the woods.
2. The speaker is dutiful and concerned about the fact that there are "promises to keep."
3. The speaker has made promises of some kind.

When you consider suggestions, you will find that there are more details to work with. The speaker seems to be alone with the horse since no one else is mentioned. The speaker seems to be sensitive to nature since he or she stops to admire the woods, even though there are many things to do. You can also guess from the manner of talking that the speaker is not a child. But, so far, the details still do not give a very clear image of the speaker. In order to bring the speaker into sharper focus you must turn to yet another source.

This source is the interpreter's *imagination* while reading the poem. Whenever you interpret a poem, you combine facts and suggestions found in the poem with other details supplied by your own imagination

Perhaps you have never thought about this process, but you use your imagination every time you see anything. Suppose, for instance, you are out for a walk and you stop to admire a particularly beautiful tree. What you actually see is only half the trunk and half the leaves. To see the other half you would have to walk around to the other side of the tree. Yet, as you stand in one place admiring the tree, you assume without thinking that the other side looks roughly the same, that the leaves on the other side are the same color and size as what you can see on this side. If you walked around the tree and discovered that lightning had sliced it neatly in two and there were no bark, limbs, or leaves on the other side, you would be amazed because you had not found what your imagination had told you to expect.

Look at these two drawings:

You will probably have no difficulty recognizing that one is a triangle and the other a heart. Yet you couldn't do this unless your imagination supplied the missing details.

In interpreting literature, you have to fill in the missing details just as you did with the heart and the triangle. But, note that any information supplied by your imagination must fit in with what you already know from the selection itself. In other words, none of the three kinds of details—facts, suggestions, or details supplied by your imagination—can contradict or disagree with one another. Your job as an interpreter is to put together all the information you can find about a fictional speaker into a clear understanding of that person.

The most vivid interpretations are those in which the performer has carefully thought out all the necessary details about the fictional speaker. Those details include not just the fictional speaker's physical appearance but his or her state of mind and *motives*—the reasons why the fictional speaker behaves and speaks as he or she does.

TEACH

"Imagination is more important than knowledge."

—Albert Einstein

● **SKILL DEVELOPMENT**

Creative Thinking
Recall the scene from the movie *Dead Poet's Society* where the teacher encourages students to look at things from a new perspective and invites them to stand on their desks. Invite students to think of at least three alternate uses for their textbook. Then discuss how their suggestions might be different if they had lived 200 years ago, or if they lived in India. Discuss how expectations of time and place influence creativity.

● **LEARNING STYLES**

Visual Learning
Some students could bring to class or create some pictures that appear to be one thing if you concentrate on one area of color and appear to be something else if you focus on another area. Discuss what the mind supplies, or imagines, in everyday situations.

APPLY

AMAZING FACTS!
The United States Library of Congress was founded in 1800 and is the largest library in the world today, with over 575 miles of shelving, 15.7 million books, and more than 5,000 employees.

• ENRICHMENT
Some students could obtain information at the local public library about the services it offers to younger children. Many children's librarians provide story hours and reading experiences for young children. These students could make a calendar of events for the coming month and share this information with the class.

• LEARNING STYLES

Beyond the Classroom
Since most libraries hold story hours for younger children, some students might prepare a tape to present as an "audition" to a children's librarian for the opportunity to present or participate in a story hour at the library or day care center.

Technology Tools
Students could interview a children's librarian to learn about the use of computer and multimedia products in the children's library. Have students develop interview or survey questions to determine what is being learned and how technology is being used by younger students.

• SKILL DEVELOPMENT

On the Job
Students could contact the children's librarian at the public library in order to inquire about the next story hour and volunteer to make puppets or other props to enhance the presentation.

CAREER CLOSE-UP

Children's Librarian

Children's librarians, working in both school and community libraries, use oral interpretation to make stories from folklore and children's literature come alive for their young listeners. A good oral interpreter helps children appreciate good literature, become better listeners, and develop a lifelong interest in reading. Most applicants for librarians' positions have a bachelor's degree and a master's degree in library science.

In selecting literature to be interpreted, librarians consider the age group of their listeners. Because children's librarians have experience working with children and have a knowledge of child development, they understand the interests, needs, and literary tastes of children. Librarians study a story before interpreting it to gain familiarity with the plot, characters, and the language. They also use this time to practice the voices and dialogue that will help them portray the characters.

While they are interpreting a story or poem, oral interpreters use their facial expressions, gestures, and voices to express the different emotions within the story, They vary the pitch and force of their voices and use expressive eye movements to convey levels of excitement.

Librarians who are skilled in oral interpretation bring a vast oral tradition of life by transforming stories into rich, vibrant tales that captivate audiences. The preparation, time, and expertise that they devote to oral interpretation are gifts that communicate a love of literature to children.

Because of their experience and academic backgrounds, children's librarians have an understanding of appropriate interests, needs, and literary tastes.

Know the Imaginary Audience

When a fictional speaker relates a story or a poem, he or she "speaks" to an **imaginary audience.** In "Stopping by Woods on a Snowy Evening" the fictional speaker is alone so you know that the speaker is talking to an audience made up only of himself or herself.

Sometimes the imaginary audience is one or more characters within the story or poem. Consider the audience in the following poem by Edward Field.

> *At the Coney Island Aquarium:*
> *"An Ode for Ookie, the Older Walrus Child*
> *or The Sibling Rival"*
>
> Do not worry, sweet little walrus, about the superior cuteness
> Of those two new babies they brought to share your pool.
>
> You keep pushing the twins out of the way
> More concerned about keeping them from getting attention
> Than having your own scrub-brush nose whiskers rubbed
> So that no one gets the chance to give you
> The endless hugs and kisses you deserve.
> It is impossible of course to be more popular than twins
> So finally you sink to the bottom and play dead
> Hoping our hearts break—mine does anyway
> And the Keeper watches anxiously, so you see it works.
> But how long can you sit at the bottom of the water
> When lungs cry for air and the heart for love?
> No, Ookie, don't seek indiscriminate love from the many
> As those two simple-minded children do
> Who have not yet met with heartbreak (although they will),
> But leap the railing right into my arms
> And squirm there fishily always, Ookie, mine alone.

In this poem, the fictional speaker is talking to a young walrus. If you were to do an oral interpretation of this poem, you would have to take into account the fact that a walrus is the imaginary audience. In other words, you would have to perform this poem as if speaking to a fictional or real walrus.

The third type of imaginary audience is the most common. Here, the fictional speaker speaks directly to the reader, as in the following passage from *David Copperfield* by Charles Dickens.

> Whether I shall turn out to be the hero of my own life, or whether that station will be held by anybody else, these pages must show. To begin my life with the beginning of my life, I record that I was born (as I have been informed and believe) on a Friday, at twelve o'clock

---

> *"How to gain, how to keep, how to recover happiness is in fact for most men at all times the secret motive of all they do, and of all they are willing to endure."*
>
> —William James

● SKILL DEVELOPMENT

Critical Thinking
Have students identify a character in a current movie or television program. Invite students to speculate on why this fictional character behaves and speaks as he or she does. Discuss how the motives, or state of mind, of the character influence a performer's interpretation of the character.

Gestures
Have students read the poem "At the Coney Island Aquarium" and make a list of at least three characteristics of the imagined audience, the walrus. Discuss what gestures the performer might use when the poem is read aloud.

● LEARNING STYLES

Cooperative Learning
You might organize small groups of students according to the number of siblings they have and ask them to discuss or share experiences of sibling rivalry. Encourage them to read the poem "At the Coney Island Aquarium" and note the words and experiences that seem most real to them.

TEACH

> *In the little world in which children have their existence, whosoever brings them up, there is nothing so finely perceived and so finely felt as injustice.*
>
> —Charles Dickens

● SKILL DEVELOPMENT

Gestures
Ask students to think of how they would create the impression of being David Copperfield to an audience. Ask them to identify the clothing, gestures, tone of voice, and accent they would use for the character. Once they have some notions in mind, ask them if any of these ideas would change if their audience were a group of senior citizens or a group of handicapped children.

● RETEACHING

Ask students to make a list of all the excerpts contained in this section and identify the fictional speaker and imaginary audience for each.

---

520   CHAPTER 16 Oral Interpretation

at night. It was remarked that the clock began to strike, and I began to cry, simultaneously.

In consideration of the day and hour of my birth, it was declared by the nurse and by some sage women in the neighborhood who had taken a lively interest in me several months before there was any possibility of our becoming personally acquainted, first that I was destined to be unlucky in life; and secondly, that I was privileged to see ghosts and spirits; both these gifts inevitably attaching, as they believed, to all unlucky infants of either gender born towards the small hours on a Friday night.

Your decision about what kind of imaginary audience is involved in a piece of literature will have a direct effect on how you perform the selection. Your performance should also reflect the kind of relationship you believe exists between this imaginary audience and the fictional speaker. You know from your own experience that the way in which people say things is greatly influenced by their relationship with their listeners. As you become even more attuned to this, look for opportunities to apply it to selections you interpret orally.

Understand the Relationship Between the Fictional Speaker and the Imaginary Audience

The kind of relationship that exists between the fictional speaker and the imaginary audience is important even when the fictional speaker is talking to himself or herself. Notice, for example, the words used when Lewis Carroll's Alice talks to herself in the following passage from *Alice's Adventures in Wonderland*.

> You ought to be ashamed of yourself...a great girl like you...to go on crying in this way! Stop this moment, I tell you!

Now compare the way Alice talks to herself with the way the fictional speaker in "Stopping by Woods on a Snowy Evening" talks to himself or herself. Though both fictional speakers are giving themselves advice, Alice advises herself rather sharply. Frost's fictional speaker uses a gentler approach. While Alice speaks to herself as a parent might to a naughty child, Frost's fictional speaker talks as if speaking to another adult. Two important kinds of relationships that can exist between fictional speaker and imaginary audience, then, are one in which the fictional speaker is in some way *superior* to the imaginary audience and one in which the fictional speaker is *equal* to the imaginary audience in some way, such as age, experience, or social status.

A third important relationship is the fictional speaker being in some way *inferior* to the imagined audience. This type of relationship is also

> *"Take care of the sense, and the sounds will take care of themselves."*
> —Lewis Carroll

SKILL DEVELOPMENT

Critical Thinking
Some students could make a chart with the categories age, experience, and social status and indicate whether the audiences in each of the selections printed in this chapter are more, less, or equal in each of the categories.

LEARNING STYLES

Cooperative Learning
Have small groups of students conduct a little experiment in understanding roles and relationships. Designate one person in each group to assume the role of parent, child, teacher, friend, and grandparent, but the students should not tell others which role they have. Ask each student to assume a gesture or facial expression that will identify their role for the other members of the group. Based on the gesture or expression, the other members of the group should identify the role. Invite students to describe the tone of voice used by each "speaker."

Interpreting Your Selection   521

found in *Alice's Adventures in Wonderland*. Alice has just fallen down the rabbit hole at the beginning of the story, and as she falls, she talks to herself:

> "I wonder how many miles I've fallen by this time?" she said aloud. "I must be getting somewhere near the centre of the earth. Let me see: that would be four thousand miles down, I think—" (for, you see, Alice had learned several things of this sort in her lessons in the schoolroom, and though this was not a *very* good opportunity for showing off her knowledge, as there was no one to listen to her, still it was good practice to say it over)—"Yes, that's about the right distance—but then I wonder what Latitude or Longitude I've got to?" (Alice had not the slightest idea what Latitude was, or Longitude either, but she thought they were nice grand words to say.)

In the last quotation Alice is showing off her knowledge, trying to impress the listener, much as a child might show off before adults. You could say that the speaker-to-listener relationship is that of a very young child speaking to an adult, or in more general terms, an "inferior" speaking to a "superior."

Following the examples given above, you can capture a major part of the speaker's attitude toward the listener by determining if the speaker's relationship to the listener is superior, equal, or inferior. Keep in mind, however, that relationships can be influenced by many different factors. For example, differences in age and differences in power can greatly influence relationships, sometimes in contradictory ways. Social rank can also have an influence on the relationships between people. The tone of your voice can help make all of these relationships between fictional speaker and imaginary audience clear to your listeners.

Know the Setting

If you wish to communicate all of the important elements of a piece of literature to your audience, you must also deal with the **setting**—the place and the time—in which the fictional speaker and imaginary audience are found.

Place: The Where of the Setting   To understand how important setting is, return to "Stopping by Woods on a Snowy Evening" on page 516. In the poem most of the details you are given concern the place where the poem occurs. In fact, place seems to be the most important single aspect of the whole situation. Even the title mentions it. In just sixteen lines Frost gives you the following details. The fictional speaker is alone except for the horse, and far from any farmhouses. The speaker

TEACH

> **❝** If I were to name the three most precious resources of life, I should say books, friends, and nature; and the greatest of these, at least the most constant and always at hand, is nature. **❞**
>
> —John Burroughs

● **LEARNING STYLES**

Visual Learning
Some students might collect photographs or illustrations of various regions of the United States to demonstrate the variety of regional settings we have.

● **CURRICULAR CONNECTIONS**

Language Arts
You might collaborate with a geography or English teacher who emphasizes the importance of setting and knowing the geography of place in establishing the setting. You might read the opening paragraph of Pat Conroy's *The Prince of Tides* to demonstrate the importance of setting.

CHAPTER 16 Oral Interpretation

In order to communicate the where and when of the setting of a piece of literature, first capture them vividly in your imagination.

is probably in a sleigh, since a harness is mentioned. On one side of the speaker is the woods, further described as "lovely, dark and deep" and on the other side is a frozen lake. You also know that the night is very dark (though there must be enough light to see the woods), that it is snowing, and that the wind is blowing gently. As an oral interpreter, you must capture the feeling of this poem by imagining these specific *vividly* during the performance.

Time: The When of the Setting Now focus your attention on the second element of setting—in Frost's poem the time when the scene takes place. Here you will find fewer details and will need to use your imagination to fill in the spaces. You are given some clues to help you however. You know for instance the season (winter) and the time of day (evening). This isn't just any evening, however. It is described as "the darkest evening of the year." Careful readers of this poem have long been fascinated by this little detail. It is a good example of a writer giving readers part of the information and demanding that they fill in the rest with their imagination. Can this detail really be true? Have you ever tried walking on a truly dark night with no starlight or moonlight to guide you? If so, you probably had difficulty even seeing the path at your feet. Frost's fictional speaker can "watch his woods fill up with snow" and can see deep into the woods as well. Perhaps, as some

522

readers have suggested, the fictional speaker intends the detail about the darkest night to describe his or her personal feeling at the time of the poem rather than the real physical setting. You may not agree with this interpretation. But, as an interpreter, what you decide will affect your performance. If you believe that the fictional speaker is going through what another writer has called "the dark night of the soul," the attraction of the speaker for the woods would be far different from the feeling involved if the speaker, in a lighthearted mood, just happens to be attracted by the woods.

Dealing with Time and Place How do you perform a setting? First, you must see the setting vividly in your imagination and second, you must believe in it throughout the performance. It is one thing to picture in your mind all the necessary elements of the setting and quite another to act as though you really are *in* that setting.

In the Frost poem, for instance, if you are the speaker, where are the woods in relation to you? Where is the frozen lake? From what direction have you come? In what direction are you going? Are you standing or sitting? Are you cold, or warmed by lap rugs in a sleigh? Answering these questions can help you see the setting in your imagination, which is the first step in making it believable to others.

When you first ask questions about the setting of a selection, you are standing outside the selection looking for clues. When you perform the selection you stand inside it. You put yourself in the place of the fictional speaker, inside the setting that you have analyzed. When you read a story or poem silently and read it well, that is, when the literature affects you vividly, you are apt to say that you are "absorbed" by it. What is meant is exactly what you must do in oral interpretation—place yourself within the setting of the story.

If you truly believe in the setting that you have imagined as you perform, those who watch you will believe in the setting too. In performing Frost's poem, if you say "whose woods these are I think I know" and look directly at the audience, you are not *in* the poem. You don't believe in the woods and no one watching you perform does either. Instead, you must look at the woods you are imagining and put yourself in the place of the poem's fictional speaker.

Fill in Missing Details

After you have identified speaker, audience, and setting, there are still likely to be some missing details. Even the most thorough descriptions in literature require a reader to fill in unmentioned details; no description can give a complete picture of the subject described. The reader and the oral interpreter must supply these missing details.

TEACH

> **"** The land is like poetry: it is inexplicably coherent, it is transcendent in its meaning, and it has the power to elevate a consideration of human life. **"**
>
> —Barry Lopez

● **SKILL DEVELOPMENT**

Critical Thinking
Have students return to Frost's poem, "Stopping by Woods on a Snowy Evening" on page 516. In addition to the information supplied in the text, ask students to add to the description of place. Ask them to close their eyes while they listen to another read the poem. Challenge them to describe what they hear in the place described. Ask them to describe what they smell, what they touch, what they feel.

Creative Thinking
Use the detail from Frost's poem about "the darkest evening of the year." Read the possible explanations for that phrase. Discuss the seasonal and the psychological interpretations of the phrase. Ask students to arrive at their own interpretations and describe how they would convey that interpretation in an oral reading.

Gestures
Ask students how they might convey the place and time of the setting for Frost's poem without saying one word. Encourage volunteers to demonstrate their interpretations.

TEACH

> **As much as 95 percent of communication is nonverbal.**
>
> —Marilyn Maple

● RETEACHING

Ask students to imagine that they were directing a junior high class where individuals were preparing to give an oral reading or a choral reading of Frost's poem. Have students write a one-page summary and checklist that those junior high students could use to prepare their reading.

● SKILL DEVELOPMENT

Creative Thinking
Have students focus on the line "But I have promises to keep" and address the question about the promises that had the power to draw someone from the beauty of the woods. Make a list of the possibilities.

15-Second Skill Opportunity
Ask students to complete the sentence, "But I have promises to keep and they are…."

CHAPTER 16 Oral Interpretation

What were the promises mentioned in Frost's poem? They are missing detail. Why didn't Frost tell the reader what those promises were? Certainly not because they are unimportant. They are the most important motive behind the fictional speaker's decision to move on. One reason for not telling readers what they were could be that Frost wanted each reader to go through what the fictional speaker experienced in this poem. In other words, Frost may have wanted you to identify with the fictional speaker and supply, yourself, the reasons for not staying. What kind of promises would draw *you* away from the beauty and attractiveness of the woods? Your answer is likely to be different from the answer given by anyone else. This is one reason why you and other people would all perform slightly different interpretations of the poem. But it is also the reason why the poem is able to affect almost everyone personally, whether they are reading, performing, or listening.

● ACTIVITY

Analyzing Literature

Choose a piece of literature that you enjoy or find interesting. Analyze your selection by answering the following questions.

1. What is the central idea or theme of the selection?
2. What are the selection's main units of thought and how are they related to each other?
3. Are there any words, phrases, and sentences in the selection that you do not understand?
4. How can you make use of pause, emphasis, pitch, inflection, rate, and volume in interpreting this selection?

If you cannot answer all of these questions, ask your classmates for help as you prepare for an oral interpretation of the selection.

● TWO FINAL STEPS: INTRODUCTION AND PRACTICE

Your work is not finished when you have completed your analysis and interpretation of your selection. You must also prepare an introduction and, perhaps most important, you must practice. As you will see, this practice involves many of the same elements found in practicing for public speech.

TEACH

▼ PORTFOLIO PRODUCTS

Have students present their interpretations for the class. These could be recorded or taped and become part of the portfolio assessment.

● TEACHING

Emphasize with the class the four purposes of an introduction for an oral interpretation of literature. Encourage students to add other functions for the introduction.

SUBSTITUTE TEACHER TIP

If possible, bring a tape recorder to class and have each student do an oral interpretation of the Frost poem or another of their choosing. Their tape segments could be part of their personal portfolio.

Two Final Steps: Introduction and Practice   525

Prepare an Introduction for Your Selection

The introduction is an extremely important part of your performance. It provides you with the opportunity to beckon the audience toward the piece you have selected and the interpretation you will bring to it. The four purposes of the introduction are to:

1. Gain the audience's attention.
2. Set the mood for the audience.
3. Give needed information.
4. Establish rapport with the audience.

An audience will not automatically give you its attention just because you are a performer. You must earn this attention. You must *work* to get the audience's interest in the introduction, or you won't *ever* get it.

An audience needs to be prepared for the mood of the material. If the material is funny, don't look serious; smile and look light-hearted. If the material is very serious, your demeanor during the introduction should be serious.

Many times you need to include information in your introduction that will help the audience understand the material. This is particularly true if you are reading only an excerpt from a much longer piece of literature. Remember that the audience only hears *once* what you have probably read dozens of times.

Among your goals in the preparation of the all-important introduction are gaining the attention of the audience and providing needed information.

AMAZING FACTS!

Imagine the consternation of the performers of the play, *Bag*, which opened to a completely empty house on Nov. 24, 1983. Things did improve slightly for the second of its two performances when a small audience was in attendance.

● SKILL APPLICATION

Introductions
Have students write an introduction that would be suitable for the oral interpretation of the literature they have selected. Once the introduction is written they should use the three points listed in the text as a checklist and make sure that all items are included in their remarks. Suggest that pairs of students work together to practice their introductions.

● LEARNING STYLES

Cooperative Learning
Once students have written and practiced their introductions with partners, you might organize small groups and have those students deliver their introductions. Then ask each group to decide which student should represent their group and give their introduction in front of the entire class. You might present the representative with a Certificate of Recognition which could also be part of his or her portfolio.

525

TEACH

> **"A word is not a crystal, transparent and unchanging, it is the skin of a living thought and may vary greatly in color and content according to the circumstances and time in which it is used."**
> —Oliver Wendell Holmes, Jr.

● **SKILL DEVELOPMENT**

Creative Thinking
Ask students to use both stress and pauses in a new way to emphasize certain words in the Pledge of Allegiance. Encourage volunteers to demonstrate the use of voice for emphasis in reciting the Pledge.

▼ **PORTFOLIO PRODUCTS**

Encourage students to make a video or tape recording of a performer who demonstrates the skills in oral interpretation described in this chapter. They should prepare an introduction to the recording that explains the topic and the reasons for their selection. This could become a portfolio product.

CHAPTER 16 Oral Interpretation

The introduction gives the audience a chance to make some kind of judgment about you as a person. They decide whether they want to listen to you or not. Your appearance, your demeanor, your whole attitude is judged by an audience very quickly. You must appear prepared, enthusiastic about your material, and glad to be there. If you appear nervous, if you lack energy, if you are not dressed appropriately, your audience will not be very interested in listening to your performance.

For a ten-minute performance an introduction should not be longer than thirty to forty-five seconds. The longer the performance, the longer the introduction can be.

Be sure then that your introduction contains:

1. An attention-getting device, such as your relating to the audience the literature's impact on you as a person.
2. Needed information to facilitate audience understanding.
3. Author and title. If possible tell something special about the author to increase audience understanding.

The introduction is so important to your performance that it should be carefully prepared. You may memorize it, but it should appear to be ad-libbed. Your delivery in the introduction should be very conversational. This effort will be worthwhile because your audience will be prepared to listen and will reward you with an enthusiastic response.

Practice Your Selection

Practice is essential to a good oral performance. Thinking about how you will sound when you perform in front of an audience is not the same as actually doing it. The best way to prepare yourself for a performance is to practice aloud again and again. Don't expect every part of your performance to be perfect the very first time you do it. You must work slowly and carefully on every aspect of your delivery.

Your voice is important in an oral interpretation. Never attempt to vary it artificially. Let the emotion of what you are performing be heard by your audience. If you feel the meaning of what you are saying, your voice will usually take on the characteristics expressed in the words. Your voice should be flexible in pitch, force, and rate so it can respond to various shades of interpretation.

One of the most important aspects of any oral delivery is the use of emphasis. There is no doubt that some words should receive more emphasis than others, but you must be very careful not to disturb the rhythm of the language. This is especially important in poetry. Poets choose their words carefully to create and maintain a particular rhythm

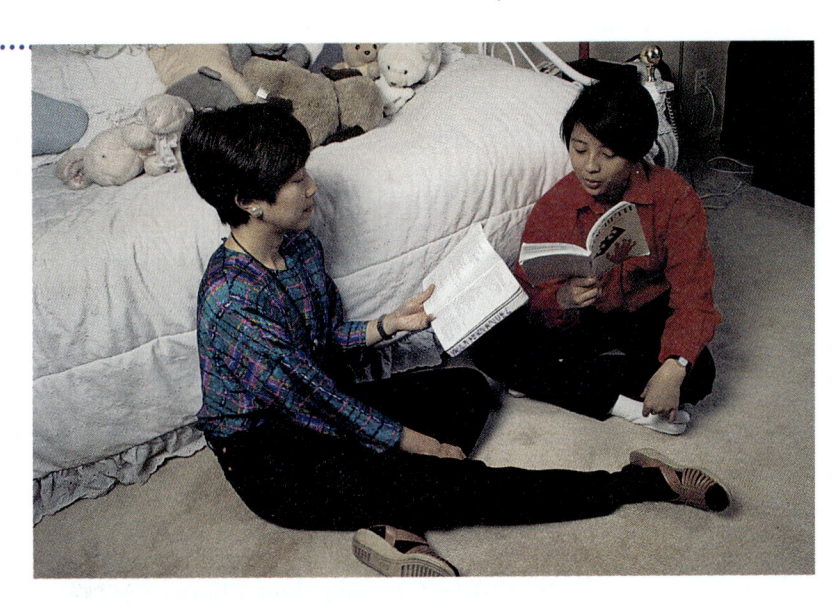

Practicing aloud, working slowly and carefully on every aspect of your delivery, is the best way to prepare yourself for a performance.

The words that should be emphasized will be stressed naturally. Skillful speakers use pauses as well as stress for emphasis. Did you ever notice that when a good speaker stops speaking for a moment the last few words seem to take on more significance? Use both stress and pauses to emphasize certain words.

Speaking rate is also important in oral interpretation. Speak slowly if the ideas you are expressing are serious or difficult to understand. Light, humorous, or urgent matters can be expressed at more rapid speeds. When dealing with a poem, look closely at its rhythm. Some poems are meant to be read slowly, while others should be spoken quickly. Examples of these different types of rhythm are found in the beginning lines of William Collins' "Ode to Pity" and William Wordsworth's "The Tables Turned."

Ode To Pity

O thou, the friend of man assigned
With balmy hands his wounds to bind,
And charm his frantic woe…

The Tables Turned

Up! Up! my Friend, and quit your books;
Or surely you'll grow double:
Up! Up! my Friend, and clear your books;
Why all this toil and trouble?

TEACH

SUBSTITUTE TEACHER TIP

You might play several segments from rap musicians and ask students to estimate how fast the words are spoken. The record for rapping is 674 syllables in less than 55 seconds. You might determine who can speak the fastest in the class.

SKILL DEVELOPMENT

15-Second Skill Opportunity
Have students pick one of the poems here and practice their timing and articulation. Ask volunteers to recite their poems.

Active Listening
After students have practiced reading their poem, ask them to memorize it. You might give them several minutes to accomplish this and then have students recite the poem from memory. Then discuss with students how they felt when they read the poem as compared to when they recited it from memory. Encourage them to assess audience rapport in both situations.

TEACH

> **"Excellence costs a great deal."**
>
> —May Sarton

● **RETEACHING**

Ask students to make a list of all the guidelines that have been suggested for the skills of oral interpretation. They could develop a chart with these guidelines. The checklist could be used to analyze and evaluate interpretations.

CHAPTER 16 Oral Interpretation

The two poems quoted above begin in very different ways. The words "Up! Up!" show that the second poem, "The Tables Turned," is to be read at a quick pace. On the other hand, the words "O thou, the friend of man…" in the first poem, "Ode to Pity," have a solemn ring to them and suggest a much slower reading.

Good articulation and correct pronunciation are both essential in oral interpretation. Don't be afraid to put your tongue, jaw, and lips to their full use in order to say words clearly and correctly. As in public speaking, your audience must be able to hear your words and understand them. In order to remember how you want to say a particular word or phrase, it is a good idea to mark the manuscript. You can develop your own system, which may or may not include underlining words you want stressed or using accent marks to remind you how to pronounce words you may have trouble with.

Above all, you must establish a rapport with your audience. Your listeners must believe that you are speaking directly to them and not to a piece of paper or to the floor. Although it is not recommended for beginners, some oral performers prefer to memorize what they perform. That way, they do not have to worry about losing their place in the manuscript or losing contact with their audience. If you do choose to memorize, be sure to have a copy of the piece you are performing

In oral interpretation, the audience members are influenced by what they see as well as what they hear.

Two Final Steps: Introduction and Practice   529

nearby. Nervousness in front of an audience can cause you to forget some or all of a selection you thought you knew well. If you do not memorize the entire selection, you should at least know it well enough that you don't have to read every word from the manuscript. This will leave you free to gauge audience feedback.

Your audience will be influenced by what they see as well as by what they hear. It is important that the nonverbal aspects of your interpretation add to the effect of your performance. As a general rule, your gestures and facial expressions should be natural. If you are genuinely concerned with getting your message across, gesture will come naturally as part of the performance. Remember though that body movement is secondary to the spoken words. Exaggerated or nervous movements can distract your listeners from what you are saying. Gestures should be used to clarify, emphasize, or reinforce what you say. The visual aspects of your performance must be appropriate to your audience, the occasion, and the selection you have chosen. Most important, the visual aspects of your performance should be natural to you.

After you have practiced reading your interpretation aloud and feel comfortable with it, try speaking into a tape recorder so that you can get an idea of how you will sound to others. If you have access to a video recorder take advantage of the opportunity to videotape your performance. Videotapes are invaluable rehearsal tools for an interpreter. Then have one or two friends listen and see you perform. In this way you will become used to having an audience in front of you. You will also get a chance to observe and interpret some audience reaction to what you are saying and how you are saying it. By performing first in front of a small audience, you begin to gain the confidence necessary to do the same before a larger group of listeners.

● **ACTIVITY**

Delivery of an Oral Interpretation

Return to the literary piece you analyzed in the previous Activity. If necessary, make cuts so that it will take no longer than eight minutes for you to perform. Write an introduction that will capture your audience's attention and prepare them to listen to your selection. Rehearse your performance several times—at least once before a mirror—until it feels polished enough to share with an audience. Deliver your oral interpretation in class.

TEACH

● **LEARNING STYLES**

Cooperative Learning
Invite small groups of students to nominate candidates for the best oral interpretation given in class. Award presentations could be planned for the class.

● **ACTIVITY**

Encourage students to practice at least three times before they indicate they are ready to deliver their oral interpretation in class. This is the culmination of the chapter and their interpretation could be recorded or taped for inclusion as a portfolio product.

ASSESS

● STUDENT PERFORMANCE COMPETENCIES

- Identifies occasions when oral interpretation is appropriate
- Identifies different types of literature suitable for oral interpretation
- Edits a selection for oral presentation
- Practices a selection using voice techniques to emphasize meaning
- Prepares and uses a checklist for oral interpretation skills
- Writes and delivers an introduction for an oral interpretation

● sca GUIDELINES

- Uses voice and gestures effectively for theatrical performance
- Represents another's viewpoint in oral interpretation
- Expresses feelings to others in small and large groups
- Performs social rituals

▼ PORTFOLIO ASSESSMENT

Standard
- Glossary of Speech Terms
- Checklist for Oral Interpretation Materials
- Written Introduction to Oral Interpretation Selection
- Tape of Oral Interpretation

Enrichment
- Staged Interpretation of Selected Material
- Audition Tape for Children's Storytelling

Challenge
- Certificate of Recognition for Oral Interpretation
- Taped Collection of Best Oral Interpretations

CHAPTER **16** REVIEW

● SUMMARY

A good speaker can perform literature just as a good musician performs music. Oral interpretation is the process by which a speaker performs literature aloud for an audience.

A Brief History of Oral Interpretation Stories were preserved orally long before they could be preserved in writing. People still enjoy practicing this tradition, and by preparing for oral interpretation they better understand a piece of literature. Listeners then share the speaker's enthusiasm and understanding of it.

Types of Material for Oral Interpretation Literature says something of lasting value and says it well. Prose is closer to everyday language than poetry and includes works of fiction and nonfiction. Poetry communicates thought and feeling through the careful arrangement of words for their sound and rhythm as well as for their meaning.

Choosing Material for Oral Interpretation Choose literature for oral interpretation that has universal appeal and offers insight, beauty, and technical quality. Choose a piece you enjoy and that fits the occasion, your purpose, your audience, and your time allotment.

Interpreting Your Selection Know the meaning and pronunciation of every word in any selection you interpret orally and research both its author and the period in which it was written. To find out about the author's fictional speaker, imaginary audience, and setting, consider facts and details in the selection and use your imagination to fill in other details. Your interpretation of these missing details will probably differ from that of anyone else, as will your performance.

Two Final Steps: Introduction and Practice An introduction for your selection should include the kind of literature it is, its title, information about its author, and its historical background. If you interpret only part of a selection, be sure to include an explanation of the selection in your introduction.

Prepare for a performance by working slowly and carefully on every aspect of your delivery, including vocal flexibility, articulation, pronunciation, gestures, and body movement. Practice your selection until you feel comfortable. Then rehearse again with a tape recorder and several friends. This will help you gain the confidence necessary to perform for a larger group of listeners.

ASSESS

● ASSESSMENT STRATEGIES

Individual Assessment
- Participates in practice activities daily or weekly
- Completes classwork
- Demonstrates knowledge of content through questions, discussion, quizzes, and Chapter 16 test
- Displays skill in oral interpretation

Group Assessment
- Sets and achieves goals
- Develops cooperative learning projects
- Supports efforts of team and class members
- Provides feedback and encouragement to members

VOCABULARY

Define each term in a complete sentence.

oral interpretation
minstrel
bard
literature
prose
fiction
nonfiction
poetry
narrative poetry
lyric poetry
universal appeal
insight
technical quality
fictional speaker
imaginary audience
setting

CHECKLIST

Oral-Interpretation Skills

1. Understand the history of oral interpretation.
2. Choose good and lasting literature for your interpretation.
3. Know the difference between prose and poetry, and use this knowledge when you interpret.
4. Practice pronunciation and learn the meaning of every word in your selection.
5. Research the background of the author of your selection.
6. Know the fictional speaker and imaginary audience.
7. Picture the setting of your selection in your imagination.
8. Be certain that verbal and nonverbal aspects of your interpretation are natural.
9. Prepare an introduction that includes information about your author.
10. Practice before a small group of friends before you perform.

REVIEW QUESTIONS

1. Define oral interpretation.
2. Name several occasions when oral interpretation may be needed.
3. Identify the value of oral interpretation for the speaker.
4. Identify the value of oral interpretation for the listener.
5. Name some types of literature that can be used successfully in oral interpretation.

● ANSWERS

See the Answer Key for more complete answers.

REVIEW QUESTIONS
1. A speaker performs literature aloud before an audience.
2. Reading a story in school, reading to a child, and reading in a religious service are common occasions for oral interpretation.
3. Oral interpretation gives the speaker a sense of pride and improves study skills.
4. The listener benefits from the speaker's understanding and develops listening skills.
5. Dramatic literature is used for oral delivery, and prose and poetry are also used.

531

ASSESS

6. The speaker needs a selection with universal appeal, insight, beauty, and technical excellence.
7. The speaker should like the work, and consider the occasion and purpose for the delivery.
8. Effective performance demands an understanding of the nature of the work, its setting, and missing details.
9. Introductions need the title of the work, the author, background information, and a summary.
10. The speaker should practice aloud, vary the voice, and use gestures.

DISCUSSION QUESTIONS

The following code is used to designate discussion questions and activities as suitable for students of varying ability levels:

▼ = below average to average
◆ = average to above average
■ = all students

1. ■ Critiques should focus on aspects that are important or difficult in oral interpretation.
2. ■ Ask if students have discussed universal appeal in other classes.
3. ■ Choose a selection to show appropriate gestures and body movement.
4. ◆ A lively debate could result from these questions.
5. ▼ Ask students to share practice experiences and observations with the class.

532

CHAPTER 16 REVIEW

6. Name and explain four characteristics of a literary work to consider when you select a piece for oral interpretation.
7. List personal elements to consider when selecting literature for oral interpretation.
8. Identify the elements within a selection that the speaker must understand in order to perform the work effectively.
9. Name several elements that an introduction to an oral interpretation should include.
10. Identify the steps that a speaker should take when practicing for oral interpretation.

? DISCUSSION QUESTIONS

1. As a class, choose a piece of literature that everyone agrees is noteworthy. Discuss the techniques used to analyze literature. Go over the chapter and list the specific features that a thorough analysis should contain. Then analyze the piece of literature that the class has chosen.
2. Literature that is best suited for oral interpretation has universal appeal. Discuss what the term *universal appeal* means. What is it that makes literature interesting to people? What does literature really tell us about? What pieces of literature have you read that possess universal appeal?
3. Discuss ways in which nonverbal communication skills support oral interpretation. What are these skills? How do they enhance the effectiveness of an oral interpretation? How do you decide on the appropriate use of these skills?
4. Discuss the importance of determining the author's intent when interpreting a poem or a piece of prose. What can you do to be sure you understand the author's message? If you did not understand the message, how would you prepare an oral interpretation for it?
5. Discuss the importance of practice in effective oral interpretation. What benefits come to someone who rehearses a selection thoroughly? Why is it important to know your exact speaking rate? How can a tape recorder help during a practice session?

CRITICAL THINKING

1. Analysis What are the steps that you would follow in choosing a piece of literature for oral interpretation? Describe the criteria that you would use in selecting a piece for oral interpretation.

2. Synthesis Imagine that you have been assigned an oral interpretation that will be from five to seven minutes long. Describe the steps you would follow from passage selection to presentation.

ACTIVITIES

In-Class

1. As a class, select a piece of literature that is suitable for oral interpretation. Discuss the selection, making sure that the author's intent is understood. Then analyze the selection carefully. Make suggestions for words and phrases to be emphasized and decide upon an appropriate reading rate for the selection. After the class has made complete recommendations for interpreting the selection, have several students read sections of it in class. The class will react to the interpretation and offer feedback.

2. Form into groups of from five to seven. Identify and practice vocal exercises for breath control, projection, stress, pitch, inflection, intonation, and articulation. Check one another for progress in voice control. Practice oral interpretation by performing short selections chosen by the group.

3. Working in groups of from five to seven, select three poems with similar themes. Discuss the poems to be sure that you understand the author's intent. Then practice interpreting the poems orally. Choose a member of the group to interpret the poems before the class. The other members of the group will prepare a general introduction explaining how the poems are related and specific introductions for each individual poem. Practice your oral interpretations for a class presentation.

ASSESS

CRITICAL THINKING
1. **Analysis** Ask students to explain the choices they made for oral interpretations.
2. **Synthesis** Students could work in groups to choose one selection or participate in a group presentation using several works that deal with a specified theme.

ACTIVITIES
In-Class
1. Students could write introductions to different parts of the selection. They could work in groups to decide on phrasing and gestures.
2. Copy and distribute oral interpretation selections for students. Have them mark selections for proper pauses and emphasis.
3. Students could use three poems by the same author or interpret the same poem from three different perspectives.

ASSESS

4. Students should identify the target audience. Comments should also refer to the process of editing the selection.

Out-of-Class
1. Students might select a short story and poem that are linked by theme or mood.
2. Fables are found in the children's section of the public library.
3. Introductions are especially important if the author is not well known.
4. Assign each type of audience to a small group. The group could choose one student to deliver the selection.

CHAPTER 16 REVIEW

4. Select a short story that you believe is suitable for oral presentation. Edit the selection so that it takes no longer than ten minutes to perform. Mark your script for pause and emphasis. Write an appropriate introduction. Practice your selection until you are confident and then perform the selection in class.

Out-of-Class

1. Select one short story and one poem that you believe possess universal appeal. In your speech notebook, analyze each selection and describe its universal appeal. Then form into small groups of from five to seven. Share your notes with the members of the group. Discuss the appropriateness of the selections for oral interpretation. Interpret your selections orally before the group and ask for reaction and feedback from group members.

2. Locate several fables that have interesting morals. Plan a presentation made up of at least five fables—one that will give listeners an idea of the fable as a literary form. As you practice, pay particular attention to the voices of any animals that appear. Experiment with different voices that help project a distinct personality for each one. Write an introduction to the fables you have chosen and give your oral interpretation in class.

3. Choose a poet whose works you enjoy. Research the poet's life by consulting as many sources as possible. Find four or five poems that seem to reflect stages in the poet's life, or that seem to have been based on actual life experiences. In your speech notebook, write an introduction to an oral presentation for the group of poems you have chosen. Then write individual introductions to each poem. These introductions should link the selections together smoothly. Present your oral interpretation in class.

4. Choose a poem or story and plan an oral interpretation for each of these audiences:
    (a) a small group of children
    (b) your classmates
    (c) a visiting theater company from Europe

Decide how you would change your presentation to perform for each audience.

CHAPTER PROJECT

As a class, discuss the various oral interpretations that have been presented in class. Vote on the best performances. Structure an oral-interpretation program that features the winners. The program could be given at a school assembly or at a joint meeting of several speech and English classes.

CHAPTER PROJECT
- This project could be pursued with English classes. Encourage students to select performances that meet the criteria they have studied. They should keep in mind the larger audience as they prepare their introductions and presentations.

Selections to Interpret Orally

TO A PRIZE BIRD

You suit me well, for you can make me laugh,
nor are you blinded by the chaff
    that every wind sends spinning from the rick.

You know to think, and what you think you speak
with much of Samson's pride and bleak
    finality, and none dare bid you stop.

Pride sits you well, so strut, colossal bird.
No barnyard makes you look absurd;
    your brazen claws are staunch against defeat.

Marianne Moore

WINDOW WASHER

And again the screech of the scaffold
High up there where all our thoughts converge:
Lightheaded, hung
By a leather strap,

Twenty stories up
In the chill of November air,
Wiping the grime
Off the pane, the windows

Which have no way of opening—
Those windows with their brooding interiors,
That figure who lets the light in,
One imponderable stroke at a time

Charles Simic

SEA FEVER

I must go down to the seas again, to the lonely sea and the sky,
And all I ask is a tall ship and a star to steer her by,
And the wheel's kick and the wind's song and the white sail's
    shaking,
And a gray mist on the sea's face and a gray dawn breaking.

I must down to the seas again, for the call of the running tide
Is a wild call and a clear call that may not be denied;
And all I ask is a windy day with the white clouds flying,
And the flung spray and the blown spume, and the seagulls
    crying.

I must down to the seas again to the vagrant gypsy life.
To the gull's way and the whale's way where the wind's like a
    whetted knife:
And all I ask is a merry yarn from a laughing fellow rover,
And quiet sleep and a sweet dream when the long trick's over.

John Masefield

TO JAMES

Do you remember
How you won
That last race…?
How you flung your body
At the start…
How your spikes
Ripped the cinders
In the stretch…
How you catapulted
Through the tape…
Do you remember…?
Don't you think
I lurched with you
Out of those starting holes…?
Don't you think
My sinews tightened
At those first
Few strides…
And when you flew into the stretch
Was not all my thrill
Of a thousand races
In your blood…?
At your final drive
Through the finish line
Did not my shout
Tell of the
Triumphant ecstasy
Of victory…?
Live
As I have taught you
To run, Boy—
It's a short dash
Dig your starting holes
Deep and firm
Lurch out of them
Into the straightaway
With all the power
That is in you
Look straight ahead
To the finish line
Think only of the goal
Run straight
Run high
Run hard
Save nothing
And finish
With an ecstatic burst
That carries you
Hurtling
Through the tape
To victory…

Frank Horne

ASSESS

I AM INDELIBLE

Some say the path to spiritual and human awareness
goes by way of humbleness and personal sacrifice
and these words are true
yet
if I am to be aware of my self, my possibilities
and my path in this world
I must recognize the uniqueness of my life and all life.
I am indelible.
From the fingerprint message of my genes
to the exact place where the stars stood at my birth.
From the number of seasons I have survived
to the memory and understanding that I keep of those times.
From all the things I have ever thought or said
to all the little pieces and parts of life I have nurtured and encouraged.
From the time my spirit came and moved in my mother's womb
to the coming time of my completion of my life's cycle…
and after,
I am indelible.
I am a part of this world,
whether I draw breath as a physical entity
or if I give my spirit form energy.
I am indelible.
I am my mother's child.

earth lodge woman/minnie two shoes

**IN HONOR OF
DAVID ANDERSON BROOKS,
MY FATHER**

July 30, 1883–November 21, 1959

A dryness is upon the house
My father loved and tended.
Beyond his firm and sculptured door
His light and lease have ended.

He walks the valleys, now—replies
To sun and wind forever.
No more the cramping chamber's chill,
No more the hindering fever.

Now out upon the wide clean air
My father's soul revives,
All innocent of self-interest
And the fear that strikes and strives.

He who was Goodness, Gentleness,
And Dignity is free,
Translates to public Love
Old private charity.

Gwendolyn Brooks

**from MACBETH
(Act V, Scene 5)**

Tomorrow, and tomorrow, and tomorrow
Creeps in this petty pace from day to day
To the last syllable of recorded time;
And all our yesterdays have lighted fools
The way to dusty death. Out, out, brief candle!

Life's but a walking shadow, a poor player,
That struts and frets his hour upon the stage
And then is heard no more. It is a tale
Told by an idiot, full of sound and fury,
Signifying nothing.

William Shakespeare

PREPARE

● CHAPTER PLANNER

Day 1	Day 2	Day 3	Day 4	Day 5
Prepare	Prepare	Prepare	Prepare	Prepare
Teach	Teach	Teach	Teach	Teach
Assess	Assess	Assess	Assess	Assess
Sub. Teacher Tip p. 544	Sub. Teacher Tips pp. 548, 549	Sub. Teacher Tips pp. 550, 552	Sub. Teacher Tip p. 557	Sub. Teacher Tip p. 565

● CHAPTER OVERVIEW

This chapter examines the following topics:
- The Nature of Drama *p. 539*
- A Brief History of Drama *p. 540*
- Developing a Character *p. 543*
- Organizing a Theatrical Event *p. 555*
- Producing a Theatrical Event *p. 561*

▽ PORTFOLIO PRODUCTS

Individual Projects
- Glossary of Speech Terms
- Theater Review
- Award Nominations
- Character Development
- Tape of Individual Performances
- Chapter 17 Portfolio Products

Group Projects
- Job Descriptions for Various Aspects of Theatrical Production
- Team Production for Event
- Publicity for Event

School Project
- Theatrical Event for School

● sca GUIDELINES

- Uses voice and gestures effectively for theatrical performance
- Expresses ideas and character clearly
- Expresses feelings to others in small and large groups
- Performs social rituals

CHAPTER

17

Drama

When you have completed this chapter you should be able to:

● Explain the elements of drama.

● Develop understanding of a character by doing background research and by analyzing the script.

● Experiment with non-verbal and verbal aspects of character development.

● Describe some of the jobs that are part of organizing a theatrical event.

● Explain the steps necessary in producing a theatrical event.

TEACH

● **LINKS TO PAST LEARNING**

Ask students to share memories of their pre-school or junior high class plays. Talk about the variety of roles, costumes, mistakes, and audience reactions.

● **MOTIVATION**

To build awareness of the importance of nonverbal communication, give each student a card or slip of paper that identifies a specific emotion. When called upon, the student should act out that emotion with facial expression, gesture, and body movement. Emotions could include: adoration, aggression, anger, anxiety, amusement, awe, annoyance, bliss, confusion, defiance, doubt, dread, fear, grief, humor, impatience, pride, sadness.

The Nature of Drama **539**

Drama is an art form. Like the art forms of painting, sculpture, music, dance, and architecture, drama has been a part of people's lives in all areas of the world throughout history. You are surrounded by these art forms every day.

Drama is special, however, because at one time or another it makes use of all the other art forms. Set and costume designers create with wood, plastic, metal, and fabric, putting materials together in colorful, pleasing designs. Musicians provide sound through which mood and thought are communicated. Choreographers devise movement for interpretation of story and emotion, and architects plan the stage space. All that is needed are playwrights, directors, actors, and audiences.

● **THE NATURE OF DRAMA**

Drama exists to provide people with entertainment, education, and feelings of spiritual uplift and joy. It studies humanity's successes and failures by exploring the relationships of human beings in the past, present, and future.

Drama has four principal elements, all of which are necessary to produce a theatrical event. First, there must be live actors. The major difference between a television show, a film, and the theatrical event of drama is that only in live theater do the actors play and respond to the reactions of a live audience. Second, there must be a plot or story. A stand-up comedy act is not drama because drama presents a story, with

Live actors are the first principal element of drama.

539

TEACH

> **"The play's the thing Wherein I'll catch the conscience of the king."**
> —William Shakespeare

● TEACHING

Emphasize the four requirements for drama. Then discuss the author's contention that drama makes use of all other art forms. Encourage students to provide examples that would support that statement. Others might present some objections to that statement.

● CURRICULAR CONNECTIONS

Language Arts
You might work with the drama or English teacher or drama club to teach this chapter. If students are presenting a school play or if they are studying a particular play in another class, you could integrate instruction to emphasize the experience of drama.

● LEARNING STYLES

Cooperative Learning
Ask groups of students to bring to class any programs from plays or other theatrical events they may have attended recently. Each student who brings in such a program could give a brief description of the event. A class bulletin board could be made based on these programs.

---

540   CHAPTER 17 Drama

a beginning, a middle, and an end. The characters must act and interrelate. Third, there has to be a theatrical area. Drama can occur on a streetcorner, in a cafeteria, or in a place specifically designed as a theater; it is essential that some space serve as a stage. Fourth, the presentation must result in a theatrical event. The term **theatrical event** means that there must be both actor and audience. Drama does not truly exist until it is viewed.

● A BRIEF HISTORY OF DRAMA

Throughout history, drama has been woven into the social and cultural fabric of human endeavor. Theatrical events have existed because people have felt the need to stand up and act out stories as well as tell them. As you will see, different themes have been favored in different eras, but the four basic elements of drama have always remained.

In ancient Greece, rituals were dedicated to the god Dionysus. In Athens, each March, Dionysian festivals were held, with choral singing, dancing, and plays. The final two or three days of the festival were reserved for play contests, at the end of which the winning playwright, or dramatist, was crowned with a wreath of ivy. Thespis won the first contest in 534 B.C. Since he is also known as one of the first actors, performers are still known as **thespians.** Your own school may have a thespian troupe or club.

Both comedies and tragedies were performed in ancient Greece. Like all good drama, the plays had their basis in human conflict. In **comedy,** the conflict was usually not serious, and the ending was generally happy. In **tragedy,** the conflict was always more serious and generally resulted in the destruction of the hero or heroine.

Greek tragedies were based on ancient myths that were well-known to the audience. The philosopher Aristotle (384–322 B.C.) identified certain rules for tragedy in his book *Poetics:*

1. Plays should inspire the audience to reform their lives through **catharsis,** or by releasing their pent-up emotions.
2. The hero or heroine, who must be of a high social standing, must possess a **tragic flaw,** or weakness of character, that leads to his or her destruction.
3. A change of fortune involving **reversal** (in which the character's actions boomerang) or **discovery** (in which the character's attitudes change from ignorance to knowledge) must be included.
4. Dignified, beautiful poetic writing must be used.

Plays of the Greek period are still performed, and some playwrights today still use the rules of Greek tragedy as a basis for their work.

TEACH

● **TEACHING**

You will want to make sure that students understand the many terms emphasized here in bold type. These could be added to their glossary of terms.

> *"One can play comedy; two are required for melodrama; but a tragedy demands three."*
> —Elbert Hubbard

● **SKILL DEVELOPMENT**

Research
Some students could obtain more information about the history of drama. The information could be presented in the form of an illustrated time line and displayed in the classroom.

Other students could look up Aristotle's *Poetics* and elaborate the guidelines for Greek tragedies.

● **LEARNING STYLES**

Visual Learning
You might show a portion of a Shakespearean drama or another classic play performed on film. If the students become involved in the performance, you might continue to show a segment each day as a way to begin class and demonstrate elements of theatrical productions.

A Brief History of Drama **541**

During the **Middle Ages** (about A.D. 500–A.D. 1450), because many people could not read or write, priests presented dramatic representations of Biblical events and parables to their congregations. During this era drama was also performed on street corners by groups of strolling players. These groups are now thought to have been the first professional acting companies. They performed only for the common people.

From A.D. 1350 to A.D. 1650 in Europe, during a period called the **Renaissance** (meaning rebirth), there were new developments in all the arts and literature. Drama changed along with everything else. Wealthy nobles and kings and queens became patrons, or sponsors, of the theater and the arts. In Italy splendid buildings were built for **operas,** a new type of musical drama that provided a social gathering place for the wealthy. At the same time, Italy's **commedia dell'arte** (comedy of art) provided comedy for the common people in productions performed without a script. Commedia actors worked with outlines called **scenarios,** from which they made up speeches, songs, dances, and pantomimes as they went along. This type of presentation is called **improvisation.** Improvisations also remained popular and are still performed today.

The **Elizabethan era** in England was the climax of the Renaissance. It occurred while Elizabeth I was queen of England (1558–1603). William Shakespeare (1564–1616) was the greatest playwright of that age. Shakespeare wrote thirty-eight plays. They include histories, comedies, and tragedies. Many of the phrases Shakespeare wrote for his characters have become common sayings. The chart on page 542 contains a list of popular ones you may have heard and the plays in which they appear.

The Renaissance came late to **French theater,** which developed in the seventeenth century primarily as drama for the court. Theatrical buildings were grand showplaces, like the Italian opera houses. The

From Greek tragedy to the Theater of the Absurd, drama exists because people have felt the need to act out stories.

541

TEACH

AMAZING FACTS!
European theater had its origins in Greek drama performed to honor Dionysius. Small theaters were built around Greece by the fifth century B.C.

● **TIME MANAGEMENT**

You might want to condense the amount of time spent on the history of drama and spend more time on the actual production of a theatrical event. To condense the time, you might ask small groups to do independent research on specific time periods or countries and report to the class.

● **LEARNING STYLES**

Multicultural Learning
In addition to the information about the history of European theater, some groups could investigate the history of drama in other areas such as China, Japan, and India. These countries also have a rich history of drama.

● **SKILL DEVELOPMENT**

15-Second Skill Opportunity
Each student could select a line from one of Shakespeare's plays and prepare to recite it for the class.

---

542   CHAPTER 17   Drama

principal dramatist of this period was Molière (1622–1673). Molière was the first French writer to raise comedy to a point where it could hold its own with tragedy as entertainment for the upper classes. He ridiculed people and ideas. Themes of hypocrisy, medicine and medical fees, and arranged marriages recur many times in his thirty-three plays.

After Molière's death the five theatrical companies existing in Paris merged into one group called the **Comédie Française** (French comedy), the first national theater in the world. Still in existence, this organization is the most important troupe in France today.

In 1660 a new era of drama began in England. Theaters that had been closed during the Commonwealth government led by the Puritans were reopened when Charles II became King. During this period

Some common sayings from Shakespeare's plays	
Hamlet	"brevity is the soul of wit" "neither a borrower, nor a lender be"
Othello	"pomp and circumstance" "wear my heart upon my sleeve"
Julius Caesar	"it was Greek to me" "masters of their fates"
Macbeth	"the milk of human kindness"
Henry IV, Part 2	"eaten me out of house and home"
As You Like It	"too much of a good thing" "all the world's a stage"
The Merry Wives of Windsor	"as good luck would have it"
The Merchant of Venice	"it's a wise father that knows his own child"

ENRICHMENT

Some students might research the life and times of William Shakespeare and report to the class. He is the subject of much research, respect, and speculation.

CURRICULAR CONNECTIONS

Language Arts
Students could compile a list of famous lines from various Shakespearean plays. This could be published with a code or index to indicate context and application to modern life.

> *"How sharper than a serpent's tooth it is To have a thankless child!"*
> —William Shakespeare

---

known as the **Restoration,** a new style of writing and acting, called the **comedy of manners,** was used to make fun of social customs of the day. Women were allowed for the first time to appear as players, and elaborate stage settings were devised. The free spirit was dampened, however, when the Puritans later regained control of the government. Restrictions then limited the number of theaters to three, making all others illegal. Plays had to pass a censoring committee before they could even be performed. Thus, the term **legitimate theater** originated. Eighteenth-century English playwrights did, nevertheless, continue to write in the comedy-of-manners style.

During the early nineteenth century, **romanticism** became the most prominent dramatic art style. People tried to escape the problems of reality through imagination and thoughts of adventure and beauty. A reaction to these attitudes took place about mid-century, when a majority of playwrights turned to **realism.** Realism in this period stressed the virtues of directness and truth. **Slice-of-life theater** developed as part of this new movement. Playwrights wrote about everyday, real-life situations, conflicts, and people. Historical works were forgotten for a time. Henrik Ibsen (1828–1906), a Norwegian called "the father of modern drama," August Strindberg in Sweden, and Anton Chekhov in Russia, were important dramatists of realism.

Further changes in theater were brought about in the twentieth century after World War II by the movement that brought the **Theater of the Absurd.** Dramatists in this movement viewed human existence as purposeless, lonely, and out of harmony with its surroundings. They opened the way for the use of very experimental theater techniques. Performances took on a laboratory approach, and experiments were made with attitudes, characters, and ways of using theatrical space.

Today, playwrights make use of all ideas and techniques that have been developed throughout the centuries. They create a great variety of theatrical events that entertain, educate, and uplift today's audiences.

DEVELOPING A CHARACTER

One of the main ways a playwright's work is brought to life is through the characters that are developed in the play. An actor must portray a character in ways that fully represent the author's intent. This section will discuss some specific steps an actor can use to develop a theatrical role. Reading the section, you will receive many ideas about how you yourself might interpret a role in a play.

Just as voice and body are used to get messages across in other communication situations, you as an actor must use your voice and body to portray a character. Facial expressions, posture, gestures,

TEACH

SUBSTITUTE TEACHER TIP

You might bring to class a pair of Greek tragedy and comedy masks or other masks. Encourage students to talk about unusual masks they have seen displayed or used. Discuss how masks and costumes enhance the performance of actors.

● **LEARNING STYLES**

Visual Learning
Encourage students to add to the chart of Shakespearean sayings. They might provide additional information such as the date the play was written, and the exact quotation and citation.

● **SKILL DEVELOPMENT**

Creative Thinking
Students could share experiences they have had with summer theater, street theater, Shakespearean theater, and drama schools. Ask them to develop a short drama that would be suitable for a junior high school audience that would emphasize the theme "Say No to Drugs."

---

544 CHAPTER 17 Drama

speech, and vocal tone combine to provide the audience with a total overview. Your first responsibility then is to interpret and visualize the playwright's words through the character you are portraying. You must also believably expand the character's personality, actions, emotions, and objectives so that the viewer has a clear understanding of what the playwright had in mind when he or she wrote the play.

Secondly, you as an actor must tell the story. This means that you must develop the storyline for the audience by speaking clearly and effectively and providing insight through vocal variety. For example, if you are creating the role of a strong, domineering person, you might want to use a loud, aggressive voice to get the character across. On the other hand, a timid person needs a totally different tone. Each of these roles would also require different postures, gestures, and distinctive clothing to separate them further.

Whether you play a lead role, an animal who speaks no lines, or a chorus part, you must believe in yourself, in the other members of the acting company, and in the project as a whole. You must be secure within yourself before you concentrate on portraying others. Obviously, when you are acting, you must block out all of your own problems before you walk onstage. The audience will not tolerate or believe an actor who bounces in and out of a role. Theater creates an imaginary world and the audience must be able to believe in this illusion of reality. The actors must become the characters while they are performing.

As an actor, your first responsibility is to interpret and visualize the playwright's words through the character you are portraying.

● **LINKS TO PAST LEARNING**

Ask students to identify some of the memorable characters from TV or movies that they consider to be "classic." Encourage them to describe the qualities of voice gestures, facial expression, and costume that contributed to the success of the portrayals.

> **TEACH**
>
> *"Character cannot be developed in ease and quiet. Only through experience of trial and suffering can the soul be strengthened, vision cleared, ambition inspired, and success achieved."*
> —Helen Keller

● **SKILL DEVELOPMENT**

15-Second Skill Opportunity
Ask each student to think of an animal and ways they could convey that animal on stage without using words. Ask volunteers to demonstrate their animal characters.

Doing Background Research

To perform a role adequately, you should begin by researching the history of the play, the playwright, the period in which the play takes place, and the type of work it represents (musical, tragedy, comedy, or other). Begin with the play itself. Frequently, scripts contain an introduction to the play and some background about the playwright and his or her ideas. Study the script carefully. It may suggest additional readings. If the play is a modern one and has been previously produced, read any critical reviews you can find. These can provide different interpretations of the play. Recordings are available in libraries of many plays, operas, and musical comedies. Many of the recordings of Shakespeare's works (and other classics) are performances by famous actors such as Laurence Olivier, Edith Evans, Richard Burton, John Gielgud, Paul Scofield, and Orson Welles. Watch newspaper announcements for film presentations of famous theater works. Attend local college and civic theater productions. Especially if you are a newcomer to acting, immerse yourself in different types of theater literature and performances as much as possible. Watching well-directed and well-performed film and television productions can provide a valuable background of acting techniques.

You should next research the era in which the playwright wrote. The social conditions and political environment of the period may be reflected in his or her writing. For example, Oscar Wilde revealed the shallowness and emptiness of much of English society during his lifetime. His analysis of hypocrisy and society's willingness to close its eyes to unpleasantness have made his plays among the most beloved of English comedies. A knowledge of Victorian society (1837–1901) will therefore help you understand Wilde's works.

Playwrights sometimes write about a period that is different from their own. Shakespeare's *Julius Caesar* was written in 1599, but takes place in Rome during Caesar's time, 100–44 B.C. In this case thorough research of both Shakespeare's time and Caesar's would help you to understand the meaning of the play.

If you are unfamiliar with the different types of theatrical works, study the style of the play you are reading. Become acquainted with the characteristics of Greek tragedy and compare them with Shakespeare's. Research comedy of ancient Greece, of the Renaissance, the Restoration, and other eras. See if you can find differences in the quality of each type. No matter what the play, the writer intended it to fall within a certain dramatic category. See if you can recognize whether it is a tragedy or comedy or **tragicomedy,** which combines tragic and comic elements.

APPLY

● **LINKS TO PAST LEARNING**

Ask students to name from memory the recipients of the best actor and best actress awards given by the Motion Picture Academy going back in years as far as they can identify. The Oscars for best actor and best actress go back to 1928. Some students might develop a list of those recipients and include it as a portfolio product.

● **ENRICHMENT**

If possible, you might ask someone who has participated in a professional or amateur theatrical production to speak to the class. Students could prepare interview questions to learn about the actor's experiences and skills.

● **SKILL DEVELOPMENT**

15-Second Skill Opportunity

Ask students to think of the best actor of all times, according to their opinion. Have them prepare a brief nomination of that actor in which the students state the reasons for their choice. Ask volunteers to nominate the best actor of all times. Once the nominations are made, see if the class can arrive at a consensus about the top three actors.

CAREER CLOSE-UP

Actors

Actors entertain audiences with their portrayals of characters in plays, films, television and other works. An acting career requires years of study, hard work, and perseverance. While drama schools and college theater programs provide important training, invaluable acting experience is gained from local theater productions, school plays, and public speaking. Acting students should include the study of speech, voice, and movement to supplement their theater courses.

To prepare for a theatrical role, actors first research the play's and the playwright's background to determine the themes and point of view. Following this scrutiny, they study their part and plan appropriate movements and gestures that will enhance the portrayal of their character.

Actors do much more than say their lines when they play a character. They communicate nonverbally by using a variety of facial expressions and gestures that depict their character's personality. By varying the pitch and volume of their voices, performers can interpret their character's emotions. As they combine these skills with the ability to articulate clearly and project forcefully, they make it possible for the audience to believe in the reality of their character.

When performers convincingly create an imaginary world, they demonstrate the power of effective communication. Their outstanding portrayals inspire audiences to a greater awareness of the influence of communication over the entire human experience. This is perhaps the greatest gift an actor can bestow on an audience—a heightened appreciation and understanding of the tragic and comic dimensions of the human condition.

In addition to "saying the lines," the actor projects a character's personality through a variety of nonverbal expressions and gestures.

TEACH

● **TEACHING**

To emphasize the importance of developing skills in creating a character, you might share stories with the class about the search for the actress to play Scarlett O'Hara for the film *Gone With the Wind*. Ask students to describe the character of Scarlett and identify ways in which the actress, Vivien Leigh, conveyed that character.

AMAZING FACTS!
The world's biggest building used for theater is the National People's Congress Building in Tiananmen Square, Beijing, China. It was completed in 1959 and covers 12.9 acres and seats 10,000 people.

● **SKILL DEVELOPMENT**

Research
Have students summarize how to conduct background research to develop a character. Invite students to select a character from any play they have seen or are studying and indicate five things they could do to conduct background research for the development of that character.

Developing a Character **547**

Analyzing the Script

It may take several careful readings to analyze a play. Try to picture in your mind a production of the play as you read it, and be sure you can answer the following questions:

- What is the theme of the play?
- What is the author trying to say?
- What is the plot?
- Where does each scene and act take place?
- What are the thoughts and problems behind the dialogue?
- What are each character's reactions to other characters?
- What emotional feelings does the play evoke?
- What family or friendship relations are presented?
- What are the social and cultural backgrounds of the characters?

If you have trouble with any of these answers, further research is probably in order.

The **structure** of the play, its form, shape, and development, must also be examined. The presentation of who, what, where, and why is called the **exposition.** The first event to take place, from which the plot develops, is called the **initial incident. Rising action** is the series of the events that develop toward the highest point of interest in the play, the **climax.** This point reveals whether the major character will succeed or fail to solve her or his problem. Events following the climax tie the loose ends together and are called **falling action.**

Analyzing Character

After you have completed your analysis of the play as a whole, begin to get acquainted with your specific character. Don't waste your time counting the number of lines or entrances you have. It is the quality of your performance—not the quantity—that counts! It may help to begin by underlining your lines or highlighting them with a yellow or pink felt transparent marker. This will help you to distinguish your lines from the others on the page more quickly. Some actors also underline their **cue lines,** the previous speaker's last few words.

Information you will want to know about an individual character includes the points on the following page.

TEACH

> **SUBSTITUTE TEACHER TIP**
>
> You might be able to show clips of famous actors such as those mentioned in the text. After each segment, ask students what qualities of voice, gesture, body language, and costume contributed to the effective portrayal of the character.

● **SKILL DEVELOPMENT**

Feedback
Have students use the questions for analyzing dramatic material to develop a checklist that can be used for understanding and developing a character for a performance.

Physical characteristics and age

Personality traits and emotional stability

Intelligence

Social and personal background

Relationship with other characters

Character, motivation, objectives, and state of mind

Strengths, weaknesses, fears, and hopes

Movement, speech, and type of clothing worn

Remember that these elements may change during the course of the action. If the script does not reveal all the answers, you may want to add interpretations of your own that will fit in with the play. A complete understanding of your character is the basis upon which a creative and memorable performance is built.

After you have become familiar with the attitudes and objectives of the character you will portray, you need to begin to study the lines themselves. Study the **dialogue,** or conversation, for emphasis, phrasing, pronunciation, and meaning. Make sure you know the author's intended purpose for every word, sentence, and paragraph. Determine your objectives or motives in each scene. For each scene you should be able to answer the following:

- Why am I here?
- Where did I come from?
- Have I been here before?
- Do I know the other people in the room?
- Why do I leave?

As you begin to memorize your part, try to think, feel, see, move, and speak with your character in mind.

Once in a while actors have to depart from the script because someone fails to make an entrance, forgets a speech, or part of the set breaks. Actors should be ready for these kinds of mix-ups and be imaginative enough to deal with them. The better you know your character, the better you will be able to cope with performance problems. Obviously, if you are on stage and another actor is supposed to enter and does not, you have a problem! Instead of repeating the cue line loudly several times, try to speak some appropriate lines which fit into the action of the play. If your character would do so, pick up a book and recite a poem, look out a window and comment on the landscape, or simply sit down

Developing a Character **549**

and wait. Whatever happens, do not panic. Backstage, the stage manager will be finding the tardy actor. If you happen to be that actor, do not suddenly rush out on stage. Listen backstage for a moment and find an appropriate time to enter.

Believability is a word which often is mentioned in connection with the theater. Keep believability in mind as you work on your role. Because the first impressions you make on the audience as your character should be believable, you must get into character long before you walk onstage. Many actors feel that the best time to do this is while applying makeup. Some actors rehearse troublesome scenes in the dressing room before a performance. Some directors require company warmup exercises. In any case, you should not wait to get into character until just before making your first entrance. Only when you are properly prepared ahead of time and are eager to share your knowledge, are you ready to go on stage.

Learning the Movements

Your nonverbal communication with your audience is also an important part of the development of your character. Start by becoming aware of how different people move, make gestures, converse, whisper, dress, relax, argue, age, and express themselves. Look around you. Concentrate particularly on facial expressions. Observe the emotions that different parts of the face can convey. Become aware of the ways you

A range of emotions including stubbornness, despair, bitterness, and cruelty is projected in the faces of these actors in *King Lear*.

TEACH

SUBSTITUTE TEACHER TIP
You might show a collection of brief film or video clips that show an actor walking. Use these segments to ask students what they imagine the character to be like and the circumstances involved in the walk.

"Generally speaking, the American theater is the aspirin of the middle class."
—Wolcott Gibbs

● SKILL DEVELOPMENT

Creative Thinking
Ask students to think of a new character for young children that might make an appearance on *The Muppet Show*. Encourage them to fill in the details mentioned here about individual characters.

Vocabulary
Ask students to imagine they are playing a specific character in a play they are studying. They should have copy for some of the script. Have students highlight their part(s) and develop cue cards for themselves. Display the various cue cards and talk about the helpful information that is included on them. Encourage students to modify their cards based on the suggestions and class discussion.

549

TEACH

SUBSTITUTE TEACHER TIP

Ask each student to write a "Trivial Pursuit" type question and answer about a favorite theater or film character. You could hold a "game show" based on the questions developed by the students.

● **RETEACHING**

Ask students to think of actors who portrayed a character who "aged" on stage. Then ask students to describe the differences in the actor's uses of movement throughout the aging process.

● **SKILL DEVELOPMENT**

Creative Thinking

To emphasize the aspect of believability that is so important to staging a performance, ask students to imagine that the classroom will become a stage to represent a forest, an ocean, or another planet for a science fiction production. Encourage students to think of ways to suggest the transformation of the classroom to make it believable for the audience.

Research

Explain to students that perhaps the best antidote to stage freight or nervousness is solid preparation. The more research, practice, and memorization they put into their part, the more self-assured they will be. Have students develop a personal list of five things they can do to reduce nervousness or stage fright. They could use the resource video to learn and practice techniques to overcome anxiety.

● **LEARNING STYLES**

Kinesic Learning

Suggest that students pantomime a physical activity to prepare them for a dramatic role. For example, take the movement of walking. Suggest that students first demonstrate how they walk naturally. Then ask them to walk as if they were one of the following: a young child going to the park, a teacher on a field trip, a bank robber approaching a teller, an injured football player, a grandparent in church.

---

550 CHAPTER 17 Drama

can use your own facial expressions by practicing in front of a mirror. See what kinds of expressions you can make using only your mouth. Try to speak holding your mouth in various positions. Then see what feelings you can show using only your eyes and eyebrows.

You might want to try the following exercise some afternoon when you have a couple of hours to spare. In a park or on a downtown street pick a person out of the crowd who interests you. The first time pick a person just a little older than yourself. Later you can experiment studying people even older. Observe carefully, following your subject as he or she proceeds with normal activities. Do not contact this person in any way. Study his or her manner of walking, arm motions, and posture. Concentrate on details. Watch how your subject carries a purse, a briefcase, a grocery bag, or a baby. After you have observed this person for as long a time as possible, write down a description of what you saw. Begin a diary of observations of different types of people. Refer to the diary for techniques of movement when preparing for a role.

As you memorize your lines, you should also work on gestures and movements to accompany your dialogue. These details should be written down in the script and memorized along with the words. Some stage movements are naturally required by the plot (Romeo must fight Tybalt, and Juliet must stab herself). Other movements are incidental to the action (Romeo must draw his sword in order to fight). Action needed to add realism are usually suggested by the plot, stage directions, or dialogue. If a line reads "please hang up my hat and coat," one of the actors will have to take the items and hang them up. If the scene calls for a family to sit around a table and eat dinner, then there will have to be food, and it will have to be eaten.

Spending time practicing unusual or difficult movements will help prevent awkward movements during a performance. If you are uncomfortable, the audience will notice it. Be sure that you time movement with the dialogue. Wrapping a package, writing a note, eating a sandwich, or putting on a coat all take longer than you think. Even if you cut out some time-consuming details, you can still suggest realistic movements. A package can already be wrapped, and you can simply add a bow. If the wrapping paper roll is placed alongside the work area, it still appears as though the total wrapping job has taken place.

Stage movements can be used to enhance a thin, empty scene. They can also be used to emphasize a dramatic moment. Think, for example, of a scene in which a young man takes out his handkerchief to wipe the tears from a child's face. Activities are often used to fill a momentary gap in the advancement of the plot—during difficult costume changes, for example. Movement also includes necessary movements across stage, the placement of actors, **choreography** (dance patterns), stage fights, love scenes, and gestures. All must be worked out to fit in with the situations and characters of the play.

TEACH

• CURRICULAR CONNECTIONS

Writing
Students could be encouraged to begin or keep a journal in which they describe various "characters" and their expressions, gestures, and walking styles. Ask students to think of various ways to keep their journal entries "organized" so that they can retrieve or refer to information when they want to.

> *"Nothing is more revealing than movement."*
> —Martha Graham

Once you are familiar with the type of character you will play, experiment with appropriate body movements outside of rehearsal. If the play is an English Restoration comedy, research and study the styles of body movement used at the time. Restoration style includes the use of fans, handkerchiefs, and formal deep bows. Tight breeches, heeled shoes, and formal curled wigs for gentlemen and tight corsets and huge skirts placed over padded hip rolls for ladies determined and restricted movements. Elizabethan hoop skirts do not fit in a small armchair. Find out what kind of clothes are called for in your role and be sure to consider the restrictions of your costume. Make sure that you rehearse in shoes and clothing that are similar to those which will be used in performance. An actor walks and moves differently in jeans and sandals than in high heels and formal clothing.

• LEARNING STYLES

Visual Learning
Display some photographs or portraits of individuals. Ask students to observe each face carefully. Suggest that they try to describe the character of each or the emotion captured in the photograph.

● ACTIVITY

Experimenting with Movement
Practice the following walking exercises at home or in the classroom. Begin your walk across the room or stage, using your body to communicate one characterization and changing it as you complete your walk. Experiment with movement, posture, and expression.

1. Start walking as a timid person and end as an outgoing one.
2. Start walking with confidence and end with defeat.
3. Start walking as though you did not want to get to your destination and finish as though you did.
4. Start walking as a toddler, taking its first steps; end as an athlete, about to run a marathon.
5. Start walking as though your body were made of steel; finish as though it were made of rubber.

Clear, expressive movements will help to define a character for you and for the audience. When rehearsing a play, write your movements down in the script. As you rehearse, they should become as natural to you as what you say.

● ACTIVITY

You might conduct this Activity as a kind of guessing game and ask the "audience" to figure out from the student's movement which of the scenarios is being presented. You could award Certificates of Recognition to those students who successfully portray their exercise.

As a variation to this activity you might invite students to add a single word to accompany their walk transformation.

● SKILL DEVELOPMENT

15-Second Skill Opportunity
Give students the opportunity to demonstrate their own natural walk and have them supply three words that they think describe their walk. Invite other students to agree or disagree with the description. Then have students demonstrate the walk of one of the character suggestions in Kinesic Learning. Discuss the differences between the two walks.

Developing Your Character's Voice

As you know, clear, expressive speech is a necessary tool for every part of life. In Chapter 2 you read about the physical aspects of proper speech. You may now want to review some of the technical aspects.

TEACH

SUBSTITUTE TEACHER TIP

You might bring to class a tape with voice segments of famous actors. Have students guess who the actors are based on the voice and speech patterns they recognize.

● **CURRICULUM CONNECTIONS**

Writing
Students could add the descriptions of actors' voices to the journal they began for character descriptions.

> *[Jimmy Durante] spoke and sang in an unmistakable voice that sounded like gravel being mixed in a food processor, and he fought a life-long battle with the English language.*
>
> —George Burns

● **LEARNING STYLES**

Audio Learning
You might ask students to tape brief segments of actors from television programs. They could play their tapes in class and ask students to identify the actors on their tape. Discuss the qualities of voice these actors have.

● **SKILL DEVELOPMENT**

15-Second Skill Opportunity
Ask students to read a single sentence into a tape recorder in three different ways. The first should be read with normal voice; the second time, in a high pitch; the third time, with a low-pitched voice. Play back the recording and compare the sounds.

---

552 CHAPTER 17 Drama

Actors in particular must become very good vocal technicians. As an actor you must learn to:

- Stand up straight with good posture so your voice will project better.
- Control your breathing.
- Change your speaking rate for variation and dramatic emphasis.
- Articulate clearly.
- Pronounce words correctly.
- Project your voice to the last rows of the auditorium.
- Have a flexible voice.
- Listen to the other characters and respond to them.

Begin your character's voice development by listening to as many voices as you can. Tape record interesting speech patterns. Listen to actors on the stage, in films, or television, and on recordings. Listen to your family and friends. Keep a diary of voices you hear the way you did with peoples' movements. Write down what you like and dislike about each voice in your diary. Does the voice make you want to listen more carefully? Can you distinguish personality, nationality, and age? Is it a monotone? Does it project vitality and energy? Is it boring? Can you recognize whether the speaker is sincere in his or her beliefs? Are emotions revealed? Is there variety in pitch, volume, and speaking rate?

As an actor you should become aware of the pitch changes caused by emotional tensions. Low pitch is usually associated with love, sincerity, or sorrow. High pitch is often caused by the emotional stress involved in anger or rage, terror, or excitement.

Three problems related to vocal pitch may arise when you are acting:

1. Your habitual pitch may be too high or too low, limiting the range of pitch changes possible.
2. Lack of variety in pitch may cause uninteresting speech.
3. Your voice may fall into a pitch pattern and thus tend to be repetitive.

An awareness of these potential problems should be very helpful. With practice, you can eventually overcome them.

Another vocal characteristic, volume, is also very important for an actor. Concentration on volume control will allow you to spread a stage whisper across a large auditorium and still maintain the necessary quiet breathy quality. Ordinarily a director will stand in various parts of the theater during rehearsals to insure that you can be heard at all times.

TEACH

● **CURRICULAR CONNECTIONS**

Writing
Once students have identified the relationships between the characters in a play, suggest that they write the "Cast of Characters" page as it might appear in a program. This page usually identifies each character by name and indicates, briefly, the relationship to other characters in the play.

AMAZING FACTS!
Sound is measured in a unit called a decibel (db). The normal speaking voice measures 60 db. Permanent deafness can occur at 150 db. A rock concert is over 110 db and headphone amplification can reach 136 db.

● **SKILL DEVELOPMENT**

Creative Thinking
Ask students to explore the relationship of characters in a play to each other. If no relationship is evident, encourage them to think of connections that link the various characters.

● **LEARNING STYLES**

Cooperative Learning
Organize students in groups that relate either to the protagonist of the story or to the antagonist. Each group should identify famous actors who have played in those roles. Discuss which role, protagonist or antagonist, is easier to play.

Pitch, volume, and rate of speaking are all aspects of the actor's vocal technique.

Like pitch and volume, your rate of speaking can be useful in suggesting changes in emotional states. Anxious or excited characters often speak rapidly. A slower, even sluggish rate might be better for a tragic or awesome passage.

Taking care of your voice, and developing variations in shading, intensity, and mood will be of great help as you begin to develop your character. Look through your diary of voices and pick several types of voices and qualities that might work with your character. Do not be afraid to experiment and overact at first. Use a tape recorder or ask a friend to listen to your ideas. Try the voice out in rehearsal. When you have established a voice that corresponds to your interpretation of the character, return to the script. Note changes of quality, pitch, volume, and speaking rate that should be used for different lines or passages. Continue to rehearse and practice your role until your movements and your voice work well with each other and with the rest of the play.

TEACH

> *Audiences? No, the plural is impossible. Whether it be in Butte, Montana, or Broadway, it's an audience. The same great hulking monster with four thousand eyes and forty thousand teeth.*
>
> —John Barrymore

● **SKILL DEVELOPMENT**

Critical Thinking
Encourage students to compare and contrast polite and enthusiastic audiences. Ask them to provide examples of each based on personal experience. Discuss what factors might be involved in changing a merely polite audience into an enthusiastic one.

● **LEARNING STYLES**

Beyond the Classroom
Ask students to imagine that they have been approached by a friend of a friend of the family who is asking them to invest $5,000 on the production of a new play that plans its debut in your city. Discuss the pros and cons of making the investment.

CHAPTER 17 Drama

Exploring Character Relationships

In order to understand your character's relationships with other characters in the play, you must study each of the other characters as well. Don't take the way they relate to each other for granted. Even if the relationship of one character to another character is a family relationship, it may be one that includes deep-rooted feelings of hatred or distrust. Characters who are not blood relatives might relate to each other in the plot through an emotional situation, a business deal, religious circumstances, or simply friendship. Whatever the relationship, you must discover the underlying feelings the characters have for one another.

Understanding the personalities of and relationships between characters helps identify their function within the plot. Each character ordinarily serves several functions, but one is usually most important. The **protagonist,** or principal character, is the one whose story is being told. The **antagonist** is the chief opponent of the principal character. Other characters revolve around these two major characters.

Recognizing the Relationship Between the Actor and the Audience

People go to the theater for a variety of reasons: to be entertained, to lose themselves in the lives of the characters, to be educated, or to see friends perform. Actors have a responsibility to provide a vital, energetic performance. As a beginning actor, you will become aware rather quickly that acting is very demanding work. Plenty of rest, good nutrition, and a full awareness of the play and your role will help fortify you as you prepare to perform.

The spark between actor and audience is what makes for good theater. You respond to the audience, and they respond to you. Many stories have been published about actors who have felt they "lost" the audience during the first scene of the performance and never got them back. Because live theater is an immediate art form, you can correct your relationship with the audience. By changing your volume or rate of speech, or by speaking more personally, you can work for audience approval.

No two performances of an actor are ever alike. Feelings, outside distractions, and energy level influence performance. In turn, differences in the makeup of each audience—age, culture, or social background—contribute to each audience's awareness of and sympathies toward the play's theme.

TEACH

● **TEACHING**

Bring a theater program to class and use it to show students the many people involved in a theatrical event. List on the chalkboard those credited. Ask students to think about which of the roles, or jobs, they would be most comfortable with in organizing a theatrical event.

AMAZING FACTS!

The longest continuous run of any show in the world is *The Mousetrap* by Dame Agatha Christie. The 16,000th performance was on May 6, 1991.

● **ACTIVITY**

Pairs of students should work together to improvise a brief skit based on the information provided. The pairs of students may choose which option they want to work with but should not reveal their choice to the rest of the class. The ability of the class to identify the roles will reveal the success or failure to establish character.

Organizing a Theatrical Event   555

● **ACTIVITY**

Developing Character Through Improvisation

Practice developing believable characters by taking part in the following improvisations. Choose a partner and improvise short scenes based on the following characters and situations. Keep your character's motivation clearly in mind as you and your partner work through each conflict to a conclusion.

1. **manager - employee** *Conflict:* Manager wants employee to work overtime; employee wants to leave early to meet grandmother at airport.
2. **doctor - patient** *Conflict:* Doctor must convince patient to lose 50 pounds for health reasons; patient believes extra weight is protection against illness.
3. **interior decorator - client** *Conflict:* Client insists house built in 1680 be decorated in modern, streamlined style; interior decorator's reputation will be ruined if modern furniture is installed in this historic house.
4. **astronaut - alien** *Conflict:* Alien wants to take astronaut on test drive of intergalactic spaceship; astronaut wants to take alien to NASA laboratory for observation.

● **ORGANIZING A THEATRICAL EVENT**

The **production organization** is the group that works together to choose, finance, cast, direct, design, construct, publicize, and perform a play. Following are some of the roles and functions that are necessary to produce a theatrical event. The Organizational Chart on page 556 shows the relationship between members of such a production organization. As you read the following descriptions of some of these jobs, think of the ones which you would most enjoy doing.

The **producer** heads the organization. This is the person who is responsible for the success or failure of the production and thus the person who has the power to make or overrule all decisions. In the professional theater the producer finances the production or convinces others to do so. Producers make or approve all decisions concerning budget, publicity, hiring, and firing. They often choose the script.

555

TEACH

AMAZING FACTS!
The smallest regularly operated professional theater in the world is the Piccolo in Hamburg, Germany. It was founded in 1950 and has a maximum capacity of 30 seats.

● **CURRICULAR CONNECTIONS**

Writing
Ask students to choose one of the jobs identified in the organizational chart and write a job description that would be suitable for that job.

● **SKILL DEVELOPMENT**

Critical Thinking
Use the organizational chart for a theatrical event and invite students to guess at the numbers of people involved in each task. Discuss those tasks that seem most important to the success of the event.

● **LEARNING STYLES**

Multicultural Learning
Have students identify movies or plays that either took place in another land or had characters from a particular region of another country. Share lists with the entire class. Discuss the role of a dialect or vocal coach in productions that call for regional or foreign accents. You might use Meryl Streep's performances in *Out of Africa* or *Sophie's Choice* as examples.

---

556 CHAPTER 17 Drama

The **director** stages the theatrical production, selecting and controlling everything that happens onstage. After a script is chosen, the director selects the cast and technical designers. The director is also responsible for arranging all movements that take place onstage, teaching dialects (possibly aided by a dialect or vocal coach), developing pace and emphasis, and, perhaps most important of all, establishing an environment of creativity, energy, and trust among all those involved. A director needs to have a thorough knowledge of literature, theatrical periods and styles, as well as scenery, lighting, and costume design.

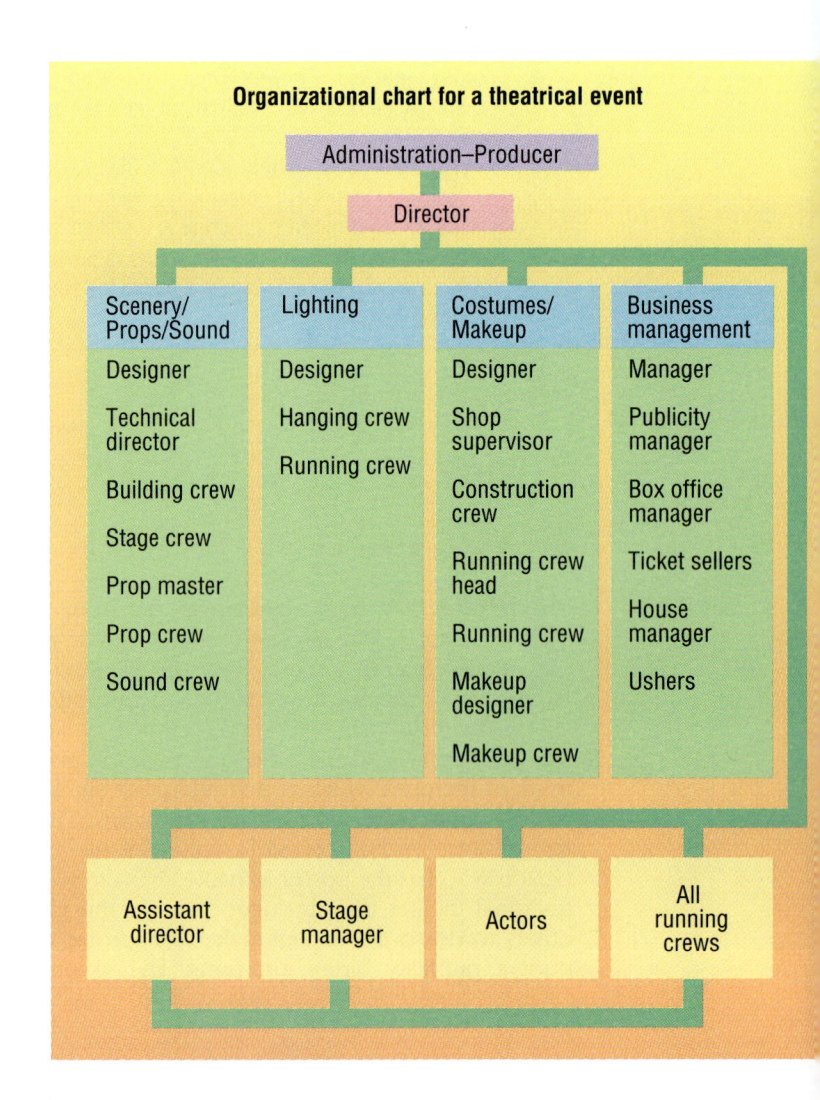

Organizational chart for a theatrical event

- Administration–Producer
  - Director
    - **Scenery/Props/Sound**
      - Designer
      - Technical director
      - Building crew
      - Stage crew
      - Prop master
      - Prop crew
      - Sound crew
    - **Lighting**
      - Designer
      - Hanging crew
      - Running crew
    - **Costumes/Makeup**
      - Designer
      - Shop supervisor
      - Construction crew
      - Running crew head
      - Running crew
      - Makeup designer
      - Makeup crew
    - **Business management**
      - Manager
      - Publicity manager
      - Box office manager
      - Ticket sellers
      - House manager
      - Ushers

- Assistant director
- Stage manager
- Actors
- All running crews

TEACH

SUBSTITUTE TEACHER TIP
If possible distribute diagrams of the school stage for students. You might ask them to design a floor plan for graduation ceremonies, or for a play the class is working on.

AMAZING FACTS!
The largest stage in the world is in the Ziegfield Room, Reno NV. It has three main elevators each capable of raising 1,200 actors and it has 800 spotlights.

● LEARNING STYLES

Technology Tools
Some students will want to learn about CAD software and could demonstrate it for the class. This technology is widely available and has widespread applications in the areas of architecture and home remodeling. Invite students to make a list of ways they expect CAD to benefit them in their adult lives.

Organizing a Theatrical Event **557**

All final technical designs—scenery, costume, lighting, graphics, sound, and properties—are in the director's hands.

The stage manager is in charge of daily organization, especially the organization needed to keep rehearsals running smoothly. The stage manager runs additional rehearsals, posts calls (asks people to attend specific rehearsals), and writes down stage instructions, changes in the script, and actor notes. A stage manager may sometimes act as prompter, reminding actors of forgotten cues or lines. The job includes making sure actors have arrived and are ready to go on stage at the proper time, supervising set-change crews, and taking care of emergencies. When the play goes into technical rehearsals (final rehearsals involving lighting and other technical aspects), the stage manager takes over.

The **scene designer** creates the backgrounds against which a play is performed. Scenery must put the audience in the correct frame of mind for the particular play. The set should, if possible, indicate the type of location, time, and economic and social position of the characters. Effective scenery will suggest a particular emotional atmosphere as well. A comedy might, for example, have scenery that is bright and cheerful. Scenery for a tragedy, on the other hand, might look more somber to reflect the mood of the play.

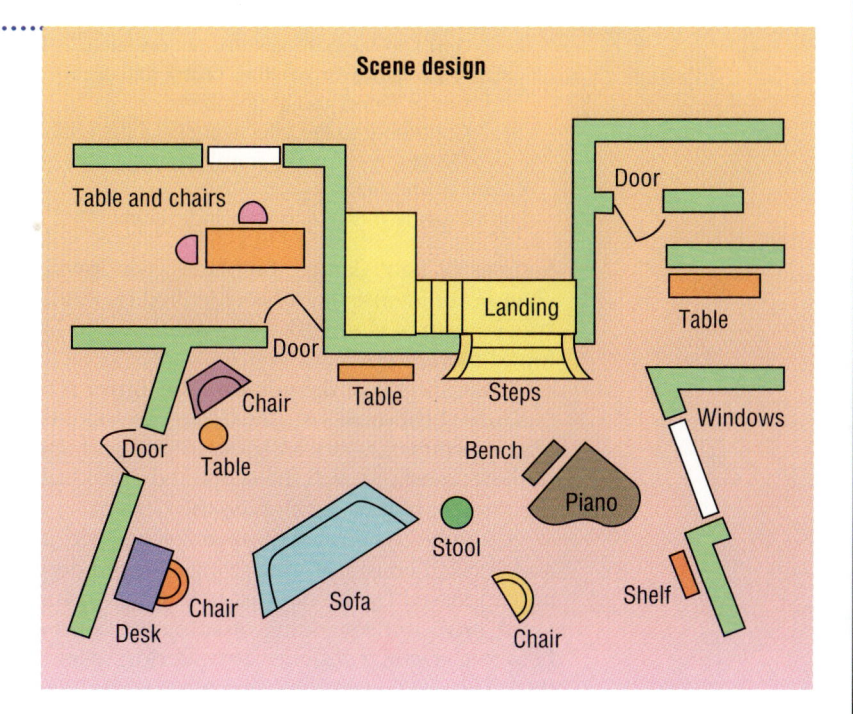

...oor plan for a scene ...sign, showing walls, ...rniture, and entrances.

Scene design

557

TEACH

AMAZING FACTS!
The largest number of costumes used for any one film was 32,000 for the 1951 movie, *Quo Vadis*.

● LEARNING STYLES

❋ Cooperative Learning
Small groups of students could focus on one of the production crews to develop a plan for set design, costumes, lightening, and sound strategies for a play the class is studying. These plans could become a group portfolio product.

● SKILL DEVELOPMENT

Research
Some students could research the Oscar winners for categories such as costume design, makeup, sound, sound effects, and visual effects. Charts could be compiled to identify the winners in these categories for the past ten years. If possible, clips from these films could be shown to help students develop a sense of the criteria used to determine excellence in these fields.

558

CHAPTER 17 Drama

The time the play takes place and the director's ideas provide the scene designer with a starting place. The designer must then research the script and time period, consult with the director, and devise a **floor plan** which the director must approve. This plan is a drawing of the position of the walls, entrances, and furniture on the stage. It is drawn from above, giving a bird's eye view of the stage. Next, sketches of the set from the audience's point of view must be produced and then drawings must be done to scale. **Scale models** of the set are often built to illustrate spatial requirements. They may include miniature furniture, props, and drapes. Directors use models when planning movement and technicians use them when constructing the set, furniture, and props. The designer must create detailed and scaled working drawings for the builders.

The **lighting designer's** chief function is to light both the actor and the set. In small theaters the same person who designs the lighting often hangs it and sometimes even runs the controls during performances.

Many aspects of lighting design are too technical to be discussed here, but the functions of effective lighting should be mentioned. Lighting design should:

    Provide maximum visibility, except where the play requirements suggest otherwise.
    Assist in suggesting information such as location, time of day, season, weather, or whether or not an offstage room is occupied.
    Create mood and atmosphere.
    Contribute to the effectiveness of the entire stage picture.
    Distribute emphasis from one stage area to another or from one actor to another.
    Provide theme and style indications.

Sources of light (lamps, fireplaces, windows), direction of light, and changes in intensity can be identified by reading the script. Necessary special events (fireworks, Christmas trees, lightning storms) can be found there, too.

The function of the **costume designer** is to help make the characters more believable visually. Costumes should show at a glance a character's occupation, social background, and age. To do this a costume designer must research the script and period and discuss concepts with the director before developing the designs.

Costume designs are done in color, accompanied by fabric swatches and detailed construction drawings. Design decisions are discussed with and approved by the director before the costumes are made.

A basic understanding of some elements of costuming can be of help to a costume designer. **Proportion** relates to the amount of something balanced against the amount of something else. In costume design

TEACH

AMAZING FACTS!
The ruby slippers, a personal prop worn by Judy Garland in the 1939 film, *The Wizard of Oz*, were sold to a mystery buyer in 1988 for $165,000.

SKILL DEVELOPMENT

Creative Thinking
Ask students to focus on a film they have all seen. You could suggest *The Wizard of Oz*, for example. Invite them to think of alternate costumes for Dorothy, the Lion, the Tinman, and the Scarecrow.

LEARNING STYLES

Visual Learning
Encourage students to bring Halloween costumes to class. Pass them out to students and have them write an appropriate line to go with the costume. Then give each costumed actor the opportunity to recite the line in front of a live audience—the other students in the class. You could award a Certificate of Recognition for the best performance.

Beyond the Classroom
Ask students to imagine that they are in charge of costumes for the pre-school production of *The Wizard of Oz*. They have 30 preschoolers and a budget of $200. They could work in small groups to develop a budget for costumes and present a plan for the use of the money and costume designs.

---

this principle is seen in the use of color and design elements. A well-proportioned design utilizes one major color, one minor color, and one accent color.

The amount and location of decorations can also make or break a costume design. Remember that the most important part of an actor is his or her face. So instead of just putting trim or a fabric flower anywhere, the designer must position it so that it will guide the viewer's attention toward the head.

Color can affect mood and atmosphere. Light, warm colors (red, orange, yellow) are better for comedy than dark, cool colors (blue, green, violet). Throughout history, specific colors have come to signify certain occupations or stations in life. Royalty is often dressed in purple and burgundy; young women, or **ingenues,** in baby pink or powder blue; devils in black and red; and angels in white or silver.

Fabric choices also can identify people. Shiny or rich fabrics such as taffeta, satin, velveteen, and velvet can be used for wealthy or flashy characters. Plain or open-weave fabrics can be associated with poor, uneducated, or common characters. The **drape,** or hang, of a fabric should also be considered. Heavy or stiff fabrics do not drape well on the body. Softer fabrics such as chiffon, lightweight cottons, and knits hang loosely. A costume designer must look at the fabric from at least ten feet away to see what it will look like from where the audience sits.

After the costumes are designed, about a week before the first dress rehearsal, a **dress parade** is held. This is the first opportunity for the designer and director to see the costumes all together on stage. It also gives the actors the opportunity to find out whether their costumes will withstand stage fights or dance routines. Dress rehearsals allow the actors time to become comfortable in their clothing. An actor who does not work enough in costume will be more likely to look and feel awkward and fidget with stiff collars, lengthy hems, or hooped skirts. The costumer or the crewhead takes care of nightly repairs, washing, and ironing during the run of the show.

Costumes often seem to be last on the list for money. A costume designer must learn to create imaginative and functional costumes with very little money. If you ever work as a costume designer for a school play, you might want to become familiar with the costumes owned by other schools and work out a borrowing arrangement. You might also ask for donations from the PTA and students at your school. Exciting costumes have been made from dyed chenille bedspreads and old curtains, so be creative!

A **publicity manager** provides the public with information concerning the production and its participants. Many weeks prior to the first rehearsal, publicity is discussed with and approved by the director and the producer. Poster designs are then created. One good way to find creative graphic designs for a high school production is to hold a poster

TEACH

> *The most amazing feature of American life is its boundless publicity. Everybody has to meet everybody, and they even seem to enjoy this enormity.*
> —Carl Jung

● **SKILL DEVELOPMENT**

Creative Thinking
Work with students to plan a publicity campaign for a school play or program. Brainstorm various ideas and strategies and make decisions based on priorities and available resources.

560

Posters that are well designed and provide all the essential information about the performance should be distributed no later than two and a half weeks before opening.

contest. Contestants should know what the play is about and create their designs so as to include:

    name of play (author if necessary)
    name of organization
    location
    dates
    time
    box office phone
    permission or royalty information
    creator's signature
    director's name

A well-designed poster catches the eye, can be clearly read, and is interesting and creative. Posters for school performances can be distributed to other schools, area retail stores, houses of worship, and local bulletin boards.

Additional publicity for a school play can take several forms. Advertisements taken out in local newspapers reach a wide range of people. Critical reviews in newspapers are a good way of letting the public know what you are doing. Play announcements might be sent to high school parents or drama teachers at other schools. School window displays can get students excited about the play. Try to present a short scene from the play at an assembly, in the cafeteria, at lunch, for a class, or at a PTA or local club meetings. Publicity stunts are particularly effective. Stage a parade, take costumed players to a local shopping mall, wear buttons or tee-shirts displaying the name of the show, or obtain time on a local television show.

560

TEACH

● **RETEACHING**

Ask students to write a memo to all people involved in a theatrical production. The memo should address the issues of who, what, when, where, and how involved in a theatrical production.

Publicity timing is important. Posters should be distributed no later than two and a half weeks before opening. Newspapers like to receive theater information two to three weeks before publication. Other publicity methods should be employed the week of the opening.

The programs for a show are also part of the publicity manager's responsibility. High school theater departments often sell program advertisements to help offset production costs. Be sure that the program is correct in all its listings of information and names!

● **ACTIVITY**

The Importance of Organizing

Invite to class people from your area, including students, who have worked on plays as producers, directors, stage managers, designers, and business managers. Ask these guests to explain what their exact duties were and how they fulfilled them in coordination with each group in the production organization. Ask them to explain in detail the decisions that they had to make and how they made them. Ask your guests to participate in a class discussion of the importance of each task to the overall success of the production.

● **ACTIVITY**

If possible, invite a local college drama teacher to speak on the topic of organization. Students could prepare interview questions before the visit. Discuss the role of teamwork and communication in the success of a production.

● **PRODUCING A THEATRICAL EVENT**

Now that you have some idea of the many people involved in producing a show, you are ready to consider some of the major steps leading up to and including opening night. The play must be cast. Rehearsals must be held. Numerous problems must be solved to insure a successful opening.

Casting

A play's cast is generally chosen through a process of two or three **auditions,** or tryout sessions. Aspiring actors should, if possible, prepare for tryouts by reading the script. Some directors require **prepared readings** from the play or another source of the actor's choice, while other auditions are improvisational in nature. After the initial auditions, most directors post **callbacks,** auditions reserved for actors whom the director wishes to hear again. Although the first consideration of casting is the ability of the actor to interpret the role, most directors are also interested in selecting a hardworking group of actors who work well together.

TEACH

> *The only thing you owe the public is a good performance.*
>
> —Humphrey Bogart

● LEARNING STYLES

Beyond the Classroom
Ask students to think of a reading that might be appropriate for them to use as an audition for a contemporary award-winning play. Students might actually prepare an audition tape and include it in their portfolio.

● SKILL DEVELOPMENT

15-Second Skill Opportunity
Ask students to imagine that they only have 15 seconds to do a live audition for a part of their choosing in a play of their choosing. Call on various students to perform their audition.

● CURRICULAR CONNECTIONS

Writing
Ask students to draft a memo announcing the rehearsal times, places, and characters for the school play. They could share their draft with a partner for feedback. They should clarify any ambiguity in the original memo and write a revision based on the feedback.

If you are auditioning for a part in a play, you should wear comfortable clothing, have your hair off your face, wear noiseless shoes, speak in a loud, clear voice, and be alert. If you do not get the part you want you should keep auditioning. There are always many reasons for not being chosen. Experience, physical build, vocal qualities, attitude, and script style all must be considered by the director. You should also not be disappointed by a small role. The old saying, "There are no small parts, only small actors," might well be engraved above every stage.

Rehearsals

During the first rehearsal the director discusses his or her **production concept** with the actors, and the cast reads through the script. This concept, the director's interpretation of the play, helps unify the actions and thoughts of director, actors, and designers. Throughout the rehearsal period the director holds **production meetings** with the staff to give people a chance to air problems and to make sure that every aspect of the production is running smoothly on schedule. Changes in concept, script cuts, additional technical requirements, and budgets are discussed at production meetings.

These terms identify different areas of the stage. They are used by directors during rehearsal to block each actor's movements.

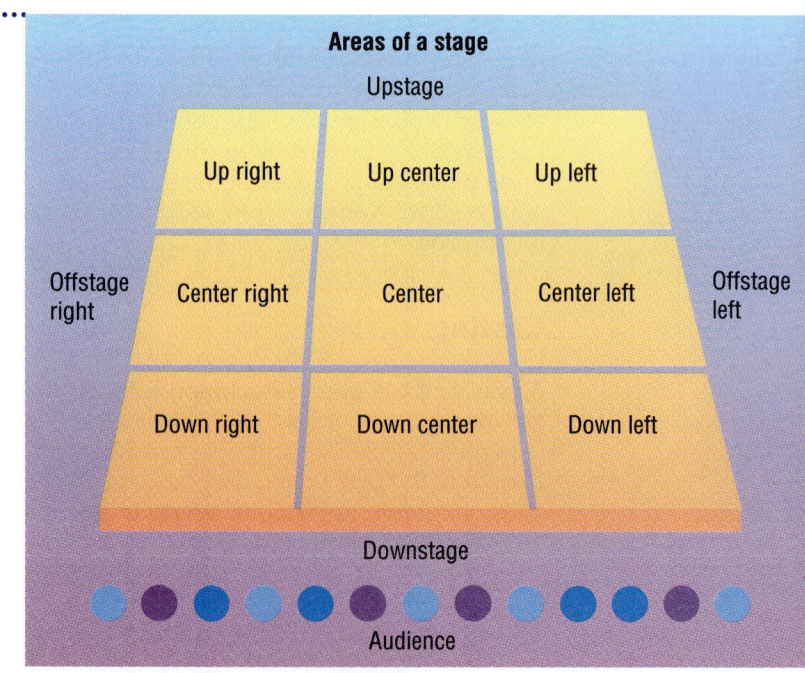

Areas of a stage

	Upstage	
Up right	Up center	Up left
Center right	Center	Center left

Offstage right — Offstage left

| Down right | Down center | Down left |

Downstage

Audience

TEACH

● ENRICHMENT

Students could make plans for a production meeting that is scheduled to last 30 minutes and to be held two nights before the dress rehearsal. Either assign roles as identified in the chart on page 556 or ask for volunteers to serve those roles. The director should develop an agenda and manage the time and discussion during the meeting.

> ❝ *Actors are cattle.* ❞
> —Alfred Hitchcock

● LEARNING STYLES

Kinesic Learning
Have students write stage directions using the diagram showing the areas of the stage on page 562. The instructions should tell the leading protagonist how to move from down center to up right within five seconds in order to answer a telephone that is used as a prop. Students could volunteer to follow the instructions that others wrote.

About halfway through rehearsals, actors must be off book; dialogue, cues, and blocking have been memorized.

A schedule of the entire rehearsal period is handed out to everyone involved in the show. The first rehearsal is a good time for designers to discuss their ideas and present color renderings. It is also a good time for making sure that all participants understand the "rules of the game" and what will be expected of them as members of the production.

When producing a high-school play, five to seven weeks of rehearsal, two to three hours per day, five days a week, is ideal. Weekend rehearsal should be reserved for the final weeks. During the week prior to opening, called **tech week,** rehearsals will generally last longer. Depending upon the play, rehearsals are usually divided into scenes, so that not all of the actors have to attend each rehearsal.

During the first few rehearsals, the director gives blocking instructions. **Blocking** is the arrangement of the movements of the actors. It includes how and when actors get onstage and off, as well as how and when they will move about while onstage. Each actor should write blocking instructions down carefully *in pencil,* and then walk through them with the other actors. A normal, full-length play takes about a week to block and set.

The language of stage blocking is not difficult but must be mastered early in the training of all theater people. The diagram on page 562 shows you the terms used for the different areas of a stage. You should also become familiar with the abbreviations used to mark blocking instructions and dialogue interpretation in the script. Some of these symbols are shown in the chart at the top of page 564 and in the sample page of marked script on page 565. Careful notation of your blocking instructions helps insure that your position and movements on stage are correct.

The next step for the actors is the memorization of their lines. Both the dialogue and the blocking should be memorized at the same time. Because it is difficult to handle stage movements with a script in hand, actors should memorize as quickly as possible. If you are acting in a play, remember to memorize your lines exactly as written, including the pauses that have been written in by the playwright. If you have difficulty memorizing, have someone help you by reading the scene with you. Be sure to become familiar with your cue lines. You may

TEACH

> *Professional jargon is unpleasant. Translating it into English is a bore.*
> —Fred Hechinger

● CURRICULAR CONNECTIONS

Writing
You might ask the drama coach to share blocking instructions with your class. Copies could be made and distributed. Discuss how these instructions should be read.

● LEARNING STYLES

Limited English Proficiency
You might use the chart, "Abbreviations for stage directions" and compare it to learning another language. Abbreviations are symbols just as words are symbols. The ability to learn new codes or languages often depends on the present need to know or learn something. Discuss in class how easy or difficult it would be to learn these and other abbreviations.

● SKILL DEVELOPMENT

On the Job
Most professions have their own special or technical words and terms. Invite students to select a career they are most interested in and develop a list of at least ten words or phrases that are unique to that profession.

CHAPTER 17 Drama

Abbreviations for stage directions			
X	Cross	3/4	Turn 3/4 away from facing center front
X)	Cross on curved line	1/4 L	Turn 1/4 away from center front toward stage left
XDR	Cross down right	PSR	Stand in profile toward stage right
↑	Voice up	—	Underline words which are to be emphasized
↓	Voice down	✕	Cut

also find that writing the lines several times helps establish them in your mind. However you memorize, spend considerable time going over and over the material. After three to five weeks of rehearsals, you should be familiar with all the lines of the play. If you try to capture the spirit of every scene in your mind, you will be better able to handle any problems that arise during performance.

About halfway through the rehearsal period actors are required to be **off book.** This means that they must have all of their dialogue, cues, and blocking memorized. They will then be able to run through a rehearsal without too much prompting. Two weeks before opening the company should be ready for **run-throughs** during which the play is gone through in its entirety so that the director can concentrate on polishing the fine details of the production.

Tech Week

The first technical rehearsal is held without actors. Often called **paper tech,** this rehearsal involves the director and technical staff. They run through the entire show, writing down specific cues and deciding set changes. During other technical rehearsals the lighting designer sets and checks lights, while the actors become familiar with the set, their costumes, and the costume changes. Finally, makeup is added, and production photos taken. During all tech rehearsals, the director and designers take thorough notes and discuss them with the cast and staff after each performance.

Opening Night and Evaluation

The director's job is not finished on opening night. He or she should continue to watch each performance and take notes. Before each

Producing a Theatrical Event   565

Sample of script marking

Scene from Act II of BETTER LATE

by Georgina Spelvin

GRADY: (Stunned) Winnie, I never said that. Never. Whoever told you that I said such a thing about you?

WINORA: (Defensive) It doesn't matter who told me—and don't call me Winnie.

GRADY: It matters to me. (Waits for her response; exasperated when he gets none. Turns and walks away; then turns back) Win--ora! What is the problem?

WINORA: (Ready to explode) I'll tell you what the problem is, Grady Bartholomew Sefton. (Turns to him, sees FOOTBALL COACH passing upstage from L to R) Hi, Mr. Wolchek. (Faces down)

GRADY: (Turns and waves to FOOTBALL COACH, then back) What is it? What's going on?

WINORA: (Struggling to find the words) It's just that—well, you seem so far away.

GRADY: What do you mean?

WINORA: (Turns right, close to tears) I always thought I could count on you—as a friend.

performance, the director talks to the cast and crews, analyzes the audience's response to the last performance, and encourages a strong, energetic performance. Actors should consider every night "opening night."

When a high-school show closes, the actors and staff generally hold an evaluation session. A discussion of strengths and weaknesses, audience reactions, and the benefits gained by the people involved will provide insights useful in future productions.

ASSESS

● **STUDENT PERFORMANCE COMPETENCIES**

- Explains the elements of drama
- Researches and analyzes script to develop character
- Describes jobs connected with producing a theatrical event
- Demonstrates verbal and nonverbal aspects of character development
- Understands a basic history of the development of drama

● **sca GUIDELINES**

- Uses voice and gestures effectively for theatrical performance
- Expresses ideas and character clearly
- Expresses feelings to others in small and large groups
- Performs social rituals

PORTFOLIO ASSESSMENT

Standard
- Glossary of Speech Terms
- Theater Review
- Award Nominations
- Character Development

Enrichment
- Tape of Individual Performances
- Job Descriptions for Various Aspects of Theatrical Production
- Team Production for Event
- Publicity for Event

Challenge
- Theatrical Event for School

CHAPTER 17 REVIEW

● **SUMMARY**

Drama is an art form that utilizes all other art forms, such as painting, sculpture, music, dance, and architecture. It has been a part of people's lives in all parts of the world throughout history.

The Nature of Drama Drama as a theatrical event exists only when the following are present: live actors, plot, theatrical space, and an audience. Through these elements drama provides entertainment, education, and spiritual uplift and joy. For the participants, drama offers great challenges, insights into history and human existence, and self-esteem.

A Brief History of Drama From the tragedies and comedies of ancient Greece, theater evolved into a medium of religious education in the Middle Ages and into a source of entertainment for common folk during the Renaissance and the Elizabethan era. During the 1600s in France and England, theater was used for comedic social commentary. In the 1800s it moved from romanticism to realism, and in the mid-1900s it began to portray a vision of human desolation.

Developing a Character Actors study vocal and body presentations of the past and present, conduct background research, and analyze the scripts and the characters they will play. They then develop the characters' voices, movements, and relationships with other characters.

Organizing a Theatrical Event The chart on page 556 shows the major jobs involved in organizing a theatrical event. Each artist—producer, director, designer—must understand and coordinate with the work of all the others in order to reach a common goal.

Producing a Theatrical Event Play production begins with a thorough study of the script. The director establishes a production concept and unifies all theatrical elements, while each actor and technician is responsible for carrying out the director's decisions.

ASSESS

● **ASSESSMENT STRATEGIES**

Individual Assessment
- Participates in practice activities daily or weekly
- Completes classwork
- Demonstrates knowledge of content through questions, discussion, quizzes, and Chapter 17 test
- Displays skills in the development of a character role

Group Assessment
- Sets and achieves goals
- Develops cooperative learning projects
- Provides encouragement and feedback to members

VOCABULARY

Define at least fifteen of the following terms in a complete sentence.

drama
theatrical event
thespian
comedy
tragedy
catharsis
tragic flaw
reversal
discovery
Middle Ages
Renaissance
opera
commedia dell'arte
scenario
improvisation
Elizabethan era
French theater
Comédie Française
Restoration
comedy of manners
legitimate theater
romanticism
realism
slice-of-life theater
Theater of the Absurd
tragicomedy
structure
exposition
initial incident
rising action
climax

falling action
cue line
dialogue
choreography
protagonist
antagonist
production organization
producer
director
stage manager
scene designer
floor plan
scale model
lighting designer
costume designer
proportion
ingenue
drape
dress parade
publicity manager
audition
prepared reading
callback
production concept
production meeting
tech week
blocking
off book
run-through
paper tech

ASSESS

● **ANSWERS**

See the Answer Key for more complete answers.

REVIEW QUESTIONS
1. The elements of live drama include live actors, a plot, a theater, and an audience.
2. Catharsis is the purging of emotions.
3. The tragic hero is a person who had a fatal flaw that led to destruction.
4. Examples are Shakespeare and Moliere.
5. Henrik Ibsen is called the "father of modern drama."
6. To develop a character, research, analysis, and mastery of voice and gestures are essential.
7. The director is responsible for cast, staff, staging, and maintaining a creative environment.
8. The stage manager is responsible for rehearsals and supervising crews.
9. A costume designer must consider characterization, historical period, proportion and the use of color and fabric.
10. The responsibilities of the business staff include publicity, ticket sales, and ushering.

DISCUSSION QUESTIONS
The following code is used to designate discussion questions and activities as suitable for students of varying ability levels:
- ▼ = below average to average
- ◆ = average to above average
- ■ = all students

1. Ask students to give specific examples that
◆ illustrate the qualities they name.

568

CHAPTER 17 REVIEW

✔ CHECKLIST

Drama Skills

1. Keep the purpose of drama in mind, whatever your role is.
2. Know your character so well that you can cope with missed lines and other mix-ups.
3. Keep a diary of observations of different types of people.
4. Use clear, expressive speech in all acting roles.
5. Practice volume control to help project your voice well.
6. Be aware of the organization of a theatrical event.
7. Prepare programs carefully for every theatrical event.
8. Dress properly for auditions.

REVIEW QUESTIONS

1. Name the four elements of drama necessary to produce a theatrical event.
2. Define *catharsis*.
3. Name two characteristics of the tragic hero according to Aristotle.
4. Name two playwrights of the Renaissance.
5. Name the playwright who is known as "the father of modern drama."
6. List the steps an actor must take to develop a character.
7. Identify the responsibilities of a director.
8. Name the responsibilities of a stage manager.
9. Describe the elements a costume designer must consider.
10. Name some jobs included on the business staff of a theatrical organization.

? DISCUSSION QUESTIONS

1. Discuss the benefits of theatrical productions to the individual and society. What qualities make theatre different from other art forms? In what sense are theatrical productions sources or reflections of human knowledge?

2. Discuss the interrelationships among the four elements necessary for a theatrical event to take place. Why does it make sense to say that theatrical drama really can't take place without an audience?

3. Discuss an actor's creative process. What does an actor bring to a role? In what ways is the actor the playwright's accomplice? Is it more accurate to say that the actor is the playwright's assistant? Why or why not? Is the actor responsible for discovering and portraying a role as the playwright intended, or may the actor depart from the playwright's original intention and interpret a role freely?

4. Discuss the Greek concept of catharsis. Why did the Greeks believe that it was a valuable emotional experience? Have you ever experienced catharsis while viewing a theatrical production? Have you ever had such an experience at other times? Do you think catharsis has a valid place in contemporary drama?

CRITICAL THINKING

1. Analysis Everyone has witnessed examples of mediocre or poor acting. How do you know when acting is not what it should be? What are the signs that the actor is failing to perform the part adequately?

2. Evaluation Compare and contrast the roles of the playwright, the director, and the actors in a theatrical production. Can they ever operate completely independently of each other? In what sense might the playwright be most distant from the actual theatrical production?

ACTIVITIES

In-Class

1. In each of the following situations, perform the appropriate nonverbal actions. Use no words as you perform each situation. Obtain reactions and feedback from your classmates. (a) You are an older person looking through a photograph album. The photographs are bringing back old memories. React to the various memories that the photographs suggest. (b) You are waiting to see the dentist. The pain of a toothache is compounded by concern about what the

---

2. Students could eliminate one element at a time to illustrate how interdependent they are.
3. Actors bring an analysis of the play and characters, experience, and talent to the stage.
4. Catharsis also occurs in real life when people undergo intense emotional experiences.

CRITICAL THINKING
1. **Analysis** Students should critique specific actors and specific performances.
2. **Evaluation** Have students refer to the discussion of these roles in the text.

ACTIVITIES
In-Class
1. Vary this activity by having students develop their own lists of situations.

ASSESS

2. This activity could be an audition for casting the play used in the chapter project.
3. Students could plan the schedule for a real production.
4. Ask students to justify their choices of cast members.

Out-of-Class
1. Encourage students to read plays that are reviewed.
2. This is a good opportunity for a class field trip. Secure necessary permissions.

570

CHAPTER 17 REVIEW

dentist is likely to do. As you wait, you hear a scream from the other room. Show your reaction and your final decision. (c) You are waiting at a bus stop with your only token in your hand, ready to pay your fare. You drop it accidentally and it rolls into a grate. Reveal how you finally retrieve the bus token.

2. With a partner, select a one-person scene or monologue from a play. Decide who will direct and who will perform the monologue. Analyze the character in the scene. Develop a blocking pattern that supports the role and the scene, and rehearse the monologue several times. Present the scene in class.

3. Work in groups of from five to seven. Choose a one-act or a full-length play and imagine that it will be performed three months in the future. Decide upon the kinds of committees you will need to produce the play. Devise a schedule to be followed in order to meet the date of performance. Make your schedule as complete as possible—from tryouts through dress rehearsal. Be sure to schedule dates for tasks such as costume fittings, publicity photos, and preparation of the manuscript for the program. Compare your schedule with the schedules developed by other groups.

4. As a class, select a play from which two or three scenes can be used for the purpose of auditioning. Discuss how the characters in each scene can be interpreted. Choose a group of five students who will, together, serve as the casting director and evaluate the auditions of the remaining students. The group serving as casting director will then choose the best actor for each part and will explain their choices. The class will discuss the group's decisions.

Out-of-Class

1. At the library, find play reviews by professional theater critics written for newspapers and magazines. Study the reviews carefully. In your speech notebook, summarize the criteria that professional critics use in evaluating plays, actors, and productions. Note the aspects of the plays and productions that these reviewers comment upon most often. Be prepared to share your findings with the class.

2. Attend a theatrical performance in your area. If there is no professional theater company nearby, you should be able to attend a high-school production, or a production presented by a college or community theater group. Evaluate all aspects of the production and write a review in your speech notebook. Be prepared to share your review with the rest of the class.

ASSESS

3. Some people avoid taking part in a theatrical production because they think they have no acting talent. In your speech notebook, write a letter to an imaginary person who holds that belief. Point out the various nonacting skills that are essential for a theatrical production. Suggest activities that a person can participate in without ever facing a live audience on stage. Be prepared to share your letter of encouragement with classmates.

4. Imagine that you have been appointed publicity agent for a theatrical production that opens in one month. Think of ways in which you might publicize the production in your locality. Find out how others have gone about publicizing theatrical events in your community and sketch out a publicity campaign in your speech notebook. Compare your campaign with those of classmates.

CHAPTER PROJECT

As a class, identify a number of one-act plays that might be suitable for a class production. Read all of the plays suggested and select one that would be possible to stage in class. Select a casting committee and conduct auditions. Name a student director and assign all other students to the various production committees. Rehearse the play and set a date for the performance. You will probably want to invite other classes as your audience.

---

3. Consider assigning characters to students
■ and having them write the letters in the characters' voices.
4. You may want students to record a radio
▼ spot or create a poster for publicity.

CHAPTER PROJECT
■ Students will enjoy putting into practice what they have learned in this chapter. They will also find out what hard work it is to organize and produce a play.

TEACH

AMAZING FACTS!

Sandburg, a poet living and writing in Illinois, became fascinated with the life of Abraham Lincoln. He researched his life and was awarded the Pulitzer prize for history for his *Abraham Lincoln— The War Years* (1939). His love and admiration for Lincoln and his work are reflected in this speech.

CURRICULAR CONNECTIONS

History

Students could review the chronology of Lincoln's life and the events surrounding the Civil War. Have students identify the places mentioned in this speech on a map of the United States. They could also trace the route of the funeral procession through the seven states from Washington DC to Springfield, IL.

LEARNING STYLES

Cooperative Learning

Have small groups of students highlight and compile the quotations and anecdotes that Sandburg uses in this speech. Let each group discuss the impact of these quotations and stories and select their favorite.

Appendix of Speeches

INFORMATIVE/COMMEMORATIVE SPEECH

Address on the Anniversary of Lincoln's Birth
Carl Sandburg

On February 12, 1959, the 150th anniversary of Abraham Lincoln's birth, American poet Carl Sandburg delivered the following address to a special Joint Session of Congress. Sandburg, the author of a prize-winning biography of Lincoln, presents in this address a noble and tragic portrait of the beloved President. Note Sandburg's use of quotations and anecdotes to make his subject come alive.

Not often in the story of mankind does a man arrive on earth who is both steel and velvet, who is hard as rock and soft as drifting fog, who holds in his heart and mind the paradox[1] of terrible storm and peace unspeakable and perfect. Here and there across centuries come reports of men alleged to have these contrasts. And the incomparable Abraham Lincoln, born 150 years ago this day, is an approach if not a perfect realization of this character.

In the time of the April lilacs in the year 1865, on his death, the casket with his body was carried north and west a thousand miles; and the American people wept as never before; bells sobbed, cities wore crepe; people stood in tears and with hats off as the railroad burial car paused in the leading cities of seven states, ending its journey at Springfield, Illinois, the home town.

During the four years he was President he at times, especially in the first three months, took to himself the powers of a dictator; he commanded the most powerful armies till then assembled in modern warfare; he enforced conscription of soldiers for the first time in American history; under imperative necessity he abolished the right of habeas corpus;[2] he directed politically and spiritually the wild, massive, turbulent forces let loose in civil war.

He argued and pleaded for compensated emancipation[3] of the slaves. The slaves were property; they were on the tax books along with horses

---

[1] **paradox** (par′ ə däks): contradiction.
[2] **habeas corpus** (hā′ be əs kôr′ pəs): in law, the right that safeguards persons against illegal detainment or imprisonment.
[3] **compensated emancipation** (kä′ pən sāt′ id i man′ sə pā′ shun): program under which slaves would be freed and slave owners would be compensated for their losses.

CURRICULAR CONNECTIONS

History
Emphasize the importance of the Mississippi River in the Civil War and all of our history. Students could share stories about the great river. Recorded music about the Mississippi could be brought to class and students might discuss the type of music that could be used as "background" to enhance the oral reading of Sandburg's speech.

LEARNING STYLES

Limited English Proficiency
Make sure that students understand the words and terms that are footnoted throughout the speech. Encourage students to identify other words that present difficulties in understanding. These terms could be compiled as a dictionary or glossary.

---

and cattle, the valuation of each slave next to his name on the tax assessor's books. Failing to get action on compensated emancipation, as a Chief Executive having war powers he issued the paper by which he declared the slaves to be free under "military necessity." In the end nearly $4,000,000 worth of property was taken away from those who were legal owners of it, property confiscated, wiped out as by fire and turned to ashes, at his instigation and executive direction. Chattel property[4] recognized and lawful for 300 years was expropriated, seized without payment.

In the month the war began he told his secretary, John Hay, "My policy is to have no policy." Three years later in a letter to a Kentucky friend made public, he confessed plainly, "I have been controlled by events." His words at Gettysburg were sacred, yet strange with a color of the familiar: "We cannot consecrate—we cannot hallow—this ground. The brave men, living and dead, who struggled here, have consecrated it, far beyond our poor power to add or detract."

He could have said "the brave Union men." Did he have a purpose in omitting the word "Union"? Was he keeping himself and his utterance clear of the passion that would not be good to look at when the time came for peace and reconciliation? Did he mean to leave an implication that there were brave Union men and brave Confederate men, living and dead, who had struggled there? We do not know, of a certainty.

Was he thinking of the Kentucky father whose two sons died in battle, one in Union blue, the other in Confederate gray, the father inscribing on the stone over their double grave, "God knows which was right"? We do not know.

Lincoln's changing policies from time to time aimed at saving the Union. In the end his armies won and his nation became a world power immersed in international politics. In August of 1864 he wrote a memorandum that he expected to lose the next November election; sudden military victory brought the tide his way; the vote was 2,200,000 for him and 1,800,000 against him.

Among his bitter opponents were such figures as Samuel F. B. Morse, inventor of the telegraph, and Cyrus H. McCormick, inventor of the farm reaper. In all its essential propositions the Southern Confederacy had the moral support of powerful, respectable elements throughout the North, probably more than a million voters believing in the justice of the Southern cause.

While the war winds howled he insisted that the Mississippi was one river meant to belong to one country, that railroad connection from coast to coast must be pushed through and the Union Pacific Railroad made a reality. While the luck of war wavered and broke and came again, as generals failed and campaigns were lost, he held enough forces of the North together to raise new armies and supply them, until generals were found who made war as victorious war has always been made, with terror, fright-

---

[4]**Chattel property** (chat' l prä' pər tē): moveable personal property.

TEACH

● **SKILL DEVELOPMENT**

Critical Thinking
Have students analyze the references in the speech to Lincoln's thoughts and policies about slavery and emancipation. Discuss what might have been done historically to be "better prepared for the new." Ask students to consider what they would like done to make themselves "better prepared for the new."

APPENDIX OF SPEECHES

fulness, destruction, and on both sides, North and South, valor and sacrifice past words of man to tell.

In the mixed shame and blame of the immense wrongs of two crashing civilizations, often with nothing to say, he said nothing, slept not at all, and on occasions he was seen to weep in a way that made weeping appropriate, decent, majestic.

As he rode alone on horseback near Soldiers' Home on the edge of Washington one night his hat was shot off; a son he loved died as he watched at the bed; his wife was accused of betraying information to the enemy, until denials from him were necessary.

An Indiana man at the White House heard him say, "Voorhees,[5] don't it seem strange to you that I, who could never so much as cut off the head of a chicken, should be elected, or selected, into the midst of all this blood?"

He tried to guide Gen. Nathaniel Prentiss Banks, a Democrat, three times Governor of Massachusetts, in the governing of some seventeen of the forty-eight parishes of Louisiana controlled by the Union armies, an area holding a fourth of the slaves of Louisiana. He would like to see the state recognize the Emancipation Proclamation,[6] "and while she is at it, I think it would not be objectionable for her to adopt some practical system by which the two races could gradually live themselves out of their old relation to each other, and both come out better prepared for the new. Education for the young blacks should be included in the plan."

To Gov. Michel Hahn, elected in 1864 by a majority of 11,000 white male voters who had taken the oath of allegiance to the Union, Lincoln wrote:

"Now you are about to have a convention which, among other things will probably define the elective franchise,[7] I barely suggest for your private consideration, whether some of the colored people may not be let in—as for instance, the very intelligent and especially those who have fought gallantly in our ranks."

Among the million words in the Lincoln utterance record, he interprets himself with a more keen precision than someone else offering to explain him. His simple opening of the House Divided speech in 1858 serves for today:

"If we could first know where we are, and whither we are tending we could better judge what to do, and how to do it."

To his Kentucky friend, Joshua F. Speed, he wrote in 1855:

"Our progress in degeneracy appears to me to be pretty rapid. As a nation we began by declaring that 'All men are created equal, except Negroes.' When the Know-Nothings[8] get control, it will read 'All men are

---

[5]**Voorhees**: Daniel Wolsey Voorhees, Senator from Indiana.
[6]**Emancipation Proclamation**: proclamation issued by Lincoln in 1862, freeing the slaves in areas of the country still at war with the Union.
[7]**elective franchise** (i lek' tiv fran' chīz): the right to vote.
[8]**Know-Nothings**: members of a radical organization dedicated to keeping out of office anyone not a native-born, white, protestant American.

created equal except Negroes and foreigners and Catholics.' When it comes to this, I shall prefer emigrating to some country where they make no pretense of loving liberty."

Infinitely tender was his word from a White House balcony to a crowd on the White House lawn, "I have not willingly planted a thorn in any man's bosom," or to a military governor, "I shall do nothing through malice; what I deal with is too vast for malice."

He wrote for Congress to read on Dec. 1, 1862:

"In times like the present men would utter nothing for which they would not willingly be responsible through time and eternity."

Like an ancient psalmist he warned Congress:

"Fellow citizens, we cannot escape history. We will be remembered in spite of ourselves. No personal significance or insignificance can spare one or another of us. The fiery trial through which we pass will light us down in honor or dishonor to the latest generation."

Wanting Congress to break and forget the past tradition his words came keen and flashing. "The dogmas of the quiet past are inadequate for the stormy present. We must think anew, we must act anew, we must disenthrall[9] ourselves." They are the sort of words that actuated[10] the mind and will of the men who created and navigated that marvel of the sea, the Nautilus and her voyage from Pearl Harbor and under the North Pole icecap.

The people of many other countries take Lincoln now for their own. He belongs to them. He stands for decency, honest dealing, plain talk, and funny stories. "Look where he came from—don't he know all us strugglers and wasn't he a kind of tough struggler all his life right up to the finish?"

Something like that you can hear in any near-by neighborhood and across the seas.

Millions there are who take him as a personal treasure. He had something they would like to see spread everywhere over the world. Democracy? We can't find words to say exactly what it is, but he had it. In his blood and bones he carried it. In the breath of his speeches and writings it is there. Popular government? Republican institution? Government where the people have the say-so, one way or another telling their elected leaders what they want? He had the idea. It's there in the lights and shadows of his personality, a mystery that can be lived but never fully spoken in words.

Our good friend the poet and playwright Mark Van Doren tells us:

"To me, Lincoln seems, in some ways, the most interesting man who ever lived. He was gentle, but his gentleness was combined with a terrific toughness, an iron strength."

How did Lincoln say he would like to be remembered? His beloved friend, Representative Owen Lovejoy of Illinois, had died in May of 1864 and friends wrote to Lincoln and he replied that the pressure of duties

---

[9]**disenthrall** (dis' in thrôl'): free.
[10]**actuated** (ak' choo wāt' id): moved or put into action.

TEACH

AMAZING FACTS!

Susan B. Anthony was born in Massachusetts in 1820 and was a suffrage advocate for women. She served as president of the National American Woman Suffrage Association (1892-1900) and was elected to the American Hall of Fame in 1950.

● MOTIVATION

Write a dictionary definition of "citizen" on the chalkboard. Ask students to identify the people in the United States who are excluded from citizenship.

APPENDIX OF SPEECHES

kept him from joining them in efforts for a marble monument to Lovejoy, the last sentence of his letter saying, "Let him have the marble monument along with the well-assured and more enduring one in the hearts of those who love liberty, unselfishly, for all men."

So perhaps we may say that the well-assured and most enduring memorial to Lincoln is invisibly there, today, tomorrow, and for a long time yet to come in the hearts of lovers of liberty, men and women who understand that wherever there is freedom there have been those who fought, toiled, and sacrificed for it.

● PERSUASIVE SPEECH

Woman's Right to Suffrage
Susan B. Anthony

Susan B. Anthony, an activist in the cause of voting rights for women, delivered the following speech after being fined for voting in the Presidential election of 1872. With impeccable logic, Anthony argues that the question of women's suffrage, believed by many to be a question of value or policy, is actually a question of fact. Her argument can be summarized as follows:

The Constitution guarantees the right to vote to all citizens.
Women are citizens.
Therefore, the Constitution guarantees the right to vote to women.

As you read the speech, note how Anthony combines this appeal to reason with appeals to emotion—to justice and fairness. Also note the various kinds of evidence that Anthony uses, including her appeals to the authority of the Constitution and to accepted definitions.

Friends and Fellow Citizens: I stand before you tonight under indictment for the alleged crime of having voted at the last Presidential election without having a lawful right to vote. It shall be my work this evening to prove to you that, in thus voting, I not only committed no crime, but instead, simply exercised my citizen's rights, guaranteed to me and all United States citizens by the national Constitution, beyond the power of any state to deny.

The preamble of the federal Constitution says:

"We, the people of the United States, in order to form a more perfect union, establish justice, insure domestic tranquility, provide for the common defense, promote the general welfare, and secure the blessings of liberty to ourselves and our posterity, do ordain and establish this Constitution for the United States of America."

It was we, the people: not we, the white male citizens; nor yet we, the male citizens; but we, the whole people who formed the Union. And we formed it, not to give the blessings of liberty, but to secure them; not to the half of ourselves and the half of our posterity, but to the whole people women as well as men. And it is a downright mockery to talk to women of

● **ENRICHMENT**

Some students could research the Susan B. Anthony dollar coin and share the information with the entire class.

● **CURRICULAR CONNECTIONS**

History
Some students could research information about Susan B. Anthony and the women's suffrage movement. The chronology could be presented as a timeline.

TEACH

AMAZING FACTS!

Barbara Pierce of Rye, NY, and George Bush married in 1945. They moved to Texas where George established an oil company and Barbara raised their children. Associated with traditional family values, Mrs. Bush campaigned for her husband and endeared herself by her active commitment to literacy.

● **SKILL DEVELOPMENT**

Critical Thinking
Have students examine the logic of Anthony's argument and point out its strengths and weaknesses. Invite students to identify the consequences of her argument.

Appendix of Speeches   577

their enjoyment of the blessings of liberty while they are denied the use of the only means of securing them provided by this democratic-republican government—the ballot.

For any state to make sex qualification that must ever result in the disfranchisement[1] of one entire half of the people is to pass a bill of attainder, or an *ex post facto*[2] law, and is therefore a violation of the supreme law of the land. By it the blessings of liberty are forever withheld from women and their female posterity. To them this government has no just powers derived from the consent of the governed. To them this government is not a democracy. It is not a republic. It is an odious aristocracy; a hateful oligarchy[3] of sex; the most hateful aristocracy ever established on the face of the globe. An oligarchy of wealth, where the rich govern the poor, or an oligarchy of learning, where the educated govern the ignorant, might be endured; but not this oligarchy of sex, which makes father, brothers, husband, sons, the oligarchs over the mothers and sisters, the wife and daughters of every household—which ordains all men sovereigns, all women subjects, carries dissension, discord, and rebellion into every home of the nation.

Webster, Worcester, and Bouvier[4] all define a citizen to be a person in the United States, entitled to vote and hold office.

The only question left to be settled now is: Are women persons? And I hardly believe any of our opponents will have the hardihood to say they are not. Being persons, then, women are citizens; and no State has a right to make any law, or to enforce any old law, that shall abridge their privileges or immunities. Hence, every discrimination against women in the constitutions and laws of the several States is today null and void.

● **INSPIRATIONAL SPEECH**

Choice and Change
Barbara Bush

When Barbara Bush was invited to give this commencement speech at Wellesley College, a number of the students at the college protested the choice on the grounds that, since she was not herself a career woman, Mrs. Bush was not an appropriate role model for the graduates. Her speech focused on the challenge facing many contemporary women: how to balance both

---

[1] **disfranchisement** (dis fran' chiz mənt): denial of the rights of citizenship, especially of the right to vote.
[2] **ex post facto** (eks pōst fak'tō) Latin: "from after the fact," a term applied to laws having a retroactive effect, especially when these laws deny previously established legal rights. *Ex post facto* laws are expressly prohibited by the United States Constitution.
[3] **oligarchy** (äl' ə gär' kē): a type of government in which power rests with a small group of people.
[4] **Noah Webster, Joseph Emerson Worcester, and John Bouvier:** lexicographers, or makers of dictionaries. Bouvier's *A Law Dictionary Adapted to the Constitution and Laws of the United States and the Several States of the American Union* was the standard legal dictionary of his day.

TEACH

● SKILL DEVELOPMENT

Storytelling
Have students read the anecdote about the mermaid and practice telling that story to members of the class. Discuss why the story is so engaging and memorable. Encourage students to evaluate storytelling techniques used by members of the class.

Creative Thinking
Ask students to analyze the second paragraph of Mrs. Bush's speech and identify the technique she uses to establish common ground with the many dubious graduates she addressed.

Review the background notes with students. Ask students how they might have tried to win over the audience.

APPENDIX OF SPEECHES

career and family responsibilities. Mrs. Bush combined humor and humility to eventually win over many of Wellesley's dubious students, and, in the process, found her speech widely circulated as a significant address.

Thank you President Keohane, Mrs. Gorbachev, trustees, faculty, parents, Julie Porer, Christine Bicknell, and the class of 1990. I am thrilled to be with you today, and very excited, as I know you must all be, that Mrs. Gorbachev could join us.

More than ten years ago when I was invited here to talk about our experiences in the People's Republic of China, I was struck by both the natural beauty of your campus and the spirit of this place. Wellesley, you see, is not just a place, but an idea, an experiment in excellence in which diversity is not just tolerated, but is embraced.

The essence of this spirit was captured in a moving speech about tolerance given last year by the student body president of one of your sister colleges. She related the story by Robert Fulghum about a young pastor who, finding himself in charge of some very energetic children, hit upon a game called "Giants, Wizards, and Dwarfs." "You have to decide now," the pastor instructed the children, "which you are: a giant, a wizard, or a dwarf?" At that, a small girl tugging on his pants leg, asked, "But where do the mermaids stand?"

The pastor told her there are no mermaids. "Oh yes there are," she said, "I am a mermaid."

This little girl knew what she was and she was not about to give up on either her identity or the game. She intended to take her place wherever mermaids fit into the scheme of things. Where do the mermaids stand, all those who are different, those who do not fit the boxes and the pigeon holes? "Answer that question," wrote Fulghum, "and you can build a school, a nation, or a whole world on it."

As that very wise young woman said, "Diversity, like anything worth having, requires *effort*." Effort to learn about and respect difference, to be compassionate with one another, and to cherish our own identity, and to accept unconditionally the same in all others.

You should all be very proud that this is the Wellesley spirit. Now I know your first choice for today was Alice Walker, known for *The Color Purple*. Instead you got me, known for the color of my hair! Of course Alice Walker's book has a special resonance here. At Wellesley, each class is known by a special color, and for four years the class of '90 has worn the color purple. Today you meet on Severance Green to say goodbye to all that, to begin a new and very personal journey, a search for your own true colors.

In the world that awaits you beyond the shores of Lake Waban, no one can say what your true colors will be. But this I know: You have a first-class education from a first-class school. And so you need not, probably cannot, live a "paint-by-numbers" life. Decisions are not irrevocable. Choices do come back. As you set off from Wellesley, I hope that many of you will consider making three very special choices.

The first is to believe in something larger than yourself, to get involved in some of the big ideas of your time. I chose literacy because I honestly believe that if more people could read, write, and comprehend, we would be that much closer to solving so many of the problems plaguing our society.

Early on I made another choice which I hope you will make as well. Whether you are talking about education, career, or service, you are talking about life, and life must have joy. It's supposed to be fun!

One of the reasons I made the most important decision of my life, to marry George Bush, is because he made me laugh. It's true, sometimes we've laughed through our tears, but that shared laughter has been one of our strongest bonds. Find the joy in life, because as Ferris Bueller said on his day off, "Life moves pretty fast. Ya don't stop and look around once in a while, ya gonna miss it!"

The third choice that must not be missed is to cherish your human connection, your relationships with friends and family. For several years, you've had impressed upon you the importance to your career of dedication and hard work. This is true, but as important as your obligations as a doctor, lawyer, or business leader will be, you are a human being first and those human connections, with spouses, with children, with friends, are the most important investments you will ever make.

At the end of your life, you will never regret not having passed one more test, not winning one more verdict, or not closing one more deal. You will regret time not spent with a husband, a friend, a child, or a parent.

We are in a transitional period right now, fascinating and exhilarating times, learning to adjust to the changes and the choices we, men and women, are facing. I remember what a friend said, on hearing her husband lament to his buddies that he had to babysit. Quickly setting him straight, my friend told her husband that when it's your own kids, it's not called babysitting.

Maybe we should adjust faster, maybe slower. But whatever the era, whatever the times, one thing will never change: fathers and mothers. If you have children, they must come first. Your success as a family, our success as a society, depends not on what happens at the White House, but on what happens inside your house.

For over fifty years, it was said that the winner of Wellesley's annual hoop race would be the first to get married. Now they say the winner will be the first to become a C.E.O. Both of these stereotypes show too little tolerance for those who want to know where the mermaids stand. So I offer you today a new legend: the winner of the hoop race will be the first to realize her dream, not society's dream, her own personal dream. And who knows, somewhere out in this audience may even be someone who will one day follow in my footsteps, and preside over the White House as the president's spouse. I wish him well.

The controversy ends here. But our conversation is only beginning, and a worthwhile conversation it is. So as you leave Wellesley today, take with you deep thanks for the courtesy and honor you have shared with

TEACH

● **MOTIVATION**

Play a recording of the "I Have a Dream" speech for the class. Pause and give a moment of silence for reflection. Discuss the impact of the speech and encourage students to think of some of the factors that contribute to its power.

● **CURRICULAR CONNECTIONS**

History
Have students identify some of the significant demonstrations for freedom in the history of our nation. Discuss King's claim that the August 28, 1963, demonstration was the "greatest."

● **SKILL DEVELOPMENT**

Critical Thinking
Have students compare the opening paragraph of Lincoln's Gettysburg address (p. 584) with King's second paragraph. Ask volunteers to read the two paragraphs out loud. Discuss what King may have been trying to accomplish with this allusion to the Gettysburg Address.

APPENDIX OF SPEECHES

Mrs. Gorbachev and me. Thank you. God bless you. And may your future be worthy of your dreams.

● **SPEECH OF INSPIRATION AND PERSUASION**

I Have a Dream
Martin Luther King, Jr.

Delivered on August 28, 1963, before a crowd of 200,000 people in front of the Lincoln Memorial in Washington, D.C., the landmark speech of Martin Luther King, Jr. dealing with freedom for "all of God's children" stands as a monument to his personal dedication to racial equality. Many speech scholars consider it one of the great speeches of the twentieth century. Before he spoke, King refined and sharpened the text until the eloquence of the language proclaimed his mission to utterly erase inequality from America.

I am happy to join with you today in what will go down in history as the greatest demonstration for freedom in the history of our nation.

Five score years ago, a great American, in whose symbolic shadow we stand today, signed the Emancipation Proclamation. This momentous decree came as a great beacon light of hope to millions of Negro slaves who had been seared in the flames of withering injustice. It came as a joyous daybreak to end the long night of our captivity.

But one hundred years later, the Negro is still not free. One hundred years later, the life of the Negro is still sadly crippled by the manacles of segregation and the chains of discrimination. One hundred years later, the Negro lives on a lonely island of poverty in the midst of a vast ocean of material prosperity. One hundred years later, the Negro is still anguished in the corners of American society and finds himself an exile in his own land. And so we've come here today to dramatize a shameful condition.

In a sense we've come to our nation's Capitol to cash a check. When the architects of our republic wrote the magnificent words of the Constitution and the Declaration of Independence, they were signing a promissory note to which every American was to fall heir. This note was a promise that all men—yes, black men as well as white men—would be guaranteed the unalienable rights of life, liberty, and the pursuit of happiness.

It is obvious today that America has defaulted on this promissory note insofar as her citizens of color are concerned. Instead of honoring this sacred obligation, America has given the Negro people a bad check—a check which has come back marked "insufficient funds."

But we refuse to believe that the bank of justice is bankrupt. We refuse to believe that there are insufficient funds in the great vaults of opportunity of this nation. And so we've come to cash this check—a check that will give us upon demand the riches of freedom and the security of justice.

We have also come to this hallowed spot to remind America of the fierce urgency of *now*. This is no time to engage in the luxury of cooling off or to take the tranquillizing drug of gradualism. Now is the time to make real the promises of democracy. Now is the time to rise from the dark and desolate valley of segregation to the sunlit path of racial justice. Now is the time to lift our nation from the quicksands of racial injustice to the solid rock of brotherhood. Now is the time to make justice a reality for all of God's children.

It would be fatal for the nation to overlook the urgency of the moment. This sweltering summer of the Negro's legitimate discontent will not pass until there is an invigorating autumn of freedom and equality. Nineteen sixty-three is not an end, but a beginning. Those who hope that the Negro needed to blow off steam and will now be content will have a rude awakening if the nation returns to business as usual. There will be neither rest nor tranquillity in America until the Negro is granted his citizenship rights. The whirlwinds of revolt will continue to shake the foundations of our nation until the bright day of justice emerges.

But there is something that I must say to my people, who stand on the warm threshold which leads into the palace of justice. In the process of gaining our rightful place, we must not be guilty of wrongful deeds. Let us not seek to satisfy our thirst for freedom by drinking from the cup of bitterness and hatred.

We must forever conduct our struggle on the high plane of dignity and discipline. We must not allow our creative protest to degenerate into physical violence. Again and again we must rise to the majestic heights of meeting physical force with soul force.

The marvelous new militancy which has engulfed the Negro community must not lead us to a distrust of all white people. For many of our white brothers, as evidenced by their presence here today, have come to realize that their destiny is tied up with our destiny. They have come to realize that their freedom is inextricably bound to our freedom. We cannot walk alone.

As we walk, we must make the pledge that we shall always march ahead. We cannot turn back. There are those who are asking the devotees of civil rights, "When will you be satisfied?" We can never be satisfied as long as the Negro is the victim of the unspeakable horrors of police brutality. We can never be satisfied as long as our bodies, heavy with the fatigue of travel, cannot gain lodging in the motels of the highways and the hotels of the cities. We cannot be satisfied as long as a Negro in Mississippi cannot vote and a Negro in New York believes he has nothing for which to vote. No, no, we are not satisfied, and we will not be satisfied until justice rolls down like waters, and righteousness like a mighty stream.

I am not unmindful that some of you have come here out of great trials and tribulations. Some of you have come fresh from narrow jail cells. Some of you have come from areas where your quest for freedom left you battered by the storms of persecution and staggered by the winds of police

---

TEACH

● **LEARNING STYLES**

Multicultural Learning
Ask small groups of students to discuss the relative appeal of King's speech to various groups in American society. Discuss the elements in the speech that give it universal appeal. Focus on the expression "we cannot walk alone" and ask students how that applies to today's world.

● **SKILL DEVELOPMENT**

15-Second Skill Opportunity
Ask students to select a paragraph from this speech and prepare to deliver it to the class. Give volunteers the opportunity to deliver the speech segment.

TEACH

● SKILL DEVELOPMENT

15-Second Skill Opportunity
Ask students to select one of the dream paragraphs and prepare to deliver it to the class.

Creative Thinking
Ask students to imagine their own dream for American society. Have them write a short 3 to 5 line statement about their dream and deliver that statement to the class.

● LEARNING STYLES

Cooperative Learning
Ask small groups of students to develop a "report card" for the nation to evaluate the progress and failures the nation has made in the area of civil rights. Have groups display their report cards and explain the reasons for the grades they gave.

APPENDIX OF SPEECHES

brutality. You have been the veterans of creative suffering. Continue to work with the faith that unearned suffering is redemptive.

Go back to Mississippi, go back to Alabama, go back to South Carolina, go back to Georgia, go back to Louisiana, go back to the slums and ghettos of our Northern cities, knowing that somehow this situation can and will be changed. Let us not wallow in the valley of despair.

I say to you today, my friends, so even though we face the difficulties of today and tomorrow, I still have a dream. It is a dream deeply rooted in the American dream.

I have a dream that one day this nation will rise up and live out the true meaning of its creed, "We hold these truths to be self-evident, that all men are created equal."

I have a dream that one day on the red hills of Georgia the sons of former slaves and the sons of former slaveowners will be able to sit down together at the table of brotherhood.

I have a dream that one day even the state of Mississippi, a state sweltering with the heat of injustice, sweltering with the heat of oppression, will be transformed into an oasis of freedom and justice.

I have a dream that my four little children will one day live in a nation where they will not be judged by the color of their skin but by the content of their character. I have a dream today.

I have a dream that one day, down in Alabama, with its vicious racists, with its governor having his lips dripping with the words of interposition and nullification, one day right there in Alabama little black boys and black girls will be able to join hands with little white boys and white girls as sisters and brothers. I have a dream today.

I have a dream that one day every valley shall be exalted, every hill and mountain shall be made low, the rough places will be made plain and the crooked places will be made straight, and the glory of the Lord shall be revealed, and all flesh shall see it together.

This is our hope. This is the faith that I go back to the South with. With this faith, we will be able to hew out of the mountain of despair a stone of hope. With this faith we will be able to transform the jangling discords of our nation into a beautiful symphony of brotherhood. With this faith we will be able to work together, to pray together, to struggle together, to go to jail together, to stand up for freedom together, knowing that we will be free one day.

This will be the day—this will be the day when all of God's children will be able to sing with new meaning, "My country 'tis of thee, sweet land of liberty, of thee I sing. Land where my fathers died, land of the pilgrim's pride, from every mountainside, let freedom ring." And if America is to be a great nation, this must become true.

So let freedom ring from the prodigious hilltops of New Hampshire. Let freedom ring from the mighty mountains of New York. Let freedom ring from the heightening Alleghenies of Pennsylvania!

Let freedom ring from the snowcapped Rockies of Colorado! Let freedom ring from the curvaceous slopes of California!

MOTIVATION

You might invite the physics teacher to speak to the class briefly about the consequences of the "Quantum Theory" developed by Max Planck.

SKILL DEVELOPMENT

Creative Thinking
Invite students to think of the most creative ideas that have influenced civilization. List their suggestions on the chalkboard. Have small groups of students identify what they consider to be the three most creative breakthroughs in history.

But not only that. Let freedom ring from Stone Mountain of Georgia!
Let freedom ring from Lookout Mountain of Tennessee!
Let freedom ring from every hill and molehill of Mississippi. From every mountainside, let freedom ring.

And when this happens, when we allow freedom to ring—when we let it ring from every village and every hamlet, from every state and every city—we will be able to speed up that day when all of God's children, black men and white men, Jews and Gentiles, Protestants and Catholics, will be able to join hands and sing in the words of the old Negro spiritual, "Free at last! Free at last! Thank God Almighty, we are free at last!"

● EULOGY

Max Planck in Memoriam
Albert Einstein

Physicist and philosopher Albert Einstein—twice winner of the Nobel Prize and formulator of the theory of relativity—gave this speech in 1948 at memorial services for fellow physicist Max Planck. Planck, father of the theory of quantum mechanics, which states that energy such as light takes the form of small packets, or "quanta," is considered by many people to be the most important physicist of the twentieth century. Einstein begins his eulogy by praising the work of Planck and explaining the significance of this work. Einstein ends by making a persuasive appeal for free and unhampered research in the sciences.

A man to whom it has been given to bless the world with a great creative idea has no need for the praise of posterity. His very achievement has already conferred a higher boon upon him.

Yet it is good—indeed, it is indispensable—that representatives of all who strive for truth and knowledge should be gathered here today from the four corners of the globe. They are here to bear witness that even in these times of ours, when political passion and brute force hang like swords over the anguished and fearful heads of men, the standard of our ideal search for truth is being held aloft undimmed. This ideal, a bond forever uniting scientists of all times and in all places, was embodied with rare completeness in Max Planck.

Even the Greeks had already conceived the atomistic[1] nature of matter and the concept was raised to a high degree of probability by the scientists of the nineteenth century. But it was Planck's law of radiation that yielded the first exact determination—independent of other assumptions—of the absolute magnitudes[2] of atoms. More than that, he showed convincingly

---

[1] **atomistic** (at' ə mis' tik): of or related to atoms, the tiny particles of which the elements constituting the world are made.
[2] **magnitudes** (mag' nə tōōdz): measurable sizes or quantities.

TEACH

AMAZING FACTS!

The man who was to introduce President Lincoln at Gettysburg was a well-known public speaker, Edward Everett. His speech of introduction took two hours. Lincoln's remarks took about two minutes, but the weary crowd barely applauded when it was finished.

● SKILL DEVELOPMENT

Decision by Committee

Have each student practice the delivery of the Gettysburg Address. Provide time for students to read the speech privately and aloud. Then concentrate on the use of voice and gestures for emphasis. Students could practice giving the speech in small groups. Then each group could nominate the best to give the speech before the entire class.

● CURRICULAR CONNECTIONS

History

Some students could provide background about the battle at Gettysburg during the Civil War. Photos of the scene could be displayed.

---

584 APPENDIX OF SPEECHES

that in addition to the atomistic structure of matter there is a kind of atomistic structure to energy, governed by the universal constant h,[3] which was introduced by Planck.

This discovery became the basis of all twentieth-century research in physics and has almost entirely conditioned its development ever since. Without this discovery it would not have been possible to establish a workable theory of molecules and atoms and the energy processes that govern their transformations. Moreover, it has shattered the whole framework of classical mechanics[4] and electrodynamics[5] and set science a fresh task: that of finding a new conceptual basis for all physics. Despite remarkable partial gains, the problem is still far from a satisfactory solution.

In paying homage[6] to this man, the American National Academy of Sciences expresses its hope that free research, for the sake of pure knowledge, may remain unhampered and unimpaired.

● SPEECH OF DEDICATION

The Gettysburg Address
President Abraham Lincoln

In the first three days of July, 1863, a crucial battle of the Civil War took place in the farmland outside the town of Gettysburg, in southeastern Pennsylvania. This battle proved to be a turning point in the war. On November 19 of the same year, a solemn ceremony was held to dedicate a new cemetery for the soldiers who had died in the Battle of Gettysburg. President Lincoln spoke briefly and simply in honor of the dead and in the hope that the Union would endure. In his speech, Lincoln said that, "The world will little note, nor long remember what we say here." Ironically, the world has in fact remembered what was said at Gettysburg, for Lincoln's speech is universally acknowledged to be a masterpiece. As you read the speech, notice the simplicity of Lincoln's word choice and the careful phrasing of his sentences. Also notice his use of the rhetorical device known as parallelism—the repetition, with slight changes, of phrases and grammatical structures.

Four score and seven years ago our fathers brought forth on this continent a new nation, conceived in Liberty, and dedicated to the proposition that all men are created equal.

Now we are engaged in a great civil war, testing whether that nation, or any nation so conceived and so dedicated, can long endure. We are met on

---

[3] h: an algebraic symbol standing for an invariant quantity of energy, used in physical calculations.
[4] **classical mechanics** (klas' i k'l mə kan' iks): in physics, the body of theory concerning motion and force derived from the work of Galileo and Newton.
[5] **electrodynamics** (i lek' trō dī nam' iks): the branch of physics that deals with electric and magnetic forces.
[6] **homage** (häm' ij, äm' ij): due honor or respect.

a great battle-field of that war. We have come to dedicate a portion of that field, as a final resting place for those who here gave their lives that that nation might live. It is altogether fitting and proper that we should do this.

But, in a larger sense, we can not dedicate—we can not consecrate—we can not hallow—this ground. The brave men, living and dead, who struggled here, have consecrated it, far above our poor power to add or detract. The world will little note, nor long remember what we say here, but it can never forget what they did here. It is for us the living, rather, to be dedicated here to the unfinished work which they who fought here have thus far so nobly advanced. It is rather for us to be here dedicated to the great task remaining before us—that from these honored dead we take increased devotion to that cause for which they gave the last full measure of devotion—that we here highly resolve that these dead shall not have died in vain—that this nation, under God, shall have a new birth of freedom—and that government of the people, by the people, for the people, shall not perish from the earth.

● COMMENCEMENT ADDRESS

Saving Our Cities
Tom Gerety

President of Trinity College, Tom Gerety in his 1992 commencement address spoke to what was for him a significant public question: Why have our cities so declined that greater and greater numbers of our people will no longer live and work in them, and what is the solution? He compares our cities to an "American South Africa, separated out into camps: to one side, the prosperous and choosing; to the other, those for whom there is no chance of prosperity and little to choose from."

I grew up in the country, or what seemed to me the country. We had fields all around our house, with woods beyond them. In the spring, Mr. Ference came with his tractor to turn the ground and plant rows of corn and potatoes. All summer we would hide in the cornrows or make our way through them to their mysterious honeysuckled borders, near the stonewall at the edge of the woods. Three giant maples stood astride the fields, perhaps a quarter mile back from our yard.

To me the country meant solitude: there was no one to play with except my own bothers. Across the street from us lived Newton Hawkins and his sister, an ancient pair in an ancient house. Because of his name, I will forever associate them with the invention and production of what to me was the most exquisite delicacy of my childhood, the fig newton. They drew their water from a well and had no plumbing. They were reported to be the last of their line; they and their ancestors farmed land that, over two centuries, had been sold down to less than an acre.

On holidays we always went to the city. New York City was to me, in those first few years after the second world war, a splendid if somewhat

TEACH

● **SKILL DEVELOPMENT**

Critical Thinking
Ask students to focus on the term "crabgrass frontier" and try to define it. Then challenge them to think of an alternate term that describes the condition the speaker refers to.

● **SKILL APPLICATION**

Trends
Ask students to identify the ten most populous cities in the United States. Then ask each student to imagine that they could make a choice about which of those cities to live in. Their decision should factor in available jobs, population trends, and economic growth, as well as educational and cultural opportunities. Ask volunteers to identify the city of their choice and the reasons for the selection.

APPENDIX OF SPEECHES

daunting gathering of people, places, zoos, skyscrapers, museums and shops. My immigrant grandparents lived there with hot pretzels and strong brogues and close neighbors.

All my life I have loved cities, loved them as only a child of the country can love them, as a convert, a yearner, a dreamer for whom they live partly in fantasy and ideal. As soon as I could get away from the country I did: to Paris for the last year of high school, to Lima, Peru, for one year of college, to New Haven and Chicago and Pittsburgh and Cincinnati—and now to Hartford. Cities have always held out to me the promise, even in their sounds and smells, of adventure, of ideas, of music and art, of market and conversation.

Few of us can be blessed with the wisdom to know more than a portion of what really goes on around us. Was it Hegel who said that what is familiar is what is hardest to see and understand? For children, time meanders among a few landmarks: the corner store, the playground, the walk or ride to school. Later, time rushes by, or seems to, no longer a rivulet but a river.

Coming back to Connecticut after years away, I had the impression, on Hartford's streets, that little had changed: the three-family houses on Crescent and Broad, the kids in the doorways, the bustle of commuters downtown; this looked to me like New Haven or Bridgeport twenty years before when I was still a student.

But in my lifetime, and in yours, a great shift has taken place in the life of cities.

My father and mother moved to the country to rear a family in green and quiet, near woods and fields. But my father was no country-person; he was a new variety of American: a suburbanite. He commuted by train to the city; all over the United States (and a little later over much of Europe) commuters in cars and trains were building houses farther and farther from the great centers of work and culture. Soon the farms began to disappear; both the Hawkins died; Mr. Ference no longer baled hay in the heat at the end of summer.

Millions and millions of us have participated in this process of transformation. What one scholar has called the "crabgrass frontier" has lured us on as irresistibly as the Western frontier did in the 19th Century.

"First, the people went to the suburbs to live," someone said to me last year. "Then the shops went to the suburbs; and now the jobs are moving to the suburbs."

What I saw as a child was a lush countryside and an equally lush, if very different, city.

What I did not see—and what now we cannot fail to see—is that the America of suburbs leaves neither the countryside nor the cities intact. And plainly it is the cities that suffer most.

Several days after the riot in Los Angeles, commentators began to compare what had happened there with the riots of the late 1960s. The photographs showed what had become of neighborhoods and streets in Newark and Detroit and Chicago, burned out and vandalized a long time ago. With few exceptions, they remain now, a quarter-century later, just as they were in the days *after* their riots. Stores that were burnt down often do not reopen; houses rarely go up again in a neighborhood destroyed in a night.

What happened in Los Angeles, in anarchy and anger, is striking and vivid to us now, as it should be. But it should be no more vivid or striking than what we see around us in nearly every city in the nation.

Those who can choose where they will live or work are choosing too often *against* cities. The result, should we let this go on much longer, will be that our cities will die. In their place will rise up "edge" cities, built up around monotonous succession of malls—for shopping, for work, for schooling, for housing, for entertainment, and, above all, for parking.

What we will lose should America lose its cities is incalculable. Some, like Jane Jacobs, the great champion of street-life, believe that without cities a nation can have no economic future. She argues from history: great cities bring together the skills and energy and markets that foster industry and invention.

It is a good argument. Still it may prove false; perhaps we can have a strong economy without strong cities.

There are even better arguments for saving our cities.

Whatever our economic future, our cultural future without cities is barren and meager. If somehow invention and industry survive without cities, will theaters and museums and symphonies? Cities provide the one ecological niche where human beings push themselves to greater and greater achievements not only in commerce but in all the arts, especially the highest and most complex.

Patriotism, too, requires of us a standard of national achievement. We cannot lose our pride in our cities without losing some measure of our pride in our nation. To say of this country that it will someday soon have no great cities, nothing to compare to Paris or Budapest, to Delhi or Cairo, is to say that we will have no settlements of cultural and economic stature to stand alongside those of other nations.

Finally, America's cities are the great integrators of our people, of the new immigrant from Laos, Haiti or Nicaragua along with the old immigrant from Poland or Italy, Ireland or England. Cities bring us together and teach us new ideas and new possibilities. They teach us to live with one another; they permit us to see close up what we all share of the human condition, of its virtues, its vices, and its variable genius for everything from baking to poetry.

When I look out on your future, leaving school as you do in a time of some uncertainty, I have no fear for you as individuals. You are a sturdy, bright, and tenacious class. If the world does not at first open its arms to you, it will, in time, if you persevere.

But I do fear for America. We seem as a nation to have fallen into cynicism and apathy; drift seems our only response to what ails us. On our urban frontiers we give way to a greater and greater divide between those who can make choices in their lives and those who cannot. In this direction

---

TEACH

● **SKILL DEVELOPMENT**

Critical Thinking
Examine the arguments for saving our cities. Make a list and summarize them. Students could discuss which arguments are the most persuasive.

Creative Thinking
Small groups of students could suggest ways to improve the quality of life in the largest city near your school. They could imagine that they are presenting a case before the local government to request a grant to implement a program they think will benefit the city.

TEACH

● MOTIVATION

Prepare students for the speech delivered by Senator Carol Moseley-Braun by explaining that her speech is considered significant for several reasons: (1) she is the first African-American woman elected to the United States Senate; 2) her speech is a eulogy for Thurgood Marshall, the first black Supreme Court Justice; and 3) this was her first speech in the Senate.

● SKILL APPLICATION

Debate
Students could debate the fate of American cities. Some could argue that our cities will become an "American South Africa, separated out into camps." Others could argue that our cities are the hope of our democracy.

APPENDIX OF SPEECHES

lies an American South Africa, separated out into camps; to one side, th[e] prosperous and choosing; to the other, those for whom there is no chanc[e] of prosperity and little to choose from. Our cities in this bleak vision will b[e] the Sowetos of our South Africa: segregated, impoverished, disordered– and without much hope.

This need not happen; we have it in our power to stop it, you and [I.] We can call America to its senses and restore its pride in *all* its settlement[s.]

I charge you, then, with the care of our cities and of their citizen[s.] Athens, said Thucydides, was the teacher of Greece. Our cities, too, teac[h] the glory and promise of America. In forsaking them we forsake the hop[e] of our democracy.

● SPEECH IN TRIBUTE

To Thurgood Marshall
Carol Moseley-Braun

On January 26, 1993, the newly elected United States Senator from Illinoi[s,] Carol Moseley-Braun, gave her first speech to the Senate. Historically, th[e] first, or "maiden," speech by a new member of a legislative branch was con[-] sidered a significant indication of the speaker's future political career. Toda[y] the importance of such a first speech is less than it once was. Still, her fir[st] speech led Illinois Senator Paul Simon to remark: "I do not know that any[-] one was aware those were her first comments on the floor of the Senat[e.] I think it appropriate that Senator Carol Moseley-Braun, who is herself [a] pioneer, should in her first remarks, pay tribute to someone who was [a] pioneer."

Mr. President, Thurgood Marshall died last Sunday of heart failure. I sti[ll] have great difficulty believing it. I know he was born over 84 years ag[o] and I know that he himself said he was "old and falling apart," but it i[s] nonetheless hard to conceive that a heart as mighty and as courageous a[s] his is no longer beating.

Thurgood Marshall epitomized the best in America; he was, in fac[t,] what this country is all about. That may seem to be an odd thing to sa[y] about him. After all, he himself was very aware of the fact that the Unite[d] States did not, and in too many instances does not, live up entirely to h[is] founding principles. He knew that the phrases of the Declaration of Inde[-] pendence, "that all men are created equal" and are endowed "with certai[n] inalienable rights," including those to "life, liberty and the pursuit of hap[-] piness…," were not, all too much of the time, the principles that gover[n] everyday life in America.

Thurgood Marshall was born in Baltimore in 1908. He lived and felt th[e] humiliation of racism, of not being able even to use the bathroom in down[-] town Baltimore simply because of the color of his skin.

But Thurgood Marshall was not defeated by racism. He knew tha[t] racial inequality was incompatible with American ideals, and he made it h[is]

Appendix of Speeches 589

life's unending fight to see that this country's ideals became true for all of its citizens.

And what a fight it has been. It took Thurgood Marshall from Baltimore's segregated public schools to Lincoln University, where he graduated with honors, to Howard University Law School, to the NAACP, to the circuit bench, to the U.S. Solicitor General's office, to become the first African-American member of the U.S. Supreme Court.

That quick biography does not begin to measure the battles Thurgood Marshall fought and won, and the strength, conviction and power he put into the fight.

Thomas Jefferson said that "A little rebellion, now and then, is a good thing, and as necessary in the political world as storms in the physical." Thurgood Marshall took Jefferson at his word, and played a key role in creating a rebellion in America, a rebellion not of violence, but of law. What Marshall did was to use the U.S. legal system to bludgeon and destroy state-supported segregation.

What Marshall did was to use the courts and the law to force the United States to apply the promises made every American in our Declaration of Independence and our Bill of Rights to African-Americans who had little or no protection under the law up until the Marshall legal rebellion. What Marshall did was to make the 13th, 14th, and 15th amendments to our Constitution the law of the land in reality, instead of just an empty promise.

The history of the civil rights movement in this country is, in no small part, the history of Marshall's battles before the Supreme Court. As lead counsel of the National Association for the Advancement of Colored People, Marshall appeared before the Supreme Court 32 times, and won 29 times. His legal skills, grounded in sound preparation and sensitivity to the evidence, helped him win such landmark decisions as Smith versus Allwright, Shelley versus Kramer, Sweatt versus Painter, and the biggest case of them all, Brown versus Board of Education.

I am somewhat reluctant to dwell on Thurgood Marshall's many successes, because I know he would not like it. He would not like it because he knew only too well that there are many more battles that must be fought and won if America's founding principles and American reality are to become one and the same for every American of every color. In his dissent in the Bakke case, Marshall said:

> The position of the Negro today in America is the tragic but inevitable consequence of centuries of unequal treatment. Measured by any benchmark of comfort or achievement, meaningful equality remains a distant dream for the Negro.

However, the fact that the battle is not yet won does not lessen Marshall's many accomplishments. He was a man who worked and fought to make a difference; he was a man who did make a difference.

He certainly made a difference in my life, opening the doors of opportunity measured only by merit. He helped ensure that I was able to attend public schools and the University of Chicago Law School, and not schools

---

TEACH

● **LEARNING STYLES**

Multicultural Learning
Ask students to identify the major historical experiences of racism in the United States and develop a timeline to identify the major events of the civil rights movement. Have students discuss what the speaker meant when she said "But Thurgood Marshall was not defeated by racism." Encourage them to provide examples of others who were not defeated by racism.

TEACH

● MOTIVATION

List the following virtues and values on the chalkboard: honesty, generosity, cooperation, teamwork, loyalty, friendship, hard work, discipline, integrity, leadership, patriotism, respect, family, and education. Ask students what they think each term means. Invite them to add to the list those virtues and values they think are also important. Invite students to share examples of each with the class. Discuss how these values are learned in our society.

● SKILL DEVELOPMENT

15-Second Skill Opportunity

Ask students to take one of the quotations of Marshall in the Bakke case and prepare to deliver that remark to the class. Have students use gestures and voice to emphasize the meaning.

APPENDIX OF SPEECHES

for blacks only. His work helped make my election to the U.S. Senate possible. He opened closed doors and created new opportunities for me and for many, many others. His life was the most convincing evidence that change is possible.

I want to close, Mr. President, by quoting Thurgood Marshall one more time. In the Bakke case, he said:

> In the light of the sorry history of discrimination and its devasting impact on the lives of Negroes, bringing the Negro into the mainstream of American life should be a state interest of the highest order.

I share his view. Elimination of racism is not just an interest of African Americans, but of all Americans. Only then will we be able to tap the full potential of our people. Only then will we live the greatness of the American promise.

I hope we will all remember Thurgood Marshall by continuing his lifetime of struggle. I hope we will all remember Marshall by dedicating ourselves to the principles and goals he dedicated himself to: making American opportunity available to every American. And as we work toward those goals, I hope we can all live our lives as completely as he did, enjoy ourselves as much as he did, and poke as much fun at ourselves as Thurgood Marshall did all of his life.

I will miss Thurgood Marshall. America will miss Thurgood Marshall. I am proud to have the opportunity, in some small way, to continue his work, and to try to build on his legacy.

● MOTIVATIONAL SPEECH

The Quest for Shared Values
Robert A. Plane

Robert A. Plane, President of Wells College, delivered this speech on December 6, 1994, to the Women's Leadership Institute of the college in Aurora, New York. Its theme is a call for a return to honesty—personal honesty as well as the societal honor that Plane sees as sorely lacking in today's world.

The real cause for many of today's social problems is a lack of shared values. We would not have lawlessness, corruption, violence, crime, child neglect, and many other maladies if we had a true sense of community. But we can't have a sense of community except by having a sense of shared values.

Many societies are held together by religion which provides a built-in set of ethical values. Our country made the wise decision to allow religious freedom when it was founded. This precluded a ready-made set of common values. For a long time the absence went unnoticed because building the country was such an all-consuming activity. Merely sustaining life required hard work. Apart from patriotism, it was the work ethic or true valuing work that became a shared value. In finding ways to praise an individual, "hard-working" was the highest accolade.

As the international role of our country became more secure and as our lives were made easier by applied technology, we became sufficiently affluent and our belief in both patriotism and the work ethic diminished. Our lack of shared values started to become painfully obvious.

Today, one of the few values we share is a belief in education. Even in our increasingly diverse society, almost all of us value learning and education. But the question arises, education for what? To what end? Shouldn't education be the tool that instills values in society? Unfortunately, we have come to accept the model of "value-free" education. I would assert that such education is "value-less." Or as my Missouri mother-in-law would have asked, "What's the good of it?" The noted American educator Robert Maynard Hutchins spoke simply and eloquently on this complex subject when he said,

> Any system of education that is without values is a contradiction in terms; a system that seeks bad values is bad. A system that denies the existence of values denies the possibility of education.

Certainly education can teach us to do things. But just as technology destroyed our common work ethic, technology and other things we learn are only as good as what they produce: above all, the values they produce. Whatever our activities, whatever we learn to do—we generate outcomes. It is critically important that those outcomes serve the common good of society. They must support our shared values. Unfortunately, we don't know what those values are; and we seem unwilling to work together to formulate common values.

I believe there is one value, although sadly lacking in all of society today, that should be cherished by every one of us and serve as the cornerstone for an ethically based society. That value is *honesty*. How can we have any society, any human institution, any educational system that is not based on personal honesty? With honesty we can accomplish much. We can truly know ourselves: our strengths and our weaknesses, emphasize the former and correct the latter. We can do the same for those around us. But without honesty, we can do little to correct our own failings or those of others.

Trust, cooperation, team work, and leadership cannot exist without honesty. Yet today it is the norm that students go to college and learn how to cheat. Fortunately, students go to Wells and a small number of other colleges and universities and learn how to live by honor codes. At Wells, living by an Honor Code builds a true intellectual community based on trust and mutual respect. Students learn to balance freedom and responsibility. They must practice honesty and discern that quality in others.

I am firmly convinced that this is the unique strength of a Wells education; and a handful of other institutions in the nation, notably the University of Virginia, also include the Honor Code as an integral part of the

TEACH

● **SKILL DEVELOPMENT**

Creative Thinking
Ask students to focus on the two questions the speaker asks. Individuals or small groups could prepare a response to those questions.

● **LEARNING STYLES**

Cooperative Leaning
Have small groups of students develop an Honor Code that would be suitable for your class or school. Discuss ways to implement this code.

---

educational process. Honor codes help establish and teach values when they are practiced in a meaningful way.

Two questions seem to plague educators concerned with value-based education. The first is, what values should we teach? And the second, can they be taught? As for the first, I cannot imagine any disagreement over the question of whether or not honesty is an important and necessary value. What is the alternative? I doubt whether anyone will speak up in favor of dishonesty, but I'm afraid there are a number of examples where it is the prime outcome of many educational programs. What else comes from thoughtlessly parroting back the professor's lecture for a multiple choice exam? I hope that once such practices are seen for what they are, they will disappear. Then we will, as a society, agree to value honesty highly enough that an Honor Code will indeed be possible for everyone.

The second question asks whether it is possible to teach values. I am pleased that the history of Wells has shown that it is indeed possible to teach honesty through living the Honor Code. It isn't always easy; the second half of the Honor Code, seeing to it that violations are reported, goes against some of the commonly held misconceptions of looking down on the tattletale rather than honoring the one who serves as the conscience of the group.

We can teach and learn all aspects of honesty. Generations of Wells women have proved that fact. The hope is that the rest of society will follow Wells by adopting honor and honesty as shared values which will make this a better society. Once society has adopted these values, others can follow. We can even develop a group sense of right and wrong. It must start with honesty.

Glossary

The glossary provides an alphabetical listing of key words or terms used in this book. The chapter or chapters in which they are treated in depth are shown in parentheses.

abstract words: words that cannot be perceived directly through the senses; opposite of concrete words. (8)
adjourn: a privileged motion to legally conclude a meeting. (14)
affirmative: the side in a debate upholding the proposition being debated; the side in a debate that has the task of attacking the *status quo* and arguing for a specific change. (13)
agenda: a list of the items to be discussed at a meeting. (14)
agreed goal: a purpose or outcome on which both the affirmative and negative sides of a debate agree. (13)
amend: to change a pending motion. (14)
analogy: in public speaking, an extended comparison (8); in debate, a proof of the truth of something by showing its similarity to something else. (13)
anecdote: a short story, often humorous, that is related to a speaker's topic and is used to capture listeners' attention. (10)
antagonist: in a play, the chief opponent of the principal character. (17)
appeal: an incidental motion that allows a member who disagrees with a ruling by the chair to put that ruling to a vote. (14)
appointed leader: a person designated before the discussion begins to perform all the leadership duties. (5)
articulation: the way in which the tongue, teeth, lower jaw, and soft palate are used to produce speech sounds; the process of forming sounds into words. (2, 9)
articulators: the tongue, teeth, lower jaw, and soft palate, which are used to form sounds into recognizable words. (2)
attention device: a technique used to gain or maintain the attention of an audience. (10)
audience analysis: learning everything you can about the background, attitudes, and interests of the people who will listen to you. (7)

audition: a tryout session, as for a play. (17)
author card: a card in a library card catalogue listing a book by the author's name. (7)

bandwagon technique: the logical fallacy that asks people to become part of the supposedly overwhelming group in favor of some person, product, or idea. (3)
bard: a professional storyteller who traveled from village to village with both news and entertaining stories in ancient times. (See *minstrel*.) (16)
begging the question: the logical fallacy of stating that an idea is true without providing proof. (3)
biased: one-sided. (5)
blocking: arranging the movements on stage of actors in a play. (17)
brainstorming: rapidly suggesting ideas without taking time to evaluate each one. (5)
brief: an outline of a debate case, written in complete sentences. (13)
burden of proof: the obligation of the affirmative side in a debate to prove what is asserted by the proposition. (13)

cable TV: a television system that allows people to improve reception and increase the number of channels through reception from a cable service for a fee. (15)
callback: an additional audition for an actor whom the director wishes to see and hear again. (17)
call number: an identification number printed on each library book and on each title, author, or subject card in a library card catalogue. (7)
card catalogue: the alphabetical listing by author, title, or subject of all books located in a library. (7)
card stacking: presenting only evidence that supports the point being made. (3)
cartoon: a visual aid consisting of a funny or satirical drawing used to make a point. (10)

case: in debate, a team's argument on any given proposition. (13)

catharsis: a purifying of the emotions or relieving of emotional tensions, especially through drama. (17)

cause to effect: reasoning from what began something to its result. (13)

central idea: a main point. (3)

chair: a name given to the person presiding over a meeting. (14)

chart: a visual aid that is a drawing showing the relationships among the parts of a whole (often relies on words rather than simply on lines). (10)

choreography: dance patterns; the arrangement of the movements of a dance. (17)

chronological pattern: an organizational arrangement of a speech that proceeds from past to present to future. (7)

cliché: a brief expression of an idea or truth, one that has become almost meaningless through overuse. (8)

climax: in a play, the turning point, which reveals whether the major character will succeed or fail in solving the problem; the point of highest interest. (17)

climax ordering: stating items in a series moving from less significant to more significant and ending with the most important item. (8)

clique: a separate, tightly knit group within a larger group. (5)

closed-group discussion: communication only among group members to solve a common problem, arrive at a decision, or answer a question of mutual interest. (5)

close-minded: refusing to consider ideas that are different from your own. (3)

code: a symbol system. (2)

cohesiveness: a uniting or sticking together; group spirit; morale. (5)

Comédie Française: the first national theater in the world. This organization still exists in France today. (17)

comedy: a drama or narrative with conflict and a happy ending. (17)

comedy of manners: a style of writing and acting, used to make fun of social customs of the day; developed during the reign of Charles II of England. (17)

commedia dell'arte: a type of Italian comedy developed in the 16th century and employing a stereotyped plot, improvised dialogue, and stock characters. (17)

commemorative speech: an inspiring address designed to recall heroic events or people. (12)

commencement speech: an address to honor graduates of a school or university. (12)

commercial television: television broadcasting financed by companies who buy air time to advertise their products. (15)

committee: a small subgroup of a larger organization, one that has been given a specific task or set of tasks to perform. (5)

common ground technique: a means of gaining listener attention by identifying interests or things the speaker has in common with the audience. (10)

communication: the process of sending and receiving messages to achieve understanding. (1)

comparative advantages case: in a debate, an affirmative case that uses the agreed goals → plan → comparative advantages form of argument. (13)

comparison: the presentation of similarities between two dissimilar ideas or situations. (7)

competence: the condition of being well-qualified or capable. (11)

compromise: a settlement in which each member or group of members agrees to give up part of the solution or decision they want, retaining some other part of the solution they favor. (5)

computerized research service: a special library resource that helps locate obscure or specialized information rapidly through the use of a computer. (7)

concrete words: words that enable the listener to perceive the idea by means of the senses. (8)

confidence: belief in one's abilities. (11)

connotation: a meaning attached to a word that goes beyond the dictionary meaning. (2)

consensus: the agreement of all discussion-group members about a solution or decision. (5)

constructive speech: in a debate, a speech used to present and develop the major points of a team's case. (13)

contrast: a language device used to point up differences between similar ideas or situations. (8)

controlled stage fright: the realization that a feeling of tension is natural and can actually sharpen thinking, so that nervousness can be regulated. (6)

conversation: interpersonal communication about matters of common interest to the people involved. (4)

costume designer: the person who plans the clothes worn by actors. (17)

critical listener: one who analyzes and interprets messages carefully. (3)

cross-examination format: in a debate, the format that provides for questioning (cross-examination) by a member of the opposing team following each constructive speech. (13)

cross-examine: to question the opposing side about its arguments. (13)

cue line: in a play, one actor's last few words before the next actor speaks. (17)

cutaway: a visual aid consisting of a model with a section of the outer covering removed to show the interior parts. (10)

Glossary **595**

databases: collections of information, stored in computer files. (7)
decision-making group: a type of discussion in which members meet with the specific goal of reaching a judgment or conclusion. (5)
decode: to translate incoming information or messages into understandable concepts. (2)
dedication speech: a speech that highlights the meaning of a new creation or endeavor. (12)
deduction: reasoning from general principles to specific cases. (13)
demonstration speech: an informative speech that demonstrates a process or procedure to an audience and that usually makes use of visual aids. (10)
denotation: the basic meaning of a word. (2)
descriptive gestures: hand and arm movements used by a speaker to indicate characteristics of an object, such as size or shape. (9)
diagram: a visual aid that relies on lines rather than words to show the relationship of parts to a whole. (10)
dialogue: a conversation; passages of talk in a play. (17)
diaphragm: a thick muscle at the base of the rib cage. (2)
director: the person who stages a theatrical production, selecting and controlling everything that happens onstage. (17)
discovery: in drama, a change in the character's attitudes from ignorance to knowledge. (17)
disinterested audience: an audience that knows about the topic but is unconcerned. (11)
distraction: anything that draws the mind or attention away in another direction. (3)
division of assembly: an incidental motion requesting that a close voice vote be retaken by a show of hands or by having members rise. (14)
division of question: an incidental motion that requests the division of a motion having two or more parts into separate debate and voting. (14)
documentary: an in-depth report on one important subject. (15)
drama: public communication that uses both language and actions to tell a story of human conflict. (1, 17)
dramatic statement: a startling, attention-getting message used during a speech. (10)
drape: in costuming, the hang of a fabric. (17)
dress parade: the first onstage viewing of all costumes by the designer and the director, usually a week before first dress rehearsal. (17)

economy of language: the use of as few words as necessary to state ideas clearly. (8)

educational television: television that is broadcast on stations set aside for instructional and culturally enriching programs. (15)
effect to cause: reasoning from a result back to what started it. (13)
electronic media: technological channels of communication, such as radio and television. (15)
Elizabethan era: the time of the reign of Elizabeth I of England (1558–1603). (17)
emergent leadership: a form of leadership in which one or another of the group members will handle each function of leadership as the need arises. (5)
emphatic gestures: hand and arm movements used during a speech to stress what a speaker is saying. (9)
encode: to put a message into symbols. (2)
enlightenment group: a type of discussion in which members meet to share information. (5)
ethos: the speaker's character in the minds of the audience (including competence, sincerity, and good will). (10, 11)
eulogy: a commemorative speech honoring an individual who has died. (12)
euphemism: a gentle expression for a harsh or unpleasant reality. (8)
evidence: raw material with which you prove or support statements. (11)
example: a specific instance of something being described. (7)
exposition: in a play, the presentation of who, what, where, and why. (17)
extemporaneous method: a type of speech delivery in which speakers prepare ideas for their speeches but do not memorize exact words. (9)

fact: an event or a truth that is known to exist or has been observed. (7)
falling action: the events following the climax of a play that tie the loose ends together. (17)
false consensus: several group members keeping disagreement to themselves, allowing the outcome to be the reverse of what they desire, and leading others to believe all are in agreement. (5)
feedback: the reactions of the receiver to the message of the sender, consisting of words or nonverbal symbols. (2)
fiction: material created in the imagination. (16)
fictional speaker: the voice you hear telling a story or poem when you read literary work silently. (16)
fields of experience: areas of knowledge, interest, or involvement. (2)
figures of speech: phrases and sentences that make a point by stating something in a way that is not to be taken literally. (8)

GLOSSARY

filibustering: the extension of debate for the sole purposes of delaying or preventing a vote. (14)
floor plan: a drawing showing the position of the walls, entrances, and furniture on the stage. (17)
flow sheet: in debate, a summary outline of how the arguments on each issue are progressing. (13)
formal debate: a type of reasoned argument between parties, which is used in school contests. (13)
forming: the infancy stage of a discussion group in which members become acquainted with one another and leadership roles are established. (5)
French theater: drama in France, which in the seventeenth century included the comedies of Molière presented at the royal court. (17)

germane: logically or directly connected with the subject. (14)
glittering generality: a fine-sounding term, so vague that the exact meaning is unclear. (3)
graph: a visual aid that gives large amounts of information (usually quantitative or numerical) at a single glance. (10)
group discussion: interpersonal communication involving three or more people with a common purpose; the meeting of three or more people to solve a common problem, arrive at a decision, or answer a question of mutual interest. (1, 5)

handout: a visual aid given to each member of an audience. (10)
hasty generalization: a type of faulty reasoning occurring when the speaker does not have adequate evidence to support the broad conclusion drawn. (3)
hearing: the reception of sound. (3)
humor: an attention-getting device utilizing something funny. (10)
hyperbole: a figure of speech that consists of exaggeration used to emphasize a point. (8)

imaginary audience: the audience to whom a fictional speaker relates a story or poem. (16)
impromptu method: a type of speech delivery in which the speaker talks "off the cuff," with little or no prior preparation. (9)
impromptu speech: a short address given with no advance notice and with only a moment or two of preparation. (12)
improvisation: composing and performing on the spur of the moment, without any preparation. (17)
incidental motion: a type of formal proposal that relates to procedures concerning the conduct of parliamentary business. (14)
induction: reasoning from specific facts or cases to general principles. (13)

informative speech: a public communication in which a speaker imparts new knowledge or more in-depth information on a specific topic to an audience. (10)
ingénue: an innocent, inexperienced, unworldly young woman. (17)
initial incident: in a play, the first event to take place, from which the plot develops. (17)
insight: a clear understanding of the inner nature of some specific thing. (16)
inspirational speech: a speech whose purpose is to exert an enlivening influence on an audience. (11)
interpersonal communication: transmission of messages between two or more people. (1)
interview: a formal kind of interpersonal communication often involving two persons with a particular or definite goal in mind. (4)
interviewee: the person being interviewed. (4)
intrapersonal communication: an inward talking to oneself. (1)
irony: a figure of speech in which the literal meaning expressed is the opposite of the meaning intended. (8)
issue: a major point of disagreement in a debate. (13)

keynote speech: an inspirational address given at the opening of a large meeting or convention. (12)
kinesics: the study of the use of body motions to communicate. (2)

lack of confidence: a feeling of inadequacy often experienced when the symptoms of stage fright are uncontrolled. (6)
larynx: the voice box. (2)
lavalier microphone: an amplification device (microphone) that hangs around the neck. (9)
lay on the table: a subsidiary motion to set aside consideration of a pending matter until some time later in the same meeting. (14)
lectern: a speaker's stand. (9)
legitimate theater: in the Restoration period, the name given to theaters whose plays were passed by a censoring committee before being performed. (17)
lighting designer: a person who designs the lighting for both actors and set and who sometimes runs the controls during performances. (17)
limit or extend debate: a subsidiary motion that either restricts the time to be devoted to discussion on a pending motion or removes any time restrictions in force. (14)
Lincoln-Douglas format: a modification of the cross-examination format in which each side is represented by only one speaker; such debates usually deal with propositions of value rather than of policy. (13)

listening: understanding and interpreting sound in a meaningful way. (3)

literature: prose or poetry considered to have permanent value and excellence of form. (1, 16)

locative gestures: hand and arm movements used by a speaker to direct the listener's attention to a place, object, or person. (9)

logical fallacies: false or faulty methods or reasoning. (3)

logos: the thinking process that allows the listener to arrive at logical conclusions. (11)

lyric poetry: "song-like" poetry expressing emotions. (16)

main heads: the major divisions of an outline. (7)

main motion: a formal proposal that deals directly with an item of business. (14)

maintenance messages: communication designed to create a positive climate by keeping relationships in a group harmonious. (5)

majority vote: a decision agreed to by over half the members of the group. (5)

manuscript method: a type of speech delivery in which the speech is read to the audience. (9)

map: a visual aid showing information of a geographical nature. (10)

mass communication: one or several senders using printed or electronic media to communicate with a large number of people who are not necessarily present; one or more senders communicating with large groups of people who may be separated from each other and from the sender by great distances. (1, 15)

memorization method: a type of speech delivery in which the manuscript is learned and then delivered word-for-word without the use of manuscript. (9)

memory: the brain's storage bin; the power, act, or process of recalling to mind facts previously learned or past experiences. (2)

metaphor: a figure of speech containing a direct comparison that omits the words *like* or *as*. (8)

Middle Ages: the period of European history between ancient and modern times; the period from about A.D. 500 to about A.D. 1450. (17)

minority: fewer than half of the members of a meeting or group. (14)

minstrel: a professional storyteller of ancient times who traveled from village to village bringing news and stories or entertainment. (See *bard*.) (16)

model: a visual aid consisting of a scaled-down version of an object. (10)

monotone: speaking successive syllables or words without a change of pitch. (9)

Monroe's Motivated Sequence: a type of speech organization consisting of five steps—attention, need, satisfaction, visualization, and action. (7)

motion: a formal proposal made by a member for consideration and action by a group. (14)

name calling: faulty reasoning that gives a person or idea a bad label without providing evidence to support it. (3)

narrative: supporting material in the form of a story, either real or imaginary. (7)

narrative poetry: poems that tell stories. (16)

nasal cavities: the passages in the nose that act as resonators. (2)

need-plan wedge case: an argument in which the negative does not attack the affirmative's need or plan directly but attacks the logical link between the two. (13)

needs case: a form of affirmative argument based on a need → plan → advantages approach. (13)

negative: in a debate, the side that supports the status quo or denies or attacks the affirmative position. (13)

neutral audience: an audience that is neither for nor against a topic and needs more information in order to form an opinion. (11)

news magazine: a publication or television program that presents informative coverage of several important subjects in some depth. (15)

nominal technique: a form of decision making sometimes substituted for group discussion that involves listing, discussing, voting, and ranking of possible solutions. (5)

nonfiction: material based entirely on truth as the author understands it. (16)

non sequitur: "It does not follow" (Latin). A remark that does not logically follow from what has just been said. (3)

nonverbal: communicating without the use of words. (1)

nonverbal symbols: any means used to encode ideas without words, including gestures, facial expressions, and movements. (2)

norming: the cohesive stage in the formation of a discussion group when members learn to function effectively as a group. (5)

note cards: information cards used by a speaker to remember major points or to read direct quotes or statistics. (9)

notice: an announcement sent to inform members when an organization plans to hold a meeting. (14)

object: a visual aid that is the actual item being referred to. (10)

objection to consideration: an incidental motion that allows an assembly to avoid debate and decision on a pending motion. (14)

off book: without a script, having memorized dialogue, cues, and blocking. (17)

one-to-one communication: interpersonal communication between just two persons; speaking with only one other person. (1, 4)

open-minded: willing to listen to all aspects of a question before making a decision. (3)

opera: a musical drama. (17)

opposed audience: an audience that disagrees with the speaker's stand on a topic (11)

oral interpretation: the process by which a speaker performs literature aloud for an audience. (1, 16)

order of business: the sequence in which various items on the agenda will be taken up during a meeting. (14)

order or precedence: a ranking system that lists the order in which motions may be made and acted upon in parliamentary procedure. (14)

overconfidence: feeling self-assured without adequate reason or preparation. (6)

panel: a group that discusses a topic in front of an audience. (5)

panel-forum: a group discussion that is opened to questions or comments from the audience. (5)

paper tech: the first technical rehearsal, held without actors, involving only the director and technical staff. (17)

paralanguage: the ways in which you say words, including volume, pitch, speaking rate, and voice quality, as well as sounds that are not words. (2)

parallelism: the beginning or ending of several nearby sentences with the same single word or short phrase. (8)

parliamentarian: an expert on rules governing meetings who serves as an advisor to a chair. (14)

parliamentary inquiry: an incidental motion that requests information on the parliamentary procedure dealing with a motion under consideration. (14)

parliamentary procedure: a set of rules used to conduct a meeting in an orderly manner; the established rules of order for conducting group meetings. (14)

pathos: a listener's personal needs, drives, and desires. (11)

pattern of ideas: the flow of the main points of the speech. (7)

pay TV: closed-circuit television broadcasts that people pay an admission fee to see in a theater, or television broadcasts received in homes with special equipment that is paid for by viewers on a per-program or a monthly-fee basis. (15)

pending motion: a formal proposal that is under consideration. (14)

performing: the final stage in the formation of a discussion group when members bond and work together effectively and harmoniously. (5)

personalizing: bringing human experience into a speech through stories, humor, and specific examples. (10)

personification: a figure of speech that gives human qualities to inanimate objects, ideas, or non-human creatures. (8)

persuasion: a means by which one person can cause another to want to believe, think, or do something. (11)

pharynx: the back part of the throat; the muscular and membranous cavity of the alimentary canal leading from the mouth and nasal passages to the larynx and esophagus. (2)

picture: a visual aid in the form of a drawing, photograph, slide, filmstrip, or film. (10)

pitch: the highness or lowness of sounds. (2)

platform movement: the movement of the entire body while speaking. (6)

poetry: the communication of thought and feeling through the careful arrangement of words for their sound, rhythm, and meaning. (16)

point of order: an incidental motion requesting the attention of the chair and the assembly to an error that has just been made. (14)

positive audience: an audience that already agrees with a speaker's basic persuasive purpose. (11)

poster: a visual aid consisting of print or lettering. (10)

postpone definitely: a subsidiary motion putting off consideration of a motion with the intention of reconsidering the motion at a specific time. (14)

postpone indefinitely: a subsidiary motion to prevent further discussion or voting on a pending main motion. (14)

prepared reading: an audition reading that has been read or rehearsed before-hand. (17)

prestige: the power to impress or influence, which comes from one's character or position. (11)

previous question: a subsidiary motion to cut off debate on a pending motion and bring it to a vote at once. (14)

prima facie case: in a debate, the first responsibility of the affirmative side to present a logical argument that would convince a neutral judge who had not heard the response of the other side. (13)

privileged motion: a type of formal proposal of such an urgent nature that it may be considered ahead of any

other class of motion; question of privilege, recess, or adjournment. (14)
problem-solution pattern: a type of speech organization in which the first part of the speech describes the problem and the second part develops solutions. (7)
process of association: the connecting of new information with something already known. (3)
producer: the person who heads all organizational components of a play and is responsible for the success or failure of its production. (17)
production concept: the director's interpretation of a play. (17)
production meeting: a group session that is held during a rehearsal period to discuss changes and/or problems in a play production. (17)
production organization: the group that works together to choose, finance, cast, direct, design, construct, publicize, and perform a play. (17)
program concept: an overall plan for a television broadcast. (15)
pronunciation: the production of correct sounds and syllable stresses when speaking. (9)
propaganda: the stating of opinions as though they were proven facts. (3)
proportion: in costume design, the balancing of one thing, such as a certain color, against another. (17)
proposition: in formal debate, a statement to be debated, which can be answered by "yes" and "no" and generally demands that some specific action be taken or not be taken. (13)
prose: the ordinary form of written or spoken language, without rhyme or meter. (16)
protagonist: in a play, the principal character. (17)
proxemics: the study of spatial communication. (2)
public communication: interpersonal communication in which one or more people communicate with an audience. (11)
public discussion: group communication involving members of the group as well as listeners outside the discussion group. (5)
publicity manager: the person who provides the public with information concerning a dramatic production and its participants.
public relations speech: a persuasive speech that promotes and creates a positive image for an organization. (12)
public speaking: communicating ideas verbally to an audience.(1)
public television: television broadcasting financed mainly by company grants and donations by viewers. (15)
purpose sentence: a sentence stating the specific intent of a speech. (7)

question of fact: a discussion question dealing with whether a situation exists, under what circumstances it exists, or how it may be defined. (5, 11)
question of policy: a discussion question directed toward some course of physical or mental action, often including the word *should*. (5, 11)
question of privilege: a privileged motion that requests immediate action on an urgent matter related to the comfort, convenience, rights, or privileges of the assembly or one of its members. (14)
question of value: a discussion question revolving around the worth of an object person, or situation. (5, 11)
quorum: the number of members that must be present before any meeting can be held or any official business conducted. (14)
quotation: the verbatim statement of a person's words or writings. (10)

realism: a dramatic art style that stresses the virtues of directness and truth. (17)
reasoning: the ability to think, form judgments, and draw conclusions; the process of putting evidence together into a logical argument. (3, 11)
rebuttal: in a debate, a speech whose purpose is to refute the opposition's major arguments. (13)
receiver: one who intercepts and decodes a message. (2)
reception: the process of receiving and decoding a message from a sender. (2)
recess: a privileged motion that calls a temporary halt to the meeting in progress. (14)
recognizing: acknowledging the right of a member of an assembly to speak. (14)
refer to committee: a subsidiary motion to submit a matter to a sub-group for further deliberation. (14)
reference section: the area of a library containing works such as encyclopedias, indexes, dictionaries, and other books used to find specific information. (7)
refute: in a debate, to prove an argument or statement to be false or wrong. (13)
Renaissance: the period from about A.D. 1350 to about A.D. 1650 in Europe; a period of "rebirth" in all the arts and literature; a revival of learning. (17)
repetition: the stating of an idea more than once using the same words. (8)
resonators: the pharynx, nasal cavities, and mouth, which act as amplifiers to increase the sound of a voice. (2)
restatement: saying something again in a different way; stating an idea again using different words. (8)
Restoration: the period during the reign of Charles II of England when theaters closed by the Puritans were reopened. (17)

résumé: a typed summary of work experience. (4)
reversal: in drama, a change of fortune in which the character's actions backfire. (17)
rhetorical question: questions that are not meant to be answered aloud. (8, 10)
rising action: the series of events that develop toward the climax of a play. (17)
romanticism: a dramatic art style seeking to escape the problems of the day through imagination and thoughts of adventure and beauty. (17)
round-table discussion: a closed-group session in which information sharing or enlightenment of those taking part is usually the object. (5)
runaway stage fright: feelings of anxiety that are so intense that one loses control; the loss of control of the feelings of anxiety experienced before or during a speech or performance. (6)
running-refutation negative case: in a debate, an argument in which the negative side attacks all parts of the affirmative case. (13)
run-through: a rehearsal, as of a dramatic or musical work, straight through from beginning to end. (17)

scale model: a visual aid consisting of a smaller version of an object; a miniature set design built to illustrate spatial requirements of the stage. (17)
scenario: in drama, an outline or synopsis of a play, opera, or skit, indicating plot, characters, and setting. (17)
scene designer: the person who creates the backgrounds for a play. (17)
second: an indication that one other member of an assembly wishes to see a motion debated and acted upon. (14)
sender: one who transmits a message. (2)
setting: the time, place, environment, and surrounding circumstances of an event, story, or play. (16)
shock technique: an attention-getting device used to demand instantaneous attention from the audience by using a hard-to-believe or upsetting statement. (10)
simile: a figure of speech that presents a brief comparison of two basically unlike things using the words *like* or *as*. (8)
simple majority: at least one more than half the people who voted. (14)
sincerity: truthfulness; genuineness; straightforwardness; honesty. (11)
slang: informal language, outside of conventional or standard usage, which often comes in and goes out of style very rapidly. (8)
slice-of-life theater: a realistic, dramatic art style in which playwrights write about everyday, real-life situations, conflicts, and people. (17)
slogan: a catchy phrase that encapsulates a main idea, often restated at the end of a speech. (10)
spatial pattern: in a speech, the organization of ideas by order in space. (7)
speaking rate: the speed at which one talks. (2)
specific purpose: the intention of a speaker; that which the speaker wants the listeners to know, think, believe or do as a result of hearing a speech. (7)
specific words: words that refer to a limited class of objects. (8)
speech communication: the transmission of information or ideas by means of vocalized words. (1)
speech of acceptance: a short speech of thanks given by a recipient of a gift or award. (12)
speech of introduction: a short speech used to build enthusiasm and interest for a guest speaker. (12)
speech of presentation: a speech honoring the recipient of a gift or award. (12)
speech to entertain: a humorous speech designed primarily to relax and amuse an audience. (12)
stage fright: the nervousness felt when appearing as a speaker or performer before an audience. (6)
stage manager: in play production, the person who is in charge of the day-to-day organization needed to keep rehearsals running smoothly. (17)
standard format: the debate format in which each of the speakers gives both a constructive speech and a rebuttal. (13)
statistic: a fact stated in numerical terms. (7)
status quo: "the state in which" (Latin); the existing state of affairs at a particular time. (13)
stereotyping: assigning qualities to people or objects because they are part of a general group, without considering individual differences. (8)
storming: the adolescent stage of a discussion group in which members challenge goals and approaches in an effort to express individuality. (5)
stress: the amount of emphasis placed on different syllables in a word or on different words in a sentence. (2)
string-of-beads pattern: a type of speech organization consisting of a series of items strung together like beads on a string and tied loosely to a central theme used mainly for entertaining. (7)
structure: in drama, the form, shape, and development of a play. (17)
subheads: the subdivisions of the main heads in an outline. (7)
subject card: a card in a library card catalogue that lists a book by its specific topic. (7)
subsidiary motion: a type of motion that allows members to change the nature of a main motion or to alter the way in which it is debated or voted upon. (14)

summary: the main part of a speech conclusion in which the basic message is briefly restated. (10)

support: evidence (facts, statistics, testimony, narrative, examples, and comparisons) used in speeches to prove the accuracy of statements. (7)

suspend the rules: an incidental motion that allows members to set aside some procedural rule so that members can do something not ordinarily allowed by that rule. (14)

suspense: an attention-getting device developed by temporarily withholding specific information from the audience. (10)

symbol: anything that stands for an idea and is used for communication. (2)

symposium: a series of short, uninterrupted public speeches, often involving a panel of experts. (5)

symposium-forum: a symposium that is opened to questions or comments from the audience. (5)

syntality: the personality of a group as a whole. (5)

task messages: communication designed primarily to help a group achieve goals or complete tasks. (5)

technical language: terms used during a speech that can be easily understood only by listeners who are very knowledgeable about a specific field of thought or endeavor. (10)

technical quality: the way a piece of literature is put together. (16)

tech week: the week prior to the opening of a play in which technical problems are resolved. (17)

tension: mental or nervous strain; apprehension. (6)

testimonial: the not-always-expert opinion of a well-known person on a particular issue. (3)

testimonial speech: an address of praise or celebration honoring living persons at occasions such as weddings, retirement dinners, or roasts. (12)

testimony: the quoting or restating of opinions of others to support a point. (7)

Theater of the Absurd: a drama movement in which dramatists viewed human beings as purposeless, lonely, and out of harmony with their surroundings. (17)

theatrical event: live actors performing a plot or story before a live audience in a space serving as a stage. (17)

theme: the main purpose or message, often restated vividly at the end of a speech. (10)

thespian: an actor. (17)

thinking: the ability of humans to understand, conceive, and manipulate ideas. (2)

title card: a card listing a book by title in a library card catalogue. (7)

topical pattern: a type of speech organization in which the subject is broken down into its natural parts. (7)

trachea: the windpipe. (2)

tragedy: a play that presents serious conflict dealing with the problems of a central character and that has an unhappy or disastrous ending. (17)

tragic flaw: a weakness of character that leads to a major character's destruction. (17)

tragicomedy: a dramatic category that combines both tragic and comic elements. (17)

transition: a word, phrase, sentence, or group of sentences that relates a preceding topic to a succeeding one. (10)

transitional gestures: hand and arm movements used by a speaker to show movement from one part of a speech to another. (9)

understatement: a figure of speech highlighting the significant by treating it as insignificant. (8)

universal appeal: common, recognizable experiences or problems with which everyone can identify. (16)

unsupported assertion: a statement made without giving any supporting evidence. (13)

VCR: a videotape recording and playback device for recording television programs or viewing films.

verbal: of or by means of words. (1)

verbal symbols: spoken or written language symbols or words. (2)

videotape: a magnetic tape on which the electronic impulses of the picture and sound portions of a television program can be recorded for later viewing or rebroadcast. (15)

vocal cords: two folds of membrane, located in the larynx, which vibrate to produce sound. (2)

vocalized pause: the habit of filling in time between words or sentences with "uh," "er," "like," "you-know," or similar sounds. (4, 9)

voice quality: the uniqueness of vocal sound that enables people to recognize others by their voices alone. (2)

volume: the loudness or quietness of sound. (2)

warrant: justification or reasonable grounds for some act, statement, or belief. (5)

withdraw a motion: an incidental motion by a member who has made a motion to remove it from consideration before a vote is taken. (14)

Index

Abstract language, 229–230
Acceptance speech, 187, 387–388
Accuracy, in conversation, 92–93
Acting, as career, 546
Active listening, 67–73
Actors. *See also* Acting
 audience and, 554
 performers and, 489
Adaptation, of oral material, 512–513
Adjournment, of meeting, 463
Adventures of Huckleberry Finn, The (Twain), 514–515
Affirmative side, in debate, 417–418, 428–429
Agenda, for meeting, 452
Agreed goal, 429
Alice's Adventures in Wonderland (Carroll), 520–521
Amend, to change motion, 458
Analogy, 241, 425
Analysis
 audience, 185–186
 of informative speeches, 331–339
 of persuasive speeches, 369–373
 of speech, 278–279
Anecdote, 297–298
Announcers, 489
Anthony, Susan B., "Woman's Right to Suffrage," 576
Appeal motion, 463
Appearance
 in nonverbal communication, 101
 during speech delivery, 265–266
Appointed leader, 139
Aristotle
 drama and, 540
 ethos of, 302, 356–357
 Rhetoric of, 350
Arm-hand movements, 98–99
Articulation, 46, 270

Articulators, 46
Association, process of, 73
Associations (organizations), keynote speeches at, 393–394
Atlases, 198
Attention, of audience, 305–306
Attention device, 296
Attitude, toward public speaking, 166
Audience
 actor relationship with, 554
 analyzing, 185–186
 applying message to, 302–303
 approaches for, 354–356
 for discussion groups, 120
 evidence and, 363–364
 interest in, 361
 issuing challenge to, 315–316
 needs of (pathos), 350–356
 for oral interpretation, 525, 528–529
 perception of stage fright, 163–164, 166
 public speaking and, 168
 types of, 352–353
Auditions, 561–562
Award ceremonies, speeches at, 386

Balfour (Lord), 383
Bandwagon technique, 75–76
Bards, 504
Bar graph, 320, 322
Barriers, to listening, 63–67
BBC. *See* British Broadcasting Corporation World Service
Beauty, of oral material, 510–511
Begging the question, 76
Beginnings, of informative speeches, 295–305
Behavior, of groups, 127–133
Bias, in questions, 136

Biographical aids, 198
Birdwhistell, Ray, 319
Blocking, 563
Board of directors, 121
Body motion (kinesics), 97–99
Body movements, 264
 and public speaking, 169–171
Body of speech, analyzing, 334–336
Brainstorming, 147–148
Breathing process, 44–45, 46
Brief, in debate, 419–420
British Broadcasting Corporation (BBC) World Service, 481
Brooks, Gwendolyn, 537
Burden of proof, in debate, 418
Bush, Barbara, "Choice and Change," 577
Business calls, 103–104

Cable TV, 483
Callbacks, 561
Cards. *See* Note cards
Card stacking, 75
Careers. *See also* Interview; Performing; Producing
 actors, 546
 children's librarian, 518
 coach, 392
 communication and, 13–15
 health services administrator, 461
 high school teacher, 18
 interpreter, 271
 lobbyist, 239
 medical secretary, 74
 park ranger, 310
 Peace Corps volunteer, 43
 political candidates, 167
 public relations specialist, 197
 radio announcer, 485
 social worker, 359

602

Index **603**

systems analyst, 137
travel agent, 107
trial lawyer, 433
Carroll, Lewis, 520–521
Cartoons, 323
Case
  in debate, 419
  supporting, 422–426
Casting, 561
Catharsis, and drama, 540
Cause-to-effect reasoning, 425
Central idea, 70–71
  reinforcing, 314–315
Chair, of meeting, 453–454
Character
  analyzing, 547–549
  in drama, 543–544
  relationships of, 554
  researching, 545
  of speaker, 302–305
  voice development for, 551–553
Charisma, 360
Charts, 320
Chekhov, Anton, 543
Children's librarian, career as, 518
Choreography, 550
Chronological pattern, of speech organization, 205–206
Churchill, Winston, 225
  eulogy for, 390
  stage fright of, 160, 162
Circle graph (pie graph), 320, 323
Civic club, speech to, 332
Clarity
  in conversation, 95
  of questions, 135
Classmates
  analyzing speeches of, 281
  informative speeches of, 337–339
  persuasive speeches of, 372–373
Clichés, 245
Climax ordering, 238–240
Cliques, 123–134
Closed-circuit pay TV, 483
Closed-group discussion, 120
Close-mindedness, listening and, 65
Coach, as career, 392
Code, 35
Cohesiveness, of group, 125
Collins, William, 527
Color, in theater, 559
Comédie Française, 542
Comedy, 540

Comedy of manners, 543
Commedia dell'arte, 541
Commemorative speeches, 388–393
Commencement speeches, 394, 585
Commercial radio, 488
Commercial television, 483, 488
Committee, 121
Common ground technique, 298
Communication. *See also*
  Conversation; Listening;
  Nonverbal communication;
  Speech communication;
  Verbal communication
  careers and, 13–15
  conversation, 90–117
  cross-cultural, 41
  defined, 5, 31
  feedback and, 50–51
  with hearing impaired, 49
  memory and, 33
  model of process, 42
  one-to-one, 90–117
  process of, 6–8, 28–57
  reasoning and, 33
  reasons for, 34–35
  reception and, 47–48
  regulation group, 141–142
  symbols and, 35–42
  telephone, 102–103
  unintentional, 41–42
  vocalizing, 44–46
Comparative advantages case, 429
Comparison
  analogy as, 425
  in research, 194
Competence, 357
Compromise, 146
Computerized research services, 199–200
Concepts, speeches about, 295
Conciseness, 135–136
Conclusion
  analyzing, 336–337
  psychological, 315–316
  question-and-answer period in, 317–319
  reinforcing central idea in, 314–315
  rhetorical question in, 316
  signaling, 312–313
  of speech, 267, 312–316
  summary in, 314
Concrete language, 229–230

Confidence, 357
  lack of, 163
  in speaking publicly, 158–181
Conflict, in groups, 142–146
Connotation, 36–37
  unintentional, 244
Consensus, 146
Constructive speeches, 431
Contest
  debate as, 416
  in public speaking, 172
Contrast, 234–236
Controlled stage fright, 162
Conversation
  defined, 91
  enjoying, 95
  in interview, 104–111
  language used in, 228
  nonverbal aspects of, 96–102
  telephone, 102–103
  verbal aspects of, 91–95
Cooperation, in group discussion, 119–120
Cosby, Bill, 513
Costume designer, 558
Courtesy, in conversation, 93–94
Creason, Joe, 398
Credibility
  analyzing, 370–371
  of speaker, 302–305
Crediting sources, 11, 203, 235
Critical listening, 75–81
Critiquing, of public speaking, 174–175
Cross-cultural communication, 41
  proxemics and, 99–100
Cross-examination format, in debate, 418, 420, 432, 440–441
Cutaways, 326

Databases, research, 200
David Copperfield (Dickens), 519–520
Daydreaming, listening and, 64–65
Debate, 9, 414–441
  formats for, 420, 431–435
  limit or extend in meeting, 460
  meeting opposition in, 435–441
  outlining case for, 423
  parliamentary procedure and, 451
  preparation for, 418–426
  reasoning in, 425–426
  strategies for, 426–435

teams for, 421–422
Decision making, 12–13
  group discussion for, 120
  in groups, 146–147
  persuasive speaking and, 367
Decoding, 31, 35–36, 48
Dedication speeches, 395–396, 584
Deduction, 425
Delivery methods, 255–259. *See also* Speech delivery
Demonstration speeches, and visual aids, 328–329
Denotation, 36
Descriptive gestures, 261–262
Diagrams, 321, 324
Dialogue, in drama, 548
Diaphragm, 44
Dickens, Charles, 519–520
Director, 556–557
Discovery, and drama, 540
Discussion
  group, 9, 118–155
  participating in, 133–138
Disinterested audience, 352
Distance, proxemics and, 40
Distractions
  listening and, 63–64
  during speech, 276–277
Division of assembly, 465
Division of question, 464
Documentary, 488
Drama. *See also* Character
  character in, 543–544
  communicating in, 548–551
  defined, 10
  history of, 540–543
  nature of, 539–571
  research on role, 545
  theatrical event and, 555–561
Dramatic statement, in conclusion, 314–315
Drape, 559
Dress parade, 559

Economy of language, 232
Education. *See* Careers
Educational television, 483
Effective language, for public speaking, 224–253
Effect- to-cause reasoning, 425
Einstein, Albert, "Max Planck in Memoriam," 583
Electronic media, 477
  development of, 478–486
  radio, 478–479

  television, 480–481
Elizabethan era, drama in, 541
Emphasis
  climax ordering for, 238–240
  contrast for, 234–236
  repetition for, 237–238
  rhetorical questions for, 236
  variety for, 233–234
Emphatic gestures, 261
Encoding, 31, 35
Encyclopedias, 196
Enlightenment, discussion groups for, 120
Entertainment
  radio and television for, 486–487
  speeches for, 187, 398–400
Environment, for group discussion, 125–126
Equipment, for visual aids, 330–331
Ethics
  in communication, 11
  crediting sources, 203
  intensity of language and image, 235
  telling whole story, 368
  in using quotations, 427
  in using visual aids, 329
Ethos, 350, 356–361
  analyzing use of, 370–371
  establishing, 303–305
Eulogies, 389–391, 583
Euphemisms, 245
Evaluation
  of informative speeches, 331–339
  of persuasive speeches, 369–373
  of speeches, 281
Events, speeches about, 294
Everett, Edward, 232
Evidence, 362, 363–364
  analyzing, 371–372
  for debate, 424, 435–436
  strength of, 235
Examples, in research, 194
Experience, 34–35
  personal, 358
Extemporaneous method, of speech delivery, 226, 255, 257, 258
Eye contact, 97–98
  in public speaking, 171
  in speech delivery, 260–261

Face, in nonverbal communication, 98

Face-to-face conversation, 51
  enjoying, 95
Facial expressions, during speech delivery, 262–263
Fact, in research, 192
Factual questions, 134, 348–349
Failure, fear of, 161
False consensus, 147
Farbes, Hubert, 241
Feedback, 50–51
  checking interpretation with, 80–81
  in conversation, 93
  defined, 31
  listening and, 71–72
  reacting to, 306–307
Fiction, 506
Fictional speaker, 514–517, 519, 520–521
Field, Edward, 519
Fields of experience, 34–35
Figures of speech, 240–244
  analogy, 241
  hyperbole, 242
  irony, 244
  metaphor, 241
  personification, 241–242
  simile, 240–241
  understatement, 244
Filibustering, 454
Flaws, and drama, 540
Floor plan, 558
Flow sheet, for debate, 437–440
Follow up, after interview, 111
Foreign languages. *See* Interpreter
Formal debate, 415
Forming stage, of group, 130–131
Forum, 122
French theater, 541–542
Frost, Robert, 516
Future Business Leaders of America (FBLA), 172
Future Farmers of America (FFA), 172

Generalities, glittering, 76
Generalizations, hasty, 76
Gerety, Tom, "Saving Our Cities," 585
Gestures, 261–263
  in public speaking, 169–171
"Gettysburg Address" (Lincoln), 205–206, 232, 388, 477, 584
Glittering generality. *See* Generalities

Goals, of discussion group members, 124–125
Goal setting, 17
Goldwater, Barry, on speaking rate, 269
Good will, 361
Grammar, incorrect, 246, 247
Graphs, 320
Greece, drama in, 540
Group discussion, 51, 118–155. *See also* Groups
　alternatives to, 147–149
　cliques and, 123–124
　defined, 9
　discussion time and, 126–127
　group size and, 123
　leading, 139–142
　member goals, 124–125
　nature of, 119–123
　outcomes of, 146–147
　participating in, 133–138
　physical environment and, 125–126
　seating arrangement and, 126
　types of, 120–121
Groups
　behavior of, 127–133
　conflict in, 142–146
　life cycle of, 130–133

Hall, Edward T., 41, 99
Handouts, 326
Hasty generalization, 76
Hayakawa, S.I., 484
Heads, in outline, 210–211
Health services administrator, as career, 461
Hearing impaired, communicating with, 49
Hecklers, 277
Heun, Linda and Dick, 226
High school teacher, as career, 18
Holmes, Sherlock, listening and, 72–73
Horne, Frank, 536
Housman, Louis, 303
Humor, 361
　as attention device, 296–297, 306
　in public speaking, 169
　at roasts, 389
　in speeches to entertain, 398–400

Humphrey, Hubert, speaking rate of, 269
Hyperbole, 242

Iacocca, Lee, 13
"I Am Indelible," 537
Ibsen, Henrik, 543
"Ich bin ein Berliner" speech (Kennedy), 185
Ideas
　pattern of, 216
　selecting central, 70–71
"I Have a Dream" speech (King), 185, 204, 580
Imaginary audience
　fictional speaker and, 520–521
　for oral interpretation, 519–520
Impromptu method, of speech delivery, 255, 258, 404–405
Incidental motions, 463–465
Incorrect grammar, 246, 247
Indexes
　to biographical aids, 198
　to periodicals, 198–200
Induction, 425
Information sources. *See also* Reference sources; Research; Sources
　library, 195–200
　radio and television, 487–488
Informative speeches, 187, 290–345
　analyzing and evaluating, 331–339
　beginning, 295–305
　of classmates, 337–339
　about concepts, 295
　concluding, 312–316
　about events, 294
　imparting message of, 305–312
　about objects, 292–293
　about processes, 294–295
　visual aids in, 319–331
Ingenues, 559
"In Honor of David Anderson Brooks, My Father" (Brooks), 537
Inspirational speeches, 354, 577, 580
Intensity, of language and image, 235
Interests, 34–35
Interpersonal communication
　defined, 8
　reception and, 47

Interpretation, checking, 80–81
Interpreter, as career, 271
Interruptions, during speech, 276–277
Interview, participating in, 104–111
Interviewee, defined, 105
Interviewer. *See* Interviews
Interviews, 51, 200
　interviewee's role in, 104–109
　interviewer's role in, 109–111
　process of, 201
Intrapersonal communication, defined, 8
Introduction
　analyzing, 333–334
　for oral interpretation, 524–526
　speeches of, 187, 383–385
Irony, 244
Issues, in debate, 419
"I've Been to the Mountaintop" (King), 236

Julius Caesar (Shakespeare), 545

Kaye, Danny, 386, 388
Kennedy, Edward
　speech by, 193, 388
Kennedy, John F., 185
　on Churchill, Winston, 225
　gestures of, 263
　interest-building technique of, 301
　speech transitions of, 308
　use of contrast, 234
Kennedy, Robert
　speech about, 388
　speech by, 193
Keynote speech, 393–394
Kinesics, 38, 97–99
King, Martin Luther, Jr.
　"I Have a Dream," 580
　speeches, 185, 204, 236
　use of rhetorical questions, 236
Klappa, Gale, conclusion of, 315–316
Knox, Frank, restatement by, 231

Lacina, Kim, eulogy by, 390–391
Language. *See also* Emphasis; Spoken language; Verbal symbols
　economy of, 232
　effective, 224–253

figures of speech, 240–244
foreign. *See* Interpeter
use of, 17
written vs. spoken, 227–228
Language in Thought and Action (Hayakawa), 484
Larynx, 45
Lavalier microphone, 275
Lawyer, as career, 433
Lay on the table, in meeting, 460
Leadership, and group discussion, 139–142
Learning, 12–13
Lectern, 274–275
Legitimate theater, 543
Librarian, career as, 518
Library, conducting research in, 195–200
Life cycle, of groups, 130–133
Lighting designer, 558
Limit or extend debate, 460
Lincoln, Abraham, 205, 232
   Gettysburg Address of, 388, 477, 584
   persuasion and, 357
Lincoln-Douglas format
   in debate, 420, 432–434
Line graph, 320, 322
Line-staff chart, 320
Listeners
   needs of (pathos), 350–356
   speaking to, 225
Listening, 15, 16, 58–87
   barriers to, 63–67
   central ideas and, 70–71
   conditions, as attention factor, 306
   critical, 75–81
   effective, 67–73
   importance of, 60–63
   nonverbal cues and, 78–79
   process of association and, 73
Literary selection, understanding, 514
Lobbyists, 239
Locative gestures, 262
Logic. *See* Logical fallacies; Logos
Logical fallacies, 75, 81
Logos, 350, 362–367
   analyzing, 371–372
Lyric poetry, 507

MacArthur, Douglas, use of climax ordering, 238
Macbeth (Shakespeare), 537

Magazines, 199
Main heads
   complete sentences as, 211–212
   in outline, 210–211
Main ideas
   restating in speech, 231
   summarizing, 314
Main motions, 457–458
Maintenance
   messages and, 128–130
   and tasks, 128–130
Majority rule, 450
Majority vote, 147
Manuscript method, of speech delivery, 255, 256, 258–259
Maps, 321, 325
Masefield, John, 536
Mass communication, 477
   defined, 10
   radio and television, 476–499
Mayer, Thom, shock technique of, 299
Media
   electronic, 477
   radio and television, 476–499
Medical secretary, 74
Medium of exchange, language as, 36
Memorization method, of speech delivery, 255, 256–257, 258
Memory, 32–33
Memory skills, listening and, 72–73
Messages, 31. *See also* Reception
   applying to listener, 69
   imparting, 305–312
   sending and receiving, 92–93
   task and maintenance, 129–130
   transmitting, 34
Metaphors, 240–241
Microphone use, 275–276
Middle Ages, drama in, 541
Minority, 450–451
Minstrels, 504
Misunderstandings, listening and, 60–61
Models, as visual aids, 326
Molière, 542
Monotone, 268
Monroe, Alan H., 207
Monroe's Motivated Sequence pattern, of speech organization, 207, 208, 400–402
Mood, personification and, 242
Moore, Marianne, 536

Morgan, Frederick, 509–510
Moseley-Braun, Carol, Speech in Tribute to Thurgood Marshall, 588
Motions
   in meetings, 455–467
   precedence, 465–467
   seconding, 456
   types of, 457–465
Movements
   in body-motion communication, 98–99
   in drama, 549–551
   and public speaking, 169–170

Name calling, 75
Narrative, in research, 193–194
Narrative poetry, 507
Nasal cavities, 45
National Park Service, career with, 310
Need case, 428
Need-plan wedge case, 430
Negative side
   in debate, 417–418, 429–431
Nervousness. *See also* Stage fright
   concentrating on topic and, 168
   controlling, 164–175
   handling symptoms of, 171, 173
   relaxation techniques and, 165–166
Neutral audience, 352
Newscasters, 489
News commentator, 489
News magazine, 487
Newspapers, 199
Nielsen Media Research Group, 484
Nominal technique, of group communication, 148–149
Nonfiction, 506
Non sequitur, 76
Nonverbal communication
   attention factors, 306
   conversation, 96–102
   defined, 6
   in drama, 549–551
   in speech-making, 261–273
   use of, 17
Nonverbal cues, recognizing, 78–79
Nonverbal symbols, 31, 37–41
Norming stage, of group, 131

Index **607**

Note cards
  and lectern, 274–275
  for research, 204
  during speech delivery, 265
Note taking, during debate, 437–440
Notice, of meeting, 451–452

Objection to consideration, as motion, 463
Objects
  speeches about, 292–293
  as visual aids, 323
"Ode to Pity" (Collins), 527
One-to-one communication, 90–117
  defined, 8
Open-mindedness, 65
Opposed audience, 352–353
Opposing views
  in group discussion, 143–144
  respecting, 144–145
Opposition, in debate, 435–441
Optimist Clubs, 172
Oral interpretation, 502–537
  adapting material for, 512–513
  audience for, 519–520
  choosing material for, 509–513
  defined, 10
  details for, 523–524
  history of, 504
  introduction to, 524–526
  material for, 506–507
  practice for, 526–529
  preference and occasion for, 511–512
  process of, 513–524
  selections for, 536–537
  setting and, 521–523
  value of, 505
Orator, responsibility of, 367–369
Ordering, for variety, 238–240
Order of business, for meeting, 452
Order of precedence, motion in, 465–467
Organization
  importance of, 16
  outlining and, 209–214
  of speech, 205–214
Outlining, 194–195, 209–214
  of case for debate, 423
  for group discussion, 136–138

Roman numerals in, 211
sample, 212–214

Panel, 122
Panel-forum, 122
Paper tech, 564
Paralanguage, 40–41
  defined, 40
  as feedback, 51
  in nonverbal communication, 101–102
Parallelism, 238
Park ranger, as career, 310
Parliamentarian, 449
Parliamentary inquiry, 464
Parliamentary procedure, 9, 448–473
  basic principles of, 450–451
  holding meeting and, 451–455
  motions, 455–467
Pathos, 350–356
  analyzing use of, 369–370
Patterns, of speech organization, 205–207
Pauses, 101–102
  during speech, 272–273
  vocalized, 269–270
Pay TV, 483–484
Peace Corps volunteer, 43
Peck, Gregory, 386, 388
Pending motion, 456
Performing
  on radio and television, 489–491
  skills needed for, 490–491
Performing stage, of group, 131, 133
Periodical indexes, 198–200
Personal experience, 358
Personalization, 311–312
Personification, 241–242
Persons, speeches about, 382–393
Persuasive speeches, 187, 346–379, 576, 580
  analyzing, 369–373
  of classmates, 372–373
  in debate, 441
  impact of, 367–369
  organization of, 207
  sources of persuasion, 350–356
  types of, 347–349
Pharynx, 45
Picture graphs, 320, 324
Pictures, 323
Pitch, 40

Place, setting and, 523
Plane, Robert A., "The Quest for Shared Values," 590
Platform movement, 170, 264
Poetics (Aristotle), 540
Poetry, 507
Point of order, 463–464
Policy questions, 135, 349
Political candidates, 167
Political conventions, keynote speeches at, 393
Politics, persuasive speaking and, 367–369
Positions, in group discussion, 143–144
Positive audience, 352
Posters, 321
Postpone definitely, in meeting, 459
Postpone indefinitely, in meeting, 458
PR. *See* Public relations specialist
Practice, for oral interpretation, 526–529
Precedence motions, 465–467
Preparation
  for listening, 68
  for public speaking, 165
  speaker competence and, 357–358
  of speech, 182–223
Prepared readings, for auditions, 561
Presentation, speeches of, 187, 386–387
Prestige, 367
  ethos and, 356–361
Preview, of topic, 301–302
Previous question, in meeting, 460
Prima facie case, 428
Privileged motions, 462–463
Problem-solution pattern, of speech organization, 206–207
Processes, speeches about, 294–295
Process of association, 73
Producer, 555
Production
  concept, 562
  meetings, 562
  organization, 555
  for radio and television, 492–493
Profit, radio and television for, 488
Program concept, 492
Pronunciation, 270–272

Propaganda, 78
Proportion, 558–559
Proposition
  analysis of, 419
  in debate, 416–417
Prose, 506
Proxemics, 38–40, 99–100
  defined, 38
Public communication, 9–10
  drama, 10
  oral interpretation of literature, 10
Public discussion, 120–121
Publicity, for theatrical event, 559–561
Publicity manager, 559–560
Public relations specialist, 197
Public relations speeches, 396–397
Public speaking, 9–10
  building confidence for, 158–181
  common problems in, 244–247
  contests in, 172
  critiquing, 174–175
  effective language for, 224–253
  feedback in, 51
  gestures, eye contact, and, 169–171
  humor in, 169
  to inform, 290–345
  listening to, 66
  political candidates and, 167
  preparing for, 182–223
Public television, 483
Purpose
  of discussion groups, 120
  of speech, 188–190
  stating, 301–302
Purpose sentence, 188
  in outline, 209

Question-and-answer period, 317–319
Question of privilege, and motions, 462
Questions
  of fact, 134, 348–349
  in group discussion, 134–136
  of policy, 135, 349
  rhetorical, 236
  of value, 134–135, 349
  wording, 135–136
Quintilian, 367

Quorum, for meeting, 452
Quotations, 301
  in conclusion, 314

Radio, 481–482
  announcer, career as, 485
  disc jockey, 489
  history of, 478–479
  impact of, 484–486
  performing on, 489–491
  producing for, 492–493
  purposes of, 486–488
  for research, 200
  and television, 476–499
Ransley, Marie, suspense technique of, 299
Reagan, Ronald, speeches by, 354–355, 389
Realism, in drama, 543
Reasoning, 33, 362
  analyzing, 371–372
  in debate, 425, 436–437
Rebuttals, 431
Receiver, 5
  defined, 31
Reception, 47–48
Recess, of meeting, 462
Recognizing members, in meeting, 454
Recording evidence, 202–204
Reference section, in library, 196
Reference sources. *See also* Information sources; Sources
  atlases, 198
  biographical aids, 198
  encyclopedias, 196
  library, 195–200
  periodical indexes, 198–200
  yearbooks, 196
Refer to committee, in meeting, 459
Rehearsing, 214–217
  alone and with friends, 216–217
  for dramatic event, 562–564
  pattern of ideas in, 216
  timing oneself, 217
Relationships, listening and, 61
Relaxation techniques, 165–166
Renaissance, drama in, 541
Repetition, for variety, 237–238
Research
  computerized services for, 199–200
  on dramatic role, 545

  for group discussion, 138
  interviews, 200
  library sources, 195–200
  radio, 200
  recording evidence, 202–204
  television, 200
  on topic of speech, 191–205
Resonators, 45
Restatement, 231
Restoration, drama and, 543
Rhetoric (Aristotle), 350
Rhetorical question
  in conclusion, 316
  for variety, 236
Roasts, 389
Robert's Rules of Order Newly Revised, 449
Role playing, of interviews, 111
Roles, leadership, 139–142
Roll-call votes, 455
Roman numerals, in outlines, 211
Romanticism, in drama, 543
Roosevelt, Franklin D., 231, 237
  speech delivery method of, 258
  use of parallelism, 238
  use of personification, 241–242
Round-table discussion, 122
Runaway stage fright, 163
Running-refutation negative case, 430
Run-throughs, 564

Sales presentations, 400–405
Sandburg, Carl, Address on the Anniversary of Lincoln's Birth, 572
Scale models, 558
Scene designer, 557–558
Schramm, Wilbur, 34–35
Script, 565
  analyzing, 547
"Sea Fever" (Masefield), 536
Seating
  as attention factor, 306
  for group discussion, 126
Second, of motion, 456
Secret ballot, 455
Sender, 5
  defined, 31
Sending, 47–48
Sentences
  length of, 233
  in main heads and subheads, 211–212

purpose, 188, 209
structure of, 233
Set, dramatic. *See* Scene designer; Setting
Setting
  and oral interpretation, 521–523
  place and, 523
  time and, 522–523
Shakespeare, William, 537, 545
  sayings from, 542
Shock technique, 298–299
Simic, Charles, 536
Similes, 240–241
Simmons, Beth, 354
Simple majority, 450
Sincerity, 358–360
Skills, for radio and television performing, 490–491
Slang, 246
Slice-of-life theater, 543
Soap operas, 479
Social worker, as career, 359
Sound, defined, 47
Sources. *See also* Information sources; Reference sources; Research
  crediting, 11, 203, 235
  listening and, 66, 77–78
  on note cards, 204
Space (proxemics), 38–40, 99–100
Spatial pattern, of speech organization, 206
Speaker, fictional, 519, 520–521
Speaker's stand. *See* Lectern
Speaking, 15. *See also* Public speaking
  impromptu, 404–405
  rate of, 40
Specialists, radio and television performers as, 489–490
Special occasion speeches, 393–400, 572–592
  commencement, 394
  dedication, 395–396
  to entertain, 398–400
  keynote, 393–394
  public relations, 396–397
Specific purpose, of speech, 188
Specific words, 230
Speech (language), figures of, 240–244
Speech(es). *See also* Visual aids
  of acceptances, 387–388
  analyzing, 278–280, 281
  commemorative, 388–393

demonstration, 328–329
eulogies, 389–391
evaluating, 281
famous, 185
informative, 290–345
of introduction, 383–385
organizing, 205–207
outlining of, 209–214
about persons, 382–393
persuasive, 346–379
of presentation, 386–387
purpose of, 187
rehearsing, 214–217
for sales presentations, 400–405
special situations for, 380–411
specific purpose of, 188–190
testimonial, 389
Speech communication
  benefits of, 12–15
  defined, 6
  group, 9
  importance of, 19–21
  ineffective, 32
  mass communication, 10
  one-to-one, 8
  public, 9–10
  types of, 8–11
  uses of, 7
Speech communicators. *See also* Careers
  famous, 16
  qualities of, 16–17
Speech contest, 366
Speech delivery, 254–287
  appearance during, 265–266
  articulation and pronunciation during, 270–272
  combining methods of, 258–259
  concluding, 267
  distractions and interruptions, 276–277
  extemporaneous method of, 255, 257, 258
  eye contact in, 260–261
  gestures in, 261–263
  impromptu method of, 255, 258
  lectern and, 274–275
  manuscript method of, 255, 256, 258–259
  memorization method of, 255, 256–257, 258
  microphone and, 275–276
  nonverbal aspects of, 260–273
  note use during, 265
  pauses during, 272–273

pitch during, 268–269
platform movement during, 264
problems of, 273–277
speaking rate during, 269–270
speaking volume, 267–268
voice during, 267
Speech organization, 205–214
  pattern of, 205–207
Speech preparation, 182–223
  focusing on topic, 184–191
  organizing and outlining, 105–214
  rehearsing, 214–217
  researching topic, 191–205
Spoken language. *See also* Language
  clarity of, 228–232
  concrete language in, 229–230
  removing unnecessary words from, 232
  restating main ideas in, 231
  specific words in, 230
  wording in, 228–229
  written language compared with, 227–228
Stage fright, 159, 160–164
  audience perception of, 163–164, 166
  causes of, 160–161
  controlled, 162
  controlling nervousness and, 164–175
  handling symptoms of, 171, 173
Stage manager, 557
Standard format
  in debate, 420, 431–432
Statistics, in research, 192–193
Status quo, and debate, 417–418, 429–430
Stereotyping, 246
"Stopping by Woods on a Snowy Evening" (Frost), 516
Storming stage, of group, 131
Storytellers, 504
Strategies, for debate, 426–435
Stress, 40–41
Strindberg, August, 543
String-of-beads pattern, of speech organization, 207
Subheads
  complete sentences as, 210–211
  in outline, 211
Subject, of speech, 184
Subsidiary motions, 458
Success, listening and, 62–63

INDEX

Summary, in conclusion, 314
Support, research as, 191
Surveys, 202. *See also* Interviewing
Suspend the rules, motion to, 463
Suspense technique, 299
Symbols. *See also* Nonverbal communication; Verbal communication
 choosing, 35–42
 defined, 36
 nonverbal, 31, 37–41
 verbal, 31, 36–37
Symposium, 122
Symposium-forum, 122
Symptoms, of stage fright, 171, 173
Syntality, 139
Systems analyst, 137

"Tables Turned, The" (Wordsworth), 527
Tarot of Cornelius Agrippa, The (Morgan), 509–510
Tasks
 and maintenance, 128–130
 messages and, 128–130
Teaching, as career, 18
Teams, in debates, 421–422
Technical language, avoiding, 309–311
Technical quality, of literature, 511
Tech week, 563, 564
Telephone
 business use of, 103–104
 communication by, 102–103
Television, 482–484. *See also* Careers
 history of, 480–481
 impact of, 484–486
 performing on, 489–491
 producing for, 492–493
 purposes of, 486–488
 radio and, 476–499
 for research, 200
Tension, stage fright and, 161
Terzian, Carl, 396
Testimonial, 76
 speeches for, 388–389
Testimony, in research, 192
Theater. *See* Drama
Theater of the Absurd, 543
Theatrical event. *See also* Drama
 opening night and evaluation of, 564–565
 organizing, 555–561
 producing, 561–565
Thespians, 540
Thespis, 540
Thinking, 33
 critical listening and, 75–81
 logical fallacies and, 81
Thoreau, Henry, 510
Time
 in nonverbal communication, 100–101
 and setting, 522–523
"To a Prize Bird" (Moore), 536
"To James" (Horne), 536
Toll TV, 483–484
Topic
 building interest in, 300–301
 of conversation, 94–95
 for group discussion, 134
 preview of, 301–302
 public speaking and, 168
 researching, 138, 191–205
 selecting, 184–190
Topical pattern, of speech organization, 206
Trachea, 44
Tragedy, 540
Tragic flaw, and drama, 540
Tragicomedy, 545
Training. *See* Careers
Transitional gestures, 261
Transitions, 307–309
Trial lawyer, as career, 433
Twain, Mark, 514–515
 on pauses, 272–273
Two-person conversation, eye contact in, 97–98

Understanding, 31
Understatement, 244
Universal appeal, of oral material, 508–509
Unsupported assertions, in debate, 435

Value questions, 134–135, 349
Variety
 for emphasis, 233–234
 in speech-making, 263
Verbal communication
 conversation, 91–95
 defined, 6
Verbal symbols, 31, 36–37
Videotape, 480–481
Viewpoints, in group discussion, 143–144
Visual aids, 319–331
 equipment for, 330–331
 judging, 331
 in speeches, 326–328
 types of, 320–326
Vocabulary
 listening and, 68
 varying, 233
Vocal cords, 45
Vocalized pause, 101–102, 269–270
Vocalizing, 44–46. *See also* Voice
Voice
 for dramatic character, 551–553
 pitch and, 268–269
 speaking rate, 269–270
 use of, 267
 volume of, 267–268
Voice quality, 40
Volume, 40
Voting, in meeting, 455

Walden (Thoreau), 510
War of the Worlds (Wells), radio broadcast of, 484
Warrants, in group discussion, 143–144
Weisensel, Kathy, speech conclusion of, 313
Welcome speech, 187
Welles, Orson, 484
Wilde, Oscar, 545
"Window Washer" (Simic), 536
Win-lose situation, 368
Withdraw a motion, 464
Wording
 concrete, 229–230
 short, 228–229
Wordsworth, William, 527
Written language, compared with spoken language, 227–228

Yearbooks, 196

Text Credits

Chapter 8
P. 226: From PUBLIC SPEAKING by Richard and Linda Heun. Copyright © 1979 by West Publishing Co. Reprinted by permission.
P. 236: From "I've Been to the Mountaintop" by Martin Luther King, Jr. Reprinted by arrangement with The Heirs to the Estate of Martin Luther King, Jr., c/o Joan Daves Agency as agent for the proprietor. Copyright 1968 by the Estate of Martin Luther King, Jr.

Chapter 10
P. 299: From "The Life and Death of Our Lakes" from CONTEMPORARY AMERICAN SPEECHES: A SOURCE BOOK OF SPEECH FORMS AND PRINCIPLES, 3E, by William A. Linkugel, R. R. Allan, and Richard L. Johannesen, eds. Reprinted by permission of William A. Linkugel.
P. 313: Excerpt from "David—A Lot of Other Neat People," by Kathy Weisensel in CONTEMPORARY AMERICAN SPEECHES, 7th Ed., edited by Johannsen et al. Copyright 1992 by Kendall/Hunt Publishing Company. Used with permission.
P. 314: From "Hug a Bat—No Way" by Mary Nielsen, speech given April 1985 at American Forensic Association Tournament. Reprinted by permission of American Forensic Association.
P. 314: From "Laser Surgery" by Randy Larsen, speech given April 1985 at American Forensic Association Tournament. Reprinted by permission of American Forensic Association.
P. 315: From "Journalism and the Anti-Media Backlash: Five Steps to Restore the Public's Respect" by Gale Klappa, © 1985. Reprinted by permission.

Chapter 12
P. 386: Gregory Peck, introducing Danny Kaye at the 1981/54th Academy Awards. Courtesy Academy of Motion Picture Arts and Sciences © 1982. Reprinted by permission.

P. 388: Danny Kaye's acceptance speech for the Jean Hersholt Humanitarian Award at the 1981/54th Academy Awards. Courtesy Academy of Motion Picture Arts and Sciences © 1982.

Chapter 16
P. 509: "I'm Nobody! Who Are You?" by Emily Dickinson. Reprinted by permission of the publishers and the Trustees of Amherst College from THE POEMS OF EMILY DICKINSON, Thomas H. Johnson, ed., Cambridge, Mass.: The Belknap Press of Harvard University Press. Copyright © 1951, 1955, 1979, 1983 by the President and Fellows of Harvard College.
P. 516: "Stopping by Woods On A Snowy Evening" by Robert Frost from THE POETRY OF ROBERT FROST edited by Edward Connery Lathem. Copyright 1951 by Robert Frost. Copyright 1923, © 1969 by Henry Holt and Co., Inc. Reprinted by permission of Henry Holt and Co., Inc.
P. 519: "At the Coney Island Aquarium" by Edward Field, Copyright © 1992 by Edward Field. Reprinted from COUNTING MYSELF LUCKY: SELECTED POEMS 1963-1992 with the permission of Black Sparrow Press.
P. 536: "To James" by Frank Horne, as appeared in LITERATURE III, Albert R. Kitzhaber Gen. Ed., Stoddard Malarkey and Donald MacRae, Holt, Rinehart & Winston, Inc., 1969.
P. 536: "Window Washer" by Charles Simic as appeared in THE VIRGINIA QUARTERLY REVIEW, Fall 1977. Reprinted by permission.
P. 536: "Sea Fever" by John Masefield from POEMS by John Masefield. Reprinted by permission of The Society of Authors as the literary representative of the Estate of John Masefield.
P. 537: "In Honor of David Anderson Brooks, My Father" from BLACKS, by Gwendolyn Brooks, © 1991. Published by Third World Press, Chicago, 1991. Reprinted by permission.

Appendix

P. 577: "Choices and Change" by Barbara Bush. Copyright © 1990 by Barbara Bush. Reprinted by permission.

P. 580: "I Have a Dream" by Martin Luther King, Jr. Reprinted by arrangement with The Heirs to the Estate of Martin Luther King, Jr., c/o Joan Daves Agency as agent for the proprietor. Copyright 1963 by Martin Luther King, Jr., copyright renewed 1991 by Coretta Scott King.

P. 583: "Max Planck in Memoriam" by Albert Einstein from OUT OF MY LATER YEARS by Albert Einstein. Reprinted by permission of the Philosophical Library, New York.

P. 585: "Saving Our Cities" by Tom Gerety delivered at Trinity College commencement, Hartford, CT, May 17, 1992. Reprinted by permission.

P. 590: "The Quest for Shared Values: Higher Education Must Lead Society" by Robert A. Plane, delivered at the Women's Leadership Institute of Wells College, Aurora, NY, December 6, 1994. Reprinted by permission.

Photo Credits

Unit 1
Richard Hutchings/Photo Edit, *3*.

Chapter 1
Richard Hutchings/Photo Edit, *4*; Charles Gupton/Stock Boston, *6*; Larry Lawfer/The Picture Cube, *9*; Tony Freeman/Photo Edit, *11*; Mark Richards/Photo Edit, *14*; David Young-Wolff/Photo Edit, *17*; Charles Gupton/Stock Boston, *18*; Mark C. Burnett/Stock Boston, *20*; Michael Newman/Photo Edit, *21*.

Chapter 2
Richard Hutchings/Photo Edit, *28*; Myrleen Ferguson-Cate/Photo Edit, *29*; Tony Freeman/Photo Edit, *30*; Myrleen Ferguson/Photo Edit, *37*; Tom McCarthy/The Picture Cube, *39*; Leslie F. Wilson, *43*; Tony Freeman/Photo Edit, *48*; Bill Aron/Photo Edit, *49*; Bob Kramer/The Picture Cube, *50*.

Chapter 3
Bob Daemmrich/Stock Boston, *58*; Richard Pasley/Stock Boston, *60*; Ron Sherman/Stock Boston, *61*; Billy E. Barnes/Stock Boston, *64*; Ron Grishaber/Photo Edit, *66*; Bob Daemmrich/Stock Boston, *69*; Myrleen Ferguson/Photo Edit, *71*; Mary Kate Denny/Photo Edit, *74*; Michael Newman/Photo Edit, *77*; Michael Newman/Photo Edit, *78*; Amy C. Etra/Photo Edit, *80*

Unit 2
J. Koontz/The Picture Cube, *89*.

Chapter 4
Richard Hutchings/Photo Edit, *90*; Tony Freeman/Photo Edit, *92*; Tony Freeman/Photo Edit, *93*; Tony Freeman/Photo Edit, *96*; Jerry Berndt/Stock Boston, *98*; Mathew McVay/Stock Boston, *100*; Michael Newman/Photo Edit, *103*; Frank Siteman/The Picture Cube, *105*; Michael Newman/Photo Edit, *107*; Robert Brenner/Photo Edit, *109*; Michael Newman/Photo Edit, *110*.

Chapter 5
Tony Freeman/Photo Edit, *118*; David Young-Wolff/Photo Edit, *120*; Charles Glipton/Stock Boston, *121*; James Shaffer/Photo Edit, *122*; Jen Greenberg/Photo Edit, *125*; Tom McCarthy/Photo Edit, *126*; Tony Freeman/Photo Edit, *137*; Michael Newman/Photo Edit, *144*; Ellis Herwig/The Picture Cube, *148*.

Unit 3
Tony Freeman/Photo Edit, *157*.

Chapter 6
Michael Newman/Photo Edit, *158*; Dennis Stock/Magnum, *161*; The Bettmann Archive, *162*; Michael Newman/Photo Edit, *164*; Bob Daemmrich/Stock Boston, *167*; Tom McCarthy/Photo Edit, *170*.

Chapter 7
Jeff Greenberg/Photo Edit, *182*; Rhoda Sidney/Stock Boston, *183*; David Young-Wolff/Photo Edit, *187*; Robert Brenner/Photo Edit, *189*; Jeff Greenberg/Photo Edit, *192*; Jim Daniels/The Picture Cube, *195*; Bob Daemmrich/Stock Boston, *197*; David Young-Wolff/Photo Edit, *198*; Michael Newman/Photo Edit, *202*; Jeff Greenberg/Photo Edit, *203*; Jeff Greenberg/Photo Edit, *210*; Richard Hutchings/Photo Edit, *215*.

Chapter 8
Michael Newman/Photo Edit, *224*; Skjold/Photo Edit, *226*; Michael Newman/Photo Edit, *227*; Mark Richards/Photo Edit, *231*; Mark Richards/Photo Edit, *233*; Mary Kate Denny/Photo Edit, *235*; The Bettmann Archive, *237*; Tom McCarthy/Photo Edit, *239*; Frank Siteman/The Picture Cube, *245*.

Chapter 9
Frank Siteman/The Picture Cube, *254*; Bob Daemmrich/Stock Boston, *256*; Tony Freeman/Photo Edit, *257*; Mary Kate Denny/Photo Edit, *259*; Mark Richards/Photo Edit, *261*; Bob Daemmrich/Stock Boston, *263*; Michael Newman/Photo Edit, *264*; Jeff

Photo Credits

Ellis, *266*; Mary Kate Denny/Photo Edit *269*; Reuters/Bettmann, *271*; The Bettmann Archive, *272*; Bob Daemmrich/Stock Boston, *275*; Robert Brenner/Photo Edit, *276*; Ellis Herwig/Stock Boston, *279*.

Unit 4
David Young-Wolff/Photo, Edit, *288*.

Chapter 10
Grant LeDuc/Stock Boston, *290*; Bob Daemmrich/Stock Boston, *291*; David Shopper/Stock Boston, *292*; David Young-Wolf/Photo Edit, *297*; Bob Daemmrich/Stock Boston, *303*; T. Prettyman/Photo Edit, *304*; Michael Newman/Photo Edit, *307*; UPI/Bettmann, *308*; David Young-Wolff/Photo Edit, *310*; David Young-Wolff/Photo Edit, *313*; Michael Newman/Photo Edit, *318*; David Young-Wolff/Photo Edit, *331*; Jeff Ellis/National Textbook Company *335*; Michael Newman/Photo Edit, *338*.

Chapter 11
Olympia/Photo Edit, *346*; Michael Newman/Photo Edit, *348*; Ron Sherman/Stock Boston, *351*; Myrleen Ferguson Cate/Photo Edit, *353*; James Shaffer/Photo Edit, *359*; David Young-Wolff/Photo Edit, *360*; Michael Newman/Photo Edit, *364*; Ron Dorsey/Stock Boston, *369*; Mary Kate Denny/Photo Edit, *373*.

Chapter 12
Tony Freeman/Photo Edit, *380*; Owen Franken/Stock Boston, *382*; Michael Newman/Photo Edit, *384*; Tony Freeman/Photo Edit, *387*; Amanda Merullo/Stock Boston, *392*; David Young-Wolff/Photo Edit, *395*; David Young-Wolff/Photo Edit, *397*; Bob Daemmrich/Stock Boston, *399*; John Coletti/The Picture Cube, *401*; Tony Freeman/Photo Edit, *403*; Michael Newman/Photo Edit, *405*.

Unit 5
Tony Freeman/Photo Edit, *412*.

Chapter 13
Bob Daemmrich/The Image Works, *414*; Bob Daemmrich/The Image Works, *416*; Bill Aron/Photo Edit, *422*; Bob Daemmrich/The Image Works, *424*; Stephen Frisch/Stock Boston, *427*; John Neubauer/Photo Edit, *433*; AP/Wide World, *434*; Robert Finken/The Picture Cube, *436*.

Chapter 14
Jack McConnell, *448*; Jeff Ellis/National Textbook Company, *450*; Paula Lerner/The Picture Cube, *453*; Jack McConnell, *457*; Preuss/The Image Works *461*; Jeff Ellis/National Textbook Company, *464*.

Unit 6
Jeff Greenberg/Photo Edit, *475*.

Chapter 15
Michael Newman/Photo Edit, *476*; Bob Kramer/The Picture Cube, *477*; The Bettmann Archive, *479*; Tony Freeman/Photo Edit, *482*; Richard Hutchings/Photo Edit, *485*; Mary Kate Denny/Photo Edit, *487*; David Young-Wolff/Photo Edit, *490*; Robert Brenner/Photo Edit, *493*.

Unit 7
Cary Wolinsky/Stock Boston, *501*.

Chapter 16
Jeff Ellis/National Textbook Company, *502*; Michael Newman/Photo Edit *503*; The Bettmann Archive, *504*; Michelle Bridwell/Photo Edit, *508*; Laima Druskis/Stock Boston, *513*; Myrleen Cate/Photo Edit, *518*; Stanley Rowin/The Picture Cube, *522*; Jack McConnell, *525*; Rhoda Sidney/Stock Boston, *527*; Tony Freeman/Photo Edit, *528*.

Chapter 17
Wayne Hoy/The Picture Cube, *538*; John Eastcott/The Image Works, *539*; McLaughlin/The Image Works, *541*; Mikki Ansin/The Picture Cube, *544*; Capital Features/The Image Works, *546*; Spencer Grant/The Picture Cube, *549*; Spencer Grant/The Picture Cube, *553*; Michael Newman/Photo Edit, *560*; John Elk III, Stock Boston, *563*.

NOTES

NOTES

NOTES

NOTES

NOTES

NOTES

NOTES

NOTES